CW01022013

The Cambridge Handbook of Stylistics

Stylistics has become the most common name for a discipline which at various times has been termed 'literary linguistics', 'rhetoric', 'poetics', 'literary philology' and 'close textual reading'. This *Handbook* is the definitive account of the field, drawing on linguistics and related subject areas such as psychology, sociology, anthropology, educational pedagogy, computational methods, literary criticism and critical theory. Placing stylistics in its intellectual and international context, each chapter includes a detailed illustrative example and case-study of stylistic practice, with arguments and methods open to examination, replication and constructive critical discussion. As an accessible guide to the theory and practice of stylistics, it will equip the reader with a clear understanding of the ethos and principles of the discipline, as well as with the capacity and confidence to engage in stylistic analysis.

PETER STOCKWELL is Professor of Literary Linguistics at the University of Nottingham, and a Fellow of the English Association.

SARA WHITELEY is Lecturer in Language and Literature at the University of Sheffield.

CAMBRIDGE HANDBOOKS IN LANGUAGE AND LINGUISTICS

Genuinely broad in scope, each handbook in this series provides a complete state-of-the-field overview of a major sub-discipline within language study and research. Grouped into broad thematic areas, the chapters in each volume encompass the most important issues and topics within each subject, offering a coherent picture of the latest theories and findings. Together, the volumes will build into an integrated overview of the discipline in its entirety.

Published titles

The Cambridge Handbook of Phonology, edited by Paul de Lacy
The Cambridge Handbook of Linguistic Code-Switching, edited by Barbara E. Bullock and Almeida Jacqueline Toribio
The Cambridge Handbook of Child Language, edited by Edith L. Bavin
The Cambridge Handbook of Endangered Languages, edited by Peter K. Austin and Julia Sallabank
The Cambridge Handbook of Sociolinguistics, edited by Rajend Mesthrie
The Cambridge Handbook of Pragmatics, edited by Keith Allan and Kasia M. Jaszczolt
The Cambridge Handbook of Language Policy, edited by Bernard Spolsky
The Cambridge Handbook of Second Language Acquisition, edited by Julia Herschensohn and Martha Young-Scholten
The Cambridge Handbook of Biolinguistics, edited by Cedric Boeckx and Kleanthes K. Grohmann
The Cambridge Handbook of Generative Syntax, edited by Marcel den Dikken
The Cambridge Handbook of Communication Disorders, edited by Louise Cummings
The Cambridge Handbook of Stylistics, edited by Peter Stockwell and Sara Whiteley

Further titles planned for the series

The Cambridge Handbook of Linguistic Anthropology, edited by Nick Enfield, Paul Kockelman and Jack Sidnell
The Cambridge Handbook of Morphology, edited by Andrew Hippisley and Greg Stump
The Cambridge Handbook of Historical Syntax, edited by Adam Ledgeway and Ian Roberts
The Cambridge Handbook of Formal Semantics, edited by Maria Aloni and Paul Dekker
The Cambridge Handbook of English Corpus Linguistics, edited by Douglas Biber and Randi Reppen
The Cambridge Handbook of English Historical Linguistics, edited by Merja Kytö and Päivi Pahta

The Cambridge Handbook of Stylistics

Edited by

Peter Stockwell
University of Nottingham

Sara Whiteley
University of Sheffield

CAMBRIDGE
UNIVERSITY PRESS

CAMBRIDGE
UNIVERSITY PRESS

University Printing House, Cambridge CB2 8BS, United Kingdom

Cambridge University Press is part of the University of Cambridge.

It furthers the University's mission by disseminating knowledge in the pursuit of education, learning, and research at the highest international levels of excellence.

www.cambridge.org
Information on this title: www.cambridge.org/9781107028876

© Cambridge University Press 2014

First published 2014

Printed in the United Kingdom by Clays, St Ives plc

A catalogue record for this publication is available from the British Library

Library of Congress Cataloguing in Publication data
The Cambridge handbook of stylistics / Edited by Peter Stockwell, University of Nottingham ; Sara Whiteley, University of Sheffield.
    pages   cm. – (Cambridge handbooks in language and linguistics)
ISBN 978-1-107-02887-6 (hardback)
1. English language – Style.   2. English language – Rhetoric.   I. Stockwell, Peter, editor.   II. Whiteley, Sara, (Professor) editor.   III. Title: Handbook of stylistics.
PE1421.C36   2014
808′.042–dc23

                                                                          2014002752

ISBN 978-1-107-02887-6 Hardback

Contents

Figures

Contributors

Marc Alexander is Lecturer in English Language at the University of Glasgow. His research interests encompass the stylistics of popular fiction, digital humanities and meaning studies. He has published widely in these fields, including co-authored contributions to *Language and Style* (ed. McIntyre and Busse, Palgrave Macmillan, 2010) and *Stories and Minds* (ed. Bernaerts et al., University of Nebraska Press, 2013).

Joe Bray is Reader in Language and Literature at the University of Sheffield. His research interests include eighteenth- and early nineteenth-century narrative style, book history, textual culture and experimental literature. He is the author of *The Epistolary Novel: Representations of Consciousness* (Routledge, 2003) and *The Female Reader in the English Novel: From Burney to Austen* (Routledge, 2009).

Beatrix Busse is Professor in the Department of English at the Ruprecht-Karls-Universität Heidelberg. Her research interests include historical English linguistics, corpus linguistics and stylistics. She is author of *Vocative Constructions in the Language of Shakespeare* (John Benjamins, 2006) and co-editor of *Language and Style* (Palgrave Macmillan, 2010).

Patricia Canning is Teaching Assistant and researcher at Queen's University Belfast. Her research encompasses cognitive stylistics, literary theory and phenomenology. She has contributed to the journal *Language and Literature* and won the Poetics and Linguistics Association Prize in 2008. She is author of *Style in the Renaissance: Language and Ideology in Early Modern England* (Continuum, 2012).

Ronald Carter is Research Professor of Modern English Language at the University of Nottingham. His research specialisms include linguistics and literary criticism; applied linguistics and language education; healthcare communication; the teaching of English in schools; grammar, discourse and corpus linguistics. He has written and edited more than 50 books and 100 academic papers in these fields.

Jonathan Charteris-Black is Professor in Linguistics at the University of the West of England. He has published extensively in the areas of figurative language, corpus linguistics, cognitive semantics and English for specific purposes. Recent monographs include *Politicians and Rhetoric: The Persuasive Power of Metaphor* (Palgrave Macmillan, 2006), *Gender and the Language of Illness* (Palgrave Macmillan, 2010) and *Analysing Political Speeches: Rhetoric, Discourse and Metaphor* (Palgrave Macmillan, 2014).

Billy Clark is Reader in English Language and Linguistics at Middlesex University London. His research centres on the fields of linguistic semantics and pragmatics, including prosodic meaning and stylistics. He has published widely on these subjects and is author of *Relevance Theory* (Cambridge University Press, 2013).

Tracy Cruickshank is Senior Lecturer at De Montfort University Leicester. Her research centres on the representation of space and place in play texts and performance, with a particular focus on contemporary British drama. She has co-authored papers in the *Journal of Literary Semantics* and *Interactive Storytelling* (ed. Aylett et al., Springer, 2011).

Barbara Dancygier is Professor in the Department of English at the University of British Columbia. Her research interests include cognitive-linguistic approaches to metaphor and literary discourse. She is co-author of *Mental Spaces in Grammar: Conditional Constructions* (Cambridge University Press, 2005) and author of *The Language of Stories: A Cognitive Approach* (Cambridge University Press, 2013).

Alan Durant is Professor of Communication in the School of Law at Middlesex University London. His research interests include the language and regulation of media. He is author of *Meaning in the Media: Discourse, Controversy and Debate* (Cambridge University Press, 2010) and co-author of *Language and Media* (Routledge, 2009).

Catherine Emmott is Reader in English Language at the University of Glasgow. Her central research interests are the mental processing of text, discourse anaphora, and stylistics. She has published widely in these areas and is the author of *Narrative Comprehension: A Discourse Perspective* (Oxford University Press, 1997) and co-author of *Mind, Brain and Narrative* (Cambridge University Press, 2013).

Olga Fischer is Professor of Germanic Languages at the University of Amsterdam. Her research focuses on historical English linguistics and language change, including grammaticalisation phenomena and iconicity. She has published widely in these fields and is the co-editor of the *Iconicity in Language and Literature* series (John Benjamins).

Joanna Gavins is Reader in Language and Literature at the University of Sheffield. Her research centres on the interactions between language, literature and the human mind. She has published widely within the disciplines of stylistics and cognitive poetics, and is the author of *Text World Theory: An Introduction* (Edinburgh University Press, 2007) and *Reading the Absurd* (Edinburgh University Press, 2013).

Alison Gibbons is Senior Lecturer in Stylistics at De Montfort University Leicester. Her research interests include cognitive poetic approaches to experimental and multimodal literature. She is the author of *Multimodality, Cognition and Empirical Literature* (Routledge, 2012) and co-editor of *Mark Z. Danielewski* (Manchester University Press, 2010) and *The Routledge Companion to Experimental Literature* (Routledge, 2012).

Christiana Gregoriou is Lecturer in English Language at the University of Leeds, and specialises in the study of mind style and the poetics of deviance. She has published widely in stylistics and has authored several books including *Language, Ideology and Identity in Serial Killer Narratives* (Routledge, 2011) and *Deviance in Contemporary Crime Fiction* (Palgrave, 2007).

Geoff Hall is Professor of English at the University of Nottingham, Ningbo, China. His research interests include literary stylistics and intercultural communication, and he has published widely in these fields. He is author of *Literature in Language Education* (Palgrave, 2005) and *Discourse Stylistics* (John Benjamins, forthcoming) and Chief Editor of the journal *Language and Literature*.

Craig Hamilton is Associate Professor in English Cognitive Linguistics at the Université de Haute-Alsace. His research interests include cognitive poetics and the cognitive rhetoric of metaphor. He has published widely in these fields, including as a contributor to *Rhetoric and Stylistics* (ed. Ulla Fix et al., Mouton de Gruyter, 2008) and as guest editor for a special edition of the journal *Language and Literature* on 'Rhetoric and Beyond' (2005).

Patrick Colm Hogan is Professor in the Department of English at the University of Connecticut. His research interests include literary theory, postcolonial and world literature, and cognitive approaches to literature and narrative. He has published over 150 academic papers and 20 books, including *The Mind and Its Stories: Narrative Universals and Human Emotion* (Cambridge University Press, 2003) and *Affective Narratology: The Emotional Structure of Stories* (University of Nebraska Press, 2011).

Lesley Jeffries is Professor in the Department of English at the University of Huddersfield. Her research encompasses the stylistics of literary and non-literary texts, in particular the style of contemporary poetry and ideology in news reporting and political discourse. She has published extensively in these fields, and her books include *The Language of Twentieth Century Poetry* (Palgrave Macmillan, 1993) and *Opposition in Discourse: The Construction of Oppositional Meaning* (Continuum, 2010).

Manuel Jobert is Professor in English Linguistics at the Université Jean Moulin Lyon 3. His research interests include English phonetics, stylistics and conversation analysis. He is President of the Société de Stylistique Anglaise and editor of *Études de Stylistiques Anglaises* (ESA). He is the author of a book on Edith Wharton (ANRP, 2004) and co-editor of *Empreintes de l'euphémisme: tours et détours* (L'Harmattan, 2010) and

Aspects of Linguistic Impoliteness (Cambridge Scholars, 2013). He co-authored *Transcrire l'anglais britannique & américain* (Presses universitaires du Mirail-Toulouse, 2009).

Rodney H. Jones is Associate Professor and Head of English at City University, Hong Kong. His main research interests include discourse analysis, health communication, and language and sexuality. His recent books include *Health and Risk Communication: An Applied Linguistic Perspective* (Routledge, 2013), the co-authored *Understanding Digital Literacies* (Routledge, 2012), a textbook in *Discourse Analysis* (Routledge, 2012) and the edited *Discourse and Creativity* (Pearson, 2012).

Marina Lambrou is Principal Lecturer in English Language and Communication at Kingston University London. Her research interests include the stylistics of literary and non-literary texts, with a focus on narratives of personal experience and the study of language and media. She has published widely in these fields, including co-authoring *Language and Media* (Routledge, 2009) and co-editing *Contemporary Stylistics* (Continuum, 2007).

Benedict Lin is Assistant Professor in the Faculty of Arts at the University of Nottingham, Ningbo, China. His research interests include applied linguistics and stylistics, their pedagogical applications, and the exploration of non-anglophone poetry in English and English translations of Chinese poetry. He has published widely in these fields, including as contributor to *Literature and Language Teaching* (ed. A. Paran, TESOL, 2006).

Bill Louw is Chair of the English Department at the University of Zimbabwe. His research interests include semantic prosody, stylistics, corpus linguistics and the philosophy of language. He has published widely in these fields, including as contributor to *Perspectives on Corpus Linguistics* (ed. Viana et al., John Benjamins, 2011) and co-author of *Literary Worlds as Contextual Prosodic Theory and Subtext* (John Benjamins, forthcoming).

Dan McIntyre is Professor of English Language and Linguistics at the University of Huddersfield. His research interests encompass stylistics, corpus linguistics and the history of the English language. He has published extensively in these fields, including the books *Language and Style* (Palgrave Macmillan, 2010) and *Point of View in Plays: A Cognitive Stylistic Approach to Viewpoint in Drama and Other Text-Types* (John Benjamins, 2006). He edits the Continuum *Advances in Stylistics* series.

Michaela Mahlberg is Professor in English Language and Linguistics at the University of Nottingham. Her main research interests are in corpus linguistics and contextual approaches to meaning. She is author of *Corpus Stylistics and Dickens's Fiction* (Routledge, 2013), editor of the *International Journal of Corpus Linguistics* and co-editor of the *Corpus and Discourse* series (Bloomsbury).

Jessica Mason is a doctoral researcher at the University of Nottingham. Her research interests bridge cognitive linguistics and education, and she is currently developing narrative interrelation theory (NIT) as a way of understanding the links we make between narratives and the impact this has upon the reading process. This includes working with schools on the application of NIT in literature classrooms.

David S. Miall is Professor in the Department of English and Film Studies at the University of Alberta. His research interests include British Romantic literature, reader response studies (in collaboration with Don Kuiken) including the role of feeling in literary reading, humanities computing and the teaching of English. He has published more than 100 academic papers in these fields and is author of *Literary Reading: Empirical and Theoretical Studies* (Peter Lang, 2006).

Sara Mills is Research Professor in Linguistics at Sheffield Hallam University. Her research interests include feminist linguistics, gender and politeness, feminist postcolonial theory and critical theory. She has published extensively in these areas; her books include *Feminist Stylistics* (Routledge, 1995), *Gender and Politeness* (Cambridge University Press, 2003), *Language and Sexism* (Cambridge University Press, 2008) and *Gender Matters: Feminist Linguistic Analysis* (Equinox, 2012).

Marija Milojkovic is Language Instructor in Contemporary English at the University of Belgrade. Her research interests include corpus stylistics and the language of poetry, as well as corpus-driven translation. She has contributed to the *Journal of Literary Semantics* and to the journal *Research in Corpus Linguistics*, and is co-author of *Literary Worlds as Contextual Prosodic Theory and Subtext* (John Benjamins, forthcoming).

Ruth Page is Reader in English at the University of Leicester. Her research interests bring together feminist narratology and the analysis of narratives in digital contexts. She has published extensively in these fields, and is the author of *Stories and Social Media: Identities and Interaction* (Routledge, 2012) and *Literary and Linguistic Approaches to Feminist Narratology* (Palgrave Macmillan, 2006).

David Peplow is Lecturer at Sheffield Hallam University. His research interests centre on linguistic approaches to social interaction, and in particular interaction within groups. He has published widely on the discourse of reading groups, including as contributor to the journal *Language and Literature* and in *Pragmatics and Literary Stylistics* (ed. Chapman and Davies, Palgrave, forthcoming).

Mick Short is Professor Emeritus of English Language and Literature at Lancaster University. His research centres on stylistic and corpus stylistic approaches to language, including the representation of perspective. He has published numerous books and papers in the field, and is co-author of *Style in Fiction* (Longman, 1981 and 2007) and *Corpus Stylistics* (Routledge, 2007) and author of *Exploring the Language of Poems,*

Plays and Prose (Longman, 1996). He co-founded the Poetics and Linguistics Association and was the founding editor of its international journal, *Language and Literature*.

Paul Simpson is Professor of English Language at Queen's University Belfast. He researches in many areas of English language and linguistics, with an emphasis on applied linguistics. His books in stylistics and critical linguistics include *Language, Ideology and Point of View* (Routledge, 1993), *Language Through Literature* (Routledge, 1997) and *On the Discourse of Satire: Towards a Stylistic Model of Satirical Humour* (John Benjamins, 2003).

Violeta Sotirova is Lecturer in Stylistics at the University of Nottingham. Her research interests centre on the narrative presentation of consciousness in modernist fiction. She has published widely in this field, and is author of *D. H. Lawrence and Narrative Viewpoint* (Continuum, 2011) and *Consciousness in Modernist Fiction: A Stylistic Study* (Palgrave, 2013).

Gerard Steen is Professor of Language Communication at the VU University Amsterdam. His main research interest is metaphor in discourse, and he also works on genre, register, style and rhetoric. He has published more than 15 books, collections and special issues, as well as about 100 articles and book chapters in these fields.

Peter Stockwell is Professor of Literary Linguistics at the University of Nottingham, and a Fellow of the English Association. Among his work in stylistics is *Texture: A Cognitive Aesthetics of Reading* (Edinburgh University Press, 2009), *Cognitive Poetics* (Routledge, 2002), and the co-edited *Language and Literature Reader* (Routledge, 2008) and *Contemporary Stylistics* (Continuum, 2007). He has also published 11 other books and over 80 articles in stylistics, sociolinguistics and applied linguistics, and he edits the Routledge English Language Introductions series.

Michael Stubbs is Professor of English Linguistics at the University of Trier. His central areas of research are English phraseology, text analysis and corpus semantics. He has published over 50 articles and chapters and is author of *Text and Corpus Analysis: Computer-Assisted Studies of Language and Culture* (Blackwell, 1996), *Words and Phrases: Corpus Studies of Lexical Semantics* (Blackwell, 2001) and co-author of *Text Discourse and Corpora* (Continuum, 2007).

Michael Toolan is Professor of English Language at the University of Birmingham. His research centres on the language of literature. He has published over 70 academic papers and his numerous books include *Total Speech: An Integrational Linguistic Approach to Language* (Duke University Press, 1996), *Language In Literature* (1998), *Narrative* (Routledge, 2nd edn, 2001), and *Narrative Progression in the Short Story: A Corpus Stylistic Approach* (John Benjamins, 2009). He is editor of the *Journal of Literary Semantics*.

Katie Wales is Honorary Professor in the Faculty of Arts at the University of Nottingham. Her research interests are wide-ranging and encompass stylistics, rhetoric, Northern English dialectology and the discourse of spiritualist mediums. She has authored nearly 100 publications in these fields and her books include *A Dictionary of Stylistics* (Longman, 3rd edn, 2011), *Personal Pronouns in Present-Day English* (Cambridge University Press, 1996) and *The Language of James Joyce* (Macmillan, 1992).

Sara Whiteley is Lecturer in Language and Literature at the University of Sheffield. Her research focuses on textual effect and interpretation in relation to contemporary literature and from a cognitive poetic perspective. She has contributed articles to the journal *Language and Literature* and her article 'Text World Theory, Real Readers and Emotional Responses to *The Remains of the Day*' won the 2012 Poetics and Linguistics Association prize.

Acknowledgements

The editors and chapter authors would like to thank the following for permission to use copyright material:

- the estate of Marin Sorescu, and his translators and editors Adam Sorkin and Lidia Vance, and Bloodaxe Books for 'Pure Pain' from *The Bridge* (2004);
- James Lasdun and publisher Jonathan Cape Ltd for 'Plague Years' from *The Revenant* (1995);
- the estate of Ted Hughes and publishers Faber and Faber for 'Hawk Roosting' from *Lupercal* (1960);
- Antjie Krog for 'Depressie 1 and 2' from *Verweerskrif* (2006);
- Benjamin Zephaniah and Bloodaxe Books for 'What Stephen Lawrence Taught Us' from *Too Black, Too Strong* (2001); and
- Billy Collins for kind permission to reproduce 'Forgetfulness' from *Questions About Angels* (1991).
- 'Going' and excerpt from 'Aubade' from *Collected Poems* by Philip Larkin; copyright 1998, 2003 by the estate of Philip Larkin; reprinted by permission of Farrar, Strauss and Giroux, LLC in the US and by permission of Faber Ltd elsewhere;
- Copyright in chapter 22 remains with the authors Catherine Emmott and Mark Alexander;
- "Student-Teacher News Is Still Key to Achievement," extract reproduced in Chapter 5. From Detroit Free Press, 9/3/2012 © 2012 Gannett-CN. All rights reserved. Used by permission and protected by the Copyright Laws of the United States. The printing, copying, redistribution, or retransmission of this Content without express written permission is prohibited.

1

Introduction

Peter Stockwell and Sara Whiteley

Stylistics is the proper study of literature. We mean this in several senses. Firstly, it is fit and apt. It is special and specialised. It is delineated by rules and principles, and by reasonable, open and honest argument. And for the evaluative sense of 'proper', we also do mean to suggest that it is ethically superior to other, non-stylistic forms of literary study. We insist that any approach to literary study that does not engage closely with the language in which the literary work appears is by definition indirect, distracted, partial and improper.

The word *stylistics* carries a strong sense of its recent etymology, inheriting a detailed interest in *style* from its French *stylistique* and German *Stilistik* ancestors in the 1950s and 1960s. Stylistics in the English language emerged as a British–American field in the late 1960s, and then developed with a northern European and Australian focus throughout the succeeding decades. There has been a steady broadening of the domain encompassed by the notion of 'style' throughout this period. Initially, stylistic features of a text were restricted to the narrow linguistic elements at the levels of phonetic arrangement, metrics and prosody, morphology and lexical choice, semantics and syntax up to the level of the clause and sentence. Even a restriction of a literary discussion to these features has never made such a discussion *formalist*, to the extent of disregarding matters of performance, utterance, artistic design and aesthetic effect. However, it was easy for others to disparage stylistics on this basis as having a narrow, decontextualised purview.

Those working in early stylistics regarded themselves very strongly as part of a European tradition of textual commentary and theory. Continuities and common concerns were perceived with the Russian Obshchestvo Izucheniia Poeticheskogo Yazyka (the Society for the Study of Poetic Language; the so-called 'Formalists'), with the Prague School and the French Structuralists, and with the New Critics in the USA. For monoglot English-speakers, the influence of the polemical positions of this last group was certainly the loudest, and prohibitions against authorial intention, creative design and artistic production on the one hand and readerly interpretation, emotional response and aesthetic value on the other were easily transferred to stylistics by its critics and also perhaps by some of its practitioners.

In the meantime, a related tradition in German-speaking and northern European countries was developing in which close relationships between rhetoric, stylistics and hermeneutic interpretation were being theorised and practised. Simultaneously in France a highly interpretative practice of stylistic explication, with an emphasis on the relationships between discourse and conscious meaning, was growing strong. These two movements – largely invisible to the monoglot – can certainly not be regarded as decontextualised or formalist at all.

As linguistics developed after the Chomskyan revolution of the 1960s, stylisticians enthusiastically picked up the latest advances in the field. The growth of text linguistics and functional grammar in the 1970s and 1980s offered analytical tools for exploring larger, longer and more complex literary works. The expansion of pragmatics and socio-linguistics around the same time offered similar opportunities for a systematic account of meaningfulness and interpretation. Generative grammar – with its focus on deep structure and relative disinterest in surface features of language – proved itself incapable of advanced stylistic analysis and disappeared from the stylistician's armoury during the 1970s, to be replaced almost exclusively until recently with systemic-functional linguistics.

Since the early 1990s, stylistics has been supercharged not only by further advances in these fields but also by the refinements of quantitative computational methods and by the cognitive turn that has affected almost all arts and humanities research. The use of computers and software programs to work efficiently through vast swathes of language data (as *corpus linguistics*) has revolutionised the study of language. Our under-standing of all aspects of language has been radically affected as a result. New grammars based on spoken forms have been produced, and new dictionaries set out not only the meanings of words as they are actually used in context but also the meanings and usages of phrases, idioms and even particular syntactic sequences. Stylisticians have been able to create digital versions of literary texts, of all the works of an author or period or genre, and devise search-mechanisms to discover features across all of this material. Corpus-stylistic studies can confirm or reject intuitive assertions made by literary scholars; they can provide measured evidence for detailed stylistic analyses; and they can even capture textual features that are so diffused across a long text that they might only be felt subliminally or subconsciously. Many researchers who have been key figures in the devel-opment of corpus linguistics have also had a central interest in literature, as stylisticians.

In parallel with these developments, work broadly in cognitive science has had a huge impact on linguistics and therefore naturally on stylistics too. Many of the advances in cognitive science have involved matters of language, thought and consciousness, and cognitive linguists and cognitive psychologists have been most significant in the development of the field. Much of the key research in cognitive linguistics focused on features that have been of interest to literary stylisticians, such as metaphor and foregrounding. Many researchers who consider themselves straightforwardly as cognitive linguists have also included several literary examples in their work. At the same time, cognitive psychologists were developing an understanding of projected situations and imagined worlds that had obvious relevance to literary fiction. A *cognitive poetics* has emerged largely as a discipline very closely associated with stylistics, to the extent that it is difficult to say which discipline encompasses the other. When stylisticians have drawn on insights from cognitive science, we have been able to offer analyses of readerly knowledge and experience, feelings and emotions, imagined worlds, metaphors, allegories, and the valuations of social significance and personal affect.

All of these traditions are represented in this *Handbook*. As you read through the surveys and discussions, arguments and practical analyses in these chapters, it should become clear that stylistics as *the* discipline of English studies has been elsewhere during the recent history of literary scholarship in the academy. While literary criticism was having a crisis of theory and methodology, especially in the 1980s, stylistics remained largely distant from these debates. Stylisticians were often also the people who taught the courses in English language and linguistics in departments of literature, and so were not regarded as active combatants by their literary colleagues. To a certain extent, this allowed stylistics to carry on unperturbed by the waves of theoretical argument that disturbed litera-ture departments, though of course most stylisticians were aware of the nature of those discussions. Many noted with either irritation or wry amusement the attempts to discuss language by critics who had never conducted a fieldwork collection of language data, never read any modern linguistics beyond the 1950s, had little inkling of work in applied linguis-tics or sociolinguistics, and never thought to engage in a descriptive account of what natural readers were doing when they read literature.

Stylistics today is probably closer to the concerns of literary scholarship in the mainstream than it has ever been. This is a mutual convergence: stylistics has developed systematic ways of addressing matters of value, aesthetics and cultural context; literary criticism has rediscovered matters of 'form' and the necessity of knowing about textuality in order to teach literature to students. However, there remains an uneasy complementar-ity. Literary criticism has largely settled into a form of cultural studies and historiography – essentially a literary branch of the discipline of history. The field of 'English' has thus been mostly vacated and left to those who draw on other disciplines: the social and cognitive sciences on the one hand, and the creative arts and industries on the other. Though stylistics largely occupies the former of these domains, the connections with creative writing in terms of stylistic choice, rhetorical patterning and readerly affect are striking and increasingly obvious. From this perspective, it is an oddity that cultural literary studies remains central in departments of English across the world, and surely this will eventually be corrected. Already it is apparent that there is a demand for an integrated language and literature curriculum being voiced from several sources including schools, students and second-language learners who see it as empowering, from governments and employers who see it as a defined set of skills and tangible training, and from academics who perhaps would like to have their work professionalised and raised in prestige.

The situation, however, is patchy around the world. Stylistics is strongest in Britain and northern Europe, with inroads across southern Europe, eastern Europe and the Middle East. It is also a strong presence generally in the English-speaking or English-using world, from Australia and New Zealand, across the Indian sub-continent, and in southern Africa, and throughout east and south-east Asia. For historical and institutional reasons that are addressed by several contributors to this *Handbook*, stylistics has remained until very recently neglected in North America and particularly in the USA. However, we must remember that stylistics goes by different names across the world, and any of the following labels usually refers to analytical practices that are recognisable as stylistics: literary linguistics, literary semantics, literary pragmatics, English language studies, poetics, rhetoric, critical linguistics, corpus stylistics, literary discourse analysis, cultural stylistics and cognitive poetics. Though stylistics is unlikely to be seen as a course title in the USA very soon, there is a great deal of activity in cognitive rhetoric, composition and cognitive approaches to literature, and towards a science of literary analysis that would certainly be recognisable to stylisticians elsewhere in the world.

As a discipline, stylistics is *progressive, systematic, transparent, replicable, evidential* and *textually grounded*. It is progressive in the sense that frameworks and approaches that are tried out and shown not to work are generally abandoned in favour of a better analysis: so in the 1970s it became apparent that generative grammar could not provide a stylistic account, and almost no one these days tries to return to it. Compare literary scholarship, where archaeological oddities or poetic expressions that have been superseded as scientific models (such as psychoanalysis, for example, or an understanding of language from the early twentieth century) are still used as the basis for apparently serious literary commentary.

Stylistics is systematic in several senses. Models for analysis tend to be part of larger methodological domains, so features of language are viewed within a generally consistent theory of language. The method of stylistics is also systematic in that the terms of the analytical framework are clearly set out first and then applied rigorously. The method does not emerge from the analysis. Furthermore, the objects of investigation (stylistic features or readerly effects) are available for investigation in the world outside the domain of stylistics: in other words, stylistic features are not constructed by the process of analysis itself. While it cannot be said that stylistics is objective (except in very narrowly restricted and non-interesting matters of linguistic facts), it is certainly an intersubjective discipline.

Stylistic descriptions have a tradition towards transparency and clarity in their exposition. This is perhaps a legacy of the pedagogic basis of many stylisticians as English-language or second-language teachers. As a stylistician you are regarded as a good practitioner if you can be clearly understood even by new students of the discipline. Obfuscation and deliberate obscurity are not well regarded, and stylisticians prefer a common currency of technical terminology rather than a personal vocabulary or the false scholasticism of 'scare-quotes' round ordinary language terms as a marker of false profundity.

Stylistic explanations aim towards a form of replicability, where possible. This represents the influence of a scientific approach to investigation, where the only valid statements are falsifiable ones. This is not straightforward when dealing with the subjective and perhaps idiosyncratic effects of foregrounding or readerly construal: two readings of the same text might generate different stylistic analyses. However, stylistics aims to be intersubjective, and analytical explanations are offered in an open and transparent articulation precisely so that later readers and stylisticians can see the working of the analysis and compare it with their own work or reading response. The aim is to present yourself not as the most interestingly eccentric and innovative reader, but as someone who presents a generalisable and recognisable explanation of literary effects.

It is self-evident that stylistics is evidential, in that stylistic arguments are only presented for verification if they are accompanied by data from the literary work or reading. The authority of the stylistician or the rhetorical skill of the account does not determine the success of the argument as stylistics. Even where stylistic work draws heavily on psychology rather than linguistics, the predominant source of the supporting evidence is grounded in the text itself, or in inferences, associations and consequences that are clearly defined as arising from the text itself. In this sense, and for all its other aliases, stylistics retains a central emphasis on style as its validating principle.

Back in 1991, one of the contributors to this volume suggested that there could not be a handbook of stylistics because, at that time, the practice had no agreed methodology, no agreed method or protocol, no clear sense of the field – in other words, it could not be said to be a discipline. In this sense, it echoed the famous distinction made by Henry

Widdowson, who observed in 1975 that English was a subject and linguistics was a discipline. Stylistics could not be encapsulated in a handbook because it was not sufficiently disciplinary, and still drew its ethos from literary scholarship, even though the two sat in an uneasy relationship with each other.

We believe this perspective is no longer true, and the *Handbook* in front of you demonstrates the proof of that. It is arranged into five parts. These reflect the slightly different audiences that might pick up the book, and we have tried to look in several directions at once. In Part I, our contributors set out and explore the discipline of stylistics. That stylistics is a coherent discipline is sometimes obscured by the fact that eclecticism is held as a central principle by many stylisticians. In other words, there has always been an artisanal edge to practice in the field, and this means that stylistic work has often proceeded on a practical basis, without being over-anxious about theoretical or philosophical issues. There has very much been a sense among stylisticians that if a particular linguistic model can contribute some insight to the literary text in hand, then it is worth pursuing. Stylisticians are sometimes wed closely to particular linguistic models or approaches, but more often than not will adapt frameworks from across the range of available linguistic scholarship. Equally, stylisticians generally do not seem to feel themselves tied to a particular literary historical period or mode, as literary critics tend to organise themselves both intellectually and institutionally. There is a risk, of course, in exploring the language of Geoffrey Chaucer one day and Raymond Chandler the next, but there are also benefits of insight and comparison to be gained, as well as a degree of intellectual agility being exercised.

Having said this, there have been many notable and serious statements over the years that seek to position stylistics as a theoretically rigorous as well as a productive practice. In the past, these have been rather defensive and reactive, often produced in response to a critique from outside the discipline. Michael Toolan opens this collection with an argument and discussion that is not at all defensive, but is perhaps more subtle and open to wider theoretical and critical viewpoints. We take this easiness and calmness as a sign of maturity in the field. Equally, Katie Wales, in her chapter, queries our remit of setting out the 'tool-kit' of stylistics, preferring again a more complex and nuanced view of the stylistic method, while recognising that there is a discernible and coherent methodological approach in the work of most stylisticians.

The other four chapters of this first section of the book turn the field over in different dimensions, viewing it from related aspects. Michael Stubbs takes the domain of quantitative methods as a major theme in stylistic work. He considers both the nature of textual evidence, and its theoretical relationship with literary reading; his thinking stands as an interesting counterpoint to the two previous chapters. Craig Hamilton considers stylistics as part of the millennia-old practice of rhetoric, delineating a direct thread from ancient observations about style and performance to our modern thinking informed by the sciences of linguistics, psychology and cognition. Lastly in this orientating section, Ronald Carter and Geoff Hall reflect on the nature of stylistics as a form of applied linguistics and as literary criticism, respectively.

Part II of the book takes the latter perspective and sets out a series of contributions on themes that are of particular interest for students and scholars of literature. We set our contributors a range of concepts commonly discussed in literary commentary, in order to gain an insight into these concepts from a rigorous stylistic perspective. In Beatrix Busse's work on genre, Patrick Colm Hogan on intertextual allusion, and Violeta Sotirova on literary production and intentionality, we can see the extent to which modern stylistics can address issues that have traditionally been considered to be far beyond the confines of textuality. These are core themes in contemporary literary scholarship. We also consider the interests of non-academic but engaged literary observers and students in addressing key notions that most people outside universities and colleges talk about: character (in Dan McIntyre's chapter), narrative voice (in Christiana Gregoriou's), and the nature of plots and their echoes in a reader's other experience (in Jessica Mason's). Lastly in this section, we return to the key foundational notion of literary defamiliarisation with Joanna Gavins and view it afresh from a contemporary cognitive stylistic angle, and we take examples of canonical literary texts and view their intensity and power through a similar approach by Barbara Dancygier.

In Part III of the book, we turn to the interests of readers primarily concerned with linguistics and its application to literary texts. We focus on stylistic techniques and key features, with an arrangement of chapters that is intended to recall classic stylistics in moving up the linguistic rank scale from phonology, morphology and lexis, to syntax and semantics, to matters of transitivity and pragmatics, up to text and discourse-level features such as metaphor, foregrounding and dialogue. Manuel Jobert begins with a reconsideration of the relationship between sound and text in an examination of paralinguistic vocal features in literature. Michaela Mahlberg uses corpus stylistics to explore the local grammars in Dickens. Bill Louw and Marija Milojkovic also draw on corpus linguistics in order to discuss subtle matters of subtextual meaning. Paul Simpson and Patricia Canning show how matters of grammatical transitivity contribute to viewpoint, actions and descriptions in a range of literary examples. Billy Clark explores inference from a pragmatics perspective. At an even more discourse-based level, Gerard Steen explores metaphor across a poem, Catherine Emmott and Marc Alexander discuss foregrounding and its opposite 'burying' in detective fiction. Mick Short distils four decades of stylistic experience in his discussion of dialogue presentation. And Peter Stockwell aims to develop a stylistic account of the most rarefied and subliminal effects of textual ambience, by drawing on both corpus linguistics and cognitive grammar.

In Part IV of the book, we adopt a perspective alongside the natural reader of literature, to explore the contextual experience of reading. Olga Fischer considers the central feature for stylistics of iconic connections between form and meaning in literary texts. Sara Whiteley develops a cognitive poetic account of how readers and characters are ethically positioned. Alison Gibbons shows that the stylistics of fictionality can offer a rich account even of experimental texts such as mobile interactive narratives. David Miall places the feelings and emotions of literary readers centrally in his empirical stylistic focus. Ruth Page shows how the analysis of narrative structure provides insight into the connections between a real-world narrative and its creative literary reflection. Tracy Cruickshank demonstrates that stylistic analysis also brings a fresh view to literary work on drama and performance. Lesley Jeffries proposes a model of communication to address again the important relationship between analysis and interpretation. And Joe Bray shows how stylistic analysis can make historical literary criticism richer and more evidential. Overall, the chapters in this section demonstrate in practical terms how the key questions for literary readers can be sharpened or resolved by a stylistic sensibility.

Finally, the last part of the book, Part V, recognises that stylistics has developed closely alongside applied linguistics and critical discourse analysis. Though the centre of gravity of the discipline has been literary stylistics, there is a great deal of work that shares the same approaches and methods in the analysis of other sorts of discourses. Some of these can be regarded as semi-literary, perhaps like certain advertising or media texts. All of the chapters in Part V demonstrate the continuities and the points of differentiation between literary and other sites of language. Marina Lambrou and Alan Durant show that a media stylistics can fruitfully adapt many of the same features and methods in evidence across the rest of this book. Rodney Jones looks at how a stylistic analysis of advertising discourse can reveal issues of genre, ethics and authenticity. Jonathan Charteris-Black takes an expansive view of the style of politicians, encompassing a close corpus analysis of deixis, pronouns and other inclusive and exclusive markers, and even taking in gender-projection as political image-making. Sara Mills explores the social differentiation of gender and power in personal relationships through a precise analysis of a contemporary novel. Benedict Lin considers the crucial importance of stylistic training in a translation of a Chinese poem. David Peplow draws on discourse analysis to show the continuities between creative and everyday patterns of conversation. It should be apparent from these examples that there is a mutually reinforcing and positive feedback mechanism between literary stylistics and its fellow-disciplines in applied linguistics, media studies and critical discourse analysis.

We end the book with a short reflective coda, in the form of an editorial dialogue about stylistics, its place in the world and its future. This format has been adopted explicitly in a few other chapters in the book: in Chapter 6, we interviewed Ronald Carter and recorded the conversation; in Chapter 18, Bill Louw and Marija Milojkovic conduct a written assertion-and-critique discussion. In truth, all of the chapters in this book have been the result of conversations, reflections, criticisms and further thinking. Our intention in presenting some chapters in the form of a Socratic dialogue is partly to reflect this co-operative endeavour in the discipline of stylistics, and also to echo the fact that the field has an ancient and rich pedigree.

Some chapters are principally theoretical and reflective in tone, and others are eminently practical. Almost all of them include an exemplary piece of stylistic analysis. The set of literary works covered is wide ranging: there is extended treatment, in order of appearance, of Raymond Chandler, Joseph Conrad, Khushwant Singh, Virginia Woolf, Dennis Potter, the crime writing and detective fiction of Agatha Christie and John Boyne, Stephen Chbosky, William Golding, Billy Collins, William Wordsworth, Edith Wharton, Charles Dickens, W. B. Yeats, David Lynch, Miranda July, Emily Dickinson, James Lasdun, Julia Darling, Marin Sorescu, Colum McCann, Seamus Heaney, John Keats, John Fowles, Ted Hughes, T. S. Eliot, Antjie Krog, Kazuo Ishiguro, Blast Theory, William Blake, Graham Greene, Benjamin Zephaniah, Richard Bean, Jez Butterworth, Peter Sansom, Jane Austen, Christos Tsiolkas and others. What is striking and astonishing about this list is its historical range, its coverage of poetry, prose, drama, hyperfiction and art installations, and its non-differentiation between high canonical and more populist literary works. There are also numerous shorter treatments or examples drawn from, among many others, early Sanskrit, Bertolt Brecht, Roald Dahl, Louis de Bernières, Henry James, James Kelman, Brett Easton Ellis, Sebastian Faulks, Lewis Carroll, D. H. Lawrence, Ian McEwan, Jack Kerouac, John Le Carré, David Mitchell, James Joyce, Bob Dylan and so on.

We have aimed to provide a handbook of stylistics that stands as a practical guide, a source of reflection and critical engagement, a reference for scholars, a showcase for the discipline, and a shining example for literary criticism, applied linguistics and in fact anyone interested in language and literature. Whenever we have taught stylistics to students encountering it for the first time, we have seen revelation light up in their faces: here is a way of approaching literary scholarship that is professional, disciplined and empowering.

Part I

The discipline
of stylistics

2

The theory and philosophy of stylistics

Michael Toolan

The theories of stylistics

A chapter on the theory of stylistics should describe 'that department of an art or technical subject which consists in the knowledge or statement of the facts on which it depends, or of its principles or methods, as distinguished from the *practice* of it' (OED definition of *theory*). What, then, are the facts or knowledge, or the principles or methods, which underpin and justify the practices of stylistics? These are the questions, I believe, that an enquiry into the theory of stylistics should address. Accordingly, I will not discuss style itself, as a concept or theory (see Lang 1987; Nagy 2005), nor attempt a full survey of stylistic history and practice (Nørgaard et al. 2010; Wales 2011), nor comment on theoretical studies of specific aspects of style (e.g. those on poetic rhythm and metre from Attridge 2005; Cureton 2001; Fabb et al. 2008). Nor do I address the theories of stylistics, or applications of linguistics in the study of verbal art that have developed even in closely related traditions such as those of French or German academia, let alone more distant ones such as in India or China. Rather, I discuss a much smaller field: those principles and assumptions that are most frequently invoked as the grounds for doing what is done, when academics using western traditions of linguistic analysis undertake stylistic analyses of literary texts written in English.

It is worth asserting at the outset that stylistics does have a theory – or that different forms of stylistics reflect different underlying theories, clearly articulated or otherwise. In large degree the theories stylisticians at least tacitly invoke are theories of language, which they inherit from the particular kind of linguistics (systemic-functional, corpus, cognitive, etc.) they chiefly employ. But like other specialist fields that occupy an intermediate position between larger disciplines (such as discourse analysis, and more especially critical discourse analysis; or forensic linguistics) stylistics has sometimes been described as all practice and no coherent theory. It is reassuring then to find that Peter Barry (2009: 203) considers this question in his popular overview of literary and cultural theory aimed at undergraduates, and decides that for all its enjoyable practical methods it is not untheoretical. Moreover he evidently regards it as theoretical enough to warrant a full chapter to itself. Likewise Terry Eagleton's widely used *Literary Theory: An Introduction* (1983) has a long chapter on structuralism and semiotics, much of it devoted to stylistics (it also begins with the Russian Formalists, and literary language – which is where quite a few stylisticians began their own theorising).

What Eagleton warns about literary theory applies equally to stylistics theory. Much as he says of literary theory, we can say of stylistics theory that it is a metadiscourse, an interrogation of a cultural and academic practice; it is not just another way of 'doing stylistics', but an attempt to consider the assumptions of those ways of doing stylistics. And, as Eagleton warns, theory 'tends to suspect that much of what is said [within the discipline or practice] is question-begging' (1983: viii). By way now of situating stylistics and its theory in relation to impressionistic literary commentary, we can turn to a few of Eagleton's comments on poems and their readers in another of his books, and see what questions these beg.

Putting impressionism in its place (before or after stylistic analysis)

At the outset of his primer for the literarily perplexed, *How to Read a Poem* (2007), Eagleton regrets the lack of close reading by students today:

> What gets left out is the literariness of the work. Most students can say things like 'the moon imagery recurs in the third verse, adding to the sense of solitude', but not many of them can say things like 'the poem's strident tone is at odds with its shambling syntax'.   *(Eagleton 2007: 3)*

Evidently in Eagleton's view it would be a good thing if students could talk about the stridency or otherwise of a poem's tone, and about shambling syntax (he doesn't here say why, and stylisticians are among those least likely to challenge him on this). But what *are* stridency of tone and shambling syntax? 'Shambling' and 'strident' are, for apprentices, too contentual, impressionistic and unverifiable as ways of talking about syntax and tone. So Eagleton needs to explain to his student readers what he means by shambling syntax, stridency and so on, in clear and coherent ways. He is a brilliant writer and critic, so he stands a chance of doing so. A rapid search of *How to Read a Poem*, however, suggests that Eagleton never returns to the terms 'shambling' and 'strident' after page 3, whereas he himself continually alludes to the 'imagery' in the texts he analyses, which contrasts sharply with the practice of John Lennard (2006: xv) in another influential primer, who finds the term *image* so vague or varied in sense as to be best avoided altogether. In fairness it should be noted that Eagleton (2007) has a brilliant closing section on imagery (2007: 138–42), despite concluding that the theory of imagery 'is in something of a mess' (2007:141).

Eagleton's discussion of syntax in poems (2007: 121–4) is more expressive than informative. The opening point, that 'A good many poetic effects are achieved through syntax', might suggest a lengthier treatment than the two-page commentary on three extracts found there. But it is clear from that commentary that Eagleton simply isn't equipped to offer a lengthier and more explanatory treatment. Of the grammar of the opening lines of Edward Thomas's 'Old Man' (the title is the name of a herb) he writes:

> The jagged, knotted syntax struggles to unpack the poet's constantly
> swerving thoughts about the plant he is contemplating. As it does so, its
> hesitations, stops and starts and doublings-back act out something of the
> convolutions and self-qualifications of his response to the herb.
>
> *(Eagleton 2007: 122)*

Enjoyable as this is to read, even its author seems to realise that it is not explanatory. Soon he is complaining that a Yeats poem 'almost deliberately provokes us into belletristic waffle', and evidently could not resist: 'The last line, with its artful change of key, is a kind of final flourish to this masterly performance, with its look-no-hands bravura' (Eagleton 2007: 123).

It is stylistics that undertakes to be precise, analytical and verifiable about the grammar that underlies and creates the literariness effects which in turn induce readers to reach for such complex evaluative terms as *shambling, strident, alienated, terse, passionate, placid* and so on. Stylisticians should not be dismissive of these powerfully synthesising and summarising evaluative terms – their existence makes stylistics possible, and wide agreement that a particular passage is strident or shambling or restless helps allay anxieties about conflictingly various textual intepretation. They have an important place in literary reading, but one that stylistics endeavours to keep distinct from that of analysis.

Nevertheless the piling up of value-laden judgements, with limited further explanation, can oppress the reader. As early as page 4 of his poetry primer, Eagleton has reached interim conclusions about the opening sentence of a famous Auden poem:

> The tone of the piece is urbane but not hard-boiled. It is civilised, but
> not camp or overbred, as some of Auden's later poetry.   *(Eagleton 2007: 4)*

The problem with this is that readers who fail to register stridency of tone are unlikely to be able to say (let alone understand) that another poem's tone is urbane, but neither hard-boiled nor camp nor overbred. So one must learn all these discriminating evaluations – and it seems that the chief way Eagleton will teach these labels is by using them in his own commentaries. In the best outcome, if you read enough Eagleton commentaries on poems and if these are consistent in their usage of these labels and if you encounter no contrasting uses of them by other critics, you may in time grasp what he means by a hard-boiled tone and a camp one. Even this uncertain understanding will not proceed smoothly, or without loss to self, if as is likely you are already familiar with these labels in various other contexts, and wonder if they are more charged than explanatory in the present text-analytical context.

In brief, Eagleton's guide is actually an autobiographical report – *How I read poems* – with innumerable subtle insights on poems' effects but few explanations. Stylistics believes such explanations are needed ('show your working', as the maths exams say), and are possible, and sets out to build them. Not without difficulty. But we stylisticians are sobered by the thought that while we may hope to be more explanatory than Eagleton, we will never produce an introduction half as entertaining as his.

Knowledge/facts

Here are some of the things that most stylisticians take as foundational knowledge or facts:

i. That as David Lodge famously said about novelists at the opening of *Language of Fiction* (1966: ix) but could be said in large part about all writers and speakers, literary or not, everything they do is done in and through language. Language is central to the meaning, or effects on readers (it is not clear that the two can be rigorously distinguished), of texts. In a world as full of texts spoken and written as ours, a rich reflexive study of all aspects of speech and writing is guaranteed. Hence our departments and institutions devoted to speech communication, speech and language therapy, literary criticism, linguistics, languages, media studies, creative writing, journalism, literary studies, and so on. And these are just the institutions concerned centrally with speaking and writing almost as ends in themselves, without sharp constraints on content, as distinct from disciplines like law and history in which writing plays a large role.

ii. That among all the linguistic communicative activities practised by a culture, a special place has arisen, especially for those whose living conditions allow them several hours per week of 'free' or leisure time, for reading and talking about literature. At one time in western culture much of that reading would have been scriptural or religious (and not quite conceived as 'leisure' activity), but that time is largely past. In the twenty-first century, and notwithstanding local wars and recessions, more members of western countries have more opportunities to spend their leisure time in more ways than ever before; and still a significant proportion read novels, go to plays, sample the odd poem, join reading groups, and flock to film adaptations of memorable stories.

iii. That literary texts can be as short and sweet as a two-line haiku, can be devoid of overt metaphor or other figures, lacking in patterning of any kind, childlike in vocabulary and syntax, but rarely are. Much more often and typically (but again, not definitionally, as necessary conditions) literary texts are complex and sophisticated creations in such terms as those just mentioned; and this is no surprise since (along with statutes and diplomatic agreements and love letters) they are among the most crafted and re-drafted texts in the culture, and usually composed by experts, desperate to get it right. If the literary author is an expert writer like the legal or diplomatic draughtsperson, they also often have the anguish and personal investment of the inexpert author of a love letter.

iv. That all linguistic communications within a linguistic community draw on that community's knowledge of linguistic forms, structures and effects as encountered in a host of situations. Since literary texts are such exceptionally considered and designed uses (or exploitations, or floutings) of those forms, structures and effects, we are justified in attending to them very closely in accounting for what those texts mean, to readers.

v. That stylisticians' consideration of the craft and design of texts and their shaping of reader response assumes the author has made multiple critical choices in the composing: they have chosen these forms and contents in preference to others (and, sometimes, relatively easily specified alternatives), and the particular choices are effective in ways that the alternatives would not have been.

vi. That the meanings readers derive from a text are not sourced in the text alone; the text is not an icon or island, despite its linguistic boundedness. Commentary is radically incomplete, without a consideration of the role of intertextuality and the reader's recognition of echoed or alluded-to texts and events, in the reading of a poem. Similarly, a reader's familiarity with different genres and their conventions, and with literary history more generally (or their unfamiliarity with all these), will clearly affect their response and interpretation. In Simpson's terms (2000: 3) stylistics 'acknowledges that utterances (literary or otherwise) are produced in a time, a place, and in a cultural and cognitive context'. These wider contexts interact with the text, so that a grammatical study of the latter always needs to be integrated with consideration of the former. Still, a grammar of the unvarying language of the text is a good deal more feasible than a grammar of its infinitely variable contexts of reception, which is why stylisticians concentrate on the former and approach the latter mostly by way of the former.

vii. That stylisticians mostly select literary texts because they are highly valued and highly crafted, deemed worthy of being the focus of university degree studies, for example. At the heart of these texts' power, we believe, is the exceptionally sophisticated deployment of linguistic resources within them, linguistic resources which scholars only incompletely understand. Additionally, even enthusiastic readers, such as committed members of reading groups or students taking literature degrees, may struggle to find a way of talking about these texts that is comprehensible to others and advances their own insight into the writing. For these reasons – to advance our understanding of literary linguistic phenomena primarily, and to share this understanding with readers of literature (a very large constituency, potentially) – stylisticians select texts or extracts as examples, test cases and forms of linguistic challenge. They do so, focusing on the text's craft and often original design, very much as musicologists and art critics develop systematic analyses of symphonies and paintings. And, like the latter, stylisticians' labours cannot come to an end: not only because the next decade's readership of Shakespeare's Sonnet 118 or audience for Bach's St John Passion may respond to these differently from earlier ones, but also because in a decade or two the theory and practices of linguistics and musicology that might be brought to bear may be different from those extant at present.

viii. That comprehensive stylistic analysis of any text is impossible; selectivity and sampling are always involved and these in turn cannot be finally rooted in high principle or an abstract theoretical position, but in the low pragmatics of finitudes of time, energy and interest. Analogously, there is no rule or theory to tell us how long to stand looking at Rembrandt's *The Night Watch* in the Rijksmuseum or how many times is 'sufficient' for listening to Beethoven's *Grosse Fuge* quartet. So stylisticians' claims about the virtues of their analyses' greater precision and detail in the description of textual effects have to be made with care: the objection that an analysis has too much detail is not always easy to rebut, although it may be rebuttable in light of the particular purposes it serves. A close-up study of a picture's surface may make it impossible to take in the picture as a whole; but if that study has a different purpose from whole-picture apprehension, such as understanding the deployment of pixels or brushstrokes, then it is justified. Generally, stylisticians avoid assuming a sharp separation between the 'lay' readers' reading and their own technical analyses, since the technical analyses derive their strongest rationale from being explanatory accounts of the effects that a text's texture works upon the ordinary reader.

ix. That stylistics has proven invaluable to students of literature, thanks to its clear, accurate, detailed, systematic and illuminating scrutiny of the language of literary texts. Stylistics has been performing that service for many decades; a few of the earliest and still useful studies include Leech (1969), Nowottny (1962) and Cluysenaar (1976); numerous publications since then have continued this work. As Lambrou and Stockwell (2007: 4) note, over and above the detailed grammatical descriptions based on explicit criteria afforded by stylistics, doing stylistics (or thinking about texts stylistically) can produce 'startling, pleasurable and perspective-changing moments in reading'. It can also prompt startling adjustments to the way you conceptualise reading more generally, and writing, and language.

x. Most stylistic analyses negotiate covertly if not overtly certain core assumptions about literary text. These include the idea that meanings will be 'more integrated' in literary texts than elsewhere (or at least that to read a text as literature is to *expect* a full and rich integration); that reader attention will be guided by textual patterns – noticeably repeated forms or the 'gap' of a noticeably absent form – to segments which are especially important in the creating of effects (i.e. foregrounded); and that there may be a degree of 'fit' between the foregrounded forms and the perceived meanings or effects so that the form may be called iconic. Iconicity in text, using language that is otherwise typically symbolic, is itself remarkable, if not an attempted impossibility. Language is symbolic in that the addressee's attention will usually turn from the signs used to the ideas and entities they represent; but when it is partly iconic, the signs seem partly to *embody* or *perform* the ideas and entities expressed, and the addressee is less impelled to turn their attention away from or beyond the form. Iconic text invites the reader/addressee to focus on the text for its own sake, to gloss – approximately – one of Jakobson's ideas in his famous article of 1960 (see Toolan 2010 for a commentary on Jakobson and equivalence, and Toolan 2011 for some proposals regarding repetition in literature).

xi. That, treated segregationally, feature by feature, a literary text is not radically different from any other linguistic act, spoken or written: it may or may not have more metaphors, more – or more complex – modality, more deixis, more transitivity, more blends, more text-worlds, more iconicity, and so on, than any given nonliterary text. A short poem may have fewer of all the aforementioned items than, say, a magazine advertisement promoting a brand of perfume but the former may still, taken as a whole, remain much more intellectually interesting. That is because, treated as the textual core of an integrated communicational event, the literary text is different, and aims to be. As our culture suggests to us, the successful poem requires a level of creativity and inspiration far beyond that of the successful advertisement; because verbally gifted as copy-writers are, those gifts are slight in comparison with the poet's; because while both texts will have been worked on, the kinds of revision and critique that attend a poem – long after its publication as well as before its completion – tend to far outreach those of the advertisement. Most importantly of all, for many in the culture, the literary text is 'religious' in ways that the advertisement or other verbal form is not. Here I use the term 'religious' to denote a host of concepts, with some family resemblance, frequently invoked when the powers and purposes of literature in modern society are alluded to: an exceptional insight into specific (invented) individuals, and by extension into the lives of real individuals, including the reader; explanations of the coherence or incoherence of human existence; verbal pictures that 'strike through the mask' of banality to probe hidden motivations; 'deep' analysis; indications of the meanings of things, including human life or glimpses of a transcendent reality or consolation.

Stylistics as grammar

Against the above background, stylisticians operate in relation to a number of further principles and difficulties. Firstly, I will argue that stylistic explanation of the relations between textual form and literary function is a specialist grammatical commentary. Accordingly, a theory of literary stylistics is at core a theory of grammar. In both these claims, I intend the term 'grammar' to be capaciously understood, so as to include synoptic description of the prominent licensed patterns of phrasal and clausal structuring (sequencing) of words in the language generally (see Sampson 2007 on grammar as the network of beaten tracks through the landscape that is a language), but also to reach much further than this to include genre- and register-sensitive norms and patternings, and departures therefrom. If the bases of the more interpretive categories that a particular stylistic study invokes (text-worlds, deictic shifts, cognitive blends, empathetic alignment, etc.) are not derived from a grammar of text (widely conceived), then the study is not a stylistic one.

By way of exploring the idea that stylistic studies are contributions towards a grammar of literary texts, I want to examine in some detail a stylistic analysis published in 1970, thus more than 40 years ago, by the distinguished linguist James P. Thorne. The essential steps in Thorne's argument are, I contend, still typical of most stylistic studies today, even though descriptive frameworks and technological affordances are greatly changed, because it attempts to trace interpretive impressions back to sources in the grammar that 'generated' the text. Thorne writes: 'What the impressionistic terms of stylistics are impressions of are types of grammatical structures' (1970: 188). Thorne was a generative linguist, and he sees an affinity between stylistics and generative grammar since both are essentially mentalistic: 'In both cases the most important data are responses relating to what is intuitively known about language structures' (1970: 44). Earlier grammars' failure to animate stylistics are said to stem from linguists' attention being restricted almost entirely to directly observable structural facts in or about language, and their neglect of mentalistic responses, and 'what is intuitively known [by poets and readers] about language structure' (1970: 188) and deep structure aspects rather than only 'those structural facts which can be directly related to what is observable in language' (1970: 189). Thorne's championing of mentalistic generative grammar has interesting echoes in more recent emphases on the psychology of the reader or on the cognitive underpinnings of linguistic choices, discussed later.

Such a distinction creates a clear mission for the stylistician: that of uncovering and bringing to attention various deep structure facts or characteristics that give the surface text the style it has and which we readers respond to. In this respect, the mission is a sophisticated variant of the more general idea that stylistics is a consciousness-raising exercise, bringing to the conscious attention of the reader those underlying or overlooked linguistic phenomena of the text that are instrumental in its subtle achievement of meanings and effects (effects that the less tutored reader may sense they are deriving, but whose source they cannot quite pinpoint). Much the same position is to be found in an article by Ronald Carter (1982) on Hemingway's story 'Cat in the Rain', an exemplary demonstration of the stylistic approach and frequently used in teaching for that reason. Much as Thorne did, Carter argues that his (our) interpretive intuitions about the opening paragraphs of a literary text such as the Hemingway story 'are to a large extent conditioned by linguistic patterning' – patternings that the linguist or stylistician is well placed to identify and describe.

Foregrounding and iconic aptness

At this point a crucial question becomes: which patterns? How do we know which patterns are the major ones involved in prompting our interpretive intuitions, rather than being only minor ones? Carter's answer is 'those that are most striking', meaning here 'striking to the analyst'. This was the essence of Thorne's answer too (see below): he was 'struck' by the frequency of *I VP-ed and I VP-ed* structures, and relied on absence of reader demurral. (Strangeness, or defamiliarisation, has long been a touchstone of formalist criticism.) The conventional metaphor of 'strikingness' is very prominent in this phase of the stylistic analysis; it is a variant of more abstract formulations in terms of 'foregroundedness' or 'prominence' or 'markedness', but they amount to the same move in the argument, which is subjective at source, even if the analyst can persuade their readers of the reasonableness of their identification of what is striking or foregrounded. Slightly more detached or abstract are formulations in terms of what is statistically or situationally prominent (a speech in which every other word is *like*), or disproportionate in frequency (a paragraph in which every verb is in the progressive), or situationally non-congruent (an insurance policy which uses slang). Thirty years later, Jeffries and McIntyre (2010) go through quite similar steps as Carter or Thorne before them with their first brief demonstration of stylistic method: they select the word *forget*, from lines in a James Fenton poem that run *How comforting it is, once or twice a year, / To get together and forget the old times* as 'unusual' (2010: 5) and foregrounded. They appeal to intuitions and collocational associations to justify this singling out, and then hazard an explanation: Fenton's marked choice makes us focus our attention on the absurdity of actively trying to forget something, they suggest.

If the subjectivity of foregrounding selections has been a weakness in stylistic studies, it is one that cognitive poetics (Stockwell 2002) may help to address. The kinds of phenomena that cognitive poetics centrally draws on in its explanations include ideas about figure and ground, prototypicality, deixis or perspective, script and schema, metaphor, text-worlds and mental spaces. A great many of these are accounts of human forms of attention, and of selective and discriminating attention, in our making sense of the world and its signs. They address the fact that whatever object or scene we contemplate, there are always a great many more differences we *could* attend to than, in all the circumstances, it is useful or appropriate for us to attend to. Any signifying complex, including a literary text, may make prominent (or foreground) some features rather than others, to direct the recipient's attention. So a calculation as to what kinds of attention to which distinguishable phenomena is merited (or relevant) is always going on, and cognitive poetics undertakes to explain some of the fundamental principles, many of them universals (underpinning non-literature cultures as much as literate ones) rather than language- or culture-specific, underpinning the sense-making faculties of human beings in their embodied existence. These principles may in time put stylisticians' decisions as to the striking patterns and foregrounding in a text on a much firmer footing.

A Spitzerian circle or spiral is sometimes said to operate: a text is read, and from that initial reading, first (verbal) impressions and responses (usually from the stylistician him- or herself, and/or from a sample of other readers) emerge; the stylistician returns to the text to identify the prominent (foregrounded) patterns or deviations, and seeks to describe and explain them in linguistic (perhaps cognitive-linguistic) detail. The analyst attempts both to identify what it is in the text's patterns (its form) that induces the impressions first noted, and to integrate these effects into an evaluation and interpretation that others might accept. These form-interpretation relations will rarely be statable as absolute free-standing rules, but a generalisable descriptive grammar of literary texts remains the long-term goal of stylistics. Attempts may be made to confirm the plausibility of the form-interpretation conjunctive statements via controlled testing of reader-subjects; but even when it is not, the stylistician's very act of presenting or publishing their analysis puts it in a public domain where every reader or listener can assay its claims. In passing, it is noteworthy that Thorne attributes 'impressionistic terms' (complex, terse, etc.) to stylistics, the implication being that linguists or grammarians can usefully unpack these impressionistic categories. Only a very few years later it became customary for stylisticians to attribute the vague, subjective and impressionistic terms to literary critics and readers, with the stylistician brought in, as expert, to explain what lay behind such terms in relation to a given text. An interesting shift in job demarcations and the characterisations of experts and amateurs evidently occurred – but the underlying steps in the analytical proceeding are unchanged.

There is one important way in which Thorne's ambitions differ from those of most stylistics today, and from my suggestion that stylistic analyses are contributions towards a grammar of literary texts. On the basis of what appear to be specific deviant rules of composition in single poems by Donne and Roethke and others, Thorne speculates that every poem has its own distinct dialect, so 'the task that faces the reader [of a poem] is in some ways like that of learning a new language (or dialect)' (Thorne 1970: 194). Stylisticians today tend to assume that a language is much less sharply determinate and bounded, and would lean far less heavily on the idea that poems are dialectally distinct from the circumambient language.

Thorne on Chandler

How in practice does Thorne proceed? His most fully worked example in the 1970 article is a grammatical analysis of a virtuoso passage in Raymond Chandler's crime novel *The Lady in the Lake* (1943). The first-person narrator is Philip Marlowe, a private detective:

> An elegant handwriting, like the elegant hand that wrote it. I pushed it to one side and had another drink. I began to feel a little less savage. I pushed things around on the desk. My hands felt thick and hot and awkward. I ran a finger across the corner of the desk and looked at the streak made by the wiping off of the dust. I looked at the dust on my finger and wiped that off. I looked at my watch. I looked at the wall. I looked at nothing.
>
> I put the liquor bottle away and went over to the washbowl to rinse the glass out. When I had done that I washed my hands and bathed my face in cold water and looked at it. The flush was gone from the left cheek, but it looked a little swollen. Not very much, but enough to make me tighten up again. I brushed my hair and looked at the gray in it. There was getting to be plenty of gray in it. The face under the hair had a sick look. I didn't like the face at all.

> I went back to the desk and read Miss Fromsett's note again. I
> smoothed it out on the glass and sniffed it and smoothed it out some more
> and folded it and put it in my coat pocket.
>   I sat very still and listened to the evening grow quiet outside the open
> windows. And very slowly I grew quiet with it.   *(Chandler 1943: 139–40)*

Thorne begins by suggesting that for much of the passage the underlying grammatical structure is highly repetitive, with in rough terms a *I VP-ed and I VP-ed* pattern (two conjoined clauses each with *I* as their subject and the following verb phrase in the past tense: *I pushed it to one side and (I) had another drink*). The pattern is only slightly masked in surface structure by the deletion of the repeated first-person pronoun in the second conjunct. Thorne claims the 'highly repetitive style' is instrumental in creating 'the mood of aimless, nervous agitation the passage conveys' (1970: 191); in contrast, the final sentence stands apart, he says, announcing a change of mood in part by being grammatically different. The grammatical exceptionality he highlights (and implies contributes to the mood change) is the fact that only the final sentence has an initial 'And', followed shortly by an overt first-person subject pronoun. Other final-sentence differences we might note include:

1. Only the final sentence thematises a manner adverbial, *very slowly*, prior to mention of the grammatical subject.
2. *Very slowly* clearly pairs, positionally and somewhat semantically with *very still*; but there are differences/modulations too: *very still* is adjectival, and stative, *very slowly* is adverbial and dynamic or developmental.
3. The final sentence 'copies' its verb from the previous sentence, but with morphological change from infinitive to past tense (*grow > grew*).
4. There is a clear echoic pattern where *the evening grow quiet* pairs with *I grew quiet*; plus the intimation, partly projected by the sentence-initial cohesive conjunction *And*, that the evening's growing quiet <u>causes</u> the I-figure to grow quiet too. The *with it* construction hints at this too: compare *I grew arrogant with success* > 'my success <u>caused</u> me to become arrogant'.

Such a commentary is typical of stylistic analysis in itself, and in being repeatedly open to challenge. To begin with the main claim, that the repetitive *I VP-ed and I VP-ed* structure is instrumental to 'the mood of aimless, nervous agitation the passage conveys', it is hard to see how that specific grammatical structure is *causative* of readers inferring that mood, as distinct from saying that on this occasion, in this matrix of conditions, it does not clash with the 'aimless agitation' message. One can easily invent *I VP-ed and I VP-ed* sentences that carry no mood of aimless agitation (*I started the engine and steered the plane onto the runway; I engaged the enemy and delivered three short bursts of deadly fire*). Even the preliminary observation that *I VP-ed and I VP-ed* sentences are dominant in the passage has to be qualified: in the first paragraph, for instance, three sentences are of that type, but seven are not; in the second paragraph, again three fit that structure while five do not. These facts have consequences for the five subsequent claims about the contrasting fourth paragraph: with respect to the first of these, for example, while it is clear that only in the final sentence is there an initial *And*, it is not true to say that only this sentence lacks a medial *and* (sentences 1 and 3 in paragraph 1 are the first of many without medial *and*).

The very possibility of corrective commentary of the kind just offered is what entitles stylisticians to argue that *parts* of the stylistic analytical procedure are inspectable, replicable, testable and falsifiable. The replicable–falsifiable opportunities apply chiefly at the level of grammatical description. When it comes to the more interpretive stage ('this frequently repeated *I VP-ed and I VP-ed* structure helps create the mood or effect of aimless agitation'), falsifiability is scarcely possible, because the 'aimless agitation' predicated of the passage has not itself been established on independent and inspectable grounds. Perhaps one can appeal to lexical evidence and presuppositions in the passage itself: the early mention of 'beginning to feel less savage' and the late mention of 'growing quiet', suggest that at first the narrator was in an angry, dangerous mood, and that the passage shows (rather than baldly tells) how he gradually calms down.

Returning to the issue touched on earlier, regarding causation vs correlation: stylisticians are not really content with claiming that identified pattern A 'helps create' claimed effect or meaning Y. They are equally uncomfortable with the suggestion that they are not doing anything fundamentally different from literary analysts after all (see Attridge 1996: 44–5, who characterises Jakobson's 'empirical' studies as ultimately aiming, like the critic, to persuade the reader). The idea that they are participants in a discourse, persuading with evidence rather than pinpointing definitive explanations, troubles them. Working on some of the most chameleon and elusive materials, still they crave scientific truth, and closure. They would much rather attain what lawyers sometimes call the 'but for' causation standard: but for the presence of this pattern A, meaning/effect Y would not have been created (or, at least, would not have been satisfactorily or fully created). In practice, however, the 'but for' causation standard is very difficult to meet, in textual commentary – unless there are underlying connections between the *explanandum* effect and *explanans* pattern from the outset.

Another foundational point to consider, in relation to the most clearly testable and falsifiable part of stylistic analysis, where grammatical description is undertaken, is that here too matters may be contested, and agreement about categories and identifications may not always be as shared and 'common ground' as is assumed, despite the emphases on what is empirical, quantifiable, objectively present. In the Chandler passage, for example, Thorne and I appear to have accepted that the graphological sentence is a stable and agreed-upon unit of analysis (since Thorne is making a point about the striking or foregrounded high frequency of graphological sentences containing a *I VP-ed and I VP-ed* structure). Another analyst might take a different line. They might point to the fact that some of the graphological sentences are not well formed by the standards of formal writing (e.g. *Not very much, but enough to make me tighten up again*), and might suggest that Thorne and I are using far too superficial a notion of sentence-hood. They might then propose and apply a more abstract definition of the sentence category, and this might lead them to treat the final paragraph as underlyingly just one sentence, not two:

> I sat very still and listened to the evening grow quiet outside the open windows, and very slowly I grew quiet with it.

In this alternative stylistic analysis, several of Thorne's and my claims about the contrastiveness of the final paragraph (e.g. about sentence-initial *And*, and the creative departure from the *I VP-ed and I VP-ed* structure) would be nullified. Thus although stylistics makes appeal to the agreed and stable public descriptions of linguistics, much of that description is not uncontroversial. Many linguistic categories and their membership are matters of potential disagreement, and not even basic categories ('sentence', 'word', to say nothing of 'modal verb', 'behavioural process', etc.) can be invoked without considering what conception of them the analyst has in mind. In the same way and for the same reasons some circumspection is needed when stylisticians claim that their studies are expressed in a common language, since the latter is more a rhetorical trope than a demonstrated entity (every analytical tradition claims to have its own shared but specialist language variety).

Stylistic practice and the return of the reader

None of the above means that the categories of sentence or word or modal verb or passive voice are arbitrary, or meaningless beyond the descriptive system in which they arise; it only means that these categories come with a rich history and, although used in accounts of the texture of texts, are themselves metonyms of complex accounts of the workings of language. That is why some of the grander flourishes of refutation contained in Stanley Fish's (1973) famous critique of stylistics misrepresent what stylisticians do – at least, they misrepresent the vast majority of stylisticians, who eschewed a purely structuralist or generativist and semantics-free grammar, a point to which I will shortly return.

In an assessment of stylistics papers of the 1960s, Fish complained that repeatedly the analysts made a leap from description of forms to attribution of value (i.e. meaning) that was arbitrary and (contrary to more recent stylistic conventional wisdom) unfalsifiable. Some analysts, he concedes, are more subtle than others, but all at base are saying 'here's a formal feature' (e.g. reduced relative clauses) 'and here's what it means' – by implication, what it invariably means. In the scenario Fish uncovers, the form must invariably carry the specific value or meaning because an alternative position threatens to end in vacuity: if the analyst says the form has meaning A in the present text, but may create meaning/effect B in the next text in its different context, meaning/effect C in a further text in yet another context, and so on, then no generalisable or constrained explanation at all has been achieved. The 1960s stylistician's direct and invariant form-meaning (or form-value) pairing, Fish suggests, is unwarranted, arbitrary, and 'a game that's too easy to play' (Fish 1973: 100), since the meaning or value arrived at is typically a version of the intuition or pre-analytic impression the stylistician began with. He declares:

> While the distinctions one can make with the grammar are minute and infinite, they are also meaningless, for they refer to nothing except the categories of the system that produced them, categories which are themselves unrelated to anything outside their circle except by an arbitrary act of assertion.   *(Fish 1973: 100)*

There is also a small irony in Fish's use of the indefinite reference *one* in the first quoted line: he no doubt had in mind the linguist or grammarian. But if we were to treat the *one* here as referring to the poet (or even the reader), then the stylistician's point is that the small distinctions a poet can make with a grammar are emphatically *not* meaningless. In any event, in sentences like that above it is clear that Fish's target is the kind of structuralist–distributionalist and generative grammars that flourished in the 1950s and 1960s which, consonant with his criticism, often claimed as a virtue that they made no appeal to meaning-bearing categories outside the system they postulated. But stylisticians since the late 1960s have almost never adopted and applied such a grammar; rather, they have tended only to use those grammars and linguistic descriptions that include commentary on the meaning-bearing or semiotic functions of structures at their core. And where one description or approach seems inadequate to the complex task – as is typically the case with works as complex as literary ones – stylisticians have been enthusiastically eclectic, as many commentators have noted. Jeffries and McIntyre (2010: 4), for example, report that stylisticians draw on both context-free formal descriptions and the contextualised linguistic descriptions found in versions of pragmatics and sociolinguistics while also recently leaning heavily on either cognitive or corpus linguistics and occasionally both together.

Some of Fish's chastisement nevertheless was justified, and in fact stylisticians from the 1970s onwards moved quite rapidly to make clear how much more guarded their claims would be, as to the *tendency*, all other things being equal and not without scope for exceptions, of particular forms to correlate with or contribute towards the achievement of particular meaning effects. They also acknowledged and addressed the fact that context can powerfully alter the effects of linguistic forms. Fish (1980) called for an 'affective stylistics', in which fuller attention was paid to the sequential processing of the text that the reader necessarily enacts, and a number of stylisticians and literary analysts in the 1980s attempted forms of 'reader response criticism'; but this has been developed far more fully in recent years, with the growth of cognitive poetic and empirical studies of reading.

A fairly standard characterisation of stylistics is the following:

> Stylistics is the principled, systematic and rigorous analysis of texts (mainly literary), using linguistic description.

It is arguable that one premise of such a stylistics is that something like a mirror-image of its self-characterisation applies to its target or only begetter, the work of verbal or literary art:

> Verbal art is the principled, systematic and rigorous creation (synthesis?) of texts (mainly literary), using tacit linguistic knowledge.

In seeking to analyse a poem into its main meaning-bearing verbal parts, stylistics is a re-tracing of some of the compositional steps taken by the author. Stylisticians spend so much time and effort on testing and revising their hypotheses about the key linguistic features or compositional steps because they believe that great ingenuity and care and discrimination has gone into the original work of literary making. Stylisticians are among the greatest respecters of literary authors, but they by no means wish to treat what those authors do as a sublime or sacred mystery, beyond analysis. On the contrary, in being the application and development of grammar (widely conceived) to literary or other texts, stylistics is explicitly intent on demystification of literature: it believes that, for all their literariness, literary texts are amenable to analysis and explanation just like any other texts. But – a balance of considerations, again – most stylisticians at least also recognise that certain literary texts may have an exceptional power for their readers. This freshness of literature, sourced in the freshness of its linguistic texture is well captured in this one-sentence summary by Simpson: 'To do stylistics is to explore language, and, more specifically, to explore creativity in language use' (Simpson 2000: 3).

Falsifiability and standards of proof

The crucial scientific characteristic of stylistics is often said to be falsifiability: genuinely stylistic claims are claims relating to the language of a text (or class of texts) that might with effort be proven to be wrong or need refinement. But falsifiability involves a prior clear and agreed articulation of the precise criteria underpinning any claim. If, for example, analysts agree as to what an English modal verb is by reference to various criteria (invariant in form or unmarked for tense; leftmost in the verb phrase; requiring, prior to ellipsis, an infinitive form of a lexical verb or *have* or *be* to their right; attracting negation; etc.) then a claim that the first sentence of this paragraph contains a modal verb (*might*) while the second sentence does not is a falsifiable claim. But in practice, since stylistics typically involves a hermeneutic circle or spiral of grammatical description and textual interpretation, it crucially brings in commentary that is not falsifiable. Many stylisticians have discussed kinds of free indirect speech and thought in narratives, for example, and have drawn up a useful list of typical indicative characteristics which, if present, usually suggest that sentences have modulated from narrator-voiced narrative to the covert voicing of a character's internal reflections that is free indirect thought (FIT). But those characteristics are not necessary conditions, and FIT may be strongly suspected even in their absence. Thus, towards the end of Joyce's 'The Dead', when the narrative text runs as follows –

> He stretched himself cautiously along under the sheets and lay down beside his wife. One by one, they were all becoming shades. Better pass boldly into that other world, in the full glory of some passion, than fade and wither dismally with age.   *(Joyce 2008: 80)*

– most stylisticians will want to say that sentences 2 and 3 report Gabriel's free indirect thoughts, while sentence 1, purely narrative, emphatically does not. But no easily stated criteria underpin that analytical judgement (rather, an awareness of other such narrative-to-FIT modulations earlier in this story and other *Dubliners* stories, and an awareness of Gabriel's thwarted and humbled mood guide the analyst, including an awareness that *the full glory of some passion* is very much the kind of phrase that Gabriel is capable of). So the FIT classification here is not strictly falsifiable, and alternative interpretations which attribute the pronouncements in sentences 2 and 3 to Joyce or a narrator cannot be proven wrong.

The essence of falsifiability is not that something is testable, but that it can be proven wrong and that efforts are made to prove it wrong. Relatively few stylistic studies centre on such efforts – perhaps because of the interest in pedagogy, where it is natural to emphasise positive proposals. In practice, then, stylisticians do typically write as advocates for the linguistic analysis they present, arguing for its relevance to the target text, and to readers' readings of that text. Even where they focus directly on falsifiability, and have made clear what their analytical categories are (the difficulty noted earlier), they grapple with texts affected by a greater variety of confounding variables than those in any other linguistic sub-discipline. Or it may be that difficulties with disproving the significance of any isolated textual feature of the context-embedded literary reading experience highlight, more vividly than other kinds of linguistic analysis, that the difficulties are actually general in linguistics.

Since scientific falsifiability may be unavailable, it is often useful to set stylistic claims and arguments by the less absolute legal standards of proof or certainty: not 'beyond a reasonable doubt' but 'on the balance of probabilities'. The more ambitious kinds of stylistic analysis often involve this lower standard: they aim to persuade others that, on balance, it is more likely than not that these linguistic phenomena are the necessary cause of that effect. But that is a low level of certainty, and this is where the 'systematicity and rigour' come in: it is not only possible but necessary that the qualified confidence of such stylistic claims be put to further tests, with the aim of raising the standard of proof from 'more likely than not' to 'quite sure'.

Disciplinary maturity

Stylistics has never been objective, definitive and rigorous along the lines of experimental sciences. It couldn't be – not simply because literary texts are variously contextualised and variously interpreted, but because language is endlessly potentially variable in forms and functions, languages are not finally codes, and human beings are not machines for processing those not-codes (Harris 1981, 1987; Toolan 1996). But it takes a long time to turn the linguistics tanker and its accompanying ferryboat, stylistics; not necessarily a 180-degree turn, but enough for linguists to recognise that progress in the brain sciences and in linguistics has been mostly incremental rather than revolutionary, that alongside the normative pressures on public language which ensure a degree of convergence and code-like iteration there is always variation and change, that change is not the same thing as improvement or progress, and that while some aspects of human life are susceptible to improvement it is doubtful that others are. There is a better understanding now of human physiology and illnesses or of meteorology than in 1600, but is there better understanding of poetry, or language? The physical and medical sciences progress, but do the humanities? If they did, we should be able to say that today's poets and playwrights write better than Shakespeare and his contemporaries, but such a claim seems wrong or absurd; and in the area of language study we should find people learning languages much faster than four centuries ago, but they don't seem to. Lack of demonstrable 'definitive' progress in an area of activity (playwriting, research into language teaching, stylistics) is not, however, an argument for abandoning the activity but for conceptualising it in different terms, where 'objective progress' is not mistakenly assumed to be the chief concern. This is why I have always argued that while stylistics aims at being explicit, methodical, using agreed categories and argumentation it is not itself a 'method' but a way of describing and explaining the linguistics of texts and their meanings for readers (Toolan 1990: 28 and *passim*). Doing stylistics is primarily participating in an ongoing discourse that reflects on the multiple functions of language in our cultures and seeks to revise and renew our shared understanding of language forms and functions.

It may once have been assumed that stylisticians needed to wait for a sufficiently mature and flexible linguistics to emerge, ready for application; in recent years some stylisticians have tired of this client status. The kinds of complexity of language-related phenomena that stylisticians increasingly recognise as playing a part in the creation of a work's meanings and effects have led them to review their various source linguistic descriptions and models more critically and questioningly. And where the proffered linguistic model is found to be a poor fit for the complex linguistic-analytical demands of the literary text, stylisticians are more willing than in the past to propose amendments and supplements to the received model.

Do competent readers (listeners, playgoers, etc.) need stylistics? We all like to be needed, so there's a temptation for stylisticians to answer in the eager affirmative, seeing that responding in the negative only encourages those who would shove us to the cultural and academic margin. A more plausible reply is that readers may or may not find stylistics useful, just as music-lovers may but do not invariably find musicologists helpful. And even if some, many, or even all lay music-lovers found musicology of no use to them, this would be no compelling argument for abandoning such studies. Cultures need to understand their own practices, and not just do them. So a culture that puts great store by complexly composed imaginative fiction (prose, drama or poetry) in *language*, such great store that they canonise and anthologise it, adapt it into non-verbal artforms, and often spend a good deal of their free time reading it and talking about it, is sure to develop evolving reflexive discourses contributory to the understanding of that literature. Stylistics is the most language-focused of those discourses; its emergence was guaranteed in advance, with the emergence of artistic writing.

3

The stylistic tool-kit: methods and sub-disciplines

Katie Wales

The previous chapter by Michael Toolan sought in a general overview to describe the theory and philosophy of stylistics. The title of this chapter contains a metaphor which appears time and again in definitions and applications of stylistics (see, for example, Carter 2010: 68; Jeffries 2010b: Introduction, ten times; Short 1996: xii, 169; Simpson 2004: v). As far back as 1981, Leech and Short's *Style in Fiction* brought to prominence the related practical notion of a 'stylistic check-list', still in evidence in the second edition of 2007: a list of linguistic and stylistic categories 'likely to yield stylistically relevant information', in this case specifically for prose fiction (Leech and Short, Chapter 3). There are also Short's own ten checksheets (1996) for prose, poetry and plays, recently discussed in Stockwell's wonderfully entitled 'The eleventh checksheet of the apoca- lypse' (2010). Culpeper (2001) also contains a useful checklist of typical linguistic 'cues' for dramatic character. Nonetheless, there is a potential danger in the use of this particular word that the unwary student might feel that 'ticking the boxes' will provide all the answers. It is also not the case, of course, that every stylistic analysis must include all the style markers, as they are called. While some stylistic publications are compre- hensive in what is chosen for description and interpretation, many focus on one feature, whether this is metaphor or speech acts or negation, for example.

While it might be tempting also to dismiss the tool-kit metaphor itself as a simple cliché, the fact remains that it does symbolise core attributes of the discipline (and its disciples), notably its empirical and pedagogic nature and its 'hands-on' approach, which also aims to be reader-friendly. This is particularly striking for the long-established sub-discipline of pedagogical stylistics in the foreign-language-learning context, where the stress is on students 'doing' the analysis for themselves, in close reading, often re-writing texts from different angles or in different forms (see, for example R. Pope 1995; Widdowson 1975). The metaphor, in sum, implies that stylistics is essentially functional, like a set of tools. Simpson (2004: 130–5) enriches this idea with his presentation of a 'workshop' on speech and thought presentation. A further reading of the metaphor also suggests that stylisticians as artisans can 'un-lock' the meaning or function of texts as verbal artefacts by using particular modes or models of analysis; or by focusing on particular (linguistic) features, their observed patterns and their potential effects. And like craftsmen (in the generic sense) they can, in Leech's words (2010: 20) 'enjoy the mastery behind [their] composition'.

Another reading of the metaphor, where the tools are garden tools, provides the further implication that stylistics demands 'spade-work': the systematic close reading and analysis of quite specific elements, whether at the levels of grammar, phonology, lexis, semantics and/or pragmatics or discourse, in order to elucidate or help interpretation. This presupposes, of course, that there is a distinct correlation between the choices and textures or patterns of those elements or style markers in their particular generic contexts, and the 'enactment of meaning' (Carter 2010: 61). While it is important not to assume a directly iconic or isomorphic relationship between form and meaning, nonetheless we can remember Short's pithy 'rule' (1996: 117): 'The shorter the chain of inference needed to establish [a] relationship, the more directly appropriate the relationship appears to be'. He also reminds us quite sensibly (1996: 8) that 'linguistic features *constrain* readers from inferring unreasonable [meanings] and *prompt* them towards reasonable ones' (his italics).

It is also a significant aspect of the 'spade-work' that not only do stylisticians not shy away from it, but that they are prepared to call a spade a spade. Impressionist or vague terms just will not do, whether it is the sound-scape of a lyric poem that is being examined, or the sentence structure of a Shakespearean speech. Stylisticians bristle if literary critics do not use even a well-known term. While Leech (2008: 195) is right to stress that stylistics is 'open to all who know the language, or who know something of how the language works', nonetheless some basic terminology is necessary. However, as the area of grammar well illustrates, there is no consensus on whose terminology to adopt. Some stylisticians, perhaps incorporating well-tried teaching methods into their textbooks, use terms which are inherited from traditional grammar (*simple, compound clauses; subject, verb, predicate*, etc); others have adopted the popular late twentieth-century terminology of the British grammarian Quirk and his colleagues (e.g. Leech and Short 1981, 2007). Even more popular in undergraduate textbooks, and very influential across the whole stylistics field, as we shall see, has proved the terminology from Halliday's (1985) systemic grammar, first formulated in the late 1960s, which broadly divides language structuring to make three major kinds of meaning: the experiential (concerned with how we represent experience), the interpersonal (how interlocutors are related) and the textual (how texts are organised).

It is important to stress here, however, for elaboration below, that stylistic analysis need by no means be as formalistic as I seem to be implying. (And Halliday's grammar itself certainly isn't.) As Carter and Stockwell (2008: 295) state, precisely because the range of stylistic activities has expanded since the emergence of stylistics as a discipline to be reckoned with in the 1960s, with an influx of influential models from neighbouring disciplines, 'more and more dimensions' have been added to the strictly formal linguistic levels – the core, so to speak – to become part of a possible tool-kit. Sub-disciplines and models either become deeply embedded, 'naturalised', or else they carry with them a particular slant which colours the analysis throughout, and may even be flaunted: as in the case of Halliday's, referred to above. That this has, in consequence, led to a proliferation of technical terms means that many textbooks now append a glossary; or call themselves a 'resource' (Simpson's subtitle 2004); or have referred readers to the three editions of my own *Dictionary of Stylistics*, for example: the latest edition (2011) itself incorporating a 'subject index' functioning as a checklist.

A keyword here is *systematic*: whatever model may be used as a framework and whatever elements are scrutinised, the overall stylistic method is to be scrupulously systematic and explicit and therefore transparent and retrievable, so that other people can understand how an interpretation or conclusion has been reached. The aim of any satisfactory stylistic analysis is to provide scrupulous insights into the workings of the language and ultimately, hopefully, to make convincing interpretations of texts to successive generations of readers. Quite often, the very process of analysis can lead to interesting modification of the initial model. There are two main methods or modes of analysis: the *deductive* and the *inductive*. Stylisticians can work deductively from the formulation of an hypothesis or ideological position to the linguistic and textual evidence and analysis; or inductively from textual analysis to the formulation of hypotheses. These are popularly referred to as the 'top-down' and 'bottom-up' approaches. Usually, a combination of both will be used. For example, it is quite common initially for a stylistician to be excited by certain, often foregrounded, features in a text and to formulate reasons for their prominence ('bottom-up'). The inductive method is particularly favoured by corpus stylisticians below, despite what might be said by them to the contrary. However, further or deeper exploration may lead to the refinement, even the jettison, of an initial hypothesis or intuition in favour of a revised one, which can lead to the need for additional textual evidence. In the writing up of an analysis, however, for publication, the presentation of any argument usually works from the general to the particular, from the 'research question' to its answer, from summary findings to detailed substantiation. It is quite common for an article or chapter to give a general interpretation of a poem or short story, for example, 'then to indicate significant stylistic features' and then to describe 'how the formal stylistic features are used as the basis for inferring the [text's] meaning and effect' (Short 1996: 17, see also 397). The deductive method is also popular among those stylisticians who wish either to 'test' a particular theoretical model, or to probe more deeply assertions about the workings of literary language or interpretations of texts made by literary critics.

As I have said elsewhere (Wales 2012: 10), it is a characteristic of stylistics overall to be open to a variety of methodologies, 'theory and practice interpenetrating, and at any one moment in time'. This eclecticism or 'boundless appetite' (Carter and Stockwell 2008: 209) is well known and documented. What is also often stated is that there has been a general move away from what is sometimes termed the formalist stylistics of the 1960s, heavily influenced by the newly discovered ideas of Russian Formalism and its most celebrated proponent, Roman Jakobson, towards a more functional and discourse stylistics, itself influenced by developments in pragmatics on the one hand, and literary reader response and Foucauldian theories on the other. What is not often appreciated, however, and which complicates the picture, is the fact that models may come into fashion but refuse to fade away, operating alongside or in conjunction with newer models, because of their continued relevance, albeit with some modifications, perhaps, along the way. Some examples of this I shall return to in due course, in relation to specific text types, but we can take foregrounding (from Formalism to Leech 1969 and van Peer 1986, 2007) and politeness theory (P. Brown and Levinson 1978, 1987) as good examples. This was not the case for transformational grammar, however, once popular in the 1960s in the work of Levin (1962) and Thorne (1965); apart from the useful concept of 'selectional restrictions' on the combining potential of lexical items. But by and large the result is that the tool-kit is ever expanding, due to the influence of the terms and ideas from many related disciplines, while remaining true to its core.

Interdisciplinarity is at the heart of stylistics, of course, as it tries to straddle the fields of language and literature, linguistics and literary criticism; and also increasingly take on board the social and cultural contexts of both texts and their readers in interaction with them. Feminist, discourse and pragmatic stylistics or pragmastylistics, for example, reflect this trend as emergent sub-disciplines. (See, for example, Mills 1995 for a detailed application of stylistic models to gender issues and discourses.) Moving even further away from text and discourse *per se*, is cognitive stylistics, properly cognitive poetics, concerned as it primarily is with the cognitive elements involved in the comprehension and processing of texts. Text World Theory (TWT), as developed in the first instance by Werth (1999, working on E. M. Forster's *A Passage to India*) and refined by Gavins (2007), can be seen as an offshoot, with a focus on the particular textual elements which activate the reader's mental construction of the particular 'world' of the text (e.g. modality, deixis, conditionals, negation).

Given the traditional emphasis on linguistic levels, however, and a deep knowledge of how language works, some would argue that stylistics is itself a sub-discipline of linguistics. Others would argue, given its practice of close reading, its goals and main subject matter or genres, that it is a sub-discipline of practical criticism, itself a sub-discipline of literary criticism, itself, alongside literary theory, a sub-discipline of hermeneutics, the art of interpretation. Parts II and IV of this volume discuss many concepts in literary criticism which have proved influential in stylistics. A central concern in literary criticism and practical criticism has been metaphor; but nowadays the strong influence of cognitive approaches initiated by G. Lakoff and Johnson (1980) has led stylisticians to replace I. A. Richards's terms 'tenor' and 'vehicle' by 'target' and 'source' respectively, particularly in discussions of conventional metaphors.

It has to be stressed, however, that although the traditional interest by stylisticians has been with literature with a capital 'L', increasingly literature with a small 'l' (manga comics, chick-lit, film subtitles); non-fiction (scientific discourse, propaganda); spoken registers (camp talk, spiritual mediumship); e-discourses (emails, text messaging, blogs) and the media (advertising, film dialogue) have all become grist to the mill. Indeed, in this last respect, stylistics could be seen as a sub-discipline of semiotics. Stylistics has also been seen as a sub-discipline of poetics, concerned as that is with theories of form and genre, and also of (classical) rhetoric (see further Hall and Hamilton, both in this volume).

Certainly this latter field of scholarship has provided stylistics with a very large and distinctive sub-set of analytical 'tools', particularly for poetry and prose, based on the long-established practice of the cataloguing of figures of speech, word- and sound-play and devices of persuasion, and so on. Verdonk (2010: 87) writes of the 'persuasive tool box of the classical rhetorician'. So in those stylistic textbooks which show the analysis of poetry at work (e.g. Gregoriou 2009; Short 1996) schemes and tropes such as alliteration, assonance, parallelism, chiasmus, metaphor and metonymy, and so on, are typically described. Rhetorical devices are frequently analysed in non-literary registers such as newspaper headlines, advertising and the political oratory of prime ministers and American presidents. Importantly, for the analysis of pre-twentieth-century literature, from the Middle Ages onwards, a knowledge of rhetorical devices so painstakingly collected in Renaissance handbooks is indispensable (see S. Adamson et al. 2001 on Shakespeare's use of rhetoric). Indeed, because of the serious attention paid to rhetoric in their various writings by stylisticians such as Verdonk (2010), Burke (2010a) and Cockcroft (2003), it could be argued that today rhetoric is best seen as a sub-discipline of stylistics, a rhetorical stylistics, or, pedantically, a sub-discipline of the sub-discipline of an historical or diachronic stylistics. It is all too easy to forget the temporal context of texts, but any student faced with the switches in the pronouns *you* and *thou* in Shakespeare's plays soon realises the value of diachronic socio-stylistic evidence. It is also easy to overlook the spatial context. Insights from sociolinguistics and postcolonialism, for example in respect of regional variation and diglossia, have enriched stylistic analyses of dialect- and world literatures, without as yet the establishment of coherent sub-disciplines. For sociolinguists, style itself is interestingly seen, as Simpson summarises (2012: 16), as 'a performative interactive practice' rather than 'a frequency of textual patterning'.

I want to look now in more detail at some of the most popular tools in the stylistic tool-kit, which at the same time will illustrate some of the general points about models and sub-disciplines I have referred to so far. I propose to look at these in relation to major genres or text types, although it must be stressed that, on the one hand, tools may not themselves be discrete categories and that, on the other, many are not genre-specific. Deixis, types of speech act and metaphor, for example, are equally discussed in poetry, fiction and verse drama; most recently point-of-view criticism has been interestingly extended from the novel to drama (see McIntyre 2006); and also narrative (see Bowles 2010). Some of these tools will be discussed again more extensively elsewhere in this volume, particularly in Part III.

Not surprisingly, since the Russian Formalists and the Prague Linguistic Circle of the early twentieth century had a lot to say in particular about poetic language and its qualities, the stylistics of poetry has been much influenced by ideas of structural and aesthetic patterning, and by the dominant function of poetry to 'de-automatise' the familiar (see further Gavins and Emmott, both in this volume). Against the norms of ordinary language, within the poetic text in particular features can be perceived as prominent or highlighted, 'foregrounded' for specific effects. Present-day cognitive linguists use a similar idea of 'figure' and 'ground': focused objects against background spaces. Even the regularised patterns of metre can be viewed as foregrounded against the ordinary rhythms of speech. Following Leech (1969), foregrounding devices have sometimes been grouped under the headings of 'deviation' and 'repetition'. Deviations are violations of linguistic norms: semantic, for example, like unusual metaphors or similes; or graphological, like the unpunctuated and un-capitalised lines of a poem by e. e. cummings. Repetition (e.g. of sound or syntax) strikes the reader's attention as being equally unusual: as with alliteration, or parallelism.

The ideas of the Russian Formalists were revived by Guy Cook (1994), in combination with schema theory from cognitive psychology and linguistics. Mentally, we store our cultural experiences in packages, as it were, but these can be 'updated'. Literature, in particular, Cook argues, tends to be 'schema-refreshing' rather than reinforcing, in that our conventional ways of perceiving the world are challenged or disrupted. Semino (1995) has an interesting application of Cook's model to the poems of Sylvia Plath (but see Jeffries 2001 for a critique).

Other popular sites of stylistic interest for poetry include, on the lexical level, methods of word formation such as affixation and compounding: well illustrated in poetic diction from Spenser to Keats and Hopkins. The interrelations of metre and syntax, sometimes termed grammetrics, is fruitfully illustrated in the device traditionally known as *enjambment*, where there can be tension between metrical pausing at line-endings and the syntax, and for particular interpretive effects. In this respect Milton's epic poem *Paradise Lost* resonates with the echoes of classical epic poetry. In contrast is the smaller canvas of the lyric poem, and, as Keith Green (1992) illustrates, the application of the tool-kit of deixis (personal pronouns, demonstratives, adverbs of place and time, tense) shows us how a poetic 'persona' can be created in a particular specific context.

What can cause problems for undergraduates new to stylistics is the necessary consideration of the metrical patterns of different kinds of poetry, as in sonnets, ballads, odes and epics, using the appropriate terms. Traditionally, the lexis of metrics or prosody has come from literary criticism and classical rhetoric. Terms such as *quatrain, couplet, rhyme* or *stanza* probably present few problems; not so perhaps terms such as *iambic* (x /), *trochaic* (/ x), *anapaestic* (x x /) and *dactylic* (/ x x). These are used for patterns of stressed and unstressed syllables in a 'foot' or unit of rhythm, and terms such as *pentameter* refer to the line pattern of five beats and/or ten syllables (*hexameter* would need six beats and/or twelve syllables). Clearly, for the verse drama of Shakespeare, as well as for poetry, a knowledge of the permitted rules and 'deviations' of iambic pentameter is indispensable. However, since these terms have come down to the present day from the metrical theory applied to classical poetry, and since syllable-counting is not native to English metre, rather the counting of stresses or accents, this traditional and rather complex terminology does not always work comfortably. Many textbooks for undergraduates therefore prefer the metrical tool-kit or model devised by Attridge that refers to 'beats' and 'off-beats' (see further Carper and Attridge 2003).

In the field of prose fiction there have been a number of popular models which have either sharpened existing tools of analysis, or which have brought tools to add to the tool-box. Well established is the notion of *point of view* or *focalisation*, terms introduced via literary criticism from continental theorists such as Stanzel, Uspensky and Genette in the early 1970s, and increasingly applied today to film. Just as the camera angle gives the spectator a temporal and spatial perspective on events, so does the narrator of a novel; but also, significantly, it gives beliefs (ideological perspective) and feelings (psychological perspective). The traditional omniscient narrator typically adopts an objective stance, notwithstanding, while first-person narrators commonly provide internal focalisation and so a subjective viewpoint. An extreme kind of such focalisation can be seen in the interior monologues of Leopold Bloom and Stephen

Dedalus, in James Joyce's *Ulysses*, each revealing idiolectal features of style, and complex and interrelated projected sub-worlds, in Text World Theory's terms (see Simpson 2004: 140). Stylisticians are interested in the linguistic devices which characterise different viewpoints – or 'mind styles', as Roger Fowler (1977) termed them – such as deixis (expressions for place and time), modality, value-laden expressions, metaphor and transitivity patterns. Simpson (1993) provides an important and detailed methodology for the modality configurations of point of view. In doing so he also raises the important issue of variation between sub-genres. Words such as 'the novel' or 'prose fiction' hide distinctions such as romance and Gothic, for instance.

Transitivity as a stylistics tool owes its continuing popularity to Halliday's systemic grammar or systemic-functional model of language, referred to towards the beginning of this chapter: in particular, to Halliday's own application as early as 1971, in the modestly entitled 'Inquiry' into the language of William Golding's novel *The Inheritors*. Carter and Stockwell (2008: 19) rightly call it one of the 'ground-breaking analyses in stylistics', and it has been much anthologised since. Transitivity patterns – involving processes, participants and circumstances – provide the model for understanding how the particular, rather limited, world view of Neanderthal man is creatively expressed. So normal transitive verbs are used intransitively (*smell along*; *grab at*); subjects of sentences are either parts of the body or even inanimate objects, rather than a person's name or personal pronoun; and, in general, there are no obvious grammatical or lexical patterns of cause and effect. Such an analysis, of course, echoes the long-standing interest of stylistics in norms and deviations, and it is certainly true that an interest in 'deviant' mind styles continues to this day. So Semino (Semino 2002; Semino and Swindlehurst 1996) has analysed the presentation of mental illness in Ken Kesey's *One Flew Over the Cuckoo's Nest*, and a criminal mind in John Fowles's *The Collector*. As she herself argues (2002), linguistic patterns are 'foregrounded', which suggests some cognitive habit or deficit. Not surprisingly, perhaps, she is able then to draw on conceptual metaphor and blending theory from cognitive stylistics: the character of the collector in the Fowles novella consistently 'mapping' the properties of an insect on to a human being.

As novels such as *The Inheritors* illustrate in general, the narrator, the one who speaks, is not always the main focaliser, the one who sees. So also, in a different way, in free indirect speech the voice of the character is typically blended with or mediated through the voice of the narrator, yet the focalisation remains that of the character. Free indirect speech or style as a marker of subjectivity has been a preoccupation of both literary criticism and stylistics in Europe for a century, since it was first discussed extensively by Bally (1909). It is now seen as one of the major devices of the representation of speech (and of thought) in classical fiction (see further Fludernik 1993). It also features in a classification system first associated with Leech and Short (1981), refined somewhat in subsequent publications, but still extremely popular. So direct (DS) and indirect speech (IS) and thought are generally easily recognisable formally, with their speech tags, pronoun shifts and presence (or absence) of quotation marks:

> 'You must leave now', she said. (DS)
> She said that he must leave at once. (IS)

Free indirect speech (FIS) lacks the tag and the quotation marks, but usually retains some of the immediacy of direct speech:

> He must leave now. (FIS)

Narrative report of speech acts (NRSA) is simply a report that a speech act has taken place (e.g. *she recommended his dismissal*). From the 1980s, also, the recently translated writings of the Russian linguist-philosopher Mikhail Bakhtin introduced into literary criticism and stylistics a more general dynamic perspective on point of view and modes of speech presentation. Ever mindful of novels by Dickens and Dostoevsky, for example, his over-arching theory was that the novel, unlike poetry and drama, was polyphonic, heteroglossic, permitting voices, registers and ideologies of all sorts to have free play. His own particular refinement on the model of speech and thought presentation was 'character zone': the idea that a distinctive narrative style could surround the direct speech of a character, to suggest his or her consciousness. What is a matter of critical interest and debate, however, is the extent to which the different modes of speech and thought presentation in general invite either empathy or estrangement in the reader.

An influential model of a different kind on shorter prose fiction such as novellas and short stories came from the American sociolinguist William Labov as early as 1967 (with Waletsky; see also Labov 1972, and Chapter 29 in this volume). The original model came out of research into the structuring of oral narratives of personal (non-fictional) experiences by Black Americans; it has also been applied to joke-telling, fables, strip cartoons and fairy tales. A short story could possibly have all six of the following components: abstract, orientation, complicating action, evaluation, result or resolution, and a coda – but not necessarily. Or they might be blended. So many modern short stories commonly begin without orientation, *in medias res*, or dispense with a coda or epilogue. 'Evaluation' is often left implicit; or moved to the end, as in a fable. At the beginning, it can create suspense or anticipation. Think of the opening sentence of Ford Maddox Ford's *The Good Soldier*: 'This is the saddest story I have ever heard.' Thus stylisticians are interested in the methodology not simply for its components, but the linguistic realisations of them, and their actual effects in context. They are also interested in what Halliday and Hasan (1976) would call the general textual structure of a work: the way units of a story might be arranged and organised explicitly (by devices of cohesion) and implicitly or inferentially (by degrees of coherence).

Overwhelmingly, it is drama as a genre which has been influenced in stylistic analysis by models drawn from the linguistic study of orality and speech, simply because there is an assumption that dramatic dialogue is for all intents and purposes an 'imitation' of real conversation. Even Shakespeare's plays, written in iambic pentameter, can be and have been analysed in these terms. (For a useful survey of significant models, see V. Herman 1995.) The move to analyse drama as discourse, as part of a general trend towards a discourse stylistics and later a pragmatic stylistics, was largely due to the publication in 1980 of Burton's book on that subject, particularly focusing on plays by Pinter and Ionesco. In itself it used a model of discourse analysis developed at the University of Birmingham (see Sinclair and Coulthard 1975) particularly for classroom exchanges, with units such as 'act' and 'move' for conversational behaviour. In the interest of how units enable further activity and exchanges, this model resembles the more influential model of conversation analysis (CA) developed by the American sociologist Sacks and his colleagues in the 1960s out of very detailed transcriptions. Turn-taking, topic selection, 'repairs' and pairs of utterances are significant tools in CA. In the interest, however, of the pragmatic functions or communicative intents of different acts, e.g. elicitation and directive, the Birmingham model also invokes the equally influential model of speech act theory, as developed by the philosophers Austin (1962) and Searle (1969). This is concerned with acts that have some social or interpersonal purpose and effect in conversation. Despite the popularity of this model, however, both in the analysis of dramatic dialogue and natural speech, there is no one classification system available, and indeed no consensus on how many speech acts there are in a language such as English. Gregoriou (2009: 145) lists only five types (declarations, representatives, expressives, directives, commissives), but directives can be sub-divided into requests and orders. What do we do with arguments and concessions (sometimes included under 'expositives')? Apologies, condolence and greetings can be labelled as kinds of 'acknowledgements'. Some speech acts are more transparent than others in the sense that there is often a precise speech act verb (*beseech, promise, warn*) or a correlation with a sentence type (question–interrogative, command–imperative). Others, however, are 'indirect': one speech act performed indirectly by what appears to be another, often out of politeness. So an apparent question ('Can you put the kettle on?') is generally perceived to be less brusque than a bald imperative ('Put the kettle on'). For drama, as indeed for dialogue in the novel, which has also been analysed in terms of speech act theory because of the assumption of mimesis, what is of significance is the effect of a speech act (e.g. promise, warning, command) on the development of the plot, and on judgements of character in their social and emotional interrelations with others.

Another extremely influential model on the analysis of dramatic dialogue as well as natural conversation, also from the discipline of philosophy, has been that of Grice developed in the late 1970s (Grice 1975): the 'co-operative principle' (CP) with its associated four maxims of quantity, quality, relation and manner. The co-operative principle is assumed to be fundamental to 'normal' communication: a kind of tacit agreement by speakers to work together rationally to achieve a coherent exchange. It has to be said that this is probably more true for dramatic dialogue than for informal chat, and hence its particular attraction for the stylistic analysis of drama. The maxim of quantity concerns the degree of information normally demanded; that of quality concerns truthfulness. The maxim of relation describes normal expectations of relevance and the maxim of manner concerns clarity. As Grice himself was quick to point out, however, these maxims are easily violated or blatantly flouted even in 'ordinary' conversation, let alone literary dialogues (Grice 1975). Many common figures of speech, indeed, flout the maxims: e.g. irony and hyperbole the maxim of quality ('That's very nice of you, I must say'; 'he's as old as the hills'). Constraints of politeness may also lead to floutings, for example, of the maxim of truthfulness. Leech (1983) believed politeness to be so important a factor in our conversation behaviour that he was moved to produce his own set of maxims as a refinement on Grice's model: tact, generosity, approbation, modesty, agreement and sympathy. There is an illustration of these in his analysis of Shaw's play *You Never Can Tell* (Leech 2008).

However, it is the politeness theory of two cultural anthropologists in the late 1970s, P. Brown and Levinson (1978), which has proved extremely influential on the stylistics of dramatic and fictional dialogue, as well as the analysis of everyday communication. Again, it was itself influenced by speech act theory, but also the work of the sociologist Goffman on 'face' (Goffman 1981). We tend to avoid tactics generally which threaten face. One set of their politeness strategies works by the appeal to 'positive face', the speaker's self-image; negative politeness strategies are oriented towards the addressee's 'negative face' needs, their preference for freedom of action. Indirectness, hedging and so on are important here. But since dialogue, like conversation, is set in a particular context, social variables of gender, age, class, ethnicity, power and so forth must always be taken into consideration. There may also be more complex nuances than the binary opposition between 'positive' and 'negative' implies. Cross-cultural, and also diachronic, variation must also not be underestimated, given that this particular model of politeness, despite the title of their publications, is largely based on twentieth-century British and American practices. (For an attempt to set up a model of im-politeness, see Bousfield 2008.)

What I think emerges also from my rather generalised summaries of these particular pragmatic models is the way they have interpenetrated each other. Not surprisingly, then, many stylisticians find themselves using tools from more than one of these models as they attempt to analyse the whole complex discourse-world of a play. But even in the real world there is a multiplicity of discourse and text types over and above 'ordinary' conversation, which demand a set of broad pragmatic tools. McIntyre and Culpeper (2010), for example, apply Gricean maxims, turn-taking, speech acts, politeness features and so on to auditions and talent shows. Discourses mediated by technology, whether television or the internet, pose interesting challenges to traditional stylistic analyses, which must respond also to different degrees of mediated audiences.

Profoundly influential on the study of non-literary and media discourses since the late 1980s to the present day has been the model of critical discourse analysis (CDA) developed by Fairclough and his colleagues at Lancaster University. Indebted to the work of the French theorist Foucault on discourse as an instrument of power and control, it struck a chord with stylisticians because of the underlying premise that linguistic choices are not neutral, but ideologically constructed. Metaphors in the discourses of gender, race, globalisation, politics, propaganda, news and advertising, for example, have been a particular focus of analysis; and once again the Hallidayan framework of transitivity has been used as a grammatical tool. In recent years, however, it has tended to move away to more contextual features. Also drawing heavily on systemic grammar as a tool-kit was the very similar movement known as critical linguistics (CL), developed at the University of East Anglia by the stylistician Roger Fowler and his colleagues in the 1980s. A good illustration of the application of systemic grammar is found in his *Language in the News* (1991). Both movements have recently been reclaimed for stylistics proper by Jeffries (2010b) as a 'critical stylistics', with chapters organised conceptually (devices for naming and describing, exemplifying and enumerating, negating, etc.). The retention of the term 'critical' hints at a political motivation in the sense that both CDA and CL have been anxious to raise 'critical language awareness' of bias, obfuscation and social inequality, and what we can see as a sub-discipline with bite certainly increasingly strikes a chord with students concerned with the representation of ecological issues in popular science and the media and the potential manipulation of world views. Ideally, CDA and critical stylistics would wish to change some discursive practices by intervention: a tool-kit with cutting-edge tools? (See also Carter 2012: 111 on 'stylistics and impact'.)

A kind of stylistics growing in popularity at undergraduate level that does have real-world impact is forensic stylistics, a branch of the well-established forensic linguistics discipline in the USA and the UK, used in the solving of legal and criminal problems. Drawing on discourse analysis, sociolinguistics and phonetics as well as stylistics, here the tools function, dare I say it, as scalpels, to 'dissect' text authorship, for example, or transcribed evidence or confessions in police statements (see further Coulthard and Johnson 2007).

The investigation of authorship has had a long history in literary criticism: the investigation of plays reputed to be by Shakespeare, and poems by Chaucer, for instance. Considerable emphasis can be placed on the analysis of linguistic features assumed to be relatively unconsciously used by an author, so forming a kind of stylistic 'fingerprint' for statistical comparison with the works of other authors or other kinds of texts. Word and sentence length, connectives and collocations are characteristic variables, traditionally collected and frequency-counted by painstaking and slow manual card-indexing. Nowadays, computational stylistics, as it is known, has been revolutionised by the computer; and a new very popular sub-discipline has emerged, corpus stylistics, aided by the technological facility of the electronic storage of ever larger amounts of text in multi-million-word databases and textfiles. Corpus stylistics has the exciting potential for the investigation of large-scale stylistic changes over time or within period genres (e.g. travel-writing or the periodical), in the field of diachronic stylistics.

Since corpus stylistics, however, is dealt with in detail by Stubbs and by Louw and Milojkovic in following chapters, my comments here are simply meant to draw attention to the way in which the tool-kit metaphor which I have laboriously dissected has actually been revitalised in the technological domain. There are literal 'WordSmith Tools' in software, for example (Scott 1996), a search tool which enables the retrieval of key words and their clusters, potential style markers, in their particular contexts. I shall also use my observations as a way of summary for this chapter, since the emergence of corpus methodologies sheds interesting light on stylistic practice in general: not only its strengths but also its potential weaknesses. For the irony is that, despite the novelty of electronic aids, some stylistic analyses run the same risk of being criticised for 'bean-counting' as in the early days of stylistics in the 1950s and 1960s: formalist for the sake of formalism. Any data must still be analysed qualitatively as well as quantitatively, subjectively as well as objectively. Frequency of words is assumed to be of functional relevance or salience, but this is not always the case. Stubbs himself has been mindful of potential pitfalls in his own analysis (2005) of Joseph Conrad's *Heart of Darkness*, much cited since then.

One of the main arguments in favour of corpus linguistic techniques and strategies is, in Carter's words (2012: 107–8) that they allow 'significant linguistic patterns to be identified that would not be normally discernible by human intuition'. These, it has to be said, are predominantly lexical: collocations and formulaic clusters or repeated sequences. Software tools are still being developed for grammar, semantics and pragmatics, as Carter himself acknowledges (but see Archer and Bousfield 2010; Walker 2010; and Louw and Milojkovic, Chapter 18 in this volume). Word-play and irony are potentially difficult to tag. And while human intuition might falter over the significant patterns to be discerned across a whole genre or a writer's oeuvre, it can nonetheless work very well, and especially at the outset, for the analysis of long narrative poems and even a whole novel, let alone a play.

Computational tools are therefore best seen as discovery procedures that can enhance existing methods, and confirm or refute a research question or hypothesis. The stylistician is at heart a critic. And as with other tools borrowed from an ever-widening array of (sub-)disciplines, some of which, like cognitive stylistics or indeed (multimodal) semiotics, have a focus away from the text itself, the aim should be use them to 'supplement, rather than supplant' (Simpson 2004: 39) existing methods of analysis. Wherever the stylistician may roam, the text must be the starting and finishing point, with interpretation as the goal. The eclectic nature of stylistics, however, means that new methods or models have the exciting potential of awakening fresh mental constructions and interpretations and of uncovering reverberations even of texts long believed familiar, literary or non-literary.

4

Quantitative methods in literary linguistics

Michael Stubbs

Computer-assisted quantitative analysis of literary texts is especially useful in studying long texts (e.g. whole novels), in comparing individual texts to text collections (e.g. comparing *Frankenstein* to a sample of Gothic fiction), and in identifying characteristics of large text collections (e.g. typical grammatical features of eighteenth- versus twentieth-century novels). A realistic long-term goal is to interpret literary texts not only against the background of other texts from the same literary period or genre, but also against general language use at the same time period as the text itself or against language use today.

Criteria for computer-assisted literary study

In a study of Jane Austen's novels, Burrows (1987: 3) argues optimistically that computer-based methods, supported by statistical analysis, 'make it possible to enter hitherto inaccessible regions of the language [which] defy the most accurate memory and the finest powers of discrimination'. Kenny (1992) is cautious and formulates two evaluative criteria: studies must provide results which could not be obtained without a computer, and which provide an original scholarly contribution to literary studies. In the early 1990s, he could find only a 'sadly small' number of such studies. Over fifteen years later, Hoover (2008) was similarly pessimistic: 'all too often quantitative studies fail to address problems of real literary significance'.

It seems evident that it is pointless to use a computer to analyse literary texts if the analysis can easily be done by hand, and also that computers can discover things (e.g. quantitative features of long texts) that could not be discovered without their help. What has certainly changed since the early 1990s is the easy availability of computer-readable texts and user-friendly software. But the question remains: do large resources lead to results of literary interest?

Fish (1973) famously criticises stylistics in general for being 'circular' and 'arbitrary', due to its selective attention to data. Either we select a few linguistic features that we know how to describe, and ignore the rest; or we select features which we know are important, describe them, and then claim they are important. Since stylisticians can neither describe everything, nor attach definitive meanings to specific formal features, they are apparently caught in a logical fork (which I will call the Fish Fork). These criticisms might seem particularly damaging to quantitative methods. First, software is restricted in what linguistic features it can easily and accurately find (see below). And second, computer-assisted methods can drown us in huge quantities of text and resulting statistics, and make it even more difficult to decide what is significant.

However, the Fish Fork applies to any study of anything. Since pure induction never leads automatically from empirical observations to valid generalisations, you have to know where to look for interesting things. No one claims that computer software provides one single analytic method: it offers a variety of exploratory techniques, which can both document more systematically what literary critics already know (and therefore add to methods of close reading), and also reveal otherwise invisible features of texts. Findings are always open to different interpretations (though some are more plausible than others), and if findings are publicly observable, then they are not created by the analysis and are, to that extent, objective. In any case, Fish's criticism is an example of the pot calling the kettle black, since literary criticism can also be circular and selective. Finally, if software finds previously unrecognised features, then the methods are not circular (Burrows 1992: 182).

Corpus linguistics and literary computing

The mutual scepticism between literary and linguistic textual scholars – so evident in Fish (1973) – is explained by fundamental differences in approach.

Literary scholars look inwards: they usually wish to interpret particular texts and/or make generalisations about a limited set of texts (e.g. from a given author or genre). The individual texts are either unique (e.g. Shakespeare's history plays) or selected from a relatively small set (e.g. Gothic fiction).

Corpus linguists look outwards: they are interested in patterns in general language use (e.g. how words and grammar distinguish fiction and non-fiction), and for this purpose any texts from an incalculably large and open-ended set may provide evidence. Since no individual text is essential, different corpora can be equivalent as valid samples (e.g. of narratives in conversation and in tabloid newspapers).

Literary scholars are often sceptical of quantitative analysis, especially if this implies that literary style can be reduced to statistics about low-level language features (usually words and grammar). They object that deeper thematic and symbolic patterns must be interpreted, not only against linguistic norms, but also against their historical and cultural background.

Linguists are sceptical of imprecise claims (e.g. 'typical of Romantic poetry', 'frequent in Dickens' novels'), and insist on standards of experimental design, comprehensive coverage of data, and replicability. In a computer-assisted analysis, both data and methods must be explicitly defined, which means that the results can be independently checked by any scholar.

For example, it is often said that English prose has shifted over time from an 'elaborate' style to a more 'colloquial' or 'plain' style. Biber and Finegan (1988) make this claim precise by studying the changing distribution of 67 linguistic features in fiction, essays and letters from 1700–99, 1800–65 and 1865–1950. To cite just one finding from their detailed study: they show that earlier fiction (e.g. by Swift) typically makes elaborate and explicit reference (e.g. in many wh-relative clauses), whereas later fiction (e.g. by Lawrence) avoids this and makes direct reference to temporal and physical context (e.g. with time and place adverbials). 'Elaborate' and 'plain' are expressed in clusters of features which occur in complementary distribution, and which can only be revealed by statistical techniques.

The linguists' criticisms could be formulated even more sharply, by demanding that literary study should apply statistical tools, in order to build 'a body of solid knowledge' based on 'evidentiary standards' of hypothesis and proof. However, I am here quoting, not a linguist, but a literary critic (Gottschall 2008a), who sees literary study as 'moribund' and 'aimless', due to its failure to learn from the natural sciences (without, however, 'abandoning the things that make literature special'). Predictably, his article provoked the response that science and art are essentially different modes of knowledge (although in his orginal article, Gottschall explicitly rejects C. P. Snow's 'two cultures' view).

Corpora

In the past, much stylistics was restricted to short texts, often poems and fragments of novels. For example, the opening of Charles Dickens's *Bleak House* (a symbolic description of London in the fog) is a favourite with stylisticians, who typically ignore the remaining 800 pages. I have done this myself in teaching stylistics, because the opening paragraphs contain unusual lexical and grammatical patterns, but a systematic analysis of the novel can hardly be based on such a small and unrepresentative sample.

Until the 1990s, it was impossible to store and search large amounts of text, and stylisticians often described what Phillips (1989: 8) ironically calls 'the extent of language that can comfortably be accommodated on the average blackboard'. This situation has fundamentally changed, given methods for studying text collections which can consist of hundreds of millions of running words. General reference corpora can contain a balanced sample of many different text types, such as casual conversation, contemporary fiction and academic articles. Specialised corpora can consist of a sample of eighteenth-century novels, all of Shakespeare's comedies, and so on, which can be searched for linguistic patterns which are inaccessible to introspection. Readers are especially unaware of patterned dependencies between words and grammar, such as the way in which clusters of features differentiate text types: this is discoverable only with statistical techniques such as multivariate analysis (Biber 1998; Biber and Finegan 1988).

The terms *corpus linguistics* and *corpus stylistics* are often used, but not well chosen, since it is not corpora which are the real object of study, but the texts which they contain. Better terms are 'empirical' or 'data-intensive' linguistics. The basic concepts and analytic methods are explained by one of the founders of the field, Sinclair (1991, 2004), and by Biber et al. (1998), G. Kennedy (1998), Partington (1998), Stubbs (2001), Tognini-Bonelli (2001) and Lindquist (2009). The application of quantitative methods to literary texts is discussed by Burrows (1992), Wynne (2006), Archer (2007), Hoover (2008), Lüdeling (2008) and Mahlberg (2012), and by articles in the journals *Computers and the Humanities* and *Literary and Linguistic Computing*.

The Gutenberg Project provides free plain-text files of 38,000 books (in 2012), both fiction and non-fiction, published before the early 1900s and therefore free of copyright (www.gutenberg.org). The Oxford Text Archive provides corpora of literary and scholarly texts from different periods (http://ota.ahds.ac.uk). Clement and Gueguen (2008) provide an annotated overview of free online resources for many genres (in English only) which allow access to literature 'in ways not possible before the digital age'. Chadwyck-Healey provide, at cost, online access to over a third of a million full-text works of poetry, prose and drama in English (http://lion.chadwyck.co.uk).

General reference corpora include the British National Corpus (BNC), 100 million words of contemporary British English from over 4,000 text samples, accessible at www.natcorp.ox.ac.uk, and via powerful user-interfaces such as BNCweb at http://bncweb.info (Hoffmann et al. 2008). American English data are available from the Corpus of Contemporary American English (COCA, http://corpus.byu.edu/coca), which consists (in 2012) of 425 million words of written texts from 1990 to 2011, and from the Corpus of Historical American English (COHA, http://corpus.byu.edu/coha), which consists (in 2012) of 400 million words of written texts from 1810 to 2009.

Initial examples: word-forms and their distribution

A simple but essential point is that such machine-readable resources can be searched fast and accurately for many kinds of linguistic patterns.

In Conrad's *Heart of Darkness*, the word *dream(s)* occurs twice at the very beginning, then several times in a cluster, when Marlow is *trying to tell* his dream, then fairly regularly throughout the rest of the story. The word *nightmare(s)* occurs once at the beginning, where there are *hints for nightmares*, and then in a cluster towards the end. This simple fact about word distribution is a textual signal that Marlow's dream turns into a nightmare.

We can also search for intertextual references. In the opening and closing paragraphs of *Heart of Darkness* we have the phrase

> waterway leading to the <u>uttermost</u> ends of the earth

The word *uttermost* is not frequent in general English (or in Conrad's other writings), but it is frequent in the King James (1611) translation of the Bible, sometimes in the phrase *uttermost part(s) of the earth*. The phrase *the ends of the earth* is also frequent in the Bible.

We can also study how a single author uses a word in different texts. Shakespeare's Sonnet 18 ('Shall I compare thee . . .') contains several words relating to the weather (*summer's day*, *temperate*) and property law (*lease*, *possession*). One might then wonder whether other words refer to maritime trading (*rough winds*, *changing course*), and whether *untrimmed* in the second quatrain refers to trimming the sails or balancing the ballast of a ship:

> . . . And every fair from fair sometime declines,
> By chance, or nature's changing course <u>untrimm'd</u>

It is easy to check whether Shakespeare uses the word in this sense elsewhere. A search of his complete works provides two clear instances, and therefore evidence that this interpretation of the word in Sonnet 18 is plausible:

> The ship is in her <u>trim</u>; the merry wind
> Blows fair from land . . . (*Comedy of Errors*, IV, i)

> As ravenous fishes, do a vessel follow
> That is new-<u>trimm'd</u> . . . (*Henry VIII*, I, ii.)

Concordances

The most important technique in studying meaning in texts is a concordance. The format of this simple display device can make visible phraseological regularities in texts, and it was recognised in the Middle Ages that this can contribute substantially to textual interpretation. Before computers, only a few texts of special religious and cultural value could justify the enormous manual labour required to construct concordances. One of the most influential, produced for biblical exegesis, was the single-handed work of Alexander Cruden (1737), who also produced an index to Milton's *Paradise Lost* (Cruden 1741). An early Shakespeare concordance was produced by Samuel Ayscough (1790).

The first use of technology was by Roberto Busa. In 1948 he persuaded IBM to begin entering the complete works of Thomas Aquinas into a computer, initially on 11 million punch cards, one for every word analysed. The eventual 20 million lines of text, in 65,000 pages (Busa 2007), was published as the *Index Thomisticus*, for which an online version with a powerful search engine is now freely available (www.corpusthomisticum.org/it/index.age). For many, his work in the 1940s defines the starting point of computer-assisted text analysis:

> The founding moment was [Busa's] creation of a radically transformed, reordered, disassembled and reassembled version of one of the world's most influential philosophies.   *(Ramsay 2008)*

James Joyce's short story *Eveline* tells of a young woman who plans to escape her dreary life in Dublin by eloping with her boyfriend to South America, but in the end she is paralysed with inaction and cannot leave home. The first word is *she*, which occurs 83 times in the story (once every 22 words on average). Figure 4.1 shows all occurrences which are followed immediately by a lexical verb. (Elsewhere, *she* is followed by *BE* (*she was tired*), modal verbs (*she would be married*), references to the past (*she used to visit*), etc.)

Alphabetising the verbs to the right of *she* makes it easy to see that they are almost all mental verbs, some repeated (e.g. *felt, heard, remembered*). Others signal inaction (e.g. *sat, continued to sit*). Only four are clear action verbs: *elbowed* (she is going shopping for her family); *stood up* (she goes to the harbour to meet her boyfriend: but *in a sudden impulse of terror*), *gripped* (she grips the rail at the harbour: but this emphasises her inability to move), and *went* (but it's only hypothetical). This clear pattern – the co-occurrence of a pronoun with a restricted set of verbs – contributes to the textual cohesion and to the interpretation that Eveline thinks, but doesn't/can't act. Stubbs (2001) and O'Halloran (2007) provide computer-assisted analyses of this short story.

It is clear that such a display technique rips textual fragments out of context, but that is precisely its purpose: to display a text differently, to act as an estrangement device, and thereby to reveal patterns which are not otherwise visible (Ramsay 2008). Literary interpretation requires more context than is visible in short concordance lines, but the concordance tells us what to look at in more detail (and most concordance software allows the context to be expanded to full sentences, whole paragraphs, etc.).

```
mined portholes. She answered nothing. She felt her
ors of the sheds she caught a glimpse of the black m
 running out but she continued to sit by the window,
y in her hand as she elbowed her way through the cro
ohemian Girl and she felt elated as she sat in an un
nswered nothing. She felt her cheek pale and cold an
 upon her heart. She felt him seize her hand: - Come
would drown her. She gripped with both hands at the
hall and outside she heard a melancholy air of Italy
 She trembled as she heard again her mother's voice
on his way home; she heard his footsteps clacking al
 in her body and she kept moving her lips in silent
ther's violence. She knew it was that that had given
t organ playing. She knew the air. Strange that it s
er favourite but she liked Harry too. Her father was
 her home. Home! She looked round the room, reviewin
ng over here! As she mused the pitiful vision of her
ming old lately, she noticed; he would miss her. Som
aze of distress, she prayed to God to direct her, to
s over nineteen, she sometimes felt herself in dange
e Hill of Howth. She remembered her father putting o
 given sixpence. She remembered her father strutting
ng as she could. She remembered the last night of he
or her. How well she remembered the first time she h
                 She sat at the window watching the
e felt elated as she sat in an unaccustomed part of
y. Amid the seas she sent a cry of anguish! - Evelin
l called to her. She set her white face to him, pass
 would save her. She stood among the swaying crowd i
Derevaun Seraun! She stood up in a sudden impulse of
final craziness. She trembled as she heard again her
. Was that wise? She tried to weigh each side of the
s love, too. But she wanted to live. Why should she
nto the mist. If she went, tomorrow she would be on
```

Figure 4.1: Occurrences of *she* followed by a lexical verb in *Eveline* by James Joyce

Similarly, in Henry James's novella *The Turn of the Screw*, we can study the verbs following the narrative 'I'. The main story is told by an unreliable, possibly mad, narrator, whose first words are *I remember*. Her unreliability is linguistically signalled by verbs of perception, listed here with their frequencies:

> I felt 45; I know/knew 32; I remember 23; I thought 12; I suppose(d) 11; I believe(d) 6; I saw 31; I see 22; I had seen 13; I could see 9

The lemmas KNOW and MEAN are frequent (in a short text of only 42,880 words):

> know 89, knew 37, known 15, knows 7, knowledge 6, knowing 4, mean 84, meaning 86, meant 82, means 1

In a study of the book (Stubbs 2008), I argue that frequent vocabulary in the semantic fields of perception and knowledge signals important themes of language and (mis)communication. But I conclude, slightly sceptically, that there are few other observable features which linguistic description can get its teeth into. Much hinges on inference and cultural knowledge which leave few traces in the surface of the text. (Alternatively, one could conclude that I was not perceptive enough to find them.)

Basic statistics and exploratory techniques

A computer can find only two things in texts: the frequency of linguistic units (words, phrases and lexicogrammatical structures) and their distribution (within an individual text or across a corpus). Many standard software programs can calculate these two things and display them in a convenient format.

An essential starting point is a *word-frequency list*, usually sorted in alphabetical or frequency order. Sorting by the order of the first use of words in a text can indicate when different topics are introduced. A reverse alphabetical sort (which brings together words with the same inflectional endings) together with a sort by word-length could show that a text contains difficult, abstract vocabulary (e.g. long words ending in *-ment* or *-tion*). Both absolute and relative frequency, and also *distribution*, are important. A word might be frequent in a novel because it is frequent in one single chapter (e.g. *fog* in the opening of *Bleak House*). Or it might be significantly more or less frequent than the norm as measured across a reference corpus: comparing word-frequency lists for a text and a corpus can help to identify *keywords* (Scott 1996).

Software can easily find orthographic word-forms. It is more difficult to identify lemmas because they are abstract categories: e.g. the lemma TAKE is the class of word-forms *take, takes, taking, taken, took*. It is also easy to produce a frequency list of *n-grams*: strings of words (2-grams, 3-grams, etc.) which are repeated verbatim. For example, frequent 5-grams in the King James translation of the Bible include:

> and it came to pass 396; it shall come to pass 120; and he said unto them 95; verily I say unto you 68

Mahlberg (2010) and Fischer-Starcke (2010) show how repeated n-grams are used by Dickens and Austen to characterise protagonists and places.

Collocation – the statistically significant tendency of words to co-occur with other words – is a relation which is essential to the concept of meaningful textual units. But collocations can also be difficult to identify automatically, because they can be variable and discontinuous. That is, words can typically co-occur, but in different forms, sequences and spans. For example, in Conrad's *Heart of Darkness*, the following variants of HEART/DARK (in text order) were identified with software written by Greaves (2009).

hidden evil, to the profound <u>darkness</u> of its <u>heart</u>
penetrated deeper and deeper into the <u>heart</u> of <u>darkness</u>
the deceitful flow from the <u>heart</u> of an impenetrable <u>darkness</u>
the brown current ran swiftly out of the <u>heart</u> of <u>darkness</u>
the barren <u>darkness</u> of his <u>heart</u>
piercing enough to penetrate all the <u>hearts</u> that beat in the <u>darkness</u>
like the beating of a <u>heart</u> – the <u>heart</u> of a conquering <u>darkness</u>
seemed to lead into the <u>heart</u> of an immense <u>darkness</u>

Searching for parts of speech and/or abstract syntactic patterns requires a corpus which is *tagged* with part of speech categories or *parsed*. Such features may seem more relevant to textual interpretation, but as the analytic categories move away from raw text, they become more dependent on the theories and assumptions of the analyst, and more liable to circularity: the analyst tags the text and then studies the tags.

Detailed discussions of measures of distribution (dispersion, range) and collocational attraction, and other statistical features of texts, are provided by Gries (2008), Evert (2008) and Hoover (2008).

Types and tokens

When we say that a short story is 1,800 words long, we are referring to *word-tokens*, some of which will probably be repeated quite frequently. The story will not consist of 1,800 different *word-types*. The *type–token ratio* is the ratio of the number of different words to the number of running words. (In Gertrude Stein's famous example, *A rose is a rose is a rose*, the ratio is 3:8). Rather similar to the type–token ratio is the *lexical density* of a text, which is usually calculated as the ratio of (high-frequency) function words to (lower-frequency) content words. Both ratios provide a measure of the diversity of vocabulary, and are generally lower in casual conversation than in written imaginative fiction.

Youmans (1990) measures the type–token vocabulary curves in a poem by Longfellow, a short story by Hemingway, a basic English version of *Macbeth*, and *Genesis*, plus *Finnegans Wake*, *Ulysses*, late and early passages of *A Portrait of the Artist*, and other literary texts. He shows that statistics on vocabulary can account for our intuitions that texts lie on a continuum between basic English and 'an upper limit for comprehension'.

Words in texts occur in bursts, and are much more likely to occur again in a text once they have occurred once (Alford 1971: 82; Manning and Schütze 1999: 547). Youmans (1991) uses this fact to identify the *vocabulary-management profile* of texts. As a text becomes longer, the type–token ratio decreases, since the number of word-tokens rises at a constant rate, but the number of word-types rises more and more slowly, as words are repeated. The writer must choose 'new' words in order to avoid too much repetition, but must also repeat 'old' words in order to make the text cohesive: this places limits on its lexical diversity. These opposing pressures operate over whole texts, and cyclically over smaller sections, to produce distributions of old and new vocabulary. If the type–token ratio is calculated as a constantly changing ratio, across segments of text, this gives a visual representation of text structure. This is illustrated by graphs in Youmans (1991, 1994) and Stubbs (2001: 136–7).

Keywords

Scott and Tribble (2006: 59–69) identify keywords in *Romeo and Juliet*, using all of Shakespeare's plays as a reference corpus. This confirms major topics (*death, lips, light, love, night, poison*), but probably adds little to a literary interpretation. Culpeper (2009) separates out the keywords in the speech of the six main characters, comparing them in each case with the speech of the other five characters. (Two tests of statistical significance gave very similar results.) The top dozen keywords with their frequencies from three of the characters are as follows:

Romeo: *me* 73, *love* 46, *more* 26, *eyes* 14, *mine* 14, *dear* 13, *farewell* 11, *beauty* 10, *rich* 7, *sick* 6, *blessed* 5, *yonder* 5

Juliet: *I* 138, *my* 92, *that* 82, *thou* 71, *be* 59, *if* 31, *night* 27, *or* 25, *would* 20, *yet* 18, *sweet* 16, *news* 9

Nurse: *you* 55, *it* 39, *day* 22, *Lady* 16, *God* 12, *Lord* 11, *Madam* 10, *he's* 9, *warrant* 7, *woeful* 6, *hie* 5, *quoth* 5

Romeo's keywords convey predominantly propositional content (e.g. *beauty, love, rich*). Juliet's keywords signal her anxiety (*if, would, yet* and subjunctive *be*). The nurse's keywords signal her emotional state (*God, woeful*), relations with people of higher rank (*Lady, Lord, Madam*), and her gossipy nature (*quoth*). Culpeper argues that findings such as the grammatical features which signal Juliet's state of mind are not obvious to introspection.

Collocations in texts, text types and corpora

Words in an individual text can be compared with their typical use in the language. The first paragraph of *A Passage to India* by E. M. Forster is a symbolic description of an Indian town in decline in the aftermath of British colonialism. Many words explicitly denote dirt, decay and disease (e.g. *filth, mud, rotting, rubbish*), but what of the word *swelling* in the final sentence of the paragraph?

the general outline of the town persists, swelling here, shrinking there, like some low form of life.

The word-form occurs 460 times in the BNC. It has medical denotations as in (a), and it has critical or threatening connotations as in (b), but it also has seemingly neutral or even positive uses as in (c) and (d).

(a) *the damaged tissues start swelling*
his eyes and hands were swelling, he was feeling nauseous
(b) *the swelling pride of Louix XIV*
Orc tribes came from the Forest of Shadows, swelling Azhag's horde
(c) *a leading figure in the ever swelling ranks of Irish singer/songwriters*
a mighty wave of sound, swelling in crescendo
(d) *admiration for her husband swelling up in her*
a slow, swelling tide that would eventually wash up on a sun-kissed beach

A few selected examples are unconvincing. However, systematic statistics show that the medical/disease use clearly predominates. The top twenty noun and adjective collocates in a span of 4:4 (using a log-likelihood statistic: see Evert 2008) were as follows:

redness, pain, shrinkage, ranks, chest, lymph, tissues, eyelids, tonsils, inflammation, breast, skin, numbers, irritation, oedema, pride, stomach, glands, tenderness, buds

marked, bruising, hypo-osmotic, facial, slight, shrinking, stinging, rapid, severe, excess, purple, burning, ugly, mild, characteristic, painful, due, gross, left, considerable

This is precise comparative evidence that the word *swelling* contributes to the textual coherence and therefore to our interpretation of the text: its connotations of disease add to the explicit denotations of other words in the paragraph.

Hanks (1988) illustrates in more detail the concept of the typical use of a word, and provides an analysis of the word *hackles*, and its slightly atypical use in a novel by Malcolm Bradbury (... *liberal and radical hackles rise* ...). Louw (1993) provides a similar analysis of the 2-gram *bent on*, and its atypical – and therefore ironic – use in a novel by David Lodge (... *bent on self-improvement* ...).

Words are, of course, used in different ways. In an early comparison of different text types, Haskel (1971) found, contrary to her expectation, that some words are used literally in fiction (e.g. *cut* collocating with *open*), but metaphorically in government documents and newspapers (e.g. *cut* meaning 'decrease'). She used a very small corpus of only a few tens of thousands of words, but I could confirm her hypothesis with a comparison of the lemma CUT in four much larger sub-corpora of the BNC. The top ten noun collocates in a span of five words to left and right were:

[1] prose fiction (16 million words): *hair, throat, voice, engine, words, knife, head, grass, way, bread*
[2] newspapers (9.4 million words): *interest, rates, rate, tax, spending, job, price, costs, jobs, budget*

[3] academic prose (15.8 million words): *expenditure, spending, government, tax, sections, costs, services, benefit, sites, education*

[4] Hansard (1.2 million words): *government, tax, defence, expenditure, training, rates, interest, services, budget, taxes*

There is a large overlap between the collocates in text types [2], [3] and [4], but no overlap at all with the top collocates in [1]. As Haskel (1971: 159) says: '[a] word of diverse meanings is defined by its co-occurrence with other words'.

A case-study – Conrad: Stubbs, Widdowson, Moon

As a final example, I will discuss three related articles on Joseph Conrad's short novel *Heart of Darkness* and its comparison with other fiction and non-fiction. This overtly political text about colonial power has been read in very different ways: it is therefore important to distinguish between objective features of the text and subjective interpretations. In addition, it has been intensively studied since its publication in 1899, so it is a good test of whether computer-assisted techniques can discover anything new.

The main story is told by a seaman called Marlow, who visits a European city, travels up a river in Africa, and becomes obsessed with finding Kurtz, an ivory trader who has apparently gone mad. Marlow finds him, but Kurtz dies on the trip down river. Marlow returns to Europe and tells of his visit to Kurtz's fiancée.

Stubbs (2005)

Critics commonly identify themes such as the hypocrisy of colonisation, and major leitmotifs which are signalled by repeated lexical contrasts, such as light and dark, appearance and reality, and they emphasise many references to Marlow's unreliable and distorted knowledge. In an analysis of the novella (Stubbs 2005), I claim that software can identify textual features of literary significance which critics have not noticed.

The computer makes it easy to find and count intratextual links, between different parts of the novella itself, such as lexical references to vagueness. The novel is very short (fewer than 40,000 words) but there are over 150 occurrences of words such as *dark/ly/ness* (52), *shadow/s/y* (21), *gloom/y* (14), *shape/s/d* (13), *smoke* (10), *fog* (9), *shade* (8), *dusk* (7), *mist/y* (7), *blurred* (2), *haze* (2), *murky* (2), *vapour* (1). These content words have certainly been noticed by critics, who nevertheless tend to ignore high-frequency grammatical words which may have the same effect. For example, there are over 200 occurrences of *something, somebody, sometimes, somewhere, somehow* and *some*, plus around 100 occurrences of *like* (as preposition),

Table 4.1 Examples of vague words per 1,000 word-tokens.
From Stubbs (2005).

	(1) HEART	(2) FICTION	(3) WRITTEN
some	2.6	1.5	1.5
something	1.3	1.0	0.4
somebody	0.2	0.1	0.05
sometimes	0.6	0.2	0.2
somewhere	0.2	0.2	0.03
somehow	0.2	0.1	0.04

plus over 25 occurrences of *kind of* and *sort of*, all often collocated with other expressions of vagueness:

> the outlines of some sort of building
> seemed somehow to throw a kind of light
> I thought I could see a kind of motion
> indistinct, like a vapour exhaled by the earth … misty and silent

If we add all this to occurrences of *seemed* (ca. 50), words expressing vagueness are very frequent (ca. 385): well over three per page. Traditional close reading could reveal such features (though it would obviously be tedious to count them), but manual analysis cannot compare these figures to the norm in other fiction or in a general reference corpus. In Table 4.1. are some statistics for vague words, normalised to occurrences per 1,000 running words, in the novella and in two small corpora of fiction and of mixed written texts (details in Stubbs 2005). Frequencies are consistently higher in HEART than in FICTION, and higher in FICTION than in WRITTEN.

I also studied phraseology, in particular the large number of phrases with the structure

> preposition + the + (adjective) + noun + of + (determiner) + noun.

The following are just a few examples.

> to the edge of the forest
> into the gloomy circle of some inferno
> into the depths of darkness
> towards the depths of the wilderness
> into the heart of darkness

They are not unusually frequent in comparison with general usage. On the contrary, the most frequent 5-grams in the BNC (frequencies per million) include:

> at the end of the 45; in the middle of the 16; at the top of the 11; at the beginning of the 9; at the bottom of the 7; on the edge of the 7.

Corpus data show that people frequently talk about the centre and periphery of spaces (geographical, social and psychological). However, Conrad's place expressions differ from their frequent use in general English. First, they are abstract and vague, and (apart from the Thames) could not be found on any map: they refer to an unnamed *forest* or *river*, to a mythical *inferno*, to an abstract *wilderness*, or to an even more abstract *darkness*. Second, these recurrent phrases are read differently because of the title of the book, the repeated references to characters who are shades and phantoms, on the threshold between this world and the next, and the last sentence, which contains two such phrases:

> to the uttermost ends of the earth
> into the heart of an immense darkness

Widdowson (2008)

Widdowson (2008) comments at length on my study (Stubbs 2005) and makes the unassailable point that

> As a text *Heart of Darkness* consists of observational data that can be analysed by computer. As a novel, however, it can only be subjectively interpreted.
> *(Widdowson 2008: 303)*

He is sceptical of corpus methods, which, by discussing only selected textual facts, presuppose a previous impressionistic literary interpretation. But he admits that these methods have discovered new facts about the text and have inspired him to look for further similar facts.

In my article, I find intratextual links between the two descriptions of the European city, before and after Marlow's journey to Africa: first, *high houses*, *narrow and deserted street* and *doors ponderously ajar*, and then *a ponderous door* and *between tall houses*. Widdowson (2008: 297) finds that these words also occur in the description of the jungle: a stretch of river is *narrow*, *straight*, *with high sides*, and there are *high walls* of trees. The word *deserted* occurs only three times, once in the description of the city, and twice in descriptions of the African scene. That is, he uses simple search techniques to discover observable lexical connections between different parts of the text. In addition, he finds that 'adjectives generally seem to be in short supply in the text': only *sombre* and *black* are in the top fifty keywords (using the BNC as a reference corpus). He then uses this fact in his own interpretation:

> One might conclude that it is a rather featureless world that Marlow describes, a monochrome world in black and white, a kind of abstraction.
> *(Widdowson 2008: 294)*

In a word, although initially sceptical, Widdowson uses the same quantitative methods to discover different objective (but not entirely clear-cut) textual facts, on which he bases subjective literary interpretations (of which I am sure Fish would disapprove). I conclude from this, as the statistician George Box famously said, 'all models are wrong, but some are useful' (Box and Draper 1987: 424).

Moon (2007)

Moon (2007) analyses word-frequency data from four corpora: fiction by Conrad, adventure fiction by other authors, factual nineteenth-century tales of exploration, and a 450-million-word corpus of general English from the late 1980s and 1990s. This provides facts which certainly could not be collected without computer-assistance, and allows her to formulate hypotheses about the relation between lexical frequency and connotative meaning.

Firstly, she provides general statistics about Conrad's vocabulary that indicate roughly how familiar Conrad's vocabulary is to a reader around 100 years later. It is notoriously difficult to estimate the vocabulary size of educated speakers, but around 20,000 word families (i.e. head-words plus their derivatives) is a common estimate. Less than 10 per cent of word-tokens in Conrad's novels fall outside the top 10,000 lemmas in the contemporary reference corpus: that is, most word-tokens in the running text are still current. However, over 50 per cent of the word-types are not among the top 10,000 lemmas: in other words, he uses a large number of relatively infrequent words (which each occur infrequently). (Bear in mind here that most text (i.e. running word-tokens) comprises a relatively small number of frequent word-types, but that most word-types occur infrequently.)

Second, she presents findings about Conrad's topics. Lexical words that are frequent in Conrad but not in the other two nineteenth-century corpora include body part nouns (*eyes*, *face*) and epistemic verbs (*know*, *seemed*). Several words which occur in Conrad, but which are rare in the large corpus, have emotive connotations (e.g. *solitude*, *sombre*, *violently*).

Third, in addition to looking at raw comparative word frequencies in the three corpora, she adopts a 'stratified approach' to see if there is 'some simple mechanism to foreground words of potential interest' (Moon 2007: 13). She groups words in the texts into three frequency bands, defined as words occurring in the reference corpus at least 50 times, 10–49 times, and 5–9 times per million tokens, and then examines the most frequent words within each band. Readers will have to consult her article for detailed statistics, but her general finding is that, as frequencies fall from band 1 to 3, there is a shift from denotation (propositional meaning) to connotation (evaluative meaning). In addition, there is a similar progression in the lexis across individual texts: words are not distributed evenly across the texts. Here she provides detailed statistics which can generalise from my observation (Stubbs 2005: 16) that there is a marked increase in the frequency of *heart*, *dark* and *darkness* towards the end of *Heart of Darkness*.

Moon admits that any set of words, identified as significant through frequency, still involves selection, and that information which is derived quantitatively is not thereby wholly objective. Nevertheless, taken together, these three studies – particularly with the inclusion of Moon (2007) – fulfil, I think, the evaluative criteria proposed by Kenny (1992). They lead to novel findings which could not be obtained without a computer and to interpretations of literary interest. Computer-assisted studies allow precise quantitative findings to be confirmed (or, of course, refuted), and allow individual observations about one text to be developed into general hypotheses about words and meaning.

Conclusion

Computer-assisted methods can find linguistic patterns in large quantities of textual data, and therefore reveal previously inaccessible aspects of literary style. Perhaps the simplest point is that analysts have a responsibility to use all available sources of information, and this includes quantitative information.

Beyond that, I have tried to take a balanced position. An aversion to quantitative methods can sometimes be due to a fear of mathematics in general, although most of the counting discussed above is of a very simple kind. Conversely, exaggerated optimism that such methods will lead immediately to new insights may be due to a naive enthusiasm for technology. Simply identifying quantitative features of text does not lead automatically to results of literary interest, since there are always non-linguistic factors, historical, cultural and psychological, and since there is always an intuitive leap from objective textual facts to subjective literary interpretation. It is clear that some information which is relevant to a literary interpretation is not quantifiable (e.g. beliefs about ghosts and witches at the time when Shakespeare wrote *Hamlet* and *Macbeth*). It is also clear that quantification is reductionist, but then that is its purpose: to reduce large amounts of information to manageable generalisations, and this is something which literary scholars also usefully do (e.g. all Jane Austen's novels are social satires about courtship and marriage).

The problem of the Fish Fork has to be dealt with. However, rather than merely rejecting or endorsing quantitative stylistics, it is more interesting to build Fish's challenge into a series of ranked criteria against which studies could be judged:

(1) Rejection. Stylistic analysis adds nothing to close reading. Worse, it is circular, since it merely describes a few things which we already knew

were important. Furthermore, the frequency of a linguistic feature does not determine its literary importance.

(2)   A weak defence. Perhaps stylistic analysis tells us nothing new, but it provides precise linguistic descriptions. Computers can count (some) things accurately across large text collections, and there is, after all, some relation between frequency and salience.

(3)   A stronger defence. Quantitative analysis can discover linguistic features which even expert scholars have not noticed and/or which cannot be discovered by a manual analysis: for example, relative frequencies of patterns in a text and in a large reference corpus.

(4)   The strongest(?) defence. A systematic stylistic analysis not only describes new things, but also helps to explain readers' literary reactions, which are based on unconscious linguistic knowledge of norms of language use and stylistic variation.

In summary: there has certainly been progress since the 1990s, but the number of convincing studies is still relatively limited, and it is doubtful if any studies have yet managed to meet the criteria in (4), and to progress, in an entirely convincing way, from descriptive to explanatory adequacy.

The use of quantitative resources in stylistics is only one small corner of a large field, which is now known as the digital humanities: a data-driven approach to large quantities of digitalised data, which can be accessed and manipulated in different ways in order to reveal patterns and connections (Schreibman et al. 2004; Schreibman and Siemens 2007). As Moulin et al. (2011: 12–13) say: 'A scholar of 19th century literature could never hope to read every book published in the 1800s – but a computer can.'

Acknowledgements

For critical comments on an earlier draft I am grateful to Achim Engels, Dorothea Halbe, Markus Müller and Bettina Fischer-Starcke.

5

Stylistics as rhetoric

Craig Hamilton

Introduction

This chapter, and the next two, define stylistics according to different traditions. The very titles of these three chapters are *A-as-B* constructions, whereby a specific term (*A*) is imagined as a generic one (*B*). Examples such as *My daughter as a bird* or *My life as a movie* offer us specific and generic terms that are *unrelated*. Daughters are daughters and birds are birds; only by a feat of the imagination can we think or speak of daughters *as* birds. Yet that feat of the mind, known as categorisation, is a vital technique of definition. That said, to define stylistics as rhetoric, applied linguistics or literary criticism, to categorise it as such, may seem odd. As I show in this chapter, stylistics comes from rhetoric, historically speaking, which makes stylistics and rhetoric *closely* related terms. Georges Molinié puts it this way in his treatise on French stylistics: 'In the beginning there was rhetoric, and since two ancestors are needed, let us say that Aristotle was the founding father' (1997: 5; my translation). As I explain elsewhere (Hamilton 2008), the other ancestor of stylistics, albeit a more recent one, is linguistics. However, in this chapter I argue that without rhetoric in the past, there would be no stylistics in the present. In what follows, I discuss the study of rhetoric and style in the ancient world, and the consequent shift from rhetoric to stylistics after the fifteenth century. Then, I briefly discuss two definitions of stylistics, before concluding with a short analysis of a recent editorial.

Studying rhetoric and style in the ancient world

The formal study of rhetoric as we know it in the west started with the ancient Greeks, who systematised it for didactic reasons. For Aristotle, rhetoric was 'the faculty of observing in any given case the available means of persuasion' (1954: 24). This is a useful definition given its broad scope which, as we will see later, encompasses style. In *Rhetoric*, Aristotle also introduced three main genres of rhetoric: deliberative, forensic, and epideictic (1954: 31–4). Deliberative rhetoric is political and involves questions about the *future*. A question such as 'Should NATO go into Syria?' is a deliberative one. Forensic rhetoric is judicial and involves questions about the *past*. A question such as 'What caused the space shuttle *Challenger* to explode in 1986?' is a forensic one, fit for a courtroom. Finally, epideictic rhetoric may be ceremonial or functional and is often concerned with the *present*. President Obama's famous eulogy in Tucson on 12 January 2011, or Sarah Crompton's encomium (2012) praising Thomas Heatherwick, the British designer who created the amazing Olympic cauldron for the 2012 London Games, are but two rather recent examples. Arguably, literature is another kind of epideictic rhetoric, and we might better understand the connection between rhetoric and stylistics if we recall the role literature played in rhetorical education.

Most teachers of classical rhetoric in the past probably aimed to help students become effective speakers and writers, rather than talented poets or playwrights. And yet, texts such as Aristotle's *Rhetoric* contain many examples from literature. This is especially true of book III of *Rhetoric*, where Aristotle discusses style. Presumably, Aristotle was not breaking new ground by including literary examples. As Jeanne Fahnestock notes, 'Rhetorical training drew on all genres and considered all texts in terms of their effectiveness. There was no special domain of "literariness" in the rhetorical tradition' (2005: 216). It thus seems that any example was useful no matter where it came from as long as it helped students learn how to compose their own texts with style in any of the three genres. As Bennison Gray maintains (1973: 508), the epic poems of Homer and Virgil were integral to education in ancient Greece and Rome, not only for the purpose of literacy but also for the purpose of commentary. Modern criticism's belief that literature should be put upon a pedestal is thus unusual given the history of western education. Whether they know it or not, scholars today in stylistics who value literature, not for its own sake but for the sake of pedagogy, are following in the footsteps of the rhetorical tradition.

Another interesting aspect of rhetorical education was its bilingual nature. As Gray states:

> From the Romans on, there is no question that education was bilingual,
> even when it ceased to be so in the sense that the child ceased in practice
> to learn Greek as well as Latin. For classical Latin literature, written on
> Greek models, with a highly Grecized vocabulary and in a very
> conservative Latin with borrowings from the archaic, produced the same
> results. The *Aeneid* was intended to resemble the *Iliad* and *Odyssey*,

and insofar as it did resemble them linguistically, it could be studied in just the way they were, even by those students for whom colloquial Latin was the native idiom.   *(Gray 1973: 508)*

Linguistic differences between students and the texts they studied was first apparent when ancient Greeks who spoke the Attic dialect studied Homer's epic poems, which had been composed a few centuries earlier, mainly in the Ionic dialect (Gray 1973: 506). Although students who spoke Latin studied in Latin later in Rome, more advanced Roman students of rhetoric also studied in Ancient Greek (Fahnestock 2011: 7). European students of rhetoric then studied for centuries mainly in Latin, which gradually became a dead language. Today, while English students may sometimes feel that the English used in texts from a few centuries ago is a foreign language, students who now study rhetoric or stylistics in foreign languages have more in common with students from the past than they may realise.

To return to the ancient world, students copied out the epic poems recited by their teachers, who had to ensure the poems were copied down properly. This is how students learned to read, write and increase their vocabulary. A *grammaticus* would have been the boys' first formal teacher, the one who taught them reading and writing – or *grammatike* in Greek and *litteratura* in Latin (Gray 1973: 506). Later, a teacher of rhetoric could then take over. In the Middle Ages, Latin translations of the Bible replaced epic literature, although the bilingual method of instruction remained intact, with the epic text on the left of the page and the student's translation and commentary on the right side. According to Gray (1973: 508), 'The type of the literary treatise from antiquity on was the commentary, which, with its line-by-line translation and linguistic description of the text, varied rarely by excursions into less verbal areas such as character consistency and allegorical justification of questionable passages, embodied the schoolroom method of literary study.' The specific study of style arguably began with these commentaries and continued with the advanced study of rhetoric (see Copeland and Sluiter (2009) for examples of Medieval commentaries). According to Fahnestock, because '[a]dvice about style in the rhetorical tradition builds on a mastery of language basics while preparing the student for life as an active citizen' (2011: 7), it seems that understanding style was important from the classroom of childhood to the active life of adulthood.

Students of rhetoric usually studied its five so-called canons, which consisted of:

(1)   invention, or knowing how to create arguments
(2)   arrangement, or deciding how to organise arguments
(3)   style, or understanding what forms and figures to use and when
(4)   memory, or mnemonic techniques for memorising speeches, for instance
(5)   delivery, or knowing how to give a speech or compose a text properly.

For many years the syllabus covered these five canons, but they developed in different ways over time. For example, Aristotle (and later Cicero) laid down rules for arrangement that were adhered to for centuries and remain useful today. Meanwhile, emphasis on memory and delivery, vital in oral cultures, waned as writing and printing grew in importance after the fifteenth century. However, the remaining two canons – invention and style – never lost their allure. Aristotle, for instance, wrote about style in book III of his *Rhetoric*, and he offered no fewer than twenty-eight common topics for inventing arguments in book II. Since then, generation after generation, finding something to say and saying it properly have remained a problem. This is obvious in the example of staircase wit, or what the French call *l'esprit de l'escalier*. This shortcoming, which befalls even the best of minds at times, refers to coming up with a witty response, unfortunately when it is too late. It is not always easy to find something to say, to say it with style, and to say it when needed; timing is crucial, as the ancient Greeks knew full well with their concept of *kairos*. Even though it is better to have staircase wit than no wit at all, this example reminds us why invention and style are still relevant.

When we compare the fates of invention and style, there apparently was a change after the Middle Ages. Walter Ong's bold claim that invention 'received the lion's share of attention' (1968: 45) in rhetorical theory may be true up to 1500, but arguably less so afterwards. Texts on invention were popular well into the fifteenth century, as the anonymous *Tria Sunt* from Oxford at that time shows (Copeland and Sluiter 2009: 670–81). But according to Fahnestock, 'of all the parts of rhetoric, style is arguably the most implicated in the others, since linguistic choice is the point of realisation for the rhetorical precepts and theories belonging to the other canons' (2011: 7). Other hypotheses about the centrality of style abound. For instance, Dan Sperber and Deirdre Wilson provocatively state:

> Rhetoric took pride of place in formal education for two and a half millennia. Its very rich and complex history is worth detailed study, but it can be summarized in a few sentences. Essentially the same substance was passed on by eighty generations of teachers to eighty generations of pupils. If there was a general tendency, it consisted simply in a narrowing down of the subject matter of rhetoric: one of its ... branches, *elocutio*, the study of figures of speech, gradually displaced the others, and in some schools became identified with rhetoric *tout court*. ... This narrowing was not even offset by a theoretical deepening. Pierre Fontanier's *Les figures du discours* does not substantially improve on Quintilian's *Institutio oratoria*, despite the work of sixty generations of scholars in between.
>
> *(Sperber and Wilson 1990: 140)*

Dismissing rhetoric is not new, of course, as Plato's critique of it in *Gorgias* and *Phaedrus* reminds us. Whether or not any intellectual progress was made between Quintilian and Fontanier is irrelevant here, but the 'narrowing' of rhetoric mentioned above is pertinent. Sperber and Wilson, who have re-shaped the contemporary study of pragmatics, make two major claims. On the one hand, they equate style with figures alone, but we need look no further than this very Handbook to see that while interest in figurative language remains strong in stylistics, topics such as phonology, semantics, dialogue and pragmatics are also important today. On the other hand, the claim that rhetoric was restricted to figures alone requires some explanation.

Moving from rhetoric to stylistics

After Rome, rhetoric continued to be taught and used by various scholars in the Middle Ages (Copeland and Sluiter 2009), but in the Renaissance, the re-discovery of classical texts, their translation into vernaculars and widespread circulation thanks to printing, helped to rejuvenate rhetoric. As Brian Vickers explains, 'Rhetoric reached its highest degree of influence, in modern times, in the great expansion of European education between 1500 and 1750. At every level of society, for every literary genre, as for the arts of painting, architecture, and music, rhetoric was an indispensable accomplishment for the civilized man or woman' (1988: 196). The sixteenth century was thus a turning point for rhetoric, which is also when its narrowing down began. Evidence for this can be seen in the reduction of the style canon itself to the study of just four main tropes: metaphor, metonymy, synecdoche and irony. Vickers (1988: 439) says he is unsure who started this practice yet nevertheless blames 'Talon (1547), Ramus (1549), Vossius (1605), Keckermann (1606), Farnaby (1625), and Smith (1657)'. Peter Ramus (1515–72) was particularly influential. As a professor in Paris, he promoted 'a curtailed rhetoric focusing almost entirely on stylistic features' (Cockcroft and Cockcroft 2005: 10). According to James Herrick, 'Rhetorical treatises after Ramus tended toward discussions of style and ornament' (2001: 163), which suggests there was a pre-Ramus and post-Ramus period in the history of rhetoric. But his 'narrowing down of rhetoric' (Cockcroft and Cockcroft 2005: 10) might have been motivated by institutional concerns. Since the history of ideas is but the history of people in specific places and times, we should remember that the aim of Ramus to circumscribe rhetoric was expressed at a time of confusion over disciplinary boundaries (Cockcroft and Cockcroft 2005: 11). The circumscription of rhetoric starting in the sixteenth century might thus be understood in this context.

Unsurprisingly, these developments had consequences. A main one was that rhetoric was 'detached from its expressive and persuasive functions, and [was] brought down finally to a handful of tropes' (Vickers 1988: 439). Herrick would agree, given his opinion that '[r]hetoric's capacity as a practical art of discourse concerned with discovering arguments toward the resolution of important issues was largely lost' after Ramus (2001: 163). Ramus is usually recalled as a controversial figure, not because he was a Protestant (and thus murdered during the infamous 1572 massacre of French Protestants), but because he was constantly criticising Aristotle, Cicero and others. His reconfiguration of rhetoric was nevertheless highly influential. As Vickers writes, 'The reforms of Ramus and Talon [his friend] may indeed have separated rhetoric from dialectic, but in their systematic development of *elocutio*, and their espousal of the vernaculars, the Ramists had a beneficial influence in applying rhetoric to literature' (1988: 206). In an odd twist of fate, then, just as literature fed into rhetoric in the past, rhetoric seems to have fed into literature from the sixteenth century onwards.

Limiting rhetoric to style, or to just a few tropes, might have started in the sixteenth century, but it took a long time. Vickers admits 'it is not easy to reconstruct the process by which this atrophying has come about' (1988: 439), but several names nevertheless stand out after the sixteenth century. For instance, Vico (1668–1744) famously emphasised metaphor, metonymy, synecdoche and irony in his work. He was a 'Professor of Rhetoric at the University of Naples for forty years' (Vickers 1988: 183) although 'he would have preferred to teach law' (C. Miller 2012: 24). The title of a recent book, *Vico and the Transformation of Rhetoric in Early Modern Europe* (Marshall 2010), implies just how important Vico was to rhetoric. His idea that rhetoric could 'be exploited for a variety of purposes, both contradictory and complementary', and his 'implementation of rhetoric for immediate purposes, including both historical reconstruction and political persuasion', were things he put into practice in Naples (C. Miller 2012: 24). In the twentieth century, the historian Hayden White claimed that Vico's four tropes inspired his own work on historiography (Vickers 1988: 440–1). After Vico in Italy, there was Du Marsais in eighteenth-century France. Gérard Genette apparently felt that 'the final process of reducing it [rhetoric] to the study of tropes took place with the publication in 1730 of the treatise *Des Tropes* by Du Marsais' (Vickers 1988: 451). Like Vico before him, Du Marsais focused on metaphor, metonymy, synecdoche and irony. However, when Fontanier re-edited the work of Du Marsais in 1818, he 'rejected irony' to focus only on metaphor, metonymy and synecdoche (Vickers 1988: 451).

Many writers in Germany, France and England in the eighteenth and nineteenth centuries – such as Goethe, Büchner, Wordsworth, De Quincey, Lamartine, Vigny, Hugo, Stendhal and Flaubert (Vickers 1988: 197–8) – studied rhetoric as students at a time when *elocutio* was gaining in significance. In the twentieth century, however, reducing rhetoric to tropes had severe consequences. The process of elimination seems to have gathered pace when Roman Jakobson decided to focus on just two tropes alone: metaphor and metonymy. Vickers, who excoriates Jakobson for different reasons, many of them methodological, notes there were things that Jakobson misunderstood. Take, for example, Jakobson's distinction of contiguity and similarity relations. The pseudo-Ciceronian *Rhetorica ad Herrennium* makes it clear that 'contiguity', according to Vickers, 'is a variant form of "similarity", not a polar opposite to it. What Jakobson does is to take the binary oppositions that he has established for linguistics – combination / substitution, code / context, paradigmatic / syntagmatic – and then forcibly impose these on the two tropes that he has picked out' (1988: 444). Jakobson's famous axes of contiguity and similarity, relied on partly to differentiate metaphor from metonymy, seem more similar than different, thus making their differentiation problematic. You cannot distinguish metaphor from metonymy in terms of contiguity and similarity if the former is but another kind of the latter. Furthermore, Jakobson's alignment of metaphor with poetry, and of metonymy with prose – which Eikhenbaum had already proposed in 1923 (Vickers 1998: 451) – is misleading. In short, trying to fit all of style or rhetoric or literature into just two categories makes them hopelessly 'malleable' and 'too vast to be usable' (Vickers 1988: 447).

Last but not least in Vickers's diatribe is Paul de Man. Several publications by de Man, notably those with the word 'rhetoric' in the title, would suggest a real interest in rhetoric. Yet Vickers explains in detail how some of the texts de Man writes about, such as Rousseau's *Essai sur l'origine des langues* or Nietzsche's 1872-3 lectures on rhetoric in Basel, seem to have been deliberately misrepresented. By going back to the texts de Man discusses in his 'rhetoric' essays, Vickers suggests that their unfair distortion was carried out to intentionally condemn rhetoric. De Man set metaphor against metonymy à la Jakobson, showed the limitations of each one, made them 'negate each other', and then reached the conclusion that since neither trope was adequate, rhetoric was hopeless and could be abandoned (Vickers 1998: 459). Because Vickers argues at length (in Chapter 9 of *In Defence of Rhetoric*) about the unfair treatment rhetoric has been subjected to over the past few centuries, his harsh critique of Jakobson, de Man and others is understandable in its context.

Moving from Ramus to Vico, from Du Marsais to Fontanier, and from Jakobson to de Man, is a brutally succinct way of saying how we went from rhetoric to style, and then from four tropes to three, from three to two, and from two to one, until we were left with almost none. But why did the circumscription of rhetoric and style occur at all? As I mentioned earlier, uncertainty over disciplinary boundaries might have led scholars to limit rhetoric to style, and then style to a few tropes or figures, to clarify divisions of labour. The complicated birth of academic disciplines after the fifteenth century, and the linguistic turn the human sciences took in the twentieth century, reveal that rhetoric underwent changes in different places at different times. A positive justification may be found in more recent research in cognitive linguistics, which shows how metaphor (G. Lakoff and Johnson 1980) and metonymy (Langacker 2008) define our conceptual and linguistic systems. Vickers suggests yet another cause as well. Deconstructionists such as de Man seem to 'be expressing modern anxieties about language, with the curiously self-satisfying claim that language is an unreliable tool,' he writes, 'but they ought not foist those anxieties on to rhetoric' (Vickers 1988: 459). Having said that, there might be some cause for hope.

Rhetorical stylistics and literary stylistics

The intense focus on figures or tropes certainly contributed to the rise of stylistics. Yet arguing that rhetoric became stylistics, or that stylistics overtook rhetoric, may be too simple. According to Molinié (1997: 5–10), there is not one kind of rhetoric but three. The first type focuses on argumentation, which began with Aristotle's *Rhetoric* and continues today in fields such as pragmatics, including the theory of relevance developed by Sperber and Wilson (1990). The second type, focusing on figures of style, began with Aristotle's *Poetics* (and, I would add, book III of his *Rhetoric*), and continues today in stylistics. The third type of rhetoric is normative and prescriptive, regarding both the production and the analysis of literary and non-literary texts. Molinié feels this third type can involve the other two, given the tendency of some rhetorical theorists to combine the first two types in their manuals about this third type (1997: 10). If he is right, this may explain how the work of Jakobson or others in stylistics in the 1950s or 1960s could coexist, for instance, with *The New Rhetoric* (Perelman and Olbrechts-Tyteca 1969).

Lest we forget, the term *stylistics* usually refers to the linguistic analysis of *literary* texts, especially in France, where there is a sharp divide between *la stylistique* (for literature) and *l'analyse du discours* (for everything else). In English stylistics, however, recent definitions carefully avoid the word *literature*. For instance, Simpson calls stylistics 'a method of textual interpretation in which primacy of place is assigned to *language*' (2004: 3), while Peter Verdonk calls stylistics 'the study of style, which can be defined as the analysis of distinctive expressions in language and the description of its purpose and effect' (2002: 4). These definitions imply that English stylistics can involve non-literary texts too. And yet, Fahnestock distinguishes 'rhetorical stylistics' from 'literary stylistics'. She notes that 'stylistics' (without a modifying adjective) normally refers to 'literary stylistics' before admitting:

> While a rhetorical stylistics can be, and often is, deployed to identify the unique features of a text or rhetorical artist, its goal is not the discovery of uniqueness per se. Its theoretical aim is rather the identification of functional features in language that have a predictable potential no matter who uses them, so that given similar purposes, it is likely that authors will choose similar functional structures.   *(Fahnestock 2011: 12)*

For Fahnestock, the goal of (literary) stylistics is to identify markers of a particular writer's style, whereas the goal of rhetorical stylistics is more general. She also notes that stylistics usually involves literary texts, whereas rhetorical stylistics typically involves non-literary texts. The difference she finds between rhetorical stylistics and literary stylistics follows from a basic distinction: students in a *Rhetoric* course aim to produce primary texts, whereas students in a *Stylistics* course aim to produce secondary texts. Granted, both students of rhetoric and students of stylistics may produce commentaries on (or analyses of) texts written (or spoken) by others. However, while students of stylistics might stop after writing *a secondary text about a primary text*, students of rhetoric may continue onward to produce their own primary texts, such as speeches or proposals. Of course, nothing prevents teachers of stylistics from having students write poems, plays or novels as part of the course, thus problematising the primary text / secondary text divide. But for Fahnestock, at least, stylistics and rhetorical stylistics use different materials and have separate aims, which leads me to my analysis.

Analysis of an editorial

Here I focus on a recent editorial from the 3 September 2012 edition of *The Detroit Free Press*. Sentences have been numbered for the purpose of analysis.

> *Student-teacher nexus is still key to achievement*

1 Michigan is logging a lot of firsts this week: the first two school districts converted to charter systems; the Detroit debut of the soon-to-be-statewide Educational Achievement Authority to buoy underperforming schools; increased opportunities for high school students to take community college classes; more charter schools; and the possibility of more cyber schools.

2 But all these systemic firsts should not detract from what matters most for the majority of Michigan's children: the first day of school, when student meets teacher and the on-the-ground activity known as education begins.

3 Set aside the politics, the debates about choice, even the impacts of budgets and policy decisions made in Lansing, and there's still the inescapable fact that it is the interaction between teacher and student that really counts.

4 The potential lying within each child is what excites parents and teachers dedicated to their profession.

5 The nurturing of that potential is often not the stuff of poetry.

6 For parents, it means instilling good eating and sleeping habits, and disciplining themselves enough to run an organized household and ensure a school-day routine.

7   Good teachers also know how to make organization and routine work to provide a backdrop where every child can learn.

8   As tumultuous as the politics surrounding schools can be, most people seem happy with their child's school (even while complaining about schools in general).

9   And, in fact, good teaching happens in schools all over the state.

10 In a study released in July (www.mackinac.org/17256), the conservative Mackinac Center assessed high school test scores against a measure of poverty to rank school performance on a more level playing field – and found charter schools and traditional district schools intermixed throughout their results.

11 Charter schools are not a panacea, and some seemingly well-off suburban districts appear to be not doing much more than going through the motions.

12 Parents and the community need to get and stay involved to ensure the schools that matter to them are making an actual difference.

13 It is also sobering to remember that Michigan has raised the benchmarks for student achievement to align better with standards for college readiness, and tests scored on those benchmarks show schools still face a big gap in boosting students onto that track.

14 There are signs of progress, but there are also signs of problems, such as a widening gap in achievement between white and minority students.

15 Parents, neighbors and policymakers alike need to remember that as Michigan's population stagnates – and grows older – each schoolchild becomes an increasingly precious resource.

16 That's what matters as school starts, and every Michigander has an investment in encouraging all students to reach their full potential.

(The Detroit Free Press 2012)

A rhetorical analysis can entail many different factors, ranging from the generic to the specific. First, this text can be classified as belonging to a specific *genre*: it is an editorial. Strictly speaking, it is neither forensic nor epideictic; rather, it is deliberative, exhorting readers to help improve schools. It thus relates more to the future than to the past, even if there are moments of praise and blame here.

Second, as for *kairos* (timing), the fact that the editorial ran on Monday 3 September is important. Every rhetorical act is a situated one, and in the USA the first Monday of September is Labor Day, a national holiday that unofficially marks the end of summer. Labor Day is the May Day of America since 1 May is not an American holiday. Traditionally, the new school year in Michigan begins on the first Tuesday of September, just after Labor Day. Therefore, it is entirely fitting to run an editorial about education on the eve of the new academic year. What is more, on the first day of the week in the first week of September before the first day of school, it is also appropriate to refer to several 'firsts' [1].

Third, apart from *kairos* there is *invention*, a canon of classical rhetoric. Common topics are one tool for inventing arguments, and at least two of them give rise to the editorial. Following Aristotle, Richard Lanham writes, just as we can argue about 'what can and cannot happen,' so too can we argue 'from consequences, good and bad' (1991: 167). The editorial mentions 'the possibility of more cyber schools' in [1], but its main focus is the *possibility* of improving schools. Exhortation occurs specifically in [12] and [15]. The common topic of *possibility* is embodied in modality: parents and the community (meaning neighbours and policymakers) 'need to get and stay involved' [12] and 'need to remember' [15] why education is so important. The fact that they 'need to' do this implies they are not now doing so. As for the negative consequences of the status quo, [13] and [14] refer to students who are unprepared for university, and to differences between white and minority students. Meanwhile, [15] implies that properly educating children should be a priority in a state with a population that 'stagnates – and grows older.' By writing about the negative consequences of the status quo, and about what is possible in the future, the authors of the editorial draw on at least two common topics from classical rhetoric for inventing arguments.

Fourth, there is *arrangement*, another canon of classical rhetoric. According to Lanham (1991: 171), an introduction – or *prooimion* in Greek and *exordium* in Latin – should be designed so that it 'catches the audience's attention'. The narration 'sets forth the facts' while the division 'sets forth points stipulated (agreed on by both sides) and points to be contested'. The proof 'sets forth the argument that supports one's case' while the refutation section 'refutes opponent's arguments'. Finally, the peroration 'sums up arguments and stirs the audience'. This kind of arrangement may seem complex, but at the very least a deliberative text will contain an introduction, a statement of the issue or narrative, a proof and a conclusion (Crowley and Hawhee 1999: 198). Although Crowley and Hawhee on the one hand, and Lanham on the other, offer slightly different ideas on arrangement, we can nevertheless see that the editorial is arranged in a particular manner. The headline and [1] get readers' attention, while the last half of [16] provides a moving conclusion. Because the case is an 'ambiguous' one, meaning 'there is some doubt about the issue' (Crowley and Hawhee 1999: 203), the decision to objectively spell out facts in the introduction seems particularly fitting. But the sentences from [2] to [15] follow an unexpected order. The 'narration' from [2] to [9] combines facts *and* opinions in order to support the claim that 'it is the interaction between teacher and student that really counts' [3]. The 'inartificial proof' or 'evidence' (Lanham 1991: 166) that 'good teaching happens in schools all over the state' [9] is provided by the Mackinac Center's report cited in [10]. The same evidence supports the argument at the end of [10] that 'charter schools and traditional district schools' have 'intermixed' results. This is meant to refute the opinion that charter schools are always better, and it supports the newspaper's opinion that 'Charter schools are not a panacea' [11]. The refutation continues from [11] to [14], where problems in all schools are mentioned, including those readers might think are good. The conclusion comes in [15] and [16], urging readers to take action in 'encouraging all students to reach their full potential'.

The fifth factor to consider is style. The series of 'firsts' in [1] is organised in a teleological way: what has already happened, what will happen soon and what might happen in the future. The more conventional pattern of listing elements from shortest to longest (Fahnestock 2011: 245) is not followed in this series. Metaphors are also used such as 'buoy' [1], 'level playing field' [10], 'panacea' [11], and 'signs of progress' [14], which is an instance of the *event structure* conceptual metaphor (G. Lakoff and Turner 1989). There are antitheses as well; for instance, [2] contrasts with [1] to mark a shift in foregrounding, while 'organization and routine' in [7] contrasts with the 'tumultuous' politics of education in [8]. Meanwhile, within [8] there is a contrast between 'schools in general' (which people dislike) and 'their child's school' (which ironically they like). Sentences also vary in length and syntactic complexity. There are 27 words on average in each sentence, much more than the Ellegard norm of 18 words reported by Leech and Short (2007: 90). The greatest syntactic complexity can be seen in [1], [2], [10] and [13], while the shortest and simplest structures can be found in [4], [5] and [9]. Perhaps the most interesting sentence is [3] given its *iconicity*: 'Set aside the politics, the debates about choice, even the impacts of budgets and policy decisions made in Lansing, and there's still the inescapable fact that it is the interaction between teacher and student that really counts.' The two halves contrast with one another, with three things to 'Set aside' listed on the one hand, and one 'inescapable fact' to face on the other. As Fahnestock notes, 'English sentences can easily carry modification to the left and right' (2011: 209), and this is what happens here. The cleft construction in the second half of [3] results from a branch to the left, while post-verbal modification of the first half of [3] reflects a branch to the right. The structure is *iconic* since its complex *form* – 4 clauses in 37 words – mimics its complex *content*. Finally, regarding register, the editorial is formal rather than informal. Lanham's rule – 'the more important the topic, the higher the style' (1991: 174) – helps explain the choice here between plain, middle or grand style. Yet the authors use some register shifts to build *rapport* with readers. While the syntax, punctuation and vocabulary ('panacea') tend to be formal, phrases such as 'the stuff of poetry' [5], 'going through the motions' [11], and 'big gap' [13] are less formal and thus more familiar. In general, the less frequent the form, the more formal it is, while the more frequent it is, the less formal it is.

The sixth and final factor involves the artistic proofs of *ethos*, *logos* and *pathos* first described in Aristotle's *Rhetoric*. In simple terms, *ethos* refers to character and *pathos* to emotions, while *logos* refers to evidence, forms and arguments. The editorial appears in *The Detroit Free Press*, a liberal newspaper read across Michigan. Some might not like the editorial, but the text is well written and contains no technical errors, which enhances its *ethos*. (By definition, an editorial has no by-line, so its authors are anonymous. Some may say that authorial anonymity defines propaganda, but the editorial board on the newspaper's masthead is not anonymous.) Shifts in register, as well as images of 'the first day of school' and 'the on-the-ground activity known as education' [2], also enhance *ethos* since the editors become more intimate and more closely identified with readers (Crowley and Hawhee 1999: 120). Furthermore, the authors seem intelligent, favourably citing a report by a 'conservative' think tank. Left-wing readers of the paper might interpret this citation of a source from the rival camp as proof that the editors are reasonable and fair, rather than dogmatic or ideological. Still, the emphasis on community in [11], [15] and [16], rather than individual students themselves, would not surprise regular readers of the newspaper. For example, a conservative reader responded online to the editorial by writing that the *Free Press* 'is speaking in liberal code words again'. But recognising that *both* teachers [3] and parents [6] help to educate school children nevertheless bolsters the editorial's *ethos*.

As for *logos*, the claim in [9] that teachers across the state do well generally is supported by the report cited in [10], showing how different schools may get the same results. While it is hard to persuade people to take action if they like the school their child goes to, yet dislike most schools in general, the text still exhorts readers to take action to improve Michigan's schools. Examples, which are a form of *logos* (Crowley and Hawhee 1999: 176–8), are used from [11] to [14] to show why the status quo is negative. Neither charter schools, nor schools in leafy suburbs, are doing as well as they might. Despite some 'signs of progress', there is a 'widening gap in achievement' and measurable 'problems' whenever strict 'standards' or 'benchmarks' are used. There are also a number of logical cause–effect relations mentioned throughout the editorial. A decision in Lansing can 'impact' students as can the teacher–student relationship [3]. The 'potential' of children 'excites parents and teachers' [4], just as parents and teachers have influence over children [6]–[7]. Going to a charter school or a 'well-off suburban' one does not guarantee success [11]; rather, it seems better to go to a school where teachers, parents, neighbours, policy-makers and the community 'get and stay involved' [12]. What is more, schools will only get better by 'encouraging all students to reach their full potential' [16], which is another implicit cause–effect relation.

Regarding *pathos*, it goes without saying that writing about children without getting emotional may well be impossible. The five 'systemic firsts' [2] might make readers proud, but mentioning the 'potential lying within each child' [4] and the 'nurturing of that potential' [5], and calling children a 'precious resource' [15], can move readers and increase their emotional involvement with the text. After all, who could possibly disagree with the idea that 'all students' should be helped 'to reach their full potential' [16]? Like the instant swimmer recipe joke – 'Instant swimmer: just add water' – there may be a failsafe recipe for *pathos* in rhetoric: 'Instant *pathos*: just add children.' Kindly writing about children is arguably the easiest way to move readers, and showing 'how the issue affects everyone' (Crowley and Hawhee 1999: 205) gets us emotionally involved. To conclude with *pathos*, we can also 'demonstrate that the state of affairs violates community values' (Crowley and Hawhee 1999: 213), and this is what the editorial does. In [12], readers are told to 'get and stay involved', and in [15] and [16] they are reminded why: bad schools are unacceptable in a state that loves its children.

Conclusion

Other experts in stylistics could undoubtedly extend my brief analysis above in many ways, but my point was to show how rhetorical stylistics involves looking at rhetoric *and* style. As I have hopefully shown in this chapter, rhetoric and stylistics are so closely related that it is not hard to see stylistics *as* rhetoric. The study of style began as a canon of rhetoric in the ancient world, then eventually came to define rhetoric as a whole after the fifteenth century. The study of style itself gradually focused on just a few figures or tropes before stylistics became a fully developed subject of its own in the late twentieth century, alongside rhetoric. If the story of how rhetoric became style, and how that canon became stylistics, seems too straightforward for some tastes, other alternatives are possible. Some may see stylistics as *part of* rhetoric; others may see it *as* rhetoric; and still others may see the two as *co-existing*. Just as work in rhetorical criticism continues (Jost and Olmstead 2004), this very Handbook shows that work in stylistics continues, too. Telling the full history of stylistics would require more space, of course, but this chapter has hopefully given readers a new understanding of the special friendship rhetoric and stylistics have. As for the rhetoric *of* stylistics, that will have to be the topic of another paper.

Acknowledgement

I thank the University of Birmingham's Department of English for its support in writing this chapter. A visiting fellowship in summer 2012 at its Centre for Advanced Research in English (CARE) enabled me to work on this project. I also thank the Colgate University Faculty Research Council for supporting this project.

6

Stylistics as applied linguistics

Ronald Carter

The *Handbook of Stylistics* interviewed Ronald Carter on the relationship between stylistics and applied linguistics.

Stylistics and applied linguistics

Handbook of Stylistics: *Can stylistics be said to be a form of applied linguistics, and would this description be accurate or appropriate? What can stylisticians learn from the main research questions and approaches in applied linguistics? And of course is there anything applied linguists should know about literary stylistics?*

Applied linguistics is commonly understood to be the investigation, both theoretically and empirically, of real-world problems in which language and communication are central issues. Applied linguistics draws centrally on linguistics but also on other disciplines too. In an institutionalised sense stylistics is a field within the broad parameters of applied linguistics and the international association for applied linguistics (AILA) (www.aila.info) has separate research networks devoted to stylistics. Since the early 1980s applied linguistics has been primarily concerned with 'real-world' problems relating to language learning and teaching and with the more transmissive and transactional aspects of human communication. More recently the field has developed to embrace, for example, work in professional and health communication, translation, the law, forensics and communication disorders, again with a primarily practical and transactional orientation. Overall, in a straightforward sense the field of study is human communication. Applied linguists are concerned with the study of human communication and the main focus of stylistics research, literary communication, is one of the most significant and highly valued forms of human communication. In this sense then there are clear commonalities; but the relationship between the two fields is not a clear-cut one.

So, yes, stylistics is a form of applied linguistics and has become institutionalised as such within the academy in professional associations and descriptions of the reach of key journals such as *Applied Linguistics*, as well as in university and college courses. This applies to both literary and non-literary modes of stylistics. But it is not entirely accurate or appropriate, at least not in the case of literary stylistics. As the study of human communication as realised in literary texts, literary stylistics is concerned with displaced communication. A world is created in literary texts that corresponds to the real world but the language used is mimetic of that world. It's not a direct or simple two-way model of human communication. And literary communication is certainly not either transmissive or transactional in any straightforward way. So stylistics as applied to non-literary texts such as media discourse or the study of scientific language or the registers of different curriculum subjects or as analysis that assists in the processes of language teaching and learning is closer to the core concerns of applied linguistics and to a definition of applied linguistics as the investigation of real-world problems. Stylistics applied to literary texts does not constitute a 'real-world' problem in this sense. For some this pushes it very much more to the margins of standard applied linguistics; for others this might mean that it can offer models for better understanding of a whole range of problems in human communication and might make it more central to the pursuit of key future applied linguistic issues. It can also mean that it follows a path that is not directly related to linguistics as such but is more closely allied to other disciplines such as psychology or sociology or philosophy.

I think we also need to recognise that the terms applied linguistics and stylistics are not discrete. Since the beginning of the twenty-first century in particular both domains have become more expansive and inclusive. Recent issues of stylistics journals have, for example, embraced areas more typically associated with applied linguistics such as empirical studies of reader response in reading groups (Swann and Allington 2009), cognitively rooted accounts of the experience of the texture of reading, while applied linguistics has expanded its domain to embrace studies of creativity in language, studies of postmodern 'styling' in the spoken discourse of young people and the uses of poetry in the foreign language classroom (for example: Hanauer 2001; Swann and Maybin 2007). Are such studies examples of stylistics or of applied linguistics in action? Standard definitions of stylistics and applied linguistics have begun to leak but in the most productive of ways. These leaks are productive because applied linguists are beginning to embrace more than the transactional and ideational forms of language and to see that representational uses of language play a key part in learning language, learning about language and in learning how to use language. In applied linguistics creative language, language play and literary language have increasingly become a part of both descriptive and applicational frameworks (for example: G. Cook 2000).

What can applied linguistics learn from stylistics and vice versa? The focus of applied linguistics continues to be 'practical' and in communicative terms remains mainly on the ideational content of the message. There has been correspondingly less of a focus on the more interpersonal, expressive, emotive texture of language. That focus is changing as more attention to more spoken data draws our focus to the interplay between the what and the how in communication and, in particular, to how the more affective components in communication work. Work in stylistics over this same period has focused on these more expressive and affective components of language and this is now assuming an even more central role within both applied linguistics and stylistics, especially within cognitive poetics within literary stylistics.

Also, within the broad frame of research in stylistics I think much can continue to be learned from research methods in applied linguistics. The history of applied linguistics supplies many paradigmatic examples of empirical research, quantitatively and qualitatively supported, that has influenced and continues to influence work in pedagogical stylistics (Watson and Zyngier 2007). Pedagogical stylistics does address 'real-world' classroom problems and synergies are ever more apparent between applied linguistics and stylistics in this area. This needs to be noted. I repeat, however, that there are both continuities and discontinuities between applied linguistics and stylistics.

Stylistics and pedagogy

Handbook of Stylistics: How do you think stylistics can be used in different sorts of classrooms – native-English school classrooms, undergraduate degree classes, EFL and ESL classrooms?

I think in much of the world literature is taught in the literature classroom without much attention to the way in which the literature works as text. The main focus tends to be on literature as history, on literature as a chronological sequence of texts, with students being required to remember and then be tested on facts about literature rather than respond to literature. Much depends of course on the language background and competencies of the students and in what context they are studying (whether it be at school or university level, for example) but the reading of texts in translation is far from uncommon and many students of literature as foreign language literature confess to not having read much literature in the target language. Pedagogic work at the interface between language and literature has attempted over a number of years to address this situation (Collie and Slater 1987; Paran 2006; Short 1989, 1996). Although it is undoubtedly on the increase at university level, literature is taught less in the language classroom world-wide in schools and language schools where it is felt, mistakenly in the eyes of some, that the emphasis should be on the more functional and utilitarian purposes of language learning and where literary communication is seen as being at one remove from standard communicative norms, even more so if it is from the past.

However, at university level in many parts of the world and where stylistics is becoming more widespread in reach and significance, I agree that stylistics will continue to have a basic (in the sense of fundamental) part to play in this particular domain of pedagogical stylistics, that it will continue to remain within the conventional remit of applied linguistics. Why is this? Why should stylistics be fundamental in this way?

Well, I would argue that this is because in a crude sense literature is made from language. And to get to the point where students can engage closely with literary texts an analysis of the language of the text is an essentially formative part of that process. I cannot see how students can begin to engage with a literary text without reference to the way language works in that text, and at a more advanced level I cannot see how any interpretation can be made replicable or falsifiable without the evidence provided by a full account of the way the language works. This is not for one minute to say that other factors such as historical context don't also help to account for our interpretation. But language use is fundamental. And in a lot of literature teaching around the world the attention to language is piecemeal, not systematic, and is often not informed by the insights of contemporary linguistics.

The tools of stylistic analysis are of course varied and different groups of students have different needs. In general stylistics carries more value for more advanced students such as native-speaking school and undergraduate students. In their case they are building on a pre-existing sensitivity to language. But it is surprising how many learners of English, both of English as a foreign language and of English as a second language, can be shown to have benefitted from reading literary texts, perhaps in part because such students are accustomed to the analysis of forms of language. And if you extend the use of the term 'literary' beyond that of canonical writers and beyond the texts published in such a way that they are indicated to be literary, the landscape changes and includes texts that have elements of language that are playful, and involve foregrounded or intricately repeated patterns. Such texts can embrace advertisements, political rhetorics, nursery rhymes, jokes and riddles. The history of integrated language and literature teaching since the 1970s furnishes numerous examples (Brumfit and Carter 1986; Carter and McRae 1996; Short 1989; Widdowson 1975). In the early days of such practices much depended on enthusiastic advocacy but increasingly empirical evidence is being brought forward to show how involvement with such uses of language can help to develop a wide range of competencies from greater stimulus to thematic classroom discussions, to sensitivity to patterns in language, to fuller awareness of how norms of language can be creatively deployed, to a fuller appreciation of the different cultural values embedded within such texts (Kramsch 1993; Kramsch and Kramsch 2000).

Handbook of Stylistics: In much of the world, literature is taught as part of English-language teaching classes – what do you think of this practice? Is it done properly? What would be the value of teaching the language of literature for analysis?

The main value of teaching the language of literature is relatively straight-forward in my opinion, though such a view remains stubbornly contro-versial. The tools of stylistic analysis provide points of entry into texts. Without a stylistic approach these texts may otherwise be seen as no more than plots, or characters or themes and, however important it may be to engage with such features of literary texts, you are not engaging with literature unless you are able to begin to demonstrate how such texts actually work. And this has to involve linguistic explanation.

Handbook of Stylistics: Stylistics is supposed to offer analytical frameworks and methods that reduce the reliance on the sensitivity or intuition of the literary reader, and so it appears useful for second-language learners with little experi-ence of literature in English. Does it actually work like this in practice? Are there differences in different parts of the world that mean that stylistics as a pedagogical practice cannot be uniformly recommended?

This is a good question and, yes, the picture is far from seamless and homogeneous. I would actually say that stylistics, if handled properly in the literature and language classroom, can enhance intuition and sensi-tivity. But it depends on the nature of the education system. Those systems in which there is a high premium placed on factual learning and memorisation are, for example, less likely to favour strategies in the classroom that may foster greater learner autonomy or the development of personal growth through more independent insights. Those systems in which authority and knowledge are invested in the teacher are also less likely to favour stylistic approaches. There is of course also considerable curricular differentiation nationally and internationally. In some curric-ula literature is the source for understanding cultural history, for some it is a window onto history, and in such contexts stylistic approaches can be seen as narrow and reductive, too text-immanent and too one-dimensional. So much depends on what is seen, more epistemologically, as the purpose of both literary education and language education.

Handbook of Stylistics: Is there a risk in taking an applied linguistics approach to literary discourse that literature is simply seen as another form of language data, and the common feeling that literature is somehow 'special' is set aside? Should literature be treated as a special form of discourse?

I see this in terms of clines and continua – which is also, of course, a form of fence-sitting. The last few years have generated numerous examples that underline that the features found in literary discourse are also present in other forms of discourse. You get parallelism, creative metaphor and rhythmic patterning in advertising language and in poetry. In some contexts, therefore, the language of advertising or the language of popular fiction may be the best starting point for the study of literature. And I would agree that in teaching poetry it can be very productive to set up classrooms where such forms are put into creative juxtaposition. For some students, to go straight into poetry can inhibit them reading poetry or, at worst, turn them off completely.

But it is naive to pretend that just because there are commonalities of this kind that there is not such a thing as very special forms that can be designated as literary nor that there is not such a thing as a literary genius (G. Cook 2011). The nature of the literary will evolve as will tastes and preferences and they will be loaded differently in different cultural contexts of literature study. The keyword 'literature' itself is, as Raymond Williams (1983) and others have shown us, highly variable in history. And it is very variable too according to the cultural relativities of different communities and different value systems (Mukařovský 1970). It is why the study of literature as conventionally practised in university departments world-wide leaves me simultaneously uneasy (if the students are only given a narrow diet of canonical texts) but also cognisant of the timelessly enduring nature of canonical texts. There is no straightforward way through such polarities. We need to learn to live productively with clines of value and value systems and to teach texts, all texts, accordingly.

Changes in stylistics

Handbook of Stylistics: *How has stylistics changed alongside the way that applied linguistics in general has changed over the last few decades? Stylistics has been traditionally based very much in an interdisciplinary state with linguistics – how far has the cognitive turn in research moved it away from the concerns of applied linguistics and towards psychology or even sociology? Or have the two disciplines of stylistics and applied linguistics moved in similar parallel directions?*

I think both stylistics and applied linguistics have fed from developments in linguistics and grown accordingly. But, as they have matured as areas of academic practice, they have become less dependent and even more interdisciplinary and begun to draw equally as powerfully from other disciplines such as psychology and sociology. I don't think the developments have been in parallel. The earliest examples of stylistics tended to embrace language as a social semiotic and to employ descriptive frameworks that had their origins in systemic-functional linguistics. Halliday's work on transitivity and stylistic analysis is a good canonical example (Halliday 1971, 1978). Latterly, however, the cognitive turn has ensured that psychological models have become more influential and more powerful as an analytical resource (Burke 2010b).

In applied linguistics the dominant research and teaching paradigm has tended to be that of language acquisition, especially second-language acquisition, and here the influence of psycholinguistics has been pervasive from the earliest days. Latterly, however, in a kind of parabola effect in relation to stylistics, social and sociolinguistic models are being taken very seriously. They are central to those traditions in applied linguistics such as professional communication and have probably always been so, but social and sociocultural theories of language learning and language development are now intersecting much more with the more cognitive models. The contexts for such research are the growing influence of Vygotskian sociocultural approaches to learning, an increasing recognition that a view of the individual 'learner' as a universal construct is limited and an acceptance that culture is best seen as something that is not a thing but an active and negotiated entity, a 'verb', a process in which learners do not simply learn new labels for what they already have but directly engage with and participate interactively and dialogically in a new reality. Add to this new non-linear theories of language development such as dynamic systems and complexity theory (L. Cameron and Larsen-Freeman 2008) and language learning becomes altogether less easily chartable and predictable in solely cognitive terms. In such an environment literature has a place in fostering self-awareness and identity in a learner's socio-cognitive interaction with a new language and culture (see Kramsch 2000; Lantolf 2000). Stylistics also has a part to play in this developing awareness (Hall 2005 contains much relevant discussion).

One concern I do have for both applied linguistics and stylistics, however they might develop, is that there are signs that people may believe that we now know as much as we need to know about language and its forms and functions and can therefore focus on bigger issues such as language and power, language and the brain, the operational nature of literary discourse and so on. In fact, there are many areas of language use that we are only just beginning to grapple with (the differences and distinctions between modality in speech and writing, for example). Spoken discourse is massively under-researched relative to written language. And some of the most vital new forms of language that are emerging under the unique pressures of digital communication are essentially hybrid in nature, combining as they do spoken and written forms in ways that we have yet to fully comprehend (Tagg 2011). It would be a serious error not to continue to interact with the very latest developments in descriptive accounts of the language. Since the 1990s, corpus linguistics has revolutionised how we do this and corpus stylistics, in particular, continues to work in synergy with these developments. But on the part of both stylisticians and applied linguists the concern with language and linguistic descriptive frameworks is not by any means universal.

Handbook of Stylistics: You once distinguished 'linguistic stylistics' and 'literary stylistics' – is that distinction still valid, with respect to the interests covered in applied linguistics?

I am not so sure about this distinction now. I think the field has changed from the 1980s when that distinction was first made. At that time I was trying to argue that stylistics needed to i) follow the lead of Crystal and Davy (1969) and embrace more than just literary texts. The importance of this position cannot be underestimated. It has led to some remarkable stylistics studies that do not mention literature. I was also recognising ii) the approach taken by John Sinclair and others (Sinclair 1966), who advocated another variety of linguistic stylistics – that is, a utilisation of everything we know about the language forms of a particular literary text in order simply to describe that text accordingly without any literary concerns being manifest such as contexts, editorial difference, evaluation and so forth. I think there still exist approaches in stylistics where the main purpose is simply to describe the language in and for itself but they are fewer now, and they were I think part of the mistaken effort to get stylistics recognised as a totalising practice. It is fair to say that many applied linguists would see that now as part of the mission of applied linguistics. Literary stylistics is linguistic analysis applied to literary texts. That is now pretty much the dominant form of stylistics internationally and it has enabled stylistics to establish itself as a significant and growing sub-discipline. So, I think the distinction still holds but much less so now.

Handbook of Stylistics: Are there other developments in the field of stylistics that you consider to be significant?

Yes. I think there has been a consistent move since the 1960s to begin better to define the nature of literary discourse. What makes literature literature, at least in terms of its textual nature, has always been a focus within the field of stylistics. Back in the 1970s stylisticians were exploring the nature of deviant discourse, patterns of parallelism and deviation in language considered to be literary (Widdowson 1975). And there were subsequently influential studies of the nature of literary and non-literary speech acts (Pratt 1977) and of the nature of literature as measured by schema theory (G. Cook 1994). And through to the early part of the current century we now have a number of studies of creativity within and across literary and non-literary discourses, some arguing that there is less of a differentiation than is assumed; others arguing that literary discourse is distinct (Carter 2004; Swann et al. 2010). There are exciting developments in Text World Theory (Gavins 2007). And studies of the aesthetic texture of the text (Stockwell 2009) continue this tradition systematically and rigorously, I think, placing such accounts even more firmly within the realm of readerly experience. What all these studies over all these years have in common is the use of tools of stylistic analysis to further the analysis of textuality, the textual nature of texts. I do think applied linguists could learn a lot from this focus on the textuality of texts.

It is fair to say, nonetheless, that such explorations seem to be of limited interest to applied linguists who remain resolutely concerned with models of communication that are 'real' and not deferred or displaced or fictive. But such pursuits are of more extensive interest within departments of literature, and several recent university appointments world-wide that would normally have resulted in stylisticians working unambiguously in the field in applied linguistics are now embedding research and teaching in stylistics within departments of literature. This is a significant develop-ment that could have long-term repercussions for the relationship between the disciplines/sub-disciplines of stylistics and applied linguistics (and I deliberately don't enter the debate here about what does or does not constitute a discipline). It may be that in future the field of stylistics no longer sees itself in relation to applied linguistics, whether as ancillary to it, parasitic upon it or separate from it, but rather establishes itself much more as a distinct investigative pursuit, in both theory and practice and creates closer links with literary studies.

Finally, I suppose we have in a way already touched on other significant developments – developments, I think, that are likely to play a part in shaping stylistics in the future:

Spoken stylistics. In such a perspective style is not simply a case of foregrounding or parallelism or of norms and deviations: style is also an interactive practice; it can be a verb as well as a noun (styling as well as style); it is essentially unstable; it can be performed as an identity marker as well as a more static mediation of meanings. The focus of stylistics over the years on language and literature and on style as a written medium has led to some neglect of these dimensions and indeed exploration of how such perspectives on styl-ing can inform the discipline. The sociolinguistic work of Coupland on style (see especially Coupland 2007) is seminal here. There is a distinct challenge here for stylistics to embrace a poetics of spoken discourse.

Cognitive poetics. For me the interesting and potentially very rich poten-tial in cognitive poetics is its focus on how readers process the lan-guage of texts. In one sense cognitive poetics represents a turn back in time, to the study of classical rhetoric but with the advantage that it draws on principles of contemporary cognitive linguistics to account for key aspects of textual processing in both production and reception (Stockwell 2002). The growth of this domain will allow us to get much closer to our experience of the textuality of texts and to our interaction with them and it will begin to allow us to talk more precisely about how we may be moved, shocked, persuaded, taken in and more generally affected by our engagement with language in many of its textual and rhetorical shapes.

Corpus stylistics. Corpus stylistics extends practical stylistics and is growing as a methodology within the world of stylistics, linguistics and poetics, enabling more developed and detailed quantitative studies of literary linguistic patterns of meaning formation. Stylo-statistical studies are, of course, not new, but for the first time in the history of stylistics contemporary corpus stylistics makes use of computer-informed searches of the language of large multi-million word databases, considerably advancing reliability in the identification of the traits of individual authors or groups of writers (for recent further discussion, see Archer et al. 2010; Culpeper et al. 2010; Hoover 2008, and for specific examples: Fischer-Starcke 2010; Mahlberg 2012; Stubbs 2005). The use of corpus linguistic techniques and strategies allows significant linguistic patterns to be identified that would not normally be discernible by human intuition, at least not over the extent of a whole novel or long narrative poems and dramas. To end more or less where we began, for me corpus stylistics at its best illustrates the best of both stylistics and applied linguistics practice: it is evidenced in language use, it is retrievable in quantitative datasets, it does not hide from qualitative human assessment and evaluation, it offers rich possibilities for language learners at all levels and it expands the frontiers of applied linguistics and literary studies, even if some literary specialists and some applied linguists may be looking in other directions.

All these developments may simply underline once again that stylistics has now reached the point where it may be more productive to talk about it in future as a separate and mature field of research and teaching that is sufficiently healthy now not to need interdisciplinary partners but is always willing to work with them as long as attention to language is central and as long as stylistics continues, as we have begun to do in our conversation here, to interrogate its own boundaries as a domain of academic research and teaching.

7

Stylistics as literary criticism

Geoff Hall

Stylistics and literary criticism

Literary criticism concerns itself with the reading, interpretation and evaluation of literary texts. As such its activities sound close to those of modern literary stylistics. One of the most eminent of current British literary critics, Bate (2010) in *English Literature: A Very Short Introduction*, emphasises the centrality of the study of 'style' to literary criticism: 'Literary criticism has traditionally involved judging pieces of writing on the basis not of *the things said* but of *the way in which they are said* ... Judgements regarding style are always subjective' (2002: 30, Bate's italics). The key difference from stylistic activity is also here spelled out in the emphasis on subjective 'judging' where stylistics generally claims to be involved in a more objective or at least replicable study of literary texts: 'The difference between practical stylistics and the looser, more discursive accounts found in practical criticism is one of degree, along a continuum, with the stylistic account seeking above all else to be made retrievable and recoverable by other readers' (Carter 2010: 61). Bate refers to 'the detailed analysis of [English] literary texts' (Bate 2002: 65) where the basis of stylistic analysis will be linguistic but he does not specify more precisely or illustrate what this might mean in practice. Evaluation of 'questions of literary style' (2002: 65–9) is the remit of literary criticism. This is the position also in classic studies such as that of Eagleton (1983) or Lodge (1966). '[L]iterary criticism typically involves grasping *what* is said in terms of *how* it is said' (Eagleton 2007: 67). One of the founders of modern literary criticism said the same thing more than a century ago: 'Our investigations will deal largely with style' (Quiller-Couch, inaugural lecture at Cambridge University, 1911, in W. Martin 2000: 289).

For a stylistician one of the most interesting sections of Bate's *Short Introduction* is a passage justifying the 'analytic' study of literature to those who might object to such an approach:

> If you are a biker, your pleasure in riding at a hundred miles an hour
> along the motorway will not be diminished – it might positively be
> enhanced – if you also learn to strip down your bike, work out how it is
> constructed, tinker with its parts and put it back together again. At the
> very least, your mechanical expertise will give you good material for
> conversations with your fellow bikers – and being part of a community of
> bikers, with a shared body of knowledge, customs and traditions,
> will give you added pleasure.   *(Bate 2002: 25)*

The argument is again one not unfamiliar to practitioners of stylistic
approaches to literature, including advocacy of pedagogical stylistics
for creative writing (e.g. R. Pope 2002). The problem for the stylistician,
however, would be precisely that the kind of dissection or analysis
typically practised in literary criticism will not actually enable you to
put that beautiful bike back together again! You will be looking perplexed at the pieces on the garage floor while your more precise and
thorough mates are out having fun. Interestingly, leading stylistician
Mick Short (e.g. 1996) insists that the key value of stylistics is in the
metaphorical 'tool-kit' it offers to users which will enable a reader to
'take a poem to pieces' (this is Sinclair's metaphor in 1966) with more
precision and a more realistic chance of putting it all back together
successfully than by shadowing the erudite literary critic. The most
valued literary critics persuade by rhetoric. The creative writing of
the literary critic can be highly stimulating, rich in intertextual and
historical references sometimes lacking in more stylistic work, but to a
stylistician will usually seem incomplete, unsystematic and impressionistic, particularly in its references to language.

I offer an example of such criticism in the second half of this chapter. For
now we note that the particularising (Bateson 1934) of literary criticism is
selective, secondary to the interpretation and evaluation which are for
critics the main ends of literary criticism, where stylistics seeks more
systematically and empirically to understand the workings of language
in literature as a particularly interesting instance of language use. As far
back as 1975, Widdowson distinguished between a linguist's interest
in text as language, the stylistician's interest in literature as discourse
(language being used to make meanings) and the literary critic's interest
in meaning and evaluation: 'stylistics occupies the middle ground between
linguistics and literary criticism and its function is to mediate the two'
(Widdowson 1975: 117). This remains a useful formulation of my concern
here to investigate the possibilities for fruitful conversations between
stylistics and literary criticism as criticism assimilates theory and stylistics
advances beyond formalism in more recent emanations. Where some
stylisticians have occasionally lost sight of the value of literary criticism,
I want to insist with Verdonk (2002) on the indispensable and complementary value of the two endeavours:

The scholarly study of literature, long established under the name of literary criticism, has yielded a vast amount of insightful commentary, both on individual works, and on the sociocultural and aesthetic trends that they exemplify. Whereas, generally speaking, literary criticism directs attention to the larger-scale significance of what is represented in verbal art, stylistics focuses on how this significance can be related to specific features of language, to the linguistic texture of the literary text.

(Verdonk 2002: 55)

Historical connections

Western literary criticism arguably begins with Aristotle's *Poetics* in the fourth century BC. In this chapter, however, I concentrate on literary criticism from the early twentieth century to the present day as it established itself as a respectable subject for study in western universities. Not coincidentally this is also the period which saw the formation and expansion of stylistics, with literary criticism sometimes virtually indistinguishable, though more often each at loggerheads with the other or at least pursuing separate paths in relative ignorance of each other's activities. Some history will help us understand the formative ideas of the two endeavours and some differences between them.

Relations have certainly not always been easy. Most notoriously in the Fowler–Bateson controversy (R. Fowler 1971; extracted most accessibly in Simpson 2004: 148–57), the upstart new kid on the block, stylistics, came to prominence in the still prestigious literary journal *Essays in Criticism*. Fowler wrote of the 'unnecessary schism between "language" and "literature" which has so long marred English studies' (see Simpson 2004: 149). He also pointed out that 'there is no single thing "criticism" any more than there is "linguistics", although literary people faced with the imagined threat of linguistics, tend to talk as if there is' (2004: 150). 'For some reason, "interpretation" ... and "evaluation" have come to be regarded as the only activities which are worth doing and which are actually done' (2004: 150). But Fowler argued there is no 'one objective in studying literature', and stylistics has much to offer in the service of a more rigorous description of the language of literary texts, which can then inform more convincing overall accounts (2004: 150).

Both stylistics and criticism have moved a long way since the Fowler–Bateson debate. Stylistics for Fowler in the 1960s as well as for Bateson seems to be largely word-level grammatical analysis of text. Similarly Bateson's talk of a mysterious 'full aesthetic response' – you are or are not 'born a literary critic' (see Simpson 2004: 151) – would be rejected by most scholars of literature today. At the same time, Fowler's position that literary uses of language remain, ultimately, uses of language, or Bateson's insistence that linguistics describes and criticism evaluates are still recognisable and respectable positions. And yet both are aware of the paradox with which I began this chapter – 'To invite the reader to look hard, really hard, at the words on the page is indeed what the modern critical doctrine of close reading amounts to, when it is reduced to its simplest terms' (according to Bateson; see Simpson 2004: 151). The suggestion is that the purposes or the ends of the looking are different. But again, as with Bate (2002), although 'style' is seen by a critic as central to the critical endeavour, a key difference seems to be whether formal training or at least awareness of linguistic findings and methods is a help to such analysis or not, and the alternative to such knowledge and expertise is not spelled out but left frustratingly implicit by the critic – Bateson on this occasion: 'Stylistic discrimination is the one indispensable prerequisite for the aesthetic appreciation of great literature' (in Simpson 2004: 153). How does this discrimination work? How might it be learned or taught? Neither Bateson, nor Bate, gives us any clues, but linguistic training is firmly rejected – 'Mr Fowler ... present[s] the study of language as a necessary concomitant to the study of literature ... this is simply not true' (says Bateson, in Simpson 2004: 153).

Characteristically the literary scholar sees ideas where the linguist sees language; the critic looks through language as through a window, the stylistician looks at it. 'One synonym is as good as another', Bateson proposes in *English Poetry and the English Language* (Bateson 1934, quoted in Lodge 1966: 13). Fowler later comes to insist 'I'm offering linguistic criticism as an alternative, an improvement on literary criticism' (1981, also in Carter and Stockwell 2008: 51) but by that time the understanding of 'linguistic criticism' was informed by sociolinguistics, discourse analysis, *Ideologiekritik*, the Bakhtin circle and more: 'linguistic criticism – a careful analytic interrogation of the ideological categories, and the roles and institutions, and so on, through which a society constitutes and maintains itself and the self-consciousness of its members' (R. Fowler 1981: in Carter and Stockwell 2008: 49). Superficially, Fowler's later characterisation sounds much like cultural materialism. The weakness and conservatism of much Formalist criticism in the 1960s and 1970s led inevitably in literary criticism to the explosion of theory and more reflexivity. In parallel, in linguistics, formalism and obsession with lexis and syntax were overtaken by discourse analysis, sociolinguistics, pragmatics and other approaches more overtly concerned with meaning-making in contexts which should be of more interest to the non-linguist reading literature.

Comments of Bateson in the debate with Fowler suggest that he was unaware of sociolinguistics, presumably due to the dominance of the Chomskyan generative paradigm at that time. He and others hostile to stylistics may understandably have had an idea of stylistics as a Jakobsonian exhaustive analysis of Shakespeare sonnets (Jakobson and Jones 1970, a book-length study of a single sonnet!) or of Baudelaire's

'Les Chats' (Jakobson and Lévi-Strauss 1962). There is little or no interest, in these papers, in readers or readings, or value or cultural significance, which would have alienated literary critics at the time, but which also makes the analyses seem curiously pointless to the modern stylistician too. Such demonstrations of the intricacy of verbal patterning of a text were later shown by Werth (1976) and others through to Carter (2004) to be operating in any stretch of language use. Stylisticians gradually came to the realisation that it was not the mere existence of patterning or parallelism or deviance that mattered as such, but rather what effects it was being used to achieve – the *use* of cliché or allusion, not its uncreative presence, as literary critic Ricks, for example, has always insisted (Ricks 1984, 2002).

Early analyses of literary texts by Halliday (1964) or Sinclair (1966) had deliberately and provocatively stopped short of any overt interpretation and evaluation, and were rightly criticised for such 'naming of parts'. But what even these analyses showed was the value of moving beyond a school-level 'parts of speech' type of common-sense analysis of the language as found in literary-critical work to more linguistically informed attention to texts. Fowler was right to insist on this (see also Short 1996 or Leech 1969). Lodge in 1966 criticised contemporary literary criticism for

> a somewhat provincial mistrust of formal grammatical analysis and description from which its own characteristically intuitive and empirical approach could benefit,

but then in turn criticised stylistics for its thin results,

> in terms of interpretation and evaluation of individual texts . . . It has not really asked itself the fundamental questions about the nature of literary discourse . . . which are the commonplaces of literary theorizing in England and America. It remains blandly convinced of a success which is not altogether apparent to an outsider.   *(Lodge 1966: 52)*

Traces of this unaware complacency or even triumphalism are not unknown in some stylistics talk and writing still today. But Lodge and Widdowson, Sinclair or Halliday would all have agreed that 'no grammatical analysis of a poem can give us more than the grammar of the poem' (Riffaterre 1966: 36, quoted by Lodge 1966: 30). Literary texts therefore came to be seen as acts of communication needing to be analysed as such – even if an unusual kind of communication, as indicated by 'deviant' features such as conversations with the dead or trying to achieve some other unusual perlocutionary end. This was the key idea of *discourse stylistics*, where context and meaning were brought into the picture as stylistics developed (notably in Carter and Simpson 1989).

Jakobson, most obviously in his much cited 1960 polemical 'Closing Statement', would have bemused or even annoyed literary scholars by his insistence on the decontextualised identifiable formal qualities of 'a verbal work of art' – notably parallelism and the 'poetic function', which he tried to separate from a reader, or the social context in which 'function' could come to be. (Compare Attridge's (1996) critique of Jakobson's exclusion of considerations of the reader). Even here, however, it is worth stressing how valuable notions like *parallelism* have been to analysts of poetic texts. Great works do often contain stimulating sets of parallel linguistic features, and the explicit recognition and examination of patterning can lead a reader on to more significant findings. The very word *parallelism* is taken from the Victorian poet Gerard Manley Hopkins, much admired by Jakobson for his startling and deviant uses of language just as he was canonised by literary critics through the twentieth century. The argument is that valued creativity originates in exploiting human propensity to pattern matching to draw readers' attention and prompt them into thought in verbal as in other forms of art. We remember the key idea of *defamiliarisation* of Shklovsky and the 'Russian Formalists', later to be followed by (say) Mukařovský's Prague Circle investigations into the nature of poetic and ordinary language in which Jakobson also personally participated and where the functionalism that formed Halliday was first elaborated, or where a 'New Critic' later to be celebrated for his aesthetic subtlety, Rene Wellek, also began to develop his ideas and understanding of literature and the workings of language. Richards spoke with Jakobson at Harvard. New Critics at Yale bred deconstruction in their wake. The imbrications of modern linguistics, stylistics, and literary criticism and theory are more complex than we sometimes remember or perhaps more than some wish to be reminded of. I return to the example of Hopkins to explore such issues later in this chapter.

Literary criticism

Standard histories of literary criticism point to two influential 'founding fathers' of modern Anglo-American criticism, I. A. Richards (British 'Practical Criticism') and T. S. Eliot, and to the related US school of 'New Criticism' (Brooks, Wimsatt). Examining the work of those who set the parameters for literary criticism in its formative period, however briefly and schematically, will highlight features and uncertainties persisting today, even through and after the high tide of literary theory which in some ways questioned, in some ways only confirmed, the contribution and standing of these early ideas. Through all this work, we note again the concern for the language of literary texts and for pedagogy shared by literary criticism and stylistics.

Richards is widely credited as a founder of modern criticism, in particular 'practical criticism', but also noted for his insistence on 'feelings' in the literary experience and for his interest in particular in overt figurative language, particularly metaphor. (See D. West (2013) for more detail on Richards's interest to stylistics.) From 1925 Richards gave lectures in 'practical criticism' to Cambridge undergraduates, and from 1926 'practical criticism' was a required paper for English undergraduates at the University (W. Martin 2000: 296). The idea that undergraduates must learn to do practical criticism has been firmly established in the discipline ever since, even though not all are agreed on how exactly it works beyond phrases such as 'careful' or 'close' reading of 'the words on the page'. The book *Practical Criticism* itself (Richards 1929) actually spends more time telling Richards's Cambridge undergraduates and wider audience what they should avoid doing when they read rather than what they really need to do, much like the New Critics' celebrated 'fallacies' of literary reading in the US 20 years later. Then as now there was an impatience with trivialising, explicit or detailed stylistic writings in university English departments, and so a reluctance to demonstrate bottom up to the neophyte the actual content of 'close reading'.

Richards made extensive use of the early (1917–24) criticism of T. S. Eliot as he and the new discipline elaborated its founding principles. Eliot was at first sight a formalist: 'When we are considering poetry we must consider it primarily as poetry and not as another thing' (*Sacred Wood*, 1920: viii; in Menand 2000: 18). Arguably this formalism screened a more ideological programme, but that is not the main issue here. With Eliot in particular originate many of the terms that were needed to fill the 'Dictionaries of literary terms' and the like that would later be produced to guarantee respectability to the new discipline, the 'dissociation of sensibility' (1921), or 'objective correlative' (1919) (Eliot 1966). Later theorists have pointed out that however authoritative these terms sound it is often difficult to see what precisely they refer to or what empirical coherence they may have. Eliot anticipates Leavis and much later mainstream literary criticism when he says 'every person of sensibility' will understand. The idea of the sensitive well-educated reader continually stands intimidatingly in the path of the student reader only later to be challenged by the unruly theorists like Eagleton (1983) who wished to undermine the implicit conservatism and elitism of such key literary-critical criteria. Eliot's criticism remains thought-provoking, well-informed and intelligent. It is classic literary criticism, not least in being so opinionated and self-assured. For present purposes here, however, we note again the incidental appeals to language as primordial but which are ultimately highly selective and impressionistic. 'At many points in Eliot's work, quotations are used not as the starting point for an analysis of language and form, but as a means of justifying evaluative comments that are presented as objective, all-encompassing truths' (Atherton 2005: 132).

Empson was Richards's student at Cambridge and began publishing brilliant literary criticism even before he had graduated. His interest here is that he exemplified for many 'close reading' at its best, in particular in *Seven Types of Ambiguity* (1930). Empson privileged ambiguity as he looked at language and looked for language uses to comment on in literary texts. He wrote on irony as a particularly valuable kind of ambiguity (see also Empson 1935). The best literary works, for Empson, are those in which complex clashes of meanings and tensions or apparent contradictions occur. His impressionistic comments on 'light thickens' in Shakespeare's *Macbeth* or Hopkins's 'The Windhover' can indeed dazzle with their ingenuity, but identification of 'irony', or 'ambiguity' or argument as to why complexity is more to be valued than simplicity is left implicit or seems rather basic not least in the light of systematic work in pragmatics since that time. One might also query the discrepancy between the possible readings concentrated attention can produce and what any ordinary reader or listener would have been likely to notice.

The algebra of *The Structure of Complex Words* (1935) is mystifying and unhelpful. '[E]ven a moderate step forward in our understanding of language would do a great deal to improve literary criticism' he muses at the outset (quoted in Wood 2000: 228), but the most fervent admirer of Empson will not be able to discern any such step here. More interesting are the key words identified purely intuitively which, when closely examined by Empson, do indeed give real insights into the literary texts in which they occur: 'wit' (Pope, 'Essay in Criticism'), 'all' (in Milton's *Paradise Lost*), 'dog' (*Timon of Athens*), 'honest' (*Othello*), 'sense' (Wordsworth's *Prelude*), 'madness' in *King Lear* and more. Empson shows how far you can go without any explicit or principled understanding of language if you have read a great deal and have unusual intelligence and leisure, but once again those less talented or privileged will not be able to produce such analyses for themselves. Indeed, the idea of keywords and the brilliance of the writing that follows may remind us of later Cambridge English Professor Raymond Williams, whose *Keywords* (1983) gave the terms of reference to early British cultural studies in a qualitative way only now to be effectively complemented by corpus linguistics (see Romaine's (2010) discussion of 'keywords' or Stubbs 2005). This literary-critical tradition is carried on in Patterson's (2009) *Milton's Words* (compare Ricks 1964), an extraordinary book to one from outside literary criticism which talks of words, style and related linguistic matters but gives no hint of methodology used or how the words discussed have been identified (see 2009: 3 in particular). The irrelevance of stylistics to the book is assumed but not discussed. If this author was aware of corpus linguistics she is not prepared to give any hint as to why she did not use its methods. Barry (2007) is another good example of this resolute gulf between stylistics and literary studies. To the stylistician it is obvious how the use of a computer could have improved his studies. No English language undergraduate would be allowed to get away with these gaps and unfounded assertions. I return briefly to Barry and to corpus stylistics below but this is a weakness of literary criticism, not unique to Barry.

Most of us read as we are taught to read, institutionally at least. In some ways the competition or mutual distrust of practical criticism and stylistics are brought about by a primary pedagogical orientation and sphere of operation, our acculturation into either literature or language studies departments. Critical theory may have delegitimated many of the founding ideas of practical criticism, but no better first approach to the language of the text has been developed from within literary criticism to replace it, and the idea of simply adopting stylistic approaches is still anathema to many literary scholars despite the growing number of 'lang-lit' degrees in British universities at least. Stylistics for those who have not read much beyond Jakobson is naive and 'positivist' (Barry 2009).

An example: Hopkins's *God's Grandeur*

It is becoming a commonplace of modern theorists and critics that students do not and cannot do practical criticism, cannot read literature closely, even though this should be basic to the discipline (Barry 2007; Eagleton 1983, 2007).

> [S]aying what the poem means, and then tagging on a couple of sentences about its metre or rhyme scheme, is not exactly engaging with questions of form ... the language of a poem is constitutive of its ideas ... It would be hard to figure out, just by reading most of these content analyses, that they were supposed to be about poems or novels, rather than about some real-life happening. What gets left out is the literariness of the work ... they treat the poem as though its author chose for some eccentric reason to write out his or her views on warfare or sexuality in lines which do not reach to the end of the page. Maybe the computer got stuck.
>
> *(Eagleton 2007: 2–3)*

Surely stylistics could offer something to the distressed literary critics in this respect? An example of an analysis of a Hopkins poem can illustrate an alternative towards the positive value of a real dialogue between literary and stylistic concerns.

God's Grandeur
The world is charged with the grandeur of God.
It will flame out, like shining from shook foil;
It gathers to a greatness, like the ooze of oil
Crushed. Why do men then now not reck his rod?
Generations have trod, have trod, have trod;
And all is seared with trade; bleared, smeared with toil;
And wears man's smudge and shares man's smell: the soil
Is bare now, nor can foot feel, being shod.

And for all this, nature is never spent;
There lives the dearest freshness deep down things;
And though the last lights off the black West went
Oh, morning, at the brown brink eastward, springs –
Because the Holy Ghost over the bent
World broods with warm breast and with ah! bright wings.

(Hopkins 1918)

A first and basic problem in reading Hopkins is usually comprehension, hence a need for close and careful slow reading, perhaps the prototypical literary reading experience. The language is very much 'foregrounded' in Hopkins's poetry. Any reader of whatever persuasion would surely agree so far. Hopkins was self-consciously concerned with and informed about linguistics, aesthetics and poetics, and his writing has always been a source of fascination to both stylisticians and literary scholars. The stylistician and literary critic will both be looking to produce an account of the poem that shows its workings and meaning. The difference is that the stylistician will approach the task more systematically and with reference to linguistic knowledge, while the critic will typically seize on some features or elements without fully explaining why these words are chosen rather than others as the basis for larger claims about meaning or the writer's work or period or genre. In fact one of the more frustrating features of much literary criticism on Hopkins is how swiftly it leaps over the obvious or apparent linguistic difficulties of the texts to larger issues of ideology, sexuality or 'indeterminacy'. To the stylistician the issue of linguistic difficulty is a primary reality to be investigated rather than mentioned on the way to more speculative explanations of this difficulty. Critics such as Barry (2007) or Eagleton (2007) deplore the lack of ability in undergraduates to study the language of a text closely, but then themselves demonstrate that even the best teachers cannot hold close to the linguistic detail of a text for long in any systematic way.

'God's Grandeur' is one of a series of eight or nine sonnets on aspects of nature produced from early 1877 where the priest–poet Hopkins perceives and urges readers to see the workings of God in or despite nature. A full stylistic account is clearly impossible within a paragraph or two, but it would include structural contrasts between the mundane and human and the celestial and cosmic, and a climactic emotional affirmation of God's 'care for' the world. The exclamations 'Oh' and 'ah' in the poem could be described with reference to the research literature on discourse markers. Hopkins is speaking to others. Jakobson can be invoked to show the significance of tensions set up by the rhyme scheme relating to the poem's main theme. Thus in the second stanza the rhyme moves from unregenerate 'things' (l.10) to more hopeful and energetic 'springs' to the comfort and peace of 'wings', which concludes the poem. Enclosure is enacted in the final line of the poem by 'World broods ... bright wings'.

Other repetitions or near-repetitions ('have trod, have trod, have trod', l.5) combined with sound symbolism in, for example, 'seared ... bleared, smeared' (l.6) again testify to the validity of Jakobson's insistence on forms driving meaning rather than meaning form in poetry, though also of course 'flame/ seared/ light' also give a semantic cohesion to the poem. 'Man's smudge' and 'man's smell' are clearly linked to each other by sound and meaning as they are linked to 'smeared' and 'soil', among others. The organisation of the poetry prompts the reader to find connections between such similar sounding terms. What is the relation between the /d/ of God and that of 'trade'? or 'God' and 'trod'? 'The world is charged' (l.1) contains two more /d/ sounds in tension. We note also the pun in 'charged', a term from physics, even warfare, but also an accusation or responsibility. The generic first copula ('is') states a fact of Christian belief; 'will' in line 2 simultaneously signals prediction and insistence. There are two present tenses in the poem, that of everyday reality, and that of eternal truth, in deliberate tension. Alliteration and assonance link God, grandeur, greatness. The paradox of apparent defeat by the world in 'Crushed' carried over from line 3 to 4 is that this crushing actually has very fruitful consequences. The stylistician might comment on marked word choices like 'shod' (l.8) which seems to carry connotations of 'shoddy', 'shed' (get rid of) as well as of humans as animals (as a horse is shod). Review of other poems by Hopkins would reveal the repetition of emotional 'dearest' (l.10) across a range of poems and indeed across intense poems by all the major Victorian poets (e.g. through Tennyson's 'In Memoriam A. H. H.'). The causal structure signalled by line opening 'Because' again presents a Christian world view unequivocally to the reader through syntax and word choice. Four lines out of six begin with 'And' as Hopkins first catalogues the difficulty of mundane life, but then shifts to religious affirmation, distorting everyday syntax as he does so. The curious thing is that at the 'volta' of the sonnet (structural move from problem to solution) Hopkins equivocates between addition, cause and concession through use of the word 'for' (l.9) before moving to the less equivocal equivocation 'though' (l.11). 'For' seems to exploit simultaneously meanings of 'because', 'but' and 'despite'. Negative 'spent' (l.9) moves to positive (or ambivalent?) 'bent' (l.13). In short, it is clear why such a text would be valued highly by critics who hunt ambiguity and complexity, as Empson performs more interpretatively on the theme of 'The Windhover' in *Seven Types* (1930) or Jakobson in 'Closing Statement' (1960) and elsewhere. The number of connections defies commentary and, in short, we understand the new critical idea that form is meaning, that a poem is ultimately irreducible and best itself at saying what it has to say. The stylistician will work more carefully and methodically than I have suggested here through sound, syntax, word choice (including archaism, Biblical influences), deviance and parallelism but we might expect critic and stylistician to notice many of the above features if describing them less or more technically and completely and with more or less reference to a wider literature. (Compare, for example, Short 1996, Chapter 2 on another nature sonnet by Hopkins, 'Pied Beauty'.)

Eagleton (2007) offers an interesting example of a modern literary critic reading this poem, in *How to Read a Poem*, his guide to close reading for the undergraduates he charges elsewhere with inability to read closely and refer to a text for evidence for their more evaluative conclusions. Would-be critics are told to read (among others) for:

5 Texture
6 Syntax, Grammar and Punctuation
7 Ambiguity
8 Punctuation [twice?]
9 Rhyme
10 Rhythm and Metre
11 Imagery

(Eagleton 2007: vi)

It is odd then that Eagleton opens his analysis of 'God's Grandeur' (2007: 154-7) with a paragraph on 'ambiguity' in the poem springing from Hopkins's Roman Catholicism, not from any observable textual source. The opening line which I called a 'generic sentence' in my own analysis is less technically 'an authoritative flourish': the more technical description arguably sounds less impressive but more helpfully points the reader to a range of other instances and texts against which to read the line, how it works rather than 'what I perceive to be its effect'. A long second paragraph then follows explaining tensions in the poem, illustrated with a single example where I spelled out many more of them, but, again, the precise words are lost in a welter of references to cultural knowledge concerning Roman Catholicism. Less historically, the analysis proceeds to claim 'ecocritically' Hopkins's status as an environmentalist before his time and disapproval of the industrial revolution. Repetition of 'have trod' (155) is reported as 'onomatopoeic' and then a mention with no examples or analysis is made of 'complex criss-crossing of assonance and alliteration'. Eagleton tells us that 'smeared', bleared' and 'smudge' suggest 'a purely surface contamination', though 'seared' is more difficult to explain in that way. Despite the wealth of features noticed in my earlier analysis, there is nothing more here on the language of the first stanza even though the analysis is offered to help those who reportedly cannot see or describe linguistic detail and its significance for themselves. These linguistic details could lead quite directly to the interpretations Eagleton offers, but he skips that stage. In the second stanza, '"for" here means "despite".' I have already suggested it has three or more identifiable meanings in fact. It is curious that 'ambiguities' can be missed by those who are supposed to value them so highly. 'Spent' and 'dearest' relate back to 'trade' as financial terms, Eagleton suggests from his Marxist perspective, and that is an interesting possibility I hadn't previously entertained. There are two more pages of analysis, but only one more linguistic remark, that 'bent' may mean 'both literally curved and morally corrupt'. The second meaning seems historically suspect to me but may be supported by the Oxford English Dictionary, even though Eagleton doesn't bother to refer to such research-based linguistic evidence. Most remarkably, the last two pages of his analysis are primarily content analysis of the kind he opened his book by condemning. A sunset is described and evaluated at length ('extraordinary image') but extended commentary and speculation are nowhere grounded in the concrete references to the poem I understood this textbook to be calling for. Eagleton's own checklist reproduced above is used implicitly and selectively at best. Bate's bike remains on the garage floor in pieces of varying size only partly understood. Call a stylistician. The argument here is that more work on the nuts and bolts level would be of benefit to the wider study of literature in promoting more nuanced, evidenced and precise understandings.

Conclusion

> At an academic conference on the humanities in general, held in 2009,
> I was surprised to find myself reluctant to attend the sessions on literature.
> This was, after all, my own discipline: I should be interested . . . I would
> agree, as I had so many times before, that Western imperialism has made
> untold havoc of indigenous cultures . . . Heterosexism, I would also readily
> concur, has obscured any number of homoerotic allusions . . . ecocritics
> [would] show that literature was green.   *(Belsey 2011: 18)*

What is wrong with such tired, repetitive and predictable criticism, in Belsey's view, is that 'analysis of the textual specificity of fiction' (2011: 27) and 'pleasure' have been lost sight of. Belsey gestures in the old vague way toward textual analysis but does not tell us how that might work. She calls for more work on 'pleasure' seemingly without awareness of developments in cognitive stylistics of affect and research on literary reading. There must be a genuine meeting and openness to the strengths of each other's insights as we forge more exciting and innovative approaches to the reading of literary texts. Stylisticians must learn to read and respect the contributions the expertise of the literary critics can bring to discussions of literary works; literary critics must be shown the value of getting their hands dirty with a little practical linguistic analysis.

There are examples that show this can work, if all too rare. Sotirova's research is an outstanding modern instance. An intriguing isolated earlier example of a moment of brave new theoretical exploration would be Connor's (1985) exploration of Dickens's realism in the light of Jakobson's (1960) ideas on metonymy. Another unusual attempt at dialogue equally unheard today was Robson and Stockwell (2005), who looked at how theory could talk to stylistics when investigating central preoccupations such as gender, race, authorship, interpretation or metaphor. Such work should be revisited and extended. More often there are missed opportunities. Das's (2005) very stimulating study on the senses in first-world-war writing would be so much richer if he had used cognitive linguistics in his analyses. Barry (2007), like many other literary critics, could enrich and expand his suggestive but sketchy analyses with just a brief excursion into corpus linguistics. Sadly, as his chapter on stylistics for beginning students of literature suggests (Barry 2009: Chapter 11), he has a very limited and dated understanding of what stylistics offers, though he has at least begun to explore narratology by 2009, if without realising it might have any connection to stylistics. Gavins, by contrast, explicitly develops a stylistic analysis to incorporate what has been learned of Yeats from literary criticism: 'failing to recognise a wealth of critical opinion or to address established readings within this community of practice is at best eccentric and at worst isolationist' (2012: 360).

Verdonk (2002) concludes his study of stylistics with the reflection that: 'the very richness of language as a resource for making meaning makes this meaning unstable, uncertain, and in the last analysis, elusive' (Verdonk 2002: 78; contrast Barry (2009: 206), who notes stylistics' 'refusal to take on board the notion ... that the meanings established through language are innately fluid, indeterminate, and shifting'). Verdonk's is a position the American New Critics and deconstructionists after Derrida also arrived at through close consideration of language use. Perhaps the space between literary criticism and stylistics is not so great after all (Hall (2008) attempts to elaborate an example of 'post-structuralist stylistics').

'There can be neither a first nor a last meaning' as Bakhtin observed in *Principles of Dostoevsky's Poetics* (1973). 'The meanings which literature conveys are of their nature elusive of precise description' (Widdowson 1975: 116). But if we don't try to describe language and account for its effects with more precision, we will not realise just how complex its workings are or in what ways and our thinking and understandings will be the poorer for that failure as we continue to talk past each other.

Part II

Literary concepts and stylistics

8

Genre

Beatrix Busse

Introduction

Genre analysis is a crucial component of both literary and linguistic investigations. Genres may be defined as different categories of texts which are determined by both formal and functional criteria (Jucker and Taavitsainen 2013). In other words, genres unite certain repetitive and generalisable features because their users in turn share certain goals and are prone to using a specific genre over and over again. In most cases, genres have labels, such as *epic*, *limerick* or *sonnet*, which are genres of poetry, or *textbook* and *review*, which are genres of academic discourse. Another example would be *recipes* – medical and culinary – which have retained many of their prototypical features throughout the history of English. Due to the fact that their purpose is to instruct us in how to make medicine or prepare food, they show, for example, a high number of imperative structures containing the verb *take* (Jucker and Taavitsainen 2013).

Existing linguistic definitions, especially, show some variety in the ways they define genre (Moessner 2001: 131). Genres may be seen as instruments for text classification and as 'cultural products and social forms of communication, conditioned by their time and social setting' (Jucker and Taavitsainen 2013). Genres and genre development have always been dynamic and procedural, as they may show variation and intertextuality in function and in linguistic realisations (Corbett 2006). Both literary and non-literary genres entail the possibility of changes: new genres and their features evolve and others disappear. Contextual factors mark and create the ways in which genres change over time and they interplay with the processes of making texts as well as processing them. Genres have the ability to create meaning because the continuum of adherence to linguistic conventions and social practices, on the one hand, and of creative deviation, on the other, direct readers' meaning inferences. Hence, one crucial issue to resolve is how particular texts function in a particular social and cultural context.

In this chapter, I will outline the major tenets and developments of communicative approaches to genre. I will also describe the points of intersection between *style*, *styling* and *genre*, drawing on systemic-functional linguistics, applied linguistics, historical pragmatics and stylistics. I argue for a cultural stylistic framework in which historical and contemporary genres, their accompanying linguistic features and functions, and their variation and change are seen as communication in a cultural context. Genres and genre studies as I understand them do not rely on frequency patterns and statistical significance alone. Rather, they overcome the modal linguistic bias of contemporary mainstream genres in an attempt to address generic materiality and mediality in their full cultural complexity and to address massive societal changes, such as the impact of the new technologies, globalisation, mobility and multilingualism. Singular places and isotopes that people have made meaningful can be patterned as well as generic. Mobile discourse profiles embrace and are construed by social styling and social practice.

Genre essentials and conventions

The conception of genre is crucial for both linguistics and literary studies and took place as early as Aristotle's *Poetics*. It is literary in origin: in the eighteenth century, the French term *genre* ('kind') was introduced as a loan word by so-called 'English commentators' (Corbett 2006: 26) or literary historians who attempted to differentiate between different types and developments of literary or artistic text production. Following the models and literary conceptions first outlined by Aristotle and Plato, they stress that literary genres and their dynamics are considered to be recognisable by their compliance with conventions of form, content and use of language (Corbett 2006: 26). Aristotle also distinguishes between the genres and characters of *tragedy* and *comedy*, focusing on the stylistic features of the different sub-genres. This basis in the Aristotelian model is enhanced by 'a metaphysics and an epistemology which derive from Aristotle's natural philosophy and the link between the philosophy of natural kinds of texts and sociocultural classes of people' (Threadgold 2001: 235). In other words, human beings have always categorised along a scale of values or a set of characteristics.

The conception of genre has been applied to a number of (linguistic) disciplines, but with different emphases. Generally speaking, categories and theories of genre initially serve the purpose of acting as descriptive and analytical, and prescriptive or pedagogical tools (Threadgold 2001: 236). At the same time, they are, however, used in models of text reception and reading and seen as forms of communication in a sociocultural context. In the twentieth century, the focus shifted from viewing genres as a fixed and absolute set of conventions to regarding them as dynamic conventions connected with changing institutions and social goals. Bakhtin (1986) refers to *speech genres*, which are forms of speaking or writing that people employ, mix or change according to particular social contexts. He shows that genres are at the centre of language use because all language usage belongs to one genre or another, and genres are essential for communication and for creating and interpreting texts. Bakhtin distinguishes between primary genres, which are everyday communication activities, and secondary genres, which are more explicitly and consciously produced, such as literary works. The evolution of genres is therefore a dialogue because new writing builds on earlier forms and creates a mosaic of quotations. Textual transmission and adjoining genres can thus be investigated through the study of intertextuality. Alastair Fowler (1982) also emphasises the blurred and fuzzy edges of genres, the dynamics of genres and their changes in the course of time. He draws on the prototype approach and illustrates that knowledge of genres is one of the prerequisites to recognising generic patterns.

Classifications of genre and their contextual embeddedness include and disclose a complex system of values of, for example, an institution, an author or a speech community: 'There have always been implicit and explicit social and aesthetic, and even moral values associated with the classification of genres' (Threadgold 2001: 235) and what counts as *canon* in the teaching of literary studies, for example (especially Bloom 1995). Hierarchies of genres are often linked with explicit or implicit social and moral values expressed in handbooks or style guides, or, more ideologically loaded, in fierce attempts to suppress minority languages as the Plain English Debate in the UK shows. As early as classical rhetoric, high, middle and low styles have been emphasised. These classifications resonate processes of sociocultural labelling of social classes based on the modes and styles that characterise them. At the same time, these labels are associated with the most powerful social and cultural institutions of government, religion, law and cultural authorities or with the label *high culture* (as opposed to *popular* or *low culture*). Analogous to the social foundation of any genre formation and evaluation are, for example, the formation of national language standards and attempts at critiquing language or at what Deborah Cameron (2012) calls 'verbal hygiene'. A standard of a language is often selected according to what is considered 'the best' by a prestigious, elitist social group. Verbal hygiene, in turn, describes active practices of improving and filtering normative patterns of language usage – that is, 'discourses and practices through which people attempt to "clean up" language and make its structure or its use conform more closely to their ideals of beauty, truth, efficiency, logic, correctness and civility' (D. Cameron 2012: ix).

The use of the term *genre* incorporates conceptions such as convention, communication and styling as well as value judgements and descriptions of the characteristics of actual texts, classes of texts, groups and systems of text classes, and descriptions of genre, which are theorised as social practice. At the same time genres may be conceptualised as reflecting human beings' cognitive schemata and world knowledge. Here genre is seen as a mental frame in people's minds which consists of their knowledge of schemata, scripts (Schank and Abelson 1977) and belief systems (Jucker and Taavitsainen 2013). People are able to understand and recognise these genres because in cultural contexts they are realised on a continuum of conventions on the one hand and creative foregrounding on the other. Genres may function as 'horizons of expectations' (Jauss 1970) for readers to know what to expect. These help guide the making, writing and processing of texts. Indeed, more recent attempts at defining genre and genre analysis have 'gone social' and see genre as 'an approach to communication which emphasises social function and communicative purpose' (Swann et al. 2004: 123). Genres are inherently 'dynamic cultural schemata used to organise knowledge and experience through language. They change over time in response to their users' sociocultural need' (Taavitsainen 2001: 129).

As such, interpersonal relations and functions of genres become more and more important because the communicative situation is one of the essential criteria in assessing why a text is written the way it is or whether it still shows some of the features of textuality outlined by de Beaugrande and Dressler (1981). Enkvist (1987) defines text strategies adopted by the genre-user according to their envisaged goals as the basic communicative principles in the broader framework of texts. Another crucial text-linguistic model which is based on communicative situations is Werlich's (1976) model of the five basic text types: descriptive, narrative, expository, argumentative and instructive. He provides prototypical linguistic realisations of these text types and stresses that they can be combined. Berkenkotter and Huckin's (1995) conceptualisation of genre incorporates this communicative and contextualised view of genre by developing a number of useful questions, which include:

1. Where does the genre come from and where is it going?
2. What does a text in this genre look like and what does it say?
3. How (and where and when and why) do people use this genre?
4. What sort of society does the genre create?
5. Who owns this genre?

In corpus linguistics, genres as well as representative extracts of text types are essential for the compilation of a corpus because linguistic features and repeated patterns, which have functional and conventional associations, are distributed in certain ways in various registers and genres. In other words, genres are one of the important parameters in compiling a representative, evenly balanced and evenly sized corpus for comparative studies of communicative phenomena (see Biber and Finegan 1988). *Register* is a related term here because it refers to situated language usage, which includes the setting, interactiveness, the mode of speaking, the goal and the theme addressed (Biber 2011: 707). At the same time, it can also be described in relation to the linguistic features used. Register would then relate to the language of advertising or the language of sports. With a focus on variation, register is at the centre of investigations in corpus linguistics and usually any corpus also includes excerpts from literary language, usually narrative fiction (see also Mahlberg, Chapter 17, this volume, on 'grammatical configuration' and the conception of 'local grammar'). For example, the *Longman Grammar of Spoken and Written English* (Biber et al. 1999) uses a corpus-based methodology to analyse how the characteristics of particular linguistic features can be described on the basis of their grammatical and structural functions and their 'behaviour' across spoken and written text types. They also have a chapter on 'lexical bundles', which describe multi-word patterns of usage that are character-istic of a particular register. In the multidimensional approach (Biber and Finegan 1988), statistical and corpus-based investigations are employed to analyse profiles of linguistic patterns that vary in register. Biber's study can be seen as one of the most important studies of genre which, in (historical) corpus linguistics and pragmatics, sparked ground-breaking genre-based quantitative investigations of linguistic patterning. From over 481 text extracts over 23 genres, Biber and Finegan (1988) chart the co-occurrence of 67 linguistic features and their functions. The dimensions of variation and stability are identified statistically by factor analysis (later cluster analysis), providing the co-occurrence patterns of linguistic fea-tures. Communicative functions are categorised along the following dimensions of styles: a) involved versus detached; b) elaborated versus situated; c) abstract versus non-abstract. Styles are simply defined in terms of the joint effects of multiple features and co-occurrence patterns.

In these approaches, *register* differs from *genre* in that the former denotes more generally a type of language use of or in a particular domain. Special emphasis is placed on the analysis of lexicogrammatical features. Genre here receives additional cultural nuances because specific profiles and conventions are known and actively produced by particular groups of people in a sociocultural context.

Genre studies since the early 1990s have focused on a number of text types, both literary and non-literary. This is due to new technologies and massive digitisation processes as well as discoveries of new texts. At the same time, genre boundaries have been moved.

Genre as communication, culture and styling

Systemic-functional linguistics
Genre studies and the identification of genres are important in a number of different linguistic approaches and fields of study, such as folklore,

linguistic anthropology, the ethnography of speaking, the sociology of language, corpus linguistics, historical pragmatics, or stylistics. The following overview is meant to be exemplary in outlining four approaches that take a communicative and social focus on the analysis of genre.

In systemic-functional linguistics (SFL) (Halliday 1994; Halliday and Matthiessen 2004), genre acts as one of the three levels of analysis of communication. The other two are register and lexicogrammar. As in SFL language usage is always meaning-making, semiotic, social and functional, genres have a communicative purpose and they are seen as an expression of language use in context. According to Halliday and Hasan (1989), a text can be defined as a genre if it includes the obligatory elements of a structural formula. Realisations of texts are determined by and vary in relation to three variables: field (the subject matter), mode (mode of delivery as spoken or written) and tenor (relation between participants). Together with the functions of genres, linguistic features are used to identify the so-called 'generic structure potential' (Halliday and Hasan 1989: 63–9). Another focus in SFL investigations of genres is that of the identification of stages, which are seen as 'realisation patterns' and as containing a generic structure potential with necessary and optional elements. The genre of a text is analysed by assuming that its overall goal is realised through a sequence of stages (Corbett 2006: 27). Hasan's (1978) investigation of service encounters at a grocery shop reveals a number of obligatory, predictable and repetitive sequences and elements, which she summarises under such headings as *sale request, sale compliance, sale purchase* and *purchase closure* (see also Ventola 1987). Eggins and Martin (1997) demonstrate that different genres are realised in different ways for different audiences and that different stages can be distinguished. Eggins and Slade (1997) illustrate that casual talk may be investigated from a genre perspective. They show, for example, that interactional speech genres are crucial in establishing, negotiating and maintaining group identity.

Genre analysis in SFL has for a long time favoured conventional and static situations for genre analysis. Even though Kress (1985) probably has a point that most situations are conventional and therefore generic, genre studies within an SFL and critical discourse analytical framework have moved beyond these fixed situational contexts. Fairclough (1995b: 14) stresses, for example, that genre is 'a socially ratified way of using language in connection with a particular type of social activity'. Fairclough (2003: 68–9) also shows that genres can be lifted out of particular networks of social practice from which they were originally developed. A situated genre is one that is specific to a certain network of practice.

In feminist and post-structuralist theory one aim is to highlight the conventional and socially constructed nature of both genre and biology and to explore, for example, the complex relations between genre and gender or genre and power (Corbett 2006). Linguistic and contextualised accounts of the functions of genre can be realised by looking at particular linguistic features of texts from a synchronic and diachronic point of view and/or by charting the linguistic colouring and stylistic effects of particular genres or clusterings and groupings of texts. These perspectives interplay with a wide variety of social practices so that linguistic patterns and functions are distributed differently in a number of genres, vary in texts and carry conventional associations for particular texts.

Applied linguistics

In the field of applied linguistics, there are a number of approaches to genre which focus on communicative purpose rather than on an increased sophistication about the categorisation of genres or on determining genre membership. J. R. Martin and Rothery's (1981) six elemental genres are criticised because their taxonomic schemes draw on classic studies such as Wittgenstein's (1958) theory of family resemblance or Rosch's (1975) concept of prototypes. Approaches in applied linguistics pay more attention to the historical development of genres (Yates and Orlikowski 1992), the process of genre production (Myers 2010) and accounts of non-literary language. Examples include Giddens's theory of structuration (1984) or the focus on context in Duranti and Goodwin (1992). Swales (1990) considers the tendency to focus on patterns of language to be homogenising. In his famous 1990 account of research article introductions in the sciences and social sciences, he shows a three-move sequence of establishing a territory, a niche and the occupation of a niche. Essential to these approaches is the notion of a *discourse community*. The underlying assumption is that similarities in speech can be accounted for by the speakers of a community who are defined by geographical space, social class, gender, ethnicity and so on. Those who belong to a particular speech community share a common set of communicative goals.

However, to determine the communicative purpose of a speech community is a complex exercise because a communicative purpose can be less easily demonstrated than recurring linguistic patterns of a text. The questions of how a communicative purpose can be used to decide if a particular text belongs to a certain genre category or not has to be incorporated in a focus on the socio-communicative context. Similarly, it is necessary to ask to what extent communicative purpose is too subjective to serve as a reliable criterion for class membership. Bhatia (1993) also introduces the psychological dimension; that is, so-called 'tactical aspects of genre constructions' (Askehave and Swales 2001: 200) where informants are needed. Genres are goal-directed and staged because communicative purposes shape the genre. Speakers know the layered communicative sets (Askehave and Swales 2001: 198), although more recent work has questioned the static nature of the discourse community as such (Corbett 2006: 29–32). Discourses can be multifunctional and discourse communities can be diffuse. Bex (1994), for example, adopts and adapts social network theory in his redefinition of genre and thereby allows genre analysts to move away from the notion of genre as being confined to rituals of speech. Recent approaches to social styling address a similar issue.

Historical pragmatics and corpus linguistics

In historical pragmatics, genres are seen as 'cultural products and social forms of communication' (Jucker and Taavitsainen 2013) that are determined by their time and the social context in which they occur including the process of reception and production. Genres have been frequently studied in historical pragmatics with the aim to identify repertoires of genres or a 'matrix of genres' (Jucker and Taavitsainen 2013) and their features in the history of English within their contextual and social situatedness. The aim of determining genre styles and conventions is based on analysing particular linguistic profiles of a text from a synchronic and diachronic perspective.

Historical pragmatics makes use of the distinction between *genres* and *text types* first introduced by Biber and Finegan in 1988 and elaborated on by Taavitsainen in 2001. Both terms are abstractions: *genre* is based on a categorisation that draws on external sociocultural evidence and *text type* refers to classifications based on internal linguistic features of a text. With the attempt to investigate historical language in use, procedures of change and the dynamic use of genres, this distinction is useful because it allows for the classification of (the same) linguistic features in different ways. It has been shown that if a genre is defined by its function (e.g. a report or a review) or audience (e.g. children's literature), it may be realised in different ways, hence including different text types (Jucker and Taavitsainen 2013). Often a variety of text types is typical of longer texts. In other words, narratives, for example, are embedded in different genres. Therefore, the separation also guarantees more analytical rigour and provides a framework of genres in the attempt to trace genre dynamics and mechanisms of change from a historical perspective. As linguistic realisations of texts within genres change over time, it is possible to trace the changing genres by drawing on a number of synchronic analyses. The comparison of texts of a specific genre at specific points in time makes it possible to establish norms, deviations, innovations and individual functions. This form-to-function mapping will also reveal co-occurrence patterns (the related concept of *register* is mentioned above). The set of genres may also change in the course of time. The Bakhtinian idea that all language use is framed in genres and that genres are integral for communication and for creating and interpreting texts is one of the bases in historical pragmatics genre research.

Methodologically speaking, qualitative methods of genre studies and corpus linguistics have been fruitfully combined (Jucker and Taavitsainen 2013). Taavitsainen (2001, 2009), for example, uses Biber and Finegan's (1988) multidimensional corpus linguistics study on the styles of contemporary written and spoken English for historical genre analysis. In a diachronic study, Biber and Finegan (1989b) illustrate that, due to sociocultural reasons, there is a tendency for the style of genres such as fiction, essays and letters to show a more oral style, to become more involved, less elaborate and less abstract.

Speech acts have been connected with genres since the beginning of speech act theory: they are 'said to arise from the codification of discursive properties relevant to a society' (Taavitsainen 2001: 148). One focus is to assess the influence of pragmatics. Another is to assess its relevance in relation to determining the contextual units (or the larger pragmatic units) that mark the genre when interpreting and analysing the realisation of speech acts. Semino and Short (2004) and Busse (2010a) have shown that discourse presentation is crucial to other than fictional genres and that the different modes of realisations as well as their accompanied narrative stretches are also marked by particular repetitive linguistic profiles.

Pahta and Taavitsainen's (2010) findings from their pioneering project on 'Scientific thought-style: the evolution of English medical writing' can be used as another example. It describes 'stylistic change in medical English in a long diachronic perspective in a multifaceted sociohistorical framework' (Pahta and Taavitsainen 2010: 2). Adopting mainly a historical socio-pragmatic and historical corpus linguistic perspective, the scholars have not only compiled the *Corpus of Early English Medical Writing* (CEEM, 1375–1800) and extensively studied a variety of medical texts to illustrate their changing and stable genre-specific and context-dependent linguistic features. They have investigated how corpus linguistic methods can be used to explain flexible and stable styles in the scientific genres of medical writing in processes of medicalisation, changing scientific paradigms, and the interplay between the significance of English as the language of science. For example, there is a development from anonymously produced texts to a more author-centred approach in the early modern period, indicated, among other things, by a marked and increasing use of reporting verbs and reference to specific classical authorities or to general categories of people (Taavitsainen 2002, 2009).

Stylistics

Stylistics is

> the study of the ways in which meaning is created through language in literature as well as in other types of text. To this end, stylisticians use linguistic models, theories and frameworks as their analytical tools in order to describe and explain how and why a text works as it does, and how we come from the words on the page to its meaning.
>
> *(Nørgaard, Busse and Montoro 2010: 1)*

In stylistics, the conception of genre has always been centre stage on a variety of analytical, methodological and theoretical levels because a communicative, contextual approach to language also includes cognitive meaning-making processes. In addition, one important basis of stylistics is that meaning is choice and that each choice is meaning-making.

Another link between genre analysis and stylistics can be seen in the latter's use of the so-called stylistic tool-kit or tool-box (see Wales, Chapter 3, this volume). These terms are used metaphorically to describe the vast number of linguistic tools available to stylisticians for their systematic, detailed and retrievable analysis of literature and other text types. With the aim to find meaning-making linguistic characteristics in these genres, tools are adopted from and adapted to respective genres and new linguistic methods, theories and paradigms as well as new text types. One result is the (sometimes controversially discussed) interdisciplinary and eclectic character of stylistics and the evolution of various branches of stylistics (functional stylistics, pragmatic stylistics, new historical stylistics, cognitive stylistics, corpus stylistics, multimodal stylistics).

The theoretical foundation and methodology of foregrounding incorporates the identification of linguistic devices in a text that stand out against the contextual background of the text in which they occur. Therefore, foregrounding and style can only be measured, described and interpreted if conventions and norms of texts are established within a complex contextual framework. Deviation and parallelism are strategies of foregrounding. Deviation refers to linguistic moves away from the conventions, and parallelism refers to an overuse of particular repetitive linguistic structures. The interplay between conventions and foregrounded aspects of a text and the creation of 'poetic effect' are particularly addressed at the reader and enhance the narrative reader progression (Toolan 2009) of texts. Complex communicative characteristics of particular genres and text types can thus be measured and described as well.

In investigating style, the analysis can be on variation according to situation (register) or, more sociolinguistically and pragmatically speaking, on the level of formality or degree of involvement, and on the style of an author or work. These dimensions interplay with one another, and style can be seen as 'the set of sums of linguistic features that seem characteristic whether of register, genre or period' (Wales 2011: 371). Stylistics finds out what makes a text or a group of texts or the words of a particular character or a writer stand out. As a more recent branch or methodology of stylistics, corpus stylistics has enhanced detailed, systematic and retrievable quantitative investigations of patterns in literature which are meaning-making (see, for example, Busse 2010a, 2010b; Mahlberg 2007a, 2012; Semino and Short 2004; Stubbs 2005). 'Stylometry' is not new, but by combining corpus linguistic method and theory with major tenets from stylistics, patterns that would otherwise have been missed can be disclosed and fresh views of (generic) norms and deviations can be explained. Corpus linguistic methods provide quantitative findings about linguistic features (Mahlberg 2007a) through concordances whose output is compared statistically with patterns in other texts. This display of words in context discloses linguistic profiles of usage in corpora of representatively sized and balanced genres. Although corpus linguistics is inherently lexically based and although there is a risk of focusing exclusively on these forms (Carter 2012), questions of how a text 'means' or how readers uncover meanings can be linked to a corpus linguistic focus on the complex relationship between meaning, function and form across different texts and different text types used for common purposes. Variation and creativity, both synchronically and diachronically speaking, can be discerned on a broader and more complex analytical scale to identify tendencies, intertextual relationships, and reflections of social and cultural contexts (Busse 2010c: 33; Mahlberg 2007a: 221).

Carter (2004) has shown that the distinction between literary and non-literary language is a myth and not productive. Literary and non-literary language are seen on a continuum, as a cline of 'literariness'. This is valid all the more for the historical investigation of style where the analyst has to rely on emergent genres and grammars and on literary discourse such as playtexts to investigate the styles of the domain of the 'spoken'. New historical stylistics (Busse 2010c) takes account of the fact that, through digitisation processes, we can exploit new ways of engaging with historical texts and literature and of sorting linguistic features systematically as well as investigating much larger amounts of historical data to analyse phenomena such as repetition, parallelism and the foregrounding of stable and changing styles in texts. However, quantitative investigations need to be supported by informed contextual qualitative stylistic analyses. Deborah Cameron's concerns about the limits of empiricism in humanities scholarship also demand an interplay between quantitative and qualitative stylistics. In an article from 2011, she expresses the concern that a more empirical approach to literature (which includes corpus methods) as proposed by Gottschall (2008b) may lead to unwelcome outcomes 'if it is used without due sensitivity to the nature of humanities scholarship' (Carter 2012: 108).

Historically speaking, the analytical focus of stylistics on specific genres is strongly related to the development of stylistics as a discipline, and, due to stylistics' focus on particular genres, checklists have been developed that are useful in an analysis of a particular genre. At the same time, what Leech and Short (2007: 61) call 'good bets' for meaning-making and stylistically relevant patterns are part of any introduction to stylistics. In the 1960s, stylistics aimed to complete the work of the Russian Formalists by making literary research more scientific through an observation of formal features with the aim to establish 'literariness'. At the same time, literature was said to have the (political) function of defamiliarisation, and their main focus was on poetry. Matters of context were increasingly addressed in the 1970s when stylistics also took part in what can be called a functional turn. Halliday's functional model of language is of particular importance for the first analyses of narrative fiction. In the 1980s and 1990s, pragmatic approaches and the analysis of play texts and other text types characterised by dialogue played a crucial role and enhanced more detailed stylistic investigations of conversation as exchange (Nørgaard, Busse and Montoro 2010: 2). Most recently, stylistic studies have investigated the function of human cognition in the creation of meaning. Meaning is created through the text and human conceptualisations of it. As such, a focus is placed on reading practices to try to account for reader responses that say more about the 'texture' (Stockwell 2009) of a text or a group of texts.

Following a transcultural framework, and as a reaction to increasing globalisation and mobility (Adey 2010; Cresswell 2006) and a view of discourse going beyond traditional notions of the text, stylistics has broadened its scope to the analysis of multimodal texts and semiotics (Busse 2010b; McIntyre 2008; Montoro 2011; Nørgaard 2010). The aim is to describe how non-linguistic modes and multimodal texts mean, along with how they can be described, how discourses as well as cultural and social contexts contribute to the ways in which videos and film are produced and received, and how they interplay with verbal discourse (Carter 2012). A bias to classic genres of mass media, such as newspaper discourse, which are often part of linguistic corpora, is no longer sufficient. With a focus on how a text means, stylistics needs to address the important role played by spoken interaction and the new media, such as blogs and wikis, and the discourse used in social networks. Stylistics needs to find out how we can measure, describe and interpret this use of language which is, according to Carter (2012: 107), 'not standard, nor simply written or spoken English but a language which allows users to give a creative expression of feeling of friendship, intimacy, resistance' and in which new modes of speaking are facilitated.

Multimodality also includes semiotic sign-making in places (Backhaus 2007; Jaworski and Thurlow 2010). For example, the city is a highly concentrated place in which a variety of social effects and agents arise and influence one another (Busse forthcoming; Warnke 2012). It is a place of movement, transformation and migration, which is visible, for example, in multilingualism in general, or texts as diverse as street art, graffiti, leaflets, street signs, films, shop names and the like. My proposed term 'cultural stylistics' is, then, able to incorporate 'blurred genres' (Geertz 1983) as well as materiality and mediality as forms of cultural identity with the aim of revealing how and in which processes culture-specific features are discursively formed. Pattern formation and the establishment of cultural profiles and identities can then be discerned not only in quantitative significance or frequencies, but also in singular historical and contemporary places or isotopes – that is, areas which people have made meaningful in interaction (Cresswell 2006).

This 'cultural stylistics' framework also embraces social styling outlined by Coupland (2007) as interactivity in (spoken) discourse. Style is not just the measurable linguistic profile that deviates from or is parallel to certain norms but must always be seen as a communicative and social practice (Carter 2012; Coupland 2007; Moore 2012). It is crucial to take account of the 'communities of practice' (rather than the speech community) in which language usage or the use of particular styles or the use of genres take place. Coupland (2007) and Moore (2012) point out that only in a specific community of practice may linguistic features become socially meaningful: 'We are now trying to understand how social meaning is reflected and created by (an accumulation of) linguistic entities' (Moore 2012: 71). This entails understanding the social concerns of a community and how they are embodied in social styles (Moore 2012: 71). Linguistic features occur in interaction with others (Moore 2012: 68). While it is always possible that speakers exhibit particular effects or characteristics outside their socioeconomic classification, the social meaning of a linguistic feature (and a genre) is typically underspecified until it enters into a speaker's or a group's social practice. The social meaning of a linguistic feature is embedded in the specific context of its use; which means we situate meaning relative to the other social or linguistic feature. To illustrate how certain forms of language in an urban place construe identity, Barbara Johnstone (2009) elaborates on the term *enregisterment*, which is used to conceptualise the ways in which certain local or dialectal words, phrases, phonological features or syntactical structures in Pittsburgh are indexically linked with (that is, they become interpreted and evaluated according to) social meanings so that their usage is ascribed with a sense of local identity and variation. Style is therefore a 'socially meaningful clustering of features within or across linguistic levels and modalities' (Moore 2012: 69). In turn, language is a resource for identity styling and not just a reflection of one's social position (Moore 2012: 69).

The Labovian (1966) interest in style and the social variable is therefore overcome because it can no longer describe a fixed 1:1 correlation between language usage and social class of a speaker with static variants, such as social class, formal versus informal and so on. It is very important to determine the linguistic practices of a community, but so far these investigations have not focused enough on variation and 'the social detail that vivifies language usage' (Moore 2012: 67); so far social meaning has been seen as exclusively tied to social groups. Stratification models are useful for our understanding of general standards but they also limit it (Moore 2012: 69). Frequency of usage plays a role in a particular community of practice in relation to the significance of the 'variants' themselves and what they mean, especially because some social variables are cognitively stored. More focus should be placed on why speakers style-shift and on the interpersonal function of style shifting (Moore 2012: 67), where other layers of social meaning would play a role. The interest lies in how styles – linguistic or multimodal – index social meanings in a cultural context.

Conclusions

Genre studies are indispensable components of research in literary criticism and for the investigation of language in use. The conception of genre refers to categories of text types and their accompanying functional and formal linguistic features which mark them. At the same time, genres are theorised as communication and as situated in their cultural contexts of usage. As such, genres play a crucial role in the production and reception of meaning. These complex genre profiles have changed throughout the history of English, resulting in speech genres that carry intertextual dimensions. Genres may also serve as mirrors of values and evaluations of a community of practice. Due to massive technological, global, political and cultural transformations, the view of genres as fixed and stable entities has given way to a more dynamic view of genre as social practice which draws attention to all sorts of multimodal (spoken) discourses. The interest in cultural stylistics lies in how styles – linguistic or multimodal – index social meanings in a cultural context.

9

Intertextuality and allusion

Patrick Colm Hogan

Literary critics and theorists in a range of traditions have been interested in the ways two texts may be connected with one another. Such connections are widely viewed as having consequences for readers' and interpreters' understanding and response. Intertextuality and allusion are, along with influence, the most widely discussed forms of such textual interrelations. Though all three concepts have a basic intuitive comprehensibility, at least two problems arise in treating them theoretically. First, it is very difficult to arrive at definitions of the terms that would be both precise and widely acceptable across theoretical orientations. The latter is particularly a problem for *intertextuality*, a term of art that arose in the context of a particular school of semiotics. Consistency across theories is less a problem for *allusion* and *influence*, since these are ordinary language terms. However, that also means that the standard usage of these terms suffers more obviously from imprecision. Moreover, this vagueness makes it difficult to determine just where allusion ends and intertextuality begins or where intertextuality ends and influence begins.

The second large problem with treating intertextuality and allusion theoretically is, in a sense, the obverse side of the first problem. It focuses on objects, rather than words – relations between or among texts, rather than the concepts bearing on those relations. Specifically, it seems that there are quite a few ways in which texts may be interrelated, not only two or three. It is undoubtedly possible to expand *allusion*, *intertextuality* and *influence* to cover the entire field. But that is only because they are vague, and that vagueness may be increased. But as vagueness and thus coverage are increased, the potential value of the concepts declines. As more and more textual relations are covered by the term 'allusion', for example, the term tells us less and less about those textual relations.

To address the issue more concretely, we might briefly consider a few examples. At one point in James Joyce's *Ulysses*, Stephen has been knocked down by a British soldier. He mutters to himself a few lines from a poem by

William Butler Yeats, a poem that we know from earlier in the book that he had sung to his mother. Gifford and Seidman (1988: 18) report that the poem 'was included as a song in the first version of Yeats's 1892 play *The Countess Cathleen*. The song, accompanied by harp, is sung to comfort the countess, who has sold her soul to the powers of darkness that her people might have food.' Thus we have a specific intertextual connection, localised in a quotation, but mediated by another textual relation internal to *Ulysses*, a connection that may draw a scholar's attention away from the text of the poem in Yeats's 1893 collection *The Rose* to the sung version in the earlier play. Elsewhere in the novel, Stephen plays with the idiom 'let the cat out of the bag' in saying that a pregnant woman has let the cat into the bag and now has to let it out (Joyce 1986: 343). This echo clearly involves a relation among texts. But it seems rather different from Stephen's citation of the poem by Yeats.

Sticking with *Ulysses*, there are numerous points in the novel where Blazes Boylan is indirectly linked with Satan. For example, his name suggests the 'blazes' of Hell, as in the expression 'hot as blazes' (1986: 629). Molly's adultery with him is often suggestive of the Fall of Eve in her seduction by the serpent. In some cases, these connections appear to bear on the account in *Genesis*. But that account is thoroughly diffused in literary and non-literary texts in Christian societies. Such diffusion makes the textual interrelation here in some ways similar to Stephen's references to letting the cat out of the bag. But it seems mistaken to see them as instances of precisely the same thing. Moreover, there appear to be some connections with specific mediating texts, such as *Paradise Lost* and Marie Corelli's *Sorrows of Satan*. Along with these more specific links, there are still broader connections as well. For example, the Christian story of the Fall and Redemption of humankind is an instance of a cross-cultural sacrificial structure (see Hogan 2011a: 133–4). Many parts of *Ulysses* clearly connect with the specifically Judeo-Christian story. But references to sacrifice (e.g. in relation to patriotism) also connect with a cross-cultural structure that extends the textual interrelations of *Ulysses* beyond that particular story, linking it with texts of which Joyce had no direct or indirect knowledge. These are just a few instances, taken more or less at random from a single book. Nonetheless, they suggest that the terms *intertextuality* and *allusion* are not adequate to cover the range of textual interrelations, even when supplemented with *influence*.

The following discussion of intertextuality and allusion will begin with two sections briefly sketching some significant theoretical uses of the two terms. The subsequent section will set aside the impossible task of isolating the putatively 'real' meanings of these terms. Instead, it will articulate some fundamental parameters in textual interrelations. These parameters may in turn be systematically manipulated to yield a set of more precisely defined varieties of textual interrelations. In connection with this, we may distinguish varieties of allusion and intertextuality, along with varieties of influence and what may be called *modelling*. On the basis of this more theoretically precise and descriptively adequate account, the third section will take up the functions of textual interrelations – perhaps most importantly, their contribution to the thematic and emotional purposes of works of verbal art. The final section will examine two somewhat more complex cases of textual interrelations, both descriptively and functionally.

Allusion

As already noted, allusion is based on an ordinary language concept and as such it is relatively theory-neutral. A concise, fairly standard definition is offered by Frye et al. (1985: 15): 'A meaningful reference, direct or indirect.' Probably the only part of this definition that may seem controversial is the clause 'direct or indirect'. It may seem that, to be allusive, a reference must be indirect. That may be the case in ordinary language usage. But in verbal art, we commonly refer to direct quotations as allusions also. For example, we are likely to take Stephen Dedalus's quotation of 'Who Goes with Fergus?' as an allusion by Joyce even though there is a direct quote. We may still distinguish explicit and implicit allusions. Thus Frye et al. explain that *paradiorthosis* is a particular 'kind of allusion, in which a writer quotes some famous line or phrase without acknowledgment and with a new context or twist' (1985: 334). We find parallel concepts in other traditions. For example, in Japanese poetics, *mommondori* is 'Borrowing or taking over more or less as it is a passage from an older work' (Miner et al. 1985: 277). Here, the idea of a 'new twist' is itself separated off into another concept, *honkadori*, which is to say 'Allusive variation', in which a 'later poet would take some diction and conception from an earlier "foundation poem" (*honka*) and vary (*-tori, -dori*) with a new conception' (Miner et al. 1985: 277).

One might also question whether the reference must be to a specific work or may be more general. Our prototypical cases of allusion do seem to be like Stephen's reference to the Yeats poem. However, Stephen's indirect reference to the idiom 'let the cat out of the bag' seems also to be a fairly clear instance of allusion. A similar point is suggested when, for example, the great fifth-century Chinese theorist Liu Hsieh includes references to texts and to facts in his chapter on the parallel concept (1959: 202–8). Indeed, Liu includes 'maxims of antiquity' (1959: 203), which may have a specific source, but undoubtedly are in many cases available more broadly in the culture.

Nonetheless, the preceding definition does not seem quite complete. Allusion may be direct or indirect, a matter of unique source texts or commonplaces. However, it cannot be fully elaborated. It must be in part a matter of suggestion, significance that goes beyond anything explicitly stated. Suppose a few years ago, a politician was planning to bring his family to stay with Bill Clinton for a week. A friend, remembering the politician's college-age daughter, wishes to caution against this. If the friend simply mentions Monica Lewinsky, then we may say that he alludes to the affair. In contrast, if he explains carefully that Clinton does not seem particularly trustworthy around young women, citing the case of Monica Lewinsky, then he is not simply alluding.

In keeping with these points, Joyce's use of the Yeats poem clearly suggests far broader relevance than is spelled out in the text. Indeed, in this case, the relevance is so broad that it is not practical to treat it here. The same general point holds for Stephen's allusion to 'letting the cat out of the bag'. However, in the latter case, the suggestions are more manageable. Specifically, Stephen aims to use his allusion for comic effect. There is a sort of crude physical mapping by which he uses the 'bag' to refer to female genitals – first the vagina, then the uterus. In the first case, letting the cat into the bag, the cat is a man; in the second case, the cat is a foetus. This is all clearly developed by Stephen. However, Stephen does not elaborate on the reasons for using this idiom. The idiom refers to secrecy. 'Letting the cat out of the bag' means revealing a secret. The joke here is that a secretive act of sex is necessarily revealed when the woman gives birth. But Stephen does not spell out this significance of the idiom. It is therefore an allusion.

Indeed, it seems that all the forms of textual interrelations that are of interest in this context are not fully elaborated. This is why theorists do not generally consider book reviews, textual commentaries, reader's guides, and the like, to be relevant to the sort of theorisation that treats allusion and intertextuality. Clearly, book reviews, and so on, are prime cases of works exhibiting textual interrelations. They are separate, however, precisely to the extent that those textual relations are extensively and explicitly spelled out (e.g. one text is an argument against the other).

Intertextuality, archetypes and influence

As mentioned above, intertextuality is a more complex and theoretical notion than allusion. It does not derive from an ordinary language concept. Rather, it is a term introduced into literary theory by the psychoanalytic semiotician Julia Kristeva (1980; see Roudiez 1980: 15). Thus, in its origins, it is closely bound up with a particular theory.

We may try to give a relatively theory-neutral statement of what intertextuality might be. The fundamental idea is that every text includes a complex set of relations to other texts. These relations include allusions. But they are not confined to allusions. Of course, it cannot be that every link is part of intertextuality. Many such ties would be contingent, ephemeral and insignificant (e.g. having an even number of words). One way of reducing the extent of such ties is by saying that intertextuality encompasses all ties that are recurring and have literary significance (e.g. for interpretation). Crucially, however, they would not need to be so specific as allusions, but could include motifs or patterns that are much more general.

Phrased in this way, the idea of intertextuality could be seen as closely related to Northrop Frye's idea of archetypes. *Intertextuality*, in that case, would refer to the linking of texts, whereas *archetype* would refer to the elements that link the texts. Specifically, for Frye, an archetype is 'a typical or recurring image ... a symbol which connects one poem with another and thereby helps to unify and integrate our literary experience'. In connection with this, 'archetypal criticism ... attempts to fit poems into the body of poetry as a whole' (1957: 99). The same point could be made for intertextual analysis. It locates individual texts in what might be called a 'discourse space' of other texts. On the other hand, there is at least a difference in emphasis here. Archetypes are more likely to have specific sources in a tradition (e.g. the Bible) as well as trajectories of dissemination. Intertextuality is often viewed as more diffuse. Indeed, in some versions it rejects the idea of a source for intertextual elements.

As these points suggest, intertextuality and archetypes are often discussed in terms of something like autonomous relations among texts in a sort of ideal or Platonic system. Putting the idea in cognitive psychological terms, we might say that everyone in a society talks and listens, communicating ideas, phrases, attitudes and so forth. This constant interaction with others and assimilation of the thoughts, words and feelings of others has effects on the content and configuration of, for example, one's mental lexicon. A person's concepts come to be interconnected in certain ways, forming recurring structures and resonances in his or her mind. When someone writes a poem or a story, he or she does so using linguistic and other resources that are necessarily marked by these 'dialogical' experiences (as Bakhtin (1981) would say). Here too, however, we do not want to count all 'dialogical' elements equally, since some are ephemeral or trivial. Those recurring patterns of literary significance are what merit our attention.

Here, we might briefly distinguish intertextuality from the more common notion of influence. In a sense, intertextuality, as defined psychologically, is a sort of influence. However, it is a diffuse influence. It is an influence that typically does not have a specific, isolatable source. It is an influence of countless small contacts with countless people and texts, producing countless recurring patterns across texts. In contrast, what we usually refer to as influence involves a much stronger, more limited and more distinctive relation between a current text and some precursor. Instead of countless 'source texts' by countless speakers and writers, an influence study looks at a limited number of source texts produced by a single writer. Rather than a diversity of recurring, non-distinctive patterns, an influence study seeks to isolate a limited number of highly distinctive patterns. Indeed, one could formulate the purposes of influence study in direct opposition to the study of inter-textuality. If intertextuality seeks broadly shared patterns, influence study seeks to isolate the patterns that are not broadly shared, but are rather distinctive of the source text or texts and the target text or texts. In cognitive terms, this is commonly a matter of internalised principles for the generation and evaluation of literary texts (for a cognitive account of influence, see Hogan 1995). For example, an influence study might concern itself with the ways in which Joyce internalised certain writing principles initially distinctive of Flaubert, then manifested those principles in *Ulysses*.

The preceding account of intertextuality is roughly compatible with Kristeva's views. However, Kristeva does not articulate her account in this way. Thus Kristeva writes that 'the *text* … is a permutation of texts, an intertextuality' (1980: 36). She goes on to maintain that 'in the space of a given text' there are 'several utterances, taken from other texts' in a process that incorporates '*citations* and moral precepts' (1980: 52). These appropriated and incorporated texts 'intersect and neutralize one another' (1980: 36) in the recipient text. The idea of neutralisation relates to Kristeva's view that texts involve tensions and oppositions (e.g. 'the thematic loops: life-death, love-hate, fidelity-treason' – 1980: 48). Different genres treat these tensions and oppositions differently. Perhaps more significantly, in keeping with trends in literary theory over the past half-century or so, she sees intertextuality as bound up with politics. Specifically, she sets semiotics (the study of signs) the task of locating 'the specificity of different textual arrangements … within the general text (culture) of which they are part and which is, in turn, part of them' (1980: 36). Any given text presents a 'materialized' (1980: 36) version of this generalised intertex-tuality of culture, making it an 'ideologeme' or minimal meaningful unit of ideology, which should be studied 'as intertextuality … within (the text of) society and history' (1980: 37).

One might dispute Kristeva's views in various ways. For example, a standard view of dominant ideology is that it comprises sets of common beliefs and goals that function to maintain exploitative hierarchies. There is no clear reason to assume that every text does this. Of course, Kristeva is free to use 'ideology' more broadly, particularly since her view of textual tensions and oppositions may suggest that the idea of 'common beliefs and goals' assumes too great uniformity. But then her use of 'ideology' seems to be nothing more than 'society and history', which seems to lose the specificity and value of the concept of ideology. Perhaps more significantly for present purposes, it is not clear that intertextuality is itself adequately specified, along the lines mentioned at the outset of this chapter.

Parameters of textual interrelations

Clearly, there are many ways in which one might differentiate connections across texts. Which is most worthwhile will depend on one's specific purposes at any given time. However, there are some patterns that seem to be more common and of more general value than others.

Before going on to these parameters, however, we need to draw a fundamental division between what might be called *autonomist* and *cognitivist* (or more broadly *psychological*) accounts of textual interrelations. Theorists of the former sort see textual interrelations as objective facts about texts in themselves. Theorists of the latter sort see textual interrelations as contingent on cognitive or affective processes. In the general cognitivist (or psychological) view, texts are not related to one another as such. Rather, texts are related to one another through the production of authors/speakers and/or through the reception of readers/listeners. This does not mean that textual interrelations need to be self-consciously chosen and manipulated. Cognitive and affective processes operate on unconscious contents and through unconscious patterns all the time. However, it does mean that textual interrelations are inseparable from cognitive structures, processes and contents. For example, in autonomist terms a text may be seen as literally alluding to another text. However, for a cognitivist, 'This text alludes to . . .' must be shorthand for 'The author of this text alludes to . . .' – again, with the proviso that the author's allusion may be self-conscious or unselfconscious.

The following discussion will adopt a cognitive account. Readers who prefer an autonomist approach should feel free to consider the correlates of the present account within autonomism. There initially appear to be problems with both approaches. For example, they both have difficulties limiting what might count as an allusion. It seems impossible to differentiate allusion from independent convergence if the relations among texts or between texts and facts are simply autonomous. For example, what prevents some parallelism in *Ulysses* from 'alluding to' the discussion of parallelism in Liu, if we do not require that Joyce have some direct or indirect connection with Liu's discussion? The problem for the cognitive approach goes in the opposite direction, given that allusive connections can be unconscious. For example, an author may derive a scene in a novel from some trivial experience that not even the most meticulous biographer would ever discover. We would not want to count this as an allusion. In the case of the cognitivist problem, however, a solution may be found in the isolation of parameters.

In the cognitive view adopted here, textual interrelations involve the following components. Framing the entire event, there is an author or speaker and a reader or listener. Within that communicative frame, there are at least two texts. Most obviously, there is the target or recipient text, the work composed by the author and read by the reader. Second, there is the source, some precursor. Finally, there is some sort of mapping relation between the source text and the target text. For example, in the simplest case, the mapping is a matter of quotation. Joyce quotes Yeats and thus 'Who Goes with Fergus?' has a mapping relation of quotation to *Ulysses* – quotation that does not occur autonomously, but is made by Joyce and recognised by readers. The preceding points may be summarised in the simple diagram:

author[source/mapping/target]reader

The section in square brackets is governed by the cognitive and affective processes of the persons outside the brackets (author and reader), with the former (roughly) producing textual interrelations and the latter (roughly) recognising (or not recognising) them.

The key variables in textual interrelations may be defined based on the source/mapping/target division. First, the crucial parameter for the source text is socially distinctive versus non-distinctive. There are some textual interrelations that bear on a unique source or limited number of sources. The lines from 'Who Goes with Fergus?' have one or two unique sources (the song in *The Countess Cathleen* and the poem in *The Rose*). In contrast, 'letting the cat out of the bag' has no socially distinctive source. Note that the important issue here is the socially distinctive source, not the contingent source encountered by the author. For example, Joyce may have learned the expression 'let the cat out of the bag' from his father, who perhaps used it frequently. He may have come upon the connection between 'Who Goes with Fergus?' and *The Countess Cathleen* in a review of the play. In both cases, the key textual interrelation, however, is to the socially available source – common usage, in one case; the play, in the other case.

It is worth pausing for a moment to say how this may be the case. As an author is composing a work, he or she is continually evaluating and adjusting it in light of a simulated audience. That simulated audience would not be aware of the author's idiosyncratic background. Rather, they would be aware of socially available texts. The author does not have to reason out any of this. Rather, he or she judges that the text will or will not produce the desired effect on readers. If an author is successful, that intuitive judgement will, in general, tacitly incorporate the relevant social adjustment. This simulated, receptive response may be identified as the *implied author*. (The idea is discussed at length in Hogan 2013.) Thus, for the biographical author, 'letting the cat out of the bag' may be linked with a distinctive (autobiographical) source. However, for the implied author, it would not – and the implied author is the relevant norm here.

It is also important to distinguish different types of non-distinctive source. One is culturally specific. The other is universal. Sources of the second type are a matter of the operation of the human mind, principles of social dynamics, and/or other cross-cultural factors. The universal genres, such as romantic tragi-comedy, would fall into this group.

A second key parameter concerns the extent of correlates between the source and the target. This is not a simple, bivalent parameter, since there are innumerable degrees of correlational extent. However, there does seem to be a broad difference between highly localised and more extended correlations. Joyce's citation of 'Who Goes with Fergus?' is highly localised, whereas his use of the story of the Fall is extended across the text. Note that this is not the same as relevance. The story of Fergus is the story of a king who gave up his kingship and whom Yeats characterised as 'the poet' of one main cycle of Irish myth (quoted in Rosenthal 1962: 237). The poem may be taken to ask who accompanies the poet, rather than the king, and to extend the novel's imagistic connections between poets (such as Milton) and the sea. Both have relevance at various points (e.g. Bloom literally goes with the poet, parting from the King's soldier). However, the precise correlates, the incorporations of the source into the target, are limited to the quotations.

Commonly, the more limited correlates are a matter of direct borrowing, the transfer of some element from the source to the target. This element may be a phrase, as in the case of Joyce and Yeats. However, it may equally be a character trait, a particular plot event, or even a feature of narrative discourse. In contrast, the more extended correlations may be a matter of a principle, rather than an element. In other words, they may result from the recipient author taking over a way of generating events from the precursor author. For example, one technique used by Flaubert involves contrasting unrealistic romances with a more realistic depiction of actual conditions, interpersonal or political. Joyce may be seen as taking up this technique in the 'Cyclops' and 'Nausicaa' chapters. In the former, he contrasts the actual conditions of an Irish patriot (or pseudo-patriot) with the mythologising rhetoric associated with some political and cultural writing of the period. In 'Nausicaa', he contrasts the actual conditions of a young Irish girl with some of the romantic writing of the period. In this way, there are extensive textual interrelations between *Ulysses* and some of Flaubert's works. However, the interrelations are a matter of assimilated principles rather than specific borrowings.

A final, crucial parameter concerns the process of mapping. Again, the author evaluates and revises the work based in part on a tacit, ongoing simulation of the response of an audience. In some cases, the source will be integrated into that response. In other cases, it will be absent from that response. Note that this is not the same as being self-conscious or unselfconscious. The presence of a precursor text may be integrated into an author's receptive evaluation of a work, and a reader's response to the work, without either thinking self-consciously that there is, say, a

Table 9.1 Alternatives for textual interrelations

Source	Correlates	Mapping	Category
Not distinctive (U)	limited	absent	universal motifs
Not distinctive (U)	extended	absent	universal structures
Not distinctive (C)	limited	integrated	cultural allusion
Not distinctive (C)	limited	absent	cultural intertextuality (ideologeme)
Not distinctive (C)	extended	integrated	cultural modelling
Not distinctive (C)	extended	absent	cultural influence (ideologeme)
Distinctive	limited	integrated	literary allusion
Distinctive	limited	absent	literary intertextuality (archetype)
Distinctive	extended	integrated	literary modelling

specific allusion. For example, I suspect that many Indian viewers of Deepa Mehta's *Water* find their response to the film enhanced by its subtle use of Kṛṣṇa/Rādhā iconography. However, caught up in the events of the film, I suspect that most of them do not remark self-consciously on the presence of that iconography.

Based on these parameters, we may generate a set of alternatives for textual interrelations, shown in Table 9.1. 'Absent' here means 'absent from receptive response,' whereas 'integrated' means 'integrated into receptive response.' 'U' and 'C' mark universal and culturally specific (non-distinctive) sources respectively. Given their nature, universal sources (e.g. cross-cultural genres) are almost necessarily of the 'absent' variety. They are part of the way we think more than something we might reference. Manipulating the three parameters adds models to the tripartite division discussed above and distinguishes between broadly cultural and distinctively literary textual interrelations. It also allows us to link particular forms of textual interrelations more closely with Fryean archetypes and with ideology, hewing a bit closer to the usual Marxist account.

For simplicity, I have left out some distinctions. Perhaps most significantly, in referring to 'integrated' and 'absent' sources, I have taken the implied author as the standard. This of course leaves out the literary critic, who may seek any type of source, from influence to biography. It also leaves out the real reader. This is perhaps not so crucial when the real reader is idiosyncratic. However, there are some cases where the response of the real reader is theoretically important. Perhaps the clearest case of this is with influence. Authors are perhaps more likely to exclude their influences from consideration, even in cases where the influence is clear to readers. Indeed, this suggests the truth in Harold Bloom's famous account of influence (Bloom 1973). Influence is likely to give rise to a degree of anxiety and misreading in authors, depending on the extent of the influence. However, it seems that authors do not so much misread their precursors as misread themselves.

A note on the functions of textual interrelation

Here one might reasonably ask: what is the point of isolating textual interrelations? In fact, there are many reasons to define and describe these connections, just as there are many reasons for authors to employ them initially. Due to constraints of space, it is possible only to sketch these briefly, based on the preceding organisation.

First, we may consider the 'absent' relations, comprising cultural intertextuality and influence, literary intertextuality and influence, and universal motifs and structures. As Kristeva's comments suggest, cultural intertextuality is likely to be the most pervasive and thus the most consequential for our thinking and response, not only to texts but also to the world. In such intertextuality, the source is absent precisely because the repeated pattern seems natural. To take a simple case, an author may draw extensively on cultural commonplaces about gender. However, there is a great difference between alluding to these common-places and drawing them into the work intertextually. In the former case, there is at least the possibility of establishing a critical attitude. If the source is genuinely absent from authorial and readerly response, however, such a critical attitude seems impossible, or at least far less likely. In the case of distinctively literary sources, the importance of studying absent sources would seem to be primarily a matter of under-standing the organisation of literature generally (Frye's project) as well as the operation of influence, itself part of the more encompassing project of understanding human creativity. The study of universal sour-ces, finally, is of considerable significance for understanding the human mind. Both literary and universal sources may have ideological implica-tions as well.

The study of integrated sources is more clearly connected with the implicit goals of the author. These generally involve fostering certain sorts of emotional response and communicating political or social themes. Thus Joyce's integration of lines from 'Who Goes with Fergus?' may bring some of the pathos of Yeats's play into the reader's response to Stephen's mourning over his mother. Moreover, it may bear on the political concerns of the novel, including to its rather critical attitude toward the anti-colonial mythologisation of the Irish past.

Allusion and modelling may also operate to fill in different aspects of the story world or to alter aspects of discourse. For example, as to the story world, the modelling of Blazes Boylan on Satan may serve to suggest his insincerity and Molly's likely disappointment in his subsequent behaviour, reinforcing literal suggestions elsewhere. As to discourse, allusion and modelling may serve to distinguish distinct implied readers, as when an author aims a text simultaneously at two separate groups. An extreme case of this comes in politically dissident works. Such works may avoid government prosecution through the use of textual interrelations that are obscure to government censors but evident to the distinct implied readership of government opponents. Sargent cites a case of this sort from thirteenth-century China. 'In response to the desecration of the Sung royal tombs at the direction of the Mongols', he explains, some poets included 'allusions to earlier poems, and historical allusions to build up a recurring pattern of references that covertly point to objects associated with the imperial corpses and their fate.' These textual interrelations served 'the purpose of expressing moral outrage' (Sargent 2001: 331) – or, more exactly, they served this purpose for one set of implied readers while being inconsequential for another.

Two examples

Khushwant Singh's 1956 novel, *Train to Pakistan*, concerns violence between Sikhs and Hindus, on the one hand, and Muslims, on the other, at the time of the partition of India and Pakistan in 1947. One of the main characters in the novel is a young Sikh man, Jugga. He is a petty criminal and often in jail. He is in love with Nooran, the daughter of the mullah at the local mosque. This love, which crosses communal boundaries, is ultimately what saves the local Muslims from destruction at the hands of the local Sikh majority.

At one point in the novel, the village leaders determine that the Muslims must leave the village the following day. Jugga is in jail at this point, in this case for a crime he did not commit. The pregnant Nooran goes to Jugga's family home. At first Jugga's mother rejects her, asking, 'What relation are you to us?' Nooran explains that 'Jugga has promised to marry me.' Jugga's mother dismisses the idea and insults Nooran. Nooran goes 'down on her knees, clasp[s] the old woman's legs and [begins] to sob' (Singh 1989: 130). The mother's attitude changes only when she hears of Nooran's pregnancy. She then promises that Jugga will come and get her when he is released from prison. Nooran then feels 'as if she belonged to the house and the house to her' (131).

This scene derives from one of the most moving scenes in Premchand's (2004) *Godān*, a paradigmatic work of Hindi fiction published originally in 1936. Gobar, a peasant youth, has fallen in love with and impregnated Jhuniyā – a forbidden mate, due to her status as a widow. He promises to marry her, but he abandons her at the last moment. She goes to Gobar's parents. Though they reject her initially, she throws herself at his father's feet, weeping and begging that they kill her rather than sending her away. This softens his heart and he addresses her as 'daughter', telling her, 'It's your house' and 'we are yours' or 'you are one of us' (2004: 152, my translation). The parallels between the two scenes seem fairly clear. Thus this is a candidate for modelling. However, the parallels are probably not salient for most readers, and perhaps were not salient for Singh himself. Thus it seems more likely that this is, instead, a case of influence, one of many affecting the novel.

Singh set out to simulate a relation of forbidden love leading to separation. In doing this, he followed the cross-cultural romantic prototype, specifying it with respect to features of scene, society and character. The separation is a variant of the usual romantic structure, where the lover is often exiled. Singh's shift here is to exile the woman, rather than the man, and to exile her entire community – a shift entailed by the conditions in which he re-imagined the romantic prototype (specifically, the location of the events in Indian Punjab at the time of partition). The pregnancy is perhaps a more common feature in the Indian tradition, as the abandonment of a pregnant beloved occurs in such paradigmatic works as *The Rāmāyaṇa* and *Abhijñānaśākuntalam*. Thus we see both the levels of universality and unselfconscious intertextuality or culture in this development. The specific scene of the young woman going to the home of the prospective in-laws, however, appears to be taken from Premchand.

Specifically, it seems likely that when Singh thought of such a scene, the most prominent instance in his memory was that of Jhuniyā and Gobar's parents. This perhaps implicit, perhaps explicit memory served to guide his simulation of what Nooran would do, how Jugga's mother would react, and what Nooran's final feeling about the house would be. Even more importantly, it served as a standard against which he could judge whether or not his scene produced the 'right' response – the sort of empathy produced by Premchand's scene. Indeed, a partial culmination of the scene in *Godān* comes when Jhuniyā calls Gobar's parents 'bāp' and 'mā' (2004: 153, *papa* and *ma*). At the culmination of Singh's scene, Nooran leaves Jugga's mother and, instead of the Muslim salutation, she uses the Sikh version, 'Sat Sri Akal' (1989: 132). Though semantically very different, the emotional impact is similar. Both suggest an overflowing of attachment that makes the beloved's family an object of deep love and respect. That feeling is presumably something that Singh carried over from Premchand as well.

An in some ways more complicated case may be found in the paradigmatic romantic tragi-comedy of Sanskrit literature, *Abhijñānaśākuntalam* (Kālidāsa 1969, from the fourth century). The story concerns a king, Duṣyanta, and a young girl, Śakuntalā, who fall in love and marry informally in a hermitage. The king returns to his kingdom promising to send for Śakuntalā. In the brief interim, Śakuntalā inadvertently insults a visiting sage who, in keeping with conventions of Sanskrit literature, curses her. The curse is that her beloved will not recognise her. When the pregnant Śakuntalā goes to the king on her own, he indeed does not recognise her. He goes on to revile her as a schemer and to criticise women generally. Śakuntalā then calls on the earth to open and receive her in death. She is led off stage and it is subsequently reported that Śakuntalā's mother, a celestial being, has taken Śakuntalā up into heaven. Years later, when Duṣyanta's memory is restored, he meets his son, then Śakuntalā herself, and the family is reunited.

Here we see several levels of textual interrelation. As already noted, there is the intertextual motif of the curse. This is part of the literary culture, whether or not it was part of the everyday culture of the time. Some aspects of the curse motif were almost certainly confined to literature – an important point for recognising that literary conventions do not invariably have ideological consequences. We also have a variation on the cross-cultural romantic plot in which social authorities interfere in the romantic union of the lovers, preventing their union. (For a fuller discussion of this and other points, see Hogan 2011a: 165–81).

More significantly for the present analysis is the relation of the story to events in the 'Uttara Kāṇḍa' of Vālmīki's *Rāmāyaṇa*. There are many connections between the two works. Some are likely to be noticed only by experts in the *Rāmāyaṇa*. But others are almost obtrusive. In any case, the connections are clear enough that they were almost certainly integrated into Kālidāsa's receptive intention. In other words, he almost certainly expected his readers to connect the events in *Abhijñānaśākuntalam* with parallel events in the Vālmīki *Rāmāyaṇa*. Specifically, in the final canto of the epic, Rāma is faced with public scandal over his wife, Sītā, having lived in the home of another man, where she had been abducted. In consequence, Rāma has Sītā taken away and abandoned in the wilderness when she is pregnant. Years later, he meets his sons, then Sītā. He agrees to accept her back 'if she should be again shown to be unpolluted before all the world' (Vālmīki 1982: 606) by passing unharmed through fire. Sītā calls on her mother the earth to receive her. The earth opens and Sītā descends, leaving the realm of human life.

The relation of these scenes nicely illustrates a particular form of self-conscious modelling. Kālidāsa was clearly guided by the *Rāmāyaṇa* in his treatment of Śakuntalā's dilemma. Moreover, he followed the source closely enough that any reader in that literary and religious tradition would be likely to recognise the relation. Kālidāsa's alterations tell us something about the way the human mind works in varying such source models. For example, the shift from earth to heaven suggests that proximity of semantic association is involved in such transformations. Though heaven and earth are opposed, they are closely linked in most people's mental lexicons. A similar point holds for the change from self-conscious rejection (by Rāma) to unselfconscious rejection (by Duṣyanta). A more subtle alteration is the one from the popular denunciation of Sītā to Duṣyanta's sexist comments on women in general and Śakuntalā in particular. This is a change from the coercive force of patriarchal social structure to the ideology that serves to rationalise that force and structure.

More significantly, the modelling has thematic and emotional purposes. Of course, the work is not entirely unequivocal on these points. But the most likely possibility seems to be that Kālidāsa is taking part in a long tradition of revising or responding to, even criticising the *Rāmāyaṇa* (see Richman 1991). He is taking up a problematic part of the great epic – Rāma's abandonment of Sītā – and reworking it. But, if the work does indeed have something like a critical purpose, that changes the way that the textual interrelation operates. Commonly, the source text functions to affect our response to the current text, as knowledge of Premchand might affect a reader's response to Singh's novel. But in cases of critical or ideologically resistant revision, the direction of the primary effect is reversed. The point of a critical revision of the *Rāmāyaṇa* is to affect the reader's or audience member's understanding of and emotional response to the *Rāmāyaṇa*. Thus the functions of intertextual modelling may move not only from source to target, but from the target (the later work) to the source (the earlier work). In this way, it is possible to think of some cases of intertextual modelling as 'counter-ideologemes' or at least as opposed to dominant ideology.

Conclusion

Intertextuality and allusion are clearly important concepts. However, they are vague as technical terms as well as being inadequate to treat textual interrelations, even when supplemented by the notion of influence. In order to solve this problem, we may distinguish several parameters of such interrelations. The first parameter concerns whether the source is or is not distinctive. There is a sub-parameter here which concerns whether the non-distinctive source is cultural or universal. The second concerns whether the correlates (or incorporations) are limited or extensive. The third concerns whether or not the textual interrelation is or is not part of the response of the implied author and the implied reader. These parameters yield a set of textual interrelations that adds modelling and that differentiates sub-types of all four kinds of interrelation (i.e. intertextuality, allusion, influence and modelling). These various kinds of textual interrelation serve different purposes. Some bear only on critical practices, such as the study of literary creation or the critique of ideology. Others, however, are important for our understanding of story and discourse, our inference of themes and our emotional response. Finally, the concluding examples show that textual interrelations are often highly complex, combining different sorts of connection and different types of function. Indeed, in some forms of textual interrelation, the new text is not only the target, but a source for re-understanding and re-evaluating the prior text. This seems to be particularly the case in ideologically critical revision of culturally paradigmatic works.

10

Production and intentionality

Violeta Sotirova

Authorial intention: the debates

For much of literary history, writers believed that the meaning of their work was inseparable from their intention; in other words, that in order to fully grasp the meaning of a text one had to uncover the intention of its author. It was in the formalist vein of analysis that intention itself became a radical problem, particularly with Wimsatt and Beardsley's essay 'The intentional fallacy' (1954). In this chapter I trace the main arguments for and against intentionality and its inclusion in, or exclusion from, critical paradigms. I also present a stylistic case-study of authorial intention.

While the assumption that intention and meaning are somehow inseparable has been regarded as natural, this is not to say that authorial intent did not enter the critical consciousness of classical and medieval authors. 'The extent to which the earlier criticism, at least until Aristotle's *Poetics*, de-emphasises authorial intent and tends to interpret poetry as contained solely within the text', because it 'is thought of as resulting from inspiration by a god' is singled out by modern commentators as an 'especially striking' phenomenon, one that shows that 'Classical criticism anticipated features of such twentieth-century developments as semiotics, hermeneutics, deconstruction, psychoanalysis, and reader response criticism' (G. Kennedy 1997: xi).

For Plato and Socrates the divinely inspired poet may not be capable of understanding the meaning of his poem: 'since poetry as such is not thought and feeling but the performance of thoughts and feelings, the poet or performer need have no proper understanding of what he says, but may as it were be aping the appropriate words' (Ferrari 1997: 104). Ferrari's modern attempt to rescue Plato from the contradiction posed by the invocation of authorial intention in some dialogues and the banished inferior status of poets proclaimed in others, when he says that 'it is not what the author but what the *work* "intends" that the Athenian insists we should know' (Ferrari 1997: 107), cannot detract from the fact that intention is very much a guarantor of meaning in Plato, albeit meaning as properly understood by the purveyors of truth, the philosophers. In some of the earlier dialogues Socrates seems to explicitly invoke the poet's meaning for a proper understanding and interpretation of a poem, as when challenged by Protagoras that a poem contains a contradiction, he suggests that they should consider 'what the poet meant' (Ferrari 1997: 100), or when he urges Protagoras to abandon poems in their discussion because 'Simonides cannot answer him back' (Ferrari 1997: 102).

The work of Aristotle spells out clearly a distinction between rhetoric and poetics. According to Halliwell, Aristotle's *Rhetoric* 'can be turned inside out to provide a system of rhetorical criticism' and if this is done, 'the basis of critical judgement becomes authorial intent and how that is transmitted by artistic techniques through the text to the audience' (1986: 191). But it is not so, Halliwell claims, in the poetic text, where 'a poet, according to Aristotle, should speak in his own person as little as possible' and should not manipulate the text 'to give it topical meaning' (1986: 191). This suggests that an advanced understanding of polyvocality is already present in Aristotle's poetic theory where rhetorical input is only allowed in the speeches of characters, and not in the direct expression of the author's own views. The three elements of Aristotelian rhetoric – 'logical argument, the impression of the speaker's moral character (ēthos) . . . and the awakening of emotion (pathos)' (Halliwell 1986: 191) – presuppose the importance of authorial intent, which should be included under ethos as an important factor in establishing the ethical stance of the author. That is why the standard characteristics of Aristotle's rhetoric are 'authorial intent as the basis of criticism, teaching of a method of composition applicable to varied situations but within a standardised notion of oratorical genre and form, interest in argumentation, character portrayal, and emotion' (Halliwell 1986: 191). The excellence of a rhetorical argument, then, is firmly based in authorial intent and moral character.

The medieval tradition leaves us in no doubt that *intentio auctoris* (*intentio scribentis*) is a basic component of meaning. This tradition goes back at least to fourth-century grammarians, who are quite explicit on this point. The prologue to the *Aeneid*, attributed to Servius, states that

> In expounding authors these things are to be considered: the intention of the writer, the life of the poet, the title of the work, the quality of the poem, the number of the books, the explanation.
>
> *(cited in Minnis 2010: 15)*

The 6th-century philosopher Boethius considered vital the following: 'the intention of the work (*operis intentio*)'; 'its usefulness (*utilitas*)'; 'its order (*ordo*)'; its genuineness; 'the title of the work (*operis inscriptio*)'; the part of philosophy to which it pertains' (Minnis 2010: 18).

The role that intention plays in determining meaning is captured in the apt metaphor of a twelfth-century scholastic philosopher:

> The reader of a work should regard authorial intention as the kernel, claimed Dominicus Gundissalinus (writing shortly after 1150): whoever is ignorant of the *intentio*, as it were, leaves the kernel intact and eats the poor shell.   *(Minnis 2010: 20)*

Significantly, Dominicus Gundissalinus worked in the Toledo School of Translators who in the twelfth and thirteenth centuries undertook to translate philosophical works of Arabic, Greek and Hebrew provenance. His insistence on the importance of intention derives from a practical engagement with the interpretation of linguistic meaning.

Gesturing towards twentieth-century reader response theories, Montaigne, the Renaissance thinker of subjectivity par excellence, says in 1580 that both in writing and in painting poetic touches slip from the hand of the artist to surprise even himself, and that

> Fortune does yet more evidently manifest the share she has in all things of this kind, by the graces and elegances we find in them, not only beyond the intention, but even without the knowledge of the workman: a competent reader often discovers in other men's writings other perfections than the author himself either intended or perceived, a richer sense and more quaint expression.   *(Montaigne 1877: 142)*

This brief historical sketch shows that the issue of authorial intention is not 'new' with the New Critics. To properly understand Wimsatt and Beardsley's position we need first to understand two aspects of historical context. The first is what it reacts against; the second, the period of literary history that has produced it. Wimsatt and Beardsley make it clear that intentionalist criticism and 'the intentional fallacy' are romantic notions – romantic as pertaining to a specific historical period and in a figurative sense – and they insist that all the 'romantic corollaries' of the 'intentional fallacy' should be questioned because 'the design or intention of the author is neither available nor desirable as a standard for judging the success of a work of literary art' (1954: 3). Their understanding of intention is as a 'design or plan in the author's mind' (1954: 4). They align the two camps of intentionalists and anti-intentionalists with 'the polar opposites of classical "imitation" and romantic expression' (1954: 3), thus firmly positioning their arguments in the history of this perennial debate and endorsing, if anything, Plato's 'reiterated mistrust of the poets' (1954: 7).

The romantic enchantment with the author as uniquely inspired original genius is shown by Wimsatt and Beardsley (1954: 6) to run through history. This insistence on the importance of the author's personality and experience is spelled out by more recent critics who claim that 'Romantic thinkers working in aesthetics and poetics … didn't look at the literary work as essentially a completed written text but as the vital embodiment of the expression of an author's spiritual individuality and uniquely personal creative experience' (Mitscherling et al. 2004: 39). When this outlook is adopted, 'we get a new conception both of the author's intention and of the reader's understanding of that intention: the author's intention is identified as the psychic experiences, especially the *emotional* experiences, undergone during the actual writing of the text, and the understanding of this intention consists in the reader's *re*-experiencing of these experiences, the experiencing of the identical "psychic states"' (Mitscherling et al. 2004: 39).

The main quarrel of Wimsatt and Beardsley with romantic intentionalism has to do with 'the use of biographical evidence', which if used wisely may 'be evidence of the meaning of [an author's] words' (1954: 11), but if misused may detract from the meaning of the work and result in 'danger of confusing personal and poetic studies' and in 'writing the personal as if it were poetic' (1954: 10). In Wimsatt and Beardsley's manifesto for a language-based interpretative criticism, the true poetic approach to the literary work is to treat it as a self-contained whole and to analyse its language as the primary evidence of its meaning. Their insistence on the centrality of language in literary interpretation belongs to a line of Formalist criticism which was crystallised in Shklovsky's dictum of 1917 that 'The technique of art is to make objects "unfamiliar", to make forms difficult, to increase the difficulty and length of perception', because 'art exists that one may recover the sensation of life; it exists to make one feel things, to make the stone *stony*' (Shklovsky 1965: 12); in other words, the aesthetic value of art is not in its particular content or in the images portrayed. Rather its significance lies in verbal technique.

It is not coincidental that Wimsatt and Beardsley's position is voiced contemporaneously with, or shortly after, the heyday of literary modernism. For Eysteinsson, 'Modernism, in its rejection of traditional social representation and in its heightening of formal awareness, would seem the ideal example of the New Critical view of the poem as an isolated whole, whose unity is based on internal tensions that perhaps remain unresolved but nonetheless do not disturb the autonomy of the work' (1990: 11–12). Accordingly, this new vein of criticism is due in no small part to the fact that 'Many Modernists have to a great extent shared the "purist" views of formalists and New Critics, and have even forcefully uttered ahistorical notions of poetic autonomy in their essays and other commentaries' (Eysteinsson 1990: 11–12). It is the formal innovations of modernism that facilitate the ahistorical and anti-intentionalist stance in criticism.

The formalist and structuralist attempts to explicate technique and linguistic construction, when taken to their (un)natural conclusion, have resulted in the extremes of post-structuralist anti-intentionalism. Famously proclaimed originally in 1969 by Foucault (1984), 'the death of the author' became a slogan adopted by the Barthesian school (Barthes 1977). The thrust of the poststructuralist argument for expurgating the author from the text rests on a newly developed understanding of language not as a means of the expression of individuality, but as already inhabited by other discourses, including the politically tainted ones of ideological dominance. If the writer does not possess language, language utters and articulates the subject and beyond the utterance there is no subjectivity, just void: 'the mark of the writer is reduced to nothing more than the singularity of his absence' (Foucault (1984: 102). While the claims of poststructuralist thinkers would be perceived by many as 'counter-intuitive', some of their political value has to be acknowledged. The dethroning of the author is seen by Barthes (1977) as an important move in shattering authority more generally, including the authority of the author.

The New Critical and Formalist positions on how most properly to conduct criticism and interpretation and where to locate textual meaning were challenged no sooner than they were first formulated. Hirsch (1967, 1976) has persistently argued that 'once the author had been ruthlessly banished as the determiner of his text's meaning, it gradually appeared that no adequate principle existed for judging the validity of an interpretation' (1992: 12). Hirsch locates the linguistic and anti-intentionalist trend in criticism in the modernist practices of criticism and writing: 'In the earliest and most decisive wave of the attack (launched by Eliot, Pound, and their associates), the battleground was literary: the proposition that textual meaning is independent of the author's control was associated with the literary doctrine that the best poetry is impersonal, objective, and autonomous' (1992: 11). Eradicating the author as the final guarantor of meaning results in locating meaning with the reader. For Hirsch, 'as soon as the reader's outlook is permitted to determine what a text means, we have not simply a changing meaning but quite possibly as many meanings as readers', and allowing this potential multiplicity of interpretations and giving them all validity is 'a *reductio ad absurdum*', ultimately denying any objectivity in interpretation (1976: 29). But, he insists, 'if criticism is to be objective in any significant sense, it must be founded on a self-critical construction of textual meaning, which is to say, on objective interpretation' (1976: 27). This objectivity in interpretation is only possible if the critic or reader in the act of interpretation tries to reconstruct as closely as possible the author's meaning: 'objectivity in textual interpretation requires explicit reference to the speaker's subjectivity' (Hirsch 1976: 48). The counter-argument, that meaning can be determined linguistically and thus that paying close attention to the text's language would allow for objectivity in interpretation, is considered by Hirsch to be nothing more than 'open[ing] the door to subjectivism and relativism, since linguistic norms may be invoked to support any verbally possible meaning' (1992: 18).

That the argument surrounding intentionality is alive and well today is witnessed by two recent publications by Mitscherling et al. (2004) and K. Mitchell (2008). Mitchell's claims in particular, formulated in the wake of Derrida (1997), put forward an anti-theory of intentionality in which 'intention and subjectivity need not be so facilely run together' and according to which it might be possible to 'conceive of some intention *after* the subject' which 'entails the re-conceptualisation of intention as material, linguistic, textual (of the text) rather than mental, subjective (of the subject)' (2008: 114). This, according to her, 'will open up the possibility of an "ethics" of the text, in contrast to the limited anthropocentric ethics of Hirsch' (K. Mitchell 2008: 114). Thus, Mitchell's argument tries to save intention not by locating it with the subject of the author, but by attributing it to the sheer textuality of a literary work, which for the deconstructionist critic is apparently capable of generating meanings by the very nature of the linguistic sign.

More recently cognitive narratologists in their drive towards a 'natural' narratology have tried to reinstate authorial intention as a vital part of any critical discussion. David Herman (2008) has argued that we have to accept as natural the human propensity to attribute meaningful intentions to any piece of language, including written and literary language. The formulations of such claims, albeit couched in unnatural terms, state that 'humans approach one another ... as intentional systems, that is as constellations of actions whose behavior can be explained and predicted by [a] method of attributing beliefs, desires, and rational acumen' (D. Herman 2008: 237). Herman illustrates this natural inclination of readers with an analysis of deixis, asserting that 'shifts among deictic centers are assumed to be *motivated*; that is, readers assume that a communicative intention of some kind drives the filtering of the action through a particular center, the shifts from one center to another, and the combined effect of sequences of shifts as a narrative unfolds' (2008: 250).

It seems to me that by this rationale any linguistic choice made by an author can be said to be motivated and so conveys some communicative intention. Why deixis places a particular demand on the reader to invoke authorial meaning and intention is encapsulated in its strong dependence on the spatio-temporal positioning of the speaker and its strong affinities with spoken discourse where context and gesture help the hearer to construe its meaning. I have argued (Sotirova 2010) that deixis requires the joint participation of author and reader in the construction of meaning. Thus, as a linguistic feature, its decipherment is dependent on a dialogical model of narrative that works through analogy with spoken discourse. Crucially, this theoretical model places authorial intention at the heart of interpretation.

It is, then, possible to integrate authorial intention in the interpretation of literary texts while also retaining the rigour of a linguistic analysis. The accusation that linguistic criticism, having its roots in Russian Formalism, has impoverished literary interpretation with its exclusive focus on the text is ill-founded. Many stylistic studies of literary texts demonstrate this union of form and content through close integration of the historical and cultural milieu of text production in the linguistic analysis. As part of this historical and cultural purview, authorial intent is not necessarily located outside of a linguistic argument. Or, to put it differently, the set of principles that define the stylistic study of literary texts (rigour, objectivity, replicability, empiricism and falsifiability, as outlined by Jeffries and McIntyre 2010: 22–4), are sometimes necessarily bolstered by the consideration given to authorial intention.

In the next section I will demonstrate how one can uncover authorial intention stylistically by tracing the revisions introduced by Virginia Woolf on early versions of the opening of her 1925 novel *Mrs Dalloway* (Woolf 1969). I show how literary intention can be brought back into our discussion and interpretation of literature without thereby compromising the accuracy of the linguistic analysis that formalism can offer. In other words, my attempt here will be to bring together the two irreconcilable foes of literary study: literary intention and formalist precision.

Intention and re-vision

It is not possible to talk about authorial revisions without making reference to the author. Authorial agency is nowhere more clearly visible than in the construction of a final text from early drafts. Grammar alone forces us to mention the author as agent, and the analysis of authorial revisions must necessarily account for intention and rationale in the changes introduced. What revisions reveal is that authors are thinking beings whose intentional meaning as expressed in words is subject to a re-visionary process. This process need not necessarily be fully consciously grasped, but it is nevertheless a process of production which shows that aesthetic aims are not always fully realised in first drafts and that they involve some careful consideration. As Redpath observes: 'when a poet changes expressions in a poem during revision, is that not sometimes because he considers that the words he is rejecting do not express as well as the new words, what he meant?' (1976: 15).

One might object that when revisions take place after a longer period of time their execution is merely testimony to a development in the author's aesthetic vision. While it is possible that this might be the case, more often revisions do not radically alter the work as initially conceived; they tend to intensify techniques already present, themes already established. Revisions are most often stylistic, rather than about plot or event, and their careful unpacking can offer evidence for an interpretation that is based on a linguistic analysis, at the same time as the linguistic analysis can illuminate their meaning in the overall conception of the work.

Woolf's novel *Mrs Dalloway* is, according to the editor of its earlier version 'The Hours', 'not "final", but is created from constant dialogue as it speaks to and out of its associate texts' (Wussow 2010: ix). These are: Woolf's short stories 'Mrs Dalloway in Bond Street' and 'The Prime Minister' written in 1922, which 'together are the first textual layer of *Mrs Dalloway*' (Wussow 2010: ix–x); an early notebook from 1922 which contains notes on the composition of 'The Hours' and part of its opening section; and, the complete manuscript of 'The Hours', begun in June 1923 and completed in October 1924. The English edition of the book from 1925 is based on a set of page proofs, now lost, but containing Woolf's latest revisions.

The dialogic formation of the published text, as Wussow describes it, does not preclude the presence of authorial intention in the composition of the text. Even if the text of *Mrs Dalloway* is not final, the linguistic forging of Woolf's technique still bears testimony to an aesthetic ideal that is pursued through different versions of the text. My exploration of Woolf's revisions and their impact on the portrayal of narrative viewpoint will focus on 'Mrs Dalloway in Bond Street', which will be compared to the opening of the finished text of the English edition. That Woolf intended to insert this earlier material in the opening of *Mrs Dalloway* is proved by the fact that in her 1923 manuscript of 'The Hours', after a very short unnumbered section at the beginning of the first notebook, she begins a new section of the book and numbers it: III. The missing parts of the opening, then, are the short stories describing Mrs Dalloway's early morning stroll around London and the episode recounting Peter Walsh's and Clarissa's meeting at her house, which was written in the notebook from 1922 (Wussow 2010).

The first significant difference between the opening of the short story 'Mrs Dalloway in Bond Street' and the published novel is found in the two passages shown in Figure 10.1. Passage (A) contains a cluster of present-tense verbs that do not stem from the direct thought of the character, but are rather the authorial present used in 'aphoristic *generic sentences*' (R. Fowler 1977: 86). The generalising meaning of the first-person plural pronouns 'we' and 'us' confirms this interpretation, as do generic statements of the kind 'there is nothing to take the place of childhood'. Authorial present, as Fowler explains, is the vehicle of narrative authority, which is why 'the generic sentence is a regular tell-tale of the intrusive, assertive, author'; its 'moralistic and authoritarian connotations' (R. Fowler 1977: 86) make it a favoured device by 'outspoken, sententious writers' (R. Fowler 1977: 89). What we see here then is Woolf adopting a narratorial position that is consistent with an earlier tradition – that of nineteenth-century realism.

The second paragraph of (A) presents a more subjectively nuanced experience of Big Ben. We find here the characteristic Woolfian disruption of perspective: the story had been oriented through Mrs Dalloway's point of view, with some narratorial interruptions, up to this point; at the start of the new paragraph we are given an external glimpse of Mrs Dalloway through the perspective of another character. But the different perspectives are nicely contained within sentence boundaries. The sentences:

(A) 'Mrs Dalloway in Bond Street'	(B) *Mrs Dalloway*

No doubt they were not all bound on errands of happiness. There is much more to be said about us than that we walk the streets of Westminster. Big Ben too is nothing but steel rods consumed by rust were it not for the care of H.M.'s Office of Works. Only for Mrs Dalloway the moment was complete; for Mrs Dalloway June was fresh. A happy childhood – and it was not to his daughters only that Justin Parry had seemed a fine fellow (weak of course on the Bench); flowers at evening, smoke rising; the caw of rooks falling from ever so high, down down through the October air – there is nothing to take the place of childhood. A leaf of mint brings it back: or a cup with a blue ring.
 	
   A charming woman, poised, eager, strangely white-haired for her pink cheeks, so Scope Purvis, C.C.B., saw her as he hurried to his office. She stiffened a little, waiting for Burthen's van to pass. Big Ben struck the tenth; struck the eleventh stroke. The leaden circles dissolved in the air. Pride held her erect, inheriting, handing on, acquainted with discipline and with suffering. How people suffered, how they suffered, she thought, thinking of Mrs Foxcroft at the Embassy last night, decked with jewels, eating her heart out, because that nice boy was dead, and now the old Manor House (Durtnall's van passed) must go to a cousin.
	She stiffened a little on the kerb, waiting for Durtnall's van to pass. A charming woman, Scope Purvis thought her (knowing her as one does know people who live next door to one in Westminster); a touch of the bird about her, of the jay, blue-green, light, vivacious, though she was over fifty, and grown very white since her illness. There she perched, never seeing him, waiting to cross, very upright.
	
	   For having lived in Westminster – how many years now? over twenty, – one feels even in the midst of the traffic, or waking at night, Clarissa was positive, a particular hush, or solemnity; an indescribable pause; a suspense (but that might be her heart, affected, they said, by influenza) before Big Ben strikes. There! Out it boomed. First a warning, musical; then the hour, irrevocable. The leaden circles dissolved in the air. Such fools we are, she thought, crossing Victoria Street. For Heaven only knows why one loves it so, how one sees it so, making it up, building it round one, tumbling it, creating it every moment afresh; but the veriest frumps, the most dejected of miseries on doorsteps (drink their downfall) do the same; can't be dealt with, she felt positive, by Acts of Parliament for that very reason: they love life. In people's eyes, in the swing, tramp, and trudge; in the bellow and the uproar; the carriages, motor cars, omnibuses, vans, sandwich men shuffling and swinging; brass bands; barrel organs; in the triumph and the jingle and the strange high singing of some aeroplane overhead was what she loved; life; London; this moment of June.

Figure 10.1: Comparison of extracts from 'Mrs Dalloway in Bond Street' and *Mrs Dalloway* (Woolf 1969: 6)

'Big Ben struck the tenth; struck the eleventh stroke. The leaden circles dissolved in the air', although using the past simple tense, can be aligned with Clarissa's perception of the clock's strokes, because of the iconic arrangement and repetition. The final sentence of this passage is most explicitly anchored in Mrs Dalloway's consciousness, with its exclamative constructions, the use of the parenthetical 'she thought', the proximal temporal deictic 'now' and the modal verb 'must', which are all indices of free indirect style. So, the technique of rendering consciousness is already fully grasped by Woolf, but its execution is within traditional boundaries.

In the revised passage from the novel cited in (B) Scope Purvis's perception of Mrs Dalloway is rendered in more complex syntax. The initial noun phrase 'a charming woman' is followed by the parenthetical 'Scope Purvis thought her' and by a non-finite clause in parentheses 'knowing her as one does know people who live next door to one in Westminster'. The perception of Scope Purvis is then resumed with two loosely connected appositional phrases: 'a touch of the bird about her, of the jay' and a series of adjectives and a subordinate clause that describe Mrs Dalloway. This syntactic construction layers loosely linked phrases, not always expanded into complete clauses, to make the processing of the syntax when presented in the written medium more difficult than the corresponding sentence in the short story. The perspective, although limited to that of one character, is frequently interrupted by asides, parentheses and appositions, and results in a more fragmented style that follows mimetically the meandering thought of the character.

The first sentence of the new paragraph opens with the conjunction 'for', ambiguously linking Clarissa's thoughts to something which is not actually present in the prior discourse but must be part of her own inner train of thought. The main clause of this sentence ('For having lived in Westminster ... one feels even in the midst of the traffic, or waking at night, ... a particular hush, or solemnity; an indescribable pause; a suspense ... before Big Ben strikes') is interrupted three times: by an aside, semantically related to the initial clause, but not syntactically integrated in the sentence ('how many years now? over twenty'), a parenthetical ('Clarissa was positive') and parentheses '(but that might be her heart, affected, they said, by influenza)'. The present tense of the main clause and the generic pronoun 'one' are here part of Clarissa's interior monologue. The sentence structure thus mimetically follows the interruptions and digressions of spoken discourse, as well as iconically mimicking the paused expectation of the chimes of Big Ben. The passage continues in the interior monologue form with verbless clauses ('There! Out it boomed. First a warning, musical; then the hour, irrevocable'). Another use of the conjunction 'for' in: 'For Heaven only knows why one loves it so, how one sees it so, making it up, building it round one, tumbling it, creating it every moment afresh' poses a semantic challenge to the reader because it does not actually provide a semantic link, and is thus only loosely attached to the foregoing discourse. The causal meaning of 'for' is only to be inferred in relation to Clarissa's train of thought, which is not made entirely explicit to the reader and which, by its nature of being thought, is elliptical and associative. This sentence returns to the present tense of Clarissa's interior monologue and, as it progresses, makes use of several parallel constructions of participial clauses: 'making it up', 'building it round one', 'tumbling it', 'creating it every moment afresh'. All of these are what Sylvia Adamson (1999) calls the free modifier: a construction characteristic of the style of the period which leaves the logical relationship between the non-finite clause and the main clause unspecified because of the lack of conjunction. The lack of logical coherence explains why the free modifier is favoured by modernist writers in their attempts to dismantle the logic of written language. This sentence also makes a deictic reference to something left vague in the surrounding discourse. Clarissa's 'it' would be clear to her in her consciousness; to the reader, however, it emerges as a more definite reference towards the end of the next sentence, some way from its first mention when we learn what she loves: 'life; London; this moment of June'. The colloquial omission of the subject in the clause 'can't be dealt with, she felt positive, by Acts of Parliament' intensifies the orality effect. The three long lists of noun phrases embedded in prepositional phrases that open the last sentence further contribute to the overall looseness and speech-like quality of the passage. The last sentence also makes another shift, less noticeable, to the past tense of free indirect style: 'In people's eyes, in the swing, tramp, and trudge ... was what she loved.'

The revisions, introduced by Woolf in this passage, allow us to discern a marked evolution from a narrator-dominated narrative which might well belong to an earlier tradition of the point-of-view novel, towards a modernist rendition of consciousness that is syntactically more verisimilar and that does away with the voice of the authoritative narrator altogether. The experimental technique of consciousness presentation in the later passage is the result of Woolf's radical disregard for syntactic norms in the written medium. Her intention, therefore, can be uncovered on the basis of the transformation of her earlier text: to render consciousness in a verisimilar way by approximating spoken discourse in its grammatical construction.

The next extract I will consider – Clarissa's meeting with her friend Hugh Whitbread – illustrates another feature that disrupts the syntactic continuity of Woolf's discourse – the embedding of one discourse within another (Figure 10.2).

The main difference between the two extracts is that, in the earlier version, Woolf reports the conversation between Mrs Dalloway and Hugh Whitbread in its entirety using direct speech, whereas the later passage exhibits more complex modes of report and embedding. The complexity in the rendering of perspective in (C) is found in the syntactic construction of the paragraph following the direct-speech exchange that records Clarissa's thoughts. The first sentence of this thought presentation contains two interruptions to its smooth syntactic surface – the parenthetical 'she thought', accompanied by a non-finite clause 'walking on' and the apposition 'fifty, fifty-two' which gives a sense of an internal dialogue conducted in Clarissa's mind. The main part of the sentence 'of course, Milly is about my age' is thus disjointed, but not incomprehensibly so. The next sentence, more fragmented, shows Woolf's accomplished method of transcribing consciousness. The arrangement of the first three clauses ('So it is probably that, Hugh's manner had said so, said it perfectly') relies not on logical linkage with a conjunction, but on asyndetic juxtaposition. A dash makes

(C) 'Mrs Dalloway in Bond Street'	(D) *Mrs Dalloway*

'Good morning to you!' said Hugh Whitbread raising his hat rather extravagantly by the china shop, for they had known each other as children.
 	
  'Where are you off to?'
  'I love walking in London,' said Mrs Dalloway. 'Really it's better than walking in the country!'
  'We've just come up,' said Hugh Whitbread. 'Unfortunately to see doctors.'
  'Milly?' said Mrs Dalloway, instantly compassionate.
  'Out of sorts,' said Hugh Whitbread. 'That sort of thing. Dick all right?'
  'First rate!' said Clarissa.
  Of course, she thought, walking on, Milly is about my age – fifty, fifty-two. So it is probably that, Hugh's manner had said so, said it perfectly – dear old Hugh, thought Mrs Dalloway, remembering with amusement, with gratitude, with emotion, how shy, like a brother – one would rather die than speak to one's brother – Hugh had always been, when he was at Oxford, and came over, and perhaps one of them (dart the thing!) couldn't ride. How then could women sit in Parliament? How could they do things with men? For there is this extra-ordinarily deep instinct, something inside one; you can't get over it; it's no use trying; and men like Hugh respect it without our saying it, which is what one loves, thought Clarissa, in dear old Hugh.
	'Good morning to you, Clarissa!' said Hugh, rather extravagantly, for they had known each other as children. 'Where are you off to?'
	  'I love walking in London,' said Mrs Dalloway. 'Really, it's better than walking in the country.'
	  They had just come up – unfortunately – to see doctors. Other people came to see pictures; go to the opera; take their daughters out; the Whitbreads came 'to see doctors'. Times without number Clarissa had visited Evelyn Whitbread in a nursing home. Was Evelyn ill again? Evelyn was a good deal out of sorts, said Hugh, intimating by a kind of pout or swell of his very well-covered, manly, extremely handsome, perfectly upholstered body (he was almost too well dressed always, but presumably had to be, with his little job at Court) that his wife had some internal ailment, nothing serious, which, as an old friend, Clarissa Dalloway would quite understand without requiring him to specify. Ah yes, she did of course; what a nuisance; and felt very sisterly and oddly conscious at the same time of her hat. Not the right hat for the early morning, was that it? For Hugh always made her feel, as he bustled on, raising his hat rather extravagantly and assuring her that she might be a girl of eighteen, and of course he was coming to her party tonight, Evelyn absolutely insisted, only a little late he might be after the party at the Palace to which he had to take one of Jim's boys, – she always felt a little skimpy beside Hugh; schoolgirlish; but attached to him, partly from having known him always, but she did think him a good sort in his own way, though Richard was nearly driven mad by him, and as for Peter Walsh, he had never to this day forgiven her for liking him.

Figure 10.2: Comparison of extracts from 'Mrs Dalloway in Bond Street' and *Mrs Dalloway* (Woolf 1969: 7–8)

the sentence veer off onto some new association in the form of interior monologue ('dear old Hugh') which is never completed, but instead the continuation of Clarissa's thoughts is rendered in internal narration ('remembering with amusement, with gratitude, with emotion, how shy, like a brother – one would rather die than speak to one's brother – Hugh had

always been'), only to be interrupted by another stretch of interior monologue between dashes. A further interruption to the subordinate clause
('when he was at Oxford, and came over, and perhaps one of them (dart
the thing!) couldn't ride') disrupts the syntactic continuity.

Woolf's style of consciousness presentation in the short story is beginning to emerge as a complex dissolved style of orality, but its execution is
not yet consistent throughout the text. When transposing the text into
the novel Woolf's revisions confirm that her authorial quest is to render
consciousness in the most fragmented and verisimilar way possible by
not only disrupting syntactic structures (the typical stylistic form for
centuries), but by also disrupting modes of thought presentation and
thereby blurring the boundaries between narratorial report of action and
character thought and experience.

The presentation of Clarissa's and Hugh Whitbread's conversation is
only partially carried out using direct speech in the later text. Most of
this conversation is presented through embedding Hugh's free indirect
speech in Mrs Dalloway's free indirect thought, thus creating more complex levels of discourse presentation. The three instances of embedding
are further complicated by the method of integrating them into the
surrounding discourse, a method that causes further disruption to the
syntactic and stylistic coherence of the text.

The first instance of Hugh Whitbread's words in free indirect speech
('They had just come up – unfortunately – to see doctors. Other people
came to see pictures; go to the opera; take their daughters out; the
Whitbreads came "to see doctors"') displays some features of the reporter's
discourse – Clarissa – and some that are explicitly attributed to the original
speaker Hugh, thus blending the two discourses. The next instance of
embedding occurs in a sentence that stems from Clarissa's point of view:
'Evelyn was a good deal out of sorts, said Hugh, intimating by a kind
of pout or swell of his very well-covered, manly, extremely handsome,
perfectly upholstered body (he was almost too well dressed always,
but presumably had to be, with his little job at Court) that his wife had
some internal ailment, nothing serious, which, as an old friend, Clarissa
Dalloway would quite understand without requiring him to specify.' The
evaluative comment on Hugh's appearance, the mocking irony at his
expense suggest that the reporter and perceiver of his words is Clarissa.
This part of the sentence is subordinated to the reporting parenthetical
'said Hugh' and makes the whole sentence digress into a series of evaluative adjectives and a clause in parentheses. We are also given a report
of the rest of Hugh's utterance, or rather intimated utterance, in what
would normally be classed as indirect speech because of the presence of a
reporting verb 'intimating' and a subordinating conjunction 'that', had it
not been for the fact that the reported part of this sentence veers off
into a looser, colloquial style that captures Hugh's unspoken words or
perhaps rather Clarissa's way of reporting them. Clarissa's experiences

are simultaneously recorded, as the half-spoken dialogue between her and Hugh unfolds ('and felt very sisterly and oddly conscious at the same time of her hat'). The incongruous pair that these two sensations make attests to the associative leaps in the syntax that capture the associative leaps in Clarissa's thoughts. In this instance of authorial revision the dismantling of the syntax is again deliberately sought in order to record character words and thoughts with a degree of orality that renders them verisimilar. The transformation of the mode of discourse presentation, from direct speech in the earlier text to free indirect speech and thought in the later, as well as the discontinuous flow of modes of presentation and the frequent shifts from one mode to another, add more layers of complexity and allow for the simultaneous rendition of Hugh's words and Clarissa's evaluative comment on them. This dual perspective is made possible by the greater degree of indirectness and distance which creates the space for irony.

The third embedded utterance occurs in the last sentence of the passage, and its positioning is perhaps the most intricate and unexpected syntactically. The sentence begins in free indirect style, giving us an incomplete glimpse of Clarissa's internal reaction ('For Hugh always made her feel, as he bustled on, raising his hat rather extravagantly and assuring her that she might be a girl of eighteen'), but we never learn how Hugh always makes her feel. The digression from the unity of the main clause in the form of three subordinate clauses is carried further in another coordinated construction which breaches the grammatical coherence of the sentence and the narrative coherence of the mode of presentation, a construction which constitutes the third embedded report of Hugh's utterance ('and of course he was coming to her party tonight, Evelyn absolutely insisted, only a little late he might be after the party at the Palace to which he had to take one of Jim's boys'). This embedding of Hugh's words within a sentence already disintegrating into a loose syntax that follows closely Clarissa's thoughts and inner states is unmatched by anything in the earlier text of the short story. After a dash, and having lost the thread of the main clause, we return to Clarissa's experience of how Hugh makes her feel, necessarily with what in spoken discourse might be classed as a repair ('she always felt a little skimpy beside Hugh; schoolgirlish'). The digressions in the syntax continue for several more clauses which form the final part of the sentence ('but attached to him, partly from having known him always, but she did think him a good sort in his own way...') and which display a semantically incongruous use of two adversative conjunctions 'but'.

Overall, then, the two passages show some similarity in the peculiarly Woolfian way of rendering consciousness, but the later passage from the novel exhibits greater complexity in the handling of syntax, a complexity that does not reside in convoluted hypotaxis, but rather manifests itself in digressions and interruptions to the grammatical coherence of sentences

(E) 'Mrs Dalloway in Bond Street'	(F) *Mrs Dalloway*
At last! Half an inch above the elbow; pearl buttons; five and a quarter. My dear slow coach, thought Clarissa, do you think I can sit here the whole morning? Now you'll take twenty-five minutes to bring me my change! There was a violent explosion in the street outside. The shop-women cowered behind the counters. But Clarissa, sitting very upright, smiled at the other lady. 'Miss Anstruther!' she exclaimed.	And she began to go with Miss Pym from jar to jar, choosing, nonsense, nonsense, she said to herself, more and more gently, as if this beauty, this scent, this colour, and Miss Pym liking her, trusting her, were a wave which she let flow over her and surmount that hatred, that monster, surmount it all; and it lifted her up and up when – oh! a pistol shot in the street outside.

Figure 10.3: Comparison of extracts from 'Mrs Dalloway in Bond Street' and *Mrs Dalloway* (Woolf 1969: 16)

associated with spoken discourse. When transposed into the written medium this looseness of syntactic construction might pose problems of intelligibility. Why Woolf would be seeking deliberately to dismantle the syntactic coherence of her sentences and discourse can be explained as a gesture towards extreme mimeticism in the presentation of human consciousness with its fleeting impressions, momentary perceptions and associative leaps. Her intention, as stated in 1925, to break the linearity of syntax in order to capture fully the non-linear nature of consciousness can be uncovered and explained as part of her aesthetic aim to record 'the atoms as they fall upon the mind' (see McNeillie 1994: 161).

One final passage recounting Clarissa's visit to the gloves/florist's shop when an explosion takes place will complete this comparison between the short story published in 1922 and the novel published in 1925 (Figure 10.3).

There is nothing unusual in the expression of Clarissa's interior monologue in (E): it uses verbless constructions to mimic the flow of inner speech, but the sentences are still grammatically coherent. The second paragraph reports in a traditional way the occurrence of the explosion using an existential construction that almost makes it too matter-of-fact, which seems to be in line with Clarissa's measured reaction.

The breaking down of sentence structure is very apparent in the extract from the novel. The passage begins with what seems like a narrative report of action, but as the sentence progresses it becomes more and more tightly bound up with Mrs Dalloway's experiential consciousness. Even if we ignore the sudden interruption in the form of direct speech ('nonsense, nonsense, she said to herself'), the expressivity and deixis in the subordinate clauses ('choosing more and more gently, as if this beauty, this scent, this colour, and Miss Pym liking her, trusting her, were a wave which she let flow over her and surmount that hatred, that monster, surmount it all') is enough to position them closer to a rendition of Mrs Dalloway's perceptions and inner states than to the narratorial reporting voice. This blending of narrative modes, I have argued (Sotirova 2013) is one of the features of the modernist writing of consciousness, perhaps most emphatically present in Woolf's writing.

But what goes further in the experimental handling of free indirect style is the digressive and discontinuous syntactic arrangement of clauses within the sentence. We have one portion of direct discourse interrupting the flow of a non-finite clause at a most unexpected juncture ('choosing, nonsense, nonsense, she said to herself, more and more gently') which is not only not syntactically integrated into the sentence, it does not seem to have much of a semantic relation to it either. And we have a similar discontinuous structure towards the end of the sentence where the temporal adverb 'when' prepares us for another subordinate clause in which we would expect a report of an action or event, only to be interrupted by the interjection 'oh' as if transcribing Clarissa's perceptions as they take place. This last interruption brings the final clause of this sentence within the boundaries of Mrs Dalloway's consciousness, thus transforming what could potentially be interpreted as a narrative report into an experiential report of events in the outside world. In contrast to the short story, here the whole narrative seems to be filtered through the experience of the character, even sentences that report her actions. This is partly achieved through the use of expressive features, such as the repetition of the adverb 'up and up', but mostly through the dissolution of distinct narrative modes: report of action, thought presentation in free indirect style or interior monologue, internal narration and so on, all of which result in syntactic discontinuities which in the written medium appear almost as disfluencies.

What in Woolf's story began as a fairly traditional presentation of consciousness that mostly observes the continuity of narrative modes and the syntactic coherence of sentences, developed in *Mrs Dalloway* into an experimental and verisimilar rendering of human consciousness that observes hyperrealistically the digressions, asides and interruptions of private thought, but also causes problems of intelligibility with its fragmented syntax and its dissolved grammatical structure. This breaking down of syntax and modes of presentation that we have observed in the examples from *Mrs Dalloway* was not an instantaneous act of literary craftsmanship; it emerged through a process of revision which forces the interpreter to acknowledge that the inconsistences in Woolf's writing are not accidental, but the result of deliberate authorial intervention and thereby intention.

The close linguistic study of authorial revisions, then, can illuminate the crucial points of the author's technique, those that the author chooses to intensify. In this way, the comparison of earlier drafts with the final text can provide strong evidence in the explication of the significance of stylistic techniques. Intention can thus be uncovered in a linguistically sustained way. Returning authorial intention to our stylistic exploration of texts would prevent us, in the words of Close when lamenting the critical fate of *Don Quixote*, from using the text, 'as a peg on which to hang the diverse preoccupations (artistic, moral, political and philosophical) of the nineteenth and twentieth [and twenty-first] centuries' (Close 1976: 174) and would save the stylistic study of literary texts from its alleged sin of ahistoricity.

11

Characterisation

Dan McIntyre

Introduction

In stylistics, characterisation commonly refers to the cognitive process by
which readers comprehend fictional characters. In effect, characterisation
is the process of forming an impression of a character in your head as
you read. This includes determining the personal qualities of the character
in question as well as other aspects such as their social and physical
characteristics. In this chapter I explain how stylistics has tackled the
issue of characterisation. I begin by discussing four different views of the
ontological status of characters. I argue in favour of the standpoint that
sees characters as mental representations in readers' heads. Consequently,
I outline a particularly influential cognitive stylistic model of characterisation proposed by Culpeper (2001). I show how this can be used to uncover
aspects of characterisation by analysing a number of extracts from prose
and dramatic texts, as well as a longer extract from Dennis Potter's 1978 TV
drama *Pennies from Heaven* (D. Potter 1996). I focus particularly on the opening scene of the first episode. Finally, I demonstrate the practical value
of understanding the characterisation process by analysing the hearing-
impaired subtitles for the scene from the *Pennies from Heaven* DVD (*Pennies
from Heaven* 1978). I show how the differences between these and the
original dialogue are likely to impact on viewers' impressions of the two
characters in the scene.

The ontological status of characters

According to Eder et al. (2010), there are four major opinions about the
ontological (i.e. existential) status of characters, none of which are without
controversy:

1 Semiotic theories consider characters to be signs or structures of fictional texts.

2 Cognitive approaches assume that characters are representations of imaginary beings in the minds of the audience.

3 Some philosophers believe that characters are abstract objects beyond material reality.

4 Other philosophers contend that characters do not exist at all.

(Eder et al. 2010: 8)

My focus in this chapter is on position 2 from the above list, since this is the view currently dominant within stylistics (see, for example, Culpeper 2001; Culpeper and McIntyre 2010; Walker 2012). Nonetheless, it will be useful to briefly outline the other three positions in order to explain how the cognitive approach differs in terms of its underlying assumptions about characterisation.

Eder et al. (2010) immediately dispense with position 4 in the list above, on the grounds that this view causes too many logical problems and essentially means that instead of discussing characters we are forced to talk instead about the texts in which they appear. In essence, position 4 suggests that it is impossible to separate out character from the other aspects of stories. Certainly, there are interrelations between characters and other story elements, such as plot, as Hogan (2011b) points out; it is because of these interrelations that adherents to position 4 would claim that characters in their own right do not exist.

Position 1 is similar but less extreme. Adherents of this position note that characters are indeed tied to stories but that this is no reason to deny their existence. From this standpoint characters are signs arising from signifiers in the texts to which they belong. In essence, this position sees characters as part of the fabric of a text. The problem with this is that if characters really are signs arising solely from textual structures then this would suggest that they are restricted to the texts in which they originate. This, though, is not the case. For example, the Elizabeth Bennett of Seth Grahame-Smith's novel *Pride and Prejudice and Zombies* is clearly intended to be the same Elizabeth Bennet as the protagonist of Jane Austen's *Pride and Prejudice*, despite the fact that the former is trained in martial arts while the latter is not. That we understand this to be the case would suggest that characters have an existence that goes beyond being purely textual elements. This is position 3, subscribed to by Reicher (2010: 132), who notes that characters 'are something over and above stories and works' and points out that it is entirely possible to create a character before creating a story (2010: 116). For an example of this, see Daniels' (2004) account of Bob Kane's creation of the comic book superhero, Batman, initially as a response to DC Comics' desire for a character to rival the popular appeal of Superman.

Reicher's (2010) work offers a convincing account of the ontological status of character from a philosophical semantic perspective. What position 2 aims to add to this is an account of how real readers comprehend characters. This is important since the experiences of readers often conflict with traditional literary-critical accounts of character. Culpeper (2001: 6–8) points this out in his summary of the distinction between what he terms humanising and de-humanising approaches to the notion of character. Humanising approaches, most famously represented by the early twentieth-century work of the literary critic A. C. Bradley (1965), proceed on the assumption that characters are essentially like real people. This leads humanising critics to speculate about the motives and intentions of characters in the same way as we might wonder about the aims and objectives of people we actually know.

One of the fiercest critics of the humanising approach was L. C. Knights, whose essay 'How many children had Lady Macbeth?' (1946) clearly lampoons the assumptions of Bradley and his ilk. Knights's argument was that speculating about the behaviour of characters outside the bounds of the text in which they appear is a fruitless critical exercise, since characters are purely textual constructs (in line with position 1 in Eder et al.'s list, above). Knights argues that any critical analysis of a text should be based on evidence found in the text itself. To take a humanising approach is to introduce extraneous elements into one's analysis and is therefore methodologically unsound. On the face of it, Knights's position seems reasonable. However, we have already seen that there are problems with the notion of characters as purely textual constructs. Moreover, when we consider how real readers talk about characters, it is clear that there is a common tendency to discuss them as if they are actual people. For example, actors in soap operas often report being on the receiving end of fans' ire if the characters that they play behave badly. And in an article for *Slate*, an online magazine, Tom Scocca writes of his frustration with fans of the US TV series *Mad Men* who talk about the lead character Don Draper as if he is real:

> Don Draper is a made-up person inside your television set. He is a pattern of lit-up dots moving in front of your eyes[.]   (Scocca 2012)

It is unlikely that Scocca really thinks people believe Don Draper to be an actual person; it is more likely that his irritation is with the humanising tendency that real readers (and audiences) display when they talk about fictional characters. But rather than dismissing the behaviour of real readers as irrational, we would do better to provide a theoretically sound account of how and why readers behave in this way. In effect, this is what cognitive stylistic accounts of characterisation try to do. In the next section, I will explain one of the most influential cognitive stylistic accounts of the characterisation process.

Culpeper's cognitive stylistic model of characterisation

Neither Bradley's (1965) nor Knights's (1946) views about character are entirely wrong. Bradley's humanising approach reflects how real readers discuss fictional characters, while Knights's de-humanising position emphasises the necessity of grounding our analyses about character in empirical evidence. As is often the case when two critical positions are set in opposition to each other, the most profitable way forward comes from taking the best elements of the two to form a middle position. This is essentially what cognitive models of characterisation attempt to do.

Culpeper's (2001) model of the characterisation process (originally outlined in Culpeper 1994) draws on the cognitive notions of top-down and bottom-up processing and assumes characterisation to occur through a combination of the two processes. In the case of characterisation, top-down processing refers to the role that prior knowledge plays in forming an impression of a character, while bottom-up processing refers to the practice of taking characterisation cues from linguistic triggers in the text itself. Schneider (2000, 2001) proposes a very similar model, in which characterisation occurs when readers combine knowledge stored in their long-term memory (i.e. prior world knowledge) with textual knowledge accumulated in their working memory. The striking similarities between Culpeper's and Schneider's approaches are indicative of the logical composition of the models. I focus on Culpeper's (2001) model since this has had most application within stylistics.

Culpeper's (2001) model is predicated on the notion that what you already know about character types will influence how you perceive characters when you read. Conversely, what you read will shape your prior knowledge. Characterisation occurs when we combine prior knowledge and textual knowledge through top-down and bottom-up processing.

Top-down processing involves the application of schematic knowledge to help us understand character. Schemas (or schemata, to use the Latin plural) can be thought of as bundles of background knowledge about the world that are stored in our long-term memories. Schemas can be formed directly (i.e. as a result of personal experiences) or indirectly (as a result of reading or watching plays, films, etc.). When we read, we use our schematic knowledge to shape our impressions of characters. For example, Umberto Eco's novel *The Name of the Rose* tells the story of a series of murders that take place in a remote Italian monastery in the Middle Ages. The hero of the story is a monk who is sent to investigate the murders and bring the murderer to justice; we only have to read the back-cover blurb to learn this. Before we even open the book, then, we are likely to have formed some sort of idea of what the hero is like. That is, learning that he is a monk is likely to activate our schema for monks, which we will use to form an impression of his character (for details of how schemas are instantiated, and for a more detailed treatment of schema theory in relation to stylistics, see Jeffries and McIntyre 2010: 127–33). Our schematic knowledge might give us an indication both of his appearance (perhaps he wears a brown tunic with a hood and is fat, like Friar Tuck in the Robin Hood stories) and his personality (maybe he is kindly and concerned, like Friar Laurence in *Romeo and Juliet*). If our schema is more detailed and sophisticated, we might know that friars tend to work among lay people while monks do not. Consequently, the images of Friar Tuck and Friar Laurence may not be foremost in our mind and instead we might have an image closer to Saint Francis of Assisi. But we also have schematic knowledge of character types (Propp 1968) and if we know that the main character is the hero of a murder mystery novel then we would expect him to display heroic characteristics. In this case, a monk in the mould of Saint Francis of Assisi is perhaps not a best fit for the context of story.

Schemas are also shaped by culture. For a reader from a non-western background, the notion of a monk may be radically different from any of those described above.

Despite the possible differences between readers' schemas for a monk, then, what should be apparent is that we are likely to have at least some impression of the main character of *The Name of the Rose* before we start reading the novel. Once we begin to read, however, these general impressions will be challenged by what we encounter at a textual level. That is, cues from the text itself will lead us to fine tune our schema. For example, in the case of *The Name of the Rose*, the hero's name turns out to be Brother William of Baskerville. Readers with any knowledge of Arthur Conan Doyle's Sherlock Holmes stories (particularly *The Hound of the Baskervilles*) are likely to see an association between Brother William and Holmes. Indeed, William turns out to be a detective very much in the vein of Conan Doyle's hero. The name of William's character thus acts as a textual trigger for characterisation which, when combined with our prior knowledge, shapes the way we imagine his character. Of course, since we also gain schematic knowledge from past reading experiences, if we have encountered characters anything like Brother William in the past then these will influence how we perceive his character. For instance, readers of Ellis Peters's Brother Cadfael murder mystery novels will notice a distinct similarity between Cadfael and Brother William.

Character names are just one of the many bottom-up indicators of characterisation identified by Culpeper (2001). In broad terms, he divides these into explicit cues, implicit cues and authorial cues. As might be expected, explicit cues are those where a character makes specific reference either to his or her own character traits or those of another character. For instance, in the extract below from Brecht's *The Exception and the Rule*, the Merchant speaks directly to the audience about his own characteristics:

The Merchant *(To his two companions, the Guide and the Coolie who is carrying his baggage)*

Hurry, you lazy mules, two days from now we must be at Han Station. That will give us a whole day's lead. *(To the audience)* I am Karl Langmann, a merchant. I am going to Urga to conclude arrangements for a concession. My competitors are close behind me. The first comer will get the concession. Thanks to my shrewdness, the energy with which I have overcome all manner of difficulties, and my ruthless treatment of my employees, I have completed this much of the journey in little more than half the usual time. Unfortunately my competitors have been moving just as fast. *(He looks back through binoculars.)* See, there they are at our heels again!   *(Brecht 1977: 38)*

The Merchant's description of himself as shrewd and ruthless constitutes explicit self-presentation, in this case in the presence of other characters (see McIntyre 2006: 74 for a discussion of the Merchant's status as a narrator). Such self-presentation is also found in soliloquies, distinguished from the above example by the absence of other characters (for example, Gloucester's opening soliloquy in *Richard III*; see McIntyre 2008 for a discussion of what this reveals about his character). What is often more common than talking explicitly about their own characteristics, however, is for characters to describe the traits of others. This is what Culpeper (2001: 171) terms explicit 'other-presentation'. The following extract from Roald Dahl's blackly comic novel *My Uncle Oswald* (1979) illustrates this:

I am beginning, once again, to have an urge to salute my Uncle Oswald. I mean, of course, Oswald Hendryks Cornelius deceased, the connoisseur, the bon vivant, the collector of spiders, scorpions and walking-sticks, the lover of opera, the expert on Chinese porcelain, the seducer of women, and without much doubt the greatest fornicator of all time. Every other celebrated contender for that title is diminished to a point of ridicule when his record is compared with that of my Uncle Oswald. Especially poor old Casanova. He comes out of the contest looking like a man who was suffering from a severe malfunction of his sexual organ.   *(Dahl 1979: 1)*

In the above example, the first-person narrator offers unambiguous statements about his uncle, the titular Oswald. Of course, as Culpeper (2001: 171) points out, the credibility of the describing character will have an effect on the extent to which we take account of the characterisation information they present. For instance, in the following example from Louis De Bernières's novel *A Partisan's Daughter*, the narrator, Chris, offers a strongly negative portrayal of his wife based on a deeply sexist generalisation:

She was one of those insipid Englishwomen with skimmed milk in her veins, and she was perfectly content to be like that. When we married I had no idea that she would turn out to have all the passion and fire of a codfish, because she took the trouble to put on a good show until she thought it was safe not to have to bother any more.   *(De Bernières 2009: 3)*

Culpeper (2001: 171) points out that research in social psychology has demonstrated that we have a tendency to overlook contextual factors when inferring character traits, such that our natural inclination is to take explicit statements about character at face value. In the case of the above example, however, the extent to which we accept Chris's description of his wife may be affected by whether we are naturally inclined (or not) to side with such a misogynistic portrayal. In any case, as the novel progresses and we begin to question the degree to which Chris is a reliable narrator, we may well reconsider his portrayal of his wife's character traits.

So far I have shown examples of the explicit presentation of character but implicit characterisation is equally important and, arguably, more common. The variety of implicit characterisation triggers identified by Culpeper (2001) includes lexis, syntax, accent and dialect, paralinguistic features, visual features, and pragmatic cues such as conversational implicature and politeness strategies. In Andrew Martin's 1905-set novel *The Blackpool Highflyer* (2004), for example, the first-person narrator, Jim Stringer, is a working-class Yorkshireman who only ever refers to his spouse as 'the wife'. It is only towards the end of the novel that we learn her first name is Lydia; and this information is revealed only in the reported speech of her friend, Cecily. Stringer's proclivity for not referring to Lydia by name works initially to invoke a schema for a subservient housewife (as well as suggesting a fairly distant relationship between Stringer and his wife, due to the lack of proximal social deictics). This characterisation stems entirely from Stringer's presentation of his wife to the reader. However, Lydia's behaviour is incongruous with the schema that Stringer's naming convention invokes: she is outspoken, in favour of women's suffrage and not inclined to have Jim's tea on the table when he comes home from work. And as if this isn't enough, she refuses to clean the front step of the house (an action likely to have made one a social pariah in 1900s Yorkshire). Part of what makes Lydia's character interesting, then, is that her behaviour clashes with the schema for the character type that is triggered by Jim's language use (as well as the fact that Jim clearly adores her, which to some modern readers might seem inconsistent with his naming practice). For readers, the clash between prior knowledge and textual knowledge is likely to foreground Lydia as a character.

The examples from Brecht and Martin indicate how characterisation can occur as a result of the linguistic choices and behaviour of characters. But significant characterisation effects also come from what Culpeper (2001) terms authorial cues. One of the most obvious triggers is an author's choice of names for characters, as we saw above in the example of Umberto Eco naming his detective monk *Brother William of Baskerville*. In this case it is the intertextual allusion to Sherlock Holmes that contributes substantially to what we are likely to infer about Brother William's character. Names, then, can convey significant characterisation information. This includes information about gender, nationality, social class, level of education and much more. In the case of *The Blackpool Highflyer*, for some readers the name *Jim Stringer* will be strongly evocative of (possibly northern) working-class origins. *Jim*, for instance, is a diminutive of the more formal *James*, while *Stringer* is an occupational surname dating back to the medieval period when it originally denoted someone who made longbow strings for a living. Of course, without this background knowledge the characterising potential of the name is lost. Indeed, a lack of relevant schematic and pragmatic knowledge can be one of the disadvantages that make reading literature in a foreign language particularly difficult.

The above division of textual characterisation cues into the categories of explicit, implicit and authorial cues might suggest that each of these methods of characterisation is distinct and unproblematic. In reality, it is eminently possible to find a number of methods operating simultaneously in a piece of text. Consider the following extract from Louis De Bernières's 2004 novel *Birds Without Wings*.

> i am philothei an i am six eveone says wat a pritty gilr an i was born lik that an so i am usd to it i am prittier that anyon else but i don't bost about it i sor ibrahim today an he was following me and I wosent sposed to see him i went with drosoula who is not pritty by ugli but she is my fren anyway an ibrahim was playign with karatavuk and mehmetçik and they were blowing thier berdwhissles an pertendin to be berds an ibrahin sed wen we are old we wil be maried an I sed yes properly   *(De Bernières 2004: 18)*

Here, the narrator, a six-year-old girl in the fictional town of Eskibahçe in 1900s Anatolia, describes both herself and her friend Drosoula. There is explicit self-presentation from Philothei ('i am prittier that anyon else but i don't bost about it') as well as explicit other-presentation ('i went with drosoula who is not pritty by ugli'). We might also interpret Philothei's claim that she does not boast about her good looks as tautological, thereby conveying implicitly that she is indeed boastful. In addition, the non-standard spelling and syntax causes a foregrounding effect which we are also likely to link to characterisation. Since Philothei's inability to spell would not be noticeable in speech, it seems likely that the example above is intended to be interpreted as something that Philothei has written rather than Philothei talking to the reader directly. As a result, the reader is likely to attribute the non-standard spelling and syntax to Philothei's age (and possibly gender, given the setting of the novel) and consequent lack of education. In this respect, the unconventional spelling and syntax constitute implicit self-presentation.

One issue with the categorisation of characterisation triggers as explicit, implicit and authorial is that, in effect, all textual cues for characterisation stem from the author and are thus authorial in nature. Culpeper (2001: 229) explains that authorial cues are those 'over which the character notionally has no power of choice'. But note that this claim implies a humanising approach to character in which characters do have choices concerning what they say and how they behave. Given that cognitive approaches to characterisation attempt to avoid the extreme positions of the humanising and de-humanising approaches in favour of explaining how readers construct mental models of characters as they read, it would perhaps be more accurate to describe all characterisation cues as authorial but to specify at which discourse level of the text they operate; in other words, whether this is the level of author addressing reader (discourse level 1), narrator addressing narratee (level 2, in the case of prose texts) or character addressing character (level 2 for plays, level 3 for prose; see Short 1996 for a discussion of the prototypical discourse architectures of the three main literary genres). This reformulation of Culpeper's categories allows us to avoid the implicit suggestion that the model is skewed towards a humanising approach to character. This slight modification thus improves the objectivity of the model. In addition, we can note that authorial triggers at the discourse level of author addressing reader can also be sub-divided into explicit and implicit cues, in the same way that self- and other-presentation can be explicit or implicit (Pfister 1988: 184; see also Walker 2012 for an alternative reformulation of the model). An example of an explicit authorial trigger at discourse level 1 would be a stage direction offering an unambiguous statement about character. An example of an implicit trigger would be a character's name.

In order to demonstrate the combined effects of the wide variety of textual characterisation cues, in the next section I analyse an extract from Dennis Potter's TV drama *Pennies from Heaven*.

A cognitive stylistic analysis of characterisation in Dennis Potter's *Pennies from Heaven*

The following extract is from the opening scene of *Pennies from Heaven*, a TV drama originally broadcast in 1978 (turns are numbered for ease of reference). If you are unfamiliar with the drama, while reading the extract, think about what characterisation triggers it contains. What information can you infer about the characters? How old are they? What do they look like? What do they sound like?

> Int. A darkened bedroom in one of the villas. Night/Dawn. A double bed, where a husband and wife are asleep. Moving into close-up of the husband, who has suddenly, and rather startlingly popped open his eyes. He swivels his eyes and stares at the alarm clock.

> 1 Arthur   Some day if luck is kind. S-s-some day!
> *Immediately the alarm bell rings, urgent and noisy. Arthur looks at it sardonically, making no attempt to silence it. Then his hand suddenly plunges down on the clock, like a bird of prey, and chokes it into silence.*
>   Hey ho!

He turns to Joan, his wife.

        Joan...?

She does not move. But we sense that she is now awake.

        Joanie. Joanie, my pet? Are you awake? Eh? C'mon, sugar.

He puts his arm around her and pulls her into himself.

2	Joan	Mmmwa...wha...?
3	Arthur	C'mon Joanie – sugar – wake up, my pigeon...

She tries to wriggle from his grasp, pushing his hands from her breasts.

4	Joan	No – Arthur – don't –
5	Arthur	Oh, now – Joan – Joanie –
6	Joan	(*Mock sleepy*) Too early – I'm not awake – there isn't time –
7	Arthur	There's always time for this. (*She has to push his hands away again.*) (*Becoming too urgent.*) Come on, Joan. Be a sport. Come on, old girl! Joan!
8	Joan	Arthur! Stop it! No, Arthur – you'll be – *Arthur*, no, I said. No.
9	Arthur	Why not? Why?

Abruptly, she pulls the cord dangling above them. The light comes on, very bright.

10	Joan	You said you wanted to get away early. That's what you said.
11	Arthur	You never want to nowadays, do you? Never.
12	Joan	Never?
13	Arthur	Not what I call want to. Not really *want* to, I mean.
14	Joan	That's a very silly thing to say, Arthur dear. And I'm not even properly awake yet.
15	Arthur	But it's best like that – nicer – when you're a bit sleepy and – Joan? Joanie – eh? Please?

Fractional pause.

16	Joan	Make us a nice cup of tea, will you, lovey?
17	Arthur	Bloody tea!
18	Joan	Language!

He stares at her, then swallows.

19	Arthur	Look here, Joan. I'm going to be away from home for the next four days and nights, and –
20	Joan	There's no need to swear, though.
21	Arthur	No, but you ain't being very –
22	Joan	(*Cutting in*) There isn't. Is there, Arthur?
23	Arthur	I was – whatdysay? – exasperated – and it wasn't much of a cuss.
24	Joan	(*Again, cutting in*) Well, I don't think it's very nice. Not in the house.
25	Arthur	Not anywhere!
26	Joan	But specially not in your own home, Arthur.
27	Arthur	Cup of char is it then, old gel?

        (*D. Potter 1996: 1–3*)

One of the long-standing methodological issues in the stylistic analysis of drama is whether the text or a performance of the text should be the object of study. Traditionally, the dominant view in stylistics has been that, since text is more stable than performance, stylistic analyses should be of the play script (Short 1996). Although there are situations where replicable analyses of performances are possible (see, for example, McIntyre 2008), generally speaking, starting with the dramatic text is a sensible methodological position to take, not least because this is a necessary starting point for actors and directors (especially in situations where the play has never been performed before). The accessibility of cognitive stylistic methods of analysis makes them particularly suitable for this task. Indeed, one of the merits of cognitive stylistics is the democratising principle on which it is founded; that is, cognitive stylistics aims to account for how real readers respond to texts. Cognitive stylistic analyses therefore aim to be transparent explanations of the reading process and the interpretative effects arising from this, rather than rarefied literary-critical 'readings'. In this respect, the cognitive model of characterisation outlined above is not only a logically sound account of how readers construct mental models of characters as they read. In addition, it offers a practical method for the analysis of character that is grounded in the structure of the text while taking appropriate account of the existing world knowledge of the reader. In the case of the *Pennies from Heaven* example, there are numerous textual triggers which allow us to infer information about context and character.

To begin with, we might consider two distinct authorial cues at discourse level 1. First, the stage directions indicate explicitly that Arthur and Joan are married ('a husband and wife are asleep'). Secondly, the names *Arthur* and *Joan* are rather old-fashioned and this suggests that the drama is a period piece. Of course, an alternative explanation is that the play is contemporary and the characters are simply elderly. In practice, though, anyone reading the script in its entirety or seeing the drama on TV is likely to have read a synopsis of the drama and will know that it is set in the 1930s. This small amount of information is enough to trigger our schematic knowledge of married couples. This, combined with the subject matter of the extract (Arthur wanting to have sex and Joan refusing), is enough to generate a range of stereotypical assumptions. For example, Arthur and Joan's marriage appears to be rather staid so they are unlikely to be newlyweds. These inferences can lead to other, indirect assumptions. When I give this extract to my students, they routinely say that they expect Arthur to be wearing striped pyjamas. This information is purely schematic, since there is nothing in the text to indicate this. Nonetheless, watch the drama (*Pennies from Heaven* 2004) and it transpires that this is indeed the case.

The initial level 1 authorial cues pertaining to the names of the two characters and their marital status are enough to invoke a basic schema for a married couple. This is then tuned as a result of the many level 2 implicit textual triggers of characterisation in the dialogue. Some of these appear to indicate permanent characteristics (for example the dialect features of Arthur's speech in turns 21 and 27; though it may also be argued that the sparse use of dialect spellings indicates Arthur momentarily playing up to a stereotype) while others appear to mark transitory characteristics (for example, the anger that can be inferred from the taboo language and exclamation mark in turn 17).

The first turn of the scene is likely to strike readers as odd. Arthur's first words on waking up are 'Some day if luck is kind'. Turn 1 is foregrounded by virtue of the fact that this is an extremely unusual statement to make on waking from a night's sleep. Grammatically, the statement is incomplete, lacking a main clause to follow the conditional subordinate clause. The significance of this line can be determined once we have access to some contextual knowledge. This is the first episode of *Pennies from Heaven*, the title of which is 'Down Sunnyside Lane'. This was also the name of a popular song from 1931, performed by Jack Payne and His BBC Orchestra, which features as the title music to the episode. Arthur's utterance is a line from the lyrics: 'Some day if luck is kind, I'll leave my cares behind.' There is an existential presupposition in the main clause that the speaker does indeed have cares (indicated by the object noun phrase; see Simpson 1993). That this is Arthur's first utterance would suggest that he does too, and that these must be at the forefront of his mind if the song is in his head as he awakes (note that we take all characterisation information as salient in drama, whereas in real life we might be inclined to dismiss some triggers as non-salient). Because only the conditional clause is uttered, the sentence is foregrounded. And if we are aware of what the main clause is, then its absence is likely to lead us to infer, via Grice's (1975) maxim of relation, that Arthur is not confident that luck will be kind to him.

Arthur then turns his attention to Joan, trying to persuade her to have sex. The variety of terms that he uses to address her (*Joan, Joanie, sugar, my pet, my pigeon, old girl*) characterise him as affectionate, though the repeated use of terms of endearment may also be seen to convey desperation and insistence. Culpeper (2001: 190) uses Taavitsainen's (1999) term *surge features* to describe the linguistic elements used for emotional outbursts. That these are transitory characteristics displayed for a particular purpose is suggested by the fact that in turn 17 Arthur's manner changes abruptly.

Aspects of Joan's character are revealed in the way she responds to Arthur's pestering. Her use of repeated imperatives to stop Arthur's attempts to initiate sex characterise her as both firm and determined. (These characteristics can also be seen in her repeated admonishing of Arthur for swearing; see turns 18, 20, 22, 24 and 26). After Arthur has relented, she then attempts to offer some explanation for her lack of interest ('You said you wanted to get away early'), perhaps in an effort to defease any alternative implicatures that Arthur might infer from her refusal (see P. Brown and Levinson's 1987 notion of off-record politeness strategies). This suggests both a degree of consideration and an element of self-protection. Readers are likely to infer that Joan feels uncomfortable with the situation and, perhaps, with her own actions.

Joan's verbal behaviour also works to characterise Arthur as somewhat downtrodden. In turn 14 she dismisses his halting efforts to initiate a discussion about what he perceives as her lack of interest in sex. She does this directly: 'That's a very silly thing to say, Arthur dear.' This casual dismissal of a serious subject is reminiscent of how parents might dismiss the naive concerns of a child, which indirectly conveys extra information about the power relations between Arthur and Joan.

In turn 15 Arthur attempts to steer the topic of conversation back to sex. However, Joan's pause and abrupt change of topic in turn 16 signals her unwillingness to discuss this. From this we might infer that she is ill at ease with the topic, and potentially also embarrassed by it. Arthur's outburst in turn 17 is another surge feature, which may be interpreted as conveying anger and/or frustration. He attempts again to return to the topic in turn 19 but is rebuked by Joan for swearing. Arthur then appears to accept the rebuke and give up on his earlier inclinations by abruptly changing the topic: 'Cup of char is it then, old gel?' (27). The term of endearment indicates social closeness and the non-standard spelling of *girl* as 'gel' is suggestive of accent and dialect. The fact that Arthur's attempts at a serious conversation about his and Joan's marriage is eventually abandoned by both of them is perhaps indicative of underlying problems which, given the nature of drama, the reader/viewer is likely to expect to have some significance later on. The reader's/viewer's initial schema for a married couple, then, is tuned as a result of the textual triggers encountered in the dialogue, demonstrating how the characterisation of Arthur and Joan is achieved through a combination of top-down and bottom-up processing.

The initial aspects of characterisation described above do indeed feed into the plot of *Pennies from Heaven*. Arthur is a sheet-music salesman in 1930s England with dreams of exchanging his humdrum existence for the kind of excitement described in the lyrics of the popular songs that he sells. His dissatisfaction with his marriage to Joan leads him to have an affair with a schoolteacher, Eileen. This causes him to be in the wrong place at the wrong time and he finds himself convicted of the murder of a young girl and sentenced to hang. The actions that cause him to end up in this situation are all the result of the frustration that he feels with his life, emotions that are conveyed from the very beginning of the very first scene of the drama.

Effects of hearing-impaired subtitling on characterisation

It should be clear from the analysis above that even in the fairly short extract from *Pennies from Heaven* there is a substantial number of textual triggers of characterisation. What the above analysis does not take into account, though, is how characterisation is likely to be different for viewers watching the drama as opposed to readers interpreting the play script itself. If we are dealing solely with the play script we may well find ourselves rereading particular lines in the light of information contained elsewhere in the text. Our impressions of character may thus be determined through post hoc rationalisation rather than online processing. If we are watching a TV drama, however, and we choose not to pause and rewind at particular points, our bottom-up impressions of character will be determined solely on the basis of those textual triggers we are able to pick up on; in other words, we may well miss some of the cues for characterisation contained in the text. Furthermore, if the cues that we fail to notice would have invoked particular schematic knowledge, missing a textual trigger can also affect our top-down processing. This becomes a particular problem for viewers relying on subtitles. In the case of foreign language subtitling, a whole range of additional non-linguistic variables can cause problems of comprehension when it comes to interpreting character (see Luyken 1991 for a comprehensive survey of subtitling practice). However, the general effect of subtitling on characterisation can be seen if we examine subtitles for hearing-impaired viewers (i.e. subtitles that are in the same language as the original dialogue). Below are the hearing-impaired subtitles for the extract from *Pennies from Heaven* discussed in the previous section. Underlining indicates additions to the original dialogue while square brackets indicate deletions:

1	Arthur	Some day.<u>...</u> I[i]f luck is kind[.].<u>...</u> S[-s-s]ome day[!]. Hey- ho.[!] Joan[...]? Joanie[.]? Joanie, my pet? Are you awake? Eh?
2	Joan	Mmm[wa]...<u>W</u>[w]hat[...]?
3	Arthur	C'mon Joanie. Wake up. [That's my girl.]
4	Joan	No, [-] Arthur. [- d]<u>D</u>on't. [-]
5	Arthur	Oh, [now – Joan –] Joanie.<u> Come on.</u> [-]
6	Joan	It's t[T]oo early. [-] I'm not awake <u>yet</u>. [-] [t]<u>T</u>here isn't time. [-]
7	Arthur	There's always time for this.
8	Joan	<u>Arthur, don't.</u>
9	Arthur	Come on, Joan. Be a sport. Please [Joan, please].
10	Joan	Arthur, no.
11	Arthur	Please!
12	Joan	I said no!
13	Arthur	Why not? Why?
14	Joan	You wanted to get away early. That's what you said.
15	Arthur	You never want to nowadays, do you? Never.
16	Joan	Never?
17	Arthur	Well, not what I call want to. Not really want to, I mean.

18	Joan	That's a [very] silly thing to say. [, Arthur dear.] I'm not [even] properly awake yet.
19	Arthur	[Yeah but] [i]It's best like that, when you're sleepy. [It's nicer. Come on.]
20	Joan	Make us a nice cup of tea, will you, lovey?
21	Arthur	Bloody tea!
22	Joan	Language!
23	Arthur	[Now] L[l]ook here.[, Joan.] I'[m]ll [going to] be away from home for the next four days and nights... [, and –]
24	Joan	There's no need to swear, though[, is there?].
25	Arthur	[No,] B[b]ut you ain't being [very –]
26	Joan	[Well] [T]there isn't, is there[, Arthur]?
27	Arthur	[No, well] I was – what d'you say? – I was exasperated. [Anyway,] [i]It wasn't much of a cuss.
28	Joan	[Well, I don't think] [i]It's not very nice. Not in the house.
29	Arthur	Not anywhere!
30	Joan	But especially not in your own home, Arthur.
31	Arthur	Cup of char [is it] then, old [gel] girl?

What is apparent from the above is that the subtitles do not include all of the textual triggers of characterisation that are in the original script. In some cases this is likely to have a significant impact on how those viewers relying on the subtitles interpret the characters. For example, in the original script (D. Potter 1996) turn 3 is: 'C'mon Joanie – sugar – wake up, my pigeon. . .'. In performance, this line was changed to: 'C'mon Joanie. Wake up. That's my girl.' The difference between the original script and the performance is that, in the latter, two vocatives which are terms of endearment are omitted ('sugar' and 'my pigeon'). Although the utterance 'That's my girl' is added, the omission of the vocatives reduces the extent to which this line characterises Arthur as both affectionate and insistent. The subtitle for turn 3 is even shorter: 'C'mon Joanie. Wake up.' The lack of any terms of endearment (save for the diminutive form of *Joan*) removes the mitigation (cf. P. Brown and Levinson 1987) of the two imperatives ('C'mon' and 'Wake up'). The effect on characterisation is that we are likely to consider Arthur to be much blunter and more forthright than if we were relying on the performed dialogue.

Similarly, in turn 18 the dialogue as it is performed is: 'That's a very silly thing to say, Arthur dear. I'm not even properly awake yet.' In the subtitles, however, this is reduced to: 'That's a silly thing to say. I'm not properly awake yet.' The omission of 'Arthur dear' from the first utterance makes the proposition much more impersonal and, potentially, more damaging to Arthur in relational terms (see Bousfield 2008 and Culpeper 2011 for revisions to P. Brown and Levinson's 1987 taxonomy of politeness). This characterises Joan as much less concerned with Arthur's feelings than she is in the original dialogue.

Elsewhere there are numerous textual characterisation triggers missing. For instance, Arthur's dialectal pronunciation of *girl* in turn 27 is not accounted for in the accompanying subtitle, nor are the discourse markers 'Now' (turn 23) and 'Well' (26, 27, 28), or the conventional implicature of 'Anyway' (27). In short, the viewing experience of anyone relying on the hearing-impaired subtitles is likely to be impoverished when compared against that of viewers who do not need the subtitles. Of course, there are technical constraints on subtitling that restrict the number of graphological characters which may be displayed on a line (see Luyken 1991), but in many cases in the above extract there is no unassailable reason for having omitted elements. One way of improving subtitling, then, would be to provide clear guidelines to professional subtitlers on the effects of particular linguistic choices on such macro-level issues as characterisation. Indeed, Luyken (1991: 65) is clear that research on the linguistic and stylistic implications of subtitling is much needed.

Conclusion

My aim in this chapter has been to indicate the importance of characterisation in stylistic analysis and to demonstrate the application of one of the most influential models of characterisation available to stylisticians. I have also pointed towards the practical value of characterisation analysis as a first step towards improving hearing-impaired subtitling for TV drama. There remain, of course, issues with current approaches to characterisation that need to be addressed. The extent to which Culpeper's (2001) checklist of textual characterisation triggers is falsifiable is an issue that would benefit from further research, since this impacts on the replicability of analyses that utilise the model. There are also, as I have suggested, refinements which could be made to the model. For instance, authorial cues can feasibly be divided into explicit and implicit triggers, as Culpeper (2001) does with self- and other-presentational triggers. Furthermore, all characterisation cues are effectively authorial and the objectivity of the model can be improved if we integrate this into the description of the different categories of triggers. Despite these issues, the model described in this chapter offers genuine insights into (i) how real readers are likely to respond to characters as they read and watch fiction, and (ii) the stylistic effects that readers are likely to perceive as a result.

12

Voice

Christiana Gregoriou

Introduction

As an art form, literature transports its readers to real or imaginary spaces, invites them to take part in ordinary or extraordinary adventures and, as Palmer (2004: 10) puts it, pleasurably shows readers what 'a variety of fictional people are thinking'. It is through access to fictional others' thoughts that literature invites readers to adopt different ways of seeing the world. This chapter focuses on this latter literary quality, taking 'Voice' to refer to language as a projection of individuals' mental functioning rather than their actual voice, in the sense of their verbal interaction/dialogue with others (for the latter, see Short's Chapter 23 in this very collection). Like in previous work of mine (see for instance, Gregoriou 2007, 2011b), I employ Roger Fowler's (1977: 76) linguistic concept of *mind style*, originally coined to refer to 'cumulatively consistent structural options, agreeing in cutting the presented world to one pattern or another', giving rise to 'an impression of a world-view'. Roger Fowler (1977: 103) then takes 'mind style' to refer to 'any distinctive linguistic representation of an individual mental self', the phenomenon in which the language of a text projects a characteristic world view, a particular way of perceiving and making sense of the world:

> A mind style may analyse a character's mental life more or less radically;
> may be concerned with relatively superficial or relatively fundamental
> aspects of the mind; may seek to dramatize the order and structure of
> conscious thoughts, or just present the topics on which a character reflects,
> or displays preoccupations, prejudices, perspectives and values which
> strongly bias a character's world-view but of which s/he may be unaware.
>
> *(R. Fowler 1977: 103)*

With Fowler's mind style premise in mind, I take a close look at the linguistic make-up of three novels which portray such more or less radical fictional 'minds', meaning minds assumed to be characteristic, unique, and even unusual and unorthodox compared to the readers' own, acknowledging of course that novels might well have a number of readerships, and therefore multiple readings. In accordance with other such mind style research (see, for instance, Bockting 1994; Leech and Short 2007; Semino 2007; Semino and Swindlehurst 1996), aspects of note here cover all linguistic areas: phonology, lexis, semantics, grammar and pragmatics. Specific features which can be used to project unique views of the world include, but are not limited to, over- and under-lexicalisation (suggestive of underlying understandings surrounding referents and their related senses), particular syntactic transitivity choices (to do with agency and responsibility), metaphors and other figurative language choices (suggestive of underlying thought structures and ideologies), and choices of particular types of speech and thought presentation (see, for instance, framework in Leech and Short 1981). It is not always easy to distinguish between narratorial and character voice/thought; as Palmer (2004, 2007) argues, the boundary between pure narrative and thought presentation is fuzzy, there is a thought–action continuum (statements found in novels often refer to action suggestive of a state of consciousness), while cognitions and emotions are too inextricably linked. Along the same lines, Bronwen Thomas (2012: 7) argues that:

> the notion that thoughts and emotions can be communicated either to others or to oneself unproblematically and coherently is often put to the test in novels that trade for the purposes of humor or suspense on the verbal inadequacies of characters or which powerfully hint at the characters' alienation from the social settings in which they find themselves.

It is such suspense-driven novels projecting the view of characters finding themselves estranged that I focus on here. I adopt the premise that textual means enable readers to take particular implied reader positionings when engaging in literary reading. Even more so, novel-reading is mind-reading (Palmer 2007: 83), meaning that readers can only understand literary texts by engaging in a process of following, and therefore understanding, the workings of their characters' minds. Since ideological viewpoint refers specifically to the attitudes, beliefs, values and judgements shared by people with similar social, cultural and political backgrounds (Semino and Swindlehurst 1996: 145), 'ideology' is also a term entangled with my definition of mind style. Nevertheless, having taken mindset-related linguistic choices to project *characteristic* world views, language here enables readers to mind-read the world via the mental functioning of the sorts of focalised characters that are rather unusual in the context of fiction. In doing so, language can prove instrumental in enabling readers to think about, even question, their own positions and grounding in the world they actually inhabit. I next analyse the mind styles of three contemporary fictional and literary character-focalisers: a child in *The Boy in the Striped Pajamas* (Boyne 2006a, the title spelling of 'pajamas' being American), an obsessive self-harmer in *Sharp Objects* (Flynn 2006), and an angel character-narrator situated in heaven in *The Lovely Bones* (Sebold 2002). All three projections received high commercial acclaim, the related books reaching various best-sellers' lists, and their authors gaining award nominations. Among others, *The Boy in the Striped Pajamas* was a New York Bestseller, *Sharp Objects* a twice CWA (Crime Writers Association) Dagger winner, and *The Lovely Bones* a number one Bestseller. *The Lovely Bones* and *The Boy in the Striped Pajamas* in particular were also adapted into major films (dir. Jackson 2009 and dir. M. Herman 2008 respectively), because of or despite these two books also generating some controversy.

A boy's mind style

Boyne's (2006a) *The Boy in the Striped Pajamas* is a historical fictional novel projecting the perspective of 9-year-old Bruno, the privileged son of a German official posted as a commandant at a house nearing the Auschwitz Nazi concentration camp. In an interview with the author published in the book's final pages, Boyne himself asserts he does not think of this as either a children's book or an adults' book (Boyne 2006b: 5). In fact, he adds he is not entirely sure he understands the difference: 'You know who these distinctions are for? They're for bookshops', he explains (Boyne 2006b: 6). Much like with other young adult fiction, *Pajamas* is focalised through a young character-narrator, whose perspective we have access to through a limited internal narrative mode, meaning a mode giving us access to the character's perceptual (or psychological), spatio-temporal and ideological standpoint on the world (for more on viewpoint, see Short 1996; Simpson 1993). Unlike some such fiction though, the narrative is here communicated through the third- rather than first-person mode. As the author himself explains in the same interview, 'I wanted to view it in the third person. To do it from Bruno's point of view, but to do it from a slight distance as well, as an observer' (Boyne 2006b: 4). Perhaps most importantly, the book's own back cover asserts that, despite its framing as 'a fable', 'this isn't a book for nine-year-olds', the reader here advised that 'sooner or later you will arrive with Bruno at a fence. Fences like this exist all over the world. We hope you never have to encounter one.' 'Fence' acquires a certainly figurative meaning here, standing for racial problems, genocides even, parting people the world wide. Boyne himself hopes that, by avoiding to specifically name 'Auschwitz' throughout, his story acquires generic dimensions; 'By removing that word, even though we are clearly there, and all the signs are there . . . by not specifically basing it there, it broadened it' (Boyne 2006b: 9).

When readers first encounter young Bruno, they meet a boy who is alert, bright and inquisitive, the over-coordination of clauses helping construct his observing, yet also childlike world view: 'The servants still came *and* washed things *and* swept things *and* cooked things *and* cleaned things *and* served things *and* took things away *and* kept their mouths shut unless they were spoken to' (Boyne 2006a: 96, my italics). The grammatical parallel-ism alongside lexical repetition of unnamed 'things' additionally suggests the monotony he experiences living in his new house. He also finds himself objecting to others' hostility, describing Nazi officials as 'plain nasty' (2006a: 77) for instance, while being, to a certain extent, unafraid to express his rather liberal ideology when confronted with fascist ideology:

> 'What do you think of all this, Maria?' he asked after a long silence because he had always liked Maria and felt as if she was one of the family, even though Father said she was just a maid and overpaid at that.
>
> *(Boyne 2006a: 17)*

> 'Who are all those people outside?' [Bruno] said finally. [. . .]
>   'Ah, those people,' said Father, nodding his head and smiling slightly. 'Those people. . . well, they're not people at all, Bruno.'
>   Bruno frowned. 'They're not?' he asked, unsure what Father meant by that.
>   'Well, at least not as we understand the term,' Father continued. 'But you shouldn't be worrying about them right now. They're nothing to do with you. You have nothing whatsoever in common with them [. . .]'
>   'Yes, Father,' said Bruno, unsatisfied by the response.
>
> *(Boyne 2006a: 52–3)*

Pragmatically speaking, Bruno of course does not define either his own liberal or his father's fascist ideology as such; he appears to lack the knowl-edge structures, otherwise known as 'schemata' (for an introduction to 'schema theory', see chapter 5.2 in Gregoriou 2009), with which to concep-tualise them as such. His Nazi upbringing does, however, creep in at times, even when Bruno appears to be admittedly uneasy with it:

> 'Well, because Germany is the greatest of all countries,' Bruno replied, remembering something he had overheard Father discussing with Grandfather on any number of occasions. 'We're superior.'
>   . . . Bruno felt a strong desire to change the subject because even as he had said the words, they didn't sound quite right to him . . . *(Boyne 2006a: 112)*

Bruno is also importantly too naive and innocent to understand what the camps actually entail, his parents deliberately protecting him from that knowledge.

Being lonely and devoid of friends his own age in his new surroundings, Bruno regularly observes concentration camp inhabitants and interacts with some. He even secretly closely befriends prisoner Shmuel, an exactly same-aged Polish boy living on the other side of the wire fence, the boy whom the book's title is in reference to. Bruno remains oblivious to the reality of the camp's use, and even wants to be inside it so he can make friends, until he meets his own tragic fate at the novel's end, when he disguises himself as a camp inhabitant and crawls into the camp so as to, ironically, help Shmuel find his 'missing' father. Much like Shmuel's dad (the readers will of course assume), the boys are murdered in a gas chamber, ironically unafraid in their naivety, and holding hands. As Osherson (2009: 256) notes, the author renders the novel a self-proclaimed fable, 'its ironic closing sentences [pointing] more dully to the author's intentions': 'Of course all this happened a long time ago and nothing like that could ever happen again … Not in this day and age' (2006a: 216). The story therefore carries a moral message for its readers. As Curry (2010) puts it, the text calls for multiracial acceptance; like its apolitical protagonist, the text invites readers to also penetrate walls, barriers and borders, increasing social awareness, and giving those marginalised among us an actual visibility and 'voice'. Having said that, others, such as Gilbert (2010: 355), instead argue that 'the blunt didacticism of Boyne's text might close down possibilities for the child reader's imaginative engagement with the ungraspable nature of the Holocaust'; Gilbert therefore questions whether 'such works do necessarily perform a progressive educative role'. Similarly, Eaglestone (2007: 53, cited in Gilbert 2010: 356) rather provocatively asserts that 'it is as risky to turn the Holocaust into a fable as it is to deny it'.

Devices in use in the novel imply Bruno's narrative unreliability, and innocent ignorance of his surrounding horrific circumstances. Naming strategies are particularly revealing. Bruno refers to his own parents with the formalised 'Father' (2006a: 17) and 'Mother' (2006a: 3), suggesting he has a perhaps distancing respect for them, while he contrastingly refers to his teasing sister Gretel as 'a Hopeless Case' (2006a: 19) or uses others' reference for her as 'Trouble From Day One' (2006a: 21), her unpleasant friends being likewise reduced to 'monsters' (2006a: 22). Limited Bruno also mistakes the camp prisoners' stripy prison outfits for comfy striped pyjamas: 'In fact [Bruno] did like stripes and he felt increasingly fed up that he had to wear trousers and shirts and ties and shoes that were too tight for him when Shmuel and his friends got to wear striped pajamas all day long' (2006a: 151–2). The under-lexicalisation of the prisoner uniform referent highlights an ironic similarity with respect to the two outfits, but also suggests a world view consisting of relaxation and game-playing with friends, an image contrasting the very real institutionalised murderous violence taking place in the prison camp. The 'striped pajamas' reference of course also shows Bruno's lack of understanding as to camp inhabitants, mistaken for farmers at first, being in fact dehumanised, kept in captivity against their will, until the time comes for them to be gassed to death. In linguistic deterministic terms (see Sapir 1921, 1929; Whorf 1956) and, as Fowler (1981: 152) puts it, under-lexicalisation spells out the crucial assumption that lacking a referent from one's lexicon (in this case 'Nazi prisoner') suggests that the individual lacks the relevant concept. Importantly, the boy wonders why these 'striped pajama people' were never invited to dinner, and forms questions suggestive of important underlying realisations he himself even is not completely aware of: 'And who decided which people wore the striped pajamas and which people wore the uniforms?' he asks (2006a: 100).

As many, such as Gilbert (2010), have noted, Bruno also revealingly phonetically mispronounces 'Auschwitz' into 'Out-With' (2006a: 25) (note that /aʊʃvɪts/ and /aʊt wɪð/ are phonetically similar), the relexicalisation interestingly alluding to the otherness of those placed 'outside' of his own surroundings yet 'within' confinement, and therefore inside the camps. The word acquires numerous meanings for readers of the text but not the character-narrator himself, or indeed his sister:

> 'Out-With?' asked Bruno. 'What's an Out-With?' . . .
> 'That's the name of the house,' explained Gretel. 'Out-With' . . .
> 'But what does it mean?' he asked in exasperation. 'Out with what?'
> 'Out with the people who lived here before us I expect', said Gretel.
>
> *(Boyne 2006a: 24–5)*

In contrast to Bruno's line of thinking, Gretel's explanation of the mis-pronounced reference is instead suggestive of an ideology approximating the fascist one, as certain races would indeed be literally 'done out/away with' in that very locale.

Bruno similarly phonetically mispronounces 'the Führer', literally meaning 'the leader', into 'the Fury' (2006a: 5) (again note /fjʊrə/ and /fjʊrɪ/ being near-homophones), Bruno's impersonal wording suggesting the Nazi leader's anger and aggressive, irrational even, behaviour toward all others, particularly since Bruno has met Hitler in person. The reference being inclusive of a definite article highlights the man's uniqueness though, through mispronunciation, Bruno appears to lack awareness as to the implications of the adjectival referent sense the article is followed by. The boy also mistakes *Heil Hitler* as another way of simply saying 'Well, goodbye for now, have a pleasant afternoon' (2006a: 54), oblivious that this salute actually has the proposition of a fascist ideology. Bruno also performs the salute-accompanying arm action ignorant of its same con-notations: 'As they left they stood in a row together like toy soldiers and their arms shot out in the same way that Father had taught Bruno to salute, the palm stretched flat, moving from their chests up into the air in front of them in a sharp motion' (2006a: 43–4). Bruno's simile linking the soldiers to 'toy' ones implies his child's game-playing world view but also perhaps hints at a belief in behaviour that is questioning and distinctive as opposed to unthinking and automatic. In any case, while reading Bruno's mind, here and elsewhere, readers are indirectly invited to read aright the signs that Bruno misreads, engaging in frame repair (Emmott 1997: 225) throughout, even when Bruno fails or is simply unable to repair his own understanding. Along the same lines if not on an ideological level, when he is asked for a spare tyre to use as a swing, Lieutenant Kotler jokingly refers to a sergeant being 'attached to his spare tyre' (2006a: 73). Literal-minded Bruno is unable to process the metaphorical meaning of the bodily-weight-related expression: 'He doesn't understand you. He's only nine', his sister Gretel says (2006a: 74). Bruno overall has age-related limitations where pragmatic processing is concerned.

Numerous such meaningfully ironic instances occur throughout. When Polish camp prisoner Pavel nurses Bruno's lightly cut knee after the boy has fallen from the swing, his mother worryingly asks to take the credit for the wound's cleaning wanting to, unbeknown to Bruno, protect Pavel in the long run. Bruno misreads his mother's kindness for selfishness: this 'seemed terribly selfish to Bruno and a way for Mother to take credit for something she hadn't done' (2006a: 85). In possible world theory terms (see Ryan 1991a, 1991b, 1998), there appears to be a conflict here between Bruno's knowledge world and his mother's (and also the adult readers'). The conflict needs resolving, and the boy's innocent framing of the circumstances needs repairing, both of which generate tension. Finally, before the boys die, Bruno tells Shmuel 'You're my ... best friend for life' (2006a: 213), neither of the boys yet knowing how literal the expression is, their lives being about to end indeed.

When Bruno and Shmuel innocently discuss the commonality or otherwise of the boys' names, Bruno notes his name being unique on his side of the fence, to which Shmuel responds with: 'Then you're lucky' (2006a: 109). On the implied and pragmatic author–reader communicative level, a question of identity arises: Shmuel, as an imprisoned mirror-image of Bruno, lacks one. While discussing how they can play without a fence separating them, Shmuel tells Bruno 'You're on the wrong side of the fence' (2006a: 132), here 'wrong', like 'lucky' in the previous example, acquiring different interpretations for the readers from the basic ones the words have for the two boys; aspects of moral ethics and fate are brought to bear on the interpretative level of the implied author and mature reader. Such momentary switches to Shmuel's viewpoint show the Polish boy to be also oblivious to his own circumstances, though perhaps not to the extent that Bruno is, the latter not appreciating how bad living conditions are on the inside of the fence. When Bruno disguises himself as a prisoner, readers are told: 'It was almost (Shmuel thought) as if they were all exactly the same really' (2006a: 204), a realisation that rings true for readers yet on a deeper semantic level than it does for the characters. Shmuel also later adds 'I never see the people after they've gone on a march' (2006a: 211), readers repairing an understanding of prisoners walking to their death in a way the boy cannot appreciate.

Gilbert (2010: 364) also notes the linguistic structure of the book's individual chapter titles themselves, 'manipulating' readers where perspective is concerned, the 'Thinking Up the Final Adventure' (2006a: 193) chapter title ironically and, in Gilbert's view distastefully, echoing the Nazi 'Final Solution' for instance. Many of the chapter titles are themselves clause-long, and indicate a perspective that is distinctively Bruno's, such as the ideologically slanted 'How Mother Took Credit for Something That

She Hadn't Done' (2006a: 67) chapter title and the increasingly subordinated and visually perceptually slanted 'The Dot That Became a Speck That Became a Blob That Became a Figure That Became a Boy' (2006a: 104). Ultimately, the second to last chapter ends when the focalised character dies, as readers no longer have any of the two boys' internal consciousness to tell the story through. The story being given in the third person also allows for a further last chapter though, a chapter given in the external mode with glimpses and blends into Bruno's surviving family members' viewpoints. While those Bruno left behind come to manage their loss, the overall style is not dissimilar to that of preceding chapters. Despite Bruno's physical absence, his mind style survives; the lexicon and sentence structure remain mostly simple, the naming strategies appropriate to Bruno's mind style still remain, as does the plain yet deeply ironic, for readers, tone: 'Father stayed at Out-With for another year . . . and he ended up sitting on the ground in almost exactly the same position as Bruno had every afternoon for a year, although he didn't cross his legs beneath him' (2006a: 215–16).

A self-harmer's mind style

Flynn's (2006) *Sharp Objects* gives voice to the dark mind of the troubled self-harming journalist Camille who, while coping with her own psychological disorder, becomes involved in a multiple-victim murder case unravelling in the Midwestern town in which she grew up. Instructed by her editor, she returns to her home town to report on the case, only to find herself interested in solving it, and even working alongside the police in doing so. In the meantime, as suggested by the title itself, Camille tries to recover from her compulsive self-cutting of her skin, which left her with the scars of written words across her whole body, a cutting that relates to the distress and emotional pain she herself experienced after the death of her young sister Marian when Camille too was young. As signalled through the mind style, Camille's troubling relationship with her neurotic mother Adora and young half-sister Amma cause her 'cutting' tendencies to worsen, all while the horrific involvement the last two have with the numerous murder cases come to be revealed.

The first hint at Camille's self-cutting past comes in the reference to her not liking showers: 'I can't handle the spray, it gets my skin buzzing, like someone's turned on a switch' (Flynn 2006: 7) the character-narrator says, the (transitivity speaking – see Chapter 19 in this volume, by Simpson and Canning) material process of her inanimate skin 'buzzing' hinting at what later is to be explained: that she has scars and/or open wounds which, in interaction with the shower spray, cause her some sort of involuntary physical or psychological reaction in the form of a 'buzz'. For the reader as yet oblivious to her body being scarred, the shower buzzing reference would be taken to be non-episodic, meaning not immediately relevant, only to later be re-classified as episodic, meaning ultimately relevant to the unfolding murder story; her scars later prove indicative where her own family's involvement in numerous murders is concerned (see Emmott 1997 for more on the episodic/non-episodic information distinction). Later on in the novel, Camille comes to write, in blue ballpoint, victims' names, among other words, on areas of her body she ensures stay hidden, conscious or perhaps paranoid of others seeing not only those words penned, but also those knifed (the reader later realises) onto her bare skin: 'I pulled my sleeves down over my hands, balled the ends up in my palms' (2006: 58).

It is not until page 63 when the narrator explicitly mentions words being 'traced' on her skin ('I traced the word *yelp* on my right palm with a fingernail'). The reader here realises that Camille indeed has words physically knife-scratched and not just visually penned onto her body, the italics graphologically indicating the body wording as such. To show her losing more and more control of her cutting tendencies, Camille's skin also starts to take personified dimensions, involuntarily taking agency over the cutting process, as do her scars, which eventually get named as such:

> I paced a bit, tried to remember how to breathe right, how to calm my skin. But it blared at me. Sometimes my scars have a mind of their own. . . .
>
> I am a cutter, you see. Also a snipper, a slicer, a carver, a jabber. I am a very special case. I have a purpose. My skin, you see, screams. It's covered with words – *cook*, *cupcake*, *kitty*, *curls* – as if a knife-wielding first-grader learned to write on my flesh. . . . The one thing I know for sure is that at the time, it was crucial to see these letters on me, and not just see them, but feel them. Burning on my left hip: *petticoat*.
>
> And near it, my first word, slashed on an anxious summer-day at age thirteen: *wicked* . . . I remember feeling that word, heavy and slightly sticky across my pubic bone. My mother's steak knife. Cutting like a child along red imaginary lines. Cleaning myself. Digging in deeper. Cleaning myself. Pouring bleach over the knife and sneaking through the kitchen to return it. *Wicked*. Relief. The rest of the day, I spent ministering to my wound. Dig into the curves of *W* with an alcohol-soaked Q-tip. Pet my cheek until the sting went away. Lotion. Bandage. Repeat.
>
> *(Flynn 2006: 75–6, author's italics)*

Camille's skin here becomes animated, and appears to be audible on some level ('blare', 'screams'), therefore taking over her perceptions on an aural as well as visual ('see these letters'), tangible ('I remember feeling that word . . . sticky across my pubic bone'), and also affecting level ('Burning on my left hip'). The sentences are simple ('I have a purpose'), or indeed minor: noun-phrased ('My mother's steak knife') and non-finite ('Cleaning myself'), hence acquire a 'stream-of-consciousness' effect, the acts appearing to be organised yet also continuous and habitual. As Camille here revisits her memory of first cutting herself, after being unable to cope with her sister's loss, she also draws on similes ('as if a knife-wielding first-grader', 'cutting like a child') to ironically compare her experience with that of a child first learning to write. The redness of lines alludes to visual blood lines, her self-injury writing growing compulsively enthusiastic. Camille, like a child, here takes pleasure in a newly learned task. It is a bit later that, having grown to be a writer, Camille explicitly links her compulsive worded self-harming with compulsive writing: 'By eleven, I was compulsively writing down everything anyone said to me in a tiny blue notepad, a mini reporter already' (2006: 77). Compulsion with words appears to haunt Camille, the cutter and the writer, everywhere. Besides, Camille does not just 'cut'; 'I cut words' she says (2006: 308).

To return to the body wording, it soon becomes personified, the words loudly and menacingly interacting with each other:

> Sometimes I can hear the words squabbling at each other across my body. Up on my shoulder, *panty* calling down to *destiny* on my right ankle. On the underside of a big toe, *sew* uttering muffled threats to *baby* just under my left breast. I can quiet them down by thinking of *vanish*, always hushed and regal, lording over the other words from the safety of the nape of my neck.   *(Flynn 2006: 78–9, author's italics)*

Taking on life of their own, the animated words attract attention to themselves somehow, Camille becoming all the more aware where exactly words are on her body and what personalities they have. The reader is here left wondering as to the meaningfulness or otherwise of what types of words she has on her body, and also what context she herself thinks of particular words in. Camille does in fact hint as to some patterns: 'Why these words? Thousands of hours of therapy yielded a few ideas from the good doctors. They are often feminine, in a Dick and Jane, pink vs puppy dog tails sort of way. Or they're flat out negative. Number of synonyms for anxious carved on my skin: eleven' (2006: 76); 'I had a dirty streak my senior year, which I later rectified. A few big cuts and *cunt* becomes *can't*, *cock* turns into *back*' (2006: 78). In terms of context, and though mostly random ('The word *tickle* flashed randomly from my right hip', 2006: 162), the words mentioned occasionally bear relevance to what actually happens in the unfolding narrative. The word '*favourite*' 'buzz[es]' (2006: 182) when Adora overly protects Amma for instance, while in '[a]ll I did was write *sick place sick place* over and over for twelve pages' (2006: 209), Camille's compulsive reaction to the place she was born clearly emerges through her pen-writing.

Elsewhere, words are described as involuntarily flashing, getting hot, blazing up and burning, suggesting a now stronger affective reaction on her part: 'A word suddenly flashed on my lower hip: *punish*. I could feel it getting hot' (2006: 120); 'I felt the word *wicked* blaze up by my pelvis' (2006: 143); '*Belittle* burned on my right hip' (2006: 153). The words are also animated in the sense of figuratively crawling from under her clothes and skin; 'I could see the word *lipstick* crawling out from my right shirtsleeve' (2006: 138); 'The words on my chest looked swollen in the fluorescent light, like worms tunnelled beneath my skin' (2006: 153). Overall, grammar plays a crucial role in the projection of Camille's mind style, as she finds herself tempted to return to 'cutting', a word that, as a verb, is here used mostly intransitively; 'I wasn't going to cut, just allow myself that sharp pressure. I could already feel the knifepoint gently pressing against the plump pads of my fingertips, that delicate tension right before the cut' (2006: 155). Here the knife acquires grammatical agency itself doing the cutting, while the nominalisation of 'pressure' and 'cut' too disguise Camille as the actor, her participation deemed almost irrelevant to the self-harming action. In other words, grammar itself suggests that Camille is overwhelmed with cutting urges; she simply cannot help herself.

As her cutting urges grow, Camille's skin and its wording become more audible in their agency: 'My skin began to quiet down' (2006: 157); '*Catfight* began thumping on my calf' (2006: 171); 'On my left calf *freak* sighed suddenly' (2006: 236). Words also become more sensationally affective in their agency: '*Sugar* flared on my thigh, *nasty* burned near my knee' (2006: 172); '*Nurse* began throbbing' (2006: 248); '*bundle* began tingling' (2006: 261), boulomaic modality more explicitly taking over: 'I wanted to cut. … I wanted to slice *barren* into my skin' (2006: 172). Words even metaphorically and eagerly are said to 'pop' (2006: 230), 'flicker' (2006: 269), 'beat' (2006: 284), unwillingly 'pant' (2006: 231), 'light up' (2006: 300) and '[catch] fire' (2006: 211), her skin 'blinking' (2006: 212). The book ends with Camille struggling to come to terms with the revelation of her mother and half-sister's murderous actions. She gives into the cutting urges: 'I slipped a knife up my sleeve … and dug it deep into the perfect circle on my back. Ground it back and forth until the skin was shredded in scribbly cuts' (2006: 320–1). The lack of a reference to an emotional reaction here suggests that Camille is only doing what feels best. It is here that she gets rescued by her editor, who takes her in, cares for, and parents her. Her skin, nevertheless, continues to 'pulse' at night (2006: 321).

An angel's mind style

A survivor herself of a brutal rape, Sebold sets her (2002) *The Lovely Bones* in the 1970s, where the raped and murdered teenager Susie Salmon watches her killer and surviving family members and friends as she looks down from heaven. Despite Susie not referring to herself as an 'angel' as such, the term appears appropriate here. Described as a postfeminist Gothic novel (Whitney 2010), *The Lovely Bones* is unlike other murder mystery novels of the 'whodunit' tradition; readers are made aware of 14-year-old Susie's murderer's identity from the novel's start, a killer who her father also finds himself suspicious of, despite being unable to prove his guilt. It was secret serial killer Mr Harvey, Susie's neighbour, and a man her own parents have interacted with on several occasions, who raped, murdered and dismembered Susie in an ice-cold cornfield. The deceased character Susie's reference to her killer with the respectful and formalised title alongside surname format 'Mr. Harvey' (2002: 6) is revealing in itself. Despite the horridness of his actions, and Susie's reference to 'his audacity' (2002: 8) on one occasion, Susie's overall tone suggests a certain level of composure on her part after the murder act. As Whitney (2010: 353) puts it, Sebold chooses elegy rather than anger for her heroine. Interspersed with extracts from Susie's life on earth, and therefore frame switching as well as mixing in Emmott's (1997) terminology, the novel appears to focus on the emotional turmoil Susie's death has had on those she left behind. Like Susie's own body, her family is also disintegrated; her mother leaves the family home for numerous years, her father suffers and is crippled by a heart attack, and her siblings find themselves emotionally distanced from their parents. It is not until the end of the novel that the heroine's family is brought back together in celebration of the joys that life can bring. Susie's murderer meets some justice also, when he dies by a blunt-force trauma caused by a falling icicle. An icicle previously appeared as Susie's murderous weapon of choice when game-playing: 'I always chose the icicle: the weapon melts away' she says (2002: 125). The second reference to the icicle finds it in an (inanimate) subject rather than an object position, and in a material event and not a material action: 'The icicle fell' (2002: 327). (Material events are, by definition, events that feature inanimate subjects, material actions featuring animate subjects instead.) The choice of structure suggests a lack of agency on angel Susie's part, the icicle's 'heavy coldness' (2002: 327) ironically linking back to the coldness of the weather in which Susie herself was kidnapped, and also Harvey's body's physical 'heaviness' and metaphorical 'coldness' in his rape and murder of the girl as well. Dismissingly, Susie directly then changes her focus to talk about 'someone special' (2002: 327), her sister Lindsey instead, suggesting that he is not special and is not worth dwelling on from then on, and certainly not worth ending her story on.

The narrative voice is in the first-person mode throughout. Uncharacteristically for such crime fiction, and also for first-person narratives, the voice is given from the perspective of a crime victim now deceased: 'My name was Salmon, like the fish; first name, Susie. I was fourteen when I was murdered' (2002: 5). An early reference to an identity now belonging to the past ('My name was Salmon') suggests that this is no ordinary character. It is not the voice of a physical Susie addressing readers, but one in fact separated and dislocated from her body, who speaks of herself in terms of 'body parts' (2002: 49), and retains access to earth even after she physically dies. References to 'my heaven' (2002: 6) suggest a universe where not only does heaven exist, but every deceased person has their own. As she later explains, 'in my heaven I can make a bonfire in the classrooms or run up and down the halls yelling as loud as I want. But it doesn't always look like that. It can look like Nova Scotia, or Tangiers, or Tibet. It looks like anything you've ever dreamed' (2002: 308). In Susie's heaven, 'intake counsellor[s]' (2002: 8), 'roommates' (2002: 17) and other 'residents' (2002: 35) help the departed manage their own death. Such first-person narration is, by definition, internal but, unlike other such character-narrators encountered in fiction, Susie is here reliable and *un*limited. Susie has omniscient, all-knowing abilities, not only having thoughts of her own after death ('After I was dead I thought about . . .', 2002: 6), and the capacity to actually relive memories, but also the ability to access the thoughts, feelings, perceptions and reactions of all others. As she puts it, she manages to '[break] through' (2002: 45) and 'fall inside' (2002: 81) others, their container-like bodies enterable by Susie's spirit. She has, for instance, access to her father's memories ('He remembered the day . . .', 2002: 47), her sister Lindsey's perceptions, knowledge and thoughts ('If the house was quiet or if she heard murmurs below her, she knew she would be undisturbed. This was when she could think of me', 2002: 59) and her mother's mind, at times even before Susie was born. The narrator even has access to her killer's ideological viewpoint, internally congratulating himself over, and celebrating, her death with a good meal, for example. She has access to his perceptions ('Mr. Harvey could see for miles', 2002: 54), his reactions ('He liked the Pennsylvania keystone [he kept as a trophy]', 2002: 54) and even senses ('and then Mr. Harvey, sensing my father had no intention of leaving, asked him if he wanted to help', 2002: 55). Like with her own mother, Susie also has access to a young, non-criminalised Mr Harvey, existing prior to Susie's birth. In these episodes he is meaningfully relexicalised into 'George Harvey' (2002: 97), the naming pointing to an as yet innocent first-named boy witnessing his mother's leaving, and hinting at later criminal behaviour towards women, possibly as a result of this event. In other words, we here get not only access to the victim but, through her, also access to the criminal mind style and his own indirect justification for his aggressive acts over the victim (for more on the criminal mind style, justification for murder, and also generic and social deviance in contemporary crime fiction, see Gregoriou 2007; for serial killer narrative discourses, including mother blaming, see Gregoriou 2011a).

When recalling her own rape, Susie resorts to similes: 'I felt like a sea in which he stood and pissed and shat. I felt the corners of my body were turning in on themselves and out, like in cat's cradle . . . How [my heart] skipped like a rabbit, and how his thudded, a hammer against cloth' (2002: 14). The experiences she draws on here hint at her innocent nature ('sea', 'cat's cradle', 'rabbit', 'cloth'), itself contrastingly attacked by violence ('pissed', 'shat', 'thudded', 'hammer'). When recalling the knife attack that followed, the knife is animated: 'He brought back a knife. Unsheathed, *it* smiled at me, curving up in a grin . . . The end came' (2002: 15, my italics). Here, the knife is personified, smiling and even menacingly grinning at the victim it is about to attack, somewhat distancing the murderer from the slashing act itself. The final sentence being a material event naturalises Susie's passing, as if inevitable and predestined rather than effected by her attacker. When Susie later watches her sister Lindsey having sex, she likens the experience to a concretised room: 'At fourteen my sister sailed away from me into a place I'd never been. In the walls of my sex there was horror and blood, in the walls of hers there were windows', metaphorically enabled to express the difference between the two girls' sexual experiences.

Susie 'hovers' (2002: 279), 'roves' where others 'rove' (2002: 232), and 'moves with' others (2002: 237). She also 'pushes' on 'the Inbetween' (2002: 180) when striving for communication with those she left behind. She even mentions being seen by family members on occasion, though it is unclear how conscious others are of seeing her. She ponders over not being able to grow, and enjoy sex when others can ('My mother had my body as it would never become', 2002: 197), but is ultimately enabled to enjoy sex with Ray, the boy she loves, through a girl she shares a strong connection with at earth, Ruth. Unaware of having fans in heaven, Ruth has an affinity with the deceased, can see them in ways others living cannot, and even has special access to the circumstances of their death. By allowing Susie access to her body, Ruth enables her to experience the one thing Susie had not, an experience that Ray too understands to be sharing with Susie and not Ruth.

Language proves instrumental for characters on a metalinguistic level as well. Deceased Susie now notes newly appreciating word meanings ('by then I knew the meaning of forever', 2002: 20; 'And they had never understood, as they did now, what the word *horror* meant', 2002: 21). Her mother struggles to come to terms with Susie's murder, and is in need of it being acknowledged, and named, as such: '"My daughter's murder," my mother said . . . "No one says it. No one in the neighbourhood talks about it. People call it the 'horrible tragedy' or some variation of that. I just want it to be spoken out loud by somebody"' (2002: 147–8). It is towards the end of the book that Susie gives another meaning to its title. Though *The Lovely Bones* could be taken to refer to Susie's actual body parts, it comes to acquire a meaning related to family connections:

> As I watched my family sip champagne [at the news of Lindsey's engagement], I thought about how their lives trailed backward and forward from my death and then, I saw, as Samuel took the daring step of kissing Lindsey in a room full of family, became borne aloft away from it.
>   These were the lovely bones that had grown around my absence: the connections – sometimes tenuous, sometimes made at great cost, but often magnificent – that happened after I was gone.   *(Sebold 2002: 319–20)*

'Lovely' does not collocate with 'bones' in everyday language. The loveliness of the 'bones' alludes here perhaps not just to Susie's remains and the 'loveliness' of her innocence, but also the eventualities of all our lives. It may even refer to the loveliness of our ability to find pleasure in pain.

13

Narrative

Jessica Mason

Introduction

Modern narratology is a highly eclectic landscape that can be characterised by a magpie-like utilisation of work in other disciplines, a concern with incorporating an authentic consideration of 'real' readers within narrative analysis and a far-reaching infiltration of the 'cognitive turn' in literary linguistics. This *postclassical model* of narrative analysis is not an abandonment of narratology's structuralist roots so much as it is the product of an explosion of the innovations and capabilities of research and a resultant evolution of traditional models to allow the field to reap the benefits of advancements in areas such as psychology, anthropology, gender studies and computer science. This takes place alongside an opening up of narratology to welcome in narrative studies in other mediums and modes, with a parallel development of approaches to accommodate this expansion.

This chapter considers how the evolutions of postclassical narratology, particularly in terms of cognitive models of reading, can contribute to an examination of Stephen Chbosky's novel *The Perks of Being a Wallflower* (1999). Framed within traditional models of intertextuality (Genette 1979, 1980; Kristeva 1981; Riffaterre 1990), this analysis draws in particular on schema theory (J. R. Anderson 1983; Bartlett 1932; G. Cook 1994; Rumelhart 1975; Schank 1982a, 1982b, 1984, 1986; Schank and Abelson 1977; van Dijk and Kintsch 1983) to show how the postclassical approach can capture, more acutely, the process of narrative interrelation in reading and assess how individual difference among readers can impact the role of intertextual reference in reading.

Narratology: from classical to postclassical

The structuralist paradigms which characterised early classical narratology placed heavy emphasis on the attempt to discover the universals of narrative experience. In some senses, it was an attempt to discover the homogenising features, the common laws and structures, which would enable us to incorporate readers into our understanding and analysis of texts by flattening them out into a collective entity which was definable and therefore manageable.

The problem with this approach is not the desire to incorporate a consideration of real readers into narrative analysis; it is the attempt to do this while clinging furiously to the idea of establishing universals. The result is an inevitably unrepresentative and inauthentic, often highly idealised, vision of 'readers'; in trying to pin down 'all readers', the result was often simply a dislocated version of the analyst themselves. This approach proves problematic.

Consider the example of intertextual references, the recognition and interpretation of which are highly nuanced and subjective. In trying to homogenise reader response in terms of how we find, understand and interpret intertextuality under the structuralist paradigm, many papers framed reading as a game of 'spot the reference'. Riffaterre, for example, casts a complete and holistic awareness of all texts to which a given narrative makes reference, the *intertext*, as a necessary component of an individual's journey to the 'correct interpretation' of a text. That is, 'an intertext is one or more texts which the reader *must know in order to understand* a work of literature in terms of its overall significance' (Riffaterre 1990: 56, my italics). Rather than trying to account for the range and degree of difference across readers regarding the recognition, or not, and interpretation of intertextual references, the classical narratological approach looked to reason away these variations, believing that the universal reading can be found if all criteria are met. At worst, this sometimes teetered dangerously close to suggesting that not only do all readers notice and consistently interpret the intended salience of intertextual references, no matter how subtle or obscure, but that anyone who fails this test of literary hide-and-seek is essentially ignorant. In his analysis of an André Breton poem, for example, Riffaterre respectively describes two references:

- 'Even the most absent-minded readers will find the thread leading to the solution' (1990: 65)
- 'The recovery of an intertext proceeds in two stages both so overdetermined that they are unlikely to elude for long any reader equipped with basic linguistic competence' (1990: 73).

These kinds of statements are indicative of how the composite aims of the earlier structuralist-based models in narratology became self-limiting. The only way to neutralise the variation across readers in order to meet the desire for universality of reading outputs is to introduce a measure of skill and competence. In essence, Riffaterre argues that, in order for Breton's poem to be read 'correctly', readers must identify the intertext as Breton intended otherwise they simply do not qualify as having read the poem properly. Any proper reading will, he argues, incorporate 'the intertextual drive'; readers' responses will be compulsory and interpretation will be universal: 'facts of reading suggest that, when it activates or mobilises the intertext, the text leaves little leeway to readers and controls closely their response' (Riffaterre 1990: 57). These initial ventures into giving proper credence to reader response inevitably led to a dissatisfaction with this treatment of 'the reader'. In this sense, *post*classical narratology is something of a misnomer; it is not so much a 'moving past' as a renovation, a reworking. This is why David Herman's (1999, 2002) definition of the postclassical seeks to incorporate, rather than reject, classical narratology as part of an evolution of the discipline.

Postclassical narratology 'prefers to consider the circumstances that make every act of reading different' (L. Herman and Vervaeck 2005: 450). The transition to postclassical narratology can perhaps best be characterised as a movement from trying to deal with the capricious 'reader' by flattening out their quirks and squeezing them into a one-size-fits-all to an acknowledgement and celebration of their difference. This shift presented narrative analysis with a new but equally difficult task: how to account for that difference.

Giving primacy to readers and all their messy, discordant behaviours, their infinitely variant backgrounds, readings and ideologies required an explosion of new approaches and methodologies as varied as the factors narratology was now tasked to explain. As a result, postclassical narratology is best described as an umbrella for a range of a diverse group of methods and approaches variously triangulating aspects of the individuality of 'the reader'. These approaches have been grouped in an assortment of ways (D. Herman 1999; Nünning 2003), but there is general consensus that the following constitute substantive strands which characterise the postclassical landscape of narrative analysis:

- *Thematic*: Many researchers group readings by ideology. Analyses adopt a 'feminist' reading, a 'postcolonial' reading, 'a queer theory' approach, to name but a few. This methodology deals with the reader subjectivity problem by tracing the readings possible via a specific ideological perspective. It uses a narrowing lens technique, generating narrative analyses which cohere with a particular viewpoint and making no claim to speak for all. This methodology selects out a certain strand of readers rather than trying to homogenise across groups. In being explicit about its biases, the thematic approach serves to both acknowledge and celebrate reading from a particular perspective in a particular context.
- *Interdisciplinarity*: Looking to other disciplines for answers which escape the remit and capabilities of our own characterises the interdisciplinary strand. Postclassical narratology casts a wide net in the quest to

make the earlier models better able to cope with the scope of factors and variables the field now seeks to account for, rather than brush over. The aim is rarely to replace many of the models and approaches that were pervasive in the classical, more structuralist, period but to use research from other disciplines to evolve the way we approach our own. David Herman terms this, 'covering blind spots' (2004: 397). Deviation and foregrounding, for example, now borrow extensively from attentional psychology (Gavins and Steen 2003; Stockwell 2002, 2009; Whiteley 2011a). Possible worlds theory, which is pervasive enough that many separate it into a category of its own, is in many senses an amalgam of narratology, philosophy and psychology. Cognitive poetics leans heavily on neuroscience, psychology, sociology and rhetoric.

- *The cognitive turn*: As becomes quickly apparent from the previous category, the nature of interdisciplinary borrowing has led to wide-spread interest in incorporating consideration of cognition processes, in what has been termed 'the cognitive turn' (D. Herman 1999; Stockwell 2002; Tsur 2008) in narrative analysis. This is perhaps unsurprising given that examining 'real readers' prompted the initial shift toward postclassical narratology in the first instance: the problem of dealing with the subjective ways in which humans think, experience and feel when they engage with narrative makes a cognitive turn the inevitable consequence. David Herman, who coined the term 'postclassical narratology' to group this new set of methodologies, championed the integration of the cognitive into existing models in particular: 'according to Herman, the key to the logic of stories and storytelling lies in the preference rules and processing strategies of cognitive (re)construction, simultaneously facilitating narrative comprehension and the creation of intelligent world models' (Herman, Jahn and Ryan 2005: 70). Fields such as cognitive poetics have historically borrowed substantively enough from the cognitive disciplines since the early 1990s to come to stand as disciplines in their own right. Cognitive poetics, as the name suggests, has become independently interdisciplinary, concerning itself as much with cognition as with literature and thus facilitating a decreased need to depend on the research of other disciplines. This is the evolutionary aim that typifies much of postclassical narrative analysis; to develop and nurture the models to a point of fully functional independence.

From intertextuality to narrative interrelation

The following analysis of Chbosky's *The Perks of Being a Wallflower* (1999) attempts to exemplify the postclassical approach via an examination of some of the novel's intertextual references. Using the more structuralist-based models of intertextuality (Genette 1979, 1982; Kristeva 1981; Riffaterre 1990) discussed above as a start-point, it exemplifies the benefits of the postclassical approach. The analysis typifies two strands of postclassical narratology, namely working interdisciplinarily, drawing on work adopted into linguistics from other disciplines in the postclassical era, notably schema theory from computer science, and incorporating a consideration of cognition. It will first highlight some of the weaknesses and 'blind spots' (D. Herman 2004: 47) in current approaches, in particular the limitations of having no mechanism by which to account for variation across different readers. It then adopts a postclassical approach to advance the capabilities of previous accounts of intertextuality prevalent in literary criticism and classical narratology (Genette 1979, 1982; Kristeva 1981; Riffaterre 1990). I propose parsing out intertextual references as they appear in narratives and narrative interrelation, the process by which readers make intertextual links, in order to more accurately account for intertextuality, its role in reading and the cognitive mechanisms by which it works.

The Perks of Being a Wallflower

The Perks of Being a Wallflower by Stephen Chbosky (1999) centres around Charlie, the protagonist and intradiegetic narrator, who reports his experiences of entering high school in the form of a series of letters sent to a character identified only as 'Dear Friend'. Charlie comes across as a fairly honest but naive narrator, with some form of unstated mental health issue. While reference is made to a significant episode Charlie has had in the past, and a number of reported incidents throughout the book, resulting in psychiatric interventions, his symptoms are never explicitly medicalised or labelled for the reader. Nonetheless, readers are privy to several 'tells'; reports of panic attacks, a sense of frequent social ineptitude and a manifest tendency to cry a lot in situations which wouldn't generally warrant such a response from a 15-year-old boy, which serve to illustrate his issues more effectively than any 'diagnosis'.

When Charlie enters high school he successfully befriends some older students, notably Sam and her gay stepbrother Patrick, who take him under their wing. Charlie also develops a strong relationship with his 'advanced english teacher', Bill, who gives him extra books to read throughout the course of the novel. Charlie frequently updates his 'Friend' on what he is reading and comments reflexively on what he thinks of the books Bill gives him, often hypothesising what Bill is trying to teach him by giving him these particular texts. Near the novel's finale, when Sam and Patrick graduate high school, Charlie divides up his copies of these books giving some to Sam and the others to Patrick:

Then, I gave Patrick and Sam their presents. I even wrapped them up special. I used the Sunday funny papers because they are in color. Patrick tore through his. Sam didn't rip any of the paper. She just plucked off the tape. And they looked at what was inside the box.

I gave Patrick *On the Road*, *Naked Lunch*, *The Stranger*, *This Side of Paradise*, *Peter Pan*, and *A Separate Peace*.

I gave Sam *To Kill a Mockingbird*, *The Catcher in the Rye*, *The Great Gatsby*, *Hamlet*, *Walden*, and *The Fountainhead*.

Under the books was a card that I wrote using the type-writer Sam bought me. The cards said that these were my copies of all my favorite books, and I wanted Sam and Patrick to have them because they were my two favorite people in the world.

When they both looked up from reading, they were quiet. Nobody smiled or cried or did anything. We were just open, looking at each other. They knew I meant the cards I wrote. And I knew it meant a lot to them.   *(Chbosky 1999: 208).*

So here we have, within the space of a few paragraphs, no fewer than twelve intertextual references. How do we begin to interpret this episode?

Problems with 'the intertext' approach

This extract highlights unequivocally the problems with trying to apply theories of intertextuality which were originally constructed as conceptual rather than practically applicable to real examples. It does not appear, either intuitively or contextually, that these intertextual references are entirely arbitrary and, more importantly, it is unlikely that many readers will interpret them as such. The problem comes with trying to parse out what Chbosky as author, or Charlie as character, is 'trying to say' about Sam and Patrick in assigning these particular texts, in this particular grouping, to each of these particular characters. Even if readers have read the twelve other novels cited here, the idea that there is a 'correct' way in which to interpret the intertext to reach the meaning Chbosky intended would require as fundamental criteria:

- consistent and homogeneous recollection of each text across readers.
- matching identification of salient features both with Chbosky and each other. That is, of each entire text, readers would need to universally know, recall and recognise which features have caused Chbosky to reference them in this context.
- consistent and homogeneous composition of a sense of the over-arching salient features of the texts as a group which reveal the 'purpose' of assigning these texts, in this group, to that character.

No small task. In fact, taking the 'intertext' model as an example, the sheer volume of material cited here makes Riffaterre's assertion that readers 'must know' all referenced works 'in order to understand a work of literature in terms of its overall significance' clearly nonsensical. This approach is not only not a viable way to comprehend the references; any product we wanted to assign the title of the universal output reading would have a threshold so high in terms of intertextual knowledge that we would know no more about how readers process this kind of episode than we did before we started.

Let us step back, then, and consider what we do need to know about reading in order to make sense of this scene.

The need for a holistic model of reading

When faced with an actual text, it quickly becomes clear that, if we want to look at intertextuality not as something that exists between texts but as a process enacted by readers, there is a need to move away from the conceptual to a more mechanistic pragmatic definition. I would therefore propose a parsing of the intertextual process into two discrete stages:

- The textual object that exists in a text which prompts a reader to make a link between that narrative and another: the *intertextual reference*.
- The process of interrelating one reading experience with another: the *narrative interrelation*.

Intertextual reference and narrative interrelation are linked processes but they are not mutually dependent. Whereas a narrative interrelation will always be preceded by some sort of intertextual link, an intertextual reference will not necessarily lead a reader to make a narrative interrelation. When readers interrelate narratives they are prompted to do so by intertextual references that are either text-driven or reader-driven. There are three discernible types: *explicit*, *unmarked* and *implicit*.

Explicit intertextual reference (EIR) is fairly self-explanatory and text-driven EIRs probably typify what most people have in mind when they think about intertextual reference. A text-driven EIR is an explicit link made by one text to another. Take, for example, this excerpt from Golding's *The Lord of the Flies*:

> Ralph went on.
> 'While we're waiting we can have a good time on this island.'
> He gesticulated widely.
> 'It's like in a book.'
> At once there was a clamour.
> '*Treasure Island* –'
> '*Swallows and Amazons* –'
> '*Coral Island* –'
> Ralph waved the conch.

'This is our island. It's a good island. Until the grown-ups come to fetch us we'll have fun.'   (*Golding 1958: 45*, italics added)

Readers are universally homogeneously exposed to text-driven EIRs. They are unchanging, concrete and enduring. Every person who has ever or will ever read *The Lord of the Flies* (assuming they read it cover-to-cover) will encounter these references and, whether it is to ignore, acknowledge and pass over, comprehend or consciously reflectively contemplate, every reader must do something with them.

Reader-driven EIRs task readers with the same decision, the only difference being that the explicit reference comes from the discourse-world, not the text itself. That is, rather than the excerpt above, a reader-driven EIR may involve a friend mentioning a link in passing: 'oh, *Lord of the Flies*, that's a bit like *Coral Island*'. An explicit reference to another narrative may appear in a review or an article – this chapter, for instance. The sources of such references are diverse, and more difficult to track and capture than their text-driven equivalents, but the fact that the reader is explicitly presented with a specific intertextual reference remains unchanged.

Unmarked reference is a trickier category to pin down. Predominantly text-driven, unmarked intertextual reference can be specified as a definite reference to another text that has not been explicitly signposted to the reader. Such references thus pass unnoticed by readers who do not recognise them for what they are; these kind of references form the basis of the 'literary hide-and-seek' version of intertextuality favoured by many critics as discussed above.

Unmarked references are the main sticking-point for structuralist approaches such as was exemplified by Riffaterre's Breton analysis. If readers must recognise unmarked references in order to reach a correct reading then they represent flashpoints for slippage away from the authorised interpretation. The reality, of course, is that unmarked references do not bother the readers who do not notice them because they are unaware that their 'literary competence' is lacking – you cannot miss what you do not know is there. While in structuralist terms the recognition of unmarked references and the correct interpretation of explicit references matters a great deal, it is unproblematic in terms of narrative interrelation because the emphasis has shifted from what readers should do with texts to what readers actually do with texts.

Implicit references are reader-driven; they occur when a reader makes an intertextual link without being prompted to do so by a deliberate reference embedded in the narrative. This is the only category in which the narrative interrelation and the intertextual reference can be said to have a fully integrated dependence because the link is generated by the readers themselves. The 'intertextual reference' is perhaps better considered as the recognition of a *point of narrative contact*, which becomes absorbed into the interrelation process. As such, it seems pertinent to refer to it as 'implicit narrative interrelation' (INI).

The line between the unmarked reference and INI is often tenuous. The distinction goes to authorial intention, a dicey concept at the best of times. Many cases are clear cut: *The Wasteland*'s 'The Chair she sat in like a burnished throne / Glowed on the marble' (Eliot 1922) is, via a simple examination of the unusual lexis and mirrored syntax, unequivocally an unmarked reference to Shakespeare's *Antony and Cleopatra*: 'The barge she sat in like a burnished throne / Burned upon the water' (II, iii, 201–2; Shakespeare 2004), even before Eliot's confessional footnotes. Often, however, readers may believe they have spotted an unmarked intertextual reference when in fact they have actually made an implicit interrelation. In a recent interview about her novel *The Casual Vacancy* (2012), for example, J. K. Rowling nearly spat out her water at the suggestion that her character Robbie, the young son of a recovering heroin addict, was a reference to Dobby, a house-elf in her Harry Potter series. What the interviewer believed to be an unmarked reference was in fact his own INI generated by his recognition of multiple points of contact between the two characters; their small and vulnerable status and the phonetic similarities between their names. This example demonstrates very effectively the need to parse out an interrelation process from the umbrella of intertextual reference; for readers, links are processed and have an equivalent ability to impact and play a role in reading no matter whether their inception point was tangibly deliberate or not. Readers rarely have the opportunity to be told that an author actually thought a character's mother was the sort of woman who might name her child because she liked Robbie Williams. The stamp of authorial approval has no real role in interrelation as a cognitive process; the imposition of validity is an external post-measure which has no power to prevent readers from making links of their own or to control how intertextual references are interpreted. The causative factor which prompts a link is when a reader identifies a *point of narrative contact* between a *base* (the text which is the initial and usually primary attentional focus) and another. This process can be instigated by texts and readers alike; the process is the same whether the link is explicit, implicit or unmarked. There is a wide degree of variation between readers regarding who makes a particular interrelation and what that interrelation looks like. This is, I suggest, because readers are not interrelating between texts but between narrative schemas.

Narrative schemas

A key factor which accounts for the differences in how people interpret intertextual references and the range and nature of the interrelations they make is that whenever we encounter a narrative, our memory of that experience is extremely unlikely to match the original narrative itself. With the possible exception of short poems or stories, and then only with concerted effort, we do not remember narratives verbatim and it would be beyond the capacity of human memory to recall whole texts even if we did (Klingberg 2009; G. A. Miller 1956). Any engagement with that narrative is also likely to individualise our reading and distort our recollections; some things we may have found particularly salient, some things we may not have understood. This same notion expands to the level of our different narrative experiences. Where one person fell asleep before the end of a film, another may have watched it fifteen times. One person skimmed a book ten years ago; another read it with great enthusiasm last night. Parts of a narrative may be forgotten; others may be remembered in acute detail. Whole passages may be memorised or complete narratives obliterated entirely. There may be books we have never read but our friend told us all about it and perhaps we read a review. We may have read another text by the same author. We may have been told a film is just like another one we have seen. Schema theory offers a way in which to account for these variations.

Initially developed in computer science as a way to provide computers with the appropriate contextual information in order to perform processing tasks, schemas were first discussed in relation to the cognition of literature by Bartlett (1932) and have since been developed by a number of other theorists, notably Rumelhart (1975) van Dijk and Kintsch (1983), Schank (1982a, 1982b, 1984, 1986; Schank and Abelson 1977), J. R. Anderson (1983) and G. Cook (1994). A schema is:

> essentially the context that someone needs to make sense of individual experiences, events, parts of situations or elements of language [which] is stored in background memory as an associative network of knowledge. In the course of experiencing an event or making sense of a situation, a schema is dynamically produced, which can be modelled as a sort of script based on similar situations encountered previously.   *(Stockwell 2003: 255)*

On a principle of efficiency, in comprehending and assimilating each new situation whether real or fictional that we encounter, we utilise our knowledge of similar things we have previously encountered, minimising the cognition effort by adapting what we already know and applying it to the current context. Schemas can be adapted via the following processes:

- Tuning – the modifications of facts or relations within the schema.
- Restructuring – the creation of new schemas.
- Schema reinforcement – where incoming facts are new but strengthen and confirm schematic knowledge.
- Schema accretion – where new facts are added to an existing schema, enlarging its scope and explanatory range.

(Stockwell 2002: 79–80)

When considering reading in the more holistic sense, especially with a view to accounting for how readers recall and interrelate between their many narrative experiences, it seems that schema theory offers a fruitful solution. Readers, it would seem, do not only have schemas for generic situations; they individuate schemas to the level of individual narratives as well. All the things you attach to a particular text form your narrative schema. Your schema, just as your knowledge of a text, can be accreted before, during and after the reading event itself, if there even is one. Things that are deemed salient are strongly represented and probably influence the shape and nature of the schema as a whole and the other features therein. If you think *Fifty Shades of Grey* (2012) is pornographic you probably also think that the book is poorly written and dominated by sex scenes, and that the story at its core is about the physical relationship between the two protagonists. If, on the other hand you think it is a love story then you might be less attentive to the quality of the writing, characterise it primarily as a novel about romance rather than sex and potentially be more inclined to view the characters more positively. The accretion of new features can cause the tuning, enforcement or decay of others; as bundles of knowledge schemas often, though not always, have a sense of a cohesive whole, just as an individual's reading and attitude towards particular narratives are rarely grossly disjunctive. 'Schemas belong to readers, not texts' (Stockwell 2003: 269) and each is unique to the individual; this accounts for all the variations listed above which impact the nature and quality of knowledge readers have about a particular narrative when they encounter an intertextual reference. As narrative experiences and encounters accrue over time we develop a *mental archive* of stories; like an internal personalised library where every book, film and tale looks exactly how you remember it.

Interrelating schemas

It is from and to this mental archive we draw down and add when we make narrative interrelations and engage with intertextual references. Interrelations occur when a reader identifies a *point of narrative contact* between two schemas, one currently being experienced (read, watched or thought about) and one, or more, in their mental archive. This initial contact can often lead to a *spreading activation* where bringing the two schemas into concurrent examination leads to further points of contact being recognised. Examining instances of such points of contact being made by readers reveals that the range and type of the interrelations subsequently made can vary significantly in terms of their salience, intensity and impact on the individual's reading experience (J. Mason 2012); however, this is beyond the remit of this chapter.

So what do we know about wallflowers?

Returning to the Chbosky extract, the first thing which seems apparent is that each set of books Charlie gives to Sam and Patrick respectively is likely to be characterised and understood according to three factors:

- *The texts for which the reader has existing narrative schemas in their mental archive are likely to take a primary role in any interpretation of this episode*; a reader cannot make points of contact with an empty schema.
- *The richer and more developed the archived schema, the more likely points of contact will be identified.* There may be some leaking from archived schemas to the newly created ones. That is, where I knew nothing about *Naked Lunch* before I encountered this scene, now I know that it is in some way similar to these other texts. I might also accrete all of these schemas with things I know about the characters they are gifted to, or by speculating about why they are given (regardless of whether my conclusions are right or wrong). I think Charlie sees Sam as naive so perhaps her books are about naive characters. She is graduating high school and leaving for college; perhaps these naive characters have new experiences and learn to find their place in the world.
- As with any explicit intertextual reference, many readers will infer a sense of intentionality in Chbosky's positioning of these texts in these groupings. That is, the referenced texts are unlikely to be considered to have been referenced arbitrarily or randomly. This means that *readers are primed to seek out salient points of contact* between their schema for the referenced text and the text which is doing the referencing (the *base*). The 'key features' of the interrelated narrative are tuned to the 'key features in relation to *The Perks of Being a Wallflower*'. Where my archived schema for *Catcher in the Rye* might normally be characterised by Holden's disillusionment, here it may be tuned to afford more salience to adolescent experience. This goes a step further in this extract because there are multiple intertextual references being grouped together. This means that any interrelations between the narratives in the set are likely to become candidates for characterising the group as a whole and to thereby be cast as the intended salient point of contact: what this point is, is subject to all the variables laid out above.

A final step: the intratextual presence of intertextual references

As the example above demonstrates, comprehending intertextual references can be a complex and layered process. This is not to say that readers will experience them as such; in fact, this is often not the case. It is widely accepted that most cognition passes below the level of human consciousness (Fauconnier and Turner 2002; G. Lakoff and Johnson 1980, 1999). What requires the dynamic employment and tuning of multiple archived schemas and several interrelations may seem to a reader to be a spontaneous occurring or the sense of some cohesive link. Indeed, much of the reader response data suggest that readers are often unaware of the particular point of contact that has led them to make an interrelation (J. Mason 2012).

The only environment in which there is likely to be widespread unity in how intertextual links are interpreted, the scenario imagined by Riffaterre as outlined earlier, is when the possible interrelations are limited by the base itself. That is, when the 'intended' points of contact are very explicit and immediately available. For instance, when the children in *Lord of the Flies* refer to *Treasure Island* because they are going to have a 'good time' (Golding 1958: 45), it is unlikely that readers will interpret this as a hope that they will encounter pirates. Even then, however, those readers with richly developed schemas for referenced texts may still stray from the outlined point of contact or experience a spreading activation effect, where additional interrelations are made. When writing this chapter, for example, I noticed when reviewing the intertextual references made throughout Chbosky's novel that Charlie starts worrying about being a 'faker' just as he mentions having read *Catcher in the Rye* (his new favourite book) three times (Chbosky 1999: 110). This caused me to contact his concerns with Holden Caulfield's frequently railing the charge that other people are 'phonies' and I wondered whether this was a subtle unmarked reference by Chbosky showing Charlie being influenced by the books Bill gives him to read, or whether it was simply an implicit interrelation caused by spreading activation. This highlights a final important consideration: the intratextual presence of intertextual references.

I have so far treated the twelve texts referenced in the extract as though readers must rely wholly on their archived schemas and their active schema for the base (*Wallflower*) to interpret them, but this is misleading: Charlie has often discussed or made reference to his own experience of reading these texts within the body of *The Perks of Being a Wallflower* itself. What we can concretely discern is a baseline for each intertextual reference: any reader who had no schema whatsoever for a referenced narrative when they began reading *The Perks of Being a Wallflower* is exposed to everything mentioned about it in the novel itself, and therefore has the opportunity to accrete from that material. The references are not entirely exophoric; they have an endophoric presence too.

The curious case of *Naked Lunch*

Readers have two available sources of knowledge when dealing with an intertextual reference:

1) Previously existing information known prior to encountering the intertextual reference, the archived schema.

2) The information about the referenced text available in the base narrative.

Naked Lunch provides an interesting example in *Wallflower* in terms of the role and scope of application of intertextual references in narrative. These references offer readers the opportunity to apply their schema to a number of different characters. *Naked Lunch*, for example, could be applied to tell readers:

- about how Bill sees Charlie – What is Bill trying to teach Charlie by giving him *Naked Lunch*? What does he think he will gain from it?
- about Bill – How does Bill see himself? Why does he give Charlie *Naked Lunch*?
- about Charlie – What does Charlie think about *Naked Lunch*? What do we learn about him through his interactions with Burroughs's novel?
- about how Charlie sees Patrick – What is Charlie trying to teach Patrick by giving him *Naked Lunch*? What does he think he will gain from it?
- about Patrick?
- about Stephen Chbosky – What does Chbosky think about *Naked Lunch*? What does his narrative schema look like? Why did he choose to include this particular text to pass across his characters?

Charlie outlines his own experiences of *Naked Lunch*. Thus by the time readers encounter it in the final extract, they have all had the opportunity to accrete their '*Naked Lunch* schemas' with the following:

- Bill deviated from his usual selection process in giving Charlie *Naked Lunch*. Charlie recognises this because 'everything Bill tells me to read or see are similar. Except the time he had me read Naked Lunch' (177). *Naked Lunch is different from the other texts we have seen Bill give Charlie.*
- Bill tells Charlie he gave him the novel to read because 'he had just broken up with his girlfriend and was feeling philosophical' (177). *Naked Lunch is the kind of book you might give someone if you were feeling philosophical, particularly if you were sad because your relationship had ended.*
- Charlie's sister offers us some biographical information about the author, telling Charlie 'Burroughs wrote the book when he was on heroin and [Charlie] should just "go with the flow"' (115). *Naked Lunch might not have a clear linear narrative. It was written by someone who was taking a lot of drugs and probably reflects that fact.*
- Charlie's impression of the novel was that he 'had no idea what [Burroughs] is talking about' (114–15). *Enforcing the previous point.* *Naked Lunch might be difficult to understand and follow.*
- Charlie interrelates *Naked Lunch* with two of the other books, eventually giving one to Patrick and the other to Sam. He tells his Friend that *The Fountainhead* 'wasn't like The Stranger or Naked Lunch even though

I think it was philosophical in a way' (181). Naked Lunch *is philosophical but not in the same way as* The Fountainhead. *It might be similar to* The Stranger.

- In this last evaluation Charlie even offers up a comparative analysis of these three texts (*The Fountainhead*, *The Stranger* and *Naked Lunch*) and the others Bill has given him over the course of the novel, an opportunity for mass schema accretion: *The Fountainhead* 'was a different book from the others because it wasn't about being a kid. And it wasn't like The Stranger or Naked Lunch even though I think it was philosophical in a way' (181). Naked Lunch *is more like* The Stranger *and* The Fountainhead *than any of the other books Bill has given Charlie. Those books are all about being a kid.* Naked Lunch *is therefore not about being a kid.*

The schema features derived from the intratextual presence of *Naked Lunch* that I have suggested here are by no means fixed. None are immediately available to readers when they encounter the gift-giving scene and many may have passed over them without any accretion of their *Naked Lunch* schema taking place. However, it seems uncontroversial to suggest that having a sort of 'authorised presence' in the base text is likely to prime many readers to tune their schema to give these particular features, if attended to, primacy in making sense of vaguer references to Burroughs's novel, such as that in the final extract.

Conclusion

Intertextual references are made by texts; narrative interrelations are made by readers. Highly explicit references which clearly delineate the preferred points of contact between a base and a referenced text may sometimes, even often, produce consistent interpretations across readers. But readers read holistically and interrelate freely. A lifetime's gathering of narrative experiences across contexts and mediums provisions readers with a library of potential contacts which can be activated impulsively and cannot always be bridled, even by the strongest of steers from a text. Readers often report their interrelations as though they have little control over them: 'this book *made me* think of. . .'; 'I *found myself* comparing this with. . .' (J. Mason unpublished).

It seems that the more limited the amount of information about a referenced narrative available in the base and the richer the schema in the mental archive, the greater the opportunity for variation in the inter-relations which result from a given intertextual reference. The vaguer the intertextual reference, the more reliant readers are on their archived or co-textual knowledge of that narrative. Consistency across interpreta-tions is likely to be attributable to intratextual information about the referenced narrative, which primes tuning for salience. However, this intratextual tuning can easily be ignored, disrupted or overshadowed by readers' archived knowledge of referenced texts.

Some may find my analysis frustratingly inconclusive. I make no apology for this: the postclassical shift in narrative analysis demands it. Seeking the 'answer' to how readers interrelate the narratives referenced in the *Wallflower* scene will only ever be an exercise in flattening out, stripping away and dulling down. The real task of exploring reading as a holistic process, which so often involves the interrelation of its parts, is to celebrate its eclecticism and, as far as possible, to account for how it occurs.

Ultimately, with Patrick I confess to having read only one of his books; it is unsurprising then, especially having engaged in such an attentive reading of Chbosky's text, that I characterise his gifts as more 'philosophical'. I read Patrick as a headstrong character who is surprisingly comfortable with himself and self-assured, but who gets a little lost. Maybe Charlie surrounds Patrick with other 'lost boys' to help him find his way. I fare a little better with Sam's selection, four out of six. *The Great Gatsby*, while a favourite of mine, does not sit well with any cohesive sense of the group I can make which still sits well with the character herself or how I model Charlie as seeing her. It takes a back seat. Perhaps *Gatsby* is the caution of not being more like Scout or Holden – inquisitive about the world and managing what it throws at them as best they can. Postclassical narratology's emphasis on how readers make meaning rather than how to get to the right one means that having read a higher or lower percentage of these referenced texts does not make a reading better or worse, only different. Intertexts, as they belong to readers, are personalised; a different intertext can yield different points of contact between narratives, interrelating, accreting and tuning each other in exciting and unpredictable ways. Thus my conclusion about the *Wallflower* passage may ring true with some because it draws on the text itself and is informed by some fairly rich schemas besides, but it is just that, my conclusion, and not necessarily the 'right' one if such a thing exists. Neither is it really conclusive. If I ever read any of those other texts I may well tune and reassess my reading, precisely because individual narrative experiences dynamically contribute to reading as a holistic endeavour.

This is perhaps the key advancement of postclassical narratology: an acknowledgement that readers are not consistent, with each other or themselves; they evolve, vary and change both as a group and as individuals. Nor are they readers of only one thing. If intertextuality wants to give such primacy to the role of other texts then it must accept that readers' narrative experiences extend beyond, and will not always include, those things concretely referenced in the text under examination, no matter how convenient that would be for researchers – more so, that this is a good thing. Movements in postclassical narratology represent a necessary and integral shift in the drive to incorporate substantive consideration of readers in narrative analysis. Recognising that readers are not stable has liberated and redirected the field to focus on the aspects which are, like the cognitive processes, cultural variations and differences in ideology which enable us to arrive at such diverse and eclectic interpretations and which allow these interpretations to happily coexist.

14

Defamiliarisation

Joanna Gavins

Art as technique

The concept of defamiliarisation has played an important role in a large number of studies of literary style since the early twentieth century. The origins of the term are normally traced back to the work of Viktor Shklovsky (1893–1984), a Russian Formalist critic who argued that the function of literary texts is the 'making strange' (*ostranenie* in Russian) of familiar, everyday experiences. According to Shklovsky, art exists in order to 'recover the sensation of life' (Shklovsky 1965: 20) and to portray the world to be discovered by the reader as if for the first time. He goes on to argue,

> In studying poetic speech in its phonetic and lexical structure as well as in its characteristic distribution of words and in the characteristic thought structures compounded from words, we find everywhere the artistic trademark – that is, we find material obviously created to remove the automatism of perception; the author's purpose is to create the vision which results from that deautomatized perception. A work is created 'artistically' so that its perception is impeded and the greatest possible effect is produced through the slowness of perception. As a result of this lingering, the object is perceived not in its extension in space, but, so to speak, in its continuity.
>
> *(Shklovsky 1965: 27)*

As van Peer (1986: 1–26) outlines, Shklovsky's ideas primarily had influence on the earliest forms of stylistics which began to develop along a formalist vein in the 1960s and 1970s (for example Halliday 1971; Leech 1966b, 1970; Short 1973) and which focused on the sorts of phonetic, lexical and syntactic analysis that Shklovsky begins by advocating above. However, the additional notion he expresses here, that literature has the ability to slow perception, also continues to resonate within some of the most current approaches to literary language and style. As I will demonstrate later in this chapter, Shklovsky's argument that the linguistic configuration of a literary text can create thought structures which possess a continuity extending beyond initial perception is one which is echoed in many stylistic analyses today, particularly those attempting to explain the experience of literary reading from a cognitive perspective.

Van Peer points out that Shklovsky's concept of art as a technique is not without its complications and inconsistencies. He notes, for example, that Shklovsky is frequently criticised for the imprecision of his ideas and the lack of systematicity in his application of them and points out that the terms employed by the Russian Formalists as a whole ('defamiliarisation', 'estrangement', 'palpability', 'perceptibility' and so on) have a tendency towards near-synonymy. He comments, too, on the slippage that exists in Shklovsky's work between formal linguistic analysis and an appreciation of the psychological effects of literary art. As van Peer explains:

> A term such as 'making strange' or 'defamiliarisation' may refer to two things. On the one hand it is meant to describe the properties of the actual text, i.e. the literary devices that can be located in the text itself. On the other hand it points to the effect such devices may have on the reader. These two meanings are in fact blended together in the terms employed by Shklovsky and several other Formalists. This can be understood in the light of their aim to develop a functional theory of literature, where text and reader both have their place.   *(van Peer 1986: 3)*

Later work in the formalist tradition, such as that of Jakobson (for example, 1960, 1966, 1968) and Mukařovský (for example, 1964a, 1970, 1976), argued more clearly that the defamiliarising effect of literature is located in the formal structure of the text and, specifically, in its deviation from certain norms of standard, non-literary language. As van Peer (1986: 14–16) explains, the stylisticians of the 1960s and 1970s developed this initial idea further towards a fully synthesised theory that deviation and parallelism bring about the foregrounding of certain elements of literary texts. He notes, too, however, that foregrounding itself is still 'at least in part a psychological phenomenon' (1986: 14), later commenting that 'although intuitively appealing, [the concept of foregrounding] is still rather speculative and on the whole rests on inconclusive evidence' (van Peer 1986: 27). Van Peer goes on to deliver one of the first attempts to test the intuitions of stylisticians about the psychological effects of foregrounding through empirical experimentation. Much of van Peer's subsequent work (for example, van Peer 1986; van Peer and Andringa 1990, van Peer et al. 2007, 2012; and with Zyngier et al. 2007) is similarly dedicated to the empirical-stylistic enterprise of providing scientific evidence for the effects of particular features of literary language on readers.

Since the early 1980s, numerous other analysts have also sought to broaden the focus of literary study beyond introspection to examine a far wider range of reader responses to literary language (see, for example,

Andringa 1996; Bortolussi and Dixon 2003; Bray 2007; Emmott et al. 2006, 2007, 2010; Hanauer 1998; Hunt and Vipond 1985; Miall 2007, 2008; Miall and Kuiken 1994, 1999, 2002a, 2002b; A. J. S. Sanford et al. 2006; Sotirova 2006; Zyngier et al. 2008). Among these, the work of Miall and Kuiken (and specifically 1994) is worthy of special attention in the present chapter for its specific concerns with the concept of defamiliarisation. Miall and Kuiken begin by reiterating Mukařovský's (1964a) argument that, although the foregrounding of particular linguistic features can occur in non-literary language, it tends to do so without systematic design. Like other stylisticians before them, Miall and Kuiken also link the textual phenomenon of systematic stylistic foregrounding in literature with the psychological effect of defamiliarisation, in Shklovsky's (1965) sense of the term, but also argue that this effect has an additional, emotional dimension:

> Briefly stated, we propose that the novelty of an unusual linguistic variation is defamiliarizing, defamiliarization evokes feelings, and feelings guide 'refamiliarizing' interpretative efforts. There seems little doubt that foregrounding, by creating complexity of various kinds, requires cognitive work on the part of the reader; but it is our suggestion that this work is initiated and in part directed by feeling.   *(Miall and Kuiken 1994: 392)*

Miall and Kuiken set out to test Shklovsky's intuitions that defamiliarisation may also lead to a slowness of perception, arguing that this may in part be due to the process of 'refamiliarization', referred to above, by which readers 'discern, delimit, or develop the novel meanings suggested by the foregrounded passage' (Miall and Kuiken 1994: 394). Their experiment began with three 'judges' (one of the researchers, plus two graduate English students) analysing three literary short stories for the presence of foregrounded stylistic features. The stories were then given to three separate groups of undergraduate university students, who rated segments of the stories for their strikingness and emotional affect. On the whole, Miall and Kuiken found that the presence of stylistic foregrounding in the stories was a predicter not only of strikingness and affect, but also of reading times: in the stories containing the greatest concentration of foregrounding, as assessed by the experiment's 'judges', participants took longer to complete their readings of the texts. These findings not only appear to support Shklovsky's notions of slowed perception but, because the groups of participants in Miall and Kuiken's study were selected for their varying levels of literary competence and interest, they suggest that such psychological effects are independent from reader's expertise in literary analysis.

Swann and Allington (2009) have pointed out, however, that many empirical studies of literary style and its effects examine readings produced in artificial reading or discursive environments by readers engaged in atypical reading behaviour and often interacting with atypical texts or textual fragments (although it must be said that this final point is not true of Miall and Kuiken's study). More recently, a greater leaning in stylistics can be identified as developing towards what Swann and Allington (2009) term 'naturalistic studies', with a focus on contextualised reading practices and on examining readers' behaviours in their usual environment, engaged in habitual reading behaviour and interacting with unmanipulated texts (see, for example, Allington 2011, 2012; Allington and Swann 2009; Gavins 2013; Peplow 2011; Sedo 2003; Stockwell 2009; Whiteley 2010, 2011a, 2011b). These studies examine a range of readers interacting with literature in a variety of contexts, including academic literary analyses and student seminar discussions, but also reading groups taking place in non-academic contexts and discussions in online literary websites of various kinds. They tend to take a qualitative approach to the data gathered in these environments, data which represent voluntarily produced and often highly detailed accounts of everyday literary interaction, unmanipulated by the observing analyst. In what follows, I will be examining defamiliarisation from a similar perspective, as a psychological effect reported by a range of readers in naturalistic reading contexts. The constraints of the present chapter mean that my investigation will necessarily be limited in scope, but I am interested in exploring at least a selection of responses from readers interacting with a highly popular text, in order to ascertain whether defamiliarisation forms an important part of what makes such texts so well liked. My aim is to provide further evidence to support Miall and Kuiken's notion of defamiliarisation as a textually based phenomenon possessing an important emotional dimension.

Defamiliarising the commonplace

Billy Collins (b. 1941) is a former US poet laureate and Distinguished Professor of English at Lehman College, New York. His numerous collections of poetry have enjoyed sales figures that are exceptionally high for the genre, regularly breaking US records in this respect. Easy access to the typical evaluations made of Collins's work by readers reading in non-academic settings is available through a number of online literary discussion websites, such as *Goodreads* (*Goodreads* 2012), *LibraryThing* (*LibraryThing* 2012), and *Shelfari* (*Shelfari* 2012). These sites currently boast millions of members situated all over the world, and they provide a means through which readers may share, discuss, rate and tag the literary works they encounter. As I have pointed out elsewhere (Gavins 2013), such websites normally offer their members the possibility of complete anonymity and it is impossible to be certain of the age, gender, occupation, ethnicity and social background of the readers involved. However, for the purposes of the present discussion, this anonymity is immaterial since what distinguishes the reading *context* of an online literary website from that of a peer-reviewed academic publication is its informal and dynamic nature, rather than the profiles of its participants. Even though the responses of academics undoubtedly form a considerable part of the discourse of online literary communities, these are nevertheless responses that are produced and shared outside the usual, highly formal-ised expectations of literary criticism and pedagogical practice.

It becomes quickly evident on examining the discourse surrounding Billy Collins's poetry on *Goodreads*, *Shelfari* and *LibraryThing* that he is an immensely popular writer. On *Goodreads*, for example, his poetry collec-tions score an average rating 4.17 out of a possible 5.00 based on 22,962 reader ratings (as a quick comparison with a canonical text, Shakespeare's sonnets score 4.24 under the same system). Reviews and discussions of Collins's work online number in their hundreds and below is a typical, if small, selection of some of the most positive responses to Billy Collins's poetry offered within online discussion environments:

1   His poems are accessible but profound, sung with a vernacular lyricism, ripe with humor and grief . . . You don't realize as you continue reading that he is carrying you farther and farther away from the quotidian and into the realm of poetic meta-ness, turning your expectations upside-down. In fact, it's not until the end of a poem, when Collins drops some perfectly phrased closing observation into your lap, that you notice he has managed to bring you to the tip of a mountain while you still sit comfortably in your armchair with your tea. His poems describe heaven and home with the same affectionate wonder (and maybe they're really the same thing after all).

(Rachel 2012)

2   More and more I appreciate the poem that brings poetry down to the familiar, even the mundane. A cup of coffee and a cigarette, or the way leaves look just before a storm. Billy Collins is a master of this kind of simplicity. He grounds you firmly in the world, and then lets the truth of it open out before you. Accessible though never simplistic, direct and dryly funny, Collins is a gem.

(TracyRowan 2009)

3   Billy Collins has this extraordinary ability to portray the beauty in every moment of life. Whether it's eating an apple, or watching a storm cleave its way across his backyard. His poems truly allow the reader to transcend ordinary life and realize the deep beauty and interconnectedness of life.   *(SunnyPetunia 2008)*

It is clear from these responses that the readers concerned have experi-enced what cognitive theorists commonly describe as psychological transportation into an imaginary world (see, for example, Brock and Green 2005; Gerrig 1993; M. C. Green 2004; M. C. Green and Brock 2000; M. C. Green et al. 2004; Nell 1988). It is also clear that for these particular readers this transportation has been highly immersive and emotionally affecting. Note, in particular, how reader (1) describes losing awareness of her surroundings while reading, a key indicator of psychological immersion according to M. C. Green and Brock (2000), who develop a fifteen-point scale on which to measure such readerly sensations. Note, too, how reader (3) describes Collins's poetry as allowing her 'to transcend ordinary life', explaining her experience of his work initially in terms of physical movement, followed by a profound renewed perception ('and to realize the deep beauty and interconnectedness of life').

In later empirical studies Kuiken, Miall and Sikora (see Kuiken et al. 2004; Miall and Kuiken 2002a) develop the initial ideas on literary effect put forward in Miall and Kuiken (1994) to categorise the feelings associated with literary reading as occurring within four key domains. The first of these they term 'evaluative feelings' and argue that these relate to the overall pleasure derived from reading. Second, 'narrative feelings' are feelings provoked by an event or situation within the fictional world and include feelings of sympathy or empathy with a character. The third category of 'aesthetic feelings' relates to a heightened interest prompted by the formal features of a text and, finally, readers may also experience feelings of 'self-modification' during or after reading, described as follows:

> Readers may experience self-modifying feelings that restructure their understanding of the text and, simultaneously, their sense of themselves. Readers commonly recognize settings, characters, or events as familiar (e.g., a story event is reminiscent of something they have directly experienced or have read before). But, at times, they also find themselves participating in an unconventional flow of feelings through which they realize something that they have not previously experienced – or at least not in the form provided by the text. At these times, the imaginary world of the text is not only unfamiliar but disquieting. One aspect of this disquietude is the possibility that the shifting experience of the world of the text may be carried forward as an altered understanding of the reader's own lifeworld.
> *(Kuiken et al. 2004: 175)*

In these studies, Kuiken, Miall and Sikora delineate the aesthetic feelings stimulated by the foregrounded stylistic features of a text from the more profound and potentially long-lasting feelings of self-modification which may or may not also be induced through literary reading. Interestingly, reader (3)'s comments, above, on the new-found realisation prompted by Collins's poetry, would seem to fit neatly into the category of self-modification, and these feelings are also described as following on from an aesthetic appreciation of the craft of the poems. Indeed, all three responses report positive feelings in both the evaluative and aesthetic domains. Even more interesting for the present discussion, however, is the fact that all three, in one way or another, make an explicit connection between these feelings and the commonplace aspects of everyday life, which frequently feature in Collins's texts. Reader (1), for example, situates the activity of reading Collins itself as typically taking place in a mundane setting ('in your armchair with your tea'), suggesting through an inclusive second-person pronoun that this might be universally true for all Collins' readers. Reader (2) describes Collins as a 'master of this kind of simplicity', bringing 'poetry down to the familiar, even the mundane', while reader (3) praises Collins's 'ability to portray the beauty in every moment of life'.

While the online readers above describe their positive emotional inter-actions with Collins's work in terms of a sudden and extraordinary sensi-tivity to the ordinary, it should not be assumed from these quotations that Collins has the same effect on all of his readers. Indeed, his work appears, more accurately, to polarise opinion much of the time. Nowhere does this polarity become more marked than when positive readings reported in a non-academic context, such as those above, are compared with some of the negative evaluations of Collins's work which have been put forward by readers reading in an academic context. Consider, for example, the following:

> When [Collins] talks about death, he does it almost flippantly. When he brings history into the equation, it becomes implicated in his own banal preoccupations. Most recently, he has begun to pontificate, in his position as America's biggest-selling poet of serious intent. Having had a taste of celebrity, Collins has stepped easily into the myth programmed for him by the literary circuit. His determination to shun greatness perhaps reflects the final stage of believing too strongly in one's own genius. Collins is disturbingly content even when raising the subject of death, his glee at managing to pose intellectual riddles overriding the tragic impulse. He is like a happy adult solving the Sunday paper's crossword puzzle, having skipped the front-page headlines, the mayhem and chaos on the planet.
>
> *(Shivani 2006: 225)*

Here, the same commonplace qualities of Collins's work, which the online readers responded to so positively, are levelled against the poet as markers of flippancy and banality. Despite the fact that Collins has won a multitude of national and international literary awards for his poetry over the years, he has also been subject to quite vicious criticism from a minority of literary academics, and another prominent feature of such critical attacks is Collins's popularity, his 'celebrity' as Shivani describes it above, and his ability to make a living from his writing. Perhaps most alarmingly, the exception taken by some literary critics to Collins's popular success appears to be rooted to a great extent in prejudices expressed along the lines of class and ethnicity:

> You open the book and step into the blunt box of a fancy-doored elevator; and there it is around you, elevator music. Collins is not without some

rhetorical skills, charm and wit; there are those fancy doors. But what he finally offers is disappointingly monotonous and slight. It's no wonder no-one seems to want to speak this truth, at least not publicly. A best-selling poet who sports blue jeans, likes jazz, and is clearly at home in the neighborhood bar as well as in the poetry workshop; an Irishman with the gift o' gab who can make audiences laugh aloud and whose all-American boyish name is Billy, Charmin' Billy. Who wants to carp, to look like envy making its usual meal on sour grapes, to be a prude at the hayride, a freeze-dried academician, a snob?... Well, why the heck not?   *(Merrin 2002: 203)*

In this example, Merrin outwardly relishes the temptation to indulge in snobbery against Collins, making several swipes at the poet's Irish-American working-class roots as well as at his ability to please his audiences. These audiences, however, far outnumber the literary critics who have expressed such indignation at Collins's success. Stockwell makes the following noteworthy comment in his analysis of Rudyard Kipling's 'If', another poem which enjoys great popularity in the UK in particular:

> there is very much a canon of acceptable 'literary talk'. It is established and fixed in the main journals in our field; it forms the specified medium of expression in the assessments we require of our students; it delineates the limits of what we should converse about in seminars, and what we ought to regard as inadmissible in talking about books. Unfortunately, it no longer bears any resemblance to the discourse on literature outside our walls. Worse, it does not even concern itself with that everyday activity. And worst of all, it sees itself as a professional discourse that has little to do with the untrained folk reading of lay people.   *(Stockwell 2005: 143–4)*

Taking Stockwell's remarks into consideration, then, the readers engaging positively with Collins's work in non-academic contexts form the most interesting subject for examination in this chapter on defamiliarisation, while responses such as those made by Merrin and Shivani may be regarded as eccentric by comparison.

Defamiliarising forgetfulness

In order best to understand the psychological impact of Collins's poetry on his most affectionate audiences, in what remains of this discussion I will explore one the poems most frequently cited in online literary discussion sites as a favourite or particularly affecting text:

Forgetfulness

The name of the author is the first to go
followed obediently by the title, the plot,
the heartbreaking conclusion, the entire novel

which suddenly becomes one you have never read,
never even heard of,

as if, one by one, the memories you used to harbor
decided to retire to the southern hemisphere of the brain,
to a little fishing village where there are no phones.

Long ago you kissed the names of the nine Muses goodbye
and watched the quadratic equation pack its bag,
and even now as you memorize the order of the planets,

something else is slipping away, a state flower perhaps,
the address of an uncle, the capital of Paraguay.

Whatever it is you are struggling to remember,
it is not poised on the tip of your tongue,
not even lurking in some obscure corner of your spleen.

It has floated away down a dark mythological river
whose name begins with an L as far as you can recall,
well on your own way to oblivion where you will join those
who have even forgotten how to swim and how to ride a bicycle.

No wonder you rise in the middle of the night
to look up the date of a famous battle in a book on war.
No wonder the moon in the window seems to have drifted
out of a love poem that you used to know by heart.

(Collins 1999: 20)

We have seen clear evidence in the extracts from online readers' reports above that Collins's poetry creates imaginary worlds that have the potential to be highly immersive. To understand the configuration of these worlds, and consequently the possible stylistic causes behind readers' emotional responses to them, the framework of Text World Theory (see Gavins 2007 and Werth 1999 for full accounts) provides an ideal analytical apparatus. The theory is rooted in cognitive linguistics and aims to understand how real-world contexts influence the production of discourse and how that discourse is perceived and conceptualised in everyday situations. It unifies text and context under one analytical system, allowing the analyst to gain both an overall understanding of the interactional nature of a discourse and to achieve a precise explanation of its textual and conceptual components. Under this approach, the mental representations created by literary texts are known as 'text-worlds' (see Gavins 2007: 10), conceptual spaces constructed in the minds of readers and initially based on the deictic markers contained within the text. These markers are known in Text World Theory as 'world-building elements' (see Gavins 2007: 35–52) and they define the spatio-temporal parameters of a text- world; they specify any characters (referred to as 'enactors' in Text World Theory) or objects present in the world, establish social and physical relationships between those entities, as well as describing time and place more generally. World-building elements include spatial deictics such as locatives, spatial adverbs and demonstratives, as well as temporal deictics such as variations in tense and aspect, temporal locatives and temporal adverbs. Crucially, Text World Theory recognises that the text-worlds readers construct in their minds based on these deictic foundations have the potential to be as richly detailed and immersive as the real world, as the information provided by the text is fleshed out with readers' real-world knowledge and experiences in a process known as 'inferencing' (Gavins 2007: 24–5). All text-worlds originate from a 'discourse-world', the immediate real-world situation surrounding the participants in any discourse (see Gavins 2007: 18–34). The discourse-worlds of literary communication are normally split, with the author and the reader occupying separate spatial and temporal locations. This means that the participants must rely even more heavily on their inferencing abilities and it is from their immediate environment, and from the background knowledge and experiences which feed into it, that the participants draw the inferences they make in relation to the language they encounter. The specific knowledge the participants need to understand the discourse at hand is regulated and defined by the text itself, according to what in Text World Theory is known as 'the principle of text-drivenness' (see Gavins 2007: 29).

Adopting a text-world perspective on Collins's text, then, the first point of stylistic interest in 'Forgetfulness' is the manner in which the construction of a coherent text-world is complicated from the very beginning of the poem. In the first stanza there is an abundant use of the definite article ('*the* name', '*the* author', '*the* first', '*the* title', '*the* plot', '*the* heartbreaking conclusion', '*the* entire novel'), which might normally be associated with familiar objects and entities and be used to aid the relatively straightforward mental representation of a deictic configuration. In the case of Collins's poem, however, these definite articles occur as part of a series of references to non-specific, abstract concepts (such as 'the author' and 'the plot'), which are in turn connected to a similarly non-specific novel. Figure 14.1 illustrates the basic structure of the text-world of the opening lines of 'Forgetfulness' using standard Text World Theory notation (see Gavins 2007, and Werth 1999 for summaries).

In Figure 14.1, the temporal signature of the text-world (in the top left of the diagram) is shown as the present, since the poem begins in simple present tense. However, the under-specificity of the objects and entities described in the first stanza makes them difficult to conceptualise as text-world-builders. They are therefore shown in greyed font as somewhat ghostly figures in the mental representation in Figure 14.1. As a means of better conceptualising the poem, readers may make recourse to an additional metaphorical mental representation in these lines. This possibility is opened up through the personification of the definite but non-specific

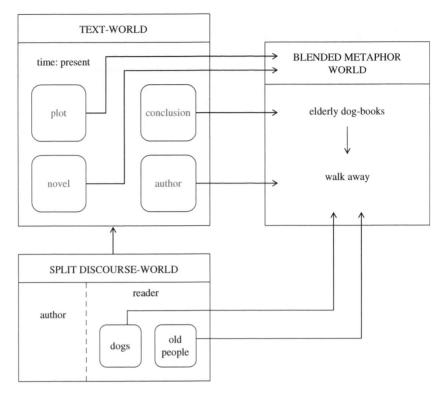

Figure 14.1: Indefinite figures and metaphor worlds in 'Forgetfulness'

name, plot, title and so on, signalled in the words 'obediently followed', which suggest that these figures may be walking away. In Text World Theory terms, metaphors such as this one create new text-worlds, formed from a blend of conceptual items initially nominated by the text but also drawn from the reader's individual background knowledge and experiences. In this regard, Text World Theory to a great extent follows Fauconnier and Turner's (2002) ideas of metaphor as arising from the integration of two or more 'input spaces' into a new conceptual space with its own emergent structure. In Figure 14.1, the input spaces generated by world-building elements in the text-world ('the plot', 'the novel' and so on) are shown feeding into the metaphor world to the right of the diagram. When I gave this poem to a group of twelve undergraduate students in a seminar at the University of Sheffield in 2012, eight students in the group reported that a mental representation of a dog had also formed an input space in the blended metaphor worlds they formed for this line of the poem, a discourse-world inference suggested by the adverb 'obediently'. Another three students in the group said that elderly people were also a component of their conceptualisation of this image, and both sets of inputs are shown in Figure 14.1 feeding into the metaphor world from the discourse-world. My student readers all suggested that the input spaces are blended together in the emergent metaphor world to form a complex mental representation of an elderly but obedient dog-book, walking away. A further transformation happens to 'the novel' later in the first stanza when it 'suddenly becomes one you have never read, / never even heard of'. The shift in tense in this line, from the simple present to the present perfect, creates what Text World Theory terms a 'world-switch' (see Gavins 2007: 48), a new world created through a shift in the deictic parameters of its originating text-world and representing a separate time-zone. In this case, the world-switch is complicated further by the fact that it is negated. In line with other cognitive-linguistic theories of negation, Text World Theory views such constructions as essentially foregrounding (see Hidalgo Downing 2000b), since the reader must first conceptualise the novel being read (at another temporal point) before then *un*conceptualising this event (see also G. Lakoff 2004).

Another embedded world of a different kind is created at the beginning of the second stanza, but it is one which nevertheless follows a similar conceptual pattern to those created in the poem's opening lines. 'As if' signals the creation of a hypothetical world, an unrealised possibility embedded within the world of the poem. Text World Theory terms all such worlds 'modal-worlds', a category which includes the mental spaces which occur as a result of the use of conditionality, those which arise from modalised forms, worlds relating to inner thoughts and feelings, alongside hypothetical worlds such as this one. All these linguistic features, Text World Theory argues, posit mental representations which are in some way ontologically remote from their originating world. In the case of the 'as if' that begins the second stanza of 'Forgetfulness', the world which is created here is a distant one and relates to another abstract concept, 'memories', represented in these lines as making a decision. The second stanza also contains a further world-switch, since the memories are described as having been harboured at a separate temporal point, indicated again by the switch in tense in 'used to harbor'. Of course, a further metaphor world is also being created in this stanza, once again through personification. This time, our notions of fishing villages, quiet southern harbours, and retirement in old age, all feed into the blended metaphor world. Note again the embedded negative in these lines, 'no phones', which once more acts to foreground an everyday object as a prominent world-building element. This complex configuration of worlds is illustrated in Figure 14.2.

There is a marked shift as the text progresses from the definite non-specific references which predominate in the first half of the poem to a proliferation of indefinite non-specific items throughout its second half (for example, '*something* is slipping away', '*a* state flower', '*an* uncle', '*whatever* it is', '*a* dark mythological river', '*a* famous battle', '*a* book on war', and so on). Rather than the poem adding clarity to the text-world as it develops, the world-building elements nominated in the text thus become increasingly difficult to conceptualise. There are also frequent further world-switches as the poem shifts backward and forward through three main

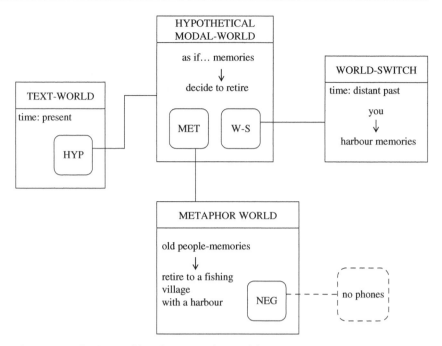

Figure 14.2: The text-world configuration of 'Forgetfulness'

temporal zones: the first and most current is the point at which 'you are struggling to remember'; the second, more temporally distant, is the point at which 'you kissed the names of the nine Muses goodbye / and watched the quadratic equation pack its bag'; and the third and most remote is the time when 'you used to harbor' memories and 'you used to know' a love poem by heart. The second-person pronoun in these examples and which runs throughout the poem is, of course, also worthy of attention here. Collins's use of 'you' in 'Forgetfulness' conforms to a type of second-person address which David Herman (1994) terms 'doubly deictic'. Herman argues that certain forms of 'you' act to conflate the text-world with the discourse-world, explaining in relation to prose fiction,

> The novel in the second person makes of the reader a fellow player, who is suspended between a fictive world and his own real world, and who stands simultaneously inside and outside the fiction ... In doubly deictic contexts, in other words, the audience will find itself more or less subject to conflation with the fictional self addressed by you. The deictic force of you is double; or to put it another way, the scope of the discourse context embedding the description is indeterminate, as is the domain of participants in principle specified or picked out by you. (D. Herman 1994: 406)

In Collins's text, the second-person pronoun is clearly situated within the text-world, indicated, for example, in the proximal temporal adverbials 'suddenly' in the first stanza and 'now' in the third. However, at the same time as it specifies a fictionalised entity at this conceptual level, the 'you' in 'Forgetfulness' also appears to reach into the discourse-world containing the reader of the text. This cross-world extension is suggested mainly through the distancing effect of the indefiniteness of the poem; it is as difficult to fix the referent of the second-person pronoun within the text-world as it is to fix any of the poem's other nebulous world-builders. Furthermore, after a series of unmodalised facts which seem clearly to relate to a fictionalised 'you' in the text-world (for example, 'you have never read', 'you kissed the names' and so on) have been defined, in the first line of the fourth stanza the pronoun suddenly becomes more generalised through the use of 'perhaps'. This epistemic modal adverbial introduces a note of uncertainty into the poem, suggesting that 'you' relates both to a fictional entity, whose inner thoughts and experiences are fully accessible to the narrating poetic voice, and at the same time to the real reader, the content of whose mind can only be guessed at by this poetic persona. This uncertainty is repeated, and the doubly deictic nature of the second person is confirmed, in the first line of the fifth stanza with 'Whatever it is you are struggling to remember'.

The pattern of negation is also repeated regularly throughout the text, either through syntactic means (for example in constructions such as 'it is not poised') or through repeated reference to objects and people leaving or disappearing (for example, 'you … watched the quadratic equation pack its bag', 'something else is slipping away', 'It has floated away down a dark mythological river'). Modal-worlds, too, figure throughout the text, all of them epistemic in nature and functioning to question or undermine the certainty of key world-building elements. According to Text World Theory, any instance of epistemic modality (for example, the use of epistemic lexical verbs such as 'believe' or 'suppose', or modal adverbs such as 'certainly' or 'perhaps') creates an embedded world which exists at a remove from its originating world and through which the relative epistemic distance of a particular proposition can be conceptualised and understood. In 'Forgetfulness' this happens in the occurrence of 'as if' and 'perhaps', as already discussed, but also in 'as far as you can recall' in the sixth stanza and with 'seems' in the final stanza. The syntactic structure of these lines is also important here as, in two of these cases (with 'perhaps' and 'as far as you can recall') the positioning of the modal at the end of a clause leads these items to act as further negation: the reader must first conceptualise 'a state flower' and a name 'beginning with L' before quickly having to relegate these to a mere possibility and a vague memory respectively.

Defamiliarisation as embodied experience

The analysis of the text-worlds of 'Forgetfulness' carried out in this chapter has examined in particular the important roles played by negation, modality, metaphor and the doubly deictic second-person pronoun in Collins's poem. Through these stylistic features, Collins captures the experience of ageing and the deterioration of memory which accompanies this universal process. In particular, Text World Theory has revealed how the linguistic structure of Collins's poem leads to the mental representation and frequent subsequent *de*representation of a series of often commonplace but elusive figures: 'The name of the author', 'the title', 'the plot', 'the heartbreaking conclusion', 'the entire novel', 'the memories', 'the names of the nine Muses', 'the quadratic equation', 'the order of the planets', 'something else', 'a state flower', 'the address of an uncle', 'the capital of Paraguay', 'Whatever it is', 'a dark mythological river whose name begins with an L', 'those who have even forgotten how to swim and how to ride a bicycle', 'the date of a famous battle', 'a love poem'. The overall under-specificity of these world-building elements helps both to universalise them and to render them tenuous, ill-defined and conceptually fragile. A proper understanding of such figures as 'thought structures compounded from words', as Shklovsky puts it (1965: 27), rather than simple linguistic items leads to a fuller comprehension of Collins's defamiliarising technique in this poem. By leading his readers through the process of perceiving and *un*perceiving over and over again in 'Forgetfulness', Collins not only represents the deterioration of memory to his readers but requires them to enact it for themselves. The experience is one which is highly engaging and material for many readers, as encapsulated in the following report offered by a reader on *LibraryThing*:

> 4. I really enjoy Billy Collins' style. It's straight-forward and unassuming. He writes as if poetry is the easiest thing in the world, and the reader is convinced it is . . . It's hard to capture emotions and moments and images in just a few lines. And yet, Billy Collins does just that. His themes are likewise real: I can relate to nearly every poem. He writes about growing older, being a professor, reading books, writing poetry, waking up in the night with insomnia. And yet, his poems are deceptively simple: behind each simple scene is emotion and struggle. He is real, and I feel I've met him.
>
> *(rebeccareid 2009)*

We have seen how many of Collins's most devoted readers appreciate, in particular, his handling of the commonplace, the everyday, and locate their most profound emotional responses to his work specifically with this aspect of his poems. As reader (4) expresses above, this dimension of Collins's work appears to encourage immersion and empathetic connection and, in some cases, to result in long-lasting self-modifying feelings. In 'Forgetfulness', I would argue that these readerly sensations are nurtured and encouraged by the fact that Collins's poem forces readers to perform the act of forgetting for themselves. Indeed, an abundance of recent empirical research in cognitive linguistics and psychology has shown that embodied physical experience underpins all human understanding of language (see, for example, Barsalou 2003, 2009; Barsalou et al. 1999; Gibbs 1992, 2003; Glenberg 1999; Glenberg and Robertson 2000; Yeh and Barsalou 2006) and that encounters with particular linguistic items provoke psychological simulations of previous physical experiences. As Barsalou explains:

> When a category is represented conceptually, the neural systems that
> processed it during perception and action become active in much the same
> way as if a category member were present (again, though, not identically).
> On conceptualising CAR, for example, the visual system might become
> partially active as if a car were present. Similarly the auditory system might
> reenact states associated with hearing a car, the motor system might reenact
> states associated with driving a car, and the limbic system might reenact
> emotional states associated with enjoying the experience of driving (again
> all at the neural level). *(Barsalou 2003: 523)*

Thus, as Collins leads his readers to conceptualise flowers, rivers, bicycles and planets he revivifies past experiences of these categories. Such experiences are embodied and tangible in their primary occurence and remain so in their re-enactment through language. 'Forgetfulness' not only demands that readers activate the neural systems associated with definite, perceptible objects and concepts, but also subsequently destabilises many of these perceptions through negation, indefiniteness and epistemic uncertainty. The defamiliarising quality of Collins's poem is realised through stylistic techniques which create text-worlds that are at once material yet nebulous, imagined yet embodied, textually driven yet psychologically experienced.

15

Intensity and texture in imagery

Barbara Dancygier

Imagery is a notoriously slippery concept. It is used widely, especially in literary pedagogy, but its specific application is often a matter of unstated assumptions. While a full account of the literature on imagery would exceed the scope of this paper, the most instructive discussion can be found in various texts by W. J. T. Mitchell (1986, 1993, 1994), though even he generally dismisses the concept of imagery as specifically useful. Mental imagery is discussed at length in Scarry (1999), and Starr (2010) highlights the multimodal nature of imagery and offers comments on different senses. Across literary scholarship, imagery can mean at least three different things – depictions of sensory perception in a text, the text's construction of a vivid image in language which evokes a mental image in the reader's mind, or any figurative use of language (see M. Abrams (2005) for a full definition). It is difficult to bring all three meanings into one cohesive concept. Still, the appeal to imagery, in which-ever sense, is pervasive in literary study, even as some authors openly reject the concepts of 'image' and 'imagery' as useful in any specific way.

Imagery and embodied cognition

How can we account for the diverse meanings of these terms and how then can we propose a usable model? It appears that the existing approaches focus on different aspects of a very complex issue which exists at the intersection of the human body, the mind, and the reality we live in. As human beings, we interact with the world on many levels. First, we rely on our bodies to orient us in real-life situations. This includes sensory perception – vision, touch, smell, taste and hearing – but also the very spatial situation of the body and its ability to move and interact with objects. In other words, our bodies are the primary source of any form of experience. At the same time, as cognitive scientists have argued, the body is also a source of conceptualisation (see, for example, Barsalou 1999; Gibbs 2005; Gallagher 2005; Pecher and Zwaan 2005b). Proponents of theories of embodiment and situated cognition claim that the mind is influenced by the body in that embodied experience and situated action are the primary sources of material for conceptualisation, including the conceptualisation of emotions and abstract concepts. Importantly, this approach also underlies an understanding of figurative language as reliant on ordinary areas of embodied experience – for example, our conceptualisation of mental processes (such as thinking) is often built on our direct experience of embodied processes, such as moving, using force, object manipulation, absorbing nutrition and so on. Lakoff and Johnson (1999) discuss numerous such examples of linguistic expression which represent thinking as moving, visualising or eating (*I need to digest this idea*; *I don't see your point clearly*; *We'll get to the next point soon*).

Embodied functioning in the world thus creates correlations between forms of mental experience and forms of actual experience. Not only do I see a view (which engages my brain primarily, not just my eyes), but I can also construe the experience in some way – this may include the recognition of specific colours and shapes, but also the recognition of objects seen, the emotion the view evokes and so on. There are many components in our appreciation of what we experience, and many of these components participate in complex knowledge structures, called frames, so that full implications of experience are part of our understanding of the concepts referred to by linguistic forms. For example, talking about *heavy clouds in the sky* (as well as seeing them) involves recognising them as clouds, perceiving colour and shape, but also perhaps understanding that they may cause rain, which in turn may prompt me to take an umbrella along if I go out.

But such conceptualisations do not always have to emerge as a result of direct experience. They can also be prompted by exposure to visual representations (such as a photograph or a painting), and, crucially, through observations of other people's behaviour, and through language (including its literary forms). I do not have to actually see the overcast sky myself to have a mental representation of it. Repeated exposure to the frames (see Fillmore 1985, 2006) involved in actually seeing heavy clouds in the sky allows me to use these frames in interpreting other situations, such as viewing pictorial representations or hearing/reading words. In fact, having experienced a situation, I can also reproduce it from memory or imagine another instance of it, one which has not actually occurred. There are many possibilities, but two points are crucial: firstly, mental imagery would not be possible without us having access to embodied frames and associated perceptual memories, and, secondly, images are structured by existing knowledge and can be prompted in our minds through many different channels.

We should also note that the concept of 'imagery', in whichever sense, assumes a subjectivity, whether real or imaginary, whose mind can be claimed to 'hold' the image. In daily interactions, we not only rely on our own experiences and their mental representations, but we can also align ourselves with the experiences of others. Watching a person in a particular situation usually evokes an understanding of how that person is affected by that situation – mentally, or emotionally, or both. Also reading a person's account of their experience, or another person's account of that experience triggers certain construals and representations of other situations in our minds. This phenomenon has been explained variously in terms of *theory of mind* skills or, at the lowest level of embodiment, through activation of mirror neurons. Importantly, however, the reader's reaction may not be identical to that of the actual experiences – while the actual experiencer may be angered, the viewer or reader maybe amused by the situation they see others in. Exposure to verbal (or visual) images comes with the same reservation: mental images evoked in readers' minds will vary widely.

Additionally, mental imagery can be used figuratively, to evoke other meanings (as in metaphor, simile, allegory, etc.). This pathway to meaning construction is in fact quite common, as the study of conceptual metaphor suggests. It seems to rely on a somewhat different pattern of evocation. Every image evokes frames of some kind, but it can evoke more than one, often based on the perceived links across different areas of experience. For example, there is a tendency for the frame of purposeful motion through space (a journey) to be used to structure an understanding of other purposeful activities, and even the very course of the human life. On the one hand, the exploitation of a concrete, embodied frame for the construal of a less directly experiential one seems to be a pervasive pattern in language use. On the other hand, given the experiential source of such construals, images rich in embodied detail can be naturally read as refer-ring to more abstract domains.

Definitions of imagery often stress the expectation that the image created be 'vivid and particularized' (M. Abrams 2005: 128). The specific meaning of this requirement is not clear, but in what follows I want to suggest that it reaches into the core of the role of imagery. I argue that the concept of 'vividness' refers to rich experiential detail, attributed to an experiencing subjectivity which the reader can align herself with. But what seems even more important is that the style should not be simply descriptive, in an objective manner, but it should evoke a subjectified response. The central idea is that the reader's mind can *experience* (as opposed to *understand*) things through the mental and emotional arousal only, not through intellectually absorbing the situation described. I argue that the contrast we should be talking about is that between 'experience' and 'description' – the effect of imagery, rather than what it depicts. Importantly, the experience evoked can be formulated through sensory perception or through other aspects of our embodied interaction with the outside world. It seems natural to include embodied experiences such as movement, the sense of weight, of proximity to other objects, of temperature and so on. In order to achieve a cohesive concept of imagery we have to define it in terms of giving verbal access to embodied experience, of whatever kind.

The processes to be captured seem to be firmly rooted in the concept of embodied cognition. Discussed in Gibbs (2005), Gibbs and Matlock (1999), Pecher and Zwaan (2005b) and many others, the embodiment hypothesis sees human mental and emotional life as directly emerging from bodily processes. The body is viewed as closely linked with the mind; in fact, it is claimed to be the source of various patterns of conceptualisation. As Gibbs (2005: 9) describes it, 'People's subjective, felt experiences of their bodies in action provide part of the fundamental grounding for language and thought.' Embodied processes are central not only to our own inner life, but also to our ability to understand the inner life of others. With the help of neural responses such as simulation (or, at a very low level, the firing of the mirror neurons), we are able to align with what others are feeling, without confusing our own experience with that of another experiencer. A broader discussion of these neural and cognitive mechanisms is beyond the interests of this chapter, but I will rely on certain general hypotheses outlined in recent research.

The use of imagery – in its embodied sense – is often connected with a specific poetic mood, and is naturally correlated with the expression of feelings. However, the way in which the connection emerges between the bodily perceptions described by the text and the feeling awakened in the reader is not clear at all. My contention is that stylistic analyses, paired with the general view of feelings as it emerges from literature on cognition, could clarify some of the sources of the connection.

As regards the very concept of 'emotion' in the context of the body, neuroscientist Antonio Damasio (1999, 2003) proposes a further distinction, between 'emotions' and 'feelings'. Emotions are ways in which our bodies respond to the environment (e.g. increased heartbeat, sense of warmth or cold, changes in the rhythm of breathing). These responses are then appreciated by our mental processes and identified as the 'feeling' of, for example, fear. Additionally, our brains can simulate the feelings of others, building on the bodily experience we have of our own emotional responses. These ideas are clearly pertinent to the question of what verbal imagery can do, especially since it has been shown repeatedly (Gibbs and Matlock 1999; Pecher and Zwaan 2005a) that words evoke simulations in our brains in ways quite similar to observing actual actions, and, as Prinz shows (2002, 2004), embodied action also prompts emotions. Although the complexity of acts of writing and reading has not been, and cannot easily be, addressed in a neuroscientist's lab, we can still rely on what we know about cognition and language to try to fill at least some of the gaps.

I argue, then, that the effects of imagery depend in equal measure on the bodily roots of experience and on the role of language in prompting conceptualisations and simulations. Specifically, descriptions of bodily responses to the environment (involving vision, touch, taste and smell, but also body posture, motion, etc.) can evoke reactions through the vocabulary of perception and movement. In what follows, I want to consider three examples of the specific linguistic means through which imagery is evoked. After some initial explanation of the concepts I will be using, I will consider three literary texts which represent interesting aspects of the use of imagery, with specific poetic effects. I will start with a classic lyric, Wordsworth's *Daffodils*, and then consider a prose example (Virginia Woolf's *To the Lighthouse*), and, finally, a contemporary poem, Philip Larkin's *Going*. These textual examples provide interesting material for a stylistic and cognitive reconsideration of how imagery achieves its effect.

Experience and subjectivity

What are, then, the means to prompt a construal of an experiencing body through linguistic choices? It does not occur entirely through vocabulary of sense perception, but also through the linguistically prompted alignment of the reader with an experiencing subjectivity. The subjectivity is roughly equivalent to what is meant by 'the poem's persona', but the latter term seems overly specific for the purposes of my discussion. The examples to be looked at below show that such a subjectivity is in fact not more than a point of view, attributed with the ability to be engaged in perception or motion (see Dancygier 2012 and the papers in Dancygier and Sweetser 2012). For simplicity's sake, I will refer to such an experiential viewpoint as an Ego (which is not a person, and has no connection to Freudian psychology). The concept of the Ego does not assume a fully profiled personhood, but it does assume an aspect of experience that a person should be capable of having. For example, saying that *The filing cabinet is to the left of the desk* typically assumes a visual viewpoint available when one is facing the desk, which is a rather common viewpoint for a desk-user, even though there is no assumption that anyone is standing in front of the desk at the moment of the utterance. I will discuss my examples in terms of such an experiential Ego's alignment with an aspect of the specific situation described.

Crucially, we need to distinguish the various possible Egos involved in a basic act of reading. The process starts with an Ego constructed by the writer, which then becomes the locus of the experience described in the text (whether it is assumed to be an experiencing person, an element of nature (flower, bird, etc.), an observer, or a narrator). In each of these cases, the experience attributed to such an Ego is different, but because personhood is not assumed, the experience itself is what determines the type of viewpoint profiled. In fact, in some cases, the experience is attributed to non-sentient entities. For example, in Wisława Szymborska's poem *Advertisement*, a tranquiliser drug speaks to the reader, assuming consciousness and agentivity.

I can take exams or the witness stand.
I mend broken cups with care.
All you have to do is take me. . .   (Szymborska 1998)

It does not matter whether a drug can in fact choose to act in specific ways, but what matters is that the Ego of the poem has been constructed in this way (for further discussion of the poem, and of the concept of Ego, see Dancygier 2012). The drug in *Advertisement* can think, act and speak, and it has expectations of its addressee. Even though we typically assume that no such powers are available to pills of any kind, we have an understanding of what a sentient Ego is like and can align it with an inanimate object. Overall, every poem constructs some Ego, though what kind of viewpoint the Ego is profiled to represent is a matter of the discourse choices made.

In the process of reading, the words of the text may then move the reader into two kinds of responses. Firstly, one aligns oneself mentally with the Ego the text profiles (so, for example, understanding what intentionality is attributed to the speaking drug, which requires mentally simulating 'being-the-drug viewpoint', as emerging from the text). Secondly, the reader needs to become another experiencing Ego by responding to the construal the poem proposes, albeit only through simulation of what the text evokes. To return to the drug example again, readers are compelled to construe themselves as addressees of the drug's tempting words. Also, they typically report feeling upset by the construal where their own power as agents is so totally appropriated by an inanimate object whose purpose is to relieve the stress of action without taking the ability to act away from us.

What should be kept in mind is that none of the reader-constructed Egos is fully predetermined by the writing. In general, when we simulate other people's responses (as in an act of empathy), what we feel is not identical to what the target of the empathy feels, as we do not map observed behaviour identically to actually experienced behaviour, but what has been experienced is needed for the observations to evoke some kind of feeling. This is what seems to be happening in reading. Readers can re-create the intentionality of the drug on the basis of their own experience of being in control of their actions, and they can understand the poetically suggested powerlessness of the drug taker, even though they may not feel generally intimidated by the power of drugs. But each reader's response may lead to somewhat different feelings (of anger at our weakness, amusement with the cleverness of the construal, vulnerability, etc.). The point is that the situation described in a poem is often a source of dual emotional response, aligned with at least two viewpoints: the text's and the reader's own.

All the ideas introduced above are naturally applicable to the construal of and response to poetic imagery, except that descriptions of experiences can be linked more directly to the kinds of feelings that emerge in reading. The point can be illustrated through a glimpse of Wordsworth's classic poem *Daffodils*. Taught in many school curricula, popularised through anthologies and family books of poems, the text has often been seen as highly representative of the romantic approach to lyrical poetry, and, especially, to feeling. In spite of its simplicity, the poem evokes an interesting set of responses to the images described.

> I wandered lonely as a cloud
> That floats on high o'er vales and hills,
> When all at once I saw a crowd,
> A host, of golden daffodils;
> Beside the lake, beneath the trees,
> Fluttering and dancing in the breeze.
>
> Continuous as the stars that shine
> And twinkle on the Milky Way,
> They stretched in never-ending line
> Along the margin of a bay:
> Ten thousand saw I at a glance,
> Tossing their heads in sprightly dance.
>
> The waves beside them danced, but they
> Out-did the sparkling waves in glee:
> A Poet could not but be gay,
> In such a jocund company:
> I gazed – and gazed – but little thought
> What wealth the show to me had brought:
>
> For oft, when on my couch I lie
> In vacant or in pensive mood,
> They flash upon that inward eye
> Which is the bliss of solitude;
> And then my heart with pleasure fills,
> And dances with the daffodils.

The poem's Ego is here aligned with a narrating voice, represented in the text by the first-person pronoun 'I', and presumably cross-linked with the 'Poet' in the third stanza. The Ego is seen here in two situations: first the past encounter with the flowers and then the present repeated situation where the memory of the flowers is reconstructed in the Ego's mind. It is thus indeed a case where the experiencing Ego is construed as having full personhood – which makes it possible for the poem to describe memories, reflect on various moods, consider the role of mental imagery in changes of feelings, and so on. Our appreciation of the Ego's feelings is mainly through vision: either the memory of what was seen, or the recalled image displayed before 'that inward eye' – the conscious mind.

But the central image I want to focus on is that of 'dancing'. Daffodils are 'dancing in the breeze', 'tossing their heads in sprightly dance'; the waves on the lake dance too, though not as joyfully as the flowers; and finally, the poet's heart 'dances with the daffodils', or rather, with their memory. The movement of a dancer is construed differently from the movement of, say, a hiker. It is not motion along a path towards a destination. On the contrary, in dance, the body posture is expected to be expressive, and loaded with emotive elements. In a sense, a dancer is somewhat like a writer: there is a construal (fully embodied, not textual) of the creative act's Ego, whose postures are aligned with any possible feeling. The viewer then, like a reader, reads the experiencing Ego's viewpoint (deciphers the emotion) and feels something in response – possibly simulating the same bodily movement and the associated emotion in her body and mind.

For flowers or waves to dance we need to construe them as having bodies that can move in expressive ways. In the case of the waves, their repeated up/down motion can be read as a pattern of certain significance, but with flowers we can assume a projection of a body posture – upright, energetic, with the head swaying to the rhythm of the wind. Flowers have a bodily structure that can easily be mapped onto a human body – the blossom being the head, and the stem being the legs and the trunk; additionally, leaves can move like arms. In the poem, the description of dancing daffodils evokes the image of joyful expressive movement of a human body, and thus the experiencing Ego is attributed to the flowers based on perception of their movement and the attribution of emotive underpinnings of such movement. The reader can then understand the Poet's sense of elation at the sight – the Poet's experiencing Ego is simulating the emotive body posture of the flowers. Finally, recreating the source of joy and the Poet's emotive response, the reader is likely to experience some sense of gaiety herself, as a result of the next step of simulation.

There is, however, one more step in the sequence. The last stanza is in sharp contrast to the first three, since the poem's Ego is described as lying down – not in an upright position suggesting activity and alertness, not moving at all, and not joyful. In this context, the 'dancing heart' is clearly not connected to bodily movement and is not (presumably) construed as moving in sync with the daffodils swaying in the breeze. What appears to be the case is that the first three stanzas describe a situation where movement of upright bodies (humans or flowers) is read as a symptom of joyous feelings, and in the last stanza the dancing movement and joy are now treated as inextricably connected. The 'dancing' heart is the consciousness that can feel joy without the body participating in the joyous act, and without even observing it in a realistic setting. Crucially, the Poet need not have danced happily before to attribute emotions to moving flowers – all it took is an embodied sense of how a specific form of movement of a fully upright body, with its head held high, can evoke the emotion of energised elation and, consequently, the feeling of joy. Then the joy can be conceived of without actually experiencing the bodily engagement, since it can now be simulated based on the experiential memory built into all human bodies (linking bodily movement and emotion). The role of 'imagery' in the poem is essentially summarised through this progression of construals: viewing bodies in a happy scene creates emotions of happiness, which our mind can preserve and reproduce based on the mental representation of the scene. Finally, it can inspire similar emotions in a reader, whose bodily sense allows her to re-simulate the feeling. Reproducing the feeling may also be paired with prompting the body into a similar state – so that we can imagine the Poet snapping out of the period of pensiveness and getting up from the couch; we can also expect the reader to feel re-energised and more optimistic – which is perhaps the whole point of reading this kind of poetry.

A disembodied subjectivity

Wordsworth's poem evokes body posture and movement to suggest action and joy. However, fine differences in the description of body posture and perception can create an image that evokes entirely different emotions and feelings, as in a fragment from Virginia Woolf's novel *To the Lighthouse*. The entire novel takes place in the summer house of the Ramsey family, located on the shore, with a lighthouse on an island nearby. In the first part, the family and many of their friends spend the summer in the house, but, to the dismay of the Ramsey children, they never reach the lighthouse. In the final part some of the members of the group return, many years later. The middle part, titled *Time passes*, is a kind of interlude, when the house, abandoned for many years because of war, deaths in the family and so forth is left to the forces of nature. The haunting emptiness of the house and the depressing events elsewhere create an atmosphere of gloom, solitude and hopelessness. And yet, the cycle of nature runs its usual course:

> In spring the garden urns, casually filled with wind-blown plants, were gay as ever. Violets came and daffodils. But the stillness and the brightness of the day were as strange as the chaos and tumult of night, with the trees standing there, and the flowers standing there, looking before them, looking up, yet beholding nothing, eyeless, and so terrible.
>
> *(Woolf 1992: 128–9)*

The description in this fragment stands in stark contrast to Wordsworth's poem, even though in both the focal point is the description of flowers in bloom, especially daffodils. Importantly, the flowers are also described in terms of upright body posture and attributed with human bodily features ('standing there, looking before them'). But the description involves a different construal of a human body – not moving and energetic, but simply standing in the 'stillness'. The effect of evoking a human body prepared for interaction (upright), but not engaged in any meaningful action is strikingly different from the 'dancing daffodils' – instead of joy and high spirits, we sense inaction, despondency, purposelessness. But the mechanism is the same – the emotion evoked reaches the reader through the described body posture. The fact that it is projected onto the flowers only makes the image more depressing, since embodied signs of mood are more readily expected of humans than of nature. Furthermore, the analogy between flowers and people is developed in a way that deprives the experiencing Ego construed of the central perceptive modality – that of vision. The flowers are first portrayed as *looking before them, looking up*, but this description applies only to projected body posture, as in fact they are *beholding nothing, eyeless, and so terrible*. At the basic embodied level, lack of vision makes interaction, object manipulation or purposeful action very difficult, and is in fact only possible when other senses compensate for the lack of visual input – clearly not what Woolf's construal suggests. Also, the adjective *eyeless* extends the projection to an image of a human face, which adds to the strange sense of a body deprived of its human features and incapable of acting or interacting.

Even more importantly, the Ego projected onto the flowers here is not in some feedback loop with a human experiencing Ego – as the 'Poet' in *Daffodils* is. The first four sections of the second part of the novel (*Time passes*) are written without an experiential engagement of any of the characters, and yet the narrative seems full of activity – though not human activity. First, darkness gradually fills the house and turns it into lifeless, colourless landscape:

> Nothing, it seemed, could survive the flood, the profusion of darkness which, creeping in at keyholes and crevices, stole round window blinds, came into bedrooms, swallowed up here a jug and basin, there a bowl of red and yellow dahlias, there the sharp edges and firm bulk of a chest of drawers.   *(Woolf 1992: 119–20)*

This description treats a static concept of darkness as if it were capable of purposeful motion and causative action (as we can see in verb forms such as *creeping, stole round, came, swallowed*). This is somewhat related to process-profiling uses such as *it became dark*, but enhances the agentless 'change of state' meaning into the presence of a wilful agency. In effect it treats imagery not in terms of states to be perceived, but in terms of actions taken. In the fragment, the experiencing Ego is aligned with the changing availability of light. But the destructive force of the darkness is in fact more tactile than visual. Objects disappear, but not only from sight. The flood of darkness feels their presence, touches them, much as a person would in the dark, and removes them out of any perceptive reach. The darkness does not experience the house as a human would, but we can project specific abilities of the human body onto its destructive presence. Imagery it is, then, but re-construed for the purpose, explicit in the whole second part, of conveying the emptiness and desolation of the house, abandoned by the summer crowd and withdrawn from their lives.

Some analysts might be inclined to simply describe this construal of darkness as 'personification' (in fact, one could quickly dismiss Szymborska's *Advertisement* in the same way, which would miss the whole complexity of construal there). I believe, though, that the category of personification is not helpful, in this as well as in other cases. It is very broad, and it relies on our ability to use words denoting inanimate objects and abstract concepts with verbs assuming agency (*the tomato sauce ruined my stomach/my dress/the meal; our beliefs give us power to endure*, etc.) or adjectives describing human feelings (*the tree looked lonesome; the house felt anxious*). The use of personification is extremely common, especially in descriptions of natural phenomena (*the wind howled; the clouds raced across the sky*). It is also not restricted to literary expression, or not necessarily more common in literary texts than in colloquial discourse.

In G. Lakoff and Turner (1989), personification is treated as an example of the EVENTS ARE ACTIONS metaphor (though this does not cover the adjectival use). Indeed, the point of most of this usage is to present what happens without any agency as if a volitional or sentient entity were involved. But this does not imply that we are indeed adding 'personhood' to our construal of an object or a phenomenon, but it is, rather, double alignment with an experiencing Ego – as in the cases described above. Sentences such as *the clouds raced across the sky* or *the house felt anxious* imply, initially, that an observer perceives the motion as determined and fast (as in a race) or the atmosphere of the house as tense. The construal is then projected onto the terms describing the objects or natural phenomena involved, and the experience felt is aligned with them, as they are the source of the perception of the observer. There is a metonymic relationship between the observer and the objects, such that the perception registered by the *recipient* is attributed to the *source* of the perception. The issue is thus directly relevant to the concept of imagery as outlined here, though in colloquial discourse the alignment of an experiencing Ego with an object is much less elaborate.

What, then, makes Woolf's narration 'literary'? There seem to be two reasons why her text goes beyond what is ordinarily referred to as personification. First, the usage is sustained through the entire passage and elaborated into a narrative – there are various 'actions' attributed to darkness and they create a dynamic story, a sequence of related events. Second, the specificity here is that there is no directly available Ego to whom the experience of seeing darkness swallow furnishings can be attributed. The only Ego in Woolf's narrative is that of the darkness itself. An interesting construal emerges that way: what could be a perception of darkness falling over the house is truly an action of darkness overtaking the house. The image emerges based on our ability to entertain two unusual conceptualisations: one, we can imagine perception without a perceiving Ego, and we can entertain an experiencing Ego without full personhood.

In further paragraphs of *Time passes* similar powers are attributed to the 'sliding lights' (passing beams of light from the lighthouse) and 'the fumbling airs', which enter the house, but, being unable to 'touch nor destroy', finally disappear. But then people leave, the house stays abandoned, and the airs return:

> So with the house empty and the doors locked and the mattresses rolled round, those stray airs, advance guards of great armies, blustered in, brushed bare boards, nibbled and fanned, met nothing in bedroom or drawing-room that wholly resisted them but only hangings that flapped, wood that creaked, the bare legs of tables, saucepans and china already furred, tarnished, cracked. What people had shed and left – a pair of shoes, a shooting cap, some faded skirts and coats in wardrobes – those alone kept the human shape and in the emptiness indicated how once they were filled and animated...
> *(Woolf 1992: 122–3)*

Here, again, is a narrative solution to a problem of how perception of change can be construed without the perceiving Ego. Besides resembling the 'darkness' example above, in that the 'airs' explore the house, allowing the reader a glimpse into its state, there is an interesting description of abandoned objects. Clothing is naturally associated with the person who wore the garment before it was abandoned, and thus the text plays not just with the current state of emptiness, but also with its past alternative, a busy summer house filled with people.

Also, the reader's expected alignment with the perspective of the wondering 'airs' has the expected effect of emotions associated with the sense of loss and emptiness. The Ego profiled is fully sentient: it can touch the objects it passes (*brushed, nibbled, fanned*), it can hear the hangings flapping loose, without anyone attending to them, and the creaking wood, making sounds, but not disturbed by a human step, and it can detect 'human shape' in the discarded objects. It 'sees' what a human would see, but there is no human to whom the experience could be attributed. Overall, the purpose of the construal seems to be primarily to create an Ego that the reader can follow in the experience of the abandoned house. But at the same time, the absence of a human experiencer contributes to the sense of emptiness in the passage.

What Woolf's text shows is that it is so natural as to be almost necessary to assume a perceiving observer in order to describe a scene. The existence of an experiencing Ego is what any description of imagery relies on, which might question the very idea that a discussion of imagery alone is in any way useful in analysing texts. But at the same time, the discussion of how various texts profile the experiencing Ego seems to be a more fruitful enquiry, involved in imagery, but not restricted to it. In the examples I have shown so far, various degrees of presence or absence and various configurations of perceiving and conceptualising Egos yield interesting poetic and narrative effects.

Experiential void and the body

My next example shows a text that refers to the senses more explicitly, though not in a straightforward description of sensory perception. Philip Larkin's short poem *Going* is a simple, yet convincing example of how the body and the senses are used in the evocation of a basic awareness of the fragility of everyday experiences. The poem begins:

 1 There is an evening coming in
 2 Across the fields, one never seen before,
 3 That lights no lamps.

 4 Silken it seems at a distance, yet
 5 When it is drawn up over the knees and breast
 6 It brings no comfort.

 7 Where has the tree gone, that locked
 8 Earth to the sky? What is under my hands,
 9 That I cannot feel?

 10 What loads my hands down?   (*Larkin 1955: 3*)

The poem's mood is dark. I often ask my students for a reaction to the first reading, and I invariably hear words such as 'depression', 'sadness', 'despair' or 'death'. The effect is achieved, again, through a depiction of the states of the body, but these states are here directly related to the senses. The most interesting suggestion seems to be that the poem is describing the experience of dying, and there are several different reasons to follow that suggestion. The poem's title, *Going*, can be read as suggesting death, via the conceptual metaphor DEATH IS DEPARTURE. This does not stand in conflict with the use of 'coming' in the first line, since the two deictic verbs suggest two different metaphorical construals of events in time – either we are moving towards them (*we are approaching Christmas*) or they are moving towards us (*Christmas is approaching*) (see Burke 2005; Dancygier and Vandelanotte 2009). There is a further metaphorical elaboration, through the word 'evening', evoking another conceptual metaphor of life and death, LIFETIME IS A DAY. The metaphor maps a life cycle onto the cycle of a day, where morning is the beginning, and evening is the approaching end of the cycle, as well as the period of darkness – which reinforces the 'death' reading, since death is often metaphorically construed as sleep or darkness.

Even independently of these metaphors, the text of the first stanza evokes a contrast between our bodily sense of 'day' – light, being active, being in control of one's actions, ability to interact with objects and other people and so on, and the embodied sense of night – lack of daylight, time of inaction, reduced mobility and limited interaction. The evening approaching us is not the familiar evening of a safe domicile ('one never seen before') and does not bring the relief of artificial light ('lights no lamps'). Such an evening can naturally be associated with a situation where inaction and lack of sensory input is forced an experiencing Ego.

The middle section of the poem evokes the sense of touch (*silken* [. . .] *to the touch*), but lines 5 and 6 disperse the sense of comfort that the word *silken* evokes. These lines also build on the embodied experience of closeness as intimacy and comfort – whether because of proximity of other people or because of a protective enclosure that separates the body from outside stimuli. The questions in the third stanza have an additional effect. First, the tree is described as *gone* (CHANGE IS MOTION), but it is also removed from the field of vision, and as a result the spatial/vertical structure of the ordinarily perceived world is shattered. The sense of cohesiveness of the surrounding world is destroyed; through these lines, a perceptive dimension is added to our embodied sense of well-being, that of predict-able directionality and spatial organisation. The next question ('What is under my hands that I cannot feel?') returns to the sense of touch, but the expected recognition of what our hands rest on is disturbed – the under-standing of the immediately surrounding world is collapsing. Both these questions build heavily on the fact that sensory perception constitutes the basic feedback on our experience – lacking an accurate sense of the situation our body is in is a clear sign of loss of the basic connection to our own life functions, our identity and our surroundings.

The final question ('What loads my hands down?') evokes yet another embodied dimension – the sense of our own weight and the resulting appreciation of our ability to move and to manipulate objects – the ability that is necessary in all life situations. Overall, the poem conveys a sense of loss of one's basic ability to use one's body, and the disturbing sense of distance between one's conscious thought and the experiencing body. Once the connection with the body is weakened, the resulting state of the diminished or severed bond between the body and the mind is possibly the most disturbing state to imagine. And yet that is what the poem forces the reader to do – to align with an experiencing Ego who/which is in fact losing its ability to experience.

Let us return briefly to the question of whether the poem describes the experience of death or some other state of inaction and withdrawal. The title of the poem was in fact changed, and the text was first known under the title *Dying Day*. While in this version there is at least some indication of death, it is in fact spurious, because of the ambiguity – it could be the day of dying or a day that is dying. The latter reading is aligned with the word 'evening' in the first line, and so the whole poem can still be read as evoking a depressing end of a day, but also, metaphorically, the end of life. Naturally, there is no point in arguing for one interpretation or the other, as both are equally valid, but whichever one we choose, we are still bound by the clear and evocative descriptions of the embodied states which we naturally connect to emotive states of inaction, lack of energy, depression, etc. The feelings thus evoked in the reader will be just those that the reader's body and mind will first suggest – of fear of death, of tiredness, of psychological trauma.

However, it has often been commented that Larkin truly feared death and struggled with the thought that it is inevitable. In another poem, *Aubade*, he expresses his fear explicitly. He describes the source of fear of death not as fear of pain or afterlife, but of 'the total emptiness forever', 'Not to be here, Not to be anywhere'. His explicit description of why death terrifies us is again appealing primarily to the senses.

> ... this is what we fear – no sight, no sound,
> No touch or taste or smell, nothing to think with,
> Nothing to love or link with,
> The anaesthetic from which none come round.   (Larkin 1977)

These words clearly match what *Going* describes, but the effect is different in the two cases. While *Going* forces us to align ourselves with the very experience of dissolving into lack of experience, into perception-less, sense-deprived nothingness, *Aubade* is a reflection on the abhorrence of such a state. The Ego of *Aubade* is a fully sentient and intellectually alert person, considering death. *Going* attempts to re-create the experience of dying and prompts an alignment of the reader's Ego with such a state, in a sense giving us a taste of what he thinks it might be. *Aubade*, for comparison, is a discourse, a reflection on death and the possible experiential aspects of its arrival. *Going* simulates the experience of dying, *Aubade* does not. In this sense, one might argue that only *Going* is a true example of the use of imagery, as it prompts an embodied alignment with the situation construed.

Experiencing imagery

In view of the above examples, imagery seems still to be a useful concept, as it allows us to distinguish the ways in which language can refer to embodied experience with different effects (descriptive or experiential). We can also attempt to explain the affective implications of image-rich texts through a better understanding of the evocative power of linguistic choices. From the stylistic perspective (properly *cognitive poetics*: see Brône and Vandaele 2009; Stockwell 2002, 2009), this approach requires a focus on the specific ways in which language can be crafted to simulate experience. While this kind of investigation may not be easily accomplished with a study of formal or grammatical means, a better understanding of the evocative power of language is a goal worth pursuing. For this to be accomplished through the study of imagery, we need to de-focus the actual matter of the *description* (what was seen, smelled, tasted, etc.), and emphasise the linguistic means that allow us to construe different *experiences* and experiencing Egos. The specific configuration of such Egos in a text and the mechanisms which invite the reader to one pattern of experiential alignment rather than another could be our primary tools. In other words, posing the question of imagery as the question of an experiencing Ego may lead to a better understanding of the processes involved and a more accurate stylistic tool-kit. The possibilities are numerous, often stylistically complex, and though poetry offers an intense example, they can be observed in any genre.

Note

I want to thank Kyle Robertson for drawing my attention to the example of Woolf's *To the Lighthouse*, and Steven Maye for pointing out the 'tactile' dimension of the 'flood' fragment to me.

Part III

Techniques of style

16

Phonostylistics and the written text

Introduction

The title of this chapter sounds like a contradiction in terms. Indeed, 'phonostylistics' implies spoken discourse and has apparently nothing to do with the written text. However, until the fourth century AD, it was customary to read texts aloud and the dichotomy between the written (*scripta*) and the spoken text (*verba*) was not as clear cut as it is today (Manguel 1997). Silent readers mentally reconstruct the fictional voices of characters that never existed. Furthermore, as Léon (1993: 29) explains:

> Any given language is spoken before it is written. That is why even the most abstract piece of writing retains some biological and physiological traces of spoken language: sounds, rhythms and intonation contours. Whether the writer wants it or not, any piece of writing betrays its oral origin. (my translation)

From this perspective, 'phonostylistics' is central to the reading process and may be used on two different planes. Firstly, a text may be seen as a potential *phonotext*; in other words, a text waiting to be read aloud. The oral rendering of a text may be studied with phonetic and stylistic tools. Secondly, a text may be seen as a *graphotext* only, with no intended vocalisation. But, even then, it contains many occurrences of spoken discourse (dialogues in direct speech) or references to spoken discourse (indirect or free indirect speech) that readers tend to read differently from narrative parts. The polyphony of literary texts (Bakhtin 1981) is actualised through the reading process. In this respect, Leech and Short (1981: 160) talk of 'the ear for conversation of a writer' on the encoding side while Raymond Chapman (1994: 15) mentions 'the inner-ear' of the reader on the decoding side of the reading process. Chapman (1994: 25) further explains that it does not really matter whether writers and readers form exactly the same phonetic representation of a character's speech; what matters is that the main deviation from unmarked speech should be made clear.

At this stage, it seems relevant to define what is meant by *phonostylistics*. Nicolaï Trubetskoy (1967), a leading member of the Prague Linguistic Circle and the father of modern phonology, coined the term *laudstylistik* to refer to the individual realisations of speech that play no part in the phonological contrasts in a given language. These features are rarely studied by phoneticians and are usually cast outside linguistic studies. Among them, *permanent features*, which denote age, sex, sociological background and so on, are to be distinguished from *relative features*, which are mainly attitudinal and which vary according to the context in which an utterance takes place. It should also be remembered that both permanent and relative features are, to some extent, language- and culture-specific.

For stylisticians, permanent features are important in terms of characterisation and ought to be taken into consideration. Nevertheless, the most precious information comes from relative features, also known as *paralinguistic vocal features* (PVFs). These may vary enormously in the course of a novel or a short story. The core of this chapter will be devoted to these interpretation-laden features.

Theoretical background

Verbal, non-verbal and multimodal communication

The interest in phonostylistics and paralinguistic features developed in the 1960s with Trager (1958) or Crystal (1963) and was mostly concerned with the phonetic component of these features. Comprehensive studies were carried out at regular intervals in Crystal and Quirk (1964), Crystal and Davy (1969), G. Brown (1990) and Poyatos (1993), but it is only recently that stylisticians have taken the possible developments of 'multimodal communication' on board (Culpeper 2001; Jobert 2003; McIntyre 2008 etc.). 'Multimodal communication' considers both the verbal content of utterances and the other layer of meaning that accompanies speech. Indeed, human interaction is not limited to the verbal content of utterances. Pragmatics has unambiguously demonstrated that linguistic messages only become meaningful in context and that inferences are necessary to interpret them successfully (Grice 1975; Sperber and Wilson 1995). The clues to make such inferences are numerous and include gestures and tone of voice that accompany, or sometimes interrupt, verbal messages. These elements are often dealt with under the umbrella term of 'paralanguage'. However, as Abercrombie (1973) points out, this term gives the impression of a coherent, well-defined and stable field, which is not the case. It is therefore better to avoid the term 'paralanguage', as its definition varies considerably from one author to the next. Crystal provides a selection of possible meanings:

A term used in suprasegmental phonology to refer to *variations in tone of voice* which seem to be less systematic than prosodic features (especially intonation and stress). Examples would include the controlled use of breathy or creaky voice, spasmodic features (such as giggling while speaking), and the use of secondary articulation (such as lip-rounding or nazalization) *to produce a tone of voice signalling attitude, social role or some other language-specific meaning.* Some analysts broaden the definition of paralanguage to include kinesic features; some exclude paralinguistic features from linguistic analysis.   *Crystal (1997: 277)*

Several linguists have tried to account for these 'non-verbal elements' in their descriptive frameworks. Joly and O'Kelly (1989: 32), for instance, present the diagram in Figure 16.1 (my translation).

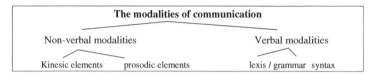

Figure 16.1: The modalities of communication

For these linguists, meaning is the sum of expression plus expressivity. Along the same lines, but from an anthropological viewpoint this time, Fernando Poyatos (1993) presents what he calls the 'basic triple structure' of communication, made up of *language*, *paralanguage* and *kinesics*. He explains the relationship between these three elements as follows:

What makes language-paralanguage-kinesics a functionally cohesive structure . . . is, first of all, their common kinetic generator, and then their combined semanticity and lexicality and their capacity to operate simultaneously, alternate with or substitute for each other as needed in the interactive situation.   *Poyatos (1993: 126)*

It could be argued that Poyatos pushes the comparison between language and kinesics too far, the two systems abiding by dissimilar rules despite many surface similarities. Nonetheless, his approach has the merit of putting these three aspects of communication on an equal footing and counterbalances the traditional bias in favour of the strictly linguistic component.

Paralinguistic vocal features (PVFs)

Gillian Brown's (1990: 112) definition of PVFs provides a sound theoretical starting point for stylisticians:

Paralinguistic features of speech are those which contribute to the expression of attitude by a speaker. They are phonetic features of speech which do not form an intrinsic part of the phonological contrasts which make up the verbal message.

1. **Para-prosodic features**
    Loudness
    Pitch
    Tempo
    Rhythm
    Pause
2. **Vocal qualifiers**
    types of tension
    – articulatory precision (precise / slurred)
    – articulatory setting (tense / lax)
    – lip setting (smiling / pursed)
    types of phonation
    – falsetto voice
    – whispered voice
    – creaky voice
    – harsh /husky voice
    – breathy voice
    peripheral modes
    – culturally coded onomatopoeia ('tsk', 'tut', etc.)
    – intentional cough / throat clearing, etc.
3. **Vocal qualifications**
    Laughter
    Crying
    Sighing

Figure 16.2: Descriptive framework for paralinguistic vocal features

Permanent features are determined by age, sex and so forth, as well as by the speaker's sociological background. These features constitute the speaker's *norm*. Although these features tend to be interpreted during verbal interaction, they do not fall into the category of PVFs, which are attitudinal. It is the *deviation* from these permanent features that will be considered as meaningful. Several descriptive frameworks exist for PVFs, and the question of 'descriptive delicacy' (Leech 2008: 12–13) is crucial as some of these frameworks are rather over-specialised. A phonetic study of PVFs may indeed imply minute distinctions between tiny acoustic differences in pitch or tempo that are often not perceived by the human ear. A study of PVFs in fiction requires a more neutral, less specialised descriptive framework. The framework presented here (Figure 16.2) is an updated version of Jobert (2003) and is an attempt to find a happy balance between theoretical soundness and simplicity of use. It derives from Crystal (1975), G. Brown (1990), Poyatos (1993) and Laver (1994).

All the items present in this descriptive framework would deserve a specific phonetic presentation. For stylistic analysis, suffice to say that they are classified along a 'scale of linguisticness' spreading from the most linguistic features (para-prosodic features) to the least linguistic features (vocal qualifications). It is important to regard all these features as belonging to the same category as they all add meaning to the verbal content of utterances. These relative features are not exclusive and are often used in combination. Some correlations can easily be anticipated (a fast tempo along with a high pitch and a falsetto voice), while others are less likely to occur, but it is extremely difficult to exclude any given combination for certain.

The combination of some of these features is typical of certain attitudes or emotions. However, there is no direct mapping between a given feature and a particular emotion. It has to be remembered that, when dealing with written texts, references to PVFs are not always straightforwardly encoded and that a certain amount of literary convention exists. Although comments of the type '"I love you", she smiled' are frequent, it is extremely rare to come across narrative comments of the type '"I love you", she said with deliberate articulatory precision'.

PVFs in fiction

Several linguists have noted that PVFs are often present in fiction, but only G. Brown (1990) gives literary examples for each and every PVF she presents. Even so, she is more interested in providing examples conveying the phonetic qualities of the different features she presents than in analysing the way they are actually encoded and, more crucially, decoded by readers. When dealing with PVFs, writers can choose to encode either the phonetic feature or the attitudinal feature. Prototypically, two cases of paralinguistic comments exist:

> *She said loudly* (phonetic feature encoded)
> *She said irritably* (attitude encoded)

In either case, a certain amount of inference is needed, and interpreting these comments is heavily context-dependent. Indeed, a loud voice can be triggered by anger or by happiness. Similarly, 'irritably' can be vocally translated as a loud voice or by its opposite, provided other phonetic features accompany the delivery. Similar examples may be found in fiction:

> 'This is beyond every thing!' <u>exclaimed</u> Elinor. [phonetic feature encoded]
> *Jane Austen,* Sense and Sensibility *(Austen 1995: 177)*

For G. Brown (1990: 138–9) 'exclaim' implies an extended pitch span and possibly a marked tempo (either slow or rapid) as well as a marked placing in voice range (either raised or lowered).

> 'Perhaps, then,' he <u>hesitatingly replied</u>, [attitude encoded] 'what I heard this morning may be – there may be more truth in it than I could believe possible at first'.   *Austen 1995: 167*

Following Brown's framework, the adverb 'hesitatingly' could evoke a lowered placing in voice range, a slow tempo, even a pause as indicated in the direct speech (DS). Sometimes, though, both types are encoded simultaneously:

'But have you not received my notes?' <u>cried</u> [phonetic features encoded]
Marianne <u>in the wildest anxiety</u>. [attitude encoded]   *Austen 1995: 149*

Gillian Brown (1990) offers a set of relationships between the reporting verbs or adverbials used and the PVFs. Obviously, these examples do not exhaust all the possibilities. Brown (1990: 114) comments:

> The fact that authors do this, that readers habitually cope with it, and that readers-aloud often adopt the same sorts of paralinguistic features to express a given emotion or attitude, suggests that there are regular, conventional, relationships between some descriptive terms and the paralinguistic features which they evoke.

Authors are pretty much aware of the problem of construing PVFs and sometimes go to great lengths in order to make clear what a particular paralinguistic comment means:

> Hitherto, <u>her voice had been hard</u>, possibly in self-accusation, <u>possibly in defiance</u>. Now it became <u>unmistakably sad</u>. 'Ah, the telegram!'.
> E. M. Forster, Where Angels Fear to Tread *(Forster 1976: 75).*

Finally, PVFs can either corroborate the actual content of an utterance (*redundancy*) or contradict it (*discrepancy*), the latter being rarer in fiction:

> 'Oh yes, I have!' Felix <u>declared, with some spirit</u>; 'before I knew better. But you don't catch me at it again' [redundancy]
> Henry James, The Europeans *(2007: 114)*

> 'Do you know I love you?' the young man said, <u>jocosely</u>, to Isabel. [discrepancy]   Henry James, Portrait of a Lady *(2003: 327)*

As Lyons (1972: 62) points out:

> It seems to be the case that, whenever there is a contradiction between the overt form of a verbal utterance and the associated prosodic and paralinguistic features it is the latter which determine the semiotic classification of the utterance. . . . It may even be the case that we should recognize more than two levels in the selection of the relevant features such as prosodic overrides verbal, so paralinguistic overrides prosodic.

As such, PVFs ought to be regarded as *illocutionary force indicating devices* (IFIDs) (Levinson 1983) and are therefore crucial in terms of characterisation. It could rightly be argued that context or word-order also triggers specific PVFs even if they are not explicitly mentioned. A further distinction could therefore be made between direct PVFs and indirect PVFs. As a first analytical approach, it is easier to concentrate on direct PVFs, what Schötz (2002: 6) calls 'paralinguistic lexica', especially when they accompany DS. It is believed there are about 600 possible substitutes for *said* after DS and that twentieth-century novelists use only about 50 of them in a given novel (Crystal 2003). There are major quantitative differences from one author to the next in the use of these 'prose stage-directions'.

Edith Wharton as a conversationalist

PVFs and style

The phenomenon of paralinguistic encoding seems to peak at the turn of the nineteenth century with authors such as Marcel Proust, John Galsworthy, Henry James or Edith Wharton. It roughly corresponds to the Victorian era in Britain and the Gilded Age in the United States. In the same period, authors were also keen to encode their characters' dialects and idiolects – in other words, their permanent features (R. Chapman 1994; G. Jones 1999). Narrators were rather intrusive and commented copiously on their characters' vocal peculiarities. There is thus a strong correlation between the presence of reporting clauses and PVFs (Bonheim 1982). Writers particularly interested in the inner lives of their characters want to make sure that the psychological portrait they pen is accurately interpreted by their readers. Direct speech is the perfect locus for such explanations provided the author is also a gifted dialogist. In *The Writing of Fiction* (1997: 55), Edith Wharton writes:

> The use of dialogue in fiction seems to be one of the few things about which a fairly definite rule may be laid down. *It should be reserved for the culminating moments, and regarded as the spray into which the great wave of narrative breaks in curving toward the watcher on the shore. This lifting and scattering of the wave, the coruscation of the spray, even the mere material sight of the page broken into short, uneven paragraphs, all help to reinforce the contrast between such climaxes and the smooth effaced gliding of narrative intervals*; and the contrast enhances that sense of the passage of time for the producing of which the writer has to depend on his intervening narration. Thus, the sparing use of dialogue not only serves to emphasize the crises of the tale but to give it as a whole a greater effect of continuous development. (my emphasis)

A cognitive stylistician would no doubt recognise the dichotomy between figure and ground applied to dialogue and narration. This is taken up by Semino (2004: 430) from a technical perspective:

> The use of DS often results in the foregrounding of the utterances it relates to, since it gives us the impression that we are listening directly to the characters' voices, apparently without the mediating interference of the narrator.

This quotation raises an interesting question: to what extent are paralinguistic comments felt as narrative 'interference'? It could be argued that short and unproblematic paralinguistic comments (corroborating the verbal message) of the 'she shouted' type pass unnoticed as they help readers in the interpretation process, whereas longer or problematic paralinguistic comments tend to distract them from the actual content of the DS and so the focus shifts from DS to the comment as such. Many paralinguistic comments tend to be in a middle-of-the-road position, and readerly attention (Stockwell 2002) can sway one way or the other. Bonheim (1982: 76–7) offers a series of statistics regarding the place of the reporting clause. It can occur before DS, after DS or even interrupt DS. It seems that reporting clauses located before DS were very frequent in the eighteenth century but less so in the nineteenth century. Interestingly, reporting clauses interrupting DS have remained rather constant since the eighteenth century. Rivara (2000: 103) discusses the effects of the three types of positioning. He claims that a reporting clause opening up on DS is 'aesthetically unfortunate' and that a reporting clause interrupting DS is more discrete. It would probably be more interesting to consider the three possibilities in the light of the figure and ground dichotomy, while keeping in mind that literary tradition also plays a role in an author's choice.

Edith Wharton's short story 'Copy: A dialogue', published in 1900, is a good starting point as it seems to have been written precisely to make readers aware of paralinguistic encoding. Indeed, the short story is presented as a dramatic script with several stage directions. It is short and there are only three characters interacting: Mrs Dale, a famous novelist; her help, Hilda; and a visitor, Mr Ventnor, a successful poet. The two writers used to be lovers but they have now drifted apart. At the beginning, the reader is simply aware that the characters are on friendly terms. They mention the letters they wrote to each other. For the sake of experiment, let us first read the passage without any stage directions:

> Ventnor.   Your letters.
> Mrs Dale.   My letters – do you remember them?
> Ventnor.   When I don't, I reread them.
> Mrs Dale.   You have them still?
> Ventnor.   You haven't mine, then?
> Mrs Dale.   Oh, *you* were a celebrity already. Of course I kept them! Think what they are worth now! I always keep them locked up in my safe over there.
> Ventnor.   I always carry yours with me.
> Mrs Dale.   You –
> Ventnor.   Whenever I go. I have them now.
> Mrs Dale.   You – have them with you – now?
> Ventnor.   Why not? One never knows –

Readers, more or less consciously, read the script in a certain way and start delineating the psychology of the two characters. If we now read the same extract with the following stage directions, our image of the relationship between the two characters is slightly altered:

Ventnor.	Your letters.
Mrs Dale (*in a changed voice*).	My letters – do you remember them?
Ventnor.	When I don't, I reread them.
Mrs Dale (*incredulous*).	You have them still?
Ventnor (*dejectedly*).	You haven't mine, then?
Mrs Dale (*playfully*).	Oh, *you* were a celebrity already. Of course I kept them! (*smiling*) Think what they are worth now! I always keep them locked up in my safe over there. (*She indicates a cabinet*)
Ventnor (*after a pause*).	I always carry yours with me.
Mrs Dale (*laughing*).	You –
Ventnor.	Whenever I go. (*A longer pause. She looks at him fixedly*). I have them now.
Mrs Dale (*agitated*).	You – have them with you – now?
Ventnor (*embarrassed*).	Why not? One never knows –

The dialogue changes and the impression is that Ventnor is still hopelessly in love while Mrs Dale simply plays with him. If fact, only one adverb has been changed: 'unguardedly' has been replaced by 'dejectedly'. If you reread the passage with the original adverb, the impression is that Ventnor is trying to deceive Mrs Dale, who is caught unaware. In the process, readers discover that the purpose of Mr Ventnor's visit is to retrieve the love letters he wrote to Mrs Dale in order to use them in his memoirs. Here is the original version in full:

Ventnor.	Your letters.
Mrs Dale (*in a changed voice*).	My letters – do you remember them?
Ventnor.	When I don't, I reread them.
Mrs Dale (*incredulous*).	You have them still?
Ventnor (*unguardedly*).	You haven't mine, then?
Mrs Dale (*playfully*).	Oh, *you* were a celebrity already. Of course I kept them! (*smiling*) Think what they are worth now! I always keep them locked up in my safe over there. (*She indicates a cabinet*)
Ventnor (*after a pause*).	I always carry yours with me.
Mrs Dale (*laughing*).	You –
Ventnor.	Whenever I go. (*A longer pause. She looks at him fixedly*). I have them now.
Mrs Dale (*agitated*).	You – have them with you – now?
Ventnor (*embarrassed*).	Why not? One never knows –
	(*Wharton 1900: 113*)

The stage directions indicate how the author intended the sentences to be read (aloud or silently). More interestingly though, they also provide information on the characters' motives. The adverb 'unguardedly' implies that Ventnor has made his first faux pas and that he may have given away the reason for his visit too early. On the other hand, 'playfully' and 'smiling' indicate that Mrs Dale has not picked up on Ventnor's blunder. This, of course, is very basic and slightly coarse precisely because the stage-direction format foregrounds the paralinguistic information to extremes. Still, this short extract shows that PVFs play a major role in information processing, and that a slight change on the paralinguistic plane may have massive consequences regarding interpretation.

In the next extract from the same short story, the density of PVFs increases:

Mrs Dale (*after a long pause*).	Am I dull – or are you trying to say that you want to give me back my letters?
Ventnor (*starting up*).	I? Give you back –? God forbid! Your letters? Not for the world! The only thing I have left! But you can't dream that in *my* hands –
Mrs Dale (*suddenly*).	You want yours, then?
Ventnor (*repressing his eagerness*).	My dear friend, if I'd ever dreamed that you'd kept them –?
Mrs Dale (*accusingly*).	You *do* want them. (*A pause. He makes a deprecatory gesture.*) Why should they be less safe with me than mine with you? I never forfeited the right to keep them.

(Wharton 1900: 117)

On top of the direct PVFs encoded, the syntax becomes more chaotic as indicated by the dashes, with questions and declarations corroborating the paralinguistic encoding. In moments of tension, like this one, the different PVFs used often become more specific, unveiling the characters' thoughts more clearly while advancing the plot.

Case-study: 'Souls Belated'

Narrative warning regarding interpretation

The short story 'Souls Belated' by Wharton, originally published in 1899 by Scribner's, will be used to study PVFs in fiction. Unlike 'Copy: A dialogue', it is written in a traditional fashion and DS is introduced by reporting verbs. As is often the case in Wharton's stories ('The dilettante', 'The last assets' or again 'The other two'), conversation is a major ingredient of the story, not only as a means of characterisation but also as a structuring theme. The plot is simple and revolves around divorce. Lydia is a married woman who has left her husband for Garnett. The entire story is devoted to their accepting this socially *risqué* liaison and the stigmas that will always remain attached to it even if she re-marries. The story opens with the two of them in a train compartment somewhere in Italy. The only other occupant gets off the train as the story begins, leaving the two lovers alone. From the very start, the difficulty to communicate is emphasised:

> He feared to speak as much as she did. It was one of the misfortunes of their situation that they were never busy enough to necessitate, or even to justify, the postponement of unpleasant discussions. If they avoided a question it was obviously, unconcealably because the question was disagreeable. They had unlimited leisure and an accumulation of mental energy to devote to any subject that presented itself; new topics were in fact at a premium. *(Wharton 1990: 81)*

This quotation – which ought to be perceived as a warning by the reader – indicates that the subtle nuances of speech and silence will have to be analysed with great care to make sense of the dialogue. Lydia, the reader is told, has a gift 'for the classification of minute differences . . . and ha[s] learned to distinguish between real and factitious silences' (1990: 82). Similar skills are also required from readers, who will have to attune their ears from the start as the different characters seem to be aware of the value of words and, as most Whartonian characters, are very articulate. Talk is meaningful only for those who can decipher the subtle social codes at work. The first instance of DS in the story is another illustration of this:

> 'Partenza!' shouted the guard [. . .]
>   The guard <u>snapped out</u> a brief *Partenza!* <u>which indicated the purely ornamental nature of the first shout.</u> *(1990: 80, underlining added)*

Not all utterances are what they seem to be, and the implicit or implied meaning is of paramount importance.

The syntax of PVFs

Before studying PVFs in context, it seems relevant to present a few occurrences to get a better picture of what readers have to process and what types are used by the author, her 'paralinguistic signature'. The sheer number of PVFs used creates a *vocalscape* readers become accustomed to as the narrator uses a wide range of possibilities – from the most straightforward to the most complex.

Subject–verb–adverb

This structure can be regarded as a prototypical way of encoding PVFs. This paralinguistic encoding is rather straightforward and can be interpreted attitudinally and/or phonetically. Several examples of the same kind are found in the story:

> ... he said pleasantly. (p.81)
> ... he exclaimed blankly. (p.88)
> ... he said sadly. (p.110)

Slight syntactic changes (subject/verb order or place of the adverb) do not alter the overall effect:

> ... she hastily explained. (p.81)
> ... she hastily emended. (p.87)
> ... said Miss Pinsent sceptically. (p.95)

Subject–verb–prepositional clause

> ... she said at length, in a tone of veiled irritation. (p.93)

The information contained in the prepositional clause is that the character is both irritated and trying to hide it. Because the information is more complex than in the previous examples, a simple adverb is not enough and the narrator has more latitude to express complex feelings with a prepositional clause. Because it is a third-person narrative, it is not clear whether this feeling is perceived by the other participant or whether it is only conveyed to the reader.

> ... he said at length, with less surprise in his voice than she had been prepared for. (p.106)

In this case, the paralinguistic information is conveyed to Lydia since it is from her perspective that the reader is told about Garnett's expression.

> ... he ventured at length, in the tone of a man who feels his way. (p.88)

This particular encoding requires the participation of the reader, as the PVFs encoded are not specified attitudinally or phonetically. There is an implicit comparison and readers are asked to use their encyclopedic knowledge to fill in the information gap. Active readerly participation is sought and the paralinguistic information proper may very well remain obscure. However, the interpretation process is not hindered.

> ... she implored, with a tearful prodigality of italics. (p.91)

Out of context, the meaning of the prepositional clause remains obscure. The purpose of such a comment is to add a humorous touch to the characterisation. The narrator metafictionally refers to authors who use italics to convey expressivity, sometimes too copiously, and does not use italics to do so. At the same time, the narrator manages to indicate that some emotion is being expressed while underscoring the fact that the written medium may sometimes be inadequate or at least too conspicuous to convey the intended meaning.

> ... that lady said, in a rich hard voice that seemed the audible expression of her gown and complexion. (p.97)

Although a clear paralinguistic feature is mentioned (*hard voice*, which defines a certain type of phonation), this first indication is only a step towards a larger, less objective type of characterisation. It is therefore not clear whether what is foregrounded is the PVF or again the clever and humorous characterisation.

Other cases

Although the structure subject–verb is very frequent, reporting clauses of the *he said* type do not provide any paralinguistic information and are therefore not regarded as prototypical. However, some reporting verbs may be enough to provide paralinguistic comments:

> ... she faltered. (p.87)

Sometimes, phrases indicate that the characters are consciously trying to use PVFs as in:

> Lydia tried to speak carelessly (p.87) *or*
> ... she cried, hiding a tremor under the laugh with which she said ... (p.94)

On top of these direct references (some more direct than others) to PVFs, there are some vocal attempts at characterisation not associated with direct speech proper:

> The English are the only people who can lead that kind of life with dignity – those soft-voiced old ladies in Shetland shawls somehow carry the British Empire under their caps. (p.92)

With a subtle hint ('soft-voiced old ladies'), the narrator manages to create a whole fictional world for the benefit of the reader. Because of this rich network of references to paralinguistic information, readers more or less consciously register them and adapt to the different degrees of complexity they display. This brief account does not exhaust the syntactic and semantic resources of paralinguistic coding. However, even this random selection is instructive. Writers usually use PVFs in idiosyncratic ways and it is always useful to know what to expect. Taking a few random examples from, say, Jane Austen's *Pride and Prejudice*, would provide a very different picture. This exercise, which can be repeated with several authors, is a very good way to attune one's sensitivity to paralinguistic phenomena.

PVFs in context

Two questions arise when trying to analyse PVFs in context:

1. What counts as a turn in the conversation?
2. How can we assess whether an utterance is marked paralinguistically or not?

A turn is defined as a stretch of discourse during which a character speaks without being interrupted by another one and without pausing (the pause being indicated by narrative comments such as *he paused* or *he added after a pause* or by a dash). An utterance is regarded as unmarked on the paralinguistic plane when the reporting phrase is neutral, like *she said*, *she asked him* or *she added*. An utterance is regarded as marked on the paralinguistic plane when some emotion is expressed phonetically or attitudinally. Occasionally though, some utterances are difficult to classify:

> 'We are together to-day because we choose to be – don't let us look any farther than that!' She caught his hands. (p.90)

It is difficult to interpret 'she caught his hands'. It is tempting to interpret it as paralinguistically significant because it is included in a network of congruent features (hesitation in the preceding DS, syntactic break and exclamation mark). Furthermore, the preceding and the following utterances are marked. What matters in fact is that analysts should be consistent in their ways of counting un/marked utterances, keeping in mind that a certain amount of subjectivity remains even with computer-mediated devices used in corpus analysis.

When reading a text and looking for paralinguistic lexica, it is obvious that PVFs are not evenly distributed. They tend to appear in clusters in particular moments of tension. In this short story, three major chunks of discourse that are particularly rich in paralinguistic encoding can be identified:

- the first conversation between Lydia and Garnett (pp.86–91)
- the conversation between Lydia and Mrs Cope (pp.97–101)
- the final conversation between Lydia and Garnett (pp.102–10).

This analysis will concentrate on the first conversation between the two main characters. A mini quantitative analysis provides the results in Table 16.1.

Out of the 42 turns in the conversation, 21 can be attributed to Lydia and 21 to Garnett. Although some of Lydia's turns are longer, there is a relative balance between the two. Out of Lydia's 21 turns, 14 carry paralinguistic information (67 per cent), 4 do not (19 per cent) and 3 are difficult to categorise (14 per cent). Out of Garnett's 21 turns, 12 carry paralinguistic information (57 per cent), 8 do not (38 per cent) and 1 has an uncertain status (5 per cent). Phonetic encoding is less used than attitudinal encoding in both cases. Quantitatively then, there seems to be a relative balance

Table 16.1 Table for 'Souls Belated'.

	Lydia	%	Garnett	%
Marked	14	67%	12	57%
Unmarked	4	19%	8	38%
Uncertain	3	14%	1	5%
Total	21		21	

between the two characters with a considerably high rate of marked utterances (well above 50 per cent).

Much more can be gleaned from a qualitative approach. The PVFs associated with Garnett go as follows:

> ... he turned to her <u>with a smile</u> (p.86)
> He looked at her <u>hesitatingly</u> (p.87) – ... he <u>hastily emended</u> (p.87)
> He <u>hesitated</u> again (p.87)
> At length he said, <u>avoiding her eye as carefully as she avoided his</u> (p.87)
> He <u>paused again</u> (p.88)
> He <u>exclaimed blankly</u> (p.88)
> He <u>ventured at length, in the tone of a man who feels his way</u> (p.88)
> He <u>suggested</u> (p.88)
> He <u>said slowly</u> (p.88) – <u>His voice had grown harsh</u> (p.89)
> ... he said <u>at length, slowly</u> (p.89)
> He <u>smiled slightly</u> (p.90)
> Garnett <u>hesitated</u> (p.90)

It is clear that Garnett uses a restricted range of PVFs. 'Hesitation' comes first with 3 direct mentions to which may be added those (4 instances) including a 'hesitant' type of delivery, such as 'at length' and 'he paused', giving a total of 7 out of 12. Three others are tentative or sympathetic (mention of 'smile' and 'suggested'). The remaining 2 appear slightly more petulant. In context though, things are more complex. The first one appears after he mentions marrying Lydia:

> 'I mean after we are married.'
>   She thrust up her chin and turned toward the window. 'Thank you!' she tossed back at him.
>   'Lydia!' he <u>exclaimed blankly</u>; and she felt in every fibre of her averted person that he had made the inconceivable, the unpardonable mistake of anticipating her acquiescence.   *(p.88)*

The adverb 'blankly', which already suggests lack of emotion, diffuses the potential face-threat of the verb 'exclaim'. In fact, it is obvious that Garnett's reaction is simply due to the surprise of being admonished by Lydia, hence his use of the vocative. In the second instance, the context helps explain Garnett's sudden shift in paralinguistic register:

> 'But I don't *want* to marry you!' <u>she cried</u>.
>   She saw that he turned pale. 'I'm obtuse, I suppose,' he said slowly. 'I confess I don't see what you're driving at. Are you tired of the whole business? Or was I simply a-an excuse for getting away? Perhaps you didn't care to travel alone? Was that it? And now you want to chuck me?' <u>His voice had grown harsh</u>. 'You owe me a straight answer, you know; don't be tenderhearted'.   *(pp.88–9)*

As in the previous instance, it is because Lydia threatens his negative face (P. Brown and Levinson 1978) that a change occurs, and his voice turning harsh is due to the fact that he is about to be faced with a reality he resents. He is in fact pleading to be told the truth.

In terms of characterisation, this brief analysis of the PVFs used by the character indicates that he is possibly weak and, in any case, irresolute. In this sense, Garnett is a typically Whartonian male character.

The PVFs associated with Lydia are different:

> ... she faltered (p.87)
> Lydia tried to speak carelessly (p.87)
> ... she objected (p.87)
> She flamed with sympathy and self-reproach (p.87)
> She faced him (p.88)
> She interrupted (p.88)
> ... she tossed back at him (p.88)
> ... she moaned (p.88)
> ... she cried (p.88)
> ... she flushed (p.89)
> ... she interrupted herself with a laugh (p.90)
> She thought she had scored a point and followed it passionately (p.90)
> She caught his hands (p.90)
> ... she implored, with a tearful prodigality of italics (p.91)

The gamut of emotions covered by Lydia is wider, as the reporting verbs indicate: *faltered*, *objected*, *interrupted*, *moaned*, *cried*, *flushed* and so on. Contrary to what a cursory glance at the PVFs might reveal, there is a clear shift in Lydia's attitude during the dialogue. In this sense, it is different from Garnett, who is rather consistent. Indeed, at the beginning of the conversation, she proves ill at ease but easy-going. Yet, 'she objected' and 'she flamed with sympathy and self-reproach' seem to stand out.

> 'But we can't travel forever, can we?'
>
>   'Oh, forever's a long word,' she objected, picking up the review he had thrown aside'
>
>   (p.87)

Her actual objection is in fact a way for her to postpone her answer rather than a way to contradict what Garnett has stated. Her gestures (picking up the magazine) indicate she is not prepared to stick to the subject. Similarly, 'she flamed with sympathy and self-reproach', although it is charged emotionally, is directed towards herself. Things change drastically when Garnett mentions marriage. From then on, the PVFs are explicitly more face-threatening, starting with 'She faced him', which literally indicates that she accepts direct confrontation. Lydia's anger increases throughout the passage. Her laugh ('She interrupted herself with a laugh', p.90) does not indicate that she distances herself from the situation but rather that she is convinced Garnett does not take the full measure of what she is actually saying. Her determination culminates at the end of the first part of the short story:

> She thought she had scored a point and followed it up passionately. 'you do understand, don't you? You see how the very thought of the thing humiliates me! We are together to-day because we choose to be – don't let us look any farther than that!' She caught his hands. '*Promise* me you'll never speak of it again; promise me you'll never *think* of it even,' she implored, with a tearful prodigality of italics.   *(pp.90–1)*

Although the PVFs used indicate she is being kinder than before ('she implored'), it makes no doubt her determination to obtain what she wants is intact, as the first paralinguistic comment makes clear: 'followed it up passionately'. This indication is actually a comment on the following statements uttered by Lydia. The others are therefore to be regarded as a way of exposing her clever rhetoric. Indeed, taking Garnett's hands and imploring are to be construed as slightly contrived. The obscure comment 'with tearful prodigality of italics', which is hard to interpret on its own, takes its full ironic dimension here. She is playing a role and over-doing it, the narrator seems to suggest. Furthermore, Lydia's tirade is framed by two narrative comments that put her utterances in perspective:

> He looked at her hopelessly. Nothing is more perplexing to man than
> the mental process of a woman who reasons her emotions.   *(p.90)*

Whartonian characters are prone to 'reason their emotions', and readers who want to have access to their minds must be prepared for this task and possess the adequate tools to decipher the tiniest vocal inflections. However, Wharton makes sure she does not side too obviously with one of her characters and she adopts an ironical perspective on both:

> They had reached that memorable point in every heart-history when,
> for the first time, the man seems obtuse and the woman irrational.   *(p.91)*

In this short story, Lydia is about to divorce her husband and although Garnett is ready to marry her, she fears the social stigmas will remain. This accounts for the fact that her behaviour should be that of a victim making desperate attempts to go on with her life. Interestingly, in the story, a woman sharing her condition is shunned by the well-to-do guests of the hotel. The woman in question, Mrs Linton, confronts Lydia about their common predicament. All of this is mostly conveyed through dialogue: society's implacable rigidity is heard in the subtle undertones voiced by the most conservative exponents of convention while individuals struggle to live the lives they have chosen. This motif is to be found in many of Wharton's short stories and novels and most remarkably so in *The Age of Innocence*.

Concluding remarks

This chapter does not exhaust all the possible uses and implications of PVFs as interpretative tools. However, several observations can be made. Theoretically, PVFs ought to be regarded as a coherent whole rather than a set of random features to be called upon if and when necessary. The descriptive framework chosen must be user-friendly even for non-phoneticians. The gap between phonetic descriptive minutia and what is usually perceived by the human ear has to be bridged. The framework used has to be adapted then to what is usually found in fiction. The discrepancy between PVFs and their written representations has to be taken into account.

Practically speaking, paralinguistic encoding is to be regarded as a dynamic process, and the analysis of short extracts shows that PVFs do not work at sentence but at discourse level. Paralinguistic vocal features can be forward or backward pointing and apply to smaller or longer stretches of dialogue. A particular paralinguistic comment may remain active over a number of turns or simply apply to the chunk of DS it is attached to. From this perspective, a quantitative analysis is often insufficient and may very well turn out to be misleading.

Paralinguistic vocal features ought to become part and parcel of the stylistician's tool-box as they are explicit emotion markers that can reveal the illocutionary force of an utterance. Some follow-up work should be carried out on the way PVFs are taken into account when reading aloud, comparing for instance a paralinguistic analysis to a recording of a text. Another field of research could also be devoted to the translation of PVFs, thus highlighting cultural similarities and differences.

17

Grammatical configuration

Michaela Mahlberg

Introduction

Research in literary stylistics analyses linguistic features of texts to explain literary or aesthetic effects as perceived by readers. The value of such an approach is, as Carter (1982: 67) points out, that 'some linguistic analysis of a literary text is essential if something other than a merely intuitive or impressionistic account of the story is to be given'. It will depend on the text under investigation which linguistic categories and frameworks are most useful for the task; as analysts, we have 'the full array of language models at our disposal' (Simpson 2004: 3). In spite of the range of choice, there are some basic units and levels of language description that are typically drawn on in stylistic analyses. For most approaches to grammar a fundamental assumption about the relationship of linguistic units is expressed through the 'rank scale'. According to the rank scale, larger linguistic units consist of smaller ones. On this scale, morphemes are the smallest meaningful units of grammar and from there units move up to clauses:

> clause
> phrase
> word
> morpheme

The linguistic units relate to the levels of linguistic description or branches of linguistics: morphology deals with the structure of words, lexicology with the vocabulary of a language, and grammar or syntax accounts for how words combine into phrases and clauses. Depending on the approach, terminology may vary as to whether something is called a noun 'phrase' or a noun 'group'. How a rank scale is perceived to continue above the clause is also a matter for debate. Sometimes sentences are regarded as units above clauses, which already highlights limitations of a neat and tidy account of grammatical units, as a definition of the 'sentence' is more readily applicable to written than to spoken language. And if the sentence was an acceptable unit, would there be any textual unit above it, so that branches of linguistics like text linguistics could be accommodated as well?

Nevertheless, basic grammatical units already have value for the analysis of literary texts. Grammatical categories are useful to label and identify features in a literary text so it is possible to make observations that, for instance, describe the preponderance of evaluative adjectives in a text, or point out that most clauses contain subordinate clauses. Such observations are only the first step and do not constitute an analysis in themselves. An analysis will seek to explain and understand the functions that are fulfilled by the grammatical categories and their configurations in the specific text under analysis. Grammar, as a set of rules about the patterns in a language, also plays a role in textual analysis by providing a norm against which particular patterns in a text can be assessed. When such patterns deviate from the general norms of the language they can create effects accounted for in stylistics by the concept of psychological foregrounding. The notion of creativity is often evoked as a typical quality of literary texts not conforming to the norms of the language. However, the 'general norms' of the language are not easily captured and creativity is more pervasive in language than its restriction to literary texts would suggest (see Carter 2004). At the same time, literary texts do not only exhibit creative language use. There are also linguistic patterns that are typical of literary texts such as novels.

What the stylistically significant units for analysis are depends on the individual qualities of a text. Still, Leech and Short (2007: 61) provide a list of categories which are 'good bets' or likely to find stylistically relevant information. This list refers, for instance, to different word classes, clause types or the structure of clauses. In this sense it is similar to the way in which other introductions to stylistics begin an overview of potentially relevant linguistic categories with reference to the rank scale (e.g. Jeffries and McIntyre 2010; Simpson 2004).

My aim in this chapter is to present examples of linguistic units and grammatical configurations that contribute to the creation of meaning in literary texts. These units might not always easily fit a rank scale in the more traditional sense but originate from a corpus-linguistic approach to the description of language. The chapter begins with a discussion of corpus views on grammar that leads to the introduction of the notion of 'local grammar'. Corpus-linguistic descriptions require a critical mass of evidence to find patterns. Hence it may not immediately be clear how corpus methods can support the qualitative analysis of a short text extract – a task that is essential to practical stylistics. To demonstrate the applicability of a corpus approach to literary analysis, the chapter first discusses a textual example before it contextualises this discussion through reference to more general literary patterns identified with the help of corpus methods. The text extract is from Dickens's *Bleak House*. It illustrates a conversation that is then interrupted by a pause. This extract serves to illustrate two functional areas that appear to be relevant to the construction of a local grammar of speech presentation.

Corpus grammar

In an article advocating the potential of corpus linguistics for the compilation of grammars, Aarts (2000: 24) observes that 'In the course of the century, a sort of canon of syntactic phenomena and their corresponding rules has come into existence, which has more or less fixed the "image of English" as perceived by grammarians'. This canon of syntactic or grammatical phenomena is also reflected in research in literary stylistics and in checklists of 'good bets'. However, the development of corpus linguistics is showing increasing impact on approaches to grammar. Biber et al. (1999) take a fresh view on canonical categories with the help of frequency information that specifically focuses on the distribution of linguistic phenomena across registers. Additionally, their grammar includes a section on 'lexical bundles' – in other words, 'the sequences of words that most commonly occur in a register' (Biber et al. 1999: 989). Lexical bundles that are common in conversation include examples such as *do you want me to* or *I don't know what*. The frequency of lexical bundles relates to the functions that they fulfil in a register. The personal pronouns in the examples from conversation reflect the interpersonal nature of casual spoken language. Examples from academic prose, such as *it should be noted that* or *there was no significant* indicate differences between the registers (Biber et al. 1999: 989). Lexical bundles are not necessarily structurally complete units so that their form points towards how they are integrated into their textual context. Biber et al. (1999: 989) see lexical bundles as representing the 'lexical end of grammar'.

An even more radical approach is the Pattern Grammar of Hunston and Francis (2000). They build their grammar on the fundamental observation that patterns and meanings are associated. They define the 'patterns' of a word as 'all the words and structures which are regularly associated with the word and which contribute to its meaning' (Hunston and Francis 2000: 37). Different meanings of a word tend to be distinguished by different patterns, and if different words have the same pattern they tend to share an aspect of meaning. On this basis, a pattern grammar is a collection of patterns of words that are grouped together and cross-referenced in a number of ways to usefully show meaning relationships. While Hunston and Francis (2000) provide the theoretical and methodological background, Francis et al. (1996, 1998) illustrate what a pattern grammar can look like for patterns of nouns, adjectives and verbs.

An example of a verb pattern is **V *at* n**, where the verb (V) is followed by a prepositional phrase, consisting of *at* and a noun group (see Francis et al. 1996: 163). The words that occur with a pattern are divided into 'meaning groups'; an example of such a group for **V *at* n** is the 'look' group, described as verbs that are 'concerned with looking at something or someone. Most of them indicate the manner of the looking or the attitude or emotion of the person looking' (Francis et al. 1996: 166). In addition to the verb *look* other members of the group include *gape, gaze, glance, goggle, peep, stare* and so on.

Another innovative approach to grammar enabled through reference to corpus data is presented by Carter and McCarthy (2006). A key feature of their grammar is the emphasis that patterns of spoken language receive so that the traditional imbalance in favour of written language as the basis for grammatical description is overcome. It is essential to Carter and McCarthy's (2006) approach that differences between spoken and written language are accounted for. So their grammar stresses that speakers and writers have choices for which the context in which the language is produced plays a crucial role. Carter and McCarthy (2006: 9–11) also argue that spoken phenomena deserve their own terminology if terms originating from the description of written language do not seem appropriate to capture spoken data. Similar to Biber et al. (1999), Carter and McCarthy (2006) also pay specific attention to sequences of words that often occur together. Although they refer to them as 'clusters' (Carter and McCarthy 2006: 15), these groups of words are similar to Biber et al.'s (1999) lexical bundles.

What all three of these approaches to grammar have in common is the emphasis they give to patterns that need the cumulative evidence from corpus data to become recognisable in the first instance or to become describable in terms of frequency. All three also illustrate that for the creation of meanings in texts (as represented in a corpus), patterns around lexical items play a more important role than more canonical grammars suggest. Such patterns require new terminology and still more research to be fully understood. Innovative corpus approaches to grammar necessarily have implications for literary stylistics. For one, they can help to provide a more detailed account of the norms of the language – and variation on the norms – against which examples from literary texts can be assessed. Additionally, new linguistic units might be added to the candidates that are likely to be useful in stylistic analysis.

Beyond these implications, a question is whether corpus approaches might change the way in which a grammar is seen to account for literary language. Biber et al. (1999) include fictional prose as one of the four registers that they refer to for frequency comparisons of grammatical phenomena. This inclusion is in line with Carter's (2004) argument that a distinction between literary and non-literary language as such is an unhelpful one. Still, it might be useful to consider how far a grammar could go in including specific linguistic phenomena that occur more frequently in literary texts, similar to the way in which Carter and McCarthy (2006) emphasise the choices that speakers or writers make and that are reflected in preferred patterns for specific contexts of use. While a more comprehensive account of the variation of grammatical phenomena across literary and non-literary texts is clearly useful, this alone does not seem to be enough. In a review of the position of literary stylistics, Sinclair (2007: 4) argues that

> There was, and is, no lack of ingenious application of linguistic categories to literary works, ... but there is no theory to explain how the patterns relate to meaning, ... no detailed, comprehensive descriptive apparatus that is flexible enough to accommodate the extremely varied language of literature.

To improve this situation, Sinclair (2007) suggests the adoption of 'local grammars'. Local grammars can be used to describe areas of the language or patterns of textual organisation that do not fit easily into a highly generalisable system of grammatical categories (Hunston and Sinclair 2000: 75). Hunston and Sinclair (2000) exemplify the concept with a local grammar of evaluation that focuses on structures in which evaluative adjectives and nouns occur. Another example is provided by Barnbrook and Sinclair (1995), who develop a local grammar for the language of the definitions in the Collins COBUILD English Dictionaries. Sinclair (2007) concentrates on a verse paragraph in Pope's 'An Essay on Man' and develops a local grammar for this paragraph. This local grammar describes the rhetorical structure of the paragraph with reference to a hierarchy that contains the units 'paragraph', 'segment' and 'passage'. Sinclair (2007) argues that this rhetorical structure organises the argumentation of the text. Although he only discusses one verse paragraph, Sinclair (2007: 19) suggests that his local grammar should be applicable to more paragraphs of this poem and other poems by Pope or even by his contemporaries. Sinclair's (2007) textual example is quite short and leaves the wider applicability of his local grammar for future research to test. In the following, I want to take a somewhat different approach to the concept of local grammar. I will discuss a short text extract, too, but with reference to local patterns that have been identified on the basis of a larger corpus.

An example of fictional speech

In this section I begin with an example from Dickens's novel *Bleak House* (1852–3). First, I focus on the grammatical configurations of the extract that appear to be most striking. Then I elaborate on these initial observations by drawing on more general patterns in *Bleak House* and a corpus of Dickens novels and other nineteenth-century fiction (Mahlberg 2013a).

However, the present section does not yet contain explanation on how these more general patterns were identified and what their wider relevance is. These points will be addressed in the following section, which begins to outline aspects of what might be developed into a local grammar of speech presentation. The division between this section and the next aims to begin with the focus on a specific text extract displaying stylistically relevant features that do not need the context of corpus research to become noticeable. Still, through reference to more general – although not necessarily obvious – patterns, it is shown how the grammatical configurations of the text extract contribute to the negotiation of meanings in this example.

The extract is from Chapter 11 of *Bleak House*. In this chapter Tulkinghorn and Krook find the body of Nemo. The extract begins when Miss Flite has just been sent to fetch Snagsby. The paragraphs of the extract are numbered for convenience.

(1)   While she is gone, the surgeon abandons his hopeless investigation and covers its subject with the patchwork counterpane. Mr. Krook and he interchange a word or two. Mr. Tulkinghorn says nothing, but stands, ever, near the old portmanteau.

(2)   Mr. Snagsby arrives hastily in his grey coat and his black sleeves. 'Dear me, dear me,' he says; 'and it has come to this, has it! Bless my soul!'

(3)   'Can you give the person of the house any information about this unfortunate creature, Snagsby?' inquires Mr. Tulkinghorn. 'He was in arrears with his rent, it seems. And he must be buried, you know.'

(4)   'Well, sir,' says Mr. Snagsby, coughing his apologetic cough behind his hand, 'I really don't know what advice I could offer, except sending for the beadle.'

(5)   'I don't speak of advice,' returns Mr. Tulkinghorn. 'I could advise—'

(6)   'No one better, sir, I am sure,' says Mr. Snagsby, with his deferential cough.

(7)   'I speak of affording some clue to his connexions, or to where he came from, or to anything concerning him.'

(8)   'I assure you, sir,' says Mr. Snagsby after prefacing his reply with his cough of general propitiation, 'that I no more know where he came from than I know—'

(9)   'Where he has gone to, perhaps,' suggests the surgeon to help him out.

(10)   A pause. Mr. Tulkinghorn looking at the law-stationer. Mr. Krook, with his mouth open, looking for somebody to speak next.

(Charles Dickens, Bleak House, *e-text from Project Gutenberg)*

Starting with the more canonical grammatical categories, the most striking passage of this abstract is its last paragraph. The paragraph contains three sentences, but none of these contains a finite verb. The first one does not even contain a verb but consists merely of a noun phrase. The second and the third sentence have a parallel structure: in each case the subject is a fictional character and the non-finite verb is *look*. However, *look* has different meanings in each sentence, as indicated by the different prepositions that follow the verb. Also the third sentence contains an additional prepositional phrase, *with his mouth open*. Because of its lack of (finite) verbs, this last paragraph recalls the opening of the novel that so frequently has served for the purpose of illustrating stylistic analyses (see, for example, Simpson 2004: 63–6). In the opening of the novel, too, there are clause patterns without finite verbs. These patterns do not indicate tense. Hence, they contribute a sense of timelessness to the atmosphere created by the all-pervasive fog. In the present example, the lack of tense indication is also relevant. The non-finite verbs emphasise the break in the conversation. Up to paragraph 9 there is a sequence of turns of character speech and finite reporting clauses, which reflect the progression of the narrative. Instead of character speech, the opening of paragraph 10 is the one-phrase sentence 'A pause.' The sentences following do not lack verbs entirely, but they lack an indication of tense. Instead of the progression of the conversation they emphasise the duration of the pause. Tulkinghorn keeps looking at Snagsby and Krook holds back speaking until the pause ends and Snagsby talks again in the paragraph that follows.

This break can be described not only in terms of the unusual structure of the sentences but also in relation to more general patterns of the presentation of fictional speech that might be argued contribute to a local grammar of speech presentation in narrative fiction. One pattern becomes apparent when Snagsby's speech is presented. In each case, the reporting clause contains circumstantial information providing detail on the manner in which Snagbsy speaks: 'coughing his apologetic cough behind his hand', 'with his deferential cough', 'after prefacing his reply with his cough of general propitiation'. In each case, the detail refers to a characteristic feature of Snagsby. When he first appears in Chapter 10 his characteristic habit is introduced: 'Mr. Snagsby, as a timid man, is accustomed to cough with a variety of expressions, and so to save words.' The striking description of character information in the text extract relates to more general patterns of body language presentation. Such patterns are often realised in the form of *–ing* clauses or prepositional phrases, which is also relevant to the final paragraph of the extract.

The sentence 'A pause' replaces the direct speech of the characters. Compare this sentence with: *There is a pause*. This existential clause would give more emphasis to the presence of the narrator, whereas *A pause* suggests the pattern of characters' speech turns is continued. As the characters do not actually say anything, there is no reporting clause. Still, there is a similarity with the grammatical pattern of reporting clauses containing descriptions of characters in the form of non-finite clauses. The second sentence of the last paragraph could be part of a reporting clause: *said Mr. Tulkinghorn looking at the law-stationer*. The non-finite *looking* seems to mainly emphasise the duration of the pause during which

Tulkinghorn is looking at Snagsby waiting for him to speak. However, it fits a larger pattern of character information for Tulkinghorn. The verb *look* often appears in patterns where the direction of gaze is accompanied with circumstantial information on the manner of the looking.

In the extract, an adverb to accompany *looking* might be for instance *impatiently*. Tulkinghorn is trying to get information from Snagsby. He already has to correct the law-stationer when he misunderstands his question and the surgeon helps finish Snagsby's sentence. So the information Tulkinghorn is after is only forthcoming very slowly. However, the fact that there is no information on the manner in which Tulkinghorn looks at Snagbsy fits the pattern with which the lawyer usually behaves. Throughout the novel he is portrayed as distant and unemotional. In the present chapter, the fact that he does not tend to show emotions is also highlighted. For instance, while Krook and the surgeon are engaged in a conversation about the dead man, Tulkinghorn stands 'aloof by the old portmanteau, with his hands behind him, equally removed, to all appearance, from all three kinds of interest exhibited near the bed'. His face is described as 'imperturbable' and 'inexpressive'. The unmodified description of his gaze behaviour can be interpreted as relating to his inexpressive face.

In the extract, Tulkinghorn's unemotional character and his loftiness are contrasted with Snagsby. Tulkinghorn's reporting clauses are only short, or there is not even a reporting clause and his speech presented in free direct form (paragraph 5). For Snagsby, in contrast, there is almost excessive reference to his cough in the reporting clauses. The cough is 'apologetic', 'deferential' or expressive of 'general propitiation', underlining in each instance Snagsby's submissive behaviour. In addition to the meanings associated with the cough its structural patterns further add to the picture. The information is twice presented in the form of a suspended question (paragraphs 4 and 8): that is, the reporting clause does not follow the character speech but interrupts it (Lambert 1981). This form of presenting reporting clauses complements the patterns of interruptions by the characters in the turn-taking of the conversation. Paragraphs 5 and 6 show how Snagsby interrupts Tulkinghorn and paragraphs 8 and 9 indicate an interruption of Snagsby by the surgeon. Both interruptions are signalled through hyphens at the end of syntactically incomplete phrases: 'I could advise—' and 'than I know—'. Functionally, the interruptions can be interpreted more as overlaps and co-operative conversational behaviour than interruptions to take the turn. In paragraph 6 Snagsby's 'No one better, sir, I am sure' shows agreement with Tulkinghorn underlined by Snagsby's deferential cough, which resembles co-operative overlaps in real speech. Tulkinghorn is not interrupted in making his point, indicated by his reformulation 'I speak of', which continues the turn he started with 'I don't speak of'. In paragraph 9, the surgeon completes Snagsby's sentence. However, what seems to be intended as co-operative behaviour on the part of the surgeon (he wants to help Snagsby) leads up to the pause in the conversation, before Snagsby is able to provide more information. Additionally, through the suspended quotations, Snagsby's speech is interrupted by the voice of the narrator. Together these patterns reflect the slow progress that Snagsby makes answering Tulkinghorn's question. Only after the pause he then begins to provide more substantial information.

A local grammar of speech presentation

Local grammars can be developed to describe grammatical structures of very specific areas of the language that are not easily covered by a general grammar. Local grammars complement and work in conjunction with a more general model of grammar. Their terminology is 'semantically suggestive' and 'indicates the area of meaning' (Hunston and Sinclair 2000: 79). Hence category labels tend to be more transparent than in highly generalised systems and indicate how the structures are part of the creation of meanings in texts. Hunston and Sinclair, for instance, are interested in the discourse functions of patterns of evaluation. They point out that '[s]tretches of texts to be handled by local grammars have to be identified in some way' (Hunston and Sinclair 2000: 78) and their work illustrates this by focusing on evaluation sentences. They also suggest that local grammars can form a useful basis for automatic parsing. The way in which I use the concept of local grammar in this chapter is slightly different with regard to the clearly defined selectiveness of the grammar and the optimism about its automatisation. In the present approach, the main features of a local grammar are its applicability to a specific area of the language and the emphasis on the kind of functional interpretation that addresses the negotiation of meanings in texts.

The presentation of fictional speech is such a specific area of the language. For one, it is limited to a specific type of text. I use 'speech' to refer to direct speech only; in other words, disregarding other forms of speech, such as indirect speech, or thought and writing presentation. Fictional speech and its presentation only fit the categories of a general grammar to some extent. It is similar to real spoken language but at the same time also fundamentally different from it. Main differences result from the fact that spoken language is affected by the pressures of real-time processing. Some of the formal reflections of these pressures (e.g. filled pauses) tend not to be represented in fictional speech unless they have a specific effect. Speech in fiction is planned and carefully edited. Structural features of the presentation of fictional speech, on the other hand, are less central in a general grammar. It is important to point out that speech (thought and writing) presentation as such is in fact relevant to registers other than fiction, as Semino and Short (2004) have clearly shown with their comparative approach based on corpus data. However, fiction contains patterns that are particularly relevant to the register. These patterns partly reflect the existence of different discourse levels in fiction. Fictional direct speech represents the communication between characters but is accompanied by patterns of presentation that show the presence of a narrator.

In this chapter, a local grammar is loosely defined as a set of local textual functions that capture a specific area of meaning. The area of meaning on which the following initial version of a local grammar of speech presentation focuses is the creation of characters. Hence this focus shapes the identification of categories and the labels used for them. It is clear that there are obvious links to accounts of discourse presentation. In the present discussion, however, these links are less central. The units that the local grammar concentrates on are instances of direct speech typically enclosed in quotation marks and their reporting clauses (or stretches of narration with similar function but that may not contain a reporting verb).

The concept of local textual functions that is central to the present version of a local grammar has been developed in the context of corpus linguistics to capture patterns of words and their functions in texts. Local textual functions describe meanings of items in texts; in this sense they are 'textual'. The functions are 'local' because they do not capture general functions, but functions specific to a (group of) text(s) and/or specific to a (group of) lexical item(s) (Mahlberg 2005, 2007b, 2013a). In Mahlberg (2013a) I have used clusters as a starting point to identifying local textual functions. While the present chapter makes reference to key findings from Mahlberg (2013), the focus for local textual functions and the associated grammar is not on clusters, but is widened to include textual patterns. While the present view is local, it is not comprehensive and other patterns and functions may be identified that fit with this initial suggestion of a local grammar. The present account is also only partial because the functions discussed here relate to the example in the previous section. Local textual functions relevant to the text extract mainly fall under the following headings.

1. Manner of speaking and body language
2. Time and timing

These functions describe how patterns of meanings work in literary texts to contribute to the creation of fictional characters. In addition to these three aspects that relate to the fictional world, the integration of the patterns into their textual contexts is described through the notion of the continuum of contextualising and highlighting functions. This continuum makes it possible to describe the functions within each category. For the following discussion it is important to note that some of the generalisations that are drawn on for explanation are based on corpus research that cannot be reproduced or summarised in the space of this chapter; for detailed discussions see Mahlberg (2012, 2013a) or Mahlberg and Smith (2010). However, I want to argue that as more patterns are studied with the help of corpus methods, the insights from this work can serve as a backdrop for the analysis of individual text extracts. A local grammar might be a way to capture and describe such relevant information and the present section suggests a first step in this direction.

Manner of speaking and body language

In the extract from *Bleak House* Snagsby's cough is referred to repeatedly. His habit of speaking with a meaningful cough fits a more general pattern of body language or non-verbal communication. When it accompanies speech, body language is commonly presented in the form of *–ing* clauses or prepositional phrases. These structures can suggest the body language and speech occur simultaneously, as is typically the case in real-life communication. Snagsby's cough is presented as a characteristic feature of his. In the extract, the repetition contributes to a highlighting function.

Examples of contextualising body language are the following. They support the meaning of what is being said without reflecting habits of a specific fictional character. Examples (1) and (2) illustrate conventional gestures and (3) practical actions.

(1) 'That was the time!' says Krook *with a nod.*

(2) 'No, guv'ner,' returns Phil, *shaking his head.* 'No, I shouldn't.'

(3) 'Now, little housewife,' said my guardian, *looking at his watch,* 'I was strictly timed before I came upstairs . . .'

In the *Bleak House* extract contextualising functions are relevant to the account of Tulkinghorn 'looking at the law-stationer'. Generally, the eyes are seen as a way of providing insights into a character's inner life and eye movement can convey a range of meanings in fictional text. Figure 17.1 is a sample of concordance lines for *looking at* in *Bleak House*. The 20 lines

```
1  ll in a day or two,' said Mr. Woodcourt, looking at her with an observant smile,
2  ther better than you know me?' she said, looking at him again. 'Yes, we happened
3  ut, George, old man!' cries Mrs. Bagnet, looking at him curiously. 'What's come
4  ds is well. 'Aye, aye?' says the lawyer, looking at him from under his bent brow
5  ter with you, Tony?' inquires Mr. Guppy, looking at him, snuffers in hand, as he
6  found you at last!' 'Jo,' repeats Allan, looking at him with attention, 'Jo! Sta
7  ow, little housewife,' said my guardian, looking at his watch, 'I was strictly t
8  ur service.' 'Let me see,' said Richard, looking at his watch. 'If I run down to
9   subdued voice, addressing him but still looking at his wife, 'I am sorry you ta
10 st place,' returns Mr. George, but still looking at Judy as if she being so old
11 blew a little dust off the pickled pork, looking at me again; 'and when ladies a
12 I made up my mind, besides,' said Caddy, looking at me hopefully but timidly, 't
13  she was so well spoken,' said the girl, looking at me with wide open eyes, 'tha
14 ing on 'em.' And Jo stands shivering and looking at the breakfast wonderingly. A
15 ss carpet. 'Sir,' returns Vholes, always looking at the client as if he were mak
16 r pleasure, day by day?' she asks, still looking at the distant sky. 'Yes, I am
17 emember, my plain dear,' I asked myself, looking at the glass, 'what Mrs. Woodco
18 Chesney Wold.' Humph!' Mr. George stands looking at these boxes a long while-as
19 y?' said my guardian, stopping short and looking at us hopefully. 'What do you t
20 e Nonpareil battalion,' said Mr. Bagnet, looking at us over his shoulder as he w
```

Figure 17.1: A sample of concordance lines for *looking at* in *Bleak House*

are all of the cases (out of a total of 89 occurrences of *looking at*) where the eye movement accompanies speech and is described in a reporting clause (or a clause without reporting verb, but with a similar function) following the speech of a character. The lines are sorted to the words on the right of *looking at*. The following observations can be drawn from this concordance sample. The direction of gaze can very simply support the turn-taking in a conversation, as in line 2. Here Lady Dedlock looked out of the window before continuing the conversation and this continuation is reflected by *looking at him again*. Line 7 is presented in greater length as example (3) above illustrating practical actions. The concordance sample also includes patterns of adverbs (*curiously, hopefully but timidly*), prepositional phrases (*with an observant smile, with attention*) or *as if* clauses (lines 10, 15) that all provide detail on the meaning of the eye language in the text.

Body language presented as contextualising can still add character information, but this information is less striking than features associated with repetitive formal patterns as in the case of Snagsby's cough – a highlighting pattern. Woodcourt's smile in line 1 is not part of such a highlighted pattern, but still it fits the overall picture that is created of Woodcourt. Line 4, produced as extended example (4), refers to Tulkinghorn and shows that contextualising and highlighting are not absolute categories but are a matter of degree. Guppy has just addressed Tulkinghorn, whose body language provides further exemplification of his arrogance and loftiness. However, the body language is not presented as a fixed or repeatedly occurring pattern. The highlighting in this context is achieved through the additional comment 'though he has no need to look again – not he', where the repetition of *not he* indicates a transition to free indirect thought.

> (4) 'Aye, aye?' says the lawyer, looking at him from under his bent brows, though he has no need to look again – not he. 'From Kenge and Carboy's, surely?'

This background of the *looking at* pattern comes into play for the meanings evoked by the final paragraph of the *Bleak House* extract. In 'Mr. Tulkinghorn looking at the law-stationer', the direction of the gaze can be interpreted as part of the turn-taking. In the previous paragraph the surgeon completes Snagsby's sentence. Tulkinghorn may (or may not) have looked at the surgeon, but he expects Snagsby to continue and answer his initial question. Because of the slow progressing conversation, an adverbial might be added to reflect Tulkinghorn's dissatisfaction with the situation – in line with the type of patterns illustrated by the concordance sample. However, it seems more fitting with Tulkinghorn's character to not provide any information on emotions. Together with the non-finite form of the verb emphasising the duration, Tulkinghorn's 'looking' appears unemotional or even compassionless, because the previous text has shown Snagsby struggling to find his way into the conversation. Additionally, Tulkinghorn's 'looking at' is contrasted with Krook's 'looking for' in the next sentence. The 'somebody' he is looking for might or might not be Snagsby and, because Krook has his mouth open, he appears to be tempted to speak himself. Eventually, however, Tulkinghorn's authority makes Snagsby end the pause.

Time and timing

The area of time meanings is highlighted in the text extract very strikingly through three sentences without indication of time. How the reader perceives the length of the pause depends partly on the cumulative effect of the preceding text. The indefiniteness of the narrated time of the pause might in part also be explained through comparison with body language patterns. When *–ing* clauses or prepositional phrases suggest that body language occurs simultaneously with the speech it accompanies, this provides an indication of the duration of the body language. In examples (1) to (3) above, the nod, the shaking of the head and the looking at the watch all appear to be relatively short. The relationship of simultaneity mainly holds for contextualising body language. In the text extract, the description of Snagsby's cough in paragraphs 4 and 8 takes up significantly more space than the speech it follows. This adds emphasis to the already repetitive description.

Paragraphs 4 and 8 of the extract further include the reporting clause in the form of a suspended quotation: an interruption of the character speech. This presentation adds extra emphasis in the overall text structure. In the discussion above, I have argued that interruptions by the narrator are contrasted with the co-operative overlaps of the characters. For the suspended quotation, the place where the interruption starts is also significant. In paragraph 2, 'Well, sir' and in paragraph 8, 'I assure you, sir' are separated from the rest of the turn. Both units are mainly characterised through their discourse functions at the beginning of the turn (rather than their content), which is also underlined through the repetition of *sir*. Hence, interpreted as contextualising, the suspended quotation helps to indicate the discourse function. Interpreted as highlighting, both discourse units are reflective of Snagsby's hesitation and deferential behaviour and work together with his cough. For the identification of contextualising functions, it is particularly important to be able to draw on data from a reference corpus. Mahlberg and Smith (2012) provide further examples of contextualising patterns in suspended quotations, including (5) below. Such examples show how suspensions support the organisation of fictional discourse. Prefaces such as 'I suppose' may add an additional thought or indicate a topic shift.

(5) 'That's all I say. And *I suppose*,' added the lofty young man, after a moment's pause, 'that visitor will ...'

(Charles Dickens, Little Dorrit, *e-text from* Project Gutenberg*)*

The discussion of the *Bleak House* example in the previous section further showed how punctuation contributes to the organisation of fictional discourse by indicating interruptions or co-operative overlaps. Punctuation as such deserves more attention or even its own local grammar but, as the extract shows, it clearly also contributes to creating time meanings.

Within the space of the present chapter, I have only discussed two functional areas of a local grammar of speech presentation. These areas were selected because they are particularly relevant to the example text extract. Other functions relate, for instance, to actual patterns in the character speech, such as clusters that reflect patterns of real speech and thus create effects of authenticity in the way fictional characters speak.

Conclusion

The present chapter suggests that local grammars might be a useful way to complement the canonical categories of grammatical description that are typically applied in the study of literary texts. The initial suggestions for a local grammar of fictional speech presentation selected patterns and functions that supported the analysis of a specific text extract. The patterns found in this text, however, were related to more general patterns that are applicable to other texts, too. The background of corpus research was based mainly on research on Dickens's novels and other nineteenth-century fiction (Mahlberg 2013a) to start with. Overall, the notion of the local grammar and its usefulness for practical stylistics needs to be tested at a larger scale. It will also be important to further investigate how different local grammars work together and work with more general approaches of grammatical description. An example is already hinted at in the present chapter. The discussion of the *looking at* pattern in *Bleak House* relates to the Pattern Grammar approach illustrated with the example of the 'look' group for the pattern **V *at* n**. Verbs in the 'look' meaning group tend to indicate the manner of the looking or emotions and attitudes associated with the looking. A concordance sample from *Bleak House* showed that one textual pattern of *looking at* is its co-occurrence with adverbials to provide character information indicating emotions and feelings. Hence patterns in fictional texts relate to more general patterns of the language, although the functions associated with formal patterns may require different interpretations. The discussion of the text extract has shown in particular how patterns of fictional texts contribute to the negotiation of meaning in the configuration of a particular text. General patterns that can be identified with the help of corpus methods and that are shared across texts indicate choices for the interpretation of meanings in a particular text. Therefore, awareness of such patterns can support a practical stylistic analysis of the grammatical configurations in a specific text.

18

Semantic prosody

Bill Louw and Marija Milojkovic

Introduction

This chapter sets out to compensate for a deficit in stylistics as a discipline: the potential for the English language to be its own *instrumentation* through the notion of *semantic prosody*. Understanding the primary meanings and subtle associations of a word can be resolved by using its typical co-text (its *collocations*) as the instrument for analysis. This instrument has been available since the first edition of John Sinclair's *Collins Cobuild English Language Dictionary* in 1987, but over a quarter of a century later, our instrumentation has barely progressed beyond the point of the merely lexicographic. Since then, no dynamic digital application of the study of collocation, upon which the dictionary was founded, has been forthcoming, though the proposed notion of *semantic prosody* (so named by John Sinclair and Bill Louw) first appeared in a fully elaborated form in Louw (1993). Corpus stylistics (the computational analysis of stylistic features) using reference corpora larger than 1 million words of running text was initiated as a discipline by Bill Louw, using the Cobuild/Birmingham University Corpus and Reserve corpora of 21 million words, also in April 1987.

The semantic prosody of a word is an exploration of the typical shadings of meaning that the word possesses, as revealed by the most common collocations with which it is found. In the years since these early beginnings, the study of semantic prosody (SP) has progressed through several phases. A very early, pre-computational, *intuitive* phase may well have occurred, but later studies testify to the fact that findings in SP are largely opaque to intuition. Contextual prosodic theory (CPT), collocational analysis and corpus-recoverable subtext approaches all fall within the compass of the study of SP. The term *prosodic* has nothing much to do here with its conventional meaning within versification studies, where it covers rhythm, stress and intonation. Instead, following

Firth (1957), prosodic patterns in meaning extend outwards from the word's location in an utterance or sentence, to its collocation with other words, within its context of situation. Meaning is thus both collocational and often hidden beyond the simple denotational value of the isolated word (Sinclair 2003: 117).

There are two main aspects to consider: SP refers to the way in which contiguous elements may affect one another by and through *proximity*, and SP effects persist in different ways and to different degrees at different *levels* of language (Firth 1957: 170). For example, at the phonetic level, Louw (1993: 159) explains why, following Bréal (1897), the vowels in the word 'Amen' are nasalised because of adjacent nasal consonants. Phonology and semantics would usually be regarded as being far apart on the scale of Firth's levels of language. Though SP operates through proximity, the negative, positive or specific attitudes affecting a word's meaning may pervade the text over very long distances, without even being consciously noticed. The fact that prosodic features work together to create an impression of unity is set out by de Beaugrande (1991), using the words of Firth himself:

> The investigation of words, pieces, and longer stretches of text leads to the prosodic approach which 'emphasises synthesis' and 'refers features . . . to the structure taken as a whole'.   *(de Beaugrande 1991: 208)*

The most recent CPT development is in the notion of *events*. In present-day metaphysics, the analysis of the concept of an event has centred on what it is for something to be '*one and the same event* . . . the individuation of events' (Mautner 2000: 184). However, as literary worlds are forms of possible worlds, our method concentrates more upon degrees of verisimilitude between events. We see states of affairs as being chunked by collocation, and so open to an SP approach. However, where collocation between things begins to give rise to states of affairs, a more compelling form of collocation is that which obtains between grammatical strings, or the text's own quasi-logic. This form of collocation is closely related to the quasi-propositional variables (QPVs) that go to make up the *subtext* (Louw 2010b), provided that the variables themselves are empirically significant in terms of their frequency (see also Glock 2005: 115). The *subtext* refers to the possible, probable and likely choices that present themselves through collocation in natural language, but which remain an unactualised presence in texts; these other associations are fully recoverable from events in reference corpora that are similar to the event under study. Hence, subtext may be entirely opaque to intuition or only dimly perceived, from the readers' point of view, to be partially 'in play' and yet proscribed for reasons of necessary meaning (Carnap 1947) or authorial choice. Subtextual meaning may be akin to that of SP. Louw's notion of subtext is founded on the logical atomism of Russell (see R. C. Marsh 1956) and Wittgenstein (see J. Griffin 1964).

The remainder of this paper will consist of an application by Marija Milojkovic of Bill Louw's stylistic theory to a poem by W. B. Yeats, 'The Circus Animals' Desertion'. The techniques set out here will allow the reader to embark upon original, individual research in corpus stylistics, without recourse to *conceptual* reasoning, in satisfaction of the Firthian criterion that meaning by collocation is not connected with the 'ideas' meaning of words (1957: 196). After Milojkovic's analysis of each section, Louw may offer comments, linking particular corpus stylistics findings to his theory and views in general. Such a dialogic approach will hopefully facilitate the reader's grasp of the method's application.

The Circus Animals' Desertion

I

I sought a theme and sought for it in vain,
I sought it daily for six weeks or so.
Maybe at last, being but a broken man,
I must be satisfied with my heart, although
Winter and summer till old age began
My circus animals were all on show,
Those stilted boys, that burnished chariot,
Lion and woman and the Lord knows what.

II

What can I but enumerate old themes,
First that sea-rider Oisin led by the nose
Through three enchanted islands, allegorical dreams,
Vain gaiety, vain battle, vain repose,
Themes of the embittered heart, or so it seems,
That might adorn old songs or courtly shows;
But what cared I that set him on to ride,
I, starved for the bosom of his faery bride.
And then a counter-truth filled out its play,
'The Countess Cathleen' was the name I gave it;
She, pity-crazed, had given her soul away,
But masterful Heaven had intervened to save it.
I thought my dear must her own soul destroy
So did fanaticism and hate enslave it,
And this brought forth a dream and soon enough
This dream itself had all my thought and love.
And when the Fool and Blind Man stole the bread
Cuchulain fought the ungovernable sea;
Heart-mysteries there, and yet when all is said
It was the dream itself enchanted me:
Character isolated by a deed
To engross the present and dominate memory.

Players and painted stage took all my love,
And not those things that they were emblems of.

III

Those masterful images because complete
Grew in pure mind, but out of what began?
A mound of refuse or the sweepings of a street,
Old kettles, old bottles, and a broken can,
Old iron, old bones, old rags, that raving slut
Who keeps the till. Now that my ladder's gone,
I must lie down where all the ladders start
In the foul rag and bone shop of the heart.   (*Yeats 1939: 236*)

The prelude: 'I sought a theme and sought for it in vain'

Milojkovic

Study the concordance in Figure 18.1.

These are 8 out of the 79 lines yielded by the corpus of the full 1995 edition of *The Times* newspaper (hereafter referred to as the Times corpus), containing 44.5 million words, for the searchline 'sought a'. If we analyse language events in the concordance lines through the Firthian context of situation we will have noticed a curious consistency: the relevant objects that are being sought, although mostly abstract (legal bans, declarations, etc.) like 'theme' in Yeats, are in the vast majority specific in detail. What makes this finding especially interesting is the presence of the indefinite article in all these contexts – despite, or because of, which the object sought is in need of extra description.

In English, therefore, what you seek is very particular and you know what it is very well. All objects of the verb 'sought' in the concordance are specified with the help of relative clauses, prepositional phrases or participle clauses. Yeats's case – or his persona's (they might be seen as one and the same person here, as Yeats's private letters show, see Sarker 2002: 289) – syntactically resembles the situation of the battered woman in line 16 who sought a divorce. (The wider context tells us that she was afterwards killed by her husband on the receipt of her

```
80 characters per entry
Sort : 1R/SW unshifted.
     9 ithin the union who have repeatedly sought a compromise with hardliners. One sen
    10 title. Last month Buckingham Palace sought a correction from Business Age over i
    11 ann, for the prosecution, initially sought a court order banning reports of proc
    12  prime radio shows after his mother sought a court ruling proving Julio was his
    13 ty moved to quash that decision and sought a declaration that Mr Oury's applicat
    14 d for the beginning of July. Truman sought a delay until the middle of the month
    15 reated for a nervous breakdown. She sought a divorce on the ground of her husban
    16 ter from her solicitor in which she sought a divorce. Relatives said Foster su
```

Figure 18.1: MicroConcord search for 'sought a'

lawyer's letter.) In the whole Times concordance there are eight cases where the sought object is specified by a preceding adjective. There are also three more cases where it remains syntactically isolated. In one, the London Underground sought a solution to a union issue, but the solution is described in a previous paragraph. In another, a married woman, in an attempt to change her life, sought a lover, but in the end went back to her children. There is one more – 'sought a mortgage', the context being a young couple where the boyfriend encounters administrative difficulties in buying their first home because he is self-employed.

A battered wife will seek a divorce, a tired one a lover (this pursuit is less justifiable on moral grounds and perhaps in need of more explanation, but the phrase occurs in a very short synopsis of a short story), and a young couple sought a mortgage. All of these are logical steps, at least no more logical than an elderly poet seeking a theme. The difference is, again, in the specificity of the thing sought. Although no explanation for divorce is given as, for example, in line 15, there is always only one divorce to be obtained; and the very situation of violence in the marriage is sufficient cause for a divorce. A mortgage is also logical when one is buying one's new home, and the particular bank and amount are of no interest in the grand scheme of things. The lover is not described, the very absence of which detail signifies that what was being sought were the usual benefits expected of lovers, personal traits being of secondary importance. But a *theme* – unspecified, and, therefore, posing a problem for the 'relevant person, personality' – is a marked deviation from the ordinary usage of 'sought a'. By choosing such a structure to express his problem the artist has foregrounded it at the very beginning (a British National Corpus (BNC) search also supported these findings). The semantic prosody of 'sought' is fractured in the poem because the Firthian context of situation is *underprovided*.

The verb 'sought' in the Times concordance above also shows determination on the part of its subject (the determination being highlighted by the very fact that the sought object is usually highly specific). The aura of determination in the poem is preserved by the adverbial 'in vain', which, as Louw (1997) noticed when discussing another poem by Yeats, carries the prosody of a goal-oriented activity.

The determined and unspontaneous nature of the action combined with its highly unspecific object contributes to the creation of the sense of paradox in the very first line. The paradox continues in the second line, where yet again re-enforced 'sought' is specified regarding how long it has lasted ('for six weeks') – the poet is so determined that he keeps a record of the time he has wasted, as if he had an urgent deadline, or was on a payroll and needed to justify his expenses – how often do poets give you this sort of data *within* poetry? After which at the end of the second line, he surprises the reader yet again by adding 'or so', before putting his first full stop. 'Or so' followed by a full stop is not rare even in written English, as the Times corpus confirms by yielding 126 lines containing it, but we would hardly require of Yeats or anyone else such a detailed account of his doings while searching for inspiration. We know that Yeats was far from given to gap-filling for the sake of metre, and yet only a child would finish an iambic verse, and a two-line sentence, with a phrase indicating that the speaker is giving an approximate amount.

It is, of course, quite clear that Yeats's wording is an expression of utter frustration and poetic impasse rather than anything else. What we have found is that the first two lines of the poem are a string of paradoxes which the reader certainly feels, but which a corpus analysis helps to interpret. A determined ('sought' is repeated three times) goal-oriented action whose goal is highly unspecific, because it is unknown, is taking place during a specific time span whose specific duration the poet cannot vouch for.

Whatever will happen next?

Louw

A major debate surrounds the point of high empiricism at which SP, as a phenomenon, begins. The indefinite article appears at position 5 in a frequency list for the English language. 'The' is the most frequent word at position 1 and occupies 4 per cent of all text; but 'a' marks the introduction of a new item into the discourse. 'Theme' sounds fairly anodyne, but the consequence of its underprovision can cause a whole man to be broken (see the next paragraph). The fractured context of situation for a writer leads to a broken writer. In the context of what Irish people call 'the troubles', a knock at the door could turn out to be lethal. It is worth noting that Yeats often uses deft forms of substitution with 'in vain'. In the poem 'Memory' we are told that 'face and charm were in vain'. The word 'efforts' is omitted, but the women to whom the persona was introduced to help him forget Maud are seen as using their faces and charm as efforts (the attitude is negative and sexist) (Hunston 2002: 129).

Milojkovic

Consider now 'Maybe at last, being but a broken man'. The search string 'but a *ed' yielded five contexts in the Times corpus (see Figure 18.2).

All these five contexts depict a degraded state of what is expected to be some sort of a more elaborated spectacle. Indeed, David Ross (2009: 68) describes the poet's 'accustomed resources' that he can no longer muster as 'the spectacle of his many masks'. Yeats's degraded show is supported by the quasi-propositional variables (QPVs) 'charred', 'ragged' and 'borrowed'. 'Folded' is perhaps an instance of the tricks that the corpus sometimes plays (language is a living thing and not mathematically arranged; a lack of such exceptions would be indicative of an incomplete

Others might argue that the new trend offers conclusive proof that rock
culture, as it totters into middle age, has finally succumbed to spontaneous combustion, leaving behind nothing **but a charred** nylon cardigan.

but in winter the theatre is dark, and the pier empty of all **but a ragged**
posse of black-headed gulls, perched on the coin-op telescopes, and a
cormorant hanging out its wings on the lifeboat slipway.

The rigour of the code, you would have thought, is why a wordless full-page
ad showing nothing **but a folded** shirt lying on a bed of nails turns out to be
for Silk Cut. Not so, says the agency behind it. It's been running it since
1983 as a coded message to the mature smoker

'Nothing **but a naked** soul. How frightening!' said the critic Mark Slonim
'The concentration of all female hysterias,' concluded Boris Pasternak.
The best critical minds of the day understood Marina Tsvetaeva's talent,
but both men and women jibbed at her character. Her

But behind the sophisticated visual interface, ISN was more modest. The
company was started by programmer Randy Adams and marketing executive
Bill Rollinson, with three employees and little to its name **but a borrowed**
Sun server and a link to the Internet.

Figure 18.2: Results of the search string 'but a *ed' in the Times corpus

picture rather than common), but Marina Tsvetaeva's 'naked' soul
resonates with Yeats's turning to his own heart in all its unattractiveness
(see the last stanza of the poem) so much that one feels that Yeats is doing
as much to explain CPT as it is at pains to interpret Yeats.

Louw

The forms of anti-climax associated with the verb 'be' followed by 'but a'
can be used by poets for the purpose of flattery, but the elements of
'elaborated spectacle' are always present. In 'The Good Morrow', John
Donne brushes aside the spectacle of the swift and successful seduction
of the lady's predecessors and presumably of herself, to declare the
predecessors 'but a dream of thee'. But the collocates that left open
any mention of the speed of seduction, 'short step', are part of the
poem, even if only subtextually. Their use is ruled out by the words
'desired, and got':

> ... If ever any beauty I did see,
> Which I desired, and got, 'twas but a dream of thee.

In the Corpus of Contemporary American English (COCA) there are 21
instances of the relevant string and 10 of them are associated with the
meaning 'short step', 5 of which are that actual phrase. Flattery does not
involve referring to the speed with which the lady in the poem was
seduced. It is the syntax of the textual world that re-creates the *logic* of
the external world. This may take the collocates 'out of play', but the
powerful empiricism of the corpus stresses their relevance (see the reference to Carnap in Louw 2010b).

Milojkovic

The very next line introduces the topic of the poet's heart to which he unwillingly turns ('I <u>must</u> be <u>satisfied</u> with my heart, <u>although</u> ...' – the unwillingness is chunked as a state of affairs by the underlined collocates), and the next two lines proceed to inform us that 'Winter and summer till old age began, / My circus animals were all on show'. What are these circus animals? The sophisticated reader of the sophisticated poet will probably not have thought of real circus animals for the simple reason that he is not reading the confessional of a ring-master. The persona, as we know from the first line, is a poet looking for inspiration. Therefore, a sophisticated reader will first have understood 'my circus animals' as a delexical expression. Then the English expression 'on show' will first be understood in its delexical meaning, 'present', and only then relexicalised because a show is what happens in a circus. The list of circus animals to follow will only reinforce the process of relexicalisation (this is the process of a delexical word regaining its full lexical meaning through co-occurrence with another collocate). In any case, the 'circus animals' in the poem are what they are understood as at first, delexically. They are what a poet, or ring-master, or dancer, or actor must have in order to keep the audience – the gift, the art, the tricks. Sarker quotes Albright (1991: 841), who mentions 'poetic themes and devices that reliably please an audience, somewhat overfamiliar to the elderly poet who has long employed them'. Apparently, Sarker himself (2002: 290) is closest to the truth when calling them 'hackneyed images and techniques'. While appreciating this focus on devices ('images and techniques') rather than themes, one must not forget that the problem is not their being 'hackneyed' or 'overfamiliar'. The problem is that old themes do not work any more because Yeats's animals are gone. As critics agree that the reference to lion and woman is reminiscent of Yeats's unrequited love Maud Gonne, I am correct in assuming that she, as the source of inspiration, is gone too.

Louw

The exhaustive (to the extent that it ends with 'and the Lord knows what') list of circus animals completes the state of affairs of the circus (a fact, as in Wittgenstein's (1958: 7) 'The world is a totality of facts'). Of course, the overprovision may not have the status of a state of affairs – it may be a list of things that fail to chunk into one through collocation. States of affairs in logic are truthful propositions, but in natural language they are judged by the external world and its logical construction (Carnap 1947). So if the poet is pessimistic, the states of affairs may feel so void of organisation as to look like lists – but even 'mounds' of refuse show signs of organisation. In philosophy there is the notion of possible worlds (Sinclair 1993: 459), but in this poem the worlds are void of life (see also the middle and final sections). It is a surreal landscape – like the heart without love in the poem's coda.

The middle stanzas: 'What can I but enumerate old themes'

Milojkovic

What can CPT contribute to existing scholarship on the three middle stanzas? It can show the subtext of the middle section of the poem and talk about devices connecting the studied text and the reference corpus. Now that literary devices have deserted the poet, he feels *driven into a corner*. He *sees the scene* of his *utter plight and helplessness*, as the empty stage is refilled by personas of the past. This is not an intuitive statement; the words in italics represent scientific findings based on the extracted subtext of the grammatical string with which Yeats begins the second section of the poem: 'what can I but *'.

The grammatical string in question is foregrounded by the mere virtue of its being extremely rare – archaic. The Times corpus, the BNC (twice its size) and the COCA (four times the size of the BNC) do not contain any examples of this line. We will see that the use of such grammatical strings is one of this poem's characteristics.

Only the Google Books corpus (googlebooks.byu.edu) assisted the investigation. The fiction part of the corpus, containing 91 billion words, provided only seventeen – as far as I could find, as many passages are repeated on the Google Books findings pages – contexts containing 'what can I but *'. The QPVs in these contexts are 'despair' (3 occurrences), 'obey' (2 occurrences), 'repeat' (2 occurrences), 'love', 'plead', 'pray', 'say', 'see', 'submit' and 'tremble'. Four contexts are translations, one into modern English. Figure 18.3 shows the key word in context (KWIC) concordance of the contexts.

The QPV 'despair' appears three times. In context 5 the husband is desperate as his young wife is dying and leaving their first new-born, in 6 a maiden has suffered at the hands of a man whom she still loves, and

1 those who won't receive it – **what can I, but** *say* my say too, & trust in God if I'm wrong
2 He flops, cries 'stand:' **what can I, but** *submit*? To fight a drunken bear, were want of wit.
3 What can I do – let doubt be dumb, – **What can I – but** *obey*? His sceptre or His rod, Who shal
4 full and just Inspires my words – **what can I but** *obey*? Yet as I stand, held fast and meshed
5 Look there On my young wife! **What can I but** *despair*? She left her tents for me — abandon'd a
6 thus oppressed with endless pains, **What can I but** *despair*?' Then rising, hopeless of relief,
7 If all my thought me helpeth nought, **what can I but** *despair*? Sorrow and sighs and dreary moo
8 all the strength of my heart, and **what can I but** *pray* for thy whole blessedness, O gentle so
9 But if Destiny to this consent, **What can I but** *my soul in sorrow bow*, With tearful eyes and
10 to your imagined throne? And **what can I, but** *see* beyond the world that is, when, faithful,
11 It is not, **What can I? but**, *What can't He?* as somebody says. Go on fearless
12 nor like the flute complain? **What can I but**, *like the ended banquet, desolate remain*? 'Fear
13 sigh for you; And knowing this, ah! **What can I But** *love* in silence, pine and die?
14 outcast from natural pride, **what can I but** *plead* the greater love I bear you as my benefact
15 *Nina* Do not cease! Say on, say on! *Doria* **What can I but** *repeat* A tale already told? *Nina*.
16 far silence touched it. **What can I but** *repeat* The vow of every mother – There is not one s
17 this swoop makes the third — And **what can I, but** *tremble* like a bird? FOOL. Give me a penny

Figure 18.3: KWIC concordance of the contexts for 'what can I but *'

in 7 a man is suffering from what we now call 'courtly love' (this is a translation into modern English).

'Obey' appears in 3, in a hymn celebrating the omnipotence of God, and in 4, where a subject is addressing his queen.

The QPV 'repeat' beautifully resonates with 'enumerate' in meaning, with two differences: one being that 'enumerate' has a routine connotation, and the other that Yeats uses it to state a repetition that is not welcome. 'Repeat' is used in the context of man–woman love in context 15, and motherly love in context 16.

'Love' comes up in a context of unrequited love with the traditional elements of the inaccessibility of the beautiful beloved; 'plead' has to do with a princess pleading with her sovereign, who is in love with her, not to marry her; 'pray' is self-explanatory; 'say' is from a letter from Thackeray to his mother, in which he asserts his faith – different from hers. 'See' has to do with a mother reading fairy tales to her daughter and seeing the world beyond reality; and 'tremble' comes from a play by none other than W. B. Yeats himself and as such will deserve special attention.

There are also two contexts (9 and 12) in which the verb appears further to the end of the clause (both are translations). In another context (11) there is a question mark after 'I' and a comma after 'but', but we assumed it has a right to its place in the concordance because of Firth's notion of collocation as abstracted at the level of syntax. These contexts will be consulted when the prosody of the string is discussed, but not checked for QPVs.

According to Louw (personal communication), the QPVs will not necessarily have one semantic feature in common, but rather each two of them will share one. The QPVs from this grammatical string can be grouped semantically in the following way:

1   'despair'
2   'obey', 'plead', 'pray', 'submit', 'tremble'
3   'love'
4   'pray', 'plead', 'say', 'repeat'

They can also be grouped thematically according to their specific contexts:

1   despairing of love: 'despair' (all three times), 'love'
2   asserting faith in God: 'pray', 'obey' (once), 'say'
3   asserting love: 'repeat' (both times)
4   new vision: 'see', 'tremble'
5   humorous: 'submit'

All contexts can be grouped into three major themes: despair (5, 6, 7, 9, 12, 13, 17), faith in God (1, 3, 11, 17), love (5, 6, 7, 9, 13, 14, 15, 16) and submission (3, 4, 9 (to fate), 14, 17). New vision is strongly present in 10 and 17.

The play *The Hourglass*, where Yeats himself uses the grammatical string in question, deserves particular attention. It is about a transition from atheism to faith. A schoolmaster (in the play called Wise Man) has asserted all his life that there is no God, nor angels, spirits, hell and so forth, condemning it all as superstition. He is widely respected and no one contradicts his views, including his pupils, wife and fellow villagers. However, he begins having dreams and visions that he has been wrong – that is the moment when this realisation prompts him to 'tremble'. God exists, and suddenly Wise Man is the greatest sinner through non-believing and teaching it to others. It is obvious that the usage of the grammatical string in *The Hourglass* expresses despair, faith in God, new vision and submission. Love is not at all mentioned in the play, and therefore cannot be considered as subtext of this line in *The Hourglass*.

Let us, however, put into words the corpus-based description of the subtext of 'what can I but *' in general terms. Provided the context of situation contains elements that warrant these headings, this grammatical string will conjure up contexts of love, despair, faith in God, submission and new vision. 'Love' is likely to be unrequited or lost (even in context 15 Nina tragically dies, unable to bear the hero's adultery). Submission is likelier to be directed to God. Despair is likelier to be caused by love and not, for example, fate, as in context 12. Interestingly, the subtext of this string bears resemblance to 'faith, hope and charity' (St Paul: 1 Corinthians 13), with the correction that charity is likely to be love unfulfilled, and, not illogically, the place of hope has been taken by its opposite, despair. When I entered 'what can I but hope' into the Google Books corpus, there were no matches.

Far from claiming that all these will be consciously used by the writer or clearly perceived by the reader, CPT nevertheless asserts that subtext deepens interpretation through being embedded in the grammatical string in the nature of the language experience of an educated adult native speaker. The theory is called 'contextual' because it relies heavily on contexts and *events* in both the studied text and reference corpora (for example, 'love' is not the subtext in *The Hourglass* because the context does not warrant it). It is called 'prosodic' because it relies on collocation, within which words imbue each other with meaning, as in the case of semantic prosodies, but also within the limits of a one-time co-occurrence. Thus, the theory is both dynamic and precise.

Let us now view the subtext of Yeats's line in 'What can I but enumerate old themes'. The archaic grammatical string collocates well with 'old themes'. According to Louw (2010b), there will be a grammatical string in the poem that will prove to carry the poem's subtext. Does the string I have been researching carry the subtext of the poem, or at least of its middle section?

Considering the context of the middle section, the subtext carried by this grammatical string is that of love (middle stanza 1), faith (middle stanza 2) and despair (middle stanza 3). Clearly the elements of subtext are not restricted to each stanza, as the second stanza is also about love, and the first about despair (it contains our string). Is love in the string's subtext unrequited? Clearly so. Has this fact produced despair in the form of writer's block? Not unlikely. Is the presence of faith in the subtext strong enough to be taken into consideration? The answer to this remarkable question is present both in stanza 1 and in stanza 3.

Stanza 1 famously ends with the delexical expression 'the Lord knows what'. Yeats never wasted words; the poem is multilayered; this delexical expression ends the whole prelude. If we accept the possibility that this expression is not used delexically only, there will be an element that will relexicalise it. The element in question could be the very string I have just analysed. The poem, in fact, runs as follows: '. . .and the Lord knows what. What can I but . . .' In the briefest possible way, 'the Lord' is relexicalised through the string that even Yeats himself has used in the past before the QPV 'tremble'.

The coda

The concluding stanza presents a change of focus. If in the preceding stanzas the focus was on what has departed, here the focus is on what has been left. If the prelude gives a mocking list of devices, and the middle stanzas a respectable description of lofty old themes, the coda suddenly shifts focus from 'the pure mind' to the squalor of the poet's heart:

> Those masterful images because complete
> Grew in pure mind, but out of what began?
> A mound of refuse or the sweepings of a street,
> Old kettles, old bottles, and a broken can,
> Old iron, old bones, old rags, that raving slut
> Who keeps the till. Now that my ladder's gone,
> I must lie down where all the ladders start
> In the foul rag and bone shop of the heart.

Similarly to the mocking list of animals, the coda contains the exhaustive, to the point of overprovision, description of utter waste that clutters the poet's heart. Unlike tricks, whether they be circus or poetic, no item of this detritus could ever serve a reasonable purpose to anyone but the rag and bone man (overprovision of uselessness) or attract so much as even a condescending smile (overprovision of disgust). Yeats's public would welcome tricks but not disgusting junk. All items in the shop are invested with the attribute of being old, like the poet himself, except 'the raving slut' (the 'broken can' is not described as old but this is easily inferred as it is broken). Interestingly, both previous sections ended with an important message whose last word and carrier of the rhyme was a grammatical word ('the Lord knows what', 'emblems of'). In the case of the concluding stanza, the last word of the concluding message and the carrier of the rhyme is the word 'heart'. The literary world of the last stanza is, however, more surreal than in the prelude: if there could exist a circus corresponding to Yeats's description, there could hardly exist a junk shop, however poor, that was run by a crazy person into the bargain ('raving' and 'keeps the till' are impossible collocates).

The progress from a reasonable and even cool comparison of literary devices and circus animals, via a sensible account of one's artistic development (containing sound judgement such as 'counter-truth' and 'heart-mysteries') towards a surreal mess of the poet's heart, which yet needs to rhyme with 'start', is paradoxical. This reminds us of the numerous paradoxes of the first stanza; however, the paradoxes are as opposite as the stanzas' moods. At the beginning the poet is so calm and collected as to insist on giving us an exact estimate of time lost on writer's block; the list of animals that follows completes the process of relexicalisation because its completeness recreates the world of the circus. By comparison, the list of items belonging to the junk shop (ostensibly having the same purpose of rounding up a metaphor) is not quite coherent. 'A mound of refuse and the sweepings of a street' are an exhaustive and disgusting enough description, but are they part of the junk shop? Hardly; rather, they are the summary of it, an exaggeration preceding the actual description of what is in itself a metaphor. Then, Yeats (the persona) must lie down in the shop ('shop' and 'lie down' are unlikely collocates). Before that, the appearance of a ladder in any shop is very likely if its point is to reach a shelf, but it is never its central feature. Ladders usually do not start (unless metaphorically); this one should obviously lead to heaven as there is nothing else in that direction.

This picture of utter underprovision is yet another 'masterful' image, 'because complete'. The image of the shop is so physical due to overprovision of disgusting items that the appearance of a 'ladder' – a traditional metaphor of spiritual growth – is almost palpable, as well as the author's intention to 'lie down' in the shop. If in stanza 1 the animals were first delexically present, and then relexicalised, here the literary world of the shop relexicalises the metaphoric notion of the ladder by co-selecting it with the till and the shop junk that have become a world. The 'ladder' is an absent collocate that becomes equated with the missing animals and the focus of the poem – in fact, its theme. The equation comes from the statement that they are both gone. Ladders do not start and not in junk shops, except metaphorically and of the heart, but by the time we have reached the mention of this one, we have taken to heart the loss and the point of the poet's new departure because of the 'completeness' of his created worlds. If the poem started with the 'ladder' metaphor, without preliminaries, the impact would have been poorer as the image in itself is almost conventional.

Let us now turn to the subtext of the stanza. Given the findings of the previously analysed string, the subtext of which was hypothesised to be love (unrequited or lost), despair, faith, new vision and submission, I will ask two important questions. Firstly, will the subtext of the middle stanzas prove plausible? 'Lie down' certainly implies submission, and 'all ladders start' certainly implies faith, as well as new vision (it will not be amiss at this point to recall St John of the Ladder). We are left with the task to prove or doubt the presence of lost love and despair. The second question stems from the first. Is the raving slut of the coda Maud Gonne?

Is the image of the slut Yeats's judgement on Maud? The poem is multi-layered, there are numerous parallelisms, and this hypothesis is not ruled out. A stylistician, however, will notice two points. Firstly, 'my dear' in the third stanza refers to Maud and the transition from 'my dear' to 'slut' would be too unjustifiably fast, even if we take into account the 'flashback' aspect of 'my dear'. Secondly, 'the raving slut' is the first item of the workshop that does not come with the epithet 'old'. In such a repetitive list describing the old poet's heart nothing would contradict the appearance of 'old' instead of 'that' except for (a) the need for the feminine image to be truly feminine, not after child-bearing age, and (b) the possibility that the reading public might *mistakenly* read Maud Gonne into the image. She was past the age of 70 at the time.

The subtext of the coda may be determined on the basis of two search lines. The grammatical string that has a bearing on the notion of the junk shop is 'but out of what'. The grammatical string that will elucidate the degree of the poet's despair and the presence (or absence) of the motive of lost/unrequited love is 'now that my * is'.

It is Louw's view that enough empiricism (namely, similar events in the corpus) allows 'text to read text' and that *the start of the event can* predict *its progress or* subvert *it into device* (Louw and Milojkovic forthcoming; see also Louw 2009 on literary devices). The findings will show that the former grammatical string ('but out of what') is an example of the event being *predicted* by corpus findings. The latter ('now that my * is') will be shown to *subvert* the event into a literary device – metaphor.

'But out of what' is a rare grammatical string. As in the case of 'what can I but', neither the BNC nor the COCA contains any examples of it. Only Google Books: Fiction, a corpus of 91 billion words, yields material for study (all searches I mention in this paper were made in September 2012). Fifty-four contexts were extracted from it.

Since 'but out of what' is syntactically capable of being followed by both verbs and clauses, the range of the potential QPVs is so huge that we should concentrate on its semantic prosody (aura) rather than subtext that is extracted through the variables of lexis. The contexts of 'but out of what' were grouped into seven categories, according to the semantic context of their occurrence. The categories are given in order of frequency, starting with the most frequent. Since three contexts quote the same thought of the same writer, I will consider the overall number of contexts to be 52:

(a)   creation (15/52, or 28.8 per cent):
  - artistic creation in 5 (the same in 13 and 46), 8, 17, 29, 51, usually followed by
    • underprovision of resources ('out of what you don't know' (5, 13, 46), 'out of what they most lacked' (17)) or
    • underprovision of the knowledge of the resources' nature (the rhetorical question 'but out of what?' (6)), 'out of what people are unpredictably going to say or do' (51)
  - Christian contexts in 7, 30, 31, 39, 54
  - philosophy in 1, 6, 26; anthropology in 6 and architecture in 43.
(b)   financial transactions, as in taxes and other payments (11/52, or 21.2 per cent) in 2, 10, 11, 12, 15, 23, 47, 48, 50, 52, 53; underprovision of resources is implied in 12, 23, 47, 48, 52 (5 contexts out of 11); in 2, 10 and 11 the theme is charity.
(c)   government and public affairs in 3, 9, 14, 27, 37, 42, 44 (7/52, or 13.5 per cent).
(d)   hedging in 18, 19, 32, 33, 34, 35 (6/52, or 11.5 per cent), e.g. 'out of what is called', 'out of what is best described as', etc.
(e)   unknown origins in 20, 21, 25, 36, 38, 45 (6/52, or 11.5 per cent).
(f)   rhetorical questions implying the absence of resources (the extreme form of underprovision) in 16, 24, 28, 41 (4/52 or 7.7 per cent).
(g)   origins of socially undesirable behaviour in 22 and 40 (2/52 or 3.8 per cent).

Two types of conclusion are to be drawn from these findings. One is that grammatical strings show specific prosodies (see also Milojkovic 2012, 2013; Sinclair 2006); therefore, in a text they may denote the beginning of a *predictable event*.

The other conclusion concerns Yeats's art. It is remarkable that he was a poet of such depth and awareness of his own language as to unwittingly (intuitively) employ a grammatical string whose main prosodies are creation and (underprovided) payment, at a point when he was introducing a metaphor of origins of creation presented as a junk shop. Paradoxically, the subtext (or semantic aura) of the string emphasises both optimism (creation) and pessimism (insufficient or unknown resources).

Louw

The notion of an event is crucial to corpus stylistics because events are re-presented in the linearity of the text. This means that when similar events are searched for by co-selection or subtext, the results from a reference corpus can be compared with the text that prompted the search in one major detail: the onset of the event to the left of the node, and the conclusion of the event to the right of the node. Part of any definition of an event will relate to the way in which the search-phrase reflects the change it has brought about in that event, e.g. but+out+of+what (see also Lombard 1998: 289). Events are prosodic because they have a duration (Sheldrake 2012: 120) and are never instantaneous. Even in a gunshot there is intentionality. The point of linear representation as prosody is that in 'desired, and got, 'twas but a' the ''twas but a' prompt is placed after 'got', so that the necessary meaning of 'short step' (although still present) is, in event-terms, already out of time. The syntax orders a preferred logic: it is Carnapian (Louw 2010a: 92).

Milojkovic

The other chosen grammatical string, 'now that my * is' turned out to subvert the event into a literary device – metaphor. There are only two such contexts in the BNC. One is religious: 'My strength is waned now that my _need_ is most'; the other comes from fiction: 'but now that my _grandmother_ is feeling better'. One is underprovided, the other more positive. The COCA has yielded 17 concordances, shown in Figure 18.4 (those examples where 'now that my * is' was followed by a grammatical word, e.g. a preposition, were considered different grammatical strings and were not included):

'Father' appears three times; 'hair' and 'job' appear twice. The quasi-propositional variables may be classified into the following subgroups:

(a)   a family member or a very significant person in 1, 2, 3, 8, 9, 10, 11, 17
(b)   body part in 6, 7, 16
(c)   significant quality in 13, 14

```
 1  Now that my father is dead
 2  Now that my father is dead
 3  now that my father is far away
 4  now that my job is done
 5  now that my job is our sole source of income
 6  Now that my hair is growing back
 7  now that my hair is turning gray
 8  now that my youngest is started school
 9  now that my wife is aware
10  Now that my sister is single
11  now that my Sandy is gone.
12  Now that my office is 10 miles from where I live
13  now that my mind is glutted
14  Now that my inability is real
15  Now that my house is uninhabitable
16  Now that my brain is empty
17  now that my beloved is gone?
```

Figure 18.4: COCA concordances for 'now that my * is'

(d)   task in 4 ('job') and 12 ('office')

(e)   significant basic necessity in 15 ('house' co-selected with 'uninhabit-able' makes the QPV dramatically necessary; 'office' could also be mentioned here).

Indeed, all the QPVs are those of basic significance to the person (personality in Firth's (1957: 182) context of situation). If we turn to the corpus of Google Books: Fiction for more data, these are the QPVs yielded: 'father' (499 occurrences), 'mind' (186), 'life' (167), 'mother' (146), 'heart' (126), 'son' (117), 'time' (110), 'husband' (107), 'brother' (104), 'hair' (87), 'innocence' (84), 'wife' (73), 'turn' (64), 'task' (63), 'name' (56), 'hand' (55), 'work' (54), 'daughter' (51), 'master' (51), 'head' (47), 'temper' (46), 'honour' (44), 'presence' (41). The classifica-tion, if attempted, would correspond to the one suggested in the dis-cussion of the COCA findings.

It would be statistically more valid but too time-consuming to check which of these occurrences are followed by a grammar word so that they could be excluded. At the time of writing it was not possible to suggest to the corpus a search string longer than five words. When I attempted to add 'gone' to it, for reasons similar to those of including 'made' in Louw (2010a), I needed to do it manually. This means I could only ascertain which QPVs become invalid after the addition of 'gone'. The invalid ones are: 'work', 'task', 'turn'; 'head', 'hand'; 'temper', 'presence'. This leaves (and it is not clear in which order of frequency, therefore I have preserved the one yielded by the first search):

| father | mind | life | mother | heart | son | time | husband |
| brother | hair | innocence | wife | name | daughter | master | honour |

These QPVs share one quality: extreme meaningfulness to the owner. If classified, there are two subgroups:

- a very significant person
- an essential quality without which life or honourable existence is impossible.

Who or what is the 'ladder'? Is it Maud Gonne? And gone she is indeed, leaving the raving slut in her place and causing greater despair than is ostensibly stated in the text. The relevant person or personality in Yeats's art whose effect was his verbal action is felt, directly or indi-rectly, in the first four stanzas of his poem, before appearing as subtext in the coda. She appears as a double absence, by not turning up in the line directly, as something like 'Now that my beloved is gone' – or, less directly – 'Now that my inspiration is gone' – and by being co-selected with the past participle 'gone', homonymous with her last name. Yeats is known to play with Maud being Gon(n)e; to what degree the pun is a part of his conscious authorial intention, we cannot tell – nor is it essential in the presence of subtext. He is about to create in a Maud-free world, despair truly great, love truly lost. No wonder he 'must' 'lie down'. There is evidence, however, that the circus animals, in a different form or shape, have announced their return. The evidence in question is the present poem.

19

Action and event

Paul Simpson and Patricia Canning

> But what is written is not all.
>
> Joseph Conrad, *Chance*

Introduction

The present chapter focuses on the representation of action and event in literature and explores the methods in style used by writers to encode the 'goings on' experienced in, and of, a fictional world. In its pursuit of a serviceable framework for action and event, the chapter takes as its principal point of departure a model of analysis that has enjoyed widespread and sustained application in stylistics. The shorthand term for this model is *transitivity*, although we want to stress at the outset that the concept has a markedly wider compass than its traditional grammatical definition as a verb that takes a direct object. Since the early 1970s, there has been a significant body of research in stylistics that has employed some form of the transitivity framework to reach insightful interpretations about patterns of meaning in fictional prose.

The particulars of the model will be addressed shortly, but the chapter has a number of additional aims and goals. Our core analysis is a stylistic exploration of a passage from Joseph Conrad's novel *Chance*, although the chapter broadens in scope as it progresses by considering the representation of action and event in a range of literary writing. It also incorporates parallel, but more recent, developments in stylistics that intersect with, and usefully line up with, the core tenets of the theoretical model that underpins this chapter. Whereas the transitivity framework accounts for the 'happenings' portrayed in literary texts, and seeks to explain how these happenings are the buttress of both plot and characterisation, one of our aims here is to account for the non-happenings, the imagined happenings and, for that matter, the imagined non-happenings in literature. To this extent the chapter develops a 'transitivity-plus' approach by locating the framework in a more broadly conceived tradition of stylistic research.

Transitivity

The impetus for this model of analysis lies with the work of M. A. K. Halliday and his followers. While various instantiations of the framework have appeared since the late 1960s, and elegant and serviceable summaries can be found in Eggins (2005), J. R. Martin et al. (1997) and G. Thompson (1996), the authoritative guide in our opinion remains Halliday's second edition of *Introduction to Functional Grammar* (1994: 106–75). This volume has admittedly been superseded by a third edition (Halliday and Matthiessen 2004) but at 132 pages, nearly double that of the 1994 version, this latter account of transitivity makes for a markedly less accessible resource for stylistic research into patterns of meaning in prose fiction. Unless otherwise indicated, reference here will therefore be to the earlier version.

The transitivity model is located in the wider scheme that is systemic-functional linguistics (SFL), the mantra of which is that the *system* of language is shaped by the *function* language serves. This social-semiotic system of language is pre-eminently semantic and context-driven in its conformation, standing in counterpoint to the syntactic and context-free foundation of Chomskyan linguistics. In SFL, grammar is organised into and by three key metafunctions: the *interpersonal* metafunction, which shows how a clause is organised as an interactive event, the *textual* metafunction, which accommodates the information-building and text-building properties of the language, and the *experiential* metafunction, which expresses the meaning of the clause as representation. It is this last metafunction which is relayed through the system of transitivity.

Much everyday experience is shaped and defined by actions and events, thoughts and perceptions, and it is an important function of the system of language that it be able to account for these various 'goings on' in the world. Reality is made up of processes and this means encoding into the grammar of the clause a mechanism for capturing activities such as thinking, saying, doing and being. Transitivity registers the way patterns of experience are encoded into text, whether spoken or written, and the way human beings make sense of what goes on around them – and indeed what goes on inside them (Halliday 1994: 106).

Six key processes make up the transitivity model and we limit the account that follows only to the most core terms, categories and criteria that make for a hands-on stylistic tool-kit. To illustrate the efficacy with which genuine portions of text can be identified and aligned with the model, we illustrate all six process types with examples from literature, although we make no critical or interpretative points about this material at this stage of the chapter. *Material* processes, the first of the six, are simply processes of *doing*:

> Sammy clutched the stick under his elbow ...
>
> James Kelman, *How Late it Was, How Late* (Kelman 1998: 83)

Associated with Material processes are two inherent participant roles. The Actor is an obligatory role and indicates the 'doer' of the process (expressed here by 'Sammy') whereas the Goal, which may not be present in a Material process, signals the entity or person affected by the process (expressed here by 'the stick'). Here, for contrast, is an example of a Goal-less intransitive Material process:

> Luis Carruthers sits five tables away from this one
> > Bret Easton Ellis, *American Psycho* (Ellis 1991: 156)

Mental processes encode sensing and thinking and unlike Material processes, which have their provenance in the physical world, they inhabit and reflect the world of consciousness. There are two participant roles present in Mental processes: the Senser (the conscious being that is doing the sensing) and the Phenomenon (the entity which is sensed, felt, thought or seen). Mental processes may also be sub-divided into the three sub-categories of *cognition* (expressed by verbs such as 'thinking' or 'remembering'), *reaction* (as in 'liking' or 'hating') and *perception* (as in 'seeing' or 'hearing'). These sub-categories are expressed, respectively, by the following three examples:

> I remember the whole beginning as a succession of flights and drops
> > Henry James, *The Turn of the Screw* (James 1994: 14)

> Our family always hated cats: nasty, low, vulgar things!
> > Lewis Carroll, *Alice in Wonderland* (Carroll 1992: 15)

> From further down the line, he could hear trench repair parties at work
> > Sebastian Faulks, *Birdsong* (Faulks 1994: 129)

The *Behavioural* process is a rather elusive, yet nonetheless important, category that sits at the interface between other types of processes. Behavioural processes can be 'Material-like' when they embody physiological actions such as 'breathe', 'cough' or 'lie down', although they are sometimes 'Mental-like' when they portray processes as states of consciousness, as in 'dream', 'stare', 'listen', 'cry' or 'laugh'. The sole participant in such processes, the conscious entity who is 'behaving', is unsurprisingly referred to as the Behaver. Here is a selection of Behavioural processes where in each case the clause-initial grammatical subject expounds this key participant role:

> He trembled with passion
> > D. H. Lawrence, *The Rainbow* (Lawrence 1986: 121)

> Henry dozed off without his supper
> > Ian McEwan, *Saturday* (McEwan 2005: 24)

> Victor takes a lonely homecoming crap in a raw toilet of tenements
> > Jack Kerouac, *Visions of Cody* (Kerouac 1980: 28)

You listened to old Cricky's crazy yarns (true? made up?)

Graham Swift, Waterland *(Swift 1992: 6)*

Importantly, the behaviour expressed in such processes is often 'dressed up' as if it were a participant (Halliday 1994: 139), extending or limiting the sense of the main verb through a structure known as the *Range* element. In other words, in a sequence like 'I take a deep breath' (B. E. Ellis 1991: 73) the noun phrase following 'take' is not a discrete, affected participant like a Goal but is part of the Range of the process as a whole. (The Kerouac example above is similarly structured). In such cases, it is often easy to re-phrase the clause to exclude the Range ('I breathed deeply'). In sum, while Behavioural processes are sometimes indeterminate and admittedly hard to classify, they normally express a psychological activity or bodily function in such a way as to imply some involuntariness or lack of will or control on the part of the Behaver.

The term *Verbalisation* describes processes of 'saying' and the associated participant roles with Verbalisation are the Sayer, who is the producer of the speech, the Receiver, the entity to whom or to which the speech is addressed, and the Verbiage, which, without any implied derogatory sense, subsumes that which gets said through the process. In this clause from *The No.1 Ladies' Detective Agency* by Alexander McCall Smith

He told me my mother's name   *(McCall Smith 1998: 7)*

the roles of Sayer, Receiver and Verbiage are expressed, respectively, by 'He', 'me' and 'my mother's name'. In the following example from the same novel, however, the Verbiage element comprises a projection:

My mother told me that my Daddy had left a long time ago   *(1998: 6)*

Here the secondary clause 'my Daddy had left a long time ago' is projected through the primary clause as a 'locution' (see Halliday 1994: 219). In clause complexes of this sort, the embedded clause is amenable to a transitivity analysis in exactly the same way as the clause that houses it. This means that the above sentence contains both a Verbal and Material process. However, because the latter is projected as Verbiage, it is debatable whether any truth-value can be ascribed to the information encoded. It is for this reason that we caution against a quantitatively biased transitivity profile that may inaccurately reflect the degree of action and event in a text when such activity is mediated through projected clauses.

Relational processes are processes of 'being', although this relatively straightforward first-level classification gives way quickly to numerous and complex subdivisions. For the present purposes, Relational processes are defined as having the specific sense of establishing relationships between two entities and come in three main types. An intensive relational process posits a relationship of equivalence, an 'x is y' connection, between two entities, while a possessive relational process plots an 'x has y' type of

connection between two entities. The third type, a circumstantial relational process, is where an element that might otherwise sit outside
the central nub of the process or which would normally form an adjunct
to the process (a prepositional phrase, an adverb of place, time or
manner) instead fulfils the role of a full participant in the process.
This relationship produces a broader range of equivalences, with the
formulae such as 'x is at y', 'x is about y', x is on y', 'x is with y' and so
on. All three patterns – intensive, possessive and circumstantial – are
realised respectively in the textual illustrations below:

> I am a rather elderly man
> > *Herman Melville,* Bartleby, The Scrivener *(Melville 1990: 1)*

> Obviously, each family possessed the strip of sand immediately in front of
> its umbrella   *F. Scott Fitzgerald,* Tender is the Night *(Fitzgerald 1986: 13)*

> This book was mostly about pirates and gold in Hong Kong
> > *Aravind Adiga,* The White Tiger *(Adiga 2008: 5)*

In these (but not all) Relational processes, the participant roles are Carrier
and Attribute, the former referring to the entity, person or concept being
described ('I', 'each family' and 'This book') and the latter the quality
ascribed to the Carrier (respectively, 'a rather elderly man', 'the strip …
umbrella' and 'pirates and gold in Hong Kong'). The Attribute therefore
says what the Carrier is, what the Carrier is like, where the Carrier is, what
it owns and so on. In view of this, it is no surprise that in prose fiction
Relational processes dominate passages of introduction or description,
often employing a variety of sub-types:

> I have a nice house with four rooms and I am very happy. To have all that
> by the time you are thirty-eight is good enough   *(McCall Smith 1998: 7)*

Existential processes, which constitute the sixth category of the transitivity model, are close in sense to Relational processes because they simply
assert that something exists. On the other hand, Existential processes
share some features of Material processes because they can also imply
that something happens or is created (see Halliday and Matthiessen
2004: 172). Existential processes typically include the word 'there' as a
dummy subject, as in

> There was a colour slide of a red tin of insecticide sitting in the out-tray on
> his desk   *John le Carré* The Constant Gardener *(le Carré 2007: 10)*

The sole participant role in such processes, the Existent, is realised here
by the whole unit 'a colour slide of a red tin of insecticide sitting in the
out-tray on his desk'.

Table 19.1 summarises the main concepts introduced thus far. In sum,
the system of transitivity probes patterns of represented action, experience and event in different kinds of texts. It serves as an analytic response

Table 19.1 Summary of main concepts.

PROCESS	PARTICIPANTS	WORLD OF . . .
Material	Actor, Goal	Physical existence
Behavioural	Behaver	↕
Mental	Senser, Phenomenon	Consciousness
Verbalisation	Sayer, Receiver, Target	
Relational	Carrier, Attribute	↕
Existential	Existent	Abstract relations

to the over-arching hub question: 'Who or what does what to whom or what?' The 'doing what' element identifies the process itself, which is picked out, as in all of the examples above, by a verb phrase. The 'who(m) or what' elements constitute different kinds of participants, and are typically realised by adjectives in Relational processes and by nouns and noun phrases in the other types of process. Supplementing the hub question are questions that probe the circumstances attached to the process, asking how, where or when it took place or was carried out. These Circumstantial elements, which are arguably less important for stylistic analysis (but see below), are typically expressed in grammatical structures such as prepositional and adverbial phrases. The Circumstantial elements in the examples from Kelman, Kerouac and Faulks, which all answer the question 'where', have been underlined:

> Sammy clutched the stick <u>under his elbow</u> . . .

> Victor takes a lonely homecoming crap <u>in a raw toilet of tenements</u>

> <u>From further down the line</u>, he could hear trench repair parties at work

Finally, the overview presented in this section is not intended to suggest that transitivity offers a complete or exhaustive explanation of all of the message-bearing components in a clause. The examples presented above contain other elements that are not captured by experiential analysis alone. For instance, Mood Adjuncts comment on the degree of probability, obligation or obviousness associated with the action or event described, while Conjunctive Adjuncts create structural links between different portions of a text. These elements have been underlined, respectively, in the examples from Fitzgerald and McCall Smith:

> <u>Obviously</u>, each family possessed the strip of sand immediately in front of its umbrella

> I have a nice house with four rooms <u>and</u> I am very happy

The section that follows puts this model to the test by exploring the ways in which transitivity can be productively employed as a model of stylistic analysis. This analytic strand is complemented and balanced by a critical overview of the theoretical issues attendant on the use of such a model.

Application

Transitivity probes the idea of 'style as choice' in that any particular textual pattern is only one from a pool of possible textual configurations. Transitivity therefore is a textual strategy that offers writers a systematic (if largely unconscious) choice about how they represent experientially the happenings of the physical or abstract world. What is of particular interest in stylistic analysis is why one type of structure should be preferred to another, how such preferences are motivated creatively, and what impact these patterns have on how the texts are experienced and interpreted.

While many studies have demonstrated the scope of the transitivity model, very few have considered the suitability of the model to event-type situations that are themselves not realised experientially, but nonetheless have narrative and conceptual significance. We are referring here to events that are imagined, counter-factual or negated – those 'what if' scenarios and the like. While these imagined happenings have no material effect in the text, they do offer an alternative narrative, a kind of 'possible worlds' criterion or projected reality against which the selected reality is measurable (see Ryan 1991a). Like the authorial language choices themselves, these experiential choices (of acting or not acting) impute an extra dimension in terms of characterisation. The following analysis therefore considers both event and non-event sequences in an extract from Joseph Conrad's novel *Chance*, in which a murder attempt is witnessed by the character Powell. The piece is stylistically significant not only for the transitivity configurations that depict the event, but also for the complementary linguistic features (such as negation, ellipsis and presupposition) that supplement this transitivity profile.

In Conrad's *Chance*, a seafarer, Captain Anthony, meets and falls in love with a young girl, Flora de Barral. Flora has had a miserable childhood, having been abandoned by her father (the self-styled 'Great de Barral') who is in prison for fraud. De Barral leaves his young daughter in the care of a cold, unfeeling governess, until the latter, having expended her hope of some monetary 'gift' from the girl's father, also abandons her. De Barral is eventually released from prison into the care of the daughter he left behind. In order to avoid creating controversy over his crime and subsequent prison sentence, de Barral is forced to adopt the pseudonym of 'Mr Smith' as he boards a boat, *The Ferndale*, captained by his new son-in-law. On the boat, he grows increasingly jealous and resentful of his daughter's marriage to Captain Anthony, and does his best to convince his daughter of her 'error' in marrying him. Having exhausted his futile disparagement of the captain, de Barral / Smith chooses instead to poison his son-in-law one night during the watch of the ship's first officer,

Mr Powell. The attempted murder scene is depicted from Powell's point of view, although, of course, the novel as a whole is narrated by Conrad's famous character, Marlowe. In the passage, the paragraph-initial inverted commas are Conrad's:

> 'The first sign – and we must remember that he was using his eyes for all they were worth – was an unaccountable movement of the curtain. It was wavy and very slight; just perceptible in fact to the sharpened faculties of a secret watcher; for it can't be denied that our wits are much more alert when engaged in wrong-doing (in which one mustn't be found out) than in a righteous occupation.
>
> 'He became suspicious, with no one and nothing definite in his mind. He was suspicious of the curtain itself and observed it. It looked very innocent. Then just as he was ready to put it down to a trick of imagination he saw trembling movements where the two curtains joined. Yes! Somebody else besides himself had been watching Captain Anthony. . . . In this state of intense antagonism he was startled to observe tips of fingers fumbling with the dark stuff. Then they grasped the edge of the further curtain and hung on there, just fingers and knuckles and nothing else. It made an abominable sight. He was looking at it with unaccountable repulsion when a hand came into view; a short, puffy, old, freckled hand projecting into the lamp-light, followed by a white wrist, an arm in a grey coat-sleeve, up to the elbow, beyond the elbow, extended tremblingly towards the tray. Its appearance was weird and nauseous, fantastic and silly. But instead of grasping the bottle as Powell expected, this hand, tremulous with senile eagerness, swerved to the glass, rested on its edge for a moment (or so it looked from above) and went back with a jerk. The gripping fingers of the other hand vanished at the same time, and young Powell staring at the motionless curtains could indulge for a moment the notion that he had been dreaming.   *(Conrad 1999: 308–9)*

Arguably, the initial feeling from reading this passage is the sense that something is missing, that information has been 'held back', but without compromising the flow of events. We instinctively 'know' that something sinister is unfolding, that somebody is doing something to somebody else. Yet, somewhat incongruously, if we examine the 'doings' of the perpetrator more closely, there is no sign of a 'holistic' human Actor at work. Table 19.2 outlines the key Material processes and relevant transitivity roles.

As this brief sketch shows, the agent responsible for the attempted murder is represented meronymically, that is, as a variety of body parts. This unusually high level of inanimacy is developed through a sequence of largely intransitive patterns in tandem with a set of verbs whose scope of reference is semantically rather broad: 'fumbling', 'grasped', 'hung', 'came', 'projecting', 'extended', 'swerved', 'rested', 'went back' and 'vanished'. As this is a report of an attempted murder it would not be unreasonable to assume that the action be communicated through a series of Material

Table 19.2 The 'perpetrator' at work.

Process type	ACTOR	PROCESS	GOAL	CIRCUMSTANCES
Material	'tips of fingers'	'fumbling'		'with the dark stuff'
Material	'they' [the tips of fingers]	'grasped'	'the edge of the further curtain'	
Material	'a hand'	'came'		'into view'
Material	'a short, puffy, old, freckled hand'	'projecting'		'into the lamp-light'
Material	'a white wrist'	[extended]		'in a grey coat sleeve, up to the elbow, beyond the elbow'
Material	'an arm'	'extended'		'tremblingly towards the tray'
Material	'this hand'	'swerved'		'to the glass'
Material	[this hand]	'rested'		'on its edge'
Material	[this hand]	'went'		'back'
Material	'the gripping fingers of the other hand'	'vanished'		

processes which directly or indirectly affect another entity; these are, after all, the most explicit way of representing 'doings'. Instead, each process takes an inanimate Actor, only two of which act on a Goal ('the tips of fingers / grasped / the edge of the further curtain'). Aside from this one instance, we are not even told what these body parts ultimately do. They appear to act on nothing and no one. The focus of the 'action' remains the curtain: 'The first sign . . . was an unaccountable movement of *the curtain* . . . He was suspicious of *the curtain* itself and observed *it*. *It* looked very innocent.' The entity responsible for moving the curtain has been elided through the substitution of the Material process 'moved', to its nominalised form, 'movement'.

Halliday observes that information is a form of discourse organisation and adds that 'any discourse is organized as a linear succession of information units' (in Kress 1976: 175). Transitivity analysis takes account of this linearity as the positioning of the constituent elements (process, participants and circumstances) is as important as the constituents themselves. As we suggested earlier, the Circumstantial element tends to carry the least focal significance. However, in a style much favoured by Conrad, the circumstances in our *Chance* extract are often at the fore, with the process and participants presented after, or between, these elements. Returning to the extract, the basic transitivity profile identified in Table 19.2 yields a sequence of Material processes. This is suggestive of narrative action and certainly accords with a narrative description of the execution of material event(s). Yet if we delve a little deeper than this decontextualised analysis to consider the linear narrative progression, we see that the Processes are often embedded within the Circumstantial information. For instance, in the sequence

> but instead of grasping at the bottle as Powell expected, this hand, tremulous with senile eagerness, swerved to the glass

the Circumstantial elements tend to slow down the arrival of the main process ('swerved') almost absorbing the Actor role. This pattern is consolidated by features of the lexicogrammar, such as the construction of nominal groups with elaborate premodifying or postmodifying elements situated around the head noun: respectively, 'a short, puffy, old, freckled *hand*' and 'an *arm* in a grey coat-sleeve, up to the elbow'.

Given that Circumstantial elements are normally 'subordinate in status to the process' (Simpson 1993: 90), we might ask the question, why are they granted such prominence in the Conrad passage? One possibility is that such constituents, by probing questions such as 'how', 'where', 'when' and 'why', are an aspect of narrative style which heightens expectation and builds suspense to what, here, is effectively very minor 'action' – action that Toolan might call 'noticeably-delayed negative-outcome foreseeability' (2009: 165). In addition, by elevating the Circumstantial adjuncts from the supplementary to the significant Conrad offers insights into the consciousness of the observer – remember that the key event is being reported from the witness's point of view – by providing a 'real-time' slow motion feel to the revelation of the crime. Consequently, Powell's observations and assessment of the situation are presented as more syntactically prominent and therefore receive greater interpretative focus than the event itself. In fact, nowhere in the extract is the attempted murder or the means of execution explicitly referred to. Such lexical under-specificity (the 'hand' engages in the following processes: 'swerved', 'rested', 'went', 'vanished') leaves the reader to make the inference that 'somebody' is up to something sinister. The impact of this omission on the transitivity analysis warrants further exploration. This will be the focus of the next section.

Transitivity-plus: 'doing' narration and negation

At the outset, it was signalled that the exploration of transitivity would broaden in scope as the chapter progresses. To this effect, we wish briefly to consider two theoretical issues that such an exploration raises. These issues relate to what we conceive here as *the plane of stylistic interpretation* and *the plane of narrative organisation*.

The first of these planes reverts to Halliday's own seminal article on William Golding's *The Inheritors* (Halliday 1971). This was the first stylistic analysis to employ the (author's own) model of transitivity, and its significance has been far-reaching for both literary critics and stylisticians.

Halliday's analysis seeks to demonstrate how the Neanderthal world of Lok and his tribespeople (the central characters in Golding's story) is conceived linguistically and in a way that is very different from our own. Lok's language is defined by a peculiar yet consistent transitivity pattern where, for example, meronymic agency ('His nose examined this stuff', 'His ears twitched') signals a markedly restricted cognitive facility on the part of the central character. The experiential dissociation of Lok and his tribe, relayed through a special set of transitivity choices, leads Halliday, in a perhaps unguarded moment, to pronounce this style 'a fair summary of the life of Neanderthal man' (1971: 350).

The problem with this type of pronunciation lies in the establishing of a direct causal link between linguistic description and critical inter-pretation, and it was this overly deterministic link that prompted Stanley Fish's attack on stylistics (1973; and see the ripostes from stylisticians in, for example, Hoover 1990; Shen 1988; Toolan 1990). Exploring the same issue, Simpson reveals that identical body-part agency, *mutatis mutandis*, dominates another of Golding's novels, *Pincher Martin*, but here the tran-sitivity patterns describe the fragmented consciousness of a drowning man (1993: 112). Indeed, other candidates for this type of marked tran-sitivity pattern are some genres of erotic fiction and horror fiction (Simpson 2004).

This aspect of the plane of interpretation may seem an impossible obstacle to overcome, but it is not insurmountable. For a start, the same problem of interpretation applies to any study of patterns in style, whether phonetic, grammatical or discoursal. What is required is that the analysts be aware that linguistic evidence *per se* does not equate to affective judge-ment; it forms part – and an accessible part at that – of the procedure by which that judgement is made. And while stylistic critique is only ever a partial exploration of text, it is at least predicated upon the rigour of a clear analytic method. This in our opinion will always offer more insight than a critique (*pace* Fish's own work) that is built on impressionism and on an unfettered trust in the wisdom and sensibility of the critic. To this end, we want to consider, further below, a more comprehensive account of transitivity that takes account of complementary stylistic features in the Conrad extract. We propose that this may lead to a more rigorously balanced interpretation than that which can be reached by a singular application of the model in isolation.

With respect to the plane of narrative organisation, an important feature of textual patterning, which has largely been neglected in accounts of transitivity, is the concept of *narrative gap* (see, for example, Hardy 2003, 2005). A narrative gap is when a specific piece of information concerning a narrative event and/or participants(s) is noticeably absent or delayed. In some senses, this has a similar effect to negation, which we discuss later, in that a narrative gap draws attention to the omission precisely because the missing information is expected (or at least, expected sooner in the event of a delay). By not narrating, the author creates a disjunction in the narrative and it is this gap that offers an extra layer of meaning. Although narrative gaps are 'non-narrated' events in the strict sense, they can be presupposed to have occurred and can be 'filled in' retrospectively because the lacuna is marked in some way. Consider this episode from David Mitchell's novel *Cloud Atlas*. Here the much put-upon elderly narrator, Timothy Cavendish, encounters three teenage girls on the streets of London. He takes issue with their dropping of litter:

> Tim Cavendish the Disgusted Citizen exclaimed to the offenders: 'You know, you should pick those up.'
> A snorted 'Whatchyoo gonna do'bou'it?' glanced off my back.
> Ruddy she-apes. 'I have no intention of doing anything about it,' I remarked over my shoulder, 'I merely said that you — '
> My knees buckled and the pavement cracked my cheek, shaking loose an early memory of a tricycle accident before pain erased everything but pain. A sharp knee squashed my face into leaf mould. I tasted blood. My sixtysomething wrist was winched back ... before my muggers could filch my wallet.   (D. Mitchell 2004:147)

The gapped event here is of course the attack by the teenagers, the import of which emerges implicitly through the immediate text that follows and more explicitly with the later appearance of the key agent noun 'muggers'. What is significant, however, is the marked absence of a transitivity process that signals the onset of the attack – along the lines, say, of 'They suddenly attacked me.' Among other things, the gap illustrates how a character may be an affected participant in an episode yet be not openly positioned as a Goal element in a Material process. Hardy makes clear the significance of 'unannounced' narrative gapping of this sort by pointing out that the presentation of gapped knowledge is 'a result of limited perception, whether that be on the part of the focaliser, the reader, the narrator, or some combination of all three' (Hardy 2005: 367–8).

In the extract from Conrad, Powell, the witness, does not quite know what to expect of the scene unfolding in front of him. His shock at the sudden realisation of events is reflected in the gapped narrative sequence 'this hand ... swerved to the glass, rested on its edge for a moment (or so it looked from above) and went back with a jerk'. From this, we are to deduce, as Powell does, that the hand contained poison, that the poison was administered and the attempt at murder successfully enacted. As a counterpoint to the Mitchell narrative above, in which the protagonist is not openly acted upon, Conrad positions the Actor (the hand) as not openly *acting* – he and his actions are subsumed by the 'when', 'how' and 'where' components, which, like the Cavendish example, reflects the limited perception, in this case, of the witness, Powell. In terms of transitivity, this gap is crucial, as it very consciously marks the absence of Goal-directed Material Processes executed by an animate Actor at the one stage in the narrative where the reader would naturally expect to encounter them. Were we to rely solely on our transitivity profile, we would struggle grammatically to locate the 'action' of the (non-)event under scrutiny. Understanding the stylistic impact of narrative gaps allows us to reconcile the apparent anomaly in the transitivity profile.

Maintaining the focus on the plane of narrative organisation, it is worth noting that applications of transitivity in stylistics have tended to apply the model in a rather linear way, plotting each process as it happens (e.g. Burton 1982; C. Kennedy 1982). As we have discussed above, what tends to be left out are the more complex shifts in narrative time, world and perspective. The Conrad excerpt exemplifies these narrative complexities and presents an interesting dynamic between events that *occur* but are not narrated, like the narrative gap discussed above, and events which do *not* occur, but which are narrated. For instance, in Kennedy's analysis of Conrad's *The Secret Agent* (1982) there is a tension between the narrative action that is under way (Mrs Verloc's approach with the knife) and Mr Verloc's projected narrative action. The latter – relayed through nominalisations, Mental processes and frequently negated Material processes – forms part of an imagined narrative world (see below on counter-factuality). This imagined world is elaborated in such detail and length that the murder of Verloc is already completed by the time we return to it, and this helps explain why our student readers often describe the passage from *The Secret Agent* as 'happening in slow motion'. Another consequence of this shift is the seeming anomaly that a character is both involved in processes of doing and not involved in processes of doing. What we propose here is a short informal account of how to tighten up the application so that it acknowledges shifts and modulations across narrative contexts.

One of the ways of addressing these narrative shifts is through a consideration of *negation* or *counter-factuality*, which, although not occurring experientially, is nonetheless present in the grammar of the narrative. If an event is reported in a text (e.g. 'Powell's only distinct aim was to remove the tumbler'), it becomes narratively significant, regardless of whether or not it is executed. Framed positively (consider the negatively framed 'Powell did not remove the tumbler') we are presented with an event-carrying clause that encodes no action. As such, these clauses will invariably factor into a transitivity profile, but not without some difficulty. What do we do, for example, with the Material action of 'remove the tumbler'? Such 'doings', actions and events, mean that a straightforward transitivity profile which accounts merely for *instances* of Material processes would skew results by throwing up 'fake' actions; grammatically, they fit the criteria for Material categorisation, but their *pragmatic* significance is ignored. It is for this reason that the area of *negation* makes for a particularly interesting intersection with transitivity analysis. Consider the effect of the final (Existential) process in the opening paragraph of Hemingway's *A Farewell to Arms*:

> In the late summer of that year we lived in a house in a village that looked across the river and the plain to the mountains. In the bed of the river there were pebbles and boulders, dry and white in the sun, and the water was clear and swiftly moving and blue in the channels. ... In the dark it was like summer lightning, but the nights were cool and there was not the feeling of a storm coming. *(Hemingway 1995: 1, emphasis added)*

In negation, the non-event becomes temporarily and locally more salient, and thus more informative (Givón 1993: 190). Moreover, Hidalgo Downing notes that the interpretation of a negative tends to require a corresponding affirmative proposition because it makes salient internal reference to the situation whose existence it denies (2000a: 70). This example of paragraph-final negation (much used by Hemingway, incidentally) consolidates the impression that the negative acts in a text as a kind of response to an implicit affirmative assumption.

Here is a pair of identical Mental processes from very different novels. In both cases, events are relayed from the perspective of a focalising male character:

> She went into the car park outside the Control Zone and got into a yellow Anglia. As she drove past him he could not see her face ...
> Bernard MacLaverty, Cal *(MacLaverty 1983: 16)*

> A woman was standing near the top of the first flight, in the shadow also. He could not see her face ... James Joyce, The Dead *(Joyce 2008: 51)*

While both processes are negated, it is implicit that some attempt at perception has been made and that both of the characters have striven to see the faces of the women who are the focus of their attention. This observation straddles Prince's concept of *disnarration*, which refers to narrative events that did not happen but whose significance is such that we are told about them (Prince 1988, 2006). This significance may be borne out by the typically full forms used for these negative particles as opposed to contracted forms such as 'there wasn't the feeling...' or 'he couldn't see her face'. Developing this further, and borrowing a term from Levinson (1983: 204), there are good grounds for describing negated transitivity processes in stories such as the three above as forms of *pragmatic presupposition*. This is because they work from shared knowledge, expectations and assumptions, rather than from a semantic core. The presupposition in this case is that the negated process is appropriately reportable and that the non-event is of narrative significance. To be sure, negation in transitivity is not readily captured by other definitions of the concept, such as those for metalinguistic negation or truth functional negation (see Carston 2012; Seuren 1988). Certainly, in *Chance*, an application of transitivity in isolation turns out to be rather complex, as a lot of the 'action' is mental or abstracted rather than experiential.

To understand how negation impacts on our analysis, we need to consider how the transitivity profile pans out as the extract progresses.

Following the administration of poison into the tumbler, Powell knows he must act to save Captain Anthony. The passage continues thus:

> Powell's only distinct aim was to remove the suspected tumbler. He had no other plan, no other intention, no other thought. Do away with it in some manner. Snatch it up and run out with it.   *(Conrad 1999: 310)*

Powell, however, is stopped by a sudden recognition of 'the safe aspect of familiar things', which leads him to experience 'a moment of incredulity as to the truth of his own conviction'. While he considers whether or not to dispose of the glass his thought process is interrupted by 'a voice', that of the victim, Captain Anthony. All Powell manages to articulate to explain his presence in the Captain's room, is the word 'Doctored', followed by, 'A hand ... a hand and the arm – only the arm – like that.' Table 19.3 summarises the full scene (Conrad 1999: 308–12) by recording the Material processes attributed to the three characters (the perpetrator of the 'crime'; the witness, Powell; and the 'victim' (Captain Anthony).

At first glance, the Table 19.3 shows an unequal distribution of Material processes between the three participants which only partly aligns with their characterisation in the text. On the one hand, the relative absence of Goal-directed Material processes obscures the ghost-like perpetrator, de Barral. On the other hand, the lack of Material action from the unsuspecting victim could be said to reflect his indifference to and or ignorance of the situation. Yet, in the context of Powell's participation, we have a seemingly anomalous abundance of Goal-directed Material processes. A total of 15 such processes are attributed to him, a character for whom, ironically, disbelief at unfolding events is *disabling*. On closer inspection, all is not as it seems: almost half of these Material processes (8) are imagined or negated, and are what we call 'non-events' (indicated by bold type). Conrad, here, presents a sequence of alternative possibilities that in themselves formulate one kind of transitivity profile in which Material action is represented as being consistent if not contiguous. The majority of these Material processes are Goal-directed. However, because most of the clauses are negated or counter-factual, we actually have a different transitivity profile, which *is* contiguous with the characters. Powell, our witness, wants to help, to be proactive, and so his *in*action is at odds with this. Conrad's use of negation signals Powell's altruistic intentions by acknowledging that alternative, proactive courses of action are open to him, lest we believe that Powell has consciously opted to do nothing out of indifference or neglect ('All he [Powell] had to do was to vanish back beyond the curtains, flee with it noiselessly into the night on deck, fling it unseen overboard. A minute or less'). Powell's inaction is explained in the narrative in the following way: 'the idea that if he did that [smash the glass] he could prove nothing'. This is interesting in terms of

Table 19.3 Summary of Material processes.

Process type	Perpetrator	Witness	Victim
Goal-directed Material Pr.	*they* [the tips of fingers] *grasped the edge of the further curtain* *it made an abominable sight*	He passed by it **Do away with it** [non-event] **Snatch it up** [non-event] **run out with it** [non event] He held the glass in his hand [All he had to do was] **to vanish … flee with it** [non-event] … **fling it** [non event] Powell … managed to lift one finger he raised the glass [he] moved his trammeled lips **Powell's only distinct aim was to remove the … tumbler** [non-event] what woke him up … was a voice **if he did that** [dash the glass on the deck] **he could prove nothing** [counter-factual event] [a voice] *fixed his feet immovably to the spot* [the idea] *that the story he had to tell was completely incredible, restrained him*	*the sight which met his eye* **The captain moved his head slightly**
Goal-less Material Pr.	*a hand came into view; a short, puffy, old, freckled hand projecting into the lamp-light, followed by a white wrist, an arm in a grey coat-sleeve, up to the elbow, beyond the elbow, extended tremblingly towards the tray.* *this hand … swerved to the glass,* [this hand] *rested on its edge …* [this hand] *went back … The gripping fingers of the other hand vanished*	he was using his eyes [Powell] entered swiftly I was coming in [Powell] found himself	Anthony advanced quietly The captain came forward slowly Anthony made himself heard **Not a feature of the captain's face moved**

transitivity as it constitutes a positively framed process ('he could prove'), albeit one that is modified by epistemic modality ('could'), yet it is both negated and counter-factual ('*if* he did that he could prove *nothing*'). By presenting these alternative proactive situations, Conrad impels us to engage in our own process of rationalisation, invoking empathy for his character; it is as if thinking about acting is almost as acceptable as physically acting. Factoring these Material processes or alternative possibilities for action into the transitivity profile, either by negation or counter-factuality, provides a more robust analysis that reflects the character's sensibilities because it permits us to 'negate and affirm at the same time' (Hidalgo Downing 2000a: 14).

If we consider the non-Material processes of the transitivity system in our extract (see Table 19.4), a pattern of non-events, in terms of perception, being and behaving, emerges more clearly. The perpetrator seems to sit outside the narrative, or at best, on its periphery, and his ghost-like status is affirmed by epistemic modification throughout ('he *must have been* startled'; 'he *must have been* thunderstruck, appalled'; 'he *must have been* concerned'; 'he *could not possibly* guess'). This type of epistemic modality, part of the *interpersonal* metafunction, transposes our transitivity profile from positive to negative. When accompanied by epistemic modal verbs ('could', 'must'), any Relational or Mental process is merely projection or presupposition. Similarly, the Relational processes isolated in our transitivity profile that are attributed to the witness, Powell, encode states of being, with some exhibiting an 'x has y' relationship ('He had no other plan'). However, such clauses are ambiguous examples as the process, like many others, is negated; what he 'had', in effect, was nothing. In transitivity terms, this clause yields nothing (literally), and you might ask where, if at all, it fits into the transitivity profile. Yet, its inclusion functions pragmatically because the negative formulation presupposes that the character should have (or could have) had a 'plan', 'thought' or 'strength'. As well as drawing attention to his character's lack of response, Conrad's use of negation offers an evaluative contrast with 'the averred actual continuation' (Toolan 2009: 148). In other words, the contrast acts as a kind of possible world, which is at times perceptually disorientating, but which reflects the character's struggle to make sense of what he believes is happening before his very eyes.

Summary

We began the latter part of this chapter by cautioning against making affective judgements based solely on linguistic evidence derived from the application of a stylistic model, however comprehensive that model may be. Without wishing to make a general ruling on the reader's interpretation of the Conrad piece, we would suggest that an intuitive response may sit uncomfortably with the transitivity profile we presented above in Table 19.2 in which the Material action is delineated. As we propose, this may be due to the ineffectiveness of the transitivity model fully to account for negative, counter-factual and disnarrated action. Thus, what we have attempted to show is that in spite of being a well-researched and frequently applied serviceable framework, transitivity can sometimes

Table 19.4 Summary of non-Material processes.

Process type	Perpetrator	Witness	Victim
Mental-Cognition Pr.	[He must have been startled] **to hear and see somebody** [non-event] **he could not possibly guess** [why I was coming] [non-event] **he must have been concerned** [non-event]	[He] observed it He saw trembling movements **Powell expected** I suppose it sounded to his ears he doubted his eyes	
Verbal Pr.		**he could prove nothing** the story he had to tell was incredible he moved his trammeled lips to form the words: 'Doctored' Powell whispered fearfully 'I am dreaming now', he said to himself Powell gasped freely	Anthony . . . had naturally exclaimed **the exclamation must have been fairly loud** [non-event] the very monstrosity of appearances silenced Anthony
Behavioural Pr.	**the old man must have been watching** [non-event] he must have been startled [non-event] **he must have been thunderstruck, appalled** [non-event] it [the curtain] looked very innocent somebody else had been watching Captain Anthony He was watching and listening its [the hand's] appearance was weird	**he had been dreaming** [non-event] He was startled to observe [proj.] the tips of fingers young Powell felt himself pierced . . . by the . . . glance of his captain He was looking at it Young Powell staring motionless He must have dreamt it **he must have looked like a man in a trance** [non-event]	
Relational Pr.		He became suspicious He was suspicious of the curtain I am certain **He had no other plan,** [he had] **no other intention,** [he had] **no other thought** He was in a sort of panic	
Existential Pr.		**Powell had no voice, no strength** There stood his second officer There he was, caught absolutely, with the glass in his hand	

fall short when it comes to interpreting the whole picture. Our own analysis uses complementary stylistic techniques to offer a way of reading action and event as well as inaction and non-event in Conrad's *Chance*. Without this, the analysis would yield an incongruous abundance of Material processes on the part of an *inactive* witness and a marked lack of human agency on the part of the perpetrator.

This of course is not to say that a stylistic analysis that explores *only* the experiential metafunction is inherently impoverished. Indeed, we have suggested that transitivity has served an important function in fore-grounding the perspective of the witness, Powell, in narrating actions and events (both real and non-real). At the same time, we have shown how the transitivity configurations represent the elusive de Barral as having no animate agency. What we want to highlight, however, is that on reading the piece we intuit a series of events and actions that seems to jar with our understanding of the transitivity profile because they are not explicitly narrated; that is, from the text we 'know' that de Barral has done something that will affect someone else unless he is stopped and we 'will' our witness to intervene. It could be argued that the disjunction between the linguistic evidence and our 'gut response' is almost *created* by the transitivity profile itself precisely because it is not equipped to deal adequately with the non-events and inaction that litter the text. To address the shortfall, we have incorporated a more varied and complementary stylistic tool-kit that offers a greater level of interpretative specificity. By exploring the phenomenon of narrative gaps we have considered what is narrated as well as what is not narrated, which we believe makes our analysis more robust and comprehensive. We have also accounted for what is narrated, but what has not actually occurred, by examining counter-factual and imagined events through the trope of negation. We believe that by acknowledging and exploiting these stylistic intersections, our linguistic evidence more strongly reflects and articulates the dynamic relationship that obtains between what we *feel* from the text and what is actually *there*. Or not there, as the case may be.

20

Pragmatics and inference
Billy Clark

> People look. And they wonder. And they make conclusions.
> And it's the same in film.
> (David Lynch in *Great Directors*, dir. Angela Ismailos, 2011)

Introduction

While he does not use the term, the process of arriving at conclusions mentioned in the above quote by the film-maker David Lynch is what psychologists describe as inference. Lynch is suggesting that people draw conclusions based on what they observe in life and also when watching films. To take a simple example, if I see a colleague at work moving very quickly down a corridor, I might conclude that they are late for an appointment. We also make inferences when people communicate with us in everyday spoken and written communications. And we make inferences when reading texts and watching all kinds of performances. Pragmatics is the field which studies inferences like this. Linguists are interested in inference because it plays a role in linguistic communication. Stylisticians are interested in inference because it plays a role in how we respond to literary and non-literary texts.

This chapter considers the nature of inferential processes, pragmatic theories which have been developed to account for them, and applications of these theories in stylistics. It points out that we make a large number of inferences very quickly in everyday situations, says something about pragmatic theories which have been developed since the work of Paul Grice (1975, 1989) and considers how these theories have been, and can be, applied in stylistics. It then considers some general theoretical questions which can be addressed to some extent by pragmatic theories. The conclusions are: that inferential processes play a significant role in the production, interpretation and evaluation of all texts; that an account of these processes is a vital part of accounts of any text or communicative act; that there are practical issues which need to be addressed when accounting for inferences; that we do not always need to refer to specific theoretical assumptions when discussing inferences, though in some cases this is useful; that pragmatics can be applied in exploring theoretical as well as analytical questions; and, finally, that there is lots of exciting work which can be carried out by looking at inference.

Inference in general

As suggested above, we make inferences all the time, whether we are communicating or not. As the pragmaticist Dan Sperber put it, in a paper on the (inferential) nature of communication:

> 'Inference' is just the psychologists' term for what we ordinarily call 'reasoning.' Like reasoning, it consists in starting from some initial assumptions and in arriving through a series of steps at some conclusion. Psychologists however are not just being pretentious in using a rarer word: when most of us talk of reasoning, we think of an occasional, conscious, difficult, and rather slow mental activity. What modern psychology has shown is that something like reasoning goes on all the time – unconsciously, painlessly, and fast. When psychologists talk of inference, they are referring first and foremost to this ever-present mental activity.   *(Sperber 1995: 194)*

It is easy to show that we reason all the time and very quickly. For non-communicative reasoning, we can see this by thinking about how quickly we react to things that we see. We might think of how quickly we infer the intentions of a car driver as we drive, walk or cycle near their vehicle. Or how quickly we adjust to other people's behaviour in crowded situations, say as we decide which checkout to head for in a busy supermarket. For communication, we might think about how quickly we react to what other people communicate in a conversation. Anyone who has studied recordings or transcripts of conversation will have noticed how often speakers overlap each other or respond before another person has finished expressing a particular proposition. Another way to see this is to think about how many inferential steps are involved in a fairly straightforward exchange. Here is an exchange I heard recently (with names changed):

(1) Andy: I just forwarded you that email about the meeting next week.
    Beth: Got it.

To understand Beth's utterance, Andy has to infer at least the following things:

a. what sense of *got* is intended (e.g. 'received' or 'understood')
b. what *it* refers to
c. who the understood subject is who has got it
d. when or in what circumstances the person has got it

Having worked out these things, Andy might represent the proposition Beth is expressing as (roughly) (2):

(2)   Beth has received the email Andy sent about the meeting next week.

This assumes that a particular set of contextual assumptions are accessed and used by Andy (roughly, those which mean that the main aim of this exchange is to establish that Beth has access to the email). If we imagine a different set of contextual assumptions, the interpretation will be different. Suppose, for example, that Andy has been trying to make sure that Beth understands something which is contained in the email (perhaps an instruction from a manager before the meeting about something Beth needs to do). In this case, Andy might represent the proposition Beth is communicating as (roughly) (3):

(3)   Beth has understood the instruction communicated in the email Andy has forwarded to her.

Up to now, we have only considered inferences involved in working out what Beth is explicitly communicating. Having worked this out, Andy has more work to do to infer what Beth is indirectly communicating (to use current terminology, the implicatures that Beth has implicated). Depending on available contextual assumptions, there might be a fairly small set of implicatures which Beth is strongly communicating (in the sense that it is fairly clear that she intends these). If, for example, Beth wants the email so she can forward it to other colleagues, Andy might infer that Beth will be forwarding the email. If the instruction in the email is important, Andy might infer that Beth will be doing what the instruction asks her to do. There may also be a range of relatively weaker implicatures such as that Beth is grateful to Andy for the help, and so on.

So far, I have pretended that things are simpler than they are. A full account of how Andy understands Beth here would take much more time and space. It would have to account not only for how Andy manages to arrive at more or less the interpretation intended by Beth when things go fairly smoothly, but also for what happens if Andy misunderstands Beth's intentions (suppose, for example, that he thinks she is communicating that she understands the instruction in the email but she only intends to communicate that she has received it).

People involved in everyday exchanges like this arrive at interpretations very quickly and tend to carry straight on with their conversation. Clearly, the inferential task is very complex, as you can see by thinking about how much I have written just to give a partial and simplified account of how this simple two-word utterance might be understood. The challenge for pragmatic theories is to explain how we do this so quickly, what is involved in each part of the process, and why we sometimes misunderstand each other.

Pragmatics

This section presents a very brief account of some current approaches to pragmatic theorising, all of which have their origins in the work of Paul

Grice. The most important source is the lecture entitled 'Logic and Conversation', which he gave as part of a series in 1967 (Grice 1975). There are two key things which Grice proposed: first, that we can distinguish between what an utterance 'says' (its explicit content) and what it 'implicates' (what it communicates indirectly); second, that we can explain implicature by assuming a set of guiding principles, which Grice termed 'maxims'. Very roughly, Grice suggested that (hearers and readers assume that) speakers and writers follow a range of maxims when formulating their utterances. These require contributions to an exchange to be informative enough but not over-informative, truthful, evidenced, relevant and formulated in an appropriate manner.

While Grice never used the term 'pragmatics', most and probably all current pragmatic theories take his approach as a starting point. However, no current pragmatic theories adopt all of Grice's assumptions. This is inevitable given that Grice proposed an outline of how a fuller account might go rather than a fully developed theory. Current theories also aim to improve on some perceived weaknesses in Grice's account. Perhaps the most significant of these has to do with the nature of explicit content (what Grice called 'what is said'). Grice said little about this and did not fully define 'what is said' beyond suggesting that it is 'closely related to the conventional meaning of the words ... uttered' (Grice 1989: 25), and that disambiguation and reference assignment are also involved. While current pragmatic theories vary with regard to how they conceive of explicit content, many suggest that pragmatic processes are involved here too, and that there is more to recovering what is said than just disambiguation and reference assignment. We can illustrate this by considering Beth's utterance in (1). First, it seems clear that pragmatic principles are involved in deciding which sense of *got* is intended and what *it* refers to (Andy will make decisions which allow the utterance to be seen as informative, relevant and so on). Second, the utterance will not be able to be seen as informative, relevant and so on if Andy does not also make inferences about the understood subject and so on.

Approaches which build on Grice's work have been distinguished in a range of ways. One division is between approaches that incorporate principles which are fairly maxim-like, and so are termed 'neo-Gricean', such as those developed by Larry Horn (1984, 1988, 1989, 2004) and Stephen Levinson (1987, 2000), and approaches such as relevance theory (Sperber and Wilson 1995; Wilson and Sperber 2004; see also B. Clark 2013), which propose principles that are not maxim-like, and so are termed merely 'post-Gricean'.

An example of a neo-Gricean principle is Horn's 'Q-Principle' ('Q' for 'quantity'), which says roughly that speakers should 'say as much as they can' and is used to explain inferences such as the one which leads from the use of *some* to the inference of 'not all':

(4)   I like some of David Lynch's movies.

This would usually be taken to implicate that the speaker does not like *all* of Lynch's movies. This follows from the Q-Principle since a speaker who is aiming to 'say as much as they can' would have said they liked all of Lynch's movies if she liked them all. Failure to use the term *all* gives rise to the implicature of 'not all'.

Another example is Horn's 'R-Principle' ('R' for 'relation') which says roughly that speakers should 'say no more than you must' and explains inferences such as the one which leads from the use of *and* to the assumption of 'and as a result':

(5)   I fell off my bike and grazed my leg.

Here the existence of assumptions about a connection between a bike accident and a grazed leg mean that the speaker does not need to spell out that the grazed leg was a result of the fall. Notice that the inference from *some* to 'not all' follows partly from the relationship between the linguistic form *some* and the equally simple and accessible form *all*, while the inference from *and* to 'and as a result' follows mainly from assumptions about the world.

Relevance theory, by contrast, does not assume any maxim-like notions. Instead, it is centred on law-like generalisations about human cognition and communication. Very briefly, the key assumption about communication is that the act of communicating ostensively gives rise to the expectation that there is an interpretation which justifies the effort involved in processing it and which does not require unnecessary effort. Given this assumption, hearers or readers can follow a path of least effort in looking for the intended interpretation and stop as soon as their expectations of relevance are met (or abandoned). The interpretation procedure is understood as a non-linear heuristic which involves accessing contextual assumptions and forming hypotheses about disambiguation, reference assignment, enrichment, accessing potential implicatures, and so on, in a process of 'mutual parallel adjustment' (Wilson and Sperber 2004: 616). This means that the various hypotheses, including those about which contextual assumptions are required, influence each other during the interpretation process. A relevance-theoretic account of (5) would suggest that the hearer quickly accesses assumptions about an individual being hurt as a result of a fall from their bike. This will give rise to enough effects to justify the effort involved in processing the utterance and so this will meet the hearer's expectations of relevance. Blakemore and Carston (2004) suggest that a key part of this involves the assumption that the conjunction is treated as a single 'processing unit' which achieves relevance as a unit – in other words, that the effects which meet expectations of relevance follow from the conjunction as a whole.

While different pragmatic theories make different assumptions about the nature of pragmatic principles, the precise nature of the semantics–pragmatics distinction and the precise nature of the explicit–implicit distinction, key assumptions shared by most current theories are that pragmatic principles govern the interpretation process and that these are grounded in rationality. These assumptions have their origins in the work of Grice.

Pragmatic stylistics

So how do we go about applying ideas from pragmatic theories in analysing particular texts? This section begins by pointing out a serious practical problem in analysing inferences and then considers a number of ways in which looking at inference can contribute to stylistics. As with other areas of stylistics, the analyses can be applied to literary or non-literary texts, but the examples here are taken from screenplays, poetry and prose.

A practical issue

If inferential processes are involved at every stage of production and interpretation, a natural assumption might be that we should simply start analysing all of them. However, this is not practical given the time and space involved in explaining even what seem like fairly straightforward inferences. Consider, for example, the following utterance (part of the first line of dialogue spoken in David Lynch's film *Mulholland Dr.* (Lynch 2001)):

(6) We don't stop here.

Let's begin by thinking about any utterance of this sequence of words. To explain how this is understood in a specific context, we would need to explain how the addressee infers a number of things, including who is the referent of *we*, where *here* is, what sense of *stop* is intended (to cease doing something, to come to a standstill, etc.), whether the stopping is a habitual action, something in the future, or some other time or circumstance, and so on. We would also need to decide whether the speaker is expressing their own thought or someone else's, making a statement or asking a question, ironic or serious, and so on. Finally, we would need to explain how the addressee works out which set of implicatures are being indirectly communicated.

In the film, this utterance is produced by the character played by Laura Harring (her complete utterance is 'What are you doing? We don't stop here'). At this stage, we do not know her name and all we know of her is what we have seen in the opening scene so far. She is sitting in the back of an oldish black Cadillac car, which we have been following as it drives in the night along Mulholland Drive in Hollywood. In this situation, most viewers will infer that she is reminding the two men in the front seat that this is not somewhere where this car is expected to stop. I have not described how this happens yet, nor said anything about the effects of contextual assumptions derived from the pre-credit sequence (with jitter-bugging couples, washed-out faces with beaming smiles looking upwards, a dishevelled red blanket) and the night-time shot looking down over a twinkling Los Angeles. Without mentioning these, I have already written over two hundred words. Describing the inferential processes would take more space. With fictional work, there is added complexity as the utterance is produced by a character whose words are determined by the author with a particular audience in mind. Inferences are also affected by a range of contextual assumptions, about the author, about the genre, and so on. In a film, there are visual images and soundtrack, which also play a role. Finally, we might consider the nature of various kinds of audiences and how their inferential processes might vary. It quickly becomes clear that it would take considerable time and space to account for the interpretation of just these four words.

However, this does not mean that we should abandon the idea of analysing inferential processes involved in producing and understanding texts. Instead, most pragmatic stylisticians will aim to account for a selection of the processes involved in particular texts. B. Clark (2009) suggests that stylisticians should be particularly on the lookout for cases where the nature of particular inferential processes becomes salient – in other words, where readers become more aware of the nature of the inferential processes they are engaged in. There are many examples in the films of David Lynch. One example is the moment in Lynch's 1997 film *Lost Highway* where the camera zooms in on the character Fred Madison (played by Bill Pullman), as he lies in a prison cell accused of murdering his wife Renee (played by Patricia Arquette) before a dissolve into a scene featuring another character, Pete Dayton (played by Balthazar Getty), and then back to the prison cell where Fred morphs into Pete. Pete is then released from prison and we follow him down a different storyline. This raises questions about what exactly has happened, what kind of film we are watching and what we are expected to make of it all. This is added to by the appearance in Pete's story of a character called Alice, who is also played by Patricia Arquette. This gives rise to a wide range of inferences about the nature of film as well as of this particular film. (For a discussion of the complexities in this work, see Buckland 2009.)

'Theory-neutral' analyses

Another reason not to give up in the light of practical difficulties with analysing inferences is that we can say a significant amount about how texts work without developing fully detailed analyses and without adopting particular theoretical frameworks.

Given the importance of inferential processes in producing and understanding texts, there has been surprisingly little work which takes such a theory-neutral approach. Among theory-specific approaches, there has been a significant amount of work based on relevance theory (for a brief survey, see MacMahon 2006; for a recent discussion, see B. Clark 2014), very little from a neo-Gricean point of view (for one exception, see S. Chapman 2012) and, surprisingly, a significant amount of work which continues to use a traditional Gricean framework (for discussion of how to apply Gricean ideas, see Lambrou 2014a). While particular theoretical frameworks may provide particular kinds of insights, it is also possible to cast a significant amount of light on particular texts without explicitly adopting a particular framework. Here is the beginning of an account of some of the effects of a short story, *The Swim Team*, by Miranda July. The story opens as follows:

(7) This is the story I wouldn't tell you when I was your girlfriend. You kept asking and asking, and your guesses were so lurid and specific. Was I a kept woman? Was Belvedere like Nevada, where prostitution is legal? Was I naked for the entire year? The reality began to seem barren. And in time I realised that if the truth felt empty, then I probably would not be your girlfriend much longer.   *(July 2007: 18)*

The character in the story goes on to tell about her time in Belvedere, the key part being that she became a swim coach giving classes in her kitchen. The swim team consisted of three elderly people who could not swim. She and her team compensated for the lack of swimmable water in the area by practising with bowls of warm salt water. She contrasts how she was in Belvedere ('I had a very different identity in Belvedere') with how she is/was known to the addressee of her story. The story also makes clear that she is a different, more assertive and more confident person while coaching. We see that the members of the swim team change as a result of their lessons. One of them, the eldest, called Jack Jack ('I don't know why Jack twice', says the narrator, 2007: 14), is 'precocious', swimming around the floor with the bowl, even doing a lap of the bedroom at one point. 'Swim to me', he would say to another team member who would look at him and 'just beam' after he had done this.

The previous paragraph describes some (far from all) of the conclusions I have made from reading the story. Clearly, a full account of all of these and other inferences made on reading the text would take a huge amount of time and space. So a pragmatic stylistic analysis will need to choose which aspects to focus on. One approach might involve listing key implicatures and discussing the evidence provided by the text for particular ones. We might, for example, look at how we infer that the narrator has changed as a result of her coaching role. A key part of the text which provides evidence for this is near the end of the story:

(8) It was just two hours a week, but all the other hours were in support of those two.   *(July 2007: 18)*

In analysing this, we could look in detail at all of the inferences involved. However, it is not likely that we will discover much by looking at certain inferences: how we infer the referent of *it*, for example. The contribution of *just* and *but* seem more important. Roughly, *just* suggests that the number *two* is comparatively small and that the proposition expressed, that 'it was two hours a week', would not be expected to implicate very significant conclusions, while *but* suggests that what follows contradicts and eliminates something which might have been inferred from the first conjunct. We might then focus on what exactly *in support of* suggests here. This would presumably not suggest that the narrator only ever did things which directly prepare for the swimming lessons but something looser than this, suggesting that the lessons are important and frequently on her mind (these conclusions are supported by other parts of the text).

We might also focus on particular parts of the text where we think a pragmatic approach would be useful. One character, Kelda, could not put her face into her bowl of water for several weeks. The swim coach reassures her that this is natural as 'It's the body telling you it doesn't want to die'. Kelda replies 'It doesn't' (July 2007: 16). A pragmatic account of this might focus on how this utterance is understood and its mildly ironic tone. The coach's utterance pragmatically presupposes (although it does not entail) that Kelda's body doesn't want to die so there would not seem to be any need for Kelda to state this. She might be doing this just to agree explicitly with the presupposition. However, particularly if we imagine a prosodic form with a marked accent on the first syllable of *doesn't*, then we might see Kelda's utterance as suggesting that the coach needs to be informed that Kelda's body doesn't want to die, hence emphasising Kelda's emotional response and the ironic tone. We could describe this in a theoretically neutral way as we have just done or we could develop an account within a particular framework. A Gricean account, for example, might suggest that Kelda seems to have said something over-informative motivating the derivation of an appropriately informative implicature. A relevance-theoretic account would focus on the process of looking for enough effects to justify the effort of deriving them.

Theory-specific approaches

In some cases, particular theoretical approaches offer accounts of particular phenomena which can be used in accounting for particular aspects of texts. This section mentions just a few examples.

Siobhan Chapman (2012) applies Horn's (1984) Q-Principle and R-Principle in discussing implicatures about misogynistic attitudes in Dorothy L. Sayers's novel *Gaudy Night*. One example she discusses concerns the use of the marked forms *undergraduette* and *Lady Head* in a London newspaper read by the main character Harriet Vane. Chapman explains this with reference to another part of Horn's approach, which he terms the 'division of pragmatic labour'. She says:

> Harriet is struck by, and writes to the paper to complain about, the terms 'undergraduettes' and 'Lady Head'. The fictitious journalist has used marked forms instead of the shorter, simpler unmarked forms 'undergraduates' and 'Warden'. According to the division of pragmatic labour, if a marked form is used, despite the impetus from the R Principle to use the simplest and shortest form possible, the Q Principle licenses the hearer to understand that the unmarked form is not used for a reason: that the situation being described is in some way not normal or stereotypical. So the implicature that Harriet objects to is that female students and wardens are not usual or normal students and wardens: that there is something 'marked' about women in these roles.　　(S. Chapman 2012: 147)

A number of ideas from the relevance-theoretic approach have been applied in developing pragmatic stylistic analyses, including relevance-theoretic accounts of metaphor (see, for example, Pilkington 2000; for a more general discussion of metaphor from a relevance-theoretic point of view, see Carston 2002), irony (MacMahon 1996 discusses irony and related concepts in developing ideas on poetic 'voice'; Morini 2010 suggests an amendment to the relevance-theoretic account; for a general discussion of irony from a relevance-theoretic point of view, see Wilson and Sperber 2012) and other specific phenomena. Here I discuss three more general notions to do with the nature of implied conclusions and the units in a text which have relevance.

Within relevance theory, there is a distinction between 'implications' (conclusions which follow logically from utterances) and 'implicatures' (the sub-set of implications which are intentionally communicated). Suppose, for example, that I don't like chocolate and you tell me as we're heading to a friend's for dinner:

(9)　Jan says she's made a chocolate dessert.

If you know that I don't like chocolate then you will implicate that Jan has made something I don't like, that this will be awkward for me, and so on. However, if you don't know that I don't like chocolate, then this will simply be an implication of your utterance. It is something I will conclude but I won't think of it as something you intend to communicate.

This distinction is useful in accounting for the difference between what authors communicate to readers and what characters communicate to each other (as well as other 'layers' of communication). When, for example, one character says something to another, we might describe some of the conclusions we derive from it as implications of the character's utterances, but implicatures of the author's writing. We might also use this notion in explaining how characters reveal things about themselves, such as some of the negative implications about the Duke in

Browning's *My Last Duchess* (discussed by MacMahon 1996). We can say that Browning is implicating some of the Duke's negative qualities while the Duke himself is providing evidence for them but merely implying rather than implicating them. We might also use this distinction in considering some of the inferences we make when reading Miranda July's *The Swim Team*. The narrator implicates some of the conclusions we derive – for example, that she enjoyed coaching her team, that this became important to her and so on – and this can be separated from what the author is implicating by having this character narrate this story in this way. This would include conclusions about how particular kinds of activity can be transformative, the power of imagination and so on. This distinction is also relevant in describing implications we derive on our own which cannot have been intended by the author (e.g. I might conclude from reading *The Swim Team* that I should change a specific aspect of my own behaviour).

Another key relevance-theoretic notion is that there is not a clear-cut distinction between communicated implicatures and implications which the addressee is solely responsible for. Rather, implicatures can be more or less strongly evidenced and it can be more or less clear that a communicator intended a particular conclusion. In other words, implicatures can be more or less strongly communicated. This can be illustrated by an everyday utterance such as (10):

(10)   Andy: Have you been following *X Factor*?
       Beth: I don't watch reality TV.

Here Beth clearly implicates that she has not been following *X Factor* (a UK reality TV show) and that she believes that *X Factor* counts as an example of reality TV. She also gives strong (but not quite as strong) evidence that she does not watch *Britain's Got Talent*, *Big Brother* and other shows which are usually considered to be examples of reality TV. There will be some shows which might less clearly count as examples of reality TV and so it will be less clear that she does not watch those. Game shows, for example, are usually considered to count as reality TV but we cannot be sure that Beth intends to include game shows when she says this. What about the assumptions in (11)?

(11) a.   Beth does not watch programmes which are not thought of as serious.
     b.   Beth disapproves of television which might be considered trivial.
     c.   Beth disapproves of people who watch reality TV.
     d.   Beth is quite moralistic.
     e.   Beth is quite judgemental.
     f.   Beth does not watch family entertainment shows.

Do you think Beth communicated these? This is less clear since it is possible for each one of them that she did not intend it. At the same time, she seems to have provided some evidence since someone who heard the exchange in (10) might think that any one of them could be true if asked questions such as *Do you think Beth watches 'Total Wipeout'?* (*Total Wipeout* is a UK game show) or *Do you think Beth would disapprove of me watching 'Big Brother'?*

An example we might discuss from *The Swim Team* concerns the use of the word *barren* in the sentence 'The reality began to seem barren'. The choice of this fairly uncommon word might give rise to weak implicatures about the word's associations with infertility. Did Miranda July intend for readers to think about these associations? I would suggest that she did. Did she strongly implicate any assumptions which connect with this association? Most readers would say no. We cannot, for example, conclude that the narrator has definitely chosen this word because of its associations with infertility.

The fact that implicatures can vary in strength can be important in accounting for textual meaning, not only because we might want to discuss this in characterising the effects of a particular text (such as those associated with the word *barren* just discussed) but also because we might want to contrast texts with regard to how strongly they create particular implicatures. Sperber and Wilson (1995) discuss this notion in their work on 'poetic effects', which they see as arising from texts that create a wide range of weak implicatures. As an example, they quote Flaubert's remark on the writer Leconte de Lisle that 'son encre est pale' ('his ink is pale'). They suggested that this provides evidence for a range of conclusions, none of which is strongly implicated but for each of which Flaubert has provided some evidence (that Leconte de Lisle's writing won't last, that it lacks passion, and so on). We can illustrate this further by considering poems such as this one by Emily Dickinson:

(12)   The brain within its groove
       Runs evenly and true;
       But let a splinter swerve,
       'T were easier for you
       To put the water back
       When floods have slit the hills,
       And scooped a turnpike for themselves,
       And blotted out the mills!   *(Dickinson 1990: 25)*

This suggests a range of conclusions which we might explore, depending, among other things, on how we conceive of the referent of *the brain*, what it means to say the brain *runs evenly and true*, whether we think it is good or bad to *swerve* it off course, and so on. None of the conclusions we entertain are strongly implicated, and an important part of an account of the poem will require an account of this wide range of weakly evidenced conclusions. We might, of course, develop a similar account of the effects of the transformation of one character into another in David Lynch's *Lost Highway* mentioned above. Another example from Lynch's work has to do with the title of the film *Mulholland Dr*. While spoken discussion of the film will tend to pronounce this as 'Mulholland Drive', Lynch's title is in the abbreviated form, which opens up the possibility of asking whether *Dr.* could be short for something else, the most likely candidate being *dream*. This in turn invites new directions for interpretation focusing on whether the film as a whole is a dream, or parts of it are. It also connects with the notion that films are dreams. (After watching a disturbing scene from the film – where a young man in a diner goes outside to the scene where he has seen a monster in his dreams – David Lynch once commented, 'A disturbing day in the city of dreams'.) Pilkington (2000) has explored the nature of effects like these, arguing that such effects play a role in giving rise to 'affective' (emotional) responses, but also that affective responses cannot be fully accounted for in terms of weak implicatures.

Another aspect of inferential conclusions which pragmatic stylisticians are interested in are those which are fairly 'local', in that they are derived on the basis of specific parts of the text, and those which are more 'global', depending on larger part of texts, or even whole texts (for discussion, see B. Clark 1996, 2009). To take a very simple example, we infer that the questions in the opening paragraph of *The Swim Team* in example (7) above (*Was I a kept woman? Was Belvedere like Nevada, where prostitution is legal? Was I naked for the entire year?*) are the narrator's representations of questions asked by the addressee (her ex-boyfriend) rather than questions being asked by the narrator herself. We can infer this using only evidence provided by the first paragraph. We also make inferences about such things as the referents of pronouns based on local evidence here. Other conclusions might depend on evidence suggested by the text as a whole. These might include implicatures mentioned above about the nature of imagination, transformative activities, and so on. Implicatures can, of course, be more or less global and be adjusted while reading and rereading the text. In this case, these might include inferences about the narrator, her reticence, her attitude to her ex-boyfriend, and so on.

Underexplored areas: production, criticism and evaluation

As with pragmatics in general, there has been relatively little work which explores processes involved in production or how meanings are negotiated in interaction between and among communicators (J. Thomas 1995 argues explicitly for the view that meanings are created by interaction rather than simply produced by communicators and received by addressees). Owtram (2010) explores inferential processes involved in academic writing, and in pedagogical contexts. Billy Clark and Owtram (2012) discuss pedagogical work designed to help writers make inferences about how readers will respond to their writing. Billy

Clark (2012) considers another stage in the production of fiction by discussing aspects of editorial work in the production of some of Raymond Carver's work (particularly those where Carver's editor, Gordon Lish, proposed and imposed significant editorial decisions which went beyond Carver's wishes). These works suggest that there is much to be done in developing models of the inferential processes involved in the production as well as the interpretation of texts.

Inferential processes are also involved in the development of literary criticism and evaluation. These are also areas which have not yet received much discussion by pragmatic stylisticians.

A theoretical question: are literary inferences different?

Pragmatic theories can also be applied in discussing more general theoretical questions. Wilson (2011) considers the role of authorial intention in literary texts, suggesting that pragmatic theories have shown that it is necessary to consider authorial intentions when understanding texts. Furlong (1996) has suggested that one way of characterising literariness is by considering the nature of inferential processes. Furlong does not suggest that literariness can be fully defined as a property of inferences but she does define a kind of inferential interpretative process which is often applied in understanding literary texts. She terms this 'non-spontaneous interpretation' and contrasts it with the 'spontaneous interpretation' processes usually involved in everyday exchanges.

Working within a relevance-theoretic framework, Furlong suggests that a spontaneous interpretation is one which involves simply following the relevance-theoretic comprehension procedure until an interpretation is found which satisfies expectations of relevance (providing enough effects to justify the effort of deriving them). Suppose, for example, that I meet a colleague in the corridor at work in the early evening and ask her if she is finished for the day. She replies:

(13)   Yeh, I'm on my way home.

I will work out that she has communicated that she is heading home and that she has taken part in a polite friendly exchange with me. I will probably then move on to think about something else, and perhaps to say something else to her – for example, to wish her a good evening.

A non-spontaneous interpretation, by contrast, is one which goes beyond the first plausible interpretation, systematically bringing all available evidence to bear and carefully developing and assessing possible interpretations. I have done something like this in thinking about the following utterance made by Bob Dylan at the beginning of a documentary about Dylan directed by Martin Scorsese:

(14)   I was born VERY far from where I'm supposed to be and so I'm on my
        way home.

(Bob Dylan, in No Direction Home, *dir. Martin Scorsese 2005)*

Dylan's utterance is clearly metaphorical and I can spend significant
effort thinking about what exactly he means by *home*, in what sense he
meant that he started his life far from there and what it means to be on his
way home during his lifetime.

While Furlong does not claim that everyday utterances cannot be interpreted non-spontaneously, nor that literary texts cannot be interpreted
spontaneously, she does suggest that non-spontaneousness is typical of literary interpretation. It would be possible for me to think 'non-spontaneously'
and at length about what my colleague might have intended by her utterance
and to think only briefly about Dylan's utterance – in other words, to
interpret it 'spontaneously'. Future work might not only explore this claim
but also consider what other ways there may be to define literary interpretations and literary texts.

Conclusion

Inferential processes play a significant role in the production, interpretation and evaluation of all texts, and an account of these processes is in
principle a vital part of accounts of any text or communicative act.
However, there are practical issues which need to be addressed when
accounting for inferences. Accounting for inferences takes considerable
time and space so it is not feasible to provide a detailed account of the
inferential processes involved in producing or responding to even fairly
short texts. Stylisticians need to develop strategies to cope with this and to
decide which inferences associated with particular texts to focus on.
Accounts of inferential processes can be developed to some extent without
relying explicitly on specific theories, but specific theories can provide
useful insights and useful accounts of specific phenomena. The above
discussion covered only a selection of the kinds of analyses which might
be developed by focusing on inferential processes. There is lots of work
still to be done in comparing pragmatic theories, exploring what they can
offer to stylisticians, and in looking at the inferences associated with
specific texts. We don't stop here.

21

Metaphor and style

Gerard Steen

The study of metaphor and style

The stylistic study of metaphor involves the idiosyncratic way metaphor is used in specific texts, by individual authors or, more broadly, sets of authors forming a school, generation or similar social groupings. Metaphor has been studied in individual texts such as Shakespeare's *Antony and Cleopatra*, *King Lear* and *Macbeth* (D. C. Freeman 1993, 1995, 1999), Patrick Süskind's *Perfume* (Popova 2003) and Ken Kesey's *One Flew over the Cuckoo's Nest* (Semino and Swindlehurst 1996), and this is typically seen as a matter of stylistics: after all, metaphor in literature is a stylistic device, and its forms, meanings and use all fall within the remit of stylistics. But is this conceptualisation of metaphor completely valid?

Since 1980, the study of metaphor has been shifted from one based in poetics, stylistics and rhetoric to one based in linguistics and cognitive science. This is due to a number of revolutionary publications that showed that metaphor was not just a matter of literature, style or rhetoric but of all language use (G. Lakoff and Johnson 1980): we speak of arguments as if they are wars that can be won or lost, love as if it is a journey that can get stranded, and understanding as if it is looking through a glass darkly. Moreover, metaphor was shown to be not just a matter of language use but of thought (Ortony 1979; Honeck and Hoffman 1980; G. Lakoff and Johnson 1980): we do not only speak in these metaphorical ways, but we conceptualise these abstract, less understood and complex topics in metaphorical ways as well, making use of our knowledge of wars, journeys and seeing to impose conceptual structure on our thoughts and texts about arguments, love and understanding. Today, metaphor is therefore not seen as a stylistic device but as a matter of thought, witness the overview of current metaphor research in the *Cambridge Handbook of Metaphor and Thought* (Gibbs 2008; see also Steen 2011a).

As a result, most metaphor occurs as a regular ingredient of the conceptual systems in our culture, and is expressed in conventionalised metaphorical language in all sorts of sociocultural domains of discourse, of which literature is only one. Moreover, most metaphor is not used as a stylistic or rhetorical device, but is simply part and parcel of the conceptual and linguistic systems we use to think and speak. The question therefore arises how metaphor should be conceptualised and analysed in relation to style. For general metaphorical language use and thought can also exhibit styles, but these are different notions of style from the idea that metaphor can be used as a stylistic device to spice up the rhetoric of a political or festive speech, to increase the intelligibility of a lecture or a business proposal, or to condense the aesthetic content of a poem into one expression. The latter seem to be deliberate metaphors, while the former are not.

It is the purpose of this chapter to make sense of these distinctions as well as their relations against the background of contemporary metaphor research. This will be done by means of a brief overview of the most important contemporary discussions in order to then illustrate the importance of some of their issues in some detailed textual analysis.

Deliberate and non-deliberate metaphor

The idea that metaphor can be used deliberately or not deliberately has aroused a controversy about the notion of deliberateness. When deliberateness is equated with consciousness, researchers object that language use is hardly ever conscious, and that a lot of cognition and behaviour are hardly ever conscious (Gibbs 2011). We do not really know how conscious poets or speech writers are when they produce their metaphors – they may be writing in a flow that is high speed and fairly automatic. The structure of a metaphor in a text does not really tell us whether it was put there while the writer was conscious of what they were doing. The same holds for metaphor in talk (see L. Cameron 2008).

However, when we make a distinction between consciousness and deliberateness, the situation changes. Even though it is possible to assert that we do not know anything about Shakespeare's consciousness when he wrote 'Shall I compare thee to a summer's day?', it does not make sense to deny that he wrote this line deliberately. Nor does it make sense to assert that he did not deliberately write the extended metaphorical comparison that follows and makes up the body of his famous Sonnet 18. Deliberate metaphor is the intentional use of metaphor *as* metaphor, and its function is to offer an 'alien' perspective (a summer's day) on some target domain (the addressee in the poem as lover). This type of metaphor is deliberate because it insists on positioning the reader in some source domain by forcing the reader to mentally attend to the source domain as a referent in its own right: 'Shall I compare thee to a summer's day?' There are particular linguistic structures that clearly signal deliberate metaphor use, including the use of a verb such as *compare* in between two incomparable entities that are each presented in their own right. The rest of the poem features comparative structures in an extended comparison ('thou art more lovely and more temperate'), and so on. Deliberate metaphor hence does not have to be conscious to be deliberate.

In fact, all language use is deliberate, in the sense of intentional in the context of some goal-directed action, but this does not also make it conscious, in the sense of the language user being aware of what they are doing linguistically when producing or receiving utterances. On the contrary, this would cognitively be far too demanding, and most language use therefore is unconscious – but not unintentional. All metaphor is therefore intentional in the general sense that applies to all language use. It is also mostly unconscious, as has been claimed by most metaphor researchers since the 1980s, and this is not a contradiction.

Metaphor only becomes deliberate when it is used *as* a metaphor. This does not happen very often. Deliberate metaphor *may* impinge on our consciousness and lead to conscious metaphorical cognition – but it does not have to, and does not often do so. Yet, when metaphor is used deliberately, it also turns into a stylistic device, while all other, non-deliberate metaphor, is simply part of a more general style of language, thought and communication.

Metaphor, fiction and other registers

An interesting reflection of this situation can be found in the results of a recent corpus project examining metaphor use across fiction, news, academic texts and conversations (Steen et al. 2010a, 2010b). In a specially constructed sample from the British National Corpus (BNC), four sets of text excerpts totalling some 50,000 words each were analysed for metaphor, making a distinction between regular metaphors on the one hand and similes and other types of direct figurative comparison on the other. The latter are all typically deliberate, while the former are typically not.

There was a massive difference between the two types of metaphor. First of all, 99 per cent of all metaphor turned out to be regular (typically non-deliberate) metaphor, with only 1 per cent being expressed as a direct metaphorical comparison (typically deliberate). Secondly, the distribution of both types of metaphor across the four registers was quite different: regular metaphor occurred most frequently in academic texts (18.5 per cent), followed by news (16.5 per cent), with fiction only in third place (13.5 per cent), and conversations (7.5 per cent) closing the rank order; by contrast, direct metaphorical comparison occurred most frequently in fiction, followed by news, with academic texts and conversations closing the rank order.

These data suggest that most regular metaphor is a non-deliberate part of a more general style of language, thought and communication, which would be typically a matter of register, and varies in intelligible ways between registers, including fiction (Biber et al. 1999). By contrast, most if not all direct figurative comparison is a deliberately used stylistic device that is most typical of fiction (Dorst 2011; Krennmayr 2011) and news (think of headlines, sports, political, financial, science and arts pages). These findings confirm and refine some of the most important intuitions and observations about metaphor and style made by Lodge (1977).

This suggests that a high density of metaphor in academic texts is not something stylistically special. It is the regular 'style' of scientific writing. It can be explained by the highly abstract content of most academic texts, which requires frequent use of conventional metaphorical models to think and talk about, for instance, organisations as machines, societies as plants, illness as wars, or time as space. Within such a register, however, some texts may display a higher frequency of instructive metaphors to help the reader understand explanations of complex conceptual models, or of entertaining metaphors to increase the level of attractiveness of the text. An example of each is provided by the following two quotations from a well-known textbook on cognitive neuroscience:

> The brain is a kind of Amazon rain forest with many undiscovered species of trees, plants, and animals. To begin we will focus only on one prototypical tree, but this is only a convenient fiction. The great diversity of the neurons in the brain is suggested by Figure...
>
> *(Baars and Gage 2010: 64)*

> Keeping up-to-date with cognitive neuroscience is much like surfing the Big Wave at Waikiki Beach. New findings keep rolling in and maintaining a stable balance is a big challenge. It is exciting, fun, and, at times, a little bit scary. But we keep climbing back on our mental surfboards, to catch the coming rollers of advancing science. This book aims to provide an overview of... *(Baars and Gage 2010: xiii)*

These *are* stylistically special, with a deliberate use of metaphor *as* metaphor (Herrmann 2013; cf. Semino 2008).

That fiction has the lowest percentage of regular metaphor among the three written text registers is also worthy of comment. Part of this is explained by the presence of dialogue, which resembles conversation in having a low number of metaphors (Dorst 2011; Kaal 2012). But fiction is also rather concrete and physical in its language use, lowering the number of metaphors used for talking about abstract phenomena in comparison with news and academic writing. This may also be dependent on perhaps a preference for showing rather than telling in the sample analysed in the project, however, which in turn may be a result of the texts included in the BNC or a preference for showing rather than telling in contemporary

British fiction. It is an interesting question for future quantitative research whether the observed tendency is more generally valid.

In addition, the fact that fiction has the highest frequency of direct metaphors, including similes and so on, is a reflection of what most people would expect about the relation between metaphor and these four registers. It may now be seen as perhaps due to the fact that direct metaphor is deliberate metaphor and may impinge on the consciousness of the reader relatively more easily or frequently than non-deliberate metaphor. If this occurs more frequently in fiction than elsewhere, this impingement may be mainly responsible for the impression that fiction is the most metaphoric of written registers (which now turns out to be incorrect).

Modelling and researching metaphor and style

The notion of deliberate metaphor and the corpus-linguistic investigation of metaphor's distribution in fiction and other registers across large sets of data are two recent foci of attention in stylistic metaphor research. They build on developments in the study of metaphor that were set in motion in 1980, and point to other controversial issues in contemporary metaphor studies. Space permits only brief indication of these other issues, with references to ongoing work suggesting where the interested reader can go for further information.

The most important aspect of metaphor revealed by the cognitive turn in the 1980s is the fact that many metaphors in language can be related to underlying metaphors in thought. These have been called 'conceptual metaphors' by G. Lakoff and Johnson (1980), and include the examples given above. Thus, many instances of metaphor in literary and non-literary texts do not appear to be novel creations of figurative comparisons, but instead represent familiar linguistic expressions of culturally shared conceptual models. Most of these linguistic expressions are so familiar that their metaphorical senses are listed in general dictionaries, showing that lexical units having to do with fighting or war, such as *defend, attack, defence* and so on are all systematically polysemous between fighting and war on the one hand and their metaphorical use in the domain of argumentation on the other. An introduction to this research has been provided by Kövecses (2010).

It is customary in metaphor research to make a distinction between these conceptual metaphors and their expression in language. The conceptual structures of metaphor in thought may be typically conventional but may also be novel, as happens in innovative poetry but just as well in copywriting for advertising or for political speeches. Independently, all metaphor in thought may be expressed in a range of linguistic forms, from regular metaphor and simile through analogy, extended comparison and thematic metaphor to text-based metaphoricity for parable and allegory. The conceptual structures as well as linguistic forms of metaphor may now also be seen to exhibit at least two distinct communicative functions: deliberate metaphor versus non-deliberate metaphor use.

One of the areas that has not been theorised very broadly yet is the interaction between all of these metaphor properties on the one hand and the presence of other figures, such as hyperbole and/or irony, on the other. One of the masters in combining metaphor and hyperbole is Jeremy Clarkson, the presenter of the BBC TV programme *Top Gear*. While he is no Shakespeare, he does have a separate page of magical metaphors on the internet. It features some of his most outrageous deliberate figurative comparisons, typically involving overstatement and humour, including 'Aston Martin DB9, that's not a racecar, that's pornography', or 'This air conditioning feels like there's an asthmatic sat on my dash-board, coughing at me.' The interaction between metaphor and irony will be illustrated in the analysis below.

Other issues in recent metaphor research include the relation between metaphor and aspects of encompassing text and context. For instance, metaphors can participate in encompassing frames that are used in politics to set up discourses about politics as family life (G. Lakoff 2004). Such frames may develop into complete scenarios, where for instance European politics is compared to love relationships between countries, including wooing, courting, divorces and so on (Musolff 2004). All of these affect the nature of texts in ways that go beyond style and have to do with the role of metaphor in, for instance, narration, argumentation and exposition as text types. Such aspects of metaphor use have also been studied as negotiated between speakers in different situations of spontaneous verbal interaction (L. Cameron 2008). Eventually all of these stylistic and non-stylistic analyses of metaphor need to be related to a genre model of discourse events to make them fully comparable across cases (Steen 2011b).

Metaphor in poetic style

In order to see some of the complexities of metaphor in action, consider the following poem by James Lasdun.

Plague Years

> 'There is, it would seem, in the dimensional scale of the world, a
> kind of delicate meeting place between imagination and
> knowledge, a point, arrived at by diminishing larger things and
> enlarging small ones, that is intrinsically artistic.'
>
> Vladimir Nabokov, *Speak, Memory*

Sore throat, persistent cough ... The campus doctor
Tells me 'just to be safe' to take the test.
The clinic protocol seems to insist

On an ironic calm. I hold my fear.
He draws a vial of blood for the City Lab,
I have to take it there, but first I teach
A class on Nabokov. Midway I reach
Into my bag for *Speak, Memory*, and grab
The hot bright vial instead. I seem at once
Wrenched from the quizzical faces of my class
Into some silent ante-room of hell:
The 'delicate meeting place'; I feel it pounce;
Terror – my life impacted in the glass
My death enormous in its scarlet grail.

James Lasdun (1995)

The simple style of this poem conceals a subtly complex structure and message. The fourteen lines, the rhyme scheme, and the turning point between lines 8 and 9 suggest that this is a sonnet. The first eight lines contrast with the last six lines in a way that is summarised by the non-metaphorical key phrases *ironic calm* (line 4) and *terror* (line 13). But there is more: the second half of the poem links back to the Nabokov epigraph, quoting *the delicate meeting place* in line 12. This is technically metaphorical, since imagination and knowledge cannot really meet, but this hardly adds significance. The meeting place does offer a unifying frame for the whole text, though: the quotation implies that the persona observes his experience of his own terror as a mixture of knowledge and imagination that is intrinsically artistic. This observation, prompted by the fact that he has to teach Vladimir Nabokov's *Speak, Memory*, not only adds a distancing layer of irony to the overt terror in lines 9–14, but it also builds a contrast with the irony insisted on by the clinic protocol in the first eight lines. The explicit link between main text and epigraph moreover suggests that the persona's experience of terror as something intrinsically artistic may be the motivation for writing the poem. The conjunction of main text and epigraph then finally needs to be linked back to the title, 'Plague Years': the interaction between imagination and knowledge has always been crucial for our experience of life-threatening diseases. The encompassing title frame of 'plague years' is mostly hyperbolic, not metaphorical, and it somewhat dampens the explicitly invoked artistic quality of the experience of the disease that is at the centre of this poem, ultimately reasserting the priority of life (and death) over art.

So what is the role of metaphor in all this? At first glance, there hardly are any prominent metaphors, with one conspicuous exception, the very last word of the poem. This clearly is a deliberately constructed artistic metaphor which forces the reader to work hard on its meaning and purport. I will first examine this metaphor in more detail, as an example of a metaphor that may be deemed typical of literary style. This may then be used as a background against which we can look at some of the other stylistic features of metaphor in this poem.

The last line presents the potentially lethal vial containing the persona's blood as a scarlet grail. This is an unexpected and in fact shocking image, since the grail is the chalice in which Christ's blood was caught. The reader could not have been prepared for this identification between the persona and Christ but it is the only possible solution to resolving the implied mapping between the concepts of vial and grail. Indeed, the only other overtly religious term in the poem is the corresponding (half-)rhyme word *hell* in line 11, but this suggests the opposite perspective and constructs the I not as Christ but as a human who is getting ready for hell.

The shock effect is not only due to the grail's association with Christ, but also by the cultural fact that the grail itself has been the object of many quests in western literature, from *Perceval* to *Monty Python and the Holy Grail*. The grail has been an object of desire throughout western history, which poses a stark contrast with the target concept it metaphorically projects onto: for the patient, the vial with its perhaps lethal content, is not exactly the thing he has been looking for throughout his life. The scarlet grail thereby becomes a highly ironic, if not sarcastic, metaphor of the I's possibly impending death.

How does this metaphor work? It can only be understood in connection with the previous line:

> . . . – my life impacted in the glass
> My death enormous in its scarlet grail.

The two lines set up two contrasting perceptions of the same situation involving the speaker's blood in a vial. Line 13 sees the blood as a metonymy of the I's life, and places it in a container depicted as just a glass object. Line 14 sees the blood as metonymically containing the cause of death and situates it in a culturally central if not holy artefact. Both work by a metonymy where the blood can stand for life (l. 13) or death (l. 14), but line 14 adds a heavily metaphorical twist that is hard to understand.

The interpretation of these lines, and of the metaphor in line 14 in particular, is textually incomplete unless the epigraph is invoked. Line 13 can be seen as an example of 'diminishing larger things', since the persona's life has been impacted in the glass of a small vial. Line 14 can be seen as an instantiation of 'enlarging small ones', since the persona's death has been made 'enormous' in nothing less than a scarlet grail. This epigraph-driven interpretation of the metaphor hence implies another conceptual frame for the experience described in the sonnet: people's deaths can be presented as small things being enlarged only if they are compared with Christ's death, which is not only culturally but also existentially the central big event in western history. The allusion is to the magnitude of Christ's sacrifice in order to redeem mankind and enable their entrance into an afterlife in heaven, not hell (the now more significant half-rhyme word in line 11). From that perspective, the I's death can be made to look enormous in its scarlet grail, the I being identified with Christ, with the understood assumption that the I's death in fact remains a small thing that is enlarged by art, the meeting place of imagination and knowledge.

The initial shock effect of the metaphor of the scarlet grail in isolation is now beginning to turn into an artistic effect of the metaphor as a hub for the entire poem's theme. It is not just a startling image and allusion as a metaphor by itself, which seems to mimic the intensity of the shock experienced by the I. The metaphor is also part of a more complex perception and conceptualisation of the same situation, expressed by the contrast between the last two lines (which are not separated by punctuation). And this complex conceptualisation in turn is part of a much more encompassing textual argument that depends on the parallelism between the last two lines on the one hand and the core of the epigraph on the other, leading to the surprising implication that the apparent enlargement of the I's imagined death in fact presupposes the opposite point of view, that people's individual deaths are small. It is the artistic moment that can enlarge them, but this should not be confused with reality. And it is the artistic enlargement into the death of Jesus Christ that by implication offers hope to those who believe in its redeeming effect. This is yet another twist to the relation between the metaphor and the poem: the comfort that may be derived from such an argument only holds for those who are Christian, or more generally religious, believers; everybody else will see this as another cruel irony of life, offering hope to those who need it whereas in fact there is none, only plague years.

The scarlet grail forms the climax of the poem. It is a striking and complex metaphor that displays many conceptual and affective ramifications. It is deceptively descriptive in a context of six lines that is full of intensity and hyperbole, as with *hell, terror* and *enormous*, but on close inspection it delivers the goods it promises as the starkly alien word in final position it is. The literary function of a metaphor does not just reside in the underlying cross-domain comparison that is the basis of every metaphor (vial is grail), or even its ironic as opposed to sincere use (your death is not something you have looked for). Metaphor in poetry is often multilayered with many relations to other aspects of the text and its language, which makes it strongly dependent on all sorts of other information throughout the poem and the knowledge it assumes, as we have seen (you are not Christ, and your death is not enormous, but this is in fact a comfort, not an existential problem – unless you do not believe, of course). All of this may be seen as highly typical of the use of metaphor in poetry.

By way of contrast, consider another metaphor that is also related to irony:

> The clinic protocol seems to insist
> On an ironic calm.

The ironic calm is the main referent of this sentence, and it is stylistically mimicked by the metaphorical expression 'the clinic protocol seems to insist'. The effect of *insist* is to turn the protocol into a human agent, taking the doctor out of the equation so that it is the protocol or the institution of the clinic that is to be held responsible for the ironic calm, not the doctor. What this in effect does is contrast the superficially ironic calm of the individual doctor to the perception of the situational, even institutional irony by the patient, who must hold the doctor responsible for what is happening. The attribution of the ironic calm to the protocol, not the doctor, is of course the patient's perception, which explains the hedge 'seems'. However, the hedge 'seems' is a double-edged sword and can also be read as pertaining to the doctor's stance, who apparently prefers a tentative and ironically calm attitude since nothing can been decided until the lab results come in.

This is a locally subtle use of metaphor by personification which is complex but much less enormous than the grail metaphor in line 14. It is, however, another typically stylistic exploitation of the potential of metaphor in literature since it attracts more than one simple conventional metaphorical meaning on the basis of the charged significance of poetic writing. Similarly deliberate exploitations of simple metaphor do not occur very often outside literature, except in language play occurring in, for instance, newspaper headlines or advertisement copy. Moreover, the thematic role of the ironic personification in relation to the massive irony at the end of the poem lends the phrase a greater reach than other less prominent metaphors, which have a purely local effect, as will be illustrated now.

Consider the verb *hold* in the ostensibly simple sentence 'I hold my fear' in line 4. On the one hand, this is a somewhat lame, submissive reflex to the ironic calm exhibited by the doctor. The sentence suggests control on the part of the patient – or at least an attempt at control. This is an element which appeals to a conventional metaphor in our language, which places us in charge of our emotions as if they are dogs or horses (Kövecses 2000).

On the other hand, the longer you look at the verb 'hold', the more the tension seems to rise. Instead of 'I hold my fear', the text reads as if it says 'I hold my breath', an expression which seems trivially metaphorical but is now revitalised in the present context. From this moment, the patient's breathing has changed into fearing. And for how long exactly will it turn out to be possible to *hold* that fear, as if it were an animal, a person or a thing, the typical direct objects associated with the verb 'hold'? For, next to control, 'hold' also has an element of voluntariness – you simply want to hold something in check, in order to prevent it from escaping but also in order to keep it and perhaps even cherish it. 'I hold my fear': fear rather than truth? But that will not work: at the end of the poem, the patient does succumb to the tension and experiences the existential angst and terror in all its enormity.

Loss of control is the turning point or volta in the sonnet. It involves the use of another inconspicuous metaphor. When the I accidentally takes the vial in his hand, in line 9, he describes it as 'hot'. But the vial has never been hot and can hardly be warm any more. Instead it is probably the cause of the patient turning 'hot'. This is a subtle exploitation of the conventional metaphor in our language that emotions are temperatures; for example, Dutch national goalkeeper Edwin van der Sar was called 'ice-rabbit' for his lack of display of emotions.

This conventional metaphor in language is due to our physical experience of emotional events, which can turn us warm or cold. In this poem this conventional metaphor is transferred outside the body and the emotions: it is not the I's body or the I's sensation that is presented as hot, but the cause of that experience, the vial with blood. In addition, the projected temperature of the vial is not called 'warm', which would imply a positive affect, but 'hot', which is negative and invokes associations with stolen or dangerous goods, something that is completely appropriate for the vial and its contents. Just like 'hold' in line 4, 'hot' is a conventional metaphor in language that is here deployed as a subtle stylistic device to give shape to the personal experience of an individual in a complex literary way.

There are other local metaphorical expressions, such as the verbs 'wrench', 'pounce' and 'impacted'. However, they all display the same interaction between local use and contextual significance, albeit in different ways, as 'hot' and 'hold'. There are different stylistics uses of metaphor in poetry which need our attention now. Consider the following poem by the late Julia Darling.

Chemotherapy

I did not imagine being bald
at forty-four. I didn't have a plan.
Perhaps a scar or two from growing old,
hot flushes. I'd sit fluttering a fan.

But I am bald, and hardly ever walk
by day, I'm the invalid of these rooms,
stirring soups, awake in the half dark,
not answering the phone when it rings.

I never thought that life could get this small,
that I would care so much about a cup,
the taste of tea, the texture of a shawl,
and whether or not I should get up.

I'm not unhappy. I have learned to drift
and sip. The smallest things are gifts.   *Julia Darling (2003)*

Metaphor works by setting up a comparison with completely different things that do not belong to the topic or situation that is the dominant target domain of a part of a text, like the grail in connection with a vial with blood. Metonymy, by contrast, zooms in on details of topics or situations that have to stand for the bigger picture. What has remained of life for this patient has been reduced in literary fashion to a number of small experiences that recur from day to day:

> a cup,
> the taste of tea, the texture of a shawl,
> and whether or not I should get up.

But here, too, the patient remains standing by means of conventional metaphor: 'the smallest things are gifts'. And here, too, it seems as if the metaphor has been used ironically: for if the smallest things are gifts, who is it that offers them to the patient, what sort of gifts are they, and how do they relate to that other, completely unwanted gift of cancer which has preceded them? These are the natural questions that often arise but are seldom heard when this conventionally metaphorical response to a lethal disease as a gift is used as a rationalisation or defence mechanism. This poem dramatises the way this metaphorical logic works on a minute but effective scale.

Perhaps it even criticises the metaphor in the same stroke, with irony. It may take some effort to accept this potentially ironic reading of the metaphor, perhaps because the last line expresses such a generally accepted and socially desirable stereotype of positive attitude. But look at that line from the perspective of the preceding one. The assertion 'I'm not unhappy' is a bomb in all its literalness; it does not take long before it denies what it affirms. And this immediately undermines the ostensibly positive purport of the last two utterances.

This also has an effect on the syntactic coordination of 'drift and sip', containing another hidden metaphor. The combination of verbs acquires a wry, almost humorous effect, as with zeugma. The metaphorical 'drift' involves a big gesture of letting go which has been acquired, probably at great pains, but its grandeur is almost completely annihilated by the metonymic 'sip', the series of daily recurring small and effortful actions that are needed for the I to keep herself alive. What kind of acceptance of cancer as a gift is this?

What we see happening in this poem is that the big thoughts by metaphor to deal with the complexities of life can be undercut or criticised by irony and metonymy. These can revitalise the underlying conventional metaphorical model and reveal its cruel ineptness (cancer is a gift?). They can also reveal and question the naturalness with which people repeat metaphorical stereotypes in natural language (I have learned to drift?). Some metaphor in poetry is therefore used not to think big, but to show how conventionalised metaphorical models in language and thought can prevent us from thinking at all – this is when they are used in their inconspicuous conventional forms in apparently innocent stylistic ways that need further interpretation and reflection because of their literary context.

The last poem to be used for illustration in this chapter goes in the other direction. It exploits the potential for big thought in metaphor to the full, displaying an extended metaphorical comparison throughout the entire text. This is another typical use of metaphor in literature, which results in a rather different style from what we have seen so far. Here is Marin Sorescu's 'Pure pain', translated from the Romanian:

Pure pain

I don't feel ill in order to feel better,
I feel ill in order to feel worse.
Like the sea with its green, treacherous waves,
You cannot sound the bottom of pain.

I dive into pure pain,
Essence of scream and despair,
And I return to the surface blue and pale,
Like a diver who lost
His oxygen tank.

To the emperor of fishes, I beg,
Kindly send me your trustworthy shark
To cut short my passing.

> *Marin Sorescu (translated by Adam J. Sorkin*
> *and Lidia Vianu; Sorescu 2004)*

This poem is an attempt to think the unthinkable. In 'Chemotherapy', illness is represented by a number of small, metonymic *slices of life*, which allude to emotions that are metaphorically expressed. Recalling Nabokov's 'delicate meeting place' between knowledge and imagination, 'Chemotherapy' works in particular by what it does not say, making an appeal to our knowledge of the situation in order to fill in our own picture. In 'Pure pain' we are moving in the direction of an appeal to our imagination by an active and explicitly formulated metaphor that presents aspects of an extended novel comparison.

We are also moving from the small or large gesture in 'Chemotherapy' to verbalised thought in 'Pure pain'. In terms of narrative theory, we are going from *showing* in 'Chemotherapy' to *telling* in 'Pure pain'. We are asked to structure the immeasurability of pure pain by means of a metaphorical comparison that we need to set up from one line to the next, requiring us to spell it out by means of our knowledge of deep-sea diving. This is a highly specific variant of yet another conventional metaphor, which represents intense experiences as something that you can be submerged in. The conventional metaphor is made special first, by using the concept of deep-sea diving, and then undermined, by imagining a sea that has an emperor of fishes who can send a trustworthy shark to shorten the diver's passage. The metaphor is extended into fantasy and grotesqueness. This is not just artistic play, but an expression of the alienating potential of pure pain.

These are a number of typical variations on the theme of metaphor in poetic style. I have shown how poets make use in varying ways of meta-phorical models in language and thought, some of which are criticised in for instance the medical humanities, following such writers as Susan Sontag (1978). On the one hand poets show how such metaphor can work, both positively and negatively, for patients and their caregivers. On the other hand poets show how the conventionalised, often stereotypical content of those conceptual and linguistic metaphors can be revealed and criticised by irony, metonymy and other stylistic devices. It some-times happens that an entire metaphor is even blown up from the inside, as with Sorescu. In some cases, life and death become 'enormous', as with Lasdun; in other cases, they become unimaginably 'small', as with Darling. Both of these options allude to another conventional metaphor in our thought, that everything important is big, and everything insig-nificant is small.

22

Foregrounding, burying and plot construction

Catherine Emmott and Marc Alexander

This chapter examines the way in which aspects of a story may be made more or less prominent for plot purposes through the use of foregrounding and burying devices. The normal expectation of readers is that foregrounding will be used to highlight significant information and that the relatively insignificant parts of a text will fall into the background. Nevertheless, for plot purposes, the reverse may often be the case. We explore this by looking at detective fiction, a genre where the intricacy of the plot is an important, or even *the* most important, part of reading. In detective fiction, the objective is to confuse the reader about the significance of information in both the foreground and background of a text, hence creating a puzzle which can subsequently be solved in a surprising way. We demonstrate how reader attention can be manipulated by foregrounding plot-insignificant items and burying plot-significant items in the background.

Foregrounding and depth of processing

The term 'foregrounding' was first used in stylistics in Garvin's (1964) translation of the work of Havránek (1964) and Mukařovský (1964a, 1964b). It generally refers to cases where the language is sufficiently deviant to draw attention to itself and thereby prompt an interpretation of extra meaning. Foregrounding is recognised as occurring at all linguistic levels, and common types are sound play, unusual graphical patterning, excessive lexical and pronominal repetition, unusual word choices, highly creative metaphors, parallelism, and breaches of the usual discourse structure. The functions of foregrounding can be various, including highlighting specific key points, producing thematic meaning, prompting an emotional response, and yielding iconic effects. Accounts of foregrounding are provided by many stylisticians including Douthwaite

(2000), Emmott (2002), Leech (2008), Leech and Short (2007), A. J. Sanford and Emmott (2012), van Peer (1986, 2007) and van Peer and Hakemulder (2006).

For some stylisticians, foregrounding is particularly important as a means of prompting literary interpretations. Miall and Kuiken (1994: 390) argue (following Mukařovský) that although foregrounding is found in everyday language, it is more 'structured' in literary texts. This is one notion of foregrounding, but nevertheless there are many non-literary texts that use extensive and 'structured' linguistic patterning for rhetorical purposes, such as advertising language, political speeches and, as we will illustrate in this chapter, popular fiction. We use the term 'foregrounding' here to cover any type of language use which may be assumed to prompt attention, regardless of whether it has literary value. Foregrounding in this sense relates simply to whether an item is likely to be noticeable or not, and our interest is in whether it has rhetorical significance generally rather than literary significance specifically.

For the forms of foregrounding, we not only include those types of *deviant linguistic usage* that are the conventional domain of foregrounding studies, but also suggest that *standard systemic choices* (choices in the language system) are important if they have some impact in terms of noticeability. So, for example, it has been well demonstrated in psychology that information that is not subordinated grammatically is more noticeable than information that is subordinated (e.g. M. Baker and Wagner 1987; see A. J. Sanford and Emmott, 2012, for a survey of relevant work). These systemic options may not be unusual as such, but may nevertheless direct attention towards one item rather than another.

The term 'foregrounding' has a degree of ambiguity because it can apply either to the linguistic devices used to create prominence or to the effect of bringing parts of a mental representation to the forefront of attention. Psychologists have shown that foregrounding affects *depth of (semantic) processing*, the extent to which a reader fully engages with the semantic content of the information presented (e.g. A. J. Sanford 2002; A. J. Sanford and Sturt 2002; A. J. Sanford and Emmott 2012). Foregrounding, in this more general sense, may involve a broader range of strategies than making micro-level stylistic choices, whether deviant or systemic. Hence, a writer may manipulate attention by anticipating a reader's processing strategies more generally, as we describe in the remainder of this section.

Firstly, an item (e.g. an object such as an ornate pen or a smart attaché case) may be given *narrative-world salience* by virtue of the fact that it has apparent importance for one or more characters in the narrative world, regardless of whether this is conveyed by unusual language. This may be simply due to the striking properties of the item, but may also be due to how the characters respond to it. So, for example, if a character in a story becomes particularly interested in an item, the reader may view that item as potentially more significant. This effect might also be enhanced if the character is deemed to be 'reliable' (Booth 1991; Zunshine 2006), hence ensuring that their interest is taken more seriously.

Secondly, *text position* may be used to present information in ways that are not linguistically unusual, but which may nevertheless affect processing. For example, if a reader is expected to make an inference from two or more pieces of information, then placing these pieces of information close together may foreground their connection and hence facilitate the ability to make that inference – the opposite of this may be that it is less easy to draw an inference if the relevant information is separated. Another example of the possible influence of text position is that a reader might be more receptive to viewing information as relevant to a puzzle if that information is given after that puzzle has been presented, when the reader is in puzzle-solving mode – conversely, information might not be so readily used in puzzle-solving if it is presented too early.

A third way of controlling information processing is to prompt *selective focus*. Psychologists have shown that readers often focus on specific aspects of an item or scene, but not necessarily on *all* aspects (e.g. Barton and Sanford 1993). Hence depth of processing can be highly differential, with the consequence that readers may not make certain inferences, particularly if they are distracted. Stylistic deviance and standard systemic choices can direct inferencing, but inferencing can also be controlled by the amount and nature of detail given before, during and after crucial points in a text. For example, Guéraud et al. (2008) have shown that if a reader is given different background information about a character before reading a passage, readers can make quite different inferences about the same reported action.

Burying

If some items are brought into the foreground, then other items are left in the background. The notion of background is little studied by stylisticians (apart from our own previous work, e.g. Emmott et al. 2013), but has been of some interest to linguists (e.g. Givón 1987; S. A. Thompson 1987) and psychologists (M. Baker and Wagner 1987; A. J. Sanford and Sturt 2002; A. J. S. Sanford et al. 2009).

Possibly stylisticians have not been interested in background because placing information in the background is not usually viewed as a major strategic choice. Nevertheless, for plot purposes, deliberately burying information in the background of a text is highly strategic. By 'burying', we mean that an item is placed in the background with the intention that it should not be easily found. It is well known that some advertisements and contracts can hide unpalatable facts in the small print and that politicians might hide unpopular details in the less prominent parts of their speeches. Our interest here is in how information which will eventually be used to solve a puzzle in a detective story is hidden until it is revealed at the end of a story as a solution, hence enhancing curiosity until that point and creating surprise.

Some of the techniques for burying an item (or burying its significance) are as follows:

(i)   Mention the item as little as possible.

(ii)   Use linguistic structures which have been shown empirically to reduce prominence (e.g. embed a mention of the item within a subordinate clause).

(iii) Under-specify the item, describing it in a way that is sufficiently imprecise that it draws little attention to it or detracts from features of the item that are relevant to the plot.

(iv)   Place the item next to an item that is more prominent, so that the focus is on the more prominent item. Hence, when foregrounding is used it may have an automatic effect of downplaying nearby items, like a spotlight that makes items around the light less noticeable.

(v)   Make the item apparently unimportant in the narrative world (even though it is actually significant).

(vi)   Make it difficult for the reader to make inferences by splitting up information needed to make the inferences.

(vii) Place information in positions where a reader is distracted or not yet interested.

(viii) Stress one specific aspect of the item so that another aspect (which will eventually be important for the solution) becomes less prominent. This may also be done *after* the original description. Psychology research shows that inferences can be more short-lived if attention is subsequently directed elsewhere (e.g. Keefe and McDaniel 1993). Moreover, research on real-life eyewitness testimony indicates that memory for events may be changed by subsequent retellings of a story (Loftus and Loftus 1980).

(ix)   Give the item a false significance, so that the real significance is buried.

(x)   Get the narrator or characters in the story to say that the item is uninteresting.

(xi)   Discredit the characters reporting certain information, thereby making them appear unreliable and giving less salience to the information they report.

We will explore these techniques in the following section.

Attention manipulation and plot construction in detective fiction

Strategies for information management in detective fiction

When attention is manipulated for plot purposes, foregrounding can be used strategically to misdirect the reader, accompanied by burying which is inherently deceptive. In our discussion of detective fiction, we will distinguish between the handling of plot-significant and plot-insignificant items. By plot, we mean here the solving of a mystery, such as a suspicious death – we are using this definition simply for ease of exposition as clearly there may be other aspects of the plot apart from the main puzzle, even in detective fiction. A *plot-significant item* is important to the solution, such as a vital piece of evidence about how a suspicious death took place, whereas a *plot-insignificant item*, by contrast, has no such importance.

We propose that the key rhetorical strategies that can be found in detective fiction are as follows. These strategies make use of the techniques for foregrounding and burying already discussed:

- *Strategy 1: At the pre-solution stage – foreground plot-insignificant items.*
  This is the classic 'red herring' of detective fiction. An item may be made to seem significant at the time of presentation, but later it seems that there was a false trail and, at the solution stage, the item turns out to be plot-insignificant.
- *Strategy 2: At the pre-solution stage – bury plot-significant items.*
  Detective writers need to introduce the items that will eventually contribute to the solution. If they did not introduce them at all, they would be accused of playing foul (Van Dine 2012 [1928]). The skill lies in mentioning these items without drawing attention to them or to their significance so that they are not suspected of being relevant to the solution.
- *Strategy 3: At the solution stage – foreground plot-significant details that were previously buried and make the solution seem credible.*
  As the solution is revealed, previously buried details are shown to have plot significance. Ideally this should be a surprise, but nevertheless a surprise which is apparently credible in retrospect. Foregrounding can heighten the sense of authority of the detective revealing the solution and add to the feeling that the solution is satisfactory.
- *Strategy 4: Throughout the text – manage the reversal in significance.*
  One important point about how these strategies work together is that they require a substantial reversal at some point in the story, as buried items are revealed and red herrings are abandoned. Not only must the solution seem credible in its own right (strategy 3) but the reversal must be either explained or glossed over (strategy 4). One option is that characters simply admit that they were wrong previously and/or take advantage of the appearance of new evidence. Throughout the text the author may also use rhetorical strategies to make the reversal plausible, such as taking care not to make too firm a commitment to a particular description at the pre-solution stage.

These four strategies can be argued to act together to form the essential schema of information management in detective fiction. An alternative to strategies 1 and 2 is the following:

- *Strategy 1-2-ALT: At the pre-solution stage – attach displaced or false significance to a plot-significant item.*

  This technique may involve both foregrounding and burying together, combining strategies 1 and 2 above. A writer can clearly identify an item (even foreground it), but draw attention to an aspect of it which is not the aspect that is relevant to solving the puzzle (displaced significance), or attach a false significance to the item. This may work if the reader is adequately distracted and/or is highly unlikely to see the real significance of the item. The item can serve as its own red herring, since some aspect or interpretation of it is misleading.

To examine these strategies, we look particularly at the work of Agatha Christie, the so-called 'Queen of Crime' (e.g. Haining 1990: 11–12). In previous studies of her work, we have focused mainly on how she presents characters and scenes (Alexander 2006; Emmott 1997; Emmott and Alexander 2010; Emmott et al. 2010, 2013). In this chapter we look largely at objects. The stories we discuss have many different plot elements, so we are selective in our presentation below and are not aiming for a full exposition of the plots. (For a fuller explanation of a Christie story, see Emmott and Alexander 2010.) Plot manipulations which might seem obvious when discussed out of context may be very difficult to spot in the original texts, where they are part of a much more complex plot structure.

Exploring strategies 1 to 4: the basic schema for information management in detective fiction

In this section, we demonstrate how Christie utilises the core strategies 1 to 4 to selectively emphasise certain parts of a scene (strategy 1-2-ALT will be examined in the next section). Christie often presents a list of items in which one or more of these items has plot significance, but the reader is left to infer which one from the description. Christie's trick is to use foregrounding to lead the reader down the wrong path at the pre-solution stage, but in a way that allows a subsequent very different interpretation of the scene at the solution stage. In 'Murder in the Mews', the following list of items on a writing-bureau occurs when Hercule Poirot, Christie's famous detective, and Inspector Japp are in the process of examining a room in a house where a dead woman has been found.

> (1a) Poirot strayed across to the writing-bureau. [. . .]
>
>   There was a somewhat massive silver inkstand in the centre, in front of it a handsome green lacquer blotter. To the left of the blotter was an emerald glass pen-tray containing a silver penholder – a stick of green sealing-wax, a pencil and two stamps. On the right of the blotter was a movable calendar giving the day of the week, date and month. There was also a little glass jar of shot and standing in it a flamboyant green quill pen.

<u>Poirot seemed interested in the pen. He took it out and looked at it but the</u> <u>quill was innocent of ink. It was clearly a decoration – nothing more.</u> The silver penholder with the ink-stained nib was the one in use. His eyes strayed to the calendar.

'Tuesday, November fifth,' said Japp. 'Yesterday. That's all correct.'

[Poirot and Japp discuss the time of death with the forensic expert.]

Poirot had turned back the cover of the blotter.

'Good idea,' said Japp. 'But no luck.'

The blotter showed an innocent white sheet of blotting-paper. Poirot turned over the leaves but they were all the same.

He turned his attention to the waste-paper basket. [He finds various old circulars and standard letters.]

'Nothing there,' said Japp. [. . .]

<u>Poirot still seemed fascinated by the writing-bureau and its appointments.</u> <u>He left the room, but at the door his eyes went back once more to the</u> <u>flaunting emerald quill pen.</u>   *(Christie 1964: 11–13, underlining added)*

The description of the green/emerald quill pen as first 'flamboyant' and then, at the end of the extract, 'flaunting' gives this item apparent narrative-world salience. The attention of a character can control the way information is presented, and may thereby control the attention of the reader. In the second paragraph, we are told that 'Poirot seemed interested' in the quill pen and we watch him examine it. At the end of this example, we learn that he 'still seemed fascinated by the writing-bureau' and the one item that is then singled out is the quill pen, with Poirot's gaze reverting to it. The text position is important here, since this provides a conclusion to the scene and is also placed right at the end of a chapter. All of these factors might be said to foreground the quill pen (using the term 'foregrounding' in the general sense of making it prominent).

In fact, Christie is using strategy 1 here since the quill pen is really a red herring. By the solution stage, interest in the quill pen will need to be dropped as the real solution is revealed, and so in Example (1a) Christie allows herself some room for manoeuvre (strategy 4). When she mentions that Poirot 'seemed' interested and fascinated this does not give full narratorial commitment to these descriptions. Either the narrator is mistaken about Poirot's interest, or, if the narrator is right, Poirot is interested in a red herring. In theory, this might not reflect well on his detective skills, but in practice there are ways round this potential difficulty in plot construction. In her books generally, Christie's detectives sometimes have revelations about the solution part-way through the story, so if their interpretation of an early scene is retrospectively seen to be unreliable it can be excused on those grounds (Poirot has a revelation of this type in 'Murder in the Mews' (1964: 40)). Moreover, Christie can rely on the fact that when a solution is provided many pages later, the reader may have forgotten exactly how information was initially presented (a text position factor) and is likely to be focusing on the solution rather than on the red herrings.

Prior to the solution, a red herring, by its very nature, diverts attention from other items in a story and may therefore make them less prominent. In the above example, Christie also uses the attention of the characters to close down interest in the other items. This is strategy 2. When the pen tray is first mentioned, the description immediately moves on to the items it contains, then the calendar. Later mention of the silver penholder is followed by Poirot's eyes straying to the calendar. Likewise, after examination of the blotter, Poirot's attention again moves on. The waste-paper basket appears to have no interest due to Japp's conclusion 'Nothing there'.

Indeed, what eventually turns out to be of interest at the solution stage is, firstly, the absence of any used blotting-paper on the blotter or in the waste-paper basket, and, secondly, the relative position of some of the items on the writing-table. These factors turn out to be plot-significant because they provide evidence that the death was suicide and not murder (one of the characters has been framed for murder). The relevant plot information necessary to understand this part of the solution (and hence Example (1b) below) is as follows: the top sheet of blotting paper has been deliberately removed to avoid showing the evidence that a suicide note had been written. In addition, the relative position of the items gives evidence that the dead woman was left-handed, since the pen tray is placed to the left of the blotter. Her left-handedness explains that she would have been able to shoot herself and thereby commit suicide, since the entry point of the wound is on the left of the head. This left-handedness is hidden from readers throughout the story since the gun was found in her right hand, supposedly making it impossible for her to commit suicide and therefore erroneously suggesting murder.

At the solution stage, Christie uses strategy 3 as Hercule Poirot reveals the solution, employing heavy foregrounding in Example (1b) to empha-sise aspects of the scene which were not previously emphasised.

> (1b) '[…] And now I come to something really interesting – I come, my
> friends, to the writing-bureau. […] That was really *very* odd – *very*
> remarkable! For two reasons. The first reason was that something was
> missing from that writing-table. […] *A sheet of blotting-paper, mademoiselle.*
> The blotting-book had on top a clean, untouched piece of blotting-
> paper. […] *it was not in the waste-paper basket.* […] A curious little problem. I
> looked everywhere, in the waste-paper baskets, in the dustbin, but I could
> not find a sheet of used blotting-paper – and that seemed to me very
> important. […] But there was a second curious point about the writing-table.
> Perhaps, Japp, you remember roughly the arrangement of it? Blotter and
> inkstand in the centre, pen tray to the left, calendar and quill pen to

the right. *Eh bien?* You do not see? The quill pen, remember, I examined, it was for show only – it had not been used. Ah! *still* you do not see? I will say it again. Blotter in the centre, pen tray to the left – to the *left*, Japp. But is it not usual to find a pen tray *on the right*, convenient to *the right hand*?

'Ah, now it comes to you, does it not? The pen tray on the *left* [Poirot here turns to speak to the accused woman] you find your friend there lying dead with the pistol clasped in her hand – the left hand, naturally, *since she is left-handed* and therefore, too, the bullet has entered on the *left side of the head*. [. . .] You take the pistol, wipe it and place it in the *right* hand.'

(Christie 1964: 51–2, original italics)

The heavy foregrounding here not only offers a re-framing of the information, but also serves to suggest the authority of the detective and the supposed obviousness and hence credibility of the solution. All the italics are Christie's and these emphasise key points (see A. J. S. Sanford et al. (2006) for psychological evidence of the foregrounding properties of italics). Since this solution is revealed in direct speech the italics can be justified as reflecting the speech stress of the speaker. The initial statements ('really interesting', '*very* odd', '*very* remarkable!') are highly evaluative, and this evaluation continues throughout Poirot's revelations ('A curious little problem', 'that seemed to me very important', 'a second curious point'). In addition, Poirot somewhat laboriously uses rhetorical questions to spell out Japp's discovery process as if no other option is possible, hence also guiding the discovery process of the reader ('*Eh bien?* You do not see?', 'Ah! *still* you do not see?', 'Ah, now it comes to you, does it not?'). There is heavy repetition ('pen tray to the left', 'to the *left*', 'The pen tray on the *left*', 'the left hand', 'she is *left-handed*') and Poirot even says 'I will say it again' to emphasise this repetition. Adverbs such as 'naturally' and 'therefore' also stress the supposed inevitability of this explanation. The negative findings about the blotter and the waste-paper bin during the original search in Example (1a) ('But no luck', 'innocent', 'Nothing there') are re-framed as being key findings, since it is now viewed as significant that these findings were negative. This is an example similar to Sherlock Holmes's observation about 'the curious incident of the dog in the night-time' (Doyle 1981: 347), where the curious incident is that the dog did nothing (Christie explicitly makes this intertextual reference in this story, although in relation to another clue). In everyday life, things are generally of interest because they are present, but in detective stories, the absence of an item can be more relevant as evidence.

The general pattern here, therefore, is to detract attention from key factors in a scene, but then to highlight their importance later. A further set of examples from 'Murder in the Mews' also follows this pattern, again using the listing technique. Hercule Poirot watches Chief Inspector Japp search a cupboard in the dead woman's house. The surviving resident, Jane

Plenderleith, is also present and her body language suggests that the cupboard may contain something suspicious (e.g. 'Poirot felt the girl at his side stiffen and stop breathing for a second', 1964: 34).

> (2a) There was not very much in the cupboard. Three umbrellas – one broken, four walking-sticks, a set of golf clubs, two tennis racquets, a neatly-folded rug and several sofa cushions in various stages of dilapidation. On top of these last reposed a small, smart-looking attaché-case.   *(Christie 1964: 34)*

Here, strategy 1 is used to foreground the attaché case. It is stereotypically the most likely item to be associated with a mystery, giving it narrative-world salience. Its description is placed in a separate sentence which psychologists have shown to have an enhancing effect (e.g. Kintsch and Keenan 1973). It is also described using extra adjectives, which again have been found to raise attention levels (A.J. Sanford and Garrod 1981). Conversely, strategy 2 is used to bury the real plot-significant item, the golf clubs. The mention of the golf clubs is placed in the middle of a list, plausibly surrounded by other outdoor equipment, and there is no extra description. As the story progresses, strategy 1 continues as the attention of the detectives focuses on the attaché case, as in Example (2b) where the 'something' is emphasised with italics then repeated and linked to the attaché case. The last statement comes from Chief Inspector Japp, who might be thought to provide a reliable opinion, but in fact is wrong here.

> (2b) 'What the – the hell was there in that cupboard? There was *something*.'
> 'Yes, there was something.'
> 'And I'll bet ten to one it was something to do with the attaché-case!'
>   *(Christie 1964: 35, original italics)*

Subsequently, Japp moves from this bet to linking the girl's body language not with the items in the cupboard generally, but specifically with the attaché case by presupposing its effect on the girl and also elevating the case (somewhat jokily) to title status.

> (2c) 'I'd like to know *why* she went all hot and bothered about that little attaché-case under the stairs [. . .] The Mystery of the Small Attaché-Case. Sounds quite promising!'   *(Christie 1964: 35, original italics)*

When the solution is revealed, as shown in Example (2d), foregrounding is used (strategy 3) to highlight the supposed inevitability of the new interpretation, the golf clubs now being recognised as plot-significant since they provide additional evidence of the left-handedness of the victim. Christie makes use here of repetition and italicisation as foregrounding devices, as in Example (1b).

> (2d) 'The golf clubs. The golf clubs, Japp. *They were the golf clubs of a left-handed person.* Jane Plenderleith kept her clubs at Wentworth. Those were

> Barbara Allen's [the dead girl's] clubs. [. . .] She tries to focus our
> attention on the *wrong object* [. . .] that, my friend, is the truth of "The
> Mystery of the Attaché-Case".'   *(Christie 1964: 54–5, original italics)*

The overall argument is made to seem more convincing by making several similar revelations at once (e.g. the left-handedness in Examples (1b) and (2d) above), whether or not explanations of specific clues are fully convincing. Poirot's delivery of the solution moves on rapidly from point to point, giving the reader little opportunity to contemplate each stage of the explanation before the next piece of evidence is presented. In case the reader has any doubts, Christie may then show the guilty person admitting the crime, hence giving the solution a real status in the narrative world, whether or not it is a very credible solution technically.

Exploring strategy 1-2-ALT: displaced and false significance

Even when an entity is clearly mentioned, it may be possible to give it a different significance from the one that it will ultimately have as part of the solution (strategy 1-2-ALT). Certain objects are important in detective fiction due to their function as evidence or to support a particular construction of events generally. However, their roles can be different depending on how their function is understood. Detective stories are exercises in lateral thinking (de Bono 1967) or its failure, as items need to be judged specifically in terms of whether or not they have a role in the crime, which may sometimes be a very unorthodox use.

For strategy 1-2-ALT, the author describes an item which has plot significance in some detail, but in a way that distracts attention from its true relevance. In Example 3 below, again from 'Murder in the Mews', Poirot draws attention to a wrist-watch that will ultimately be shown to be significant because it is on the right hand, a fact that might seem unusual if the wearer is right-handed, but makes more sense if the wearer is left-handed (further evidence of the left-handedness of the victim, as discussed above).

> (3) [Poirot] was still staring down at the body.
> 'Anything strike you?' Japp asked.
> The question was careless but his eyes were keen and attentive.
> Hercule Poirot shook his head slowly.
> 'I was looking at her wrist-watch.'
> He bent over and just touched it with a finger-tip. <u>It was a dainty jewelled affair on a black moiré strap on the wrist of the hand that held the pistol.</u>
> 'Rather a swell piece that,' observed Japp. 'Must have cost money!' He cocked his head inquiringly at Poirot. 'Something in that maybe?'
> 'It is possible – yes.'   *(Christie 1964: 11, underlining added)*

Although the characters draw attention to the watch itself, the fact that it is on the right hand is buried in the third post-modifying prepositional phrase, with the details under-specified (it is described as 'the hand that held the pistol' not 'the right hand'). Moreover, attention is diverted from the watch's position. The discussion of the characters centres on the expense of the watch, placing the focus of interest on the description of the watch given earlier in the noun phrase (its 'jewelled' nature). Hence, the appearance of the watch seems likely to attract the greatest depth of processing, rather than its position. The lack of clarity about the location of the watch due to under-specification is also enhanced by text position. If the description of the watch had come directly after the description of the body (where it is made quite clear that the pistol is in the right hand) (1964: 10–11), then it might have been more evident, but Christie ensures that there is over two-thirds of a page of intervening text (including a dramatic disclosure) so that the inference cannot be so easily made.

Example (4a), from Christie's *Hallowe'en Party*, also shows displaced significance (strategy 1-2-ALT), this time in relation to an incident in which a vase is broken. This incident is described at length so is reasonably prominent in the text – the interest lies in which specific aspects of the scene are emphasised.

(4a) '[. . .] [Mrs Drake] was carrying a large vase of mixed autumn leaves and flowers. She stood at the angle of the staircase, pausing for a moment before coming downstairs. She was looking down over the well of the staircase. Not in my direction. She was looking towards the other end of the hall where there is a door leading into the library. It is set just across the hall from the door into the dining-room. As I say, she was looking that way and pausing for a moment before coming downstairs. She was shifting slightly the angle of the vase as it was a rather awkward thing to carry, and weighty if it was, as I presumed, full of water. She was shifting the position of it rather carefully so that she could hold it to her with one arm, and put out the other arm to the rail of the staircase as she came round the slightly shaped corner stairway. She stood there for a moment or two, still not looking at what she was carrying, but towards the hall below. And suddenly she made a sudden movement – a start I would describe it as – yes, definitely something had startled her. So much that she relinquished her hold of the vase and it fell, reversing itself as it did so so that the water streamed over her and the vase itself crashed down to the hall below, where it broke in smithereens on the hall floor.'

'I see,' said Poirot. He paused a minute or two, watching her. Her eyes, he noticed, were shrewd and knowledgeable. They were asking now his opinion of what she was telling him. 'What did you think had happened to startle her?'

'On reflection, afterwards, I thought she had seen something.'

'You thought she had seen something,' repeated Poirot, thoughtfully.

(Christie 1972: 70–1, underlining added)

Here, two aspects of the scene are highlighted in the subsequent discussion between Poirot and the witness reporting this incident (only the first few lines of this subsequent discussion are shown here, but it lasts for over a page and a half in the text). In the report of the incident, the witness suggests repeatedly that Mrs Drake sees something in the hall below and mentions that this may have startled her. Poirot then discusses this extensively in his questions since there is the possibility that she may have seen someone opening the door of the library, where the murder occurred. In addition, the consequence of the vase smashing (i.e. that the glass had to be swept up) is discussed. Again, these aspects of the story are red herrings. The key plot-significant fact is that Mrs Drake (who is in fact herself the murderer) was soaked with water since, as Poirot points out at the solution stage (1972: 182), she drowned the victim and therefore may have needed to fabricate some alternative reason for being wet.

In this case, the main strategy is to emphasise other aspects of the incident, so that the reader may focus on those aspects and consequently give them greater depth of processing than the plot-significant aspect. The speaker's telling of the story is given greater credibility by Poirot himself since he views her as having 'shrewd and knowledgeable' eyes – we have elsewhere termed this *reliability vouching* (Emmott and Alexander 2010) since a supposedly reliable individual vouches for the reliability of a witness, even though that witness is in fact mistaken in her interpretation of the scene. Also, in the witness's reported story itself, the plot-significant fact is only mentioned briefly and is somewhat buried in a list of consequences since it is followed by the dramatic breaking of the vase. In a later pre-solution re-telling of the incident by Poirot in Example (4b), the water element of the incident is entirely omitted. It may be that Poirot has not yet recognised its significance, but nevertheless his omission (and another lengthy discussion about the vase shattering and the possibility of being startled) serves to downplay that aspect of the scene until the solution is presented.

> (4b) 'But I understood that there was an accident. That the vase slipped out of your hand and it fell to the hall below and was shattered to pieces.'
>
> *(Christie 1972: 112)*

By the time of the solution, the story is again re-framed, but this time with the emphasis on wetness (Example (4c)). The description of the soaking of Mrs Drake is placed alongside the description of the wetness of the murder, the words 'wet' and 'water' are foregrounded by repetition (strategy 3), and the extra details in the story are reduced so that the flooding of Mrs Drake has more prominence. This gives the argument a sense of inevitability, important if the reader is to see it as a credible explanation. This information was available from the prior story when the scene was first presented in Example (4a), but for that example Christie relied on the reader not making the connection when the wetness of the murder and the wetness of the vase incident were separated by several pages and not explicitly pointed out.

> (4c) 'Water. I wanted someone who was at the party and was *wet*, and who shouldn't have been wet. Whoever killed Joyce Reynolds would necessarily have got wet. You hold down a vigorous child with its head in a full bucket of water, and there will be struggling and splashing and you are bound to be wet. So something has got to happen to provide an innocent explanation of how you got wet. [...] And so Joyce was killed and her murderer was fairly well soaked with water. There must be a reason for that and she set about creating a reason. She had to get a witness as to *how* she got wet. She waited on the landing with an enormous vase of flowers filled with water. [...] Mrs Drake pretended to start nervously, and let the vase go, taking care that it flooded her person as it crashed down to the hall below.'
>
> *(Christie 1972: 182, original italics, underlining added)*

In Example (4c), the argument is made more forceful by the use of a generic which sounds as if it is an unarguable law of nature ('You hold down a vigorous child ...') but may not always be true. The lack of speculative modal verbs such as 'might' and 'could', even though this is speculation, and the use of strong modal verbs such as 'must' and expressions such as 'so', 'necessarily', 'bound to', 'has got to' and 'had to', serve to reinforce the argument.

The above examples involve re-directing attention, so that the reader does not notice the important details. Another version of strategy 1-2-ALT is to quite blatantly foreground a clue, but to give it a false significance. In the following example from Christie's *Dumb Witness*, the dead woman, Miss Arundell, was present at a séance the night before her death, and two witnesses describe an unusual manifestation over her head. This is foregrounded by italics and repeated mentions.

> (5a) '[...] And you know we saw – we all three saw – *most* distinctly, a kind of *halo* round Miss Arundell's head.'
>
> *'Comment?'*
>
> 'Yes. It was a kind of luminous haze.' She turned to her sister. 'Isn't that how you would describe it, Isabel?'
>
> 'Yes. Yes, just that. A luminous haze gradually surrounding Miss Arundell's head – an aureole of faint light. It was a *sign* – we know that now – a sign that she was about to pass over to the other side.'
>
> *(Christie 1958: 96, original italics, underlining added)*

Later, the manifestation is again described by a third witness, although in somewhat different form, again with some repetition and italicisation.

> (5b) '[Ectoplasm] proceeds, you know, from the medium's mouth in the form of a *ribbon* and builds itself up into a *form*. [...] On that evening I

distinctly saw a *luminous ribbon* issuing from dear Miss Arundell's mouth! Then her head became enveloped in a luminous mist.' *(Christie 1958: 134–5, original italics, underlining added)*

Normally in a detective story evidence from three witnesses would be fairly conclusive, but the narrator repeatedly casts doubt on the credibility of this testimony as spiritualist nonsense. The narrator here is overriding the foregrounding by *unreliability vouching*, by which we mean a supposedly reliable individual vouching for the unreliability of a witness (although in fact the speakers here are reporting a real event, even though their interpretation is wrong). Later, the true facts are explained by Poirot (1958: 245–6), using expert knowledge – the dead woman was killed by phosphorus poisoning and this, we are told, can cause the breath to glow in the dark. Few readers are likely to have this knowledge, so are unlikely to consider this possibility.

Although Examples (5a) and (5b) are largely characterised by foregrounding, there may still be a small amount of burying linked to text position. The details of the luminous manifestation change somewhat between Examples (5a) and (5b). Poirot himself comments on this (1958: 245) and dismisses it as just different versions of the same fact, but this change might be argued to have a rhetorical role. Possibly Christie strategically leaves the more explicit mention of the mouth in Example (5b) until this group of witnesses has been discredited, since there might be more risk of the reader linking a manifestation from the mouth with poisoning than a 'halo'.

Conclusion

The strategies discussed in this chapter reflect the core aspects of designing detective fiction plots, but also apply to plot construction in general. Writers of plots with surprise endings use foregrounding and burying to carefully direct readers in the hope of controlling their attention and thereby achieving rhetorical manipulation.

In addition to presenting a study of key strategies in creating plots in detective fiction, our chapter demonstrates the following points: (a) structured foregrounding is often discussed as a literary phenomenon but can be heavily used for rhetorical purposes in popular fiction, (b) in certain types of writing, the background of a text deserves study as well as the foreground, and (c) prominence may be achieved by a wide range of means other than linguistic deviance. This may include standard systemic choices used for contrastive purposes, and such factors as narrative-world salience, text position and the way in which inferences are controlled. In these respects, the view of foregrounding in this chapter differs somewhat from traditional accounts in stylistics, but fits in well with current psychological theories of attention control in text.

23

Analysing dialogue

Mick Short

Introduction

In this chapter I will consider how to analyse dialogues in novels and plays. The text I will use to illustrate this kind of analysis is from a story called 'Miró, Miró, on the wall', from Colum McCann's *Let the Great World Spin* (2009). I am using prose rather than a dramatic extract so that I can also explore the interaction between dialogue and character thought in prose texts and the choices in mode of speech and thought presentation which novelists have available to them. The stage directions of play texts can be seen as a more limited equivalent of narration in fictional prose, and written play dialogue can be seen as the rough equivalent of one kind of speech presentation in the novel, direct speech. But fictional prose is more sophisticated than dramatic text in the presentation of character speech and thought.

The extract I have chosen has only 15 spoken turns and 51 graphological words of direct speech out of a total of 392 graphological words in the passage as a whole. The rest of the passage is mainly the presentation of the thoughts of one of the characters. Character thoughts, especially if they are presented in the direct form (what I will call direct thought), as they are here mainly, are often compared to speech and so I will also look at these thoughts and how they are presented too.

I give the text for analysis in the next section. In the third section, I will begin my analysis by using the techniques that linguists and sociologists have developed to analyse spoken conversation to explore the patterns in the character speech. The areas we will need to look at are:

1. turn-taking
2. speech acts
3. politeness phenomena.

Normally I would include another analytical section when analysing dialogue, on inferring what is meant from what is said. But this dialogue is relatively straightforward, as we will see, and most of the things I need to say in this area relate more to the interaction between the speech and the thought in the passage than the speech itself. So I will make remarks on inferential matters throughout the whole chapter. Because I think the jury is still out on which of the competing forms of pragmatic analysis – Gricean, neo-Gricean or relevance theory – are best for text analysis, I will make my remarks on inference relatively atheoretical.

Even though the speech in the extract is relatively straightforward and simple, I will adopt a checksheet format of questions and answers within each of the above analytical modes, as they are the main focus of this chapter. The idea is to help show how I strive to be systematic in my analytical approach to dialogue analysis (for other checksheets, see Leech and Short 2007: chapter 3; Short 1996: chapters 1 and 3–11; and Stockwell 2010). Then, in the final sections, I will turn to patterns of discourse presentation in the text (speech and thought presentation in this case) and also consider, to some degree, the interaction between the speech and thought presentation in the extract. I will adopt a 'checksheet of questions' approach here too, but in a different way, to save space and focus a bit more on interpretative matters. The final analysis will be less exhaustive as we will be moving from the analysis of character dialogue into the analysis of thought. A complete stylistic analysis of the passage would involve, at the very least, more work on the thought presentation and an extended discussion of narrative viewpoint and character worlds, among other things.

I will look at each analytical area in turn to help emphasise the kind of careful and systematic analysis needed to do stylistic analysis well, because, as I have said elsewhere (Short 2012) the devil (and the angel too) is always in the detail. If I were providing, instead, a complete stylistic analysis of the passage, I would almost certainly choose a somewhat different structure, to help bring out what I think is most important about the passage interpretatively. Perhaps the significant point to make here is that there is an important difference to be made between what I call the research phase of an analysis and the writing-up phase. Keeping the two phases separate helps stylisticians to make sure they don't miss anything significant in their research-phase analysis and then, later, be able to concentrate better on how to present their findings to their readers when they move to the writing-up stage.

Because the dialogue in the passage is not very extensive and rather straightforward, at first it may seem that it is perhaps not worth analysing systematically and precisely. But, as I hope to show later in the chapter, we need to analyse the detail of the interrelations between the simple speech and the more complex thought if we are to understand the function of the relatively straightforward dialogue in the passage as a whole.

The text and its context

Colum McCann's *Let the Great World Spin* (2009) is a collection of short stories whose actions all take place on the day in 1974 in which, in real life, Philippe Petit, a French tightrope walker, famously performed a daring and illicit high-wire tightrope walk between the Twin Towers in New York (James Marsh's Oscar-winning film *Man on Wire* (2008) documents this feat). The stories in the collection have multiple protagonists, and in 'Miró, Miró, on the wall', the story from which our extract comes, the protagonist is Claire Soderberg, a wealthy American woman whose son has been killed in the American war with Vietnam. Claire, who we infer is married to a rich American Jewish businessman called Solomon, has become involved with a small self-support group of bereaved mothers of Vietnam-war victims. She has clearly gained much solace from the group but she is also very aware that she is much more privileged, financially and socially, than the other grieving mothers.

The women have meetings in each other's houses and they are about to gather in Claire's penthouse flat for the first time. The title of the story, which alludes both to the expensive paintings she has on her walls and the queen in 'Snow White', who, like Claire, also spends time looking in her mirror to assess her appearance, helps us to understand the metaphorical tightrope Claire is trying to walk, as she welcomes her new-found friends while fearing that the social chasm between her and them will destroy the bond which has become so important for her in coping with her grief. The story takes the form of a present-tense, third-person narration, and in this passage we see Claire worrying about how best to present herself to the women while giving instructions to Melvyn, the doorman on duty at the entrance to her apartment building (themselves clear indicators of her wealth and social status). Her conversation with Melvyn also shows her awareness of the social divide she is trying to traverse.

For ease of reference, below I have numbered the graphological sentences in the passage.

A quick shiver splits through her: the doorman. (1)
　　Wonder, will he question them too much? (2) Who is it today? (3) Melvyn, is it? (4) The new one? (5) Wednesday. (6) Melvyn, yes. (7) If he mistakes them for the help? (8) If he shows them to the service elevator? (9) Must call down and tell him. (10) Earrings! (11) Yes. (12) Earrings. (13) Quick now. (14) In the bottom of the box, an old pair, simple silver studs, seldom worn. (15) The bar a little rusty, but no matter. (16) She wets each stem in her mouth. (17) Catches sight of herself in the mirror again. (18) The shell-patterned dress, the shoulder-length hair, the badger streak. (19) She was mistaken once for the mother of a young intellectual seen on television, talking of photography, the moment of capture, the defiant art.

(20) She too had a badger streak. (21) *Photographs keep the dead alive*, the girl had said. (22) Not true. (23) So much more than photographs. (24) So much more. (25)

Eyes a little glassy already. (26) Not good. (27) Buck up, Claire. (28) She reaches for the tissues beyond the glass figurines on the dresser, dries her eyes. (29) Runs to the inner hallway, picks up the ancient handset. (30)

– Melvyn? (31)

She buzzes again. (32) Maybe outside smoking. (33)

– Melvyn?! (34)

– Yes, Mrs. Soderberg? (35)

His voice calm, even. (36) Welsh or Scottish – she's never asked. (37)

– I have some friends dining with me this morning. (38)

– Yes, ma'am. (39)

– I mean, they're coming for breakfast. (40)

– Yes, Mrs. Soderberg. (41)

She runs her fingers along the dark wainscoting of the corridor. (42) *Dining?* (43) Did I really say *dining*? (44) How could I say *dining*? (45)

– You'll make sure they're welcome? (46)

– Of course, ma'am. (47)

– Four of them. (48)

– Yes, Mrs. Soderberg. (49)

Breathing into the handset. (50) That fuzz of red mustache above his lip. (51) Should have asked where he was from when he first started working. (52) Rude not to. (53)

– Anything else, ma'am? (54) Ruder to ask now. (55)

– Melvyn? (56) The correct elevator. (57)

– Of course, ma'am. (58)

– Thank you. (59)

She leans her head against the cool of the wall. (60) She shouldn't have said anything at all about a correct or incorrect elevator. (61) A *bushe*, Solomon would have said. (62) Melvyn'll be down there, paralyzed, and then he'll put them in the wrong one. (63) *The elevator there to your right, ladies.* (64) *In you go.* (65) She feels a flush of shame to her cheeks. (66) But she used the word *dining*, didn't she? (67) He'll hardly mistake that. (68) *Dining* for breakfast. (69) Oh, my. (70)

The overexamined life, Claire, it's not worth living. (71)

(McCann 2009: 78–9)

Conversational patterns

Turn-taking patterns

Looking at turn-taking patterns is usually a good way to see the overall character relations in a conversation. To do this, the first thing I did was to isolate the turn-taking between Claire Soderberg and Melvyn from the rest of the text, so that I could do basic quantitative work on the data. Although the patterns shown will be helpful, it is important to bear in mind that the small amount of data means that the quantitative patterns shown cannot be statistically reliable. So I have not performed any statistical significance tests on the data. Below I include questions from my check-sheets which are not particularly revealing for this particular text (where the spoken interaction between the two characters is not at all extraordinary), as they may well be significant when other texts are being analysed. We will see that the answers to the various questions push incrementally in the same interpretative direction, strengthening and 'fleshing out' the characterisation I provided when introducing the passage. In this passage the spoken interaction is, by and large, rather unremarkable; but there are, nonetheless, some lessons which can be learned from analysing it systematically and, indeed, its very unremarkableness has some significance in the context of the whole passage, as we shall see.

Who has most turns?

Claire has 8 speech turns and Melvyn 7, a difference which is clearly not significant. The answer to this question would be more revealing in terms of power and other character relations when analysing conversations with three or more people. Two-party dialogues are bound to give roughly equal turn-quantity results, whatever the character relations. The beginning of the dialogue is a little unusual in that Claire's initial turn is non-verbal (she presses the buzzer on the intercom to summon Melvyn) and, as Melvyn does not respond to her first verbal turn, she follows this with two more adjacent turns, one verbal and one buzzer turn. So arguably Claire has 10 turns to Melvyn's 7, a pattern which suggests her ineffectual behaviour more than her power over her employee. This unusual pattern is further foregrounded by Claire's inference, which in turn suggests her hyper-awareness, that Melvyn does not respond straight away because he is outside having a smoke.

Who speaks the most words?

The easiest way to get a sense of turn volume is to calculate the average number of words per turn for each character and to look for significant variations within each character's pattern of turn-lengths. The easiest way to do this is to use the word count facility in Word or some other software. It is worth remembering that Word counts *graphological* not *morphological* words (i.e. character strings with spaces, or a space and an appropriate punctuation mark, on either side). Hence, 'you'll' will count as one word, not two. Which kind of word count you perform is not usually significant though, as long as you use the same counting method for each character.

In this passage, the turns are all pretty short, with no significant variations, as what is being discussed is not complex. Claire says briefly what she wants and Melvyn, even more briefly, accedes to her wishes.

Nonetheless, in proportional terms Claire has more than 25 per cent more words per turn than Melvyn (3.9, as opposed to 2.9), suggesting that she is the most powerful speaker.

Who initiates and who responds?

The power relations between the two characters becomes clearer when the initiation/response pattern is considered. Claire is the main initiator and Melvyn the main responder. Claire begins the conversation, and 7 of her 8 speech turns can be characterised as initiations (though sentence 57 is arguably ambiguous between initiation and response); Claire's one clear response turn is when she says 'thank you' in sentence 59 and brings the conversation to a close. Six of Melvyn's 7 turns are responses, all of which are straightforwardly supportive of Claire's initiations, and even his one initiation (54) is supportive of her.

There is one particularly interesting sequence, from sentences 38 to 49, where Claire re-initiates again and again to 'patch up' what she sees as her own communicative mistakes. Sentence 38, 'I have some friends dining with me this morning', arguably says all that is needed for Melvyn to identify the group of women and know that he has to treat them respectfully. But in sentence 40 Claire feels the need to correct her 'dining' in 38 with 'for breakfast', suggesting that she feels she has made a terminological, and so possibly a referential, *faux pas*; in 46 she checks up on whether Melvyn will welcome the visitors, something his job schematically demands and in 48 she states how many women there will be, suggesting, as in 40, that she is being over-punctilious communicatively, leading to the inference that she is very nervous about the visit.

Who interrupts whom?

Interruptions (which are usually marked textually by incomplete syntax in the interrupted turn and a turn-final long dash or ellipses) often indicate conversational power, particularly in adversarial interactions, where more powerful interlocutors typically interrupt the less powerful. (Overlaps are signalled in dramatic performance by extensive speech overlap and appropriate prosodic and kinesis signals). In this extract, where Claire, as one of Melvyn's employers, is institutionally as well as conversationally powerful, there are no interruptions whatsoever. This pattern reflects the fact that Melvyn conforms very straightforwardly, and in very few words, to Claire's stated wishes.

What address terms are used?

Address terms are typically used when opening conversations and, in multi-party conversations, sometimes medially to pick out which individual is being addressed. Powerful people typically use first name (FN) to less powerful interactants and get title + last name (T+LN) or an honorific in return. Given that our text involves just two interactants, there should in theory be no need for more address terms than one each. However, Claire uses 'Melvyn' 3 times in 8 turns and Melvyn uses an address term in each turn: 'Mrs. Soderberg' (3 times) and the status-marked honorific 'ma'am' (4 times). Melvyn is thus clearly involved in polite employer-to-employee 'facework'. Claire's address terms are more interesting. At the beginning, she has to use 2 attention-getters to establish communication with Melvyn and she then feels the need to use another in 56, even though it does not appear to be communicatively necessary. Why this is so becomes clear when we consider the surrounding co-text:

> – Yes, Mrs. Soderberg. (49)
>   Breathing into the handset. (50) That fuzz of red mustache above his lip. (51) Should have asked where he was from when he first started working. (52) Rude not to. (53)
>   – Anything else, ma'am? (54) Ruder to ask now. (55)
>   – Melvyn? (56) The correct elevator. (57)
>   – Of course, ma'am. (58)

Claire is clearly worrying about her relationship with Melvyn in 52–3, something which is schematically unnecessary. That she continues this worrying in 55 suggests that, although there seems to be very little speech time in between Melvyn's initiation in 54 and hers in 56, she perceives it as longer, presumably because of her own distraction, and so feels the need to check that Melvyn is still listening before she insists on the particular elevator he is to show her guests into. Claire's instruction also suggests that there are (at least) two elevators, equivalent in function to the front and back doors of wealthy houses, one for guests and one for servants/delivery people.

Who controls the topic of talk?

Claire, the powerful person, controls the topic of talk (how her guests are to be treated) throughout. Even when Melvyn initiates in 54, he stays on her topic, showing in this respect, as in others, what a co-operative servant he is.

Who allocates turns to whom?

Turn allocation typically only applies in conversations with three or more interactants and where some person has the power to determine who takes a turn when (e.g. in TV chat shows), and so this factor is not relevant in this text.

Any interesting turn-taking relations between the turns?

Practitioners of what is usually referred to as conversational analysis look carefully at the relationships between the turns involved in small-scale conversational exchanges, a style of analysis which often reveals, for example, that the second pair part in a two-part exchange is dispreferred in some way (e.g. that the response to a question does not actually answer the question asked). Dispreferred responses have meaningful consequences (e.g. an inference that the second speaker may be being obstreperous). In other texts, conversational analysis can be highly revealing of numerous and significant unstated meanings. Here, however, the relation between Melvyn's 6 responses and the initiations from Claire which prompt them is remarkably neat and tidy. Without exception, Claire commands and Melvyn agrees unreservedly to do as she asks.

Speech-act patterns

Unsurprisingly, the speech-act patterns in this conversation are also pretty simple and reflect the clear differentiation in roles between the two characters. Claire politely orders Melvyn to do things and he agrees to do so.

What speech acts are used by the different characters?

As we have already seen in turn-taking terms, 5 of Melvyn's turns constitute straightforward acceptances of the instruction that Claire has given him – for example, 'Yes, Mrs. Soderberg' (49), 'Of course, ma'am' (58) – showing his unreserved acceptance of his institutional role. His other turns are (i) a querying response 'Yes, Mrs. Soderberg?' (35) to her unnecessary attention-getter in 34, inviting her to give him her instructions, and (ii) 'Anything else, ma'am?' (54), an elliptical initiation which performs the same function and explains my characterisation of it above as a supportive initiation.

Apart from her 3 attention-getters in 31, 34 and 57, and her expression of thanks which ends the conversation, the rest of Claire's speech acts are polite commands to which Melvyn accedes, reflecting her control and his acceptance of it.

Are any of the speech acts ambiguous?

Melvyn's are not, apart from his initial 'Yes, Mrs. Soderberg?' (35), as he is merely agreeing to what he is told throughout. The question mark in 35 indicates that his response is not just phatic language but would be spoken with rising intonation, constituting an invitation for her to tell him what she wants. However, 6 of Claire's speech acts are ambiguous between commands and requests. This, along with her consistent use of FN only when addressing Melvyn, reflects her politeness: although she is institutionally in control, she 'gives face' to her employee by using directive speech acts which are not bald commands. We will follow this up when we consider politeness below.

Are any of the speech acts indirect?

Again, Melvyn's are not, reflecting the simplicity of his conversational position. But Claire is more indirect, reflecting her politeness. Her typical strategy is to make statements which are interpretable indirectly as commands/requests. An example is 'I have some friends dining with me this morning' (38). The statement has the indirect force of 'look out for them and assist them when they arrive'. Sometimes the statements are elliptical in form, and at the beginning of the conversation the meanings of Claire's indirect instructions can be a little unclear; but as the dialogue progresses the function of these elliptical speech acts becomes clearer. 'The correct elevator' (57) is a good example of an elliptical statement in which the content of the indirect speech act is considerably more specific, compared with 38. Although she is being polite to Melvyn overall, we can infer that Claire's anxiety concerning the welcome for her friends makes her polite demands more 'pushy' as the dialogue progresses. 'You'll make sure they're welcome?' (46) appears to be a question at first sight because of the question mark, but its declarative structure makes the 'request' arm of the command/request ambiguity of the indirect speech act less likely, increasing its command feel, another indicator of Claire's increasing worry about how her new friends will be treated (and so how they will think of her).

Anything interesting about the felicity conditions for the speech acts?

Clearly the preparatory conditions for commands and requests vary in their assumptions concerning the power disparity between the participants. We know that Claire actually has considerable institutional power over Melvyn but her indirect command/request speech acts appear to assume a less clear-cut relationship, thus reflecting her wish to be polite to Melvyn in spite of her anxiety.

Do the intended perlocutionary effects of the speech acts succeed?

Unlike in many fictional conversations, where we see tensions between interlocutors, here Claire's speech acts achieve their intended perlocutionary effects rather straightforwardly. Melvyn agrees to do everything she asks. The only exceptions to this 'rule' are her unsuccessful attempts at the very beginning of the passage to open the conversational channel. It could be argued that Melvyn does not achieve his intended perlocutionary effects, as he does not completely set Claire's mind at rest by his highly co-operative answers.

Politeness patterns

The most popular form of analysis used in politeness analysis is that set out by P. Brown and Levinson (1987), though I personally prefer the Leechian approach to politeness, as I find it easier to integrate with Gricean-style pragmatic analysis (Leech 1983: Chapter 6, 1992, 2006). Here, I provide an atheoretical discussion, as the politeness behaviours of the characters are rather straightforward. We have already noted that Claire

is polite to Melvyn even though she has the power institutionally to dominate him and Melvyn is scrupulously polite in return, as indicated by his use
of direct address terms.

Are the characters' politeness behaviours reciprocal?

In the general sense that they are both polite to one another, the answer
to this question is yes; though it is worth bearing in mind that Claire
could have been more polite earlier in their relationship, by showing
more interest in Melvyn (i.e. paying more attention to her positive face,
in P. Brown and Levinson's (1987) terms), as she herself recognises in
37 and 52. In addition, even though it is the doorman's job to act in
ways that Claire and the other occupants of the apartment block require,
Claire needs to make specific requests and she tries to mitigate these
face-threatening acts (FTAs) on Melvyn's negative face.

In what ways, if any, are face-threatening acts mitigated?

Claire uses FN-only to show interest in Melvyn and she tries, initially at least,
to make her requests indirect. So, in 'I have some friends dining with me this
morning' (38), she does not tell Melvyn to treat her friends well but makes a
statement about their imminent arrival from which he can easily infer what
he should do when they arrive. But, as we saw above, this strategy of indirectness means that she cannot be sure that she has achieved her perlocutionary
aim (even though it is pretty transparent for us and so, presumably, for
Melvyn too) and so she moves from that implicated request to 'I mean,
they're coming for breakfast' (40) and finally 'You'll make sure they're
welcome?' (46). The request FTA becomes more on-record in 46, as indicated
by the declarative grammatical structure 'mixed' with the question mark.
In 57, Claire even feels the need to specify which elevator Melvyn is to show
the women into. This suggests that she is failing, in Leechian terms, to take
proper account of the agreement maxim (minimise disagreement between
self and other) and the sympathy maxim (minimise antipathy between self
and other). In politeness terms, Melvyn is impeccably polite throughout.

Are there any examples of impoliteness?

In spite of the fact that Claire thinks she is making a bit of a mess of things,
there are no straightforward indications of impoliteness, of the sort that
others (e.g. Bousfield 2007; Culpeper 1998) have commented on in more
adversative conversations. Impoliteness is common because it reflects
character disequilibrium and generates reader interest.

Discourse presentation

I will begin this section with a set of discourse-presentation questions
that I find helpful to ask when analysing texts.

1. Is the segment of text you are looking at narration or the presentation of discourse?
2. If discourse is presented, is that discourse speech, thought or writing (don't forget there can be ambiguities, e.g. between speech and thought)?
3. What mode of presentation is it (e.g. direct, indirect, free indirect – again watch out for ambiguities e.g. between narration and free indirect thought (FIT))?
4. What general sorts of effects or meanings do you associate with each particular mode on the relevant presentation cline?
5. How do those general effects relate or play out in the particular context the presentation occurs in?
6. Are there any special effects associated with unusual ordering of the reporting signal (e.g. 'she said'), if there is one, in relation to the discourse presented?
7. Are there any examples of discourse embedded inside other discourse which need to be considered (e.g. speech embedded inside speech or speech embedded inside thought)?

In answer to question 1, this text contains speech presentation and thought presentation but not writing presentation. To save space, I do not spell out individual answers to the other questions below but instead provide answers to them via my general discussion of the speech and thought presentation in the passage. It should be noted that there is a multitude of work in this area, and categories and descriptions have changed from time to time as knowledge has developed and scholarly positions have been debated. For the latest statement of my own position, see Short (2012) and (2007). Also relevant are Leech and Short (2007: Chapter 10), Fludernik (1993), Short (1996: Chapter 10), Toolan (2001: Chapter 5) and Semino and Short (2004).

Speech presentation

The speech presented in our dialogue is all in the direct speech (DS) mode, with no ambiguities. Some undergraduates I have used this text with have been confused into thinking that DS is not being used, because of the absence of quotation marks. Instead, the beginning of each speech turn is marked by a line-initial long dash. But this typographical indicator of DS, though less common than inverted commas, is merely a graphological variant used by different (Irish-American?) publishing traditions. So there is nothing unusual in the speech presentation, no presentational ambiguities and no interesting variations in presentation between the turns or in terms of the relationship between the content of what is said and how it is presented. (For example, compare the mismatch between the content and the indirect speech (IS) presentation in the following, from David Lodge's *How Far Can You*

Go? (Lodge 1980: chapter 2). Edward and Tessa, two Catholic first-year undergraduates, have just made love, clumsily and without contraception, for the first time: 'Afterwards, he was aghast at what he had done, but Tessa covered his face with kisses and told him it had been wonderful. . .'. The mismatch between the content and the IS presentation form for Tessa's speech clearly prompts us to infer that Tessa is exaggerating to help Edward get over his feelings of guilt.) In 'Miró, Miró', there are no interesting effects created by varying the standard 'DS followed by reporting signal' of direct speech because there are no reporting clauses or equivalent reporting signals linked syntactically to the DS string. The relationships among the speech turns all have to be inferred from the prototypical adjacency-pair relationships and the surrounding context and co-text. All this reflects the ordinary, transactional nature of the interaction presented; and yet, at the same time, the DS mode, especially given its lack of associated reporting signals, dramatises the interaction to its fullest extent, suggesting that it is important even though, as we have seen, it is pretty straightforward conversationally. This apparent paradox becomes more understandable when we consider the relations between the speech and the thought presentation in the passage.

Thought presentation

I have demonstrated again and again above how unremarkable, by and large, the conversation between Claire and Melvyn is. Its significance is in the contrast we can see between the relatively straightforward speech and Claire's anxious thoughts surrounding, and interspersed with, the dialogue. My word count indicates that Claire's thought presentation takes up some 255 words of the 392-word passage, compared with the 51 words of speech, a 5:1 proportional contrast that shows the importance of Claire's inner world compared with her external dialogue with Melvyn. (This quantification cannot be entirely accurate as there are some ambiguities concerning whether particular sentences are narration or thought presentation. Sentences 36 and 37 are good examples: 'His voice calm, even. Welsh or Scottish – she's never asked' (they could be narration or FIT), as are the first two sentences of 50–52: 'Breathing into the handset. (50) That fuzz of red mustache above his lip. (51) Should have asked where he was from when he first started working. (52)' The final sentence is clearly DT but the first two could be narration, DT or FIT).

The large majority of thought presentation is in the DT mode, thus dramatising it in a way that parallels the DS presentation. A good example is the 161-word stretch from sentence 2 onwards, of which 145 words (all except sentences 16–17) are DT, if we include the italicised remembered speech in 22:

Wonder, will he question them too much? (2) Who is it today? (3) Melvyn, is it? (4) The new one? (5) Wednesday. (6) Melvyn, yes. (7) If he mistakes them for the help? (8) If he shows them to the service elevator? (9) Must call down and tell him. (10) Earrings! (11) Yes. (12) Earrings. (13) Quick now. (14) In the bottom of the box, an old pair, simple silver studs, seldom worn. (15) The bar a little rusty, but no matter. (16) She wets each stem in her mouth. (17) Catches sight of herself in the mirror again. (18) The shell-patterned dress, the shoulder-length hair, the badger streak. (19) She was mistaken once for the mother of a young intellectual seen on television, talking of photography, the moment of capture, the defiant art. (20) She too had a badger streak. (21) *Photographs keep the dead alive*, the girl had said. (22) Not true. (23) So much more than photographs. (24) So much more. (25)

The DT presentational choice enables the thought presentation to be as 'dialogic' as the speech. Claire is apparently thinking consciously 'to herself' (a common effect associated with DT) and her inner world seems to predominate over her conversation with Melvyn. Sentences 2–5 are questions Claire 'asks' of herself, and 6–7 evoke the rapid thought process by which confirms the presupposition of her 'interactive' reverse-polarity tag question 'Melvyn, is it?' (4). Clearly we use the pragmatic maxim/principle of relation/relevance to infer this relationship between the sentences and we can already see that McCann is beginning to create an effect which is stream-of-consciousness-like. This effect becomes even clearer with 'Earrings!' (11), which marks a dramatic topic shift from the previous sentence 'Must call down and tell him' (10).

What we see in this first part of the extract is repeated throughout the passage. Claire's 'internal dialogue' is markedly more lively than the dialogue between her and Melvyn. In addition, at times there is a clear interaction between the external speech and the internal 'speech', such as:

> – Yes, Mrs. Soderberg. (49)
>   Breathing into the handset. (50) That fuzz of red mustache above his lip. (51) Should have asked where he was from when he first started working. (52) Rude not to. (53)
>   – Anything else, ma'am? (54) Ruder to ask now. (55)
>   – Melvyn? (56) The correct elevator. (57)

Sentences 49, 54, 56 and 57 are speech presentation. (It is important analytically to note that the notion of internal 'speech' is a metaphor here. Otherwise considerable confusion can arise.) Other sentences arguably all present thoughts which relate to the speech. Sentences 52–3 are elliptical DT presentations of Claire's thoughts concerning what she should have said earlier but omitted, and 55 clearly determines what she does *not* say in 56–7. This interaction between the speech and the thought is reminiscent of the writing of James Joyce, Virginia Woolf, Katherine Mansfield and others. The extensive use of ellipsis both in the speech presentation and the thought presentation also brings out the dialogic, interactive nature of Claire's thoughts and their inter-connections with what she says and hears. (My undergraduate students often assume that the use of DT and/or FIT guarantees stream-of-consciousness writing. But there is plenty of vivid thought presentation which is not in the stream-of-consciousness mode (as in Jane Austen's novels, for example). Stream-of-consciousness writing seems additionally to need features such as the ellipsis and dramatic topic shifts seen in this passage (which is by no means the most extreme example of such writing), features which in turn call for harder inferential work on the part of the reader.)

Although the majority of Claire's thought presentation is in DT, there are a few sentences which are FIT, for example 'But she used the word *dining*, didn't she?' (67), where the pronominal choice is not appropriate for self-referential DT here (though the past tense is, as Claire's act of remembering is being evoked). The use of FIT, which also presents thoughts dramatically, provides cohesion with sentences of narration and relates to just (parts of) 5 of the passage's 71 sentences. There are no other examples of thought presentation forms apart from DT and FIT, and no speech presentation forms apart from DS. Essentially this means that none of the less direct presentational forms are used for either speech or thought, a clear indication of the dramatised nature of the speech presentation, thought presentation and their interaction. Given that all the thoughts in the passage are Claire's, we are clearly being led to sympathise with her plight even more strongly than we might otherwise have done.

Embedded speech presentation

The mainly DT extract from the beginning of the passage which I quoted above also contains an example of speech presentation (in sentence 22) embedded inside the thought presentation:

> She was mistaken once for the mother of a young intellectual seen on television, talking of photography, the moment of capture, the defiant art. (20) She too had a badger streak. (21) *Photographs keep the dead alive*, the girl had said. (22) Not true. (23) So much more than photographs. (24) So much more. (25)

Claire's noticing of the badger streak in her hair prompts her to remember someone with a similar streak in her hair, talking on television. McCann presents what the young woman said in italics, helping us to understand its status as remembered embedded speech and it is also in the DS form, helping us to infer that Claire's memory of what the young intellectual said is vivid (and indeed she disagrees with what was said (23)).

McCann uses italics to signal speech embedded inside Claire's thoughts on other occasions too:

> She runs her fingers along the dark wainscoting of the corridor. (42)
> *Dining?* (43) Did I really say *dining?* (44) How could I say *dining?* (45)

Here she remembers her inappropriate use of the verb 'dining' from the immediately preceding conversation, something which she has already corrected in her conversation with Melvyn. The repetition of the word in each of the three questions above helps to show her agitation at what is, after all, a minor lexical error.

The most extended use of embedded speech in Claire's thoughts relates to the next social error she makes, in specifying to Melvyn that her friends should be shown into the correct elevator, something which she would never feel the need to say, presumably, if her guests were more genteel:

> She shouldn't have said anything at all about a correct or incorrect elevator. (61) A *bushe*, Solomon would have said. (62) Melvyn'll be down there, paralyzed, and then he'll put them in the wrong one. (63) *The elevator there to your right, ladies.* (64) *In you go.* (65) She feels a flush of shame to her cheeks. (66) But she used the word *dining*, didn't she? (67) He'll hardly mistake that. (68) *Dining* for breakfast. (69) Oh, my. (70)
> The overexamined life, Claire, it's not worth living. (71)

The word 'bushe' is Yiddish (helping us, along with his name, 'Solomon', to infer that Claire's husband is Jewish), with a meaning roughly equivalent to 'faux pas'. Unlike the previous examples of embedded speech, this one-word embedded DS is not a memory but hypothetical speech – what Claire thinks Solomon *would* have said *if* he had witnessed her interaction with Melvyn. (For discussions of hypothetical discourse see Semino et al. 1999 and Semino and Short 2004: 159–71). Then, in 64–5, we have more embedded hypothetical DS, helping us to infer that Claire is imagining a situation in which her 'bushe' accidentally pushes Melvyn into doing the opposite of what she intends. This in turn leads her to re-remember her lexical mistake concerning 'dining', bringing the embedded repetition of the speech up to five occurrences, indicating how much her recognition of this tiny lexical error has affected her. Finally, in 71, we are led to infer that she has herself realised that her obsession with getting everything exactly right is over the top.

Overall, we can see that the DS embedded in Claire's thoughts, all signalled graphologically with italics, is all used systematically, whether it is remembered or hypothetical speech, to signal Claire's hyper-awareness of her minor speech errors.

Thought 'turn-taking'

Thinking is not normally a dialogic activity and so it usually makes no sense to apply turn-taking analysis to thought presentation. But the fact that the majority of Claire's thoughts are presented in the DT mode does provide the potential for creating an 'interactive' feel to the flow of thoughts, and McCann makes use of some of the features we saw above to help create such a feel for Claire's thought processes. This can be seen clearly in the 'badger-streak' paragraph which I re-quoted in the section above.

Sentences 2–5 of the passage are internal questions, which lead to the inference that Claire is seeking answers mentally to these questions. Sentence 7 is clearly the answer to sentence 4, and 5–6 can be seen as the mental steps which get Claire from question to answer. Sentences 8 and 9 are also questions, used to word worries Claire has about how Melvyn might treat her friends, and 10 can be seen as the answer she works out to those questions.

We can also see analogical equivalents to the 'question and answer' character of Claire's thoughts. Sentence 11, which we have already noted for its dramatic, stream-of-consciousness-like, topic shift from sentence 10, is not a question but an exclamation, representing another worry. In turn, sentences 12–16 provide the mental steps and mental (and, indeed, physical) solution to the problem posed. Sentences 22–5 represent Claire's mental rejection of what she remembers the woman on the TV programme claimed, as presented in the embedded DS of 22.

It is not surprising that this sort of thought presentation is sometimes referred to by critics as 'dialogic' (though it is important to remember that the word is being used metaphorically here, not literally). I do not have the space here to map out all of the 'dialogic' aspects of McCann's presentation of his character's thoughts but hopefully this discussion will help to prompt others to use conversational analysis not just for spoken dialogue but also analogically, where appropriate, to explore stretches of extended DT, and even FIT, in other texts.

24

Atmosphere and tone

Peter Stockwell

Literary features and literary effects

Literary criticism is a broad practice that ranges far beyond the professional sphere of academic books and journals; it also encompasses the blogosphere of enthusiasts, lists of favourite books and partisan views, and all points of literary journalism, recommendations, reading group discussions and notes in between. At almost every level of this vast field of human commentary, observation, opinion and argument about literature, the words *atmosphere* and *tone* can be found being used to describe a wide range of phenomena. From professional academic discourse to everyday commentary, both terms tend to be used in an equally vague, impressionistic sense, roughly covering the notion that a particular passage of a literary work has a discernible ambience, a quality that is often qualified by an emotional effect: sinister, positive, melancholy, playful, elegiac, sunny and so on. Such usages are of interest to the stylistician, firstly because their widespread adoption suggests a sociotextual reality that is significant for readers, and secondly because the specification of vagueness and the establishment of descriptive precision are the stock-in-trade for stylistics.

When *atmosphere* is used non-literally (that is, not to refer to the air surrounding the Earth), a search of the British National Corpus (BNC) reveals that it is almost always pre- or post-modified, and these functional slots are filled with a large variety of types of words and phrases. This suggests that the word invokes a sense that is relatively semantically empty or vacuous, denoting an emotional or ambient space that requires specification or filling in with the intended ambient quality. Almost all non-literal usages feature *atmosphere* as pertaining to a place or a located event: a room, building, location, classroom, party, sports event and so on. It is clear that there is a strong spatial and locative element to its meaning. The term appears frequently in advertising discourse ('pub atmosphere',

```
                    as convention would have it, those of one who has lost another. The atmosphere which
is evoked in the reading of the poem is one of hopelessness, of
its overall effect and uses to its best advantage various language features to evoke an atmosphere of
grandeur and magnificence conveying the author's passion for something which would otherwise remain
                              of the first. It is in this new phase that the train and the atmosphere of the
poem come alive. It is almost as if she
                    aware of their presence and sees them as' simply a part of the familiar atmosphere of the
room, a background which does not touch her preoccupation'. Although
                    been written on the subject of the' awful' school dinners and the general atmosphere of
school. For instance the joke: Q' What's the difference between
                    as' unfriendly, watched, gibbets, sour' help to create a sinister atmosphere as they
are all oppressive words dealing with being shut out, death, and
    witches appearing around Macbeth Banquo is a lot younger than in other play Much more atmosphere and
reality than in play Macbeth is not happy to see Ross etc, as
                    at all, just plain coloured backgrounds. Makes the film lose a sense of atmosphere.
Duncan's religiousness is being very heavily emphasized He is meant to have been
                    and the wind that shrills in the wasteland. Overall there is an atmosphere of
dispossession which again is full of sorrow. And, as it were one
    companions fight; and Pandarus is also present, soaking up and intensifying the sensual atmosphere. He
sings sordid lines, celebrating the' tickling' and' dying of
            infected Troy. Even the love of Troilus and Cressida is debased by the Trojan atmosphere, and
misplaced values. They make long and elegant speeches before Pandarus leads them
        in which Golding described the act was much more realistic than Ballantyne's. The atmosphere in
Ballantyne's book was very relaxed and optimistic, but in Golding's it
        At the beginning Dickens piles up adjectives in order to set the scene and build atmosphere as is
shown when he writes in the first chapter The marshes were just a
```

Figure 24.1: Results for 'atmosphere' in school essays in the BNC

'relaxed atmosphere', 'happy family atmosphere') and political journalism ('atmosphere of the House', 'intimidating atmosphere' 'atmosphere of pressure'), but it is its deployment in literary commentary that is of interest here. School essays in the BNC return results such as those shown in Figure 24.1.

In these and other examples, the most common modifying word or phrase is an abstract noun or adjective (*hopelessness, grandeur, sensual, relaxed* and *optimistic*), often indicating an emotional or aesthetic quality. The atmosphere of a place is a quality not only inherent in the place itself, but is an experiential quality that strongly presupposes the presence of the experiencing consciousness. In other words and in terms of literary reading, a piece of writing can be 'atmospheric' if the description it presents seems to draw the reader in and engage in the ambient feeling of the world denoted. Crucially, *atmosphere* and *atmospheric* generally point to the world-focused content of the writing, and point to a direct and integrated relationship between the reader and that world.

The use of the word *tone* is contrastively slightly different. A passage of writing has a *tone* that in fact seems to retain its literal, denotational auditory sense of a 'tone of voice'. It therefore gestures not so much at the content of the literary world as at the medium of the writing itself. Since noticing the tone of a passage serves to foreground the compositional function of the writing, *tone* seems to be attached not to the evoked world but to the authorial or narratorial voice. In the BNC, among the most common collocates (within five words either side of the word *tone*) after the literal ones of 'tone of voice', 'musical tone' and such are: *mocking, dismissive, conversational, aggressive, mild, neutral, gentle, cool, scathing, sarcastic, smooth, sardonic, sympathetic, hostile, patronising* and so on. Tone stands as a

```
second line onwards until the end of this stanza the poem has a nostalgic tone
                                    here the tone changes. It is as if Owen
                              This tone continues to the end of the stanza.
                                  nostalgic tone with the use of the phrase
                      This book ends on a heavy tone of
       original ending because it keeps up the style and tone of the rest of the novel
                            the contrast in the tone between the stanzas
                                    The tone is that of the narrator
                          disenchanted tone of many of his editorial pronouncements
                   Frazer's Comtian, progressive tone. Shaw's book, however
                                    The tone is abject, but Eliot
                            The reverential tone of Levin's text
                            hectoring tone of their documents
```

Figure 24.2: Results for 'tone' in the BNC's 'school essays' and 'academic arts writing' contexts

quality of the voice of the writing, and strongly indexes a mood, characteristic or trait of the writer's personality.

Both in the BNC's 'school essays' context and in the 'academic arts writing' context, the word *tone* often collocates in nearby co-text with references to the text, book or poem in hand, or to the author. Examples include those in Figure 24.2.

Contrastively, then, *atmosphere* pertains to the perceived quality of the literary world from a readerly perspective, whereas *tone* pertains to the quality of the meditating authorial or narratorial voice. The tone of a passage is a relatively autonomous object (in Ingarden's 1973 terms), in the sense that it has an existence and features that can be described if not exactly objectively then at least without special peculiar reference to the observing consciousness of the reader. By contrast, we would not tend to talk of the atmosphere of a passage of text but rather of a scene or episode, and so the atmosphere of a literary work is more like what Ingarden would call a heteronomous object – one that exists principally by the interaction of the phenomenon with an observing reading consciousness. In this respect, *tone* can be described in more text-stylistic terms than *atmosphere*, which requires a more cognitive poetic account, and this distinction is the organising principle of this chapter. I will explore atmospheric and tonal aspects of literature together, firstly in terms of stylistic word choice and then in terms of their cognitive effect, before finally considering their interdependent nature.

Diction and register

When a literary commentator – whether literary critic or fan – describes a poem as 'atmospheric', it almost always means that there is something about the scene that is evoked that is suggestive rather than denotative, something mystical, mysterious, oblique or somehow enigmatic or ineffable. Attempts to find articulation tend to include a heavy reliance on abstract nouns, and often a paradoxical combination of semantic contraries. Here, for example, is how the poet Michael Woods describes Seamus

Heaney's well-known 'Mid-term break', an elegy for his younger brother, killed in a car accident, and which was first published in the *Kilkenny Magazine* in 1963:

> This beautiful lyric poem is certainly enormously moving. It presents an elder brother having to deal with a terrible trauma. As is frequently the case with Heaney, there is an arresting amalgam of manliness and tenderness in the writing that lends it both warmth and astringency at the same time. This poem is powerfully moving because of its emotional restraint and control of tone. Heaney concentrates on observed details and it is the accumulation of these details that helps to make the poem so memorable.
>
> An elegiac tone is established at the beginning [. . .] The poem opens with a line that might easily describe any child but the second line introduces a darkly foreboding atmosphere:
>
> > 'I sat all morning in the college sick bay
> > Counting bells knelling classes to a close.'
>
> The word 'knell' is appropriate in the context of a poem about death because it is the sound of a funeral bell. We do not normally associate school bells with death but this day was to prove horrifically different for the poet. The rhythm and alliteration also reinforce the mournful tone. The 'c' and 'l' sounds, as well as the internal rhyme of 'bells' and 'knelling' help to suggest both the idea of finality and of time seeming to slow down.
>
> *(Woods 2013)*

The poem itself ends:

> Next morning I went up into the room. Snowdrops
> And candles soothed the bedside; I saw him
> For the first time in six weeks. Paler now,
>
> Wearing a poppy bruise on his left temple,
> He lay in the four foot box as in his cot.
> No gaudy scars, the bumper knocked him clear.
>
> A four foot box, a foot for every year.   *Seamus Heaney (1990: 7)*

As Woods intuitively notices, the tone is established firstly by the lexical choices and reinforced by phonological and prosodic features. Vocabulary choice in literature is traditionally called *diction*, a term like *tone* that also has echoes of its origins in speech performance. Here, the recalled perspective is of the elder brother (14 years old, biographically) but the diction and *register* (grammatical arrangement) is of the adult poet. There is thus a reflective tone in evidence: the boy would not choose such atmospheric words as 'knell', nor select the alliteration of the /k/ in 'college sick ... counting ... classes ... close', nor would arrange the memory into three-line stanzas. All of these features are retrospective patterns that indicate the compositional deictic centre of the adult poet looking back.

Atmosphere and tone are collectively a matter not so much of denotational semantic value as connotative or associative effects. The denotational (narrow, 'dictionary definition') meaning of the first two lines of the poem are something like: *I sat all morning in the school sickbay, listening to the bells at the end of each lesson.* However, this bald proposition does not convey the atmosphere of the scene in which the boy finds himself, nor the tone of the poet looking back. Instead, there is a strong connotation in 'knelling' already of death: the BNC lists 62 occurrences of 'knell', almost all of them collocating in 'death knell'; the only use of 'knelling' comes from a lawsuit document of 1629. So, both the lexical choice (*knell*) and the archaic choice of form (*knell-ing* – to chime with *morn-ing* and *count-ing*) are aspects of the poetic tone of voice, recreating the atmosphere felt vaguely by the boy. The tone of deathliness in *knell* is a strong connotation, perhaps strong enough to be regarded as part of its denotation.

There are other suggestions offered by some of the diction that are more tenuous or delicate. For example, the first mention of 'morning' might not suggest a phonetic echo of 'mourning', but perhaps the second use of it towards the end of the poem might do this. But the close occurrence of 'morning' and 'sick' would probably not suggest 'morning sickness' to any reader, not even perhaps one currently suffering from it in pregnancy. This connection would not be a connotation, nor even perhaps more loosely a faint association, but would be dismissed I imagine by most people as an irrelevant accident of text, given the context of the rest of the poem. Or would it? I have just looked at the middle section of the poem and found, back at the house, 'the baby cooed and laughed and rocked the pram', and later, his mother who 'coughed out angry tearless sighs'. If there is a faint, idiosyncratic association here, for me now it adds an extra painful memory for his mother, grieving for the loss of her child.

As can be seen from this account, dividing denotation from other, more rarefied senses (first connotation and then loose association) is not a distinction that is precise or principled enough. It is a distinction that is not maintained in cognitive linguistics, where any semantic value at all is always regarded as part of a prototypical domain, in which the most likely and expected senses are most readily available, with a radial gradation of looser, less likely, or unusual senses. Furthermore, every such frame or domain (Evans and Green 2006: 210; Fillmore 1982, 1985; Langacker 1987) is constituted according to the context of situation in which it is used. 'Morning', here, only suggests 'mourning' in the funereal context, and is absent in 'never glad confident morning' (Browning), or 'great morning of the world' (Shelley), or 'I caught this morning morning's minion' (Hopkins). Situation is everything. Whereas the plain, eventful meaning of the poem is mainly carried in the most central (or denotational) values of word choice, it seems apparent that the atmosphere and tone of the poem are carried mainly by the less central semantic values of the lexis. And of course we might say that it is this atmospheric meaning that in fact stands as the primary effect of the poem. The bare facts of the story are not as emotionally affecting as the tonal richness in which it is portrayed.

It is obvious, then, that atmosphere and tone are matters primarily of diction (lexical choice) and register. In linguistics, *register* largely encompasses diction, in the sense that register refers to lexicogrammatical patterns used in an appropriate social context (Halliday and Matthiessen 2004). The focus in analysing register is not only on the lexical choice, in other words, but on how those and other matters of syntactic and discursive structures are patterned in context. Earlier in this discussion, I made the distinction between the perceiving boy and the recalling adult, and noted that most of the lexical choices belong to the adult mindset: it is the adult, poetic register that established the tone of the poem, and recalls the atmosphere of the time in which the boy attends his brother's wake.

Ambience

So far, I have been talking about atmosphere and tone as phenomena that are similar to one another, but distinguished on the basis that the former pertains mainly to world and the latter to the utterer. We have seen that it is difficult to pin down the sense of atmosphere and tone very precisely to either a particular lexical choice or to a compositional principle of register. This is because the two concepts of atmosphere and tone are closely related and thus have a fuzzy boundary, and also because the traditional linguistic account of diction, lexical semantics and the systemic-functional version of register are not adequate for our needs here. An alternative, cognitive poetic account might begin by regarding atmosphere and tone as the global effects of *ambience*. By this I mean the delicate sense of a halo of associations, some barely conscious, some subliminal but coalescing cumulatively across a stretch of discourse. A word, phrase, syntactic sequence, verse placement, poetic form, rhyme or extended varied metaphor (and so on) might all contribute to a sense of ambience.

For example, as I mentioned above, the compositional aspects of the poem are part of its general register as a piece of poetic recall. The placement of 'Snowdrops' – capitalised at the start of the sentence but also standing alone at the end of the line – is rendered with extra significance: the word and its initially verbless placement create the atmosphere of stillness, establish the setting as a winter scene, which thus evokes coldness, and sets up the bleaching-out of colour, along with the (proto-typically white) candles, culminating in 'Paler now'. The candles, of course, also bring the religious ritual to the foreground. There is a further, even more delicate subtextual progression, in the citation of numbers from 'ten o'clock' when the ambulance arrives, to seeing his brother for the first time 'in six weeks', diminishing towards the final 'four' foot box and four years at the end. There is a subliminal inexorability about this arithmetic progression. Part of all this is atmospheric in the scene; part of it is tonal in the poetic arrangement – altogether a particular ambience is created in the reader's mind.

All of these effects are, to a greater or lesser degree, delicate, subtextual, and difficult to identify. They are matters not just of lexical choice but also of a more distributed arrangement of register, encompassing syntax and verse-arrangement. However, although they seem delicate and rarefied when described stylistically as here, there is little doubt for me that these effects are real. Part of the analytical difficulty is that the act of describing them raises them to a level of foregrounding that they did not naturally possess in undisturbed context. For example, it occurs to me that the strik-ingness of 'poppy bruise' is partly because the colour at the forefront of attention has been bleached into paleness, so the redness associated with the poppy has contrastively all the more impact. Many readers report this effect. Similarly, almost every commentary on the poem mentions the associative value (in a British context, at least) of the poppy as a symbol of the remembrance of the armistice of the 1914–18 Great War in Europe, with all of its associations of bloodshed and the loss of youth and innocence. This association seems generally real as well. I have not come across anyone associating 'left temple' (of the head) with the religious sense of temple, but of course it would be consistent with the general ambient sense of a reli-gious texture generated by the poem.

Ambience is a superordinate term encompassing atmosphere and tone. It can be distinguished from *resonance* (strikingness and persis-tence in memory: see Stockwell 2009) by the fact that it is even less articulatable and tangible. Resonance is what a reader takes away from a striking reading – a definite thread of sensation that persists strongly after the text has been put aside. Ambience is much more mistily defined: it is the cognitive effect of cumulative but diffused associations across discourse.

We have seen above that an attempt to locate the source of ambience in lexicogrammar cannot work adequately. This is a consequence of the discreteness of the traditional linguistic rank scale. By contrast, in cognitive linguistics (Langacker 2008), the difference between lexical choice and grammatical organisation is a matter of continuous *schema-tisation*. In other words, the most abstract sense of the clause is a *type*, carried in mind as a constitutive schema of all similar unspecified situations. For example, the third-last line of the Heaney poem is roughly schematically *X stative-verb in Y like Z*. The grammaticisation of this schema, and the lexical, prepositional and pronominal choices which are then made, render the schematic form as a specification: an *instance* of the type. The instantiation of the sentence 'He lay in the four foot box as in his cot' specifies 'four foot box' as a coffin (this would in traditional terms be a denotation) and invokes the boy's young age (the connotation or association of 'cot'). The emotional ambience of the line is not simply an isolated matter of the meanings of the words, but is a cumulative effect of these, their looser associations, their experiential value for the reader, as well as the end-stopped line, its position towards the end of the poem, the reader's sense of Heaney, Ireland, car-crashes, children's funerals and so on.

This account threatens to present the matter of ambience in literary reading as being too complex for any sort of useful analysis. However, we can proceed further by exploring the source of ambience at a micro-level as well as over a whole text. A first useful point of departure was briefly suggested in Stockwell (2009: 179–81), which drew on Langacker's (2008: 83–4) *reference point* model and the notion of *dominion*. Any unit of language has potential for meaning: this can be a single word, a phrase, an idiom, a prefabricated expression or formulaic sequence, or even a syntactic pattern, or echoic cohesion across a text – in fact, anything that is an instantiation in the sense above. Evans (2006) calls these *lexical concepts*, though they are not always individual words. Lexical concepts, in Evans's (2009) theory, provide the language user with access points to more schematised *conceptual models*, and in the process of activating the link, meaning is generated. One useful aspect of this approach is that meanings in each context of utterance are singular and unique.

The reference point of an entity often provides the attentional starting point conceptually in a clause. Consider the line which begins the last full stanza of the Heaney poem: 'Wearing a poppy bruise on his left temple'. With *wearing* as the reference point, a set of possible links and connections will instantly be available for the reader, drawing in, most probably, an expectation that the next few words will draw information from the domains of clothes, cosmetics, hats, footwear, jewellery or flowers (just about every occurrence of the 4,768 examples of *wearing* in the BNC collocates with one of these domains, and this list is given in order of frequency). These domains are all of the potential *targets* of the reference point. 'A particular reference point affords potential access to many different targets. Collectively, this set of potential targets constitutes the reference point's *dominion*' (Langacker 2008: 83–4). A dominion, then, maps the cloud of possibilities potentially available from a reference point, a sort of aura of latent associations around the symbolic unit that become available for quick resolution, depending on the immediately following text (see Figure 24.3, in which the circles and arrows represent

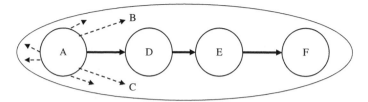

Figure 24.3: Ambience as dominion tracing

the advancement of the clause). If the order of frequency suggested by the BNC has any significance (let's assume it does, for the sake of argument), then there is likely to be the strongest expectation of the domain of clothing subliminally in the mind of the reader of the poem. The actual text follows 'Wearing' (element A in Figure 24.3) with 'a poppy', which is not the most expected domain (element D) but is within the parameters of normality. However, the addition of 'bruise' turns 'poppy' from a noun target in its own right to a pre-modifying element of a different target *bruise*. This is less usual, and this disruption in itself can generate a striking and more explicitly violent impact.

What happens, then, to all of the unrealised potential targets, the paths not taken in the dominion of the reference point (elements B and C and others unnamed, in the diagram)? It might be plausible to suggest that they leave a faint effect, a delicate association felt only as a cloud of possibility, or a rich textured ambience in the detail of the line.

Of course, this suggested effect is difficult to test empirically. I cannot devise a controlled experiment that is delicate enough to get at the phenomenon without disrupting the very object of investigation (see Stockwell 2012 for a consideration of this 'reader's paradox', but see also I. Lerner et al. 2012). However, at a more qualitative and inter-subjective though perhaps anecdotal level, a group of my Masters students all reported imagining the boy lying in the coffin, wearing a formal suit or uniform. This is nowhere stated in the text, but it might be plausible to surmise that the military associations of the 'poppy' and the lingering presence of the clothing domain in the dominion of the line are collectively responsible for their shared experience.

Where can we look for a more concrete form of validation of the notion of ambience? Within corpus stylistics, phenomena that appear to be very similar to the effects sketched above can be found. Hoey (2005, 2013) defines *lexical priming* in terms that are almost identical to the discussion of dominion effects above. For Hoey, corpus-linguistic explorations have produced certain familiar collocations so that the occurrence of a particular word is highly likely to be followed by a predictable set of associated words or of words from particular semantic and pragmatic domains.

This brings us to what is arguably the most important claim about priming and certainly the claim most capable of misinterpretation. This is that all the features we subconsciously attend to have the effect of priming us so that, when we come to use the word (or syllable or word combination) ourselves, we are likely (in speech, particularly) to use it in one of its characteristic lexical contexts, in one of the grammatical patterns it favours, in one of its typical semantic contexts, as part of one of the genres/styles with which it is most associated, in the same kind of social and physical context, with a similar pragmatics and in similar textual ways.

(Hoey 2013)

The priming effect can thus be seen to operate over a distant stretch of co-text, and up through different text and discourse levels of context.

Also from corpus linguistics comes the notion of *semantic prosody* (Louw 1993; Louw and Milojkovic, Chapter 18, this volume): the idea that syntactic formulations and other multi-lexical sequences can have a meaning as part of their structure. So phrases such as 'set in' are found to collocate almost always with unpleasant states of affairs (Sinclair 1991: 74), such that *unpleasantness* or *negativity* can be regarded as meaningful aspects of the phrase, at a loose, non-denotational level. Louw and Milojkovic (Chapter 18, this volume) refer to the effect of a linguistic element's semantic prosody as its 'aura of determination'. This sounds rather close to my account of ambience above, suggesting that there is evidence for the phenomenon not only in readers' introspective intuitions but also in computational analysis across large bodies of texts.

Hoey (2013) cites some older psychological experiments on lexical priming (such as McRae and Boisvert 1998), but ends by admitting that there is as yet insufficient empirical evidence from psychology to support the precise claims of lexical priming theory. However, as I. Lerner et al. (2012) observe, there has been a great deal of work demonstrating that semantic priming in general (much of it lexical in nature) seems to be a reasonably sound assumption. The fact that words seem to suggest semantically or phonologically associated words has long been established: as *spreading activation* (Sternberg 2011). And the evidence of repeated and widespread uses of priming as a cohesive feature showing up in semantic prosody studies (see Stewart 2010 for a critical overview) also points to the existence of the phenomenon.

The construal of presence

However, spreading activation and semantic priming test the conditions necessary for ambience, not the ambient experience directly, and I think the subliminal effect as I outline it remains difficult to test straightforwardly (as suggested above). As a further triangulating alternative, the stylistic analyses offered below provide some further evidence for a systematic account of ambient effects. Keats's 1819 poem 'La Belle Dame Sans Merci' is often cited by readers as a particularly atmospheric text. It portrays a wandering knight, 'haggard and so woe-begone', who falls in love with a beautiful enchantress, who seduces him and feeds him intoxicating food in her elfin cavern. The poem ends:

> And there she lulled me asleep
>   And there I dreamed – Ah! woe betide! –
> The latest dream I ever dreamt
>   On the cold hill side.
>
> I saw pale kings and princes too,
>   Pale warriors, death-pale were they all;
> They cried – 'La Belle Dame sans Merci
>   Hath thee in thrall!'
>
> I saw their starved lips in the gloam,
>   With horrid warning gaped wide,
> And I awoke and found me here,
>   On the cold hill's side.
>
> And this is why I sojourn here
>   Alone and palely loitering,
> Though the sedge is withered from the lake,
>   And no birds sing.
>
> (Keats 1973: 335–6)

Most literary-critical treatments of the poem focus on Keats's biographical circumstances, and resolve the enigmas in the text against features in the poet's life (see Kelley 1987); this approach is assisted by the fact that this original version was substantially altered for first publication in 1820, leading to a great deal of biographical speculation. Alternatively, the knight, the woman and all of the objects in the world of the poem are given allegorical status either in relation to biography or to Keats's poetics, or to Romanticism in general. My interest here is in how the enigmatic ambience of the poem allows these sorts of readings in the first place.

There are a few places in the poem where key experiences are evoked. The first stanza reproduced above focuses on the dream, and it is extraordinarily emphatic: 'lulled', 'asleep', dreamed', 'dream', 'dreamt' are all repetitive to the point of risking clumsiness. That the effect seems deliberate is underscored by the phonetic repetition of the voiced and unvoiced dentals (/d/, /t/) and the voiced, unvoiced and nasalised bilabials (/b/, /p/, /m/). At first the repetition of the spatial deictic 'there' seems redundant, but it becomes clear that there is a shift inside the knight's dreaming mind; so that when he awakes the 'here' on the cold hillside and the 'here' by the silent lake act as successive shifts outwards.

The usual dominion associations of a *dream* are almost universally positive (across all 4,400 occurrences in the BNC). More intuitively, dreams are associated with happy, vivid scenarios, imagined in the comfort of a warm bed at night. In the poem, however, even though the instantiation of *dream* is so emphatic, the description that follows is more like a nightmare (see Giovanelli 2013). The 'cold hill side' is not an expected dominion trace, and the figures are emphatically 'pale', unfriendly, 'starved', 'horrid' and ghostly. It is not even fully night-time, but a murky twilight 'gloam'. All colours are leached out, in contrast to the sensual overload of the stanzas previous to the excerpt above, and, after they have delivered their warning, the ghouls are motionless and silently open-mouthed.

The lexical and reference-point repetition creates ambience, but each new context alters it slightly, turning the dream contrastively into an even more horrid nightmare, the kings, princes and warriors not in finery but skeletal, the beautiful lady (in courtly French) without mercy or compassion. The disjunction results in a personality split – the narrating consciousness 'found me' (this reflexive form was archaic by Keats's day, and though it echoes the fifteenth-century French original poem of the same name, the jarring effect is likely to be prominent, in context, for contemporary and recent readers). The bleaching of colour and the lonely, exiled atmosphere of the dream are sustained in the final stanza, where the proximal deictics ('this', 'here') remind us that the poem is addressed to a hearer. The trajectory is outward towards the reader's world.

In the Keats poem, the final stanza is an almost exact repetition of the first stanza, with the intervening narrative the knight's explanation for why he is wandering alone. However, repetition is not exact repetition because of the modifying effect of the poem's ambience. The gradual immersive structure into the knight's narrative, and then into his seduction, and finally into his dream/nightmare is effected not only by the deictic shifts, but also by the increasingly vivid and sensual ambience of the deepest immersion; the sharp contrast then with the pale, bleak ambience of the ending is all the more keenly felt.

The readerly distancing and then immersion into the knight's tale, and the outward trajectory towards the reader's life at the end is not only an effect of the deictic shifts and the evocative effects of ambience, but also a matter of the subjective construal foregrounded for the reader by the first-person narration, with its perceptual and emotional content prominent (see Langacker 2008). In this last passage for brief illustration, from John Fowles's (1977) novel *Daniel Martin*, the eponymous focaliser of the narrative is presented in third-person form, yet there is still a sense of preceptual presence in the passage. This is a matter not just again of subjective construal, but of the nature of the ambient description.

> The boy sets the first two sheaves, the founders, of a new stook. They
> stand, then start to topple. He catches them before they fall, lifts them to

set them firm again. But old Mr Luscombe shocks his pair down six feet away, safe as houses. His founders never fall. He smiles lopsidedly with his bad teeth, a wink, the cast in his eye, the sun in his glasses. Bronze-red hands and old brown boots. The boy makes a grimace, then brings his sheaves and sets them against the farmer's pair. The insides of his forearms are sore already, his fingers not being strong enough to carry the sheaves far by grasp. If the stook is some way off, he hoicks them up against his side, under his arms, against the thistles. But he likes the pain – a harvest pain, a part of the ritual; like the tired muscles the next morning, like sleep that night, so drowning, deep and swift to come.

(Fowles 1977: 9)

This passage from the opening scene is often cited by fans of the book as an example of Fowles's atmospheric writing style. A close stylistic analysis of the novel is presented by Whitehead (2008), but some illustrative observations are worth making here.

Tone and atmosphere are prominent. In the world which is presented here – a memory of 1940s childhood in Devon, England – the rural dialect terms ('stook', 'founders' and the colloquial 'hoicks'), the vivid colour and the quick character-sketch of the old farmer all serve to create an atmosphere of the world with which the older, remembering Hollywood screenwriter narrator is absorbed. And this absorption also extends to many readers, not only because of this vivid atmosphere but also because the tonal quality of the passage combines (in a manner similar to the Heaney poem above) the boy's perception with the adult's lexical and phrasal choices – especially in the final sentence. The appositional structure and modified poetic repetition ('the pain – a harvest pain'), the switching from verbal 'likes' to analogous 'like the tired muscles … like sleep', and the echoic alliteration and other sound-patterns are all compositional associations with the poetic adult voice, rather than the perceiving boy.

Though some of the dialect and agricultural lexis might not be familiar to many readers, the context and the positioning of the unfamiliar words in the passage make it relatively easy to understand what they mean. The use of unfamiliar words in fact prioritises connotation over denotation, since the latter is simply not available and the sense is consequently more vague. This associative vagueness rather than precise denotation allows for a more diffuse and even richer ambience.

In a study of Fowles, Vieth (1991: 219) describes such 'intensities of imagistic insight' with reference to Walter Benjamin's 1930s notion of 'aura'. Here, he is talking about the effect of a photograph on the viewer:

Aura is the experience in which irreality seems to reach out and include, engage with and enfold the reader:

> What is aura, actually? A strange weave of space and time: the
> unique appearance or semblance of distance, no matter how close
> the object may be. While resting on a summer's noon, to trace a range
> of mountains on the horizon, or a branch that throws its shadow on
> the observer, until the moment or the hour become part of their
> appearance – that is what it means to breathe the aura of those
> mountains, that branch.   *(Vieth 1991: 230, quoting Benjamin 1979: 250)*

Vieth points out that the Fowles passage can be read as a cinematic
vision of nature (Tarbox 1988) or as a narrativised version (Alter 1986).
Both of these of course are aligned with the thematic trajectory of the
novel, and both reflect a reading for atmosphere (world of filmic representation) or for tone (the perceptive filtering of the narrating voice), as
set out in my discussion above. Furthermore, 'aura' in Benjamin's usage
here resonates with Louw and Milojkovic's (Chapter 18, this volume)
corpus-linguistic use of the same term above. Benjamin means something a bit more ethereal, perhaps, than my sense of ambience, but what
is prominent in his concept is the notion of readerly absorption in the
object of art.

The Fowles passage, like the poems by Heaney and Keats briefly considered above, draws the reader in by the careful manipulation of the
ambience of presence. All three of these works have been considered
by literary historians as examples of either straightforward or playful
autobiography, but none of them presents a direct recalled account. Each
of them, in different ways, presents a memory of the past in layered form,
with textural differences in the ambience of the different moments
across time. The experience of reading these works is delicate, rarefied,
subliminal and perhaps subconscious. Traditionally these senses in
reading have been difficult to articulate in anything other than vague
and impressionistic terms. As I hope to have shown, however, the consequences of atmosphere and tone might be subconscious at the local
level, but accumulate to a palpable if diffused sense over the course of a
reading. Atmosphere and tone – together, *ambience* – can be examined
both in corpus-stylistic terms and in cognitive-poetic terms (and for a
further, recent example of the latter, see Deggan 2013). Ambience,
then, is not exactly subtextual but, in its diffused quality as a feature of
discourse, can better be regarded as supertextual.

Perhaps more importantly, ambience – in terms of atmosphere and
tone – is a feature of literary experience that is prominent for readers.
As stylisticians, it is our task to explore this feature and offer an account
of it in systematic and principled terms, and in a way that does not
simply appeal to shared implicit intuitions: these intuitions are part of
the phenomenon to be studied, not the analytical account for its explanation. It is also essential to avoid a simple structural or typological
scheme of 'types of ambience' or a generalised set of elemental ambient

patterns. The diffused and subliminal effect of ambience across texts tells us that the ambience of a particular poem, novel or short story is part of the singular and particular nature of that literary work. A study of ambience, then, is centrally a matter of literary criticism, and one that should not be neglected. After all, ambience in literary works is often regarded by both natural readers and literary scholars as being as important as plot, character and theme, but it has until now received little proper attention.

Part IV

The contextual experience of style

25

Iconicity

Olga Fischer

Introduction

Iconicity is a term used to indicate the strong drive human beings have to describe their world by means of *signs* (pictures, gestures and, in language, sounds, words and phrases), which are seen or felt to have a natural connection with the object or concept (often termed the *signified* or the *referent*) that the sign (more narrowly, the *signifier*) refers to. An iconic sign or *icon* is a natural sign in the sense that its physical (auditory, articulatory or visual) shape resembles the object or idea that it describes. Pictures (photographs, drawings, paintings), and to a lesser extent also gestures, are the most straightforward and direct iconic signs. Such signs, however, are rare in language use (except in signed languages), because spoken language consists of articulatory and acoustic sounds which cannot easily draw or mimic an object or concept. The best-known example of an icon in spoken language is therefore an onomatopoeic sign, where the sound of the utterance reflects the sound made by the object in question. Since most objects and activities (and even less so, abstract concepts!) do not make a sound, such icons are necessarily rare. For this reason, it is not surprising that there are more possibilities for 'icons' in visual (i.e. written and signed) language, where the shape, the relative position and order of words, and in written texts also the colour, the choice of font, the use of blank space and so on may help to picture or mimic the object or activity focused on (see, for example, A. Fischer 1999; Nänny and O. Fischer 2006; Goh 2001; van Peer 1993; Wolf 2005).

As already indicated, a linguistic icon never mimes its object directly, it can only express partial similarity since the auditory nature of spoken language and its one-dimensional, strictly linear order can never capture all the features of the referent. Thus the word *peewit* (a common colloquial expression for 'lapwing') conveys the sound the bird makes, but not its colour, its size and its distinctive crest. And even the representation of its sound cannot be accurate because humans and birds produce sounds with different organs, while the sound structure itself is subject to and restricted by the language-specific phonological system that the language user has internalised in the course of acquiring his or her language (see Masuda 2003). This also explains why the same bird or its sound may be referred to by different iconic signs in different languages (e.g. *peewit* in Dutch is *kievit*, and the sound a rooster makes is *cockadoodledoo* in English, *kukeleku* in Dutch, *cocorico* in French and *chicchirichi* in Italian and Spanish – although spelled differently in the latter). The situation is somewhat different in signed language because its system is three-dimensional, it can mime objects visually and it can express simultaneity as well as chronological order. On the other hand, also in this case, language signs can only partially picture an intended referent, due to its own specific system restrictions and economy.

Of much greater significance, linguistically, than the above iconic signs (often termed *imagic* icons because they replicate part of the 'image' that they represent) are the so-called *diagrammatic* icons. Here the similarity between sign and referent is of a more abstract nature: the *relation* between the linguistic signs approximates the *relation* between the referents. In other words, the iconic diagram always involves a combination of signs or words; there is no direct similarity relation between each separate sign and its referent. Such diagrams can be spatial or temporal, making use of order, distance and proximity between words, but the relation may also be subjective, reflecting the way our mind conceptualises the order in the world (this is often termed *experiential iconicity*, see Tabakowska 1999; Wolf 2001). For instance, a temporal sequence of actions is reflected in the sequence of verbs in Caesar's famous dictum *Veni, vidi, vici*: here the phrase as a whole reflects the order of the activities performed by Caesar (i.e. he 'came, oversaw the situation, and then conquered'). A different order would express a different idea, as Sylvia Adamson (in a talk given at the University of Jena in 2001) once jokingly remarked by alluding to *Vidi, vici, veni* as a possible iconic order in a sexual context.

The dictum *Veni, vidi, vici* can also be used to show yet a different kind of iconicity (termed *second-degree* or *endophoric* iconicity; see Johansen 1996 and Nöth 2001 respectively). This is iconicity of an internal kind in that the iconic sign does not refer diagrammatically to a concept in the external world but rather points to an iconic relation with a similar sign in the same text or in another text (i.e. intra- or intertextuality). Thus the formal similarity between *veni, vidi* and *vici* (all three forms begin with the same sound, end with the same sound, have two sylla-bles of equal length, and are all relatively short) and its asyndeton (i.e. lack of linkage between the three verbs) 'expresses a sense of achievement, the consciousness of a series of actions swiftly and expertly performed' (Müller 2001: 306), each action being as short and easy as the previous one. Second-degree iconicity is found

Figure 25.1: Three types of iconicity

extensively in poetry in the form of repetition, but also in slogans and advertising, while it plays a crucial role too in folk etymology (see R. Coates 1987), in word formation, and in sound symbolism. In folk etymology, for instance, we often see that language users change the shape of a non-transparent word to make it look more like another, more common word that happens to be close to it in meaning; thus Earlier English *bride-goom* became *bride-groom* because *goom* was no longer understood, and in Modern Dutch many users refer to a round-about as *rontonde* rather than (the originally French loan) *rotonde* because the referent happens to be *rond* 'round'.

Diagrammatic relations (whether external or internal) are no longer strictly semiotic in that there is no longer a relationship of *similarity* between the signs and the objects/concepts in the world in a direct, imagic sense. This also applies to metaphor: here a diagrammatic *semantic* relation is perceived between the vehicle and the tenor, and this is expressed on the linguistic level by using the same *formal* sign; there is then no direct semiotic ('imagic') connection between the sign and its referent. Thus, when someone is called a *fox*, it is because the person referred to shows behaviour that is associated with a fox, but for which behaviour there is no separate sign; hence the sign *fox* is used to fill this gap.

The three types of iconicity (image, diagram, metaphor) can best be illustrated by Figure 25.1, where ↕/↔ indicates a direct connection and ╪ an indirect one.

Linguistic research in the twentieth century has shown that iconicity operates at every level of language structure (phonology, morphology, syntax) and in practically every known language, and literary criticism has confirmed that iconicity is pervasive in the literary text: from its prosody and rhyme, its lineation, stanzaic ordering, its textual and narrative structure to its typographic layout on the page. It needs to be stressed, however, that the perception of iconicity in language and literary texts depends on an interpreter and on the context in which it is uttered, as no sign-function is self-explanatory. In addition, iconic diagrams in everyday spoken language may have become so entrenched (so much part of the conventional system) that they are hardly noticed: they have become 'symbolic'. Johansen (1993: 227) indeed notes, as have many others, that iconic signs play 'a minor part in language as a system' but 'a leading character in literature, especially in poetry'. The awareness of its presence hence depends on how much it stands out in its context, on foregrounding and defamiliarisation.

An important occurrence in the new development of interest in iconicity was the publication of the collected papers of the philosopher and logician Charles Sanders Peirce in the early twentieth century. His division of icons into *images* and *diagrams* (and also *metaphors*) broke new ground for the study of iconicity. (In fact, Peirce refers to *hypo-icons*, rather than icons, because true icons cannot exist: nothing can resemble something else 100 per cent.) His contemporary in the 1920s, Ferdinand de Saussure, who is strongly associated with the idea that linguistic signs are arbitrary, concentrated on single morphemes, and hence did not realise the potential of iconicity – that is, of *diagrammatic* iconicity. When he describes (in 1922, on p. 101) the objections that 'might be brought against the principle that linguistic signs are arbitrary' (Saussure 1983: 69), he only mentions the exceptions formed by onomatopoeic words and exclamations such as 'ouch' (which in fact would be indexical in Peirce's terms rather than onomatopoeic); these are indeed 'rather marginal phenomena' (Saussure 1983: 69). In most recent literature on iconicity, however, it is the pervasiveness of the iconic diagram that is emphasised (see Haiman 1980, 1985, the articles in Simone 1994, Landsberg 1995, Fischer and Nänny 2001 and Nänny and O. Fischer 1999).

For this chapter, we will concentrate on diagrammatic iconicity since this plays a much more crucial role in language than imagic iconicity. We will compare 'ordinary' language use with literary language to discover the effect of iconicity. The mould into which writers and poets pour language often serves to enhance the meaning of a text. In literature, language works 'at full stretch' (Nowottny 1962: 85) by being 'hypersemanticized' (Cureton 1980: 319): in other words, iconicity plays a much larger role because it promotes the 'palpability of signs' (Jakobson 1960: 356). The purpose of this is to make us more aware. By inverting conventional language patterns, for instance by bringing them closer to 'natural' patterns or by using a painterly style, we may be made to see familiar things with fresh eyes, as if new. However, it is important to stress that the use of iconicity is not confined to literary language. The difference between everyday and literary language in this respect is one of degree, not of kind. Kiparsky has made this abundantly clear:

> 'figures of language' studied by poetics, such as alliteration, rhyme, parallelism, and metrical form ... and the regularities which may govern their distribution in a work or body of literature, are grounded in the human language faculty; this is why they always involve linguistic categories of the sort that play a role in the grammars of languages, and why the rules governing them obey principles that also apply to linguistic rules and representations.   *(Kiparsky 1987: 186, emphasis added)*

A similar suggestion was made by Lecercle (1990: 130), who distinguishes between the rules of grammar and the rules of what he has termed the 'remainder' ('the area outside the map made by the cartographers [i.e. linguists], the uncharted territories', 1990: 19). Both types of rules are intertwined in the production of language; the rules of grammar are normative and have a general application, while those of the remainder are idiosyncratic, the result of playing around with the normative rules.

Diagrammatic iconicity in syntax

Diagrammatic iconicity is especially common in the area of syntax because syntax is all about the way linguistic elements are positioned or arranged. A good reason to concentrate on syntax for this volume is also because syntax is the Cinderella in stylistic analyses of poetic texts. Usually most attention is paid to metre, rhyme (including assonance and alliteration), sound symbolism and metaphor. To begin with, I will list ways in which syntax may be used to shape meaning. After this I will show, by means of a number of poetic texts, how these devices can be or have been applied. By using the verb 'apply', I do not wish to suggest that writers or poets always do this consciously (except when they are following certain poetic conventions in choice of rhyme scheme, stanza form, etc. – but even these may be used iconically). What makes poets good poets is their instinct for the right phrase or the right sound in the right place. It is telling that these iconic devices can be used with various effects, because it is the combination of device and context that decides the effect in each case, as I indeed hope to show below.

Syntactic iconic devices

It is useful for our discussion to recognise some of the mechanisms involved in iconicity. Haiman (1980) distinguishes three types of iconic syntactic principles or motivations:

1. the 'principle of quantity' (i.e. the use of many (or few) words to express differences in size, duration, or degree of complexity);
2. the 'principle of proximity' or 'distance' (i.e. the degree to which words 'belong' together or are syntactically (and hence semantically) linked to each other); and
3. the 'principle of sequential order' (the mimicking of the chronological or the experiential order in which events occur).

These three principles have mostly to do with (i) the position or arrangement of signs in a clause. Other important syntactic devices (often involving morphology and lexis too) are (ii) the omission of words, such as cases of *ellipsis*, or of loosely connected or disconnected sentences (*enjambment* and *asyndeton* belong here), and as a kind of opposite, (iii) the repetition of lexical elements or syntactic patterns, such as cases of *parallelism, polysyndeton, chiasmus, epistrophe* (word repeated in end position) and *anadiplosis* (last word repeated at the beginning) (see Müller 2001). A repetition of patterns can also be found on a more abstract morphosyntactic or lexical level: for instance, a text may be shaped by the fact that it consists mainly of monosyllabic words (whose shortness then also involves the principle of quantity), or of abstract rather than concrete nouns (which may be said to involve the principle of distance in a mental sense), or makes use only of intransitive or stative verbs, of animate active subjects rather than inanimate passive ones, or of nominalisations rather than more active verbal constructions.

Even though I have tried to formulate categories here, it must be clear that the morphosyntactic devices mentioned under (ii) and (iii) are often intimately connected with the devices mentioned under (i), which themselves are related to principles (1)–(3). They are, in turn, also connected to other ways of formally foregrounding meaning; that is, as done by the 'misuse' of syntax: using a transitive verb, for instance, as if it is intransitive, or putting a verb or verbal argument in a position where it doesn't normally occur.

We will analyse three poems to show these various devices at work. Some use the same devices with a similar outcome, but it is interesting to observe that a device may also have a radically different effect, depending as it does on the context, both in terms of its semantic pragmatic content and the way a device may interact with other formal patterns used in the poem. Often other non-syntactic iconic devices strengthen the syntactic ones. Where useful, this will also be indicated.

Three examples of the use of morphosyntactic patterns in poetry

Ted Hughes, 'Hawk Roosting': morphosyntax conveying firmness and strength

(1)   I sit in the top of the wood, my eyes closed.
      Inaction, no falsifying dream
      Between my hooked head and hooked feet:
      Or in sleep rehearse perfect kills and eat.

(5)   The convenience of the high trees!
      The air's buoyancy and the sun's ray
      Are of advantage to me;
      And the earth's face upward for my inspection.

      My feet are locked upon the rough bark.
(10) It took the whole of Creation
      To produce my foot, my each feather:
      Now I hold Creation in my foot

Or fly up, and revolve it all slowly—
I kill where I please because it is all mine.
(15) There is no sophistry in my body:
My manners are tearing off heads—

The allotment of death.
For the one path of my flight is direct
Through the bones of the living.
(20) No arguments assert my right:

The sun is behind me.
Nothing has changed since I began.
My eye has permitted no change.
I am going to keep things like this.

This poem shows a lot of repetition of elements and patterns. What strikes us most is the repetition of the first person: 'I' being the very first word of the poem. The world is seen through the eyes of a hawk; the author is completely absent. This is in itself noteworthy because we normally do not or cannot know what a hawk thinks. The pronouns 'I' and 'me' are everywhere (they are found, even when not repeated, in co-ordinated clauses, as in lines 4 and 13), and so are the corresponding possessives 'my' and 'mine'. Together they occur twenty-one times in a poem of just twenty-four lines long – plus six hidden, because co-ordinated, instances. Also hidden but emphasising by its echo the importance of 'I/my/mine', is the manifold repetition of the /ai/ sound all through the poem in such words as 'eye(s)', 'high', 'right', 'fly/flight', which are themselves also words used in an assertive sense.

The hawk himself is centred because he functions frequently as the subject of the finite verb, or, if the hawk himself is not the subject, then often part of his body or his behaviour serves as subject ('My feet' (9), 'My eye' (23), 'My manners' (16)), which, being parallel with 'I', seem to personify the hawk as a whole, showing in addition the strength of each separate part. Even when the subject is not 'I', the subject of the sentence is often subjected to 'I' – as in lines 6–7 ('The air's buoyancy and the sun's ray / Are of advantage *to me*'), 10–12 ('It took the whole of Creation / To produce my *foot* ... / Now I hold Creation *in my foot*'), 21 ('The sun is *behind me*') – or the subject is negative or verbless, showing that it has no effect on the 'I', as in (2) 'no falsifying dream', (15) 'no sophistry', (20) 'No arguments' and (22) 'Nothing', while a finite verb is missing in lines 2–3, 5 and 8, taking the action out of the clause.

The power and strength of the I-figure is further enhanced by the use of proportionally many monosyllabic words: only five words out of thirty in the first stanza do not consist of a monosyllable; in combination with the repeated consonant cluster /kt/ and other sharp voiceless plosives

/k, t, p/ in the first stanza, this produces a staccato effect rather than one of 'soft flowing'.

It is also to be noted that the verbs connected with the subject 'I' are mostly basic, concrete verbs, such as 'sit' (1), 'eat' (4), 'hold' (12) and 'kill' (14). Strangely enough, even though 'eat' and 'kill' are telic verbs of action, the verbs here do not convey actual activity because they are in the 'eternal' present and belong to the hawk's inner monologue. In addition, many finite verbs are forms of TO BE, as can be seen in lines 7, 9, 14, 15, 16, 18, 21 and 24, expressing stasis or permanence rather than activity. This paradoxical situation of both activity and stasis is further foregrounded by the interesting use of the word 'inaction' (2) early in the poem, suggesting both inactivity as well as being '(in) action'. This is epitomised in the last three lines, which more than anything else indicate that the hawk allows no change. Like God, he is on top of the world, nothing can affect him, the world revolves around him, or, rather, he revolves the world (12–13), while the earth looks up to him (8). All the world serves him alone, both the air and the sun (6), and the whole of creation (10).

What makes the poem so striking is the image we are given of the hawk. A bird that sits absolutely still but yet is full of fierce energy: the body completely tense, with his 'hooked head and hooked feet' (3), 'rehears[ing] perfect kills' (4), always ready to kill (14) and tear (16) but yet with eyes closed (1) and feet locked (9). A bird that is its own master, in fact is God himself, who allows no one or nothing to interfere with his life as if he is not bound, like every other creature, to the rules of nature. All this is conveyed by the semantic choice of words that describe him, but even more, but more indirectly, by the form of the words (monosyllabic), the syntactic patterns used (choice of subject, use of verb) and the extreme brevity of the lines. The sentences in the poem are almost all main clauses; they are concise and usually fit within the short tetrameter lines. The stanzas themselves are stocky too, consisting of only four lines each. Most striking here is the last stanza, which contains four full sentences within four lines, each rounded off by a full stop.

T.S. Eliot, 'The Hollow Men': morphosyntax conveying weakness and loss

My second example concerns a poem which uses syntactic devices rather opposite to 'Hawk Roosting', creating an effect of looseness, lethargy and loss rather than strength, energy and purpose. Due to lack of space, I will only quote the first part here, and refer with line references to the other four parts, the text of the poem being freely available on the internet.

Mistah Kurtz – he dead.
A penny for the Old Guy

I

(1) We are the hollow men
    We are the stuffed men
    Leaning together
    Headpiece filled with straw. Alas!
(5) Our dried voices, when
    We whisper together
    Are quiet and meaningless
    As wind in dry grass
    Or rats' feet over broken glass
(10) In our dry cellar

    Shape without form, shade without colour,
    Paralysed force, gesture without motion;

    Those who have crossed
    With direct eyes, to death's other Kingdom
(15) Remember us – if at all – not as lost
    Violent souls, but only
    As the hollow men
    The stuffed men.

A completely different 'feel' is created by the syntactic forms used in Eliot's poem. The choice of words and the subject discussed convey an atmosphere of waste, emptiness and infertility, a disembodied world. This is enhanced by the formal shape of the poem. The forms used provide a good contrast with Hughes's poem. To illustrate this contrast more clearly, I will concentrate on similar syntactic devices and patterns, and lexical forms.

The first difference that strikes the eye are the long, drawn-out sentences containing a lot of finite and non-finite subordination. The sentences do not stick to the lines but crawl over them in a loose fashion, and this is further emphasised by the almost complete absence of punctuation within and sometimes even across the stanzas and sections. The very frequent use of enjambment – not only with syntactically looser, prepositional phrases but also with more direct verbal arguments such as direct objects, complements separated from the finite verb, subjects separated from the predicate, and, within the noun phrase, adjectives separated from their head noun, or even conjunctions separated from the rest of the clause (e.g. 5–6, 15–16 [where the isolated 'lost' is literally 'lost'], 31–2, 41–2, 42–3, etc.) – also conveys a sense of looseness and indirection, of a broken-up state. The stanzas themselves are also loose: the number of lines differ in each case, and line-length is far from fixed.

In Hughes's poem, we saw that negatives, when they occur (there aren't many) were used to strengthen the power of the hawk, to further delineate his domain by negating or denying other possible forces. In Eliot, there are many negatives, which, however, all add to the feeling of emptiness, of nothingness. Negative forms are encountered both semantically inside words ('hollow' (1, 17, 55, etc.), 'dried voices' (5), 'paralysed' (12), 'broken' (23), 'fading' (28), 'avoid' (59), etc.), lexically in prepositional phrases ('without form, without colour' (11–12), 'between ... and' – i.e. nowhere – in (72–3, 74–5), repeated five times more) and, more explicitly, as bound morphemes inside words ('meaning*less*' (7), 'sight*less* un*less*' (61)), or syntactically (there are nine negative clauses in the poem, which are often extra foregrounded by repetition ('let me be no nearer', 'no nearer' (29, 36); 'the eyes are not here', 'there are no eyes here' (52–3)).

When we compare the type of verbs being used, it is noticeable that Eliot's poem does not contain many telic activity verbs (such as 'eat' and 'kill' in 'Hawk Roosting'). In main clauses, which normally convey the action or provide the plot, the most common finite verb is a form of TO BE, which is a linking verb and empty of meaning. Finite forms of TO BE occur twenty-one times in main clauses (and once in a subordinate clause (48)). When used as a copula, it often comes very close to an existential verb because of enjambment and/or the use of some existential phrase such as 'there' or 'this', as in '*There*, the eyes *are* / Sunlight on a broken column' (22–3); 'And voices *are* / In the wind's singing / More distant and more solemn / Than a fading star' (25–8); '*This is* the dead land / *This is* cactus land' (39–40); '*Thine is* / Life *is* / For thine *is* the /' (92–4), stressing the existence of emptiness. Mere existentiality comes still more to the fore when TO BE is used as an auxiliary of the progressive or passive, because it is then often separated from the non-finite verb by either enjambment ('At the hour when we *are* / Trembling ...' (48–9)), or some other intervening phrase ('We *are* the hollow men / We *are* the stuffed men / *Leaning* together (1–3)), or accompanied in addition by an existential pronoun ('*There is* a tree *swinging*' (24); '*Here* the stone images / *are raised*' (41–2)).

Few other verbs occur in main clauses, I have only counted eleven full lexical verbs and three auxiliaries. The full verbs are either close to copulas ('appear' (21), 'form' (51)) or rather passive or intransitive ('remember' (15), 'receive' (42), 'grope' (58), 'avoid' (59), 'falls' (76, 82, 90), 'go' (68, 70), which do not constitute an effect or lead to some achievement as transitive telic verbs do. In other words, all these full verbs are low in transitivity in the sense of Hopper and Thompson (1980). Also noticeable in terms of transitivity is the much more frequent occurrence of inanimate subjects compared to animate ones. In the whole poem, only seven main clause subjects are animate, and these are all pronouns ('we' and 'I'); all other subjects are inanimate, but quite often part of a human body ('eyes' (22, 52, 62), 'voices' (25), 'lips' (50)) again stressing the broken-up state. Note that this is very different from the use of body parts in 'Hawk Roosting': there, they serve as a *pars pro toto* for the hawk, and are thus fully animate, while in Eliot the eyes, lips and voices are elements separated from the body, not clearly belonging to anyone. Full verbs occur more often in non-finite form in infinitival, participal or periphrastic constructions, or as verbs in subordinate clauses, but these are by their very position descriptive rather than truly active or plot-advancing. Again, they do not show any strong (telic) activity (e.g. the participle 'filled' (4), 'whisper' (6), perfective 'have crossed' (13), 'behaving', 'behaves' (35), 'waking' (47), the participle 'gathered' (60), etc.). In addition, the number of clauses without any verb is also quite high (e.g. 8–10, 11–12, 37–8).

Another device that highlights description and stasis rather than activity is the use of attributive adjectives or participles and adjectivally used nouns. In 'Hawk Roosting', there are only four (three in the first stanza, and one in line 9) constituting 2.4 per cent of the total text, while in 'The Hollow Men' there are as many as forty-nine (e.g. 'hollow', 'stuffed', 'dried', 'broken', 'rats' [feet], 'dry' in the first stanza alone), making up 11 per cent of the total. Attributive adjectives, in contrast to predicative ones, tend to denote inherent qualities (stasis) rather than stage-level activities.

Finally, as to the morphological shape of words, the use of monosyllabic words is much less noticeable in Eliot's poem. Rather – and highly noteworthy – we find the occurrence of many Latin-derived abstract nouns, which create distance and take away the emotion (see the totally insipid last lines: 'This is the way the world ends / Not with a bang but a whimper'), and make the situation nebulous and shapeless. This is especially clear in part V, as can be seen from the use of polysyllabic Latinate words such as 'reality', 'motion', 'conception', 'creation', 'emotion', 'response', 'potency', 'existence', 'essence' and so on. Even though part V starts with a clear activity: 'Here we go round the prickly pear' (the only one in the poem!), at the same time this is undermined in that it echoes the lines of a nursery rhyme, making the activity look rather childish and ineffective. This effect is exacerbated by the fact that the words in the original ('mulberry bush'), which at least contain some warm rounded sounds /m, b, u/, are replaced by 'prickly pear' with sharp plosives /p, k/ and high front vowels /i, ɛ/. The rest of part V is taken up by taking apart the Lord's Prayer, replacing its positive line 'the power and the glory, for ever and ever', by the tedious remark: 'Life is very long' and interspersing it with totally lifeless activities that are all overshadowed and in vain. Not only is the 'Fall[ing] Shadow' (with the heavy stress on 'Falls' in initial position) a shadowy presence, also the places *between* which (note, not 'on which'!) it falls (seven times!), are all abstract ideas, not concrete places. No wonder this world ends with a whimper!

Antjie Krog 'Depressie 1' and '2': syntactic devices in opposition

My last example is a poem consisting of two parts by the Afrikaans poet Antjie Krog from her volume *Verweerskrif* (2006). It shows some of the same devices already discussed above. Some used with a similar effect, but, interestingly enough, some used with an almost opposite effect. This

Depressie	Depression
1	1
dis asof jy al hoe meer binne-in jou oë wegraak asof jou voorkop al donkerder jou wange al hoe beweegloser jou mond verder word as wat enige iets nog ooit van my was jou lyf so deursigtig asof my hand deur jou steek as ek probeer keer dat jy verdwyn jy beweeg tussen ons maar het kontak verbreek aan jou hande kan ek sien hoe verbete jy soms nog vas- hou die naels in jou vingers raak uitgewis dis asof ek langs 'n oewer hardloop en reddingsboeie uitgooi en toue en takke en buite myself skreeu dat jy moet uithou en vashou dat ek jou sal uitswem dat ek my in jou plek sal gee dat ek die Here God self uit die hemel sal pluk dat ek alles alles sal prysgee om jou veilig tebring in jou oë terug	it's as if you are disappearing more and more within your eyes as if your forehead grows darker your cheeks more motionless your mouth further than anything has ever been from me your body so transparent that my hand goes right through you if I try to prevent you from disappearing you move among us but have broken all contact from your hands I can see at times how fiercely you hold on the nails in your fingers become erased it is as if I run down a riverbank throwing life-buoys and ropes and branches I am beside myself I yell that you should hang on hang in there I will salvage you I will give myself in your place I will rip up God Almighty Himself from heaven I'll give anything to bring you back safely into your eyes
2	2
dis vreeslik om jou so te sien. hoe kry ek jou. dis vreeslik om. hoe kry ek jou terug. kon dit dalk. as ek maar. had ek liewer. dis vreeslik om. kyk hier staan ek. ek skeur. ek probeer skeur.	it's terrible seeing you like this. how will I ever find you. seeing you so terrible. how do I get you back. if only I had. if I'd rather. why didn't I. it's terrifying. see, here I stand. I tear. I try to tear.
. . . . . .	. . . . . .

Figure 25.2: 'Depressie 1' and an extract from 'Depressie 2' by Antjie Krog with author's English translation

shows the strong effect of context. Simultaneously, this poem also shows how difficult it is to translate iconic devices into another language, which the English translation, made by the author herself, makes abundantly clear (many of the devices of sound, syntax and repetition are difficult to transfer). To save space I will only give 'Depressie 1' in full, and provide only the first lines of '2' (Figure 25.2).

There are a number of very interesting formal differences between the two 'Depressie' poems, which could be said to be linked to a difference between the two poems already discussed. '1' has no punctuation at all, a bit like Eliot's poem, but more strongly so, while '2' has a full stop in every line, sometimes even more than one, making it similar to 'Hawk Roosting'.

This difference reflects similar emotions: '1' represents a stage where the speaker still tries, but without much effect, to draw the beloved out of the swamp of his or her depression. This slow sinking, this inevitable falling away into nothingness, is well represented by the lack of sentence structure, the continuous stream of words, a stream that drowns all attempts at rescue: there is no stick, no life-buoy to hold on to. On the other hand, '2' depicts the feeling of complete loss: the line between the speaker and the beloved seems completely severed. This impotence, this being torn apart, can be felt in the halting, broken-up lines. No sentence here is complete. The speaker is all alone. There is an unbridgeable distance between the two personae. This aloneness is well captured by the stone-like phrases, and thus, even though this is not seen as positive, it resembles the stony aloofness of the Hawk.

There is also a clear difference between 'Depressie 1' and 'The Hollow Men' in that in '1' the situation of loss and emptiness is counteracted by very strong expressions of activity by the speaker. She or he (henceforth *she*) does not want to be sucked in, doesn't want the beloved to be sucked in, so she tries with all her might to counter the situation. There is no lethargy, as there is in Eliot's poem. This is clear from the very different type of verbs and clauses used by the speaker, and also from a difference in the use of sounds. In '1', there are concrete, very physical verbs, such as *hardloop* (run-fast) and *skreeu* (yell) and telic, transitive verbs, such as *uitgooi* (throw-out), *uitswem* (salvage; literally 'swim-out'; note the heavy use of telic *uit* 'out' – also in 13, 17, 20, all in initial position) and *pluk* (rip-up). The verbs depict the speaker's fight and her energy (cf. the similar effect of this in the 'Hawk Roosting' poem), but at the same time, because they are couched in subordinate clauses (*asof* (as if)), they also show that the speaker does not advance, does not succeed. The sounds express strength too, there being an overload of plosives (I am looking at the last nine lines here, but they occur everywhere) such as /p/ (*hardloop, pluk, prysgee*), /t/ (repeatedly in *uit-, toue, takke, buite*) and /k/ (*takke, skreeu, ek* (four times), *plek, pluk*). This provides a clear contrast with Eliot's poem, where the most regular consonants – considering only the first stanza, but the tendency continues throughout – are twenty-five liquids /l, r/, six semivowels /w/ and thirteen nasals /m, n, ŋ/, all representing the least forceful consonants.

The idea of being sucked in, as it were by a maelstrom, is expressed through the long clauses without a break, through the enjambments, through the heaping up of subordinate clauses one after the other, all of the same shape (*asof*), as if the speaker cannot get her breath, cannot stop. The first sentence streams on, it seems, as far as the middle of line 13: *dis* (it is) syntactically starts a new clause, with a new subject *dis*, but by using no full stop there, and by putting it in the middle of the line it is as if the sentence simply flows on. On a closer look, one can discern other sentences, but, as with the *dis*-sentence, they are hidden. *Jou lyf* (your body) also looks like a new subject, but since the clause has no verb, it is not truly a new sentence. *Aan jou hande* (from your hands) again starts a new clause, but here the fact that it is not itself a subject hides its structure. Similarly, *die naels* (the nails) starts a new clause but is semantically very narrowly linked to *hande*, making this new clause also less visible.

I have already noted the repetition of *asof*, introducing most subordinate clauses in the first thirteen lines of the poem. The repetition of *dis asof* divides the poem into two parts, the first part being a description of the gradual disappearance of the beloved (note words such as *wegraak/verdwyn/ uitgewis* (disappear), *beweegloser* (more-motionless), *deursigtig* (transparent), *verbreek* (break-off)), while the second part, from line 13 onwards, describes the desperate attempts of the speaker to hold on to the beloved. Here the many subordinate clauses no longer start with *asof* (only the main clause does) – emphasising too, by the way, that the speaker cannot really accept reality yet – but with *dat* (that) (five clauses in all), as if to stress that these *dat*-clauses are still facts, real possibilities. Very effective is also the end of the poem: the lines chiastically refer to the beginning (ab–ba), circling the whole poem, emphasising the spiral, the maelstrom, from which there is no escape:

(a)   te bring
(b)   in jou oë terug
(b)   binne-in jou oë
(a)   wegraak.

Yet, paradoxically, they express a contrast: the speaker hopes to *bring* the beloved *back* into his eyes (*te* (bring) *in jou oë terug*), the eyes which she was *disappearing* into in the first two lines. The chiasmus makes clear that there can be no escape, that the speaker is trapped.

The two-part structure also becomes visible from the shift in the use of pronouns. Up to line 13, *jy/jou* (you) is the pronoun used most (twelve times, against only three occurrences of *ek* (I)), while in the second part, *ek/my* (six times) is more frequent, but still *jy/jou* occurs there too (five times). It shows a change of perspective. The speaker realises that the *jou* is disappearing, and all she has left is herself to cope with the situation. This also marks a sharp change when we look at 'Depressie 2'. This is likewise divided into two halves: the first half runs to line 10; then we have two bridging lines, where *jou* and *ek* are closely combined; the second part then starts at line 13. In the first part we see eleven instances of *ek* as subject (once *my*), whereas *jou* occurs only four times, and all in object position. In the last part, we see *jou/jy* twelve times (first only as object, then also as subject), and *ek/my* only twice.

All activity is lost in '2'. This is clear from the fact that in the first half (of which only six lines are given here) we no longer encounter physical activity or telic verbs, as we did in '1', and, when we do, they are framed by *interrogative* clauses introduced by *hoe (kry ek)* (how get I) (occurring nine times in the poem, four times line-initially) thus denying their effectivity. In the affirmative clauses we see copulas (*dis* in 1, 2, 5, etc.), or epistemic modal verbs (*kon* (could), *[w]as*, *had* (3, 4), or stative non-telic verbs *kyk ... staan* (see ... stand) (5)). The normally telic verb *skeur* (6) 'tear', has even been turned into a stative one by making it intransitive.

In the second half from line 12 onwards (not shown here) the speaker tries to force herself back into action by using a deontic modal (*moet* (must)) followed by affirmative *dat*-clauses, and by employing imperatives (*wees* (be)). The effect of the more active, factual *dat*-clauses is, however, counteracted in that they contain no verbs or lack essential syntactic arguments. And again as in 'Depressie 1', the poem ends with the same words but this time not arranged chiastically, but in a broken-up order: abc–bca, with the (a)-clause even broken up internally.

(a)   *dis vreeslik om jou so te sien* (it's terrible to see you like this)
(b)   *hoe kry ek jou.* (how do I get you.)
(c)   *dis vreeslik om.*
(b)   *hoe kry ek jou*
(c)   *dis vreeslik om.*
(a)   *dis vreeslik te sien./jou so te sien.*

Some brief concluding remarks

We have seen that the three poems discussed often use similar syntactic iconic devices with the same effect, but they can also be given a different slant by the surrounding context, both the syntactic and lexicosemantic. Short clauses, and a preponderance of main clauses with full, end-stopped punctuation generally create a sense of aloofness, hardness or distance. That this is perceived as positive and powerful in the perspective of the 'Hawk Roosting', and as negative with a sense of loss in the case of 'Depressie 2' is related to the way it is combined with other syntactic devices, such as, for instance, ellipsis in 'Depressie 2'. In a similar way the stative and missing verbs in the case of the 'Hawk Roosting' emphasise the power of the hawk's (in)activity, whereas in Eliot's poem they more straightforwardly foreground emptiness, the local difference being created by the use of animate subjects in Hughes's poem versus mostly inanimate ones in Eliot's. Similar verbs may get a different reading when they occur in main clauses rather than subordinate clauses, as we have seen in the use of concrete telic verbs which work positively and energetically in the main clauses in 'Hawk Roosting' but paradoxically emphasise the absence of achievement in 'Depressie 1' because they are confined to subordinate clauses. The same can be said for the use of negative elements. In 'Hawk Roosting', they affirm the hawk's strength by negating the power of others, while in 'The Hollow Men' they enhance the layer of emptiness already pervasively present in its other forms.

I hope to have shown by this close analysis how looking at syntax, especially looking at the 'misuse' of syntax or the overuse of certain forms and patterns, helps to shape the meaning and impact of the poems.

26

Ethics

Sara Whiteley

Introduction

Literature has long been recognised as having the potential to reflect, engage and influence our beliefs and values. Questions which are often asked of literary texts' production and reception, such as: *Why did the author write this? Should the characters have acted that way? What does this work mean? How do I feel about it?* are all questions with ethical components (Schwartz 2001: 3). Davis and Womack (2001: x) describe the study of literary ethics as a broad field incorporating a number of different perspectives. Some ethical criticism focuses on the life of the author or a literary work's ethical content and status in society. These areas have been of particular interest in literary criticism, where ethical concerns have enjoyed renewed popularity recently (e.g. see J. Adamson et al. 1998; Arizti and Martinez-Falquina 2007; Eskin 2004; Gregory 1998). Other forms of ethical criticism involve the close reading of a text and the situations it represents or consideration of the ethical experience of the reader 'beyond the margins of the text' (Davis and Womack 2001: x). These areas are of particular interest within narratology and stylistics.

Some of the most significant work on the ethics of literature has been carried out by rhetorical narratologists such as Phelan (1996, 2001, 2004, 2005, 2007a, 2007b; see also Booth 1988 and Newton 1995). Rhetorical approaches view narrative as a 'multilayered event' involving the establishment of relations among tellers, audiences and the story which is told (Phelan 2007b: 203). As they involve both emotions and values, these relations are viewed as inherently ethical.

Through narrative technique, readers are positioned in relation to the author, narrator, characters and audiences of a particular narrative, and these positionings influence and guide readers' ethical and emotional experiences (Phelan 1996, 2001, 2005: 23; Rabinowitz 1998). In his analyses, Phelan conducts close reading to examine how specific narrative techniques create ethical and emotional effects (e.g. see Phelan 2001, 2005). The approach taken in this chapter has affinities with Phelan's, but while he is concerned with the development of narratological typologies, in this chapter I take a stylistic, cognitive poetic approach to the analysis of ethical positioning.

In general, stylistic frameworks are particularly useful for the detailed, systematic analysis of the representation of characters and events in literature. Ethical issues are implicit in stylistic analyses which examine the literary representation of marginalised groups, such as the work of Leech and Short (2007: 162–6) and Semino (forthcoming) on the mind style of characters with learning disabilities, Gregoriou (2011a) on the representation of criminal minds, and Mills (1995) on the representation of women in romance novels. Within the stylistic sub-discipline of cognitive poetics, the way stylistic features impact upon readers' ethical experience is a key focus. The cognitive poetic framework Text World Theory (Gavins 2007; Werth 1999) is particularly well suited to the examination of ethical issues in literary reading (Stockwell 2009: 160), because it is concerned with tracing the interaction between textual worlds and readerly context. Literary texts are seen to present alternate world(s) for comparison with the world of a reader, and, drawing on the work of Phelan described above, the act of reading itself is also regarded as inherently ethical, because it involves the establishment of relationships between a reader and the entities (author, narrator, characters) represented in a text.

This chapter presents a Text World Theory analysis of two extracts from *Never Let Me Go*, a novel by contemporary British author Kazuo Ishiguro published in 2005. This novel is set in England in the 1990s (a counterfactual version of the past) and is narrated by Kathy, a 31-year-old human clone bred for organ harvesting. Like many of Ishiguro's narrators, Kathy is primarily concerned with recounting and interpreting her life, and the novel details her childhood at a charity-run institution for clones called 'Hailsham', and her friendships and relationships into adulthood. The ethical dimensions of this novel have already received attention within literary criticism (e.g. Black 2009; Jerng 2008; Toker and Chertoff 2008). Jerng, for instance, notes that the novel departs from the conventions of clone narratives and 'foregrounds an ethical project to discover how cloning might change how we relate to each other' (2008: 391). Ishiguro's first-person style has also been recognised as ethically interesting in narratology (Phelan 2005: 31–65). I seek to contribute to these existing discussions of Ishiguro's work with some detailed analysis of the language of this text and its influence on readers' emotional and ethical experience.

I will begin by outlining some of the basic parameters of Text World Theory with reference to the opening of the novel. Then I will analyse ethical positioning in relation to an extract from the novel's penultimate chapter. During my discussion I draw on my own introspective responses to the text in addition to the comments of reviewers and members of a reading group I recorded discussing the novel. Readers often report conflicting feelings about Kathy, which have interesting implications for the novel's ethical effect, and I will examine the textual cues for these conflicts and discuss their influence on reader experience.

The text-worlds of *Never Let Me Go*

Text World Theory is a cognitive-linguistic model of human discourse processing, which views all instances of linguistic communication as pre-supposing at least two conditions. Firstly, they occur within a situational context, which is called the 'discourse-world'; secondly, they involve a conceptual domain of understanding, which is jointly constructed by the producer and recipient(s), known as a 'text-world' (Werth 1999: 17). These two levels and their interaction form the foundation of a text-world analysis.

The discourse-world must involve two or more human participants engaged in linguistic communication, and also incorporates all the perceptual, linguistic, experiential and cultural knowledge that these participants draw upon during discourse comprehension. In written communicative contexts, the reader and author typically do not communicate in a shared discourse-world, instead it is 'split' (Werth 1995: 54–5). This means that the text itself is the only means that readers have of reconstructing the communication between the author and themselves.

Text-worlds are the mental representations that participants form in order to comprehend linguistic communication (Werth 1999: 87). They are conceptual or cognitive spaces that are constructed through the combination of linguistic cues and the participant's knowledge and inferences (Werth 1999: 7). Text-worlds are ontologically distinct, yet they share a structural similarity with the discourse-world in that they are spatio-temporally defined and contain entities, known as 'enactors' (Emmott 1997; Gavins 2007), and objects involved in situations. Text-worlds can be fleeting and undeveloped representations, but also have the potential to be richly detailed. Most discourse requires participants to imagine multiple, related text-worlds.

At the discourse-world level, *Never Let Me Go* features two discourse participants: Kazuo Ishiguro and a particular reader, but because the discourse-world is split, readers use the text to reconstruct communication between the author and themselves. Readers may imagine the author at the text-world level, as an 'implied author', and attribute some meaning creation to their mental representation of him. This is reinforced, I would argue, by the presence of textually deictic titles in the novel such as 'Chapter One' and 'Part One', which foreground an author's

organisation. Thus, upon opening the novel, readers may imagine fleeting and relatively undeveloped text-world containing the implied author
(their imagined version of Kazuo Ishiguro). An implied author automatically implies the existence of an 'implied reader', who readers may
imagine to be themselves.

The title-page of the novel reads 'England, late 1990s', and this cues the
creation of another text-world, this time set in the past and in a particular
country. As the main body of the narrative begins, this text-world becomes
the main focus of the discourse and is richly detailed. The opening lines of
the novel read:

Extract 1

My name is Kathy H. I'm thirty-one years old, and I've been a carer now for
over eleven years. That sounds long enough, I know, but actually they
want me to go on for another eight months, until the end of this year.
That'll make it almost exactly twelve years...   *(Ishiguro 2005: 3)*

This establishes the presence of a first-person narrator who is 'telling' the
story, and this automatically presupposes the existence of a narratee:
someone who is being addressed (Prince 1987; see also Lahey 2005;
Phelan 2005). From this point on, *Never Let Me Go* establishes a series of
text-worlds which are temporally remote from the discourse-world.
Typically, readers assume that the world represented by the text operates
in the same ways as the discourse-world until they are presented with
information to the contrary. This is known as the 'principle of minimal
departure', a cognitive mechanism for efficiency in understanding alternate worlds (Ryan 1991a; see also Emmott 1997: 129; Gavins 2007: 12;
Stockwell 2002: 96). At the novel's publication in 2005, readers were likely
to have lived through the 1990s and have some direct personal experience
to draw upon when imagining the worlds of the text. However, several
features of the opening of *Never Let Me Go* suggest this assumption of
similarity may not wholly apply. For instance, Kathy describes herself as
'carer' who is in charge of looking after 'donors', without really explaining
what these terms mean. As the novel progresses, it becomes evident that
'carer' and 'donor' are neosemes; words which exist in the discourse-world
but have taken on a new, and in this case euphemistic, meaning in the
context of the text-world (Stockwell 2002: 119–22). Kathy works as a 'carer'
for other clones who have begun donating their vital organs to medical
science, and she cares for them until they eventually die (or 'complete').
She will begin donations herself within a year. In this counter-factual
version of the past, clones have existed since the 1950s and their organs
have become staple supplies in medical science. The precise explanation
of these terms and the existence of clones is only revealed slowly,
around a quarter of the way into the book, and given further detail in
the final chapters (Ishiguro 2005: 79–81, 251–67).

Through its representation of an alternate version of the 1990s, *Never Let Me Go* presents, for ethical comparison, an alternative state of affairs in which cloned humans exist. Furthermore, this entire world is represented through the eyes of a cloned narrator via fixed focalisation. Stockwell (2009: 162) notes that some novels have a 'prototypically ethical reading' which is highly preferred in their linguistic 'texture', and this is also the case with *Never Let Me Go*. Overall, the novel represents human cloning as undesirable and Kathy as a sympathetic character. Many reviewers and literary critics regard the novel as a contribution to bioethical debates and an illumination of the moral dangers surrounding cloning (e.g. Mirsky 2006; Montello 2005; Roos 2008; Sim 2006; Toker and Chertoff 2008). It would be highly eccentric to reach the end of the novel seriously convinced that human cloning should be implemented immediately, for instance. But critics also regard the novel as more than just an anti-cloning narrative: Harrison (2005), for instance, asks: 'Who on earth would be "for" the exploitation of human beings in this way?' The cloning scenario is seen by some as a useful setting for Ishiguro's examination of more universal themes, such as the human condition in general. In such readings the plight of Kathy and the clones is seen as distinctly similar to the plight of everyday non-cloned humans: both facing a certain death and yet preoccupied with seemingly trivial day-to-day details (e.g. Harrison 2005; Montello 2005; Robbins 2007; Roos 2008; Toker and Chertoff 2008).

Central to both these critical interpretations of the text is the question of the extent to which Kathy and the other clones are recognisably 'human', or 'like us'. The message of the novel is dependent upon the establishment of relationships between the reader, the narrator, and a number of other textual entities. From a cognitive perspective, the ability to imagine another's perspective (projection) and the comparison between oneself and another (identification or disassociation) are crucial in the novel's meaning and effect. Below, I will argue that the language of *Never Let Me Go* can promote interesting and complex effects in this respect.

Ethical positioning in *Never Let Me Go*

Text World Theory draws upon a text-as-world metaphor which is fundamentally spatial. Worlds which depart from the discourse-world in time and space are conceived as more 'remote' than those which have more affinities with the immediate context of communication. Worlds which are created through the use of modality (e.g. It *might* work; I *wish* I was there) are also more conceptually remote, as their contents are unverifiable from the discourse-world (see Gavins 2007: 91–125). Human relationships and emotional and ethical issues are also often figured spatially. Expressions such as 'we're really close' or 'she's being really distant', for instance, draw on the ubiquitous conceptual metaphor

EMOTIONAL RELATIONSHIP IS DISTANCE BETWEEN TWO ENTITIES (Kövecses 2000; Stockwell 2005: 148).

Recent work on emotional response within Text World Theory has capitalised on the notion that, during discourse, inhabitants of the discourse-world and text-world levels form relationships which can be thought of spatially. In the discourse of literary fiction, the positioning of the reader in relation to the other entities in the text-worlds is thought to be key in the creation of emotional effects and also in the ethical dimensions of a narrative (Gavins 2007; Lahey 2005; Stockwell 2009; Whiteley 2011a; see also Phelan 2005: 23). The reader's position is influenced both by the personal traits, beliefs and values of an individual reader – the discourse-world 'resources' (Stockwell 2009) which they bring to their interpretation of the text – as well as by the language of the text itself.

Positioning is typically achieved through processes of psychological projection and identification. Psychological projection is a development of the linguistic notion of 'deictic projection', which is the ability to shift one's deictic centre from its anchorage in the 'I', 'here' and 'now' in order to create or comprehend certain linguistic expressions. For instance, when giving directions and uttering 'Its on *your left*', a speaker shifts their deictic centre into that of someone else (see Bühler 1982; see also Duchan et al. 1995; K. Green 1995). In literary narrative discourse, which creates worlds that depart from the spatio-temporal parameters of the discourse-world, readers are thought to 'take a cognitive stance within the world of the narrative and interpret the text from that perspective' (Segal 1995: 15). In Text World Theory, projection is understood as a process of cross-world metaphorical mapping between discourse-world participant and text-world enactor (Gavins 2007; Lahey 2005; Stockwell 2009). This means that features of the reader in the discourse-world are thought to be mapped or transferred onto entities in the text-world during reading, and this establishes the relationships previously discussed. Stockwell characterises projection as part of the general human cognitive capacity for 'taking one domain and mapping it onto another in order to gain access or understanding of the new domain' (2009: 9; see also G. Lakoff and Johnson 1980). In other words, aspects of the readers' 'self' become implicated in the text-worlds they create as they read (Kuiken et al. 2004).

I have argued elsewhere (Whiteley 2011a) that psychological projection can involve varying degrees of mapping. At a basic level, a reader can project their sense of space and location into a text, and this facilitates the experience of immersion or engagement in a narrative (see Gerrig 1993). A broader level of projection, which I have called 'perspective-taking projection', goes beyond this purely spatio-temporal anchorage so that other aspects of a particular entity's perspective, including their world view, attitudes, emotions, goals and so on, are imaginatively reconstructed by the reader. Perspective-taking projection involves the mapping of particular human characteristics onto text-world enactors in order to flesh out their representation, and enables readers to treat text-world entities as 'real', life-like people (Gavins 2007: 42–3; see also Palmer 2004; Zunshine 2006).

Processes of identification represent a further degree of psychological projection, which refers more specifically to the involvement of a reader's 'self-aware personality' in the mappings between discourse-world and text-world (Stockwell 2009: 88; see also Gavins 2007; Kuiken et al. 2004; Lahey 2005). Identification involves acts of comparison and recognition on the part of the reader in relation to a text-world entity. Readers may recognise aspects of their own experience, emotions or world view in characters, for instance, and identification can perhaps be seen as foundational in the development of empathy or sympathy for characters (see Keen 2007; Sklar 2013; Stockwell 2009). The strength of identification is dependent on the extent of the mappings between the reader and text-world entity. It is, of course, possible to compare yourself with others in a negative way – surmising that you are *not* like them – and I refer to this reverse identification as 'disassociation'. It involves the same processes of comparison and recognition as identification, but with a distancing rather than connecting effect.

The text-worlds of *Never Let Me Go* contain a number of positions, henceforth referred to as 'roles', for readers to negotiate at the different communicative levels of the narrative (Lahey 2005; Phelan 2005). As noted above, conceptualising an implied author also involves the conceptualisation of an implied reader who is being addressed. Readers may project into this role to varying degrees (see Jeffries 2001; Rabinowitz 1998). The presence of a first-person narrator also evokes the role of a narratee. Readers will be positioned in relation to this first-person narrator and also the narratee role during their text-world construction. Finally, other characters in the narrative also provide possibilities for projection and identification. Thus, as Stockwell explains: 'readers position themselves in different places relative to the minds they are modelling in the text world', and these positions have both emotional and ethical implications, correlating with 'the degree of support, acquiescence or resistance' in the reading (Stockwell 2009: 160; see also Phelan 2005: 18–23). In a novel such as *Never Let Me Go*, which is about what it means to be human, or how 'human' is defined (Black 2009: 785; Griffin 2009: 653–4; Jerng 2008: 370), these ethical positionings, which occur out of a projection from 'self' to 'other', take on further thematic significance.

Interestingly, reviewers, literary critics, and participants in a reading group who I recorded discussing the novel all express an interesting sense of partial-identification with and partial-disassociation from the protagonist Kathy. For instance, Robbins (2007: 293) recognises similarities between himself and Kathy when he writes: 'like Kathy, I depend for my daily dose of contentment on a blinkering of awareness'. Yet he also describes a sense of identification with the un-cloned which is 'so deep as to make the reader wonder which side Ishiguro is on. And which side we're on' (2007: 293). Kerr (2005) notes how 'familiar' Kathy's childhood memories feel, and writes 'it's like a stripped down haiku version of children everywhere' (2005: 1), but then expresses similar conflict when she remarks: 'we root for Kathy – which is not quite the same as identifying with her ... by definition she is personality challenged' (2005: 2). In a generally negative review of the novel, Kermode (2005) describes Kathy's narrative style derogatively as 'dear diary prose' but acknowledges some experience of sympathy for her. And Black (2009: 792) notes that the novel complicates our identifications with Kathy 'in disturbing ways'.

Similarly mixed responses also featured in the reading group discussion about *Never Let Me Go* that I recorded as part of my investigations into the novel's effects. In the extract below, three participants (A, C and E) are discussing the style and content of Kathy's narrative – in particular her detailed recounting of quite trivial or mundane memories from her childhood, when the following exchange takes place:

Extract 2

A: ... each time there was something like that Kathy would refer to 'oh and when this happened' and then tells a little tale of something happening and on most occasions you were kind of thinking 'nothing really did happen', it was all ... kind of little events which seemed to be a big deal to her or to the people involved but were fairly kind of incidental events.

C: I suppose *that's what you remember though isn't it*, **that's the sort of things that I remember** from my own childhood, little kind of stupid things when so and so said something to somebody else but it didn't really mean anything.

E: That's it, yeah, I thought that because *it did remind me a bit ... of the sort of stuff that you get obsessed about when you're at school and you'd think was really important* ... **I could probably think of some childhood memories I've got that are like she has** when you have stupid arguments about hairbrushes or whatever, but you'd never sort of sit and tell someone about them would you, whereas she's like a 31-year-old woman and she sort of thinks that's an appropriate topic of conversation for a whole book basically (*laughs*)

The use of pronouns in Extract 2 and what they signal about the identifications which are being performed here are particularly interesting. For instance, in the utterances which are italicised ('that's what *you* remember though isn't it' and 'the sort of stuff *you* remember when you're at school'), participants C and E are using the second-person 'you' to express identification with Kathy. The second person functions to include the speaker, the other discussion group participants, and Kathy in the same group, as similarities between them are recognised (Kuiken et al. 2004). Participants

C and E also explicitly declare their similarity to Kathy using the first person, indicated in bold ('that's the sort of things that *I* remember', and '*I* could probably think of some'), which indicates close identification with the character. In the underlined utterances in Extract 2, however, the second-person pronoun is being used slightly differently: when Participant A says: '*you* were kind of thinking "nothing really did happen"' and Participant E says: 'but *you*'d never sort of sit and tell someone about them would *you*'. In these instances, the 'you' seems to express identification with a group of people which specifically *excludes* Kathy. The speakers identify characteristics of Kathy; namely, the opinion that trivial childhood memories are an important thing to discuss, which they cannot map onto themselves. Thus Participants C and E explicitly disassociate themselves from Kathy in these utterances. In fact, in the space of a single conversational turn, Participant E expresses identification with and disassociation from Kathy: she identifies with Kathy's experiences of childhood but takes issue with her narration of such seemingly trivial memories.

I wish to argue that the language of *Never Let Me Go* contains features which both promote and problematise identification with Kathy and the clones and underpin the effects described by these readers. This complex positioning has interesting implications for the text's ethical affect, because although the novel is 'anti-cloning', it also seems to prevent straightforward, close identification with Kathy, the cloned protagonist.

Positioning in the narrator–narratee roles

One interesting aspect of reader positioning in the novel occurs in relation to the narrator and narratee roles. As noted above, the first-person narrative at the opening of the novel (see Extract 1) presupposes the existence of a narratee who is being addressed. Lahey (2005) argues that readers are likely to assume they are being directly addressed by a narrator, and project into the narratee role, unless textual cues indicate otherwise. But in *Never Let Me Go*, the identity of the narratee seems to fluctuate at different points in the novel, making it difficult for readers to maintain a stable position in relation to this role.

In the opening lines of the text, the presence of unexplained terms such as 'carer' and 'donor', and the mention of unfamiliar places and referents, suggest that Kathy assumes a certain degree of shared knowledge on the part of her narratee, which readers in the discourse-world do not possess. Indeed, until Chapter 8, Kathy often directly addresses the narratee (using the second-person pronoun 'you') as if they were a fellow clone and a graduate of an institution like Hailsham. For example, she says 'I don't know if you had "collections" where you were' (Ishiguro 2005: 38) or, 'I don't know how it was where you were, but...' followed by a fact about Hailsham, such as 'at Hailsham we had to have some form of medical almost every week' (2005: 13), 'at Hailsham the guardians were really strict about smoking' (2005: 67), 'at Hailsham we definitely weren't at all kind towards any signs of gay stuff' (2005: 94). These textual cues suggest that Kathy is addressing a specific narratee who has a certain set of knowledge and experiences which a discourse-world reader does not share. Therefore, readers are likely to find it more difficult to project into the narratee role at these points in the text. While some readers may make attempts to 'imaginatively enact' the role of Kathy's narratee, and 'take on what he or she perceives to be the relevant schemata' of that entity (Lahey 2005: 286; see also Black 2009: 790; Fludernik 1995; Jerng 2008: 390–1; Toker and Chertoff 2008), others may instead feel shifted from a position of direct address to one of observation at a greater emotional or ethical distance (see Phelan 1996: 145–52, 2007b: 210). Either way, I would argue that in the moment of reading, a certain distancing or alienating effect is created as the reader adjusts their position in relation to a specific narratee whose identity differs from their own.

Elsewhere in the novel, however, it is easier for readers to project into the narratee role and feel directly addressed by Kathy. For instance, in the opening lines of the novel, Kathy introduces herself to her narratee, supplying them with her name, age and occupation. This creates the impression that she is addressing someone she doesn't know, and when processing these initial sentences it may be quite easy for discourse-world readers to project into the narratee role (as they also have not 'met' Kathy before). This projection is also possible when Kathy makes more general attributions of thoughts or opinions to the narratee. For example, when attempting to justify her complicity in a joke designed to humiliate her friend Tommy, she addresses the narratee directly and says: 'you've got to remember I was still young, and that I only had a few seconds to decide' (Ishiguro 2005: 85). She also uses rhetorical questions such as 'So why had we stayed silent that day?' (Ishiguro 2005: 69) and 'What was so special about this song?' (Ishiguro 2005: 70), demonstrating an awareness of the narratee's desire for particular details, which may or may not accord with those of the actual reader. Kathy is very attentive to the needs of her addressee, and often signposts her narrative with markers such as: 'I should explain about…' (Ishiguro 2005: 15) or 'What I'm saying is…' (Ishiguro 2005: 274). These forms of address contribute to the sense that readers *are* being directly addressed by the character at these points.

Throughout the novel, then, readers' ability to comfortably project into the narratee role shifts depending upon the mode of address used within the narrative. I propose that this fluctuation can also encourage or problematise identification with Kathy the narrator, as readers feel closer or more distant to her act of narration. For example, when Kathy is describing her childhood at Hailsham she explicitly calls on the narratee to search their memories for experiences and emotions which may match hers, with utterances such as:

> I'm sure somewhere in your childhood, you too had an experience like
> ours that day, similar if not in the actual details, then inside, in the
> feelings.   *(Ishiguro 2005: 36)*

> like a lot of things at that age; you don't have any clear reason, you just do
> it … when you're asked to explain it afterwards, it doesn't seem to make
> any sense. We've all done things like that …   *(Ishiguro 2005: 19)*

Here the reader is being invited to project themselves into the narratee role, and, by extension, imagine themselves in Kathy's role too. The text also nominates aspects of the readers' personal experience which should be compared with that of Kathy, promoting processes of identification. Whether identification is experienced is of course dependent upon the actual reader: their inclination, their personal memories, and their shared cultural knowledge about childhood. Another aspect of the text which facilitates identification with Kathy is the way information about the existence of clones is withheld from the reader until a quarter of the way into the novel. Toker and Chertoff (2008) argue that readers come to a slow realisation of Kathy's cloned status in a way which mirrors Kathy's own realisation of this in her childhood. They argue that this similarity between the experience of the reader and the experience of Kathy reinforces identification with the narrator.

Never Let Me Go encourages further complexity in positioning in relation to different *versions* (or 'enactors') of Kathy. For instance, in Extract 2 above, participants in the reading group discussion seem to be making a distinction between their response to two different enactors of Kathy. The first enactor, Kathy[1], is the 31-year-old narrator who talks about her childhood memories. In doing so, she creates text-worlds which are set in the past (remote from the time of narration), and, within them, Kathy[2], is the enactor which experiences that childhood. The reader remarks considered above seem to demonstrate close identification with Kathy[2] through their shared childhood experiences, but disassociation from Kathy[1] through their different perceptions of newsworthy material. This suggests that different enactors of Kathy are capable of attracting different levels of projection, identification and disassociation from readers, which adds further complexity to readers' engagement with the narrative. At times, the language of the text appears to promote projection into the narratee role and identification with Kathy[2], but the fluctuation of this narratee role, meaning that readers feel directly addressed at points in the narrative and distanced at others, may also work to promote a certain level of disassociation from Kathy[1].

Positioning in the implied reader role

So far I have referred quite generally to the mode of narration throughout the novel and argued that textual cues encourage readers feel both close to and distant from Kathy the narrator, which has implications for their emotional and ethical responses to the text. In this section I will go on to discuss multiple projection in relation to a particular extract from the novel, broadening my discussion to include the level of communication between the implied author and the implied reader.

This extract comes from the opening of the third and final part of the novel. Though not a particularly climactic moment, it stood out as poignant in my reading of the text because it evoked markedly mixed emotions, and I will draw on my introspective experience of the text here. For me, this extract evokes both a sense of admiration for and affinity towards Kathy, coupled with a sense of underlying sadness and pity. I wish to argue that these mixed emotions are indicative of the complex projections involved imagining the text-worlds of the passage.

Kathy has been explaining the main features of her job as a 'carer', such as the long hours and exhausting travelling (the donors she cares for are kept in a number of centres across the country). She has also discussed the need for carers to keep their spirits up when their donors inevitably 'complete', and the solitude involved (carers do not work in teams). Throughout this description, Kathy sets herself and other competent carers apart from those carers who she believes cannot cope with the job. She explains that although she has suffered all the hardships of working as a carer, she has 'learnt to live' with them. She goes on to say:

Extract 3

(1) Even the solitude, I've actually grown to quite like. (2) That's not to say I'm not looking forward to a bit more companionship come the end of the year when I'm finished with all of this. (3) But I do like the feeling of getting into my little car, knowing for the next couple of hours I'll have only the roads, the big grey sky and my daydreams for company. (4) And if I'm in a town somewhere with several minutes to kill, I'll enjoy myself wandering about looking in the shop windows. (5) Here in my bedsit, I've these four desk lamps, each a different colour, but all the same design – they have these ribbed necks you can bend whichever way you want. (6) So I might go looking for a shop with another lamp like that in its window – not to buy, but just to compare with my ones at home.

(Ishiguro 2005: 204, my sentence numbering*)*

The text-world established at the beginning of the novel, containing Kathy and her narratee, still underpins the text-worlds created in Extract 3. There are further, multiple text-worlds created here through the use of modals (e.g. *like, will, might*), hypotheticals (*if*), negatives (*not*) and spatio-temporal shifts, which I do not have space to detail here (see Gavins 2007 for an overview of world creation, and Whiteley 2010 for more detail about this extract).

More relevant to the present discussion is the way in which Text World Theory handles the knowledge and other discourse-world resources that readers utilise in their comprehension of discourse. Following established terms used in cognitive science and linguistics (e.g. Schank and Abelson 1977; Fillmore 1985; G. Lakoff 1987) Text World Theory regards participants' knowledge as being organised into 'frames', which are collections of knowledge about a particular aspect of the world (such as people, objects, situations and events, and how they interact – see Stockwell 2002: 75–90 for an introduction). Discourse-world participants have a potentially vast store of knowledge upon which they can draw, and Text World Theory focuses only on the knowledge which is cued as relevant for the particular discourse by the language of the text. For instance, when reading a novel by Thomas Hardy readers need only activate areas of knowledge which are specifically required by the text, such as those regarding farming in the nineteenth century, human relationships and the Dorset/Wessex countryside, for instance. Readers' knowledge about football matches or how to reboot a computer will remain redundant (Gavins 2007: 29). Participants use their knowledge frames to flesh out their text-world representations with inferences (Werth 1999: 148). In order to construct text-world representations of Extract 3, for instance, a reader's knowledge frames relating to: driving, English motorways, English weather and provincial towns, desk lamps and window shopping become relevant, among others. As noted above, the perception of shared knowledge or experience is important in establishing relationships of identification between readers and textual entities, and in this extract the role of readers' cultural knowledge is also significant in their ethical positioning.

In my interpretation of Extract 3, I experience quite close identification with Kathy the narrator. I recognise my own experience of driving in her descriptions here, and despite the fact that she uses quite vague expressions such as 'the roads', 'the big grey sky', 'a town somewhere' and 'shop windows' to describe her journey and the places she visits, I am able to draw on my rich knowledge of English roads, towns and weather (I have lived in England for my whole life) to imagine and recognise the scenes she describes. I also know exactly the type of desk lamps with 'ribbed necks' which she refers to (there is one on my desk as I type), and this also, however trivially, establishes a sense of recognition between me in the discourse-world and her text-world enactor.

For the majority of Extract 2, I also feel directly addressed by Kathy, suggesting that I can project into the narratee role here. Phrases such as 'that's not to say' indicate that Kathy is shaping her narrative with an intended listener in mind, but further details regarding the identity of this listener are not specified. This projection into the narratee role is destabilised, however, by the introduction of deictic information 'here in my bedsit' in sentence 5, which again suggests shared knowledge (or perhaps a shared spatio-temporal location) between Kathy and her narratee. This has a distancing effect similar to the examples I have discussed above, and means my sense of identification with Kathy is not fully sustained throughout the passage.

So far I have discussed reader positioning in relation to the narrator and narratee, but this extract demonstrates the impact of positioning in relation to the role of the implied reader too. Readers' projection into the role of the implied reader is highlighted here when there is a disjunction between the discourse-world knowledge frames evoked by the text and the content of Kathy's text-worlds. For instance, the reference to a 'big grey sky' in sentence 3 fits in with my knowledge of typical English weather, facilitating identification with Kathy – but it also evokes a connection with my linguistic and cultural knowledge of the more commonly collocating phrase 'big blue sky'. In my cultural knowledge, blue skies are viewed as having more positive connotations than grey skies (people who are sad or angry are said to be 'under a black cloud' for instance). Kathy is trying to present her day-to-day experience positively in this extract, but her mention of the 'big grey sky', with its bleak and depressing connotations, clashes with the positive attitude which she is expressing.

Another type of clash occurs at the end of Extract 2. In sentence 4 Kathy describes how she likes to go 'wandering about looking in the shop windows' in order to pass the time. However, Kathy's view of window shopping, expressed in sentence 6, departs considerably from my cultural and experiential knowledge of this pastime. Window shopping tends to involve browsing for items which are both desirable and unattainable, perhaps due to cost or practicality. But Kathy is window shopping for a mundane household item, which she already possesses. There is a noticeable disjunction between my knowledge frames and Kathy's representation of her activities here.

Both of these clashes suggest that the narrator and the narratee in the text-world do not share elements of my knowledge about grey skies and window shopping. This has implications for my ethical positioning, as it serves to highlight that the novel is a communication between an implied author and implied reader who *do* share cultural knowledge of the discourse-world. The sense of a conflict or clash here arises from my projection into the implied reader role.

My emotional and ethical experience of this passage arises from the amalgamation of positioning relative to multiple entities at the text-world level. My positive emotions and affinity towards Kathy seem to originate from my projection into the narratee role and identification with the narrator. But my sense of sadness and pity seem to be associated with my projection into the role of the implied reader, as the cultural knowledge I share with the implied author allows me to recognise Kathy's poverty, misery and restricted world view. Though projection into the implied reader role creates a disassociative 'pull' which undercuts identification on other communicative levels, it also serves to reinforce the novel's ethical 'message' about the undesirability of cloning, because in my experience it serves to maintain the distance which enables sympathy towards Kathy (Sklar 2013; Stockwell 2009).

Through the above analyses, I hope to have demonstrated that readers' complex state of partial-identification with and partial-disassociation from Kathy can be explained to some extent by the multiple positions which readers are encouraged to adopt by the language of the text. These positionings have ethical implications as they impact upon readers' response to the events and characters represented within the text. Rather than being able to view Kathy as uncomplicatedly like yourself, the novel promotes a more sophisticatedly nuanced positioning in which the notion of what it means to be human can be explored.

Conclusion

In this chapter I hope to have shown that even macro-linguistic issues such as ethical experience can benefit from close, stylistic attention to the language of a text, and detailed consideration of the experience of readers. The idea I have proposed here – that readers can simultaneously experience both identification and disassociation due to the influence of various textual features in a particular moment of reading – actually presents a challenge to more established stylistic assumptions about distancing or estrangement in narrative. For instance, first-person narration is often thought to make readers feel closer to the characters (Leech and Short 1981: 275). And Simpson's (1993) modal grammar claims that narratives with a preponderance of epistemic modality, such as *Never Let Me Go*, have an estranging and alienating feel (Simpson 1993: 53, 75). My claim regarding the subtle and sometimes contradictory influence of textual features over readerly positioning adds a greater cognitive complexity to these grammatical models. It also problematises the tendency within stylistics to categorise the experiential 'feel' of a text based solely upon its linguistic features, without a detailed consideration of readers in interaction with those features. Cognitive poetic approaches have the potential to extend our understanding of how ethical meaning and experience are created in literary discourse.

27

Fictionality and ontology

Alison Gibbons

Introduction

'The struggle to define fictionality', Punday (2010: 55) claims, 'is an inherent part of the institutional construction of contemporary writing'. What he means by this is that the proliferation of the fictive in contemporary society, including ways in which the real itself is narrativised, makes the distinction between reality and fiction rather fluid. In his words, 'the traditional institutional and disciplinary boundaries separating news and entertainment, fiction and politics have become blurred' (2010: 11). Such enhanced permeation between actuality and virtuality in literature and culture makes fictionality a central issue for contemporary stylistics and narratology.

The focus of this chapter is a Text World Theory analysis of *Ulrike and Eamon Compliant* by Blast Theory, a group of artists who create stories using interactive media. *Ulrike and Eamon Compliant* is a mobile narrative, a genre hitherto unexplored in stylistics. Since participants engage with the story through mobile technology, the boundary between fiction and reality becomes increasingly convoluted.

Fictionality: style, ontology and readers

To consider fictionality using a stylistic method, it would be tempting to offer a taxonomy of linguistic features that mark a text as fictional. This is, in many ways, the approach taken by the narratologist Cohn (1990, 1999), who places linguistic style at the centre of fictionality. In a 1990 article, Cohn contrasts fictional narratives with historical narratives through the examination of three criteria: levels of narrative (story and discourse), narrative situations (voice, mode, and point of view), and narrative agents (authors and narrators). Cohn concludes that there are qualitative differences in the form of generic features, for instance privileged access to characters' thoughts is a typical attribute of fiction.

Studying linguistic markers alone, however, would be a flawed approach, as Prince (1991) points out. He claims (1991: 546) that classical narratological investigations have been too text-driven and should instead consider truth values:

> I could, after all, begin a biography of Napoleon or Richelieu (entirely consonant with the truth and written for children or intended to highlight the legendary nature of characters) with 'once upon a time.'
>
> *(Prince 1991: 546)*

Prince advocates instead a modal logic or possible worlds model (Ryan 1991a) in which propositions are validated according to their truth conditions in relation to the fictional world(s). This therefore enables a spatialised ontological map of fiction(s).

Presenting disparate though not entirely polarised views, both Cohn's stylistic 'signposts of fictionality' and Prince's call to arms in the consideration of ontological spaces are useful for the stylistic analysis of fictionality, yet even together they still present an incomplete picture. In theorising fictionality, both approaches neglect the contextual interpretations of a reader or receiver of narrative. Working in the reader-response school of criticism, it is unsurprising that it is this readerly aspect of the fictional process that most interests Iser. In *The Fictive and the Imaginary*, he states:

> The literary text is a mixture of reality and fictions, and as such it brings about an interaction between the given and the imagined. Because this interaction produces far more than just a contrast between the two, we might do better to discard the old opposition of fiction and reality altogether, and to replace this duality with a triad: the real, the fictive, and what we shall henceforth call the imaginary. It is out of this triad that the text arises...
>
> *(Iser 1993: 1)*

For Iser, then, it is from the interaction between fiction and reality that the imagined world(s) of literary narratives emerge. A text is constituted through what he calls 'fictionalising acts'. There are three varieties: *selection*, *combination* and *self-disclosure*. Selection is concerned with setting the parameters of the text in social, historical, cultural and literary terms – selecting in other words from referential reality and literary compositional systems; combination is the organisation of the text into linguistic and semantic patterns, while self-disclosure occurs when the text reveals its own fictionality. All of these processes involve the crossing of boundaries (in terms of the ways in which they extend beyond the limits of fiction).

While Iser's approach draws on literary anthropology, it offers a valuable precedent to contemporary narratological and stylistic accounts of fictionality. Iser's triad is particularly important since it considers the relationships between fictional, actual and reader-centric imaginary as well as gesturing towards the potential impact of this imagined world on the reader.

As the next section makes clear, the reader is at the heart of contemporary stylistic analyses of fictionality. These are interested in how the reader creates fictional text-worlds from the compositional fabric of the text, including integrating information from the actual discourse-world (style and cognition); how the reader experiences the landscapes of fictional text-worlds including the division between actual and virtual (ontology); and how the reader engages with characters in fictional text-worlds (psychological projection).

Metaleptic crossings and a stylistics of engagement

Stylistics has always been concerned with readers, but the growing interest in fictionality may, in part, be understood as a consequence of the increased fusion between fictive and real in contemporary narratives, discussed in the opening to this chapter. The idea of a 'semipermeable membrane' (McHale 1987: 34–5) between the actual discourse-world (reality) and the reader's text-world (in fiction) underlies many stylistic accounts of fictionality. Linguistically, this has often meant a consideration of narrative address, particularly metaleptic second-person address from a fictional text-world enactor to the reader in the discourse-world. Working within Text World Theory, Gavins (2007) argues that second-person address leads to one of two possibilities: if the reader shares the characteristics of the 'you' described in the novel, they may process the narrative assertions as being directly addressed to them. Thus, 'the text-world entity who is using the second-person pronoun to address the reader transcends the ontological boundaries of the text-world in order to enter the reader's half of the split-discourse-world' (2007: 85). However, readers may not identify with 'you' (either because the 'you' is not a descriptive match for the reader or through the reader's deliberate resistant reading) and as such engagement is one of projection into the second-person deictic centre without assuming a self-identical persona. More recently, Whiteley (2011a) has proposed three forms of narrative projection into addressee or character roles which develop in terms of the degree of a reader's psychological involvement: *deictic projection*, based on the linguistic mechanics of the text and involving a reader's deictic shift into the spatio-temporal parameters of the text-world; *perspective-taking projection*, in which a reader also fleshes out characters through the attribution of psychological characteristics; and *self-implication* or *identification*, whereby readers implicate their own personalities into the addressee or character role and thus their sense of self is involved in trans-world mapping between the actual discourse-world and fictional text-world.

David Herman's (2002) theory of *contextual anchoring* is also concerned with second-person narrative address. He suggests that, in some cases, narratives may offer concurrent deictic projections that are at once distinct and multiplex. He writes:

> Contextual anchoring is my name for the process whereby a narrative, in a more or less explicit and reflexive way, asks its interpreters to search for analogies between the representations contained within the two classes of mental models [the story world and the reader's actual world].
>
> *(D. Herman 2002: 331)*

Contextual anchoring is a cognitive process, triggered by the linguistic composition of the text, whereby the space-time parameters of the fictional text-world and the space-time parameters of the discourse-world in which reading takes place are seen to be simultaneously referenced and thus appear to coincide. In Herman's *doubly deictic you*, second-person address signals two deictic referents at once: a 'you' character internal to the fictional text-world and a 'you' external and thus present in the actual discourse-world. Such double referentiality blurs ontological clarity between fictional and actual, text-world and discourse-world, character and reader, leading to complex projection relations. In terms of psychological engagement then, projection relations with doubly deictic 'you' cannot be neatly classified. Readers self-implicate into the 'you' role which they feel apostrophically addresses them while also experiencing degrees of deictic projection, perspective-taking projection or indeed further self-implication, depending on their psychological engagement with the character in the context of the textual moment.

Multimodal, multimedial and hypertext fictions engender not only forms of psychological projection such as those encouraged by second-person address, but also actualised and physical responses from reader-users (see Alice Bell and Ensslin 2011; Ensslin and Bell 2012; Gibbons 2012a, 2012b). My own work, for instance, has considered the way in which multimodal and multimedial texts create double deixis when readers are required to perform concrete activities that are subjectively aligned with the actions of characters in the text-world. Such subjective resonance between text-world and discourse-world referents involves a similar superimposition in the form of doubly deictic subjectivity. Moreover, performative activity on the part of reader-users may create what I have called a *figured trans-world* (Gibbons 2012a) in which trans-world projection occurs between reader and character through an embodied and enactive resonance.

Breaches of the semipermeable membrane between fiction and reality, text-world and discourse-world, are ultimately illusory. The ontological planes of each remain intact, yet it is in the realm of the imaginary, in the reader's experience of the narrative, that the stylistics of fictionality shows up the complexity of reader-users' projection relations and the ways in which these may lead to a powerful sense of psychological involvement. To demonstrate, in this chapter I present a Text World Theory analysis of a contemporary mobile narrative, with a particular focus on deictics.

Blast Theory's *Ulrike and Eamon Compliant*

Blast Theory's *Ulrike and Eamon Compliant* is a mobile narrative and a form of art installation: within the context of a city, participants are guided through the streets as the narrative unfolds. As in mobile narratives generally (see Raley 2010), communication is, for the most part, unidirectional. Through a mobile phone, a narrative voice addresses and instructs participants, although responses are required at key points. Discussing the innovative nature of mobile narratives, Benford et al. (2006: 427) state, 'Mobile experiences that take place in public settings such as on city streets create new opportunities for interweaving the fictional world of a performance or game with the everyday physical world.'

There are two key aspects of mobile narratives that are of interest in the stylistic analysis of fictionality. Firstly, since mobile narratives take advantage of the immediacy of spoken discourse and take place in real time and in real-world locations (e.g. city streets), the context in which the narrative is received is used as the backdrop or as a world-building element for the text. Secondly, the participant is not only the receiver of second-person direct address during mobile phone calls, they are required to respond physically (e.g. by following instructions). As Raley (2010: 303) puts it, 'Participating in a mobile narrative is ... precisely that – physical participation that is also understandable as performance.' Raley's choice of the word 'performance' here is particularly telling, since it implies that while psychological engagement with literary narratives is understood in stylistics through the metaphors of readerly TRANSPORTATION and PERFORMANCE (Gerrig 1993), mobile narratives actualise such metaphors in ways that make projection relations between discourse-world participants and text-world enactors considerably involving, in terms of the degree of self-implication. As such, the very nature of *Ulrike and Eamon Compliant* as mobile narrative suggests that David Herman's (2002: 345) notion of contextual anchoring is at play with an 'ontological interference pattern'.

Ulrike and Eamon Compliant was originally commissioned for the 53rd Venice Biennale in 2009 and later taken to the Seoul International Media Art Biennale in 2010 and the international Sheffield Doc/Fest in 2011. (While the published script for the work refers to its original production, having participated in the mobile narrative during Doc/Fest any self-reflexive comments made during analysis are in reference to my own experience of the work in Sheffield). It is structured as a series of telephone calls that lead participants through the city, addressing and engaging them in the second person and *as* a character in the narrative. There are two possible narratives, 'Ulrike' and 'Eamon', both based upon the real lives of two terrorists. The Ulrike narrative tells the tale of left-wing German radical Ulrike Meinhof, a leading member of the Red Army Faction committing various bank raids, shootings and bombings; the Eamon narrative focuses on IRA member Eamon Collins who, upon arrest and interrogation in 1982, gave details of IRA operations to the state, which he later retracted. While the two narratives differ in terms of character and content, over a 30-minute series of eight or twelve calls (depending on a choice made by the participant at a key narrative fork) they are structurally alike and therefore contain some overlapping text. In order to experience *Ulrike and Eamon Compliant*, participants must first choose between Ulrike and Eamon.

Call 1: Are you Ulrike or Eamon?

Starting *Ulrike and Eamon Compliant*, participants are given a mobile phone and must press the call button. A voice asks, 'Are you Ulrike or Eamon?' and gives the instructions to dial 1 for Ulrike or 2 for Eamon. This determines the choice of narrative and the character as whom the participant will be addressed. They are then directed out onto the streets; once they reach the instructed destination, they must call the narrator back. In the Ulrike narrative, the narrator answers 'Hallo Ulrike, thanks for coming', while Eamon's narrator utters, 'Hallo, it's me'. In both texts, the narrator continues (Blast Theory 2009: 10 and 23):

> You and I are going on a walk together but before we start, let's take a minute. Now stand in the middle of the bridge and turn to look at the church towers. Can you see them? If you can see them nod your head slowly.

Both narratives open with direct and immediate deictics. The fictional text-world is aligned with the discourse-world of the participant through definite spatial references ('the bridge', 'the church towers') that relate to the city in which the mobile narrative is taking place, and temporally through present tense (continuous and simple) and the adverb 'now'. Similarly, a sense of intimacy is quickly established with the pairing of the interpersonal pronouns in the construction 'You and I' and the adverb 'together'. A metaleptic illusion is therefore created in which the narrator appears to transcend the semipermeable membrane of the fiction in order to talk, via mobile phone, with the participant. Moreover, the deception of a shared world-space between narrator and participant is heightened in the question 'Can you see them?' and the conditional directive 'If you can see them nod your head slowly.' The implication of the latter statement is that the narrator is in fact observing the participant and their actions.

Participants who fulfil the directive by nodding are psychologically adopting the (false) premise of shared world-space. It is the first of many occasions throughout *Ulrike and Eamon Compliant* in which performative actions promote the participant's self-implication with 'you' and increasingly with Ulrike or Eamon also.

After this psychologically involving aperture, the narratives diverge briefly in terms of content, both providing biographical introductions to the main characters Ulrike or Eamon. In Eamon's narrative, the narrator instigates a deictic shift: 'Outside it's 1973, dark, cold. It's late and the young man has been drinking with friends. He's a legal student and is back home on the farm for the Easter break' (p. 23). The participant's psychological involvement with narrative and character becomes more distal across temporal, spatial and perceptual deictic fields: it is a temporal shift into the past (1973), a spatial shift to a rural landscape in which the point of view is disconnected from the narrative action which is happening 'outside', and a perceptual shift from second- to third-person address with the introduction of 'the young man'. Alongside these deictic shifts, readers are thus moved from self-implication with 'you' to deictic projection into this scene. Despite the temporal shift to 1973, the narrative is in present-perfect continuous ('has been drinking') and present tense, maintaining a degree of immediacy. This is important since, as the narrative continues, the deictics become increasingly proximal: 'You know what lawyers can be like, right? Priggish little fools, some of them. This one smokes a pipe if you don't mind. Oh, you know the type alright. You know this one' (p. 23). Second-person address returns, reconnecting narrator and participant. The colloquial register (rhetorical question, relational deixis, conversational collocations) suggests an intimate knowledge about 'you' on the part of the narrator. Moreover, the utterance 'Oh, you know the type alright. You know this one' implies that that 'the young man' is well known to 'you', that in fact it is 'you'. The narrative resumes, 'You walk up the street toward the door or the house. One hand on the latch and you see...', thus marrying the deictic co-ordinates of 'the young man' with a textual 'you'.

The effect of these deictic shifts from distal narrative to a narrative adjacent with 'you' is to encourage the participant's identification with 'you' as Eamon (though, at this point, projection is likely to involve perspective-taking). Similar linguistic strategies are employed in Ulrike's narrative. *Ulrike and Eamon Compliant*, therefore, initially enables self-implication through contextually anchoring the discourse-world as setting for the prominent text-world. The introduction of the main characters, however, starts distally yet is increasingly brought closer to the 'you' in order to aid the participant to project not only into an apostrophic 'you' role (as in the beginning) but to also accept the deictic and psychological positioning of the 'you' character of Ulrike or Eamon.

In the first telephone call, Blast Theory has one more tactic to secure the participant's psychological engagement with character. In both narratives, Call 1 ends in the following way:

> As everyone moves past you as you stand on the bridge, I would like to know how you describe your ability to make decisions. Are you a decisive or a hesitant person Ulrike/Eamon?
>
> Now please record your answer. Start by saying 'My name is Ulrike/ Eamon' and then tell me, are you a decisive or a hesitant person?
>
> When you have finished your recording, hang up. I'm going to start recording now.   *(Blast Theory 2009: 10 and 24)*

In deictic terms, the spatio-temporal co-ordinates are returned to the participant's here and now, on the bridge, yet they continue to be addressed not only in second person but as Ulrike/Eamon. The act of speaking and recording is significant in terms of participant engagement. The initial act of nodding the head was a performance which signalled the acceptance of shared world-space, contextually anchoring the prominent fictive text-world within the participant's discourse-world reality. The act of recording takes such contextual anchoring even further through a performative act that signals the acceptance of a trans-world identity: the participant identifies with and self-implicates into the character role. They must utter, 'My name is Ulrike/Eamon. I am a decisive/hesitant person'. The first assertion ('My name is Ulrike/Eamon') is a locutionary act that marks the participant's adoption of the character, while the second ('I am a decisive/hesitant person') enables the participant to map their own subjective personality traits onto Ulrike or Eamon. Thus while the biographical narratives instigate world-switches, such switches occur as definite temporal and spatial shifts. Perceptually, the reader is involved in a gradual strengthening of projection relations with Ulrike/Eamon, from deictic to perspective-taking to a doubly deictic self-implication whereby they maintain their own identity as 'you' in the discourse-world and psychologically integrate it with 'you' as Ulrike/Eamon of the text-world.

The participant's verbal utterance as a performative act signals trans-world identity and double deixis through the phenomenological conflation of 'you' as participant in the discourse-world in which *Ulrike and Eamon Compliant* is taking place (e.g. Venice, Sheffield) with the 'you' character of Ulrike or Eamon in the story world. It therefore works to generate what I have called a *figured trans-world* (Gibbons 2012a: 79–80). A figured trans-world emerges when a participant's performative actions in the discourse-world map onto characters in the text-world and are indicative of active involvement. Such acts are concrete performances that create subjective resonances with characters and blur the boundaries between text- and discourse-world.

By saying 'My name is Ulrike/Eamon. I am a decisive/hesitant person', the participant effectively enters into a contract with Blast Theory.

They commit to the narrative and to positioning themselves double deictically as Ulrike or Eamon. They maintain their own identities in the discourse-world walking around the city while simultaneously accepting the Ulrike/Eamon identity. The semipermeable membrane between fiction and reality in *Ulrike and Eamon Compliant* is exactly that – semipermeable. Text-world and discourse-world appear to have been compressed and the ontological distinction is troubled in experiential terms.

Calls 2–3: I see you; who do you see?

After an initial greeting, the second phone call starts with walking directions and the narrator assuring participants, 'I'll stay on the line while you walk' (pp. 11 and 25). The notion that the narrator has the participant in eye-line is sustained with the instructions, 'Keep your eyes open, act natural'. Both narratives in phone call 2 offer details of an act of insurgence. In Eamon's narrative, it is the 1981 murder of Major Ivan Toombs of the Ulster Defence Regiment, which Eamon Collins was directly responsible for planning; in Ulrike's narrative, it is a violent protest against the Shah of Iran outside the Berlin Opera House in 1967.

The stylistic construction of Ulrike's tale is particularly interesting since, while a deictic shift occurs into Ulrike's past, the narrator's words simultaneously serve to remind the participant of their discourse-world location. The narrator relates:

> I see you in the crowd at the Opera House when the Shah visits. I see you behind the police and Iranian Secret Agents. The Shah and his wife go inside. Within seconds, the Iranians turn on you with long wooden clubs and start to smash heads. Blood flows while the cops stand and do nothing. And when they finally rouse themselves they don't help: they join in with smashing the demonstrators. I see you split and run with the others. I see the policeman draw his pistol. I see Benno Ohnesorg shot in the back of the head from half a metre away... *(Blast Theory 2009: 11)*

The repetition of the phrase 'I see you...', and later 'I see...' at the violent climax of the narrative, functions on one hand to suggest the vivacity of the (supposedly shared) memory. However, it also works to foreground the participant's self-awareness: can the narrator *really* see them? Blast Theory collected participant feedback from *Ulrike and Eamon Compliant* on their microsite and many of the comments demonstrate that suspicion about being under observation is a significant part of the experience. Several comments mention 'paranoia' while one participant admits, 'I felt watched constantly.' Such responses suggest that a sense of surveillance in mobile narratives may serve to make the experience psychologically intense in terms of heightening their self-consciousness in the discourse-world context.

At this point in Call 2, the participant is faced with a decision. The narrator states, 'Now if you want me to carry on just stay on the line. But if you want to take a different turn hang up now' (pp. 11 and 25). In Ulrike's narrative, the narrator underlines this, 'Right now'. In Eamon's narrative, the narrator instead says, 'I'm going to count to ten. If you are still on the line when I get to ten then I'll know where I stand.' The counting, however, additionally narrates the violent climax to Eamon's tale of Major Toombs's murder:

One:	the two killers ride into Warren point on a motorbike.
Two:	they switch the engine off allowing the bike to glide the last 20 metres so as not to raise the alarm.
Three:	once inside, Iceman goes down the corridor into Toombs' office.
Four:	he takes up a firing position with arms outstretched.
Five:	his gun jams giving Toombs enough time to reach for his own weapon.
Six:	Iceman leaps onto him and the two men struggle.
Seven:	The second gunman comes running down the hall and shouts 'Stand back.'
Eight:	Iceman lets go and the second man fires several shots into Toombs.
Nine:	Iceman clears his weapon.
Ten:	he pumps several more rounds into Toombs as he lies dying.

(Blast Theory 2009: 25)

The participant must choose whether to stay on the line or to hang up either immediately after (Ulrike) or during (Eamon) a violent description. Their decision therefore becomes somewhat loaded, since it appears to imply either acceptance of the act or condemnation. For participants who stay on the line, the narrator responds, 'Ok I understand. In which case, you and I can speak freely' (pp. 11 and 25). As such, this decision suggests complicity on the participant's part with Ulrike or Eamon as characters and with their actions. It is, in other words, another performative act that binds participants psychologically closer to characters. Moreover, the detail in both narratives in terms of world-building elements and function-advancing propositions point to the fact that these accounts are stylised representations of real-world events. Not only does this add a further sense of slippage in terms of the narrative's fictional status, it adds sombre weight to participants' potential connivance with the actions of Ulrike Meinhof or Eamon Collins.

There are two different versions for Call 3 of each narrative, differing only in opening depending on whether participants previously stayed on the line or hung up. Unbeknown to participants, then, their decision makes very little difference. Crucially in terms of narrative engagement, the act creates a false impression of control – that the participant is empowered and their actions have some bearing on the narrative. This is important since it makes *Ulrike and Eamon Compliant* seem more of a dialogue than it actually is. Participants who continued to listen receive assertive greetings (pp. 12 and 26):

Hallo Ulrike.

You are clear, you are direct. I know you can hear it all and I can tell it all.

Hallo Eamon.

Ivan Toombs is dead. The first successful IRA kill of 1981. It's a lot to think about.

Both greetings exhibit strong epistemic certainty on the part of the narrator, through the use of categorical assertions and epistemic verbs ('know', 'think'). Coupled with the sense of compliance felt by the participant having stayed on the phone, the narrator's words suggest confidence in the participant as Ulrike/Eamon. Alternatively, participants who hung up hear the following (pp. 12 and 26):

Hallo Ulrike.

So, you hung up? Some things are hard to hear. Some things are hard to say. That's why we're here isn't it?

You hung up.

Second thoughts, eh? There'll be plenty of time for those, don't you worry about that.

Again, both narratives have similar functions. Both start with acknowledgement of the participant's choice and both aim at emotional provocation. The rhetorical questions 'That's why we're here isn't it?' and 'Second thoughts, eh?' both imply that, by hanging up, the participant made a cowardly choice, attempting to hide from a truth that they need to confront.

At the end of Call 3, the narrator commands (pp. 12 and 27):

Now I want you to pick a person as they walk past you. Choose someone and give them a name. Look carefully at them before they go. Now think about their home. Think about a treasured possession that they may have on their shelf.

Who is it that they love? Stare down at the canal and hold that person in your mind for a short while.

In this series of directives, the narrator asks participants to imaginatively construct a narrative for a passing stranger. It is an act of perspective-taking by which the participant's empathy for the stranger is evoked through the personal investment of subjective imaginings. Creating an identity for the stranger begins with the act of naming and through the imagining of concrete objects (home, treasured possession, their loved ones). The reference to 'their home' creates a deictic shift whereby the participant moves in imaginative terms from the city streets into that person's home. In my own experience of *Ulrike and Eamon Compliant*, this moment was very powerful. The deictic shift into their home felt almost like a breach of personal space. Moreover, the prepositional phrase 'on their shelf' offers specificity (although hedged with the epistemic modal 'may') to the treasured possession, making such imaginings seem strikingly vivid and thus more real.

This exercise of make-believe is another of Blast Theory's tactics to evoke empathy from participants. The group has already exploited your feelings of identification and compassion with their central characters. Here, they offer only guidance: it is the participant's own subjective storytelling which creates the felt sense of subjective connection. Indeed, this layering of empathetic relationships is deliberate. As artist Matt Adams admits in interview (2009):

> How attuned and sensitive can you be to the people around you in the world without losing a sense of focus or perspective? If you're able to empathise with a dictator or a mass murderer, at what point does that blur your ability to discriminate and think clearly?

Psychological engagements such as this act of perspective-taking projection with a stranger in the real world show up the fragility of fictionality and of the border between fiction and actuality. The imaginary identities of these strangers are no more real than those of characters in a novel. Yet, for participants, the personalisation of this act makes the subjective experience startlingly sincere and affecting.

Call 5: What is it that you can do?

In Call 5, the narrator warns: 'In a moment, I'm going to ask you to make a recording for me' (pp. 14 and 29), after which the participant hears another tale from Ulrike or Eamon's past, both of which feature situations in which the characters are forced to contemplate how their actions can be used for the progression of their causes. The narrator then says:

> Now you need to tell me this: as you sit looking at the windows and the alleys, what is it that you can do right now for the people around you? Don't be shy; it's a question we all have to answer from time to time. And today, here on this bench, it's your turn. What can you do for the people around you?
>
> When you have finished your recording, hang up. There's no rush at all.
> I'm going to start recording now. *(Blast Theory 2009: 15 and 29)*

Deictically, the narrative has shifted back (Ulrike was in Frankfurt, Eamon in Northern Ireland) to the participant's discourse-world with the repetition of the temporal adverb 'now', definite spatial references ('the windows', 'the alleys') and the locative adverb and prepositional phrase 'here on this bench'. Recording the message, though, raises questions as to exactly *who* the participant is supposed to speak as – themselves or Ulrike/Eamon? Indeed, in my own response, I found myself using emotive and politically charged lexis (such as 'freedom') not dissimilar from that I'd been hearing throughout the narrative. The tactics employed by Blast

Theory have had a powerful effect. They have created a doubly deictic alignment so strong that it becomes difficult to divide the text-world and discourse-world identities of 'you'. In making the recording, participants are therefore both speaking as themselves, through self-implication with the 'you' of the text-world that has been contextually anchored in the discourse-world, and as Ulrike/Eamon through either perspective-taking projection or further self-implication. Contextual anchoring, the participant's actualised responses, and the creation of a figured trans-world have ultimately worked to problematise the participant's recognition of the narrative's fictionality. In experiential terms, the division between their discourse-world and text-world identities appear to have collapsed; the deictic positioning from which they speak as they record their message is double.

Calls 7+: Now you need to make a very important choice

Call 7 provides the central deciding moment for participants in terms of how the narrative will end. The narrator urges:

> Now you need to make a very important choice. You can head for the room where questions get asked. Or you can take the easy way out and head home. . . .
>
> If you hang up within the next 30 seconds then I will know that you have taken the easy route and are ready to quit. If you want to quit, hang up right now. I will sit quietly while you decide.
>
> But if you stay on the line then your state of mind is clear to me.
> [PAUSE FOR 25 SECS]   (Blast Theory 2009: 17 and 31)

This is an intense moment for participants and the importance of their decision is stressed by the narrator through clear deontic modality ('need') and the intensifier 'very'. The narrator's words are also emotionally charged: the repetition of 'easy' in the colloquial collocations 'easy way out' and 'easy route' and of 'quit' in the verb phrases 'ready to quit' and 'want to quit' imply that hanging up represents an inferior choice.

If a participant does hang up, they receive one final call (7b) in which they are directed back to their starting location, where they return the mobile and the narrative ends. During the walk, the narrator first reacts to the act of hanging up and then completes the story. Participants in Eamon's narrative initially hear: 'So, there is not much more to say. You've taken the easy route. You spilled your guts to the British. Names, dates, details. Everyone who ever came near you got fingered by your evidence' (p. 32). In this sequence of categorical statements, the narrator's tone has certainly changed. It is accusative, using 'easy' to reinforce the inferiority associated with hanging up. Additionally, the repetition of the second person in subject position is used to apportion blame, setting a pattern from which it then deviates in order to cast the new grammatical subject

'Everyone' as your victims. In Ulrike's narrative, participants are similarly berated: 'OK, you have chosen to say nothing. I'm disappointed. What are our actions if we cannot explain them? And once the actions are over – once no more action is possible – what, then, are we left with Ulrike?' (p. 17). The narrator poses a series of emotive rhetorical questions. Still addressed to Ulrike, they are designed to make the participant question whether they have made the right choice. Moreover, the use of inclusive first-person 'we' suggests that, in hanging up, the participant has 'disappointed' not just the narrator but a larger subjective group – all of the people around you for whom you said in your recording there was something you could do to help in some way, including the person with the treasured possession and their loved one.

In the remainder of this final call, participants are told of Ulrike's/ Eamon's death. This is an eerie experience and one which becomes too incompatible with the participant's own circumstances in order to maintain doubly deictic alignment. Participants in Eamon's narrative are told: 'When they found your body it was so battered that they thought you'd been hit by a car. It was only later that they could establish that your attackers had used hammers to kill you' (p. 33), while participants in Ulrike's narrative hear: 'You are 41 years old when you tear a towel into long thin strips, weave them into a rope, thread them through the bars in your cell and tie them around your neck. Then you kick away the stool. It is May 9th 1976. Mother's Day' (pp. 17–18). Although both narratives continue to use second-person address, they foreground a past temporality which eases participants out of such strong connection with character. In Eamon's narrative, this is the first consistent use of past tense whereas in Ulrike's narrative, despite maintaining the historical present tense, the date is explicitly mentioned as is Ulrike's age which is likely to differ from the participant's thus allowing the mismatch to aid in the process of dis-identification. Nevertheless, I suggest that, since the participant has been subject to an intense process of psychological projection through doubly deictic self-implication and perspective-taking, the deaths of these characters is nevertheless poignantly felt.

The room: what would you fight for?

Participants who choose, at the end of Call 7 to stay on the line, are warned at the start of Call 8: 'Ulrike?/Eamon? You've made your choice. I hope you're sure about this' (pp. 18 and 33). Over Calls 8–12, they hear more stories from Ulrike and Eamon's lives and are directed to a new location where they meet with a stranger (from the *Ulrike and Eamon Compliant* team) who leads them into a concealed wooden room. This is when the interview begins. Blast Theory describe this interview in the introduction to the narrative's text in the following way:

> The interviewer invites you to sit down and asks you their first question: 'What would you fight for?' They do not refer to you using the name Ulrike or Eamon. Over the next few minutes they explore whether you would kill. They may ask, 'what would you do if people came into your area and killed your friends and neighbours?' or 'are your beliefs rational or emotional?' They probe for inconsistencies in your stance and the gap between your ideas of social engagement and the reality of your lifestyle. The last question they ask is, 'are you a hesitant or a decisive person?'
>
> (Blast Theory 2009: 7)

The interview is unsettling, for it once again causes conflict for participants in terms of whether they should speak as themselves or in character. This ambiguity is deliberately exploited by Blast Theory, as is evident in the fact that the interviewer does not address participants by name (character or otherwise). Having enlisted your compassion for, even self-implication and empathy with, a militant terrorist, the interview compels participants to reflect upon the morality and ethical implications of this identification.

For participants who struggle to detach the doubly deictic alignment of their own identities with the character of Ulrike or Eamon, this interview is therefore highly disconcerting. For instance, I found myself at times repeating phrases from Ulrike's narrative, words she (I?) had supposedly said: 'If you set fire to a car, it's a crime. If a hundred cars are set on fire that's political.' I recall trying to utter these words with conviction yet found myself experiencing misgivings, doubts. Reflecting on the purpose of this final stage of *Ulrike and Eamon Compliant*, Adams (2009) comments that in the context of the narrative it is designed to

> engage you in thinking about your relationship to these two extreme characters and invite you into a world or into a place where it's inherently complex and uncomfortable. You know, you cannot either disregard them as complete psychopaths nor can you in any way condone the choices they've made in their lives. And so you have to try to position yourself in relation to them, and for us [Blast Theory] that's a very interesting thing to do personally and politically.

Ultimately, then, in *Ulrike and Eamon Compliant* Blast Theory play with the boundaries between text-world and discourse-world, with the participant's anchoring and investment of self and with their (non-)recognition of the fictionality of the mobile narrative not simply to provide an aesthetically absorbing and interactive experience. On the contrary, their aesthetics are inherently political. They are testing your compliance. Thus, the final question, 'Are you a hesitant or decisive person?' does not merely recall the narrative's opening for neat stylistic symmetry. The act of answering reminds you just how compliant you are.

Conclusion

As with all approaches to fictionality, stylistic accounts are concerned with the ability to distinguish between the fictive and the real. Crucially, stylistics is able to explore fictionality not merely as a state created by linguistic devices or ontological borders. It acknowledges these and more. A stylistics of fictionality considers the ways in which readers interpret textual structures in order to create fictive worlds, including their ontological borders. By focusing on readers' contextual understandings, stylistic accounts are able to recognise how such fictional worlds are not only experienced but how closely related or how far divorced those fictional worlds seem to be from readers' realities.

The semipermeable membrane of fiction has always allowed for readers to feel transported into fictional worlds or to feel as though narrators or characters transcend fiction's limits in order to escape into conversation with readers in the discourse-world. These illusions, however, are more striking in texts (such as multimodal, multimedial or hypertextual works) where readers must engage physically with the narrative. Mobile narratives set in real-world locations and in which readers seemingly respond through embodied actions to the text and/or its narrators make this deception all the more convincing. This analysis of *Ulrike and Eamon Compliant* has shown the ways in which second-person metaleptic address can be utilised in order to contextually anchor the fictive text-world within the participant's discourse-world.

Blast Theory cleverly overlay text and context in order to disguise much of *Ulrike and Eamon Compliant*'s fictionality. In doing so, the narrator appears to breach the semipermeable membrane in order to share the reader's world-space while the reader forges such a strong doubly deictic identity with character that they appear to both remain in the discourse-world and penetrate the text-world. Blast Theory artist Matt Adams claims (2009: 'What participants experience') that 'by crossing that threshold and by putting yourself into this world where you're exposed to some degree, you have a very powerful relationship. And what that means is that the work is heavily tailored to you as an individual.' If, in participating in an interactive mobile narrative, you feel as though you are part of the fictional world, a stylistics of fictionality, unlike other approaches to fictionality, is capable of showing you how you got there.

28

Emotions, feelings and stylistics

David S. Miall

The primacy of feelings

The recent turn to an embodied conception of cognition brings with it several significant implications for understanding literature and the processes of reading. I will begin with three important points made by Ralph Ellis (2005) in *Curious Emotions*, who puts these forward as foundational. First, he emphasises the primacy of emotions: 'fully intentional emotions, whether conscious or not, actually ground and shape all other conscious states' (2005: 4). Emotion is thus not, as it is commonly understood, a reaction to a prior cognitive appraisal of a situation, but an already functioning stance towards the world, interpreting the environment in pursuit of our existing aims – such as the insights we often gain about ourselves from the emotional experience of empathising with a character in a narrative. Second, beyond the pervasive functioning of homeostasis, Ellis develops the concept of 'extropy': this, as he puts it, is 'the maintenance of a suitably complex and higher-energy pattern of overall activity for the organism' (2005: 4). Through extropy we pursue and may realise our aims, enabling us to identify and benefit from more elaborate conceptions – through the aroused process of literary reading, for instance, when we enjoy the complexities of bringing together setting, character, and narrative stance. Third, the cognitive system seems primarily designed for action. As Ralph Ellis points out, the occipital lobe that processes vision only begins to do so some 200 milliseconds after the mid-brain and cerebellum have already triggered the motor cortex. 'When we then reflect on why we feel the way we do, the feeling reveals itself as already having been intentionally directed to the action affordances of an object or environmental situation' (2005: 25). While we are reading there is, of course, no possibility of realising the movement called for by a description of action, but this has potential literary implications for a reader: in Ellis's account, 'when we actually perform an action, we do not pay much if any conscious attention to the action imagery. It is when we inhibit the motor command that we are most fully conscious of the action image as a mental image' (2005: 42–3). This helps to account for the vividness of narratives that present themselves through the reader's mental imagery for action.

These three issues – primacy of emotion, extropy and images of action – do not supersede cognition as vehicles for understanding the processes of literary reading – that is, cognitive concerns such as deixis, worlds theories or conceptual metaphor – but they do appear to argue for revising our set of priorities in seeking to understand the processes of response in literary reading, and how the literary may differ in significant ways from other forms and modes of reading. These three issues also effect a significant change in the discourse about a literary text: where this has been dominated until now by the insistence on interpretation – for example, Stanley Fish's (1980: 355) comment that 'interpretation is the only game in town' – a shift has been taking place towards our experience of literature; that is, its impact on our feelings, imagery, autobiographical memory, selfconcept issues and the like. Among the aims of the present chapter is to remind readers of the experiential resources that they can bring to bear on a literary text, and to outline ways in which an awareness of these and an ability to articulate them can facilitate appreciation of a text.

To provide an illustration of some of these possibilities, I will offer brief comments on the following well-known poem by Blake, from *Songs of Innocence and Experience* (1794):

O Rose, thou art sick!
The invisible worm
That flies in the night,
In the howling storm,

Has found out thy bed
Of crimson joy:
And his dark secret love
Does thy life destroy.

To begin with the metre, there is a striking contrast in pace of movement, if we compare the first line with the following three or four lines: at first the Rose, devoid of movement, is immobile and stately, although this is soon qualified by the term *sick*. This first line, which obliges us to pronounce it slowly, has three evident stresses (O *Rose*, *thou* art *sick*!), but also has a fourth, unvoiced stress, at the end of the line. Here in this apparently blank moment the feelings that are generated create a space for all the (so far) unnamed implications of sickness to be guessed at. The feelings this calls into play seem ahead of our ability to understand the predicament of the Rose. The next line is pronounced much more rapidly – to be precise, twice as fast. Where the first line has four stresses, the next line has only two but accommodates six syllables, as does the first if the unvoiced stress is counted. This gives the worm a striking rapidity in its transit through the night.

But look again: the worm is invisible. Not only is the imagery of our response to the worm's action inhibited in representing its flight, which makes it the more vivid, but where it should be on the inner mental radar it cannot be seen, giving it an uncanny presence. Note that, in the case of negatives, the brain creates the object in question first, then cancels it, just as the worm is both there and not there. The potency of this uncanny worm is increased, of course, by its ascendency over night and storm, a power through which its threat to the Rose is portended. The impact of this power is the greater for the main verb in this sentence, 'Has found out', being delayed until the second verse. The emotions in play by now are likely to be complex and conflicting. A principle part of extropy is the active nature of our current emotions: as Ellis notes, 'Emotions are not responses to stimuli, but instead are ongoing, holistically motivated processes that attempt to use environmental affordances to further their self-organizational aims' (2005: 47). Thus by now the individual reader has probably already experienced, although perhaps not in full consciousness, feelings both for the predicament of the Rose and feelings of threat due to the worm's affordances as antagonist – and found that these embody conflict. Extropy includes the monitoring of such threats, which for a given reader may envisage the worm as an identity for Satan, as a representation of a plague, or one or other of the individual's acquired or invented meanings for such a portentious worm. But with the arrival of the main verb, 'Has found out', the poem baulks at stating a clear meaning to the conflict, since 'found out' can mean either an act of discovery (e.g. I *have found out* where you keep your money) or an attribution of guilt (e.g. I *have found out* that you stole the money). Such an ambivalence develops the affordances of Rose and worm; in particular it projects back to the status of the Rose and the worm, and forward to the 'bed / Of crimson joy', which raises its own conflicts of feeling: is the bed the site of a rape by the worm; or is it the site of an illegitimate desire to which the worm has found its way? Our sense (driven by the conflicts of feeling) is that large issues are at stake, but that now, and perhaps for all time, they are unresolvable. The 'dark secret love' works its destruction, but whether this is due to the Rose being sick with desire or whether the worm is the prime agent in introducing the sickness, we cannot decide – and, given the issues at stake, this is evidence of the power of this poem as a literary text.

Thus we note how the poem, through evoking conflicts in feeling, projects several possible larger meanings – meanings that seem uncountable and inexhaustible. The emphasis I have placed on feelings is due to several factors: first, the evidence (Griffiths 1997; Panksepp 1998) that emotions do not comprise one large system, but that each emotion is active through its own neural circuits. This finding is evident in many literary texts where a given feeling may often conflict with a subsequent feeling. We have previously noted (Miall and Kuiken 2002a) that Aristotle's model of catharsis, where pity and fear conflict, is one example of a conflict between feelings. Second, feelings project a state of emotion that brings with it its own history of individual and socially situated meanings, and as a central organising principle a state that can be regarded as a prototype (e.g. Hogan 2003: 86–9) – that is, how a given emotion is typically felt. In this respect feelings embody narrative-like scripts that inform us where a feeling has emerged and what it has meant in the past, as well as anticipatory intuitions about what the feeling might mean in the future. In this respect emotions seem likely to play a primary role in our experience as literary readers, shaping response, staging conflict, marking the limits of understanding. Third, depending on context, emotions are to some degree distinctive to the individual. As readers we bring to bear our own emotion prototypes and the links they have forged to the concerns of the self-concept, our autobiographical memories, and how emotions serve to recall a given memory as Bartlett (1932: 53–4) showed; and how, based on these, the narratives about our progress through life that we compile explain ourselves to ourself and to others. In various ways literary reading draws upon, and may help to reorganise, our arrays of feelings, memories and concerns.

In reading 'The Sick Rose' we paid attention to certain words or phrases that seemed important to shaping response to the poem: the significance of some of these can be restated as follows. The term 'sick' forms a striking conclusion to the first line, helping to personify the Rose (a stance already suggested by the initial apostrophe, as though the Rose was capable of understanding if spoken to). The 'worm' that is 'invisible' intimates a dimension of the universe beyond the mundane (especially when tracked through a 'howling storm'), a dimension that already seems to connote a threat. To have 'found out' the Rose, in either sense of the term, signals a feat of navigation that further develops the uncanny resources of the worm. I point these terms out in particular, because they seem among the most striking words or phrases in the poem for two reasons: first because they play a central role in developing the cluster of feelings that dominates at least a first reading of the poem; and second because they demonstrate a pattern of foregrounding in the poem that is important for motivating the reader's sense of significance, shaping experience of the poem as a whole. The motivation to read the poem through the network of feelings and foregrounding can be termed extropic, defined by Ellis as a 'preference for high-energy states' (R. D. Ellis 2005: 14); a will, we can say in the present case, to pursue the indefinable fate of the Rose, wherever that might lead, and to whatever degree we might find that pursuit uncomfortable or troubling.

These suppositions about reading the poem, however, call for empirical verification with real readers: one procedure would be to ask readers to identify the words or phrases that seem the most important in the poem, or that seem the most striking or evocative. These are not the same question: importance points to the words that lead most convincingly to an understanding of the poem; those that are striking or evocative make the greatest contribution to the reader's felt experience of the poem. Would readers, given either question, point to the words that I have been discussing and which I have found the most striking?

To return to the question of the extropic is to approach an answer to the question why we read literary texts such as 'The Sick Rose' and find them both important and troubling. In Ellis's terms 'we need to have *novelty*, because novelty affords extropic activity'; to read a poem is to 'find ways to further concretely *embody* our conscious states so as to *amplify* them, which entails symbolization' (2005: 125). Hence the symbols of the Rose and the invisible worm, which function so as to elicit that sense of the uncanny and to elaborate it, giving rise to perspectives that we seem only to half-comprehend however often we reread the poem. And central to this experience is the role of feelings and emotions. How are we to understand more systematically what feeling contributes, when and how it acts as a principal vehicle for the literary experience? In the next section I describe several studies that give some purchase on a particular aspect of feeling and how it supports a literary response.

Three empirical studies of feelings and texts

The first study I describe (Miall 2006: 60–5) was with readers of a short story by Virginia Woolf (1989), 'Together and Apart'. It showed how feelings play a primary role in developing readers' understanding, in particular how feelings contrast or at times conflict. In this brief story Miss Anning and Mr Serle are introduced at a party and try to engage in conversation. In the opening section of the story (about one page) the phrases of the story can be placed in one of two categories: either indicating a possible relationship of the two characters, or describing the setting (which includes the sky and the moon). In the study, all the readers read the opening section of the story first; they then received a version of the opening divided into phrases (fifty-six in all) for the purpose of rating. One group of readers rated the phrases for intensity of feeling on a six-point scale; then they attempted to recall as many phrases as they could. A second group of readers rated the phrases for importance (also on a six-point scale), then went on on to read the rest of the story, after which they rated the opening set of phrases for importance a second time. Readers also made written comments about their responses before completing the ratings.

Results showed that the understanding of the first group was dominated by the prospect of a relationship between the two characters. These readers, who rated for feeling, recalled an average of 14.65 phrases, but 'relationship' phrases were recalled significantly more frequently than 'sky and setting'. In contrast, the sky and setting phrases were generally recalled by only half or fewer of these participants. For the second group, however, who rated for importance before and after reading the whole story, the 'relationship' phrases, also rated as more significant at first, declined in rated importance at a second reading. Yet several of the sky and setting phrases rated for feeling by the first group received ratings as high as those for the relationship phrases. It seems likely that the intensity of feeling in such phrases became available to readers later in their reading: as the relationship faltered so readers were able to draw upon the sky and setting phrases for their felt potential in re-construing the meaning of the story. The strong feeling attached to such phrases, in other words, tended to predict their subsequent importance in understanding the story. Some readers showed an awareness of an undercurrent created by references to the sky and setting, which might either support or cut across the relationship. As one put it, having only read the opening section, 'the introduction of the idea of futility, insignificance. Although only shown so far in relation to the vastness of the sky, I feel the author may well take this further, bring it down to a more internalised level with all its attendant dangers.' By the end of the story the failure of the potential relationship has become the main concern for readers, and some refer back to the setting phrases to bring this into focus: for example, 'Moon and sky – awesome, tend to show the unimportance of people's lives. They are not particularly romantic symbols – emotion is stunted and undeveloped.'

The study shows that feelings in response to the Woolf story were driven by two major perspectives. At first most readers gave prominence to only one – the prospective relationship. But, after the possibility of this declines on the second or third page, responses by the end of the story showed that readers had turned to the sky and setting descriptions to provide an alternative construal of the story. At the same time the traditional romantic associations of the moon have had to shift: the sky and moon now signified emptiness and the impossibility of genuine communication. The feelings central to the two perspectives have been found to conflict, and the second essentially cancels the first, or (depending on the reader) modifies it in such a way that its familiar meanings, while still in play, are rendered ineffectual. Readers who began by investing in the relationship perspective were likely to find themselves troubled by its evacuation as the story progresses. And, for some, it was this sense of conflict unresolved that remained: as one reader put it, 'Story is about communication and the rejection of it, or inability to accept it and its implications. Love akin to dislike – preconceived notions being destroyed.' This suggests one way of approaching the literariness of a text: through the conflicts or ambiguities of feeling that it makes evident.

The second study I will describe is based on the premise that words or phonemes have a relatively stable affective meaning, if this is examined over a large enough corpus of text. In her work Cynthia Whissell (2001) compiled a *Dictionary of Affect in Language* by obtaining ratings of words on a scale of 1 to 3 from several participants, where ratings were for pleasantness, activation and imagery. The resulting *Dictionary*, consisting of 8,700 words, provides a score of the words in a given text based on an emotional space in which all words can be placed. The space is defined by two dimensions: Pleasantness-evaluation and Activation. Whissell made a study of Blake's volume *Songs of Innocence and Experience* (1798/1794). She predicted that the Blake poems would evoke more imagery than materials relating to standard English (comparisons were made to a sample of English from a number of media consisting of 350,000 words), and she predicted that there should be emotional differences as measured by the *Dictionary* when comparing the *Innocence* with the *Experience* poems. She found that *Innocence* was significantly more pleasant than *Experience* (1.94 to 1.88), and both were higher than the normative corpus (1.85). Also, *Innocence* was higher on activation (1.69 to 1.67). Imagery scores (1.67, 1.68) did not differ, but were significantly higher than the corpus (1.53). Overall, words high in emotion constituted 33 per cent of the normative corpus, but were 40 per cent of Blake's writing. For example:

> A scan of the poem The Sick Rose … indicates the presence of several extreme emotional words of different types. 'Sick', 'worm', 'howling', 'storm', 'dark', and 'destroy' are the unpleasant words which create the mood of the poem. They do this, however, when placed in juxtaposition to 'rose', 'joy', and 'love', which are their counterpoints.
>
> *(Whissell 2001: 465)*

The method is effective in drawing attention to the relative emotionality of a text. One limitation of the dictionary approach, as Whissell notes, is that 'the meaning of a word cannot be modified by the context in which the word occurs' (2001: 466). 'Rose' may mean the flower; or it may be a verb, as in 'He rose to the surface.' Over a large sample, however, the problem of multiple meanings is unlikely to seriously skew the findings.

In another, recent study (Whissell 2011), Whissell develops a wider range of categories: pleasant–unpleasant, cheerful–sad, active–passive, nasty, soft. These are used to score passages from Milton's *Paradise Lost*; but now resorting to counting phonemes where these are reckoned to convey a particular affective meaning derived from the words in which they occur. This is to suggest that words may have an intrinsic meaning, which has not been a popular view among scholars who, following Saussure, argued for the arbitrariness of the sound of words. But Whissell suggests some counter-examples: the long-e (phonemically /iː/) that occurs in words for happiness (happy, peace); the /əʊ/ sound of sad words (lonely, low); the /g/ that characterises a sense of disgust (grasp, guilty). The plosives /p/ and /t/ occur more often in words judged to be active. With this extended scheme Whissell demonstrates how poems can be scored in terms of their distinctive usage of the different classes of sound (2011: 258). In this way, as A. Pope (1980: 67) puts it, 'The sound' will 'seem an echo to the sense'.

For the study of *Paradise Lost*, phonemes are separately scored for occurrences of previously coded feelings (such as the presence of pleasant phonemes, /ə/, /v/, /ɪ/, etc.), and the presence of each feeling is then compared to the norms for the poem overall. In this way, a sample of lines can, for example, be judged less pleasant and more active (Whissell 2011: 259). The pattern of pleasant and passive sounds reveals three successive narratives within the poem, derived from marked changes in the frequencies of a class of feelings from high to low or low to high. For instance, she notes that 'The central narrative [Books IV to IX] has an unhappy ending and is tragic in form. It begins with Adam and Eve in the Garden and descends to a trough for the use of Pleasant sounds in Book IX, where the two succumb to temptation' (Whissell 2011: 264). Such results 'confirm that the sound narrative of *Paradise Lost* enhances the poem's story narrative, and that those listening to a verbal rendition of the poem would be exposed to appropriate emotional sounds at various points of the narrative' (2011: 265). The value of being able to identify the shifts of feeling inherent in such patterns of sound is suggested by T. S. Eliot (1964). In his definition of the 'auditory imagination' he describes it as 'a feeling for syllable and rhythm, penetrating far below the conscious levels of thought and feeling, invigorating every word; sinking to the most primitive and forgotten and returning to the origin and bringing something back, seeking the beginning and the end' (1964: 118–19).

Whissell's work employing these and related techniques includes study of a Dickens novel, Pope's translation of Homer, the poetry of Emily Dickinson, and the lyrics of the Beatles (Whissell 2006, 2004a, 2004b, 1999). Each of her studies depends on one form or another of the *Dictionary of Affect*, which presupposes that words and phonemes have a fixed affective meaning.

A third study of feelings to be outlined here is based on the observation that certain classes of words connote an affective stance or attitude. Biber and Finegan (1989b) looked at various linguistic indicators of speaker's affect (i.e. feelings, emotions or moods) and signs of evidentiality, as they termed it (i.e. a speaker's attitude, its reliability or adequacy). Markers of evidentiality and affect were counted in four grammatical categories – verbs, adjectives, adverbs and modals – where these showed affect (positive or negative) or evidentiality (certainty or doubt). The texts studied were restricted to those presented in the first person. One other restriction noted was that, in the case of the spoken sample, intonation and other paralinguistic features were not included in the analysis. Among the categories of words included were: doubt verbs (disbelieve, expect, feel), certainty adjectives (impossible, true, undeniable), positive affect expressions (enjoy, hope, prefer), negative affect adjectives (alarmed, irritated, shocked), hedges (almost, maybe, sort of), possibility modals (may, might, could), and predictive modals (will, would, shall).

The occurrences of these words in a wide sampling of texts in twenty-four different genres were counted by computer. The counts were then subjected to cluster analysis, which brings together texts where the same features tend to co-occur in several larger clusters. Among their findings, analysis showed that overt expressions of affect were largely confined to one cluster: these include 'frequent emphatics, certainty verbs, doubt verbs, hedges, and possibility modals'; and the genres of texts primarily involved were personal letters, face-to-face conversations and telephone conversations. Otherwise just one romance fiction occurred in this grouping, but no other fiction. Fiction more generally occurred in a second cluster, which they termed the 'Faceless stance', since stance features were markedly absent: 90 per cent of general fiction was grouped as faceless, also 92 per cent of adventure fiction, 85 per cent of mystery fiction, 100 per cent of science fiction, and some romance fiction (38 per cent). The reason for the faceless finding is said to be that fiction is expressed largely in an expository mode, emphasising the information being presented as if it were factual – that is, demonstrating a largely neutral style without markers of affect or stance (romance fiction being marginally different).

I describe this study here not only to present some of its findings, which seem surprising, but also as an example of a valuable methodology that might be adapted for other types of inquiry. The 'Faceless' finding seems at odds with the common assumption that reading literary fiction will usually be an emotional experience. Recall, however, that the fiction sampled was limited to first-person narratives: a different profile might emerge from extending the sampled texts to those in the third person (a follow-up study by Watson (1999) included second- and third-person texts and found increased affect as a result). The present approach misses examples of free indirect discourse, which typically conveys affective experiences by merging character and narrator points of view. It must also miss the evaluative comments typical of many third-person narrators (as in the fiction of Jane Austen or George Eliot).

The empirically based studies reviewed so far were based on the premise that affect plays an important role in reading. In the study of Miall (2006) it was suggested that two contrasting sources of feeling were a key to the development of a literary response to the Woolf short story. The several Whissell studies and that of Biber and Finegan (1989b) demonstrated top-down methods for identifying and classifying the presence of feeling, and, in the examples of Whissell, also providing insights into the structure of a literary text. The emphasis on the affective colouration of words and phrases in each of these studies is intended to draw attention to the primacy of feeling while reading; feeling appears to form a key part of the response to the verbal experience that is prior to its cognitive construal (the given-new construct, the installation of a schema, the drawing of inferences, and so on). This is supported by studies in evoked response potentials (ERP) studies that track the brain's first responses to a word or phrase: studies have shown that the detection of feeling occurs 150–200 milliseconds following the encounter with verbal prosody; the valence of feeling (i.e. whether positive or negative) is detected at 130–180 milliseconds (see Miall 2011 for a review). These findings, while not based on literary reading, present the possibility that feeling originates and helps determine the subsequent course of a literary response, including the selection and shaping of cognitive resources. This will be examined in the last section of this chapter.

Feelings in 'The Innocent'

A fourth study will now be presented in more detail, one that is currently under way, which aims to investigate the place of feeling in response to the discourse of an unreliable narrator. In brief, the argument to be pursued is whether the indeterminacy experienced in relation to the narrator's conflicting account of himself and the events of the story necessitates the reader's recourse to feeling as a mode of understanding. An initial report on this project has recently been published in the Italian journal *Fictions* (Miall 2012), which outlined the theoretical issues raised by the unreliable narrator and presented a report of an empirical study focusing in particular on the responses of readers to the first-person narrator of a short story by Graham Greene, 'The Innocent' (1973). This first contribution to the study will be summarised next, followed by a more detailed analysis of one reader's responses to the story and how far this casts light on the role of feeling and the question of its primacy in response.

That literary texts contain alternative perspectives is a common observation (see, for example, Schmidt's 1982 polyvalence thesis); the reader's response may be characterised by uncertainty, in which reflections on different possible meanings are indexed by feeling. The unreliable narrator contributes to this by providing, for instance, conflicting versions of an event, more than one way of accounting for the behaviour of a character, or an inadequate meaning for an action; these uncertainties occur as a consequence of a narrator whose understanding of what he or she relates appears to be limited or deficient. Thus a reader is impelled to attempt a framework for the narrative which accounts for its disparities. Critical discussions of the unreliable narrator have suggested that readers achieve such a frame by recourse to the supposed norms of an implied author, or by importing an interpretative frame of their own. The unreliable narrator, however, is motivated by the implied author, and may be a symptom of some larger problem that the implied author sets out to present. Resolving such issues by appeal to norms implies an objective world, which it may be the object of the text to challenge. The implied author can also be seen as the origin of decisions such as whether to present the narrative in first or third person, what style of discourse (e.g. ironic) is to be used, whether to include interior views of a character's subjective states, and the like. Such issues as they are first encountered by readers, given the uncertainties they raise, are likely to be installed as feelings – feelings that evolve and become more complex as the narrative progresses.

Readers will have resort to their feelings when encountering further uncertainties, seeking analogies in their own experience, memories or other texts to generate insights. At times, perhaps, the frame brought to bear proves inadequate and is itself modified in the light of the current narrative. Thus, I suggest, the issues raised by the unreliable narrator 'represent a class of problems whose larger significance it is the peculiar facility of the literary text to present'. The text is not designed to resolve such problems by resort to norms: 'Norms are what the literary text puts in question' (Miall 2012: 44).

This is the main question raised by our empirical study with the Greene story: to what extent readers notice norms and their violation in the discourse of the unreliable narrator, and what role feelings appear to play. To specify this in terms of textual features and readers' responses to them, we look particularly at ambiguities, plurisignations, vagueness and other modes of uncertainty, whether present in the text or created by the reader. For the reader, in Iser's terms, response to such features is central: 'the vital process of consistency-building is used to make the reader himself produce discrepancies, and as he becomes aware of both the discrepancies and the processes that have produced them, so he becomes more and more entangled in the text' (1978: 130).

'The Innocent' by Graham Greene (1973) consists of approximately 1,900 words. In it the narrator describes arriving back in the town where he grew up. He is with Lola, evidently an escort he had picked up in a bar and had paid five pounds to accompany him for the night. On an impulse, wanting to visit the country, they have come to this town, but the memories of his childhood are so strong that the narrator regrets having brought Lola here with him. He leaves her at the hotel bar and goes out to revisit the streets he used to know. Seeing a group of children coming down one street after dancing lessons he is reminded that he too took lessons at the same house when he was eight, and formed an intense love for the girl who partnered him. Convinced that she also loved him, but unable to get close to her, he recalls leaving a message for her in a hole in the garden gate. He finds the paper is still there, and to his surprise the message turns out to be an obscene picture of a man and a woman. Later that night he convinces himself that the picture is innocent. In his last comment in the story, he says 'I had believed I was drawing something with a meaning and beautiful; it was only now after thirty years of life that the picture seemed obscene.'

The story was reviewed for ambiguities in the strict sense as defined by Shlomith Rimmon; that is, two opposing propositions that 'remain equitenable and copresent' (Rimmon 1977: 9). We found three. Firstly, in describing his childhood the narrator remarks, 'they had been ordinary years'; whereas later he claims in reference to the girl that he knew from the dancing lessons, that 'I loved her with an intensity I have never felt since.' Secondly, speaking of the birthday parties they both attended, he says 'she always kept out of my way'; yet he also states that 'She liked me too.' Finally, perhaps the major ambiguity of the story, he remarks later that night that 'I began to realize the deep innocence of that drawing.' Do readers become 'entangled' in these ambiguities, and if so do they play a significant part in developing their sense of an unreliable narrator and an overall meaning for the story? And to what extent do readers respond in terms of feelings evoked by the unreliability of the narrator?

To collect responses to the story we solicited volunteers from senior classes in English and Comparative Literature at the University of Alberta. We obtained responses from over thirty readers in all. Readers were asked to read the Greene story on computer, one section at a time (the story was divided into twenty-two sections), and to think aloud as they did so. Their comments were recorded on tape for later transcription and analysis. In addition, readers were asked to respond to a questionnaire. First, before reading, they were given the title of the story and asked to suggest what the story might be about. After reading they were asked to choose three passages for specific comments. Finally they were asked several questions about their view of the characters and of the drawing that the narrator finds.

In the analysis that follows I focus on the comments of one female reader (I will call her J). J responds first to the title, 'The Innocent'. Her opening comments show her bringing to bear several quite complex concepts that might provide a first perspective on the story: she suggests a trial of someone as guilty who is actually innocent; she refers to pre-war persecution of Jews; and she says 'he' will accept the verdict 'along with all the others' because of his innocence. The use of such a term as 'The Innocent' as the title is certainly auspicious; but her comments already suggest several potential themes involving a life story, inflected in part by a sense of history. At the same time her comments are fraught with uncertainty, such as the odd locutions 'obviously maybe', 'he never really wanted to maybe save himself', 'it almost seems like', and a single reference to 'all the others'. J's resort to history also indicates her sense that the term 'innocence' lacks present-day currency except in carefully framed legal contexts.

So far, however, J's comments elaborate potential frames for the story; no feelings are mentioned. In response to the story itself, however, she comments on all but one of the twenty-two sections; of these, 20 of her comments mention feeling (12 refer to feelings of the reader, while 14 refer to feelings of the narrator, and of these 5 refer to both), and, among her 20 feeling comments, 13 specify ambiguities or uncertainties of some kind. In the earlier part of the story the feelings of the reader predominate: J feels that the two characters are running away from something, but finds it ambiguous whether in running to this small town they are starting anew or have come somewhere familiar. This sets up for the reader a central contrast of the story, since it turns out that for the narrator the town is familiar: he grew up here. For Lola the almshouses are 'grim'; for the narrator they are like 'music'. Yet for the narrator the visit is problematic, since he begins to recover some forgotten memories and wishes that Lola was not with him to distract him, especially, as the reader puts it, 'he remembers that that's the time that he felt innocent and didn't do anything wrong'. That the reader has some trouble here points to what will be the central ambiguity of the story: the reader is building on this remark of the narrator, 'I thought I knew what it was that held me. It was the smell of innocence.' Since in response to the next section she says, it 'now makes me think that he doesn't feel so innocent anymore being back to this place where he was before, or brings him back to an innocent time when everything seemed to make sense.' This begins to ask what the feelings of the narrator mean, and seems to bring into question his sense of innocence. Following her remarks on the title the reader has been alerted to ask this wider question, which represents perhaps the first indication of the unreliability of the narrator.

Following this opening phase of the story, which has established for the reader a tentative frame for understanding it, I will mention two other moments that develop this response. The narrator mentions leaving Lola at the hotel and setting out on his own to explore the town in the light of his memories. He remembers the girl he loved at dancing class as he stands outside the same house and hears a dancing lesson in progress. The narrator remarks, 'There *is* something about innocence one is never quite resigned to lose.' He then mentions how he aimed to leave a message for her in a hole on the gate outside, but that she never retrieved it and it was forgotten. The complex of feelings here is troubling for the reader, as shown by the broken syntax of her comments: 'I get a sense of regret now because the speaker didn't really get to express his feelings even though he was so young because there was really – you're not supposed to really, at that age, it seems like, so I get this feeling of regret.' It is as if the story at this point has expressed something too complex for the reader to articulate.

Finally the paper is retrieved by the narrator, and to his intense surprise he sees that it is an obscene picture of a man and a woman. The story now raises the question of its innocence. How is it to be judged? The reader appears to find particularly interesting the lack of a definite conclusion on the part of the narrator, since she seems to accept that the picture is open to alternative understandings. The ending shows, she says:

> that you've grown a bit but also maybe that innocence from when we're
> younger, its kind of nice, because you're not understand[ing] exactly,
> I mean you can interpret it different ways and other people can interpret it
> when you're that young because everybody sees things quite differently
> and quite out of the box compared to when you're older and an adult.

The term 'nice' in this comment suggests an aesthetic response, a feeling for the shape of the story as a whole; that despite the unreliability she has indicated in a number of her comments, the story is not just confusing, but that it intrigues her by offering alternative meanings. The reader has oriented herself through feeling at many points of the story where she has encountered or expressed uncertainty, among the most frequently occurring evidence for this being her empathy for the narrator. This can often be identifed through the use of the second-person pronoun, which seems to refer to both the reader and the narrator. For instance, when referring to the narrator's childhood love for the girl, the reader says: 'you know they [the girl] feel the same way about you but you just can't express it at such a young age so you can't really say anything but just go with it.'

We have analysed just a few of the comments of one reader here, and suggested how feeling underlies a sense of the narrator's unreliability in 'The Innocent'. This is shown in several ways. For example, feeling is implicated in the three conflicting perspectives that help to motivate the issues of the story: that of the narrator in the present; that of the narrator of the past, when he was a child growing up in the town; and that of Lola, who dislikes the town. We have already mentioned some of the conflicts that occur in the narration. Other problems of intepretation are also raised by the question whether the young girl liked the narrator, whether his love was returned – the boy and the girl seem to have had differing under-standings of this that creates contradictions in the narrative over how they regarded each other. In addition, at the end of the story we are faced with the narrator's hesitations over whether the drawing is innocent or not. What if the narrator's boyish interest in picturing human mating was known to the young girl? That would account for her keeping her distance. At a number of other points in the story other ambiguities occur which contribute to the sense of the narrator's unreliability – too many to men-tion here. Beyond the comments of the reader that we have reviewed we might also consider the figure of the implied author as a way of asking what issues are raised by the design of the unreliable narrator in this story, how far the language of feeling in the story seems likely to frame the reader's response, and what 'entanglements' occur in a reader's responses to the ambiguities of the story and in what ways are these productive. Further research would triangulate on these questions about literary reading: how far ambiguity is characteristic or even essential to a literary text such as this; or, more specifically, whether the reader's concept of the unreliable narrator is an agent for the feelings of the reader. There is much more to learn about the role of feelings in literary response. One aim of this chapter has been to show how empirical study of feelings offers an important vehicle for research on this topic.

29

Narrative structure

Ruth Page

Narrative and story

Storytelling is a pervasive activity that people use to make sense of themselves and their surrounding world. Stories occur in literary forms (such as poetry, prose, drama) or non-literary genres (such as life-writing, news media and advertisements), and can narrate fictional or 'real-life' events (or versions of events which blur the boundaries between such categories). Although narratives are often told using words, narrative analysis takes into account a wide range of multimodal resources, such as image, sound and gesture (Page 2010) and the many kinds of media used to transmit stories (Grisakova and Ryan 2010). In his seminal essay on narrative structure, Barthes (1977) reflected on the expansive nature of storytelling, concluding with the bold assertion that, 'Caring nothing for the division between good and bad literature, narrative is international, transhistorical, transcultural: it is simply there, like life itself' (1977: 79). Barthes's essay was just one of many attempts to uncover the universal patterns that set apart narrative as a distinct genre. From the 1960s onwards, academic interest in narratives and their structure has increased exponentially.

In what has been described as the 'narrative turn', it is not just narratives that appear to be everywhere, but also interpretations of their form and function. Within stylistics, narratives have been explored from phenomenological (Ricoeur 1984), cognitive (Turner 1996), sociolinguistic (Labov 1972) and literary perspectives, to name but a few. One outcome of the transdisciplinary expansion of narrative research is that what counts as a 'narrative' from these different perspectives can vary a great deal and, as Ryan (2006: 6) suggests, the meaning of the term 'narrative' has become considerably diluted. From the outset, it is important to distinguish between narrow and liberal uses of the term 'narrative'. At its most liberal, narrative has come to be quasi-synonymous with the concept of the 'script' or 'interpretive pattern', as in 'cultural narratives' or 'election narratives'.

While useful at an interpretive level, this rather general use of the term lacks semantic precision required for close textual analysis typical of stylistics. At the other end of the spectrum, 'narrative' can have very specific terminological referents, especially within the fields of narratology and poetics.

In these opening paragraphs, I have used the term 'story' and 'narrative' as if they were interchangeable. Classical narratology differentiates between these two terms. Building on the Saussurean separation of *langue* and *parole* (the underlying linguistic system and its individual realisation by particular speakers), narratologists distinguish similarly between *story* (the underlying event structure) and narrative *discourse* (the representation or narration of the events). Porter Abbott puts it like this: 'story is an event or sequence of events (the action), and narrative discourse is those events as represented' (2002: 16). The distinction between story and narrative discourse is useful insofar as it provides vocabulary for describing multiple narrations of the 'same story'. But there are many criticisms of the structuralist distinction – for example, that stories are themselves a representation, and that it is the narration which evokes the mental construction of a storyworld (rather than documenting pre-existing story events). Even in cases of adaptation or multiple retellings of a recognised account, Hutcheon (2006) cautions against assuming that there is an 'original', underlying story which can be retrospectively uncovered from the narrative discourse. The illustrative examples of narrative analysis provided later in this chapter return to this distinction and the problems that it poses.

In between the liberal and narrow definitions of 'narrative', there have been many attempts to establish the semantic and textual characteristics of narrative as a distinctive analytical category (as opposed to other categories such as expository discourse or instructional texts). The structural properties of a text are one of the criteria used in this definitive process. However, narratological and sociolinguistic traditions of narrative research articulate these structural criteria in slightly different ways (for example, with reference to various units such as clauses, or events, or episodes) and with rather different emphases. Given the literary-linguistic hybridity of stylistics, I will outline two examples of influential definitions of narrative: one which emerged from the literary-critical traditions of narratology, and one situated within sociolinguistic work on narrative.

Prince defines narrative as 'the representation of at least one event, one change in a state of affairs' (1999: 43). Based on this definition, eventhood is the minimum criterion for a text to be deemed a narrative, and the sentence 'Stephen Lawrence was murdered' would constitute a narrative, while 'Stephen Lawrence was a Black British teenager from Eltham, south-east London' would not. Beyond this primary criterion, Prince suggests that the connection between the narrated events can produce different kinds of narrativity, where causal connections are a preferred condition. Hence, 'Stephen Lawrence was murdered. Two men were convicted for the crime' is judged as showing more narrativity than the apparently disconnected pair of events 'Stephen Lawrence was murdered. Lawnmowers were on sale in all British gardening stores.' Furthermore, causally connected events should be combined into 'autonomous whole[s] (with a well-defined and interacting beginning, middle, and end) which involves some kind of conflict' (Prince 1999: 45). These structuring principles of eventhood, causality and plot-like sequencing are taken to be definitive of narrative (as a universally applied category), used to interpret texts which vary in length from a few sentences to more complex examples, such as short stories, novels or plays.

Classical narratology took folk tales (Propp 1968), myth (Lévi-Strauss 1955), and European literature (Barthes 1977; Genette 1980) as its object of study. In response (and reaction) to this literary focus, the sociolinguist William Labov claimed that we would know more about such complex narratives once 'the simplest and most fundamental narrative structures' were taken into account: oral narratives of personal experience (Labov and Waletzky 1967: 12). As part of his study of African American Vernacular English, Labov analysed a corpus of many hundreds of narratives elicited in interviews with the prompt question, 'Were you ever in danger of death?' Based on these narratives, Labov proposed the minimal definition of narrative as 'one method of recapitulating past experience by matching a verbal sequence of clauses to the sequence of events which (it is inferred) actually occurred' (Labov 1972: 359–60). This definition is at once more precise and narrow than that offered by Prince: constraining narrative to events told using past-tense verbs, focusing on the unit of the clause, and requiring that the temporal sequence of the narration match the sequence of the story events.

Labov's description of a 'fully formed' narrative is also more precise than Prince's description of narrative as an 'autonomous whole'. Rather than a general description of a 'beginning, middle and end', Labov outlined the larger, cohesive narrative structures into which narrative clauses are organised, where six narrative components of a 'fully formed' narrative could be glossed as follows:

Abstract:	what was this about?
Orientation:	who, when, what, where?
Complicating Action:	then what happened?
Evaluation:	so what?
Result:	what finally happened?
Coda:	returns the listener to the present time

(Labov 1972: 370)

It is only the Complicating Action that need be present in order for a text to fulfil the criterion of temporally sequenced events necessary to be classed as a narrative, but Labov argued that, for a narrative to be successful, it must also be reportable. Labov's concept of Evaluation (the means by which the narrator makes their telling engaging and meaningful to the audience), included a description of grammatical forms (such as intensifiers and comparators) which occurred typically in his dataset as a means of making a story more vivid. Labov regarded these devices as an open set, and later work has suggested that there may be other, culturally specific or modally restricted means of marking Evaluation (for example, through prosody or typography). While this grammatical typology of devices reflects the sociolinguistic interests of Labov's project (and has mostly been taken up in discourse-analytic traditions of narrative research that followed), his notion that a narrative must be tellable is in some respects similar to classical narratologists' observations that narratives should entail a disruption from the norm, often in the form of conflict which would later be resolved. However, classical narratologists such as Chatman (1978) and Prince (1999) argued that determining whether or not a narrative was 'tellable' was distinct from a text's perceived narrativity. After all, a narrative might not be a highly reportable narrative, but it can still be a narrative. Nonetheless, Evaluation plays an important structural role in Labov's description, and was used to demarcate the climactic turning point from Complicating Action to Resolution.

Taken together, the literary-critical and discourse-analytic definitions and descriptions of narrative suggest that the genre entails core structural features (it must contain events which are sequenced in time), and non-obligatory patterns of storytelling preferences, where narratives might be more or less tellable and follow a problem-solution trajectory towards a defined point of closure. Later narrative research has moved away from attempts to define a universal structure that can account for any and all narratives. Instead, the narrowness of definitions such as Labov's have been replaced by more flexible and relativist positions. In literary-critical approaches, discussions have moved towards the scalar concept of narrativity (the features which might prompt the perception of a text as more or less like a narrative). Discourse-analytic narrative research has followed a somewhat different path. Through analysis of many examples of narrative discourse beyond Labov's original corpus, linguists have documented a range of different dimensions of narrative (Ochs and Capps 2001), which include structural concerns (in Ochs and Capps's terms, 'linearity'), but set these alongside factors related to the context of narration itself, such as tellership and how far a story can be detached from the broader conversations in which it is told. Other work, such as J. R. Martin and Plum's (1997) systemic-functional study, identified a range of cognate story genres that sit alongside Labov's narratives of personal experience. These story genres are identified on the basis of the story's pragmatic function (for example, whether the story is told to entertain or to make a moral point), and also, crucially, on where the evaluative comment from the narrator is placed.

Unlike the Labovian paradigm with its climactic mid-point, Recounts are factual reports of events, and do not contain an evaluative focus. In further contrast, Anecdotes are told to build solidarity by prompting an affectual response from the narrator's audience, and are hallmarked by the presence of an evaluative punch-line that comes at the close (and not the mid-point) of the narrative sequence.

In the rest of this chapter, I will explore how far the core and non-obligatory elements of narrative structure occur in two texts which provide different responses to the same story: the murder of British teenager Stephen Lawrence. The analyses of these texts provide contrasting case-studies which test the structural definitions of narrative, and exemplify varying narrative genres. Finally, the case-studies illustrate the place of narrative structure in reaching interpretive conclusions of literary and non-literary texts, and suggest that these structural features can provide the basis for judgements about the function of particular narratives in their wider social and cultural contexts.

The murder of Stephen Lawrence: an outline of events

Stephen Lawrence was a Black British teenager, who lived in a suburb of south London. On the evening of 22 April 1993 he was attacked while waiting for a bus by five white youths shouting racial insults. He collapsed and bled to death on a nearby pavement, while trying to run away. Despite witnesses to the crime, no convictions were secured in the initial investigation. A civil inquiry followed two years later, which failed to reach a verdict on the grounds of insufficient evidence. It was not until January 2012, eighteen years after the attack, that two members of the gang (Gary Dobson and David Norris) were convicted of murder. At the time of writing, three members of the gang remain unconvicted for their involvement in events.

In the intervening years, the quest to achieve justice for Stephen Lawrence and his family achieved significant national impact. In 1998, a public inquiry was ordered by the Home Secretary, resulting in what became known as the Macpherson Report (1999). The report found significant failings on the part of the Metropolitan Police (including incompetent treatment of evidence in the initial investigation and inadequate responses at the scene of the crime) exposing 'institutional racism' and calling for reform not only in the police force but in government and the legal system. Although the report made plain the involvement of the five youths suspected of the attack, they could not be tried again until changes in the law took place in 2005. In 2006, under a cold-case review, new evidence resulting from forensic tests was brought to light, leading to the later trial (and conviction) of Dobson and Norris in 2011–12.

There have been many reports of and responses to Stephen Lawrence's murder and its aftermath. The national media in the United Kingdom covered each landmark event, to the point of saturation by the time of the Macpherson Report (Reinelt 2006). The growth of social media in the first decade of the twenty-first century led to further documentation and public response, with commentary of the 2011–12 trial published by bloggers, on the micro-blogging site Twitter, collated on a Facebook page (Justice for Stephen Lawrence) and an entry on Wikipedia. The events of the Macpherson inquiry were reworked as a play (*The Colour of Justice*, 1999) which later formed the basis of a 2006 BBC television documentary (*The Murder of Stephen Lawrence*). In 2006, Duwayne Brooks (the friend who was with Stephen when he was killed) published an autobiographical account, as did Doreen Lawrence (Stephen's mother). Poetic tributes included Benjamin Zephaniah's 'What Stephen Lawrence Has Taught Us' (2001) and Carol Ann Duffy's (2012) 'Stephen Lawrence'.

The complexity of the reports and responses to the Stephen Lawrence case which emerged over time illustrate neatly the problem of trying to define 'narrative' in narrow and liberal senses. The events of Stephen Lawrence's murder and its aftermath contain many elements that imply narrativity. The events took place in a temporal sequence; they self-evidently entail conflict, and the need for a resolution (for instance, in a quest for truth and for justice). Reinelt (2006) points out that the protagonists in the events fall readily into the narrative roles typical of an Aristotelian plot. Drawing on Propp's structuralist typology, we might describe Stephen as the victim, his parents as the heroes seeking justice, the members of the gang as villains, with the Macpherson report and attendant lawyers who acted on behalf of the Lawrence family cast as 'helpers'.

But it is less than easy to draw boundaries around the events that constitute the 'story' of the Stephen Lawrence case. Writing in 2012, at least four options are possible. The story could equate to the events that took place on 22 April 1993: the murder of Stephen Lawrence. In a narrow definition of narrative, this event alone is all that is required. But the murder itself was only the start of a series of events. In terms of a plot, the problem is only the initiating element of a narrative sequence (in Longacre's (1983) terms, the 'inciting moment'). In this case, the murder (the events of 22 April) was (and still is) part of a larger 'autonomous whole' which required a resolution in the identification and conviction of the killers. A third interpretation of the 'story' locates the murder of Stephen Lawrence within a trajectory of events that focuses instead on police behaviour, where the 'problem' to be resolved is not just the murder inquiry, but issue of 'institutional racism' in the Metropolitan Police, as addressed through the recommended reforms of the Macpherson report, and their relative success. Lastly, the case of Stephen Lawrence is part of a wider, cultural narrative of exposing and contesting racism, injustice and social inequality, where drawing discrete boundaries around particular events in isolation ignores the broader issues at stake.

Although there is no question that the murder of Stephen Lawrence happened, the 'story' of that event proved recoverable only through the narrative discourse found in the reports that followed: eyewitness accounts, police documents, inquiries, media reports and so on. These accounts exemplify the partial and selective nature of narrative, for the 'story' of Stephen's murder varied considerably according to the narrator in question. For example, Duwayne Brooks's (2006) account of the events of the evening of 22 April 1993 is quite different from those given by the suspected killers in the controversial BBC *Tonight* interviews with Martin Bashir screened in 1999. The serial unfolding of both the story events and the narrative discourse in time troubles the distinction between 'story' and 'narrative discourse' further, for the narration of the Stephen Lawrence murder in turn became part of the ongoing pursuit of the killers, the wider stories of reforming the Metropolitan Police and the call for social justice more generally. For example, in 1997, British tabloid the *Daily Mail* ran a front-page headline accusing the suspects of murder, and inviting them to sue the newspaper if they were innocent (the suspects did not). The Macpherson Report called for the legal reforms that later enabled Dobson and Norris to be tried for murder in 2011–12. At a micro-level, the narratives of eyewitness accounts were part of the police investigation, and were later retold within the mainstream media and books (such as Cathcart 2003). In the face of these many, sometimes conflicting accounts, which have evolved over time, it is clear that there is no single text or interpretation that will narrate the 'complete' story of the Stephen Lawrence case. Instead, I will take two examples that tell the story of Stephen Lawrence in very different ways, illustrating how an analysis of the narrative structure can help us understand differences in narrative genre and the different 'stories' in which the Stephen Lawrence case was embedded.

Wikipedia article: 'The Murder of Stephen Lawrence'

Social media genres have provided many different platforms to circulate information about and responses to the Stephen Lawrence case. One source of information is the Wikipedia article headed 'The Murder of Stephen Lawrence'. A Wikipedia article might seem an unlikely site for narrative discourse, and better suited to the expository discourse more typical of encyclopedia entries. I have argued elsewhere that the kinds of collaborative writing required for conventional narrativity are ill-suited to the bottom-up editorial practices of wiki-writing, where anyone can add their own content, change or remove the content written by someone else (Page 2012a). But given the chronological timeline that underpins the events which followed the murder of Stephen Lawrence, and the inherent narrativity of those events, the material collectively organised on the murder of Stephen Lawrence page does exhibit many narrative qualities.

Like other wikis, Wikipedia consists of web pages which anyone with access to the internet can edit. Every saved revision to a Wikipedia page is archived and can be retrieved in the history of that page, which records when the revisions were made, by whom, and may also include a summary of the changes that have been made. The article for 'The Murder of Stephen Lawrence' was first written on 4 November 2003. Between that date and 11 March 2012, it was edited 1,293 times by 594 different Wikipedia users. Not all of those users contributed to the creative process equally: over half the revisions were made by 10 per cent of the users (59 users), and, of those most frequent contributors, it is two users in particular who are responsible for most of the activity: FT2 and Graham87 both made over 100 revisions each. It is most likely that the article for Stephen Lawrence in Wikipedia will continue to evolve, and further changes will be made. Here I compare two versions: the initial stub written in November 2003 and the version most recent to the time of writing in March 2012. The stub published in November 2003 was relatively brief, consisting of 344 words. This is not unusual: most Wikipedia articles begin with a similarly brief outline to which more material can be added. Its relative brevity should not be regarded as a lack of interest or knowledge about the events on the part of the users who contributed. However, it does provide a starting point from which to trace the narrative development of the article in later years.

There are many different types of revisions made in the 9 years since the Stephen Lawrence Wikipedia article was started. These include adding new information or details that had been unavailable previously, revising the style of the article, correcting details, removing vandalism, providing further citations, and organising the material into headed sections. These processes of revision are typical of Wikipedia articles more generally (Myers 2010), and the editorial behaviour of FT2 and Graham87 reflects typical patterns of contributing to a wiki, where FT2 primarily contributed new material while Graham87's revisions tend to be more minor, correcting links and errors (B. Mason and Thomas 2008). But the history of the article's revisions tells a story of its own, which is interwoven with key turning points in the timeline of bringing about the convictions of the suspected killers between 2003 and 2012. Editing activity and the addition of new material to the article are not evenly distributed over time. Instead, new material began to be added more frequently after July 2006, once the cold review re-opened the case and when a further investigation into police corruption took place. But the most significant increase in editing and the addition of new material occurred in November 2011, when the trial of Dobson and Norris commenced. In this sense, the evolution of the article reflects the points at which the Stephen Lawrence case was most newsworthy, perhaps because, during these periods, more information about the case circulated in the mainstream news and was available as a source for the verifiability of the article (51 of the 75 sources cited in the references section of the article are from news reports). In turn, this suggests that while Wikipedia's principle for contributors might include 'neutral point of view', in fact the narrative development of the article might be shaped by wider news values which promote a particular event as more or less tellable at a given point in time.

Narrative structure of the article subheadings

Both versions of the Stephen Lawrence article are sub-divided into sections, which organise material into topics with subheadings which allow the reader to navigate through the entry. A summary of the table of contents for the 2003 and 2012 versions of the article is given in Table 29.1.

Clearly, the subheadings are not clauses that can form a narrative: they are noun phrases presented in a numerical list. However, they do refer to narrative events, or key elements in the story, such as its central protagonist: Stephen Lawrence. In both versions, the subheadings structure material so that the events are reported in an order which matches the chronological sequence in which they occurred (so conforming to Labov's definition of a narrative). The material is punctuated throughout by dates

Table 29.1 Table of contents for 2003 and 2012 versions of the Stephen Lawrence Wikipedia article.

2003 stub	2012 version
1. Stephen Lawrence	1. Stephen Lawrence
2. Macpherson Report	2. Murder
3. External Links	3. Trials
4. See also	3.1 Witnesses
	3.2 Initial investigations and prosecutions
	3.3 Private prosecution
	3.4 Subsequent events
	3.5 Cold case review and new evidence
	3.6 2011–2012 trial
	3.7 Immediate aftermath of trial
	3.8 Appeals
	4. Other inquiries and investigations
	4.1 The Stephen Lawrence inquiry
	4.2 Other public complaints and investigations
	4.3 2006 investigation into police corruption
	5. Legacy and recognition
	6. See also
	7. References
	8. Bibliography
	9. External links

which establish the timeline for events. For example, the 2003 section 'Stephen Lawrence' begins with his birth, 'Born in Britain in 1974 to Jamaican parents', and concludes with the *Daily Mail*'s intervention, 'In February 1997 the *Daily Mail* newspaper sensationally labelled the five suspects "Murderers".' The second 2003 section, 'Macpherson Report' follows this chronological sequence, opening with 'After two police inquiries found no cause for concern, the new Home Secretary Jack Straw ordered a public inquiry in 1977' (an incorrect date later corrected to 1997), ending with a statement of the report's outcome, 'Macpherson found that the police were institutionally racist, and made a total of 70 recommendations for reform in his report dated February 24, 1999.'

The headed sections in the 2012 revision follow a similarly chronological sequence. However, there are obvious differences between the narrative structures implied in the two versions. The timeline implied by the 2012 subheadings extends further to include events which occurred subsequent to 2003, such as the cold-case review, the 2011–12 trial, further investigation of the police corruption (sections 3.5–3.8, section 4.3, section 5), and the awards and charitable initiatives carried out in Stephen's memory. The timeline for the sub-sections also provides more detail about the events that took place, and separates the different narrative strands (the different 'stories') that were initiated by the murder in 1993. Section 2 provides a detailed account of the day of the murder, section 3 documents the event line related to the murder inquiry and the final conviction of the suspects, while section 4 deals with the national events that evolved in response to the problem of the police inquiry.

The narrativity implied by the sequenced sections in the 2012 version of the article also contrasts with that of the 2003 stub, especially regarding the extent to which the material is shaped into an 'autonomous whole' with a defined, value-laden end point. In 2003, the events of the case were still in process, and although Reinelt (2006) suggests that the Macpherson inquiry provided a climactic endpoint, there was much that remained unresolved. The narrativity of the 2003 article sequence is weak, for the 'plot-line' of the murder inquiry had not been completed. Hoey's (2001) description of the problem–solution pattern indicates that until a point of positive evaluation (signalling that the narrative's problem has been resolved) occurs, a reader's expectation is that the narrative pattern will continue to be recycled.

By the time that the article was revised in 2012, the 'beginning, middle and end' of the story of the murder inquiry, at least, could be told in full, culminating in the sentencing of Norris and Dobson (a positive outcome to the quest for justice). Likewise, the ongoing investigations into police corruption had reached at least a temporary end point, with a quotation stating: 'No further action will be taken against the two men arrested following concerns identified by the internal Metropolitan police service (MPS) review of the murder of Stephen Lawrence.' Moreover, the final section of the entry (5. Legacy and recognition) reinforces a sense of narrative closure by focusing on the positive legacy of the Lawrence case. The content of the final section appears to function as a Labovian coda, by bringing the reader back to the present time with a description of the ongoing charitable work carried out by the Stephen Lawrence Charitable Trust. The narration moves from past- to present-tense verbs:

> The Stephen Lawrence Charitable Trust is a national educational charity committed to the advancement of social justice. The Trust provides educational and employability workshops and mentoring schemes. It also awards architectural and landscape bursaries. In 2008 the Trust, with architects RMJM, created the initiative Architecture for Everyone to help promote architecture and the creative industries to young people from ethnic minorities.
>
> (underlining indicates hyperlinks in the original article)

The sense of positive evaluation is reinforced by the quote included from Doreen Lawrence, whose words are reported in direct speech:

> I would like Stephen to be remembered as a young man who had a future. He was well loved, and had he been given the chance to survive maybe he would have been the one to bridge the gap between black and white because he didn't distinguish between black or white. He saw people as people.

The undeniably tragic story of Stephen Lawrence's murder is thereby given a final outcome with a redemptive end point: one which speaks to the wider cultural narrative of racial injustice and recasts Stephen as the hero, rather than the victim of the events.

Narrativity: developing Evaluation

The changes made to the subheadings which organise the Wikipedia article suggest that revisions to that material have developed the story's narrativity, where the later version is more complex (signalling the multiple stories initiated by the Stephen Lawrence case) and appears more complete, with an implied point of closure. The evolving narrativity of the Wikipedia article is also apparent at the micro-level development of the text within each sub-section. A sentence-by-sentence analysis of the full article is beyond the scope of this discussion. Instead, I focus on the opening lines of the 2003 stub and the version available in March 2012.

Like all Wikipedia articles, 'The Murder of Stephen Lawrence' begins with a short summary which precedes the table of contents. The text presented in the opening summary is similar to a Labovian Abstract, insofar as it provides a concise account of what the following material will be about. In the case of the murder of Stephen Lawrence article, the summary found in both the 2003 and 2012 revisions follows a narrative structure. There are various differences between the two versions. Unsurprisingly, and in keeping with the evolution of the structure of the article as a whole, the summary of the 2012 version is longer than the one given in 2003 (in fact, five times longer). Also unsurprisingly, the 2012 summary makes reference to events that took place subsequent to 2003, such as the changes in the law in 2005 to allow a retrial, the cold-case review, and the 2011–12 trial and sentencing of Dobson and Norris. More importantly, the addition of new Evaluation material that makes a further contribution to the developing narrativity of the story that is told.

The first two paragraphs of each summary are reproduced below.

2003: opening summary

(1)   Stephen Lawrence was a black British teenager living in London, UK, who was murdered on April 22, 1993, aged 18.
(2)   While waiting at a bus stop he was attacked and stabbed by a number of white teenagers.
(3)   Whilst not the first such attack, but the publicity it received turned the case into a major national issue that threatened to cause civil disturbance and severely damaged relations between the Afro-Caribbean community, the Police and justice system.

2012: opening summary

(1)   Stephen Lawrence (13 September 1974 – 22 April 1993) was a Black British teenager from Eltham, south east London, who was murdered in a racist attack while waiting for a bus on the evening of 22 April 1993.
(2)   Witnesses said he was attacked by a gang of white youths chanting racist slogans. (3) After the initial investigation, five suspects were arrested but not convicted. (4) It was suggested during the course of that investigation that the murder was racially motivated and that Lawrence was killed because he was black, and that the handling of the case by the police and Crown Prosecution Service was affected by issues of race. (5) A public inquiry was held in 1998, headed by Sir William Macpherson, that examined the original Metropolitan Police Service (MPS) investigation and concluded that the force was 'institutionally racist'. (6) It also recommended that the double jeopardy rule should be abrogated in murder cases to allow a retrial upon new and compelling evidence; this became law in 2005. (7) The publication in 1999 of the resulting Macpherson Report has been called 'one of the most important moments in the modern history of criminal justice in Britain'. (8) The then-Home Secretary Jack Straw commented in 2012 that ordering the inquiry was 'the single most important decision I made as Home Secretary'. (9) In 2010 the case was described as being 'one of the highest-profile unsolved racially-motivated murders'.

(underlining showing hyperlinks)

The opening summary of the 2003 stub begins with Orientation (sentence 1), which describes the central protagonist, moving on to the Complicating Action in sentences two and three. The final sentence opens with a comparator, 'Whilst not the first such attack', and contains the intensifier 'severely' to indicate the national impact of the case on relations between 'the Afro-Caribbean community, the Police and justice system'. But in terms of Labov's framework, there is no external Evaluation from the narrator to signal why the events are significant, or to demarcate the transition between the Complicating Action and Result. In part, this might be because in 2003 there was no final result: the case was unresolved. However, the absence of Evaluation in the 2003 summary suggests that this narrative is closer to a Recount (J. R. Martin and Plum 1997) than the 'fully formed' Labovian narrative outline.

The summary given in the opening of the 2012 version similarly opens with Orientation (sentence 1) and then moves on to an account of the events in a section of Complicating Action (sentences 2–6). In contrast to the 2003 stub, the 2012 version is rich in Evaluation. The evaluative statements are clustered in sentences 7–9, where the Macpherson Report is described as 'one of the most important moments in the modern history of criminal justice in Britain'; the ordering of the report as 'the single most important decision I made as Home Secretary'; and the case as 'one of the highest-profile unsolved racially-motivated murders'. These superlative forms 'most important' and 'highest-profile' establish the tellability of the case in relation to national events with legal and political ramifications, where decisions made by leading politicians changed the 'history of criminal justice in Britain'.

Given that the events which are evaluated in the opening summary of the 2012 version had taken place several years prior to 2003, it is all the more notable that the original stub does not contain such Evaluation. One reason for this might be that the three evaluative statements are all quotations from material that was published after 2003: a BBC news report (2004), and articles from *The Times* (2012) and *The Independent* (2010) newspapers. The tellability of the events has become apparent retrospectively, as the narrative's level of significance emerged over time. The sources for the evaluative statements in this instance are quite different from that found in Labov's corpus. In keeping with Wikipedia's principles of 'neutral point of view' and the requirement that every statement must be verifiable (Myers 2010: 149), the tellability of the Stephen Lawrence case draws on external material, rather than appraisal made by a first-person narrator. Nonetheless, the position of the evaluative statements appears at the climactic turning point between identifying failure in police behaviour and the 'resolution' of the murder inquiry in the later trial and sentencing of the suspects. The inclusion of the evaluation thus turns a narrative Recount (without resolution) to a 'fully formed', tellable, narrative sequence.

In summary, the analysis of the Wikipedia article shows that both earlier and later versions are narratives (according to a narrow definition), for they document a series of events that emerged over time, matching the reporting of events to the sequence in which the events occurred. But the analysis of the structure of these articles suggests that their narrativity is somewhat different. The later revisions transform the narrative Recount found in the stub to a more complex account, with narrativity that conforms to a conventional, plot-like sequence that moves from complication to resolution. The structural organisation of the later revision reflects the multiple event lines generated by the story of Stephen Lawrence's murder: the murder inquiry, exposure and remedy of police corruption, and a wider cultural narrative of contesting racism and social injustice. The tellability of these stories is marked throughout, but the evaluative statements incorporated into the opening summary of the later revision suggest that it is the national-level legal and political reforms brought about by the Macpherson Report that in retrospect are most significant and form the pivotal turning point that enabled the resolution in at least two of the story strands.

What Stephen Lawrence has taught us

Published in 2001, Benjamin Zephaniah's poem is less a reconstruction of the story of Stephen Lawrence's murder, and more a reflection on those events, or more specifically, 'What Stephen Lawrence Has Taught Us'. In this response, it is less easy to establish a clear timeline of events, for there are no dates and times that document the story. Although the poem alludes to the setting for the murder itself ('the tedious task / of waiting for a bus'), the inquiry ('watching his parents watching the cover-up'), failure to convict the suspects ('They paraded before us / Like angels of death / Protected by the law') and police corruption ('institutionalised racism'), these allusions are not sequenced in the poem to match the order in which the events actually occurred: the murder scene is not mentioned until stanza three, and instead the poem opens with the statement that 'We know who the killers are.' The first four stanzas of the poem are reproduced below.

What Stephen Lawrence Has Taught Us

We know who the killers are,
We have watched them strut before us
As proud as sick Mussolinis,
We have watched them strut before us
Compassionless and arrogant,
They paraded before us,
Like angels of death
Protected by the law.

It is now an open secret
Black people do not have
Chips on their shoulders,
They just have injustice on their backs
And justice on their minds,
And now we know that the road to liberty
Is as long as the road from slavery.

The death of Stephen Lawrence
Has taught us to love each other
And never to take the tedious task
Of waiting for a bus for granted.
Watching his parents watching the cover-up
Begs the question
What are the trading standards here?
Why are we paying for a police force
That will not work for us?

The death of Stephen Lawrence
Has taught us
That we cannot let the illusion of freedom
Endow us with a false sense of security as we walk the streets,
The whole world can now watch
The academics and the super cops
Struggling to define institutionalised racism
As we continue to die in custody
As we continue emptying our pockets on the pavements,
And we continue to ask ourselves
Why is it so official
That black people are so often killed
Without killers?

While Zephaniah's poem tells a story of racial injustice, it is difficult to argue that the text is a narrative, in the narrow definition of the term. The past tense is used sparingly, occurring only in one line: 'They paraded before us, / Like angels of death / Protected by the law.' Instead, the poem favours the present perfect ('has taught us', 'have watched them'), non-finite forms ('Watching his parents', 'waiting for a bus', 'struggling to define') and present-tense verbs (such as 'know', 'have', 'is', 'begs', 'endow', 'watch'). Rather than a temporal sequence of clauses in the past tense, the temporality of the poem refuses to establish exact time frames and establishes a context which extends beyond particular events to a wider, ongoing situation.

At a surface level, this stylistic choice can be explained by the historical context of the poem. In 2001, the story of the murder inquiry and police corruption had not been resolved (even partially). Instead, the outcome that Zephaniah sets out is one of continued racial inequality, where the repeated refrain of 'The death of Stephen Lawrence / Has taught us' is followed by multiple morals, such as 'That we cannot let the illusion of freedom / Endow us with a false sense of security as we walk the streets' and 'that racism is easy'. In terms of narrative structure, it would seem that Zephaniah's poem is functioning more as a Labovian coda than a narrative in its own right. It brings the speaking voice and audience back to the present moment, with the repeated adverb, 'now', and, like other forms of narrative closure, makes a clear moral point. But the moral of Zephaniah's poem is that there is no closure to the story of racial inequality: the pursuit of justice for Stephen Lawrence, his family and for people of colour was, and is, ongoing.

The lack of narrative resolution is underscored by the use of Evaluation. Zephaniah's poem is rich in the devices that Labov described as internal evaluation, most notably comparators. Comparators imply duality, function by evaluating what happened with what might have happened, but did not. Examples of comparators include the use of modality, negation, questions, metaphors and similes, all of which abound in 'What Stephen Lawrence Has Taught Us'. Similes liken the killers to fascist figures, 'like sick Mussolinis' and 'angels of death'. Comparative statements point to ongoing racial injustice, 'They just have injustice on their backs / And justice on their minds'; 'the road to liberty / Is as long as the road from slavery'. Perhaps most pointedly, the questions asked at the ends of stanzas two and three are not given an answer:

> What are the trading standards here?
> Why are we paying for a police force
> That will not work for us?

> Why is it so official
> That black people are so often killed
> Without killers?

Comparators are an apt evaluative device in this context, for they construct parallels between what has happened (the murder of Stephen Lawrence) and what has not (justice at specific and societal levels). The evaluation thus clearly draws attention to aspects of the Stephen Lawrence murder case, but positions these within a wider, cultural narrative of racial injustice: a story which remains unresolved and ongoing, even after the convictions of Dobson and Norris in 2012.

Conclusion

The discussion of the story of Stephen Lawrence's murder in relation to the Wikipedia articles and Zephaniah's poem points to the ongoing value of narrative analysis in stylistics. Narrative structure can be defined in a narrow sense to identify which texts are more like narratives than others, and also used in a more liberal fashion to articulate the relationship between particular texts and wider cultural narratives. The differences in the versions of the Wikipedia article remind us that narrative genres can vary from unmodulated accounts of events (Recounts) to more plot-like sequences, where the tellability is shaped by the changing value of the story in a wider social context. Even when a text (like Zephaniah's poem) is less like a narrative (in its strictest definition), a close reading of the formal features typical of narrativity (such as the choice of verb tense or the use of Evaluation) is a valuable strategy for articulating how the text makes its 'point' to tell a broader story which reaches beyond the boundaries of a single text in isolation.

30

Performance

Tracy Cruickshank

Introduction

Claiming that performance is neglected by stylistics is certainly not new. While there are notable exceptions, existing stylistic analyses of drama and performance tend, necessarily perhaps, to ignore the performance event itself in both practice and theory. Examples of the drama in such work, furthermore, tend to be drawn from television and film rather than play texts or other writing for performance. There are, of course, sound reasons for such omissions. The performance event in practice is ambiguous and inaccessible after the fact, and its interpretation individual and in flux at levels of both production and reception. Film and television scripts are dramatic without the complicating shadow of liveness; their realisations, by and large, recordable and somewhat more firmly fixed. Stylistic vocabularies and critical frameworks, however, are useful and pertinent for studies in drama and performance, allowing for us to actually account for the performance event and the cognitive behaviour of its audience. Also, as discourse events rely as much on performative behaviours as linguistic, an analysis that is seen, at least in part, from the perspective of performance, might be of some interest and use to the field.

Where, traditionally, stylistics concentrates on dramatic dialogue, recent work in the broader field points to more embodied concerns. In *The Way We Think* (2002) Gilles Fauconnier and Mark Turner note how, in dramatic performance, spectators and actors deliberately 'live in the blend' of a network of mental spaces; an ability, they stress, that 'provides the motive for the entire activity' (2002: 266–7). Though not concerned themselves with drama and performance *per se*, their work on conceptual blending has influenced recent work in cognitive studies. At its most basic level conceptual blending theory (CBT) allows us to account for and to understand complex processes of thinking and imagining, and in the theatre such processes are explicit. Taking knowledge from the three mental concepts of actor, character and identity, spectators 'create an actor/character'; a selective process with which an actor similarly engages (McConachie 2008: 42–3). It is a process that can also be extended to explain theatre more broadly and, in particular, the peculiar 'doubleness' of performance where objects, words and bodies exist and operate in two places – one real and one imagined – all at once.

The theory is still in its infancy as an area of study, but Bruce McConachie and F. Elizabeth Hart (2006) point to the possibility for future research in the area in their collection of essays on theatre and the 'cognitive turn'. They claim that CBT validates and extends models of acting and performance put forward by Richard Schechner (1985) and Bert O. States (1985), although it is not an area that significantly features in their study. Amy Cook, however, bases her essay in *Stylistics and Shakespeare* (2011) on CBT in her analyses of *Hamlet* and *Richard III*, illustrating how the linguistic as well as cultural structures of a community affect interpretation, understanding and thinking. Any application in the present chapter of CBT is far more rudimentary and is used by way of developing an analysis of the representation of dramatic and fictional space and place in drama and performance. Begun with reference to Text World Theory (TWT), this exploration is based on the acceptance of different world types at the level of the text that, in turn, allows us to mentally inhabit a performance space (see Cruickshank and Lahey 2010; Werth 1999).

This chapter, then, looks to recent and established positions in the fields from which stylistics and performance might respectively be plucked and offers, with further reference to cognate critical theories, an analysis of Richard Bean's play *England People Very Nice* (2009) and Jez Butterworth's *Jerusalem* (2009). Beginning with a discussion of the performance and representation of England in the staged and fictional worlds of the plays, analysis later focuses on Mark Rylance's performance as Johnny Rooster Byron in the closing minutes of the 2011–12 production of *Jerusalem* at The Apollo Theatre, London (dir. Rickson 2011).

Staging the nation

Butterworth's 'dystopian hymn', *Jerusalem*, lends itself to analysis in a number of contexts (Coveney 2009). Hailed as 'a bold, ebullient and often hilarious State-of-England or (almost) State-of-Olde-England play' Butterworth's portrait of England is far from subtle, but it is a portrait that reflects concerns of national identity (Nightingale 2009). Bean's *England People Very Nice* similarly acts as a platform for discussion, debate and analysis but is itself a critique of various representations of place through its sometimes flagrantly derisive account of the history of England and its people. Both are plays in which boundaries and borders are crossed, between town and country, and between rural and urban territorial markers (visible and invisible) that constitute historical and cultural space and place. Both too are plays in which the construction, destruction and value of home are questioned in a variety of different, often conflicting, ways, and the plays have also been staged in theatres and by companies that are home to British writing and performance. Such homes are also implicitly and explicitly framed by notions of national identity. In both plays specific homes are defended, from a street in Bethnal Green to a rundown caravan in a clearing in a wood. But these homes are depicted in recognisable and atypical representations of England: the East End of London and the county of Wiltshire. As such they act as metaphors for an England both on and off the stage. The England represented in these two plays is an ambiguous one and is as ambiguously framed. It is a place of shifting identities where local, national and international relationships are negotiated and played out.

England People Very Nice and *Jerusalem*, then, are concerned with identity from a national perspective and question, or ask us to question not only the nation's place in the world but the defining qualities of those who belong to it. A discussion of them together provokes further questions about the nature of this nation: where England is more apt a location for the world represented and performed in *Jerusalem*, Britain is very much the geographical space and place conjured in relation to *England People Very Nice*, in spite of the play's title. In *Jerusalem*, of course, both England and Englishness specifically are celebrated and, in part, lamented. This is certainly not the case with *England People Very Nice* and, while the categorisation of plays about England as plays overly concerned with heritage and nostalgia is unhelpful, the performance of these in *Jerusalem* is striking: 'the Flintock Fair; Wesley's Morris dancing; the gang's anti-council protest; Byron's oral folkloric storytelling. *Jerusalem* is, in many ways, England (old and new) performed' (Harpin 2011: 66). At the start of the play we are confronted with quite visible signs of England, with faded flags and a 'rusted' railway sign for Waterloo (Butterworth 2009: 6). But these representations of an old world order are made somewhat more elderly than ancient by other ecologically unsound objects littering Byron's clearing in the wood: an American-style fridge and 'four Coca-Cola plastic chairs' (Butterworth 2009: 6). This is, on the one hand, a local play with national concerns but these items, as well as dating the clearing back to the 1980s and 1990s, remind us of England's place on far larger stages.

In *England People Very Nice* characters question what it is to be English directly, but this is the least English of the two. In not supplying, or even attempting to supply, coherent answers to the questions raised about identity, Bean highlights, perhaps, the arbitrary nature of the politics of groups claiming to defend the country from the negative effects of immigration and asylum. But in the play-within divisions and tensions are drawn on almost entirely racial grounds and, throughout the play, the cultural and economic lives of those at risk from invasion are never clearly defined. What it is to be English for the fictional inhabitants of this East London, therefore, is confused and confusing. There is a conscious irony here, of course, but in the context of the National Theatre, and in spite of claims that the playwright is trying 'to force [his] audience to engage with histories of prejudice' this consciousness is not quite enough to protect Bean from criticism (J. Abrams 2010: 9).

This England

Bean's crowded and chaotic portrait of a nation is framed by a recognisable dramatic device: 'inmates', as Charles Spencer puts it, of an immigration centre put on a play about immigration while they await the letter that may, or may not, grant them permission to stay in Britain (Spencer 2009). It is, in effect, a play within a play, and the framing of it is as politically charged as the content itself. The play does nothing, it should be noted, to address the troubled and problematised question of British immigration policy; those seeking asylum throughout the play, for example, are never clearly distinguished from those who are not. As James Moran notes, the play 'seeks to flatten … distinctions, to create a narrative in which immigrant groups are shown as being fundamentally the same as one another' (2012: 19). Nevertheless, Spencer sees 'wisdom and humanity' in it; Michael Billington merely 'a procession of types' (Billington 2009; Spencer 2009). The play told by the Nigerian, Azerbaijani, Palestinian, Kosovan, Yemeni and Serbian players is a somewhat ironic take on a conventional love story framed by the history of British immigration. It is a boy-meets-girl tale told four times by characters whose idiosyncrasies are derived from stereotypes not unfamiliar in the British tabloid press: Philippa, the intolerable (and intolerant) director mixes prototypical theatre-speak with an unmasked rudeness; Elmar, the Azerbaijani film-maker, litters the play with seemingly inappropriate and out-of-context sayings; and Taher, a Palestinian theatre worker, makes constant anti-Israeli remarks and corrects the inaccuracies and inconsistencies in the history presented with reference to an online encyclopedia famed for inaccuracies and inconsistencies. Iqbal, from Yemen, shaves off his beard but makes a false one from the hair for the character he plays (somewhat too predictably a mad imam). While shown to be respected by the others, and held in regard particularly by Taher, the false beard adds a ridiculousness to him that is difficult to resolve. These characters are part of the core cast for the prologue and epilogue and constitute, in part, the cast for the play-within that begins in seventeenth-century Spitalfields.

Bean here is consciously, albeit controversially, playing with both the real and imagined East End of London, a place of disputed boundaries in relation to class, race and to space. It is a space-less place, located only imaginatively, but importantly so. In his investigation into the cultural construction of the East End, Paul Newland explains how, due to 'the continued existence of a spatial idea of the East End, ideological divisions between classes, ethnic groups and religions can be conveniently placed, positioned, named, and worked-through' (Newland 2008: 9). It is, he writes, a place 'defined not only in terms of class but also in terms of race, and, specifically, the imaginative impact of immigration' (2008: 25). The imaginative space of the East End is commented on throughout the play by its fictional characters. Each depicted community, for example, claims ownership of the houses and streets in which they live. Far less subtle are the patronising appraisals of the area and the characters offered by St John and Camilla. It is a place not unaccustomed to sending itself up, although this too is an easy stereotype with, for example, the familiar evocation of stock East End figures: 'Are you' asks Barry of Ida 'what the sociology books call an East End matriarch?' (Bean 2009: 91).

The play presents what has been termed a 'riotous' history of Britain, punctuated by the arrival of various communities into Bethnal Green (Bean 2009). In addition to the play within a play Bean uses a variety of dramatic devices to reflect the supposed cyclical nature of British behaviour, policy and social environment through a history as fictional, in places, as the people represented. A violent male mob recurs throughout, for example, and other characters in the play-within recur in various guises, a pattern that is mirrored by stories, phrases and jokes. The boy lover begins the play as Norfolk Danny, is hanged and is later re-incarnated as Carlo the Italian Priest (who is stabbed to death) and is, by 1888, Aaron the Jewish Printer (whose death, we might assume, is interrupted by a fifteen-minute break). It is as Mushi, on his first night in Britain in 1941, that he utters the line that gives the play its title and later, having lost his own faith at the Natural History Museum, looks on in disbelief at the actions of his children as radical Islamists. Where the boy lover, then, begins, as it were, 'British' his later 'selves' are outsiders seeking Catholics, asylum and work, respectively. The path of the girl lover runs almost in the opposite direction: an immigrant (on religious and then economic grounds, as Camille and Mary respectively) until she becomes Ruth, an English Jewish aristocrat, and, later still, Deborah, a would-be East End Gracie Fields.

Just as the corner pub plays a crucial part in 'the construction of an imagined East End' so does it play its part in Bean's more conscious 'imagined community' (Newland 2008: 116; see also B. Anderson 1983). Ida (the pub barmaid), Laurie (the landlord) and Rennie (a regular) are, like the pub they occupy, constant characters whose language and beliefs reflect changing historical contexts but act also as a through line, almost a leitmotif. The love story between Laurie and Ida runs in parallel to that of the boy and girl lovers, and this relationship is mirrored through the dialogue in an often playful manner. Laurie, for example, continually finishes Ida's sentences that recur, structurally, throughout the play. Rennie's language is more obvious in its irony. Originally from Barbados (to where he returns at the end of the play), Rennie frequently makes reference to Enoch Powell's so-called 'Rivers of Blood' speech from 1968: 'There'll be rivers of blood boy! War, across Europe!' (Bean 2009: 18). And later, at the arrival of the Irish: 'The rivers of London will run with blood boy!' (Bean 2009: 35). Finally, in a deeply problematic celebration of the London tube bombings of 2007 alongside the unresolved (and arguably irresolvable) evocation of the phrase employed by far-right groups following Powell ('Enoch was right'): 'Rivers of blood! Ha, ha! Enoch Powell was right boy! He only got one thing wrong! It's not us boy! It's not us! Ha, ha!' (Bean 2009: 107). One of Bean's most dubiously drawn characters, a Black British Nationalist from the Commonwealth, 'as British', according to BNP Barry, 'as hot tea in a flask', Rennie leaves England when it no longer feels like home (Bean 2009: 107).

Where *England People Very Nice* is unapologetically brash and provocative, Jez Butterworth's play *Jerusalem* is as much metaphor as myth. It is perhaps too obvious to point out that the play takes its name from the preface to Blake's epic poem *Milton*, set to music by Parry a century later, and the hymn is directly referenced in the play through the character of Phaedra's recital of it in the Prologue. The reference seems to operate primarily at surface level, reminding us of a green, pleasant and ancient land. Its revolutionary spirit is also echoed in the play and, through tradition, the hymn refers us to the day on which the play is set. It's 23 April (St George's Day); in the text of the play it is 2002. The play's protagonist, Johnny Rooster Byron, lives in a mobile home in a forest on the edge of a new estate. His home is frequented by the local 'youths', used for late night parties and hang-outs. Byron, it transpires, provides them with drugs and alcohol, as he did their parents before them.

In the play we meet Ginger (a disciple of sorts) and a slightly younger crowd: Lee (on the eve of his unlikely departure to Australia), Davey, Pea and Tanya. The Professor, while not a regular party-goer, is clearly well known to the others, and, with Lee, Davey, Pea and Tanya, forms an army of sorts that rally, or at the very least purports to rally, around Byron. Other characters include: Wesley, a contemporary of Byron's, the local pub landlord and much maligned Morris dancer; Marky, Byron's 6-year-old son, and Marky's mother Dawn. Phaedra, who opens the play, is the reigning May Queen, looked for by her stepfather, Troy. While we are asked, at times, to think about the social responsibility of the adults in the play towards the young people in their charge, this is not a play that preaches, but Johnny's role in the community is a complicated and contradictory one and we are, as reader and as audience, made very aware of this.

Rooster Byron is a king of a crumbling castle, the last mythical giant, protector of a corner of England being subsumed by the spoils of capitalism and suburban banality. Kennet and Avon Council, the establishment represented in the play by the dowdy figures of Fawcett and Parsons, have been trying to evict Byron for 27 years. On the morning of 23 April he is given his final notice, and a forcible eviction looms. So too does an eviction of a different kind. Johnny's status as 'Puckish merrymaker' is also under threat from the changing nature of the village whose outskirts he skirts and the changing attitude towards him by its inhabitants, inhabitants from whom he is increasingly marginalised (J. Abrams 2010: 11). The relationship between the character of Byron, then, and concepts of space and place is important. His is a space under attack; his place, perhaps, in the process of being erased. Newland reminds us how 'places can become vessels of ideology', pointing us to the expression 'knowing one's place', noting how this implies 'not only spatial meanings but also political meanings' (Newland 2008: 28). Byron's place is somewhere, we realise, he has ceased to know.

While Byron's place, framed by fantastical stories, is located in the historical (and often fictional) past, other characters are rooted more firmly in the present, defined by their relationship to the village:

Lee: You're David Dean.
Davey: Yes, mate.
Lee: David Dean from Flintock.
Davey: Absolutely.
Lee: Nothing else.
Davey: Nothing but.   (Butterworth 2009: 89)

Throughout the play there are a variety of references to off-stage worlds. In *Jerusalem*, these references serve, at times, to emphasise the smallness of Byron's own world and plight in relation to the rest of the country, as is summed up in an argument about local BBC news:

Davey: ... You ask me, BBC Points West has lost its way.
Ginger: What?
Davey: Points West used to be solid local news. First they've done the cuts, merged with Bristol, now it's half the bloody country.

[And]

Pea: Local is Bedwyn. Local is Devizes.
Davey: You want to gas yourself in your garage in Gloucester, be my guest. How could I possibly care less?
Tanya: Show me a good house fire in Salisbury. Now, *that's* tragic.
                                                   (Butterworth 2009: 59–60)

Throughout the play we are confronted with not only the tensions between England on an international stage versus its national performance but the representation of a local England, an England in decline. The last ancient kingdom is threatened, perhaps, by what Owen Hatherley calls, with a nod to J. B. Priestley, the fifth Britain: 'the post-1979 England of business parks [and] Barratt homes' (Hatherley 2010: xxxv).

The loss of England as local place is a cause of great anxiety to the characters in the play and a source of much of its humour:

> Davey: I've never seen the point of other countries. I leave Wiltshire, my ears pop. Seriously. I'm on my bike, pedalling along, see a sign says 'Welcome to Berkshire', I turn straight round. I don't like to go east of Wootton Basset. Suddenly it's Reading, then London, then before you know where you are you're in France, and then there's countries popping up all over. What's that about?
>
> *(Butterworth 2009: 24)*

But this locality is as ambiguous as the national representation of England. Depicted most prominently by Thomas Hardy, Wessex is the home of King Alfred, Jane Austen, Stonehenge and, indeed, of England. Wiltshire is where the play is set, in the fictional village of Flintock (somewhere near Devizes in the 'real' world) but Wessex, or at least the idea of Wessex, frames the play: 'The old Wessex flag (a golden Wyvern dragon against a red background) flies from one end. An old rusted metal railway sign screwed to the mobile home reads "Waterloo"' (Butterworth 2009: 6). It also, importantly, frames the fair: 'The Annual St George's Day Pageant and Wessex Country Fair in the Village of Flintock sponsored by John Deere Tractors and Arkell Ales' (Butterworth 2009: 46). Wessex (itself now an imaginary place) here becomes associated with a brewery and an American tractor firm, a not-unexpected commodification of legend and myth. The West Country has become what Newland might call 'a mythic space, a spatial metaphor, a socio-cultural and historical referent and a symbolic territory' (Newland 2008: 18). It is a country, a place, imagined.

Where the England *of England People Very Nice* is presented as a cyclical, often brutal reaction to 'the other', the England of *Jerusalem*, while certainly sharing some of these traits, also takes a defiant, if ultimately futile, stand against change. *Jerusalem* can also be read as a play that celebrates the confused and ambiguous character of the nation but, through the nature in which it is framed and the language with which it is represented, there is another way of thinking about England here, one that is far less optimistic. This is mirrored also in Bean's confused and chaotic portrait of Britain in *England People Very Nice*, a play that has both provoked and reflected anxiety in its non-fictional equivalent. While this has much to do with content and with character the language (or languages) with which the various textual worlds are presented, is equally problematic. These worlds are, at times, complicated and complicating.

The fictional world of *England People Very Nice* has two aspects: Britain in the present tense and a Britain of the past; the Britain that houses the 'players' and the Britain depicted by the players. While the two places overlap (the characters from one inhabit the other) they are framed as distinct, right from the beginning. The character lists, for example, are separated into 'Recurring characters' (for the play-within) and 'Core cast' (for the prologue and epilogue). Problematising further the fictional world is a distinction Bean makes between the representations of different locations within the representation of Britain: 'The Play requires a large stage with the facility to fly in flats, or use still, or video projections, to establish locations as required. The process should be playful and non-naturalistic. The only constant location is the pub, which can be naturalistic' (Bean 2009: 7). There are different overlapping representations of places, then, within relatively confined locales that, while imaginary, also have equivalents in the real world. Act III, for example, begins in 1888 and ends with the players from the immigration centre in the present. In between these places action shifts, from outside the pub, for example, to 'The Docks', to 'The revolutionaries flat in Whitechapel', a 'sweatshop' and in 'the pub' (Bean 2009: 48, 53, 55, 65). For all its chaos, however, the play hardly ever makes reference to itself *as* a play. With the exception of a number of 'enters' and 'exits' the only references to the stage as a stage occur in prologue-mode and there is some ambiguity concerning the status of even some of these directions, as the stage to which Bean is referring here could be the fictional one of the world inhabited by the players. Bean's England, consequently, is an anxious one, because of not only the nature of the world represented, but also the nature in which it is represented: the sometimes ill-defined overlap of fictional worlds that leads to difficult reading and the seeming refusal to engage with this world as a staged world, ironically so given that the story of Britain is framed by such a staging.

In a similar way to Bean in *England People Very Nice*, Butterworth frames his representation with the dramatic device of a play within a play. *Jerusalem* forgets its staged-ness far more often than *England People Very Nice* but it is still presented as such, with two prologues that interrupt the fictionalised performance of England and its defenders:

> *A curtain with the faded Cross of St. George. A proscenium adorned with cherubs and woodland scenes. Dragons. Maidens. Devils. Half and half creatures. Across the beam:*
> *– THE ENGLISH STAGE COMPANY –*
> *A drum starts to beat. Accordions strike up. Pipes. The lights come down. A fifteen-year-old girl, PHAEDRA, dressed as a fairy, appears on the apron. She curtsies to the boxes and sings, unaccompanied.*   (Butterworth 2009: 5)

And:

> *Spotlight. PHAEDRA appears, again dressed as a fairy. She sings 'Werewolf' by Barry Dransfield. As she finishes, the curtain rises on. . .*   (Butterworth 2009: 47)

At the level of the text what Butterworth first presents us with is a representation of England as a stage with a faded flag. On this stage the players in a fictionalised corner tell their tales of giants defeated and defiant.

If the prologues take place in a different England then it is not one to which we are returned. In this sense the play is not complete, as we are instead left waiting in the mythical England conjured by Byron's call 'Come, you giants!' at the end of the play (Butterworth 2009: 109). If the England of the prologues is a place we inhabit then we are, as Byron is, displaced. In performance, however, the blending of these two worlds allows for a more ambiguous interpretation.

On stage, in performance, the faded flag of St George is framed by the clearing in the wood; its contents spilling over onto the apron in front of the backdrop (Apollo Theatre 2011 production). The second fictional world of the play invades the first, the world inhabited by Phaedra and the world we, as the audience, might consider as being part of our own. Emerging from Byron's trailer at the end of the second of three acts, then, Phaedra's appearance in the play-proper, over and above a disturbing realisation in the context of the fictional narrative itself, can also be read as a telling merger or a blending of worlds of an altogether different kind: this England is our England. The beam, however, inscribed with *The English Stage Company*, remains intact and visible throughout the performance. The inscription reminds us of the play's first (and spiritual) home, The Royal Court. It is a reminder also of this additional dramatic frame: there is a play within this play.

In performance the place of the audience is also questioned, and this is seen most clearly in the mock building of battlements, and also in the final scene. At the beginning of Act II, the characters prepare as if for battle:

> *On the side of the trailer is a big bedsheet stretched out which reads 'FUCK OFF*
> *KENNET AND AVON'* . . . *Nearby PEA is carefully painting on the last letter to another*
> *bedsheet sign which so far reads 'FUCK OFF THE NEW ESTAT'.*
>   *Enter the PROFESSOR from behind the caravan, sleeves rolled up, whistling,*
> *pushing a wheelbarrow full of gnomes.*   (Butterworth 2009: 47)

In performance the defences built by the actors are initially pointed at us; the characters defending themselves against a threat as real as it is imagined. The use of the audience space in the performance is ambiguous, and our roles as spectators shift: we are the forest and the 'wild garlic and May blossom' (Butterworth 2009: 99). At other times we are, more simply, the audience of a performance of *Jerusalem*. The actors, and Mark Rylance in particular, play with the presence of the audience; Phaedra sings to us. We are acknowledged, then, as belonging to both of the fictional worlds and to our own.

The final scene is more challenging in this respect. Byron, bloodied and bruised, branded with crosses, calls forth the Byron boys of old to their place behind him. This call is not directed to the audience and not even, where we might also expect, to stage left towards the village, but to stage right towards the forest. This is a call back: into the forest, into the past. In the text there is some ambiguity as the detail suggests that Byron's face can be seen. In performance, however, the pose Rylance takes, beating his drum in time with Byron's call, suggests a far less determined enemy than the ones so far invoked by the language of the play (the council, the new estate, change and uncertainty) and earlier images (the audience as enemy).

Where we might, to use Paul Werth's (1999) term, 'toggle' between the spaces both of and represented by the performance at some level, we also inhabit them at the same time. It is perfectly possible to simultaneously admire Rylance's performance and be moved by Byron's futile stand, just as it is possible to see the character as representing, if not England, then an image of England created by the play. What we see in performance is an actor (Rylance) and a character (Byron) and a metaphor of an altogether different kind (England). The very notion of a blended space, then, operates at a number of levels: it describes the process of acting and watching acting; it tells us how things mean in addition to what they might mean; and it allows us to account for and experience different representations of space and place, real and imagined, all at once.

31

Interpretation

Lesley Jeffries

Introduction

The question of how texts make meaning has been a source of continuing fascination in stylistics. The charge against stylistics that it generates meanings automatically from texts (Fish 1973) is now outdated, and for many years stylistics has been assimilating developments that have emanated from linguistics, cognitive science and literary and cultural studies. Many of these disciplines have emphasised the importance of the reader in producing meaning from texts, largely, though not comprehensively, to the exclusion of the notions of authorial and text-initiated meaning that were predominant in earlier times. Developments in cognitive stylistics (Stockwell 2002) in the late twentieth and early twenty-first centuries were at the forefront of this changing focus, though in recent times the rise of corpus approaches to stylistic analysis has somewhat mitigated this movement towards a wholly reader-centred view of meaning by providing a corrective emphasis on the textual construction of meaning.

In this chapter, I will attempt to explain how we interpret texts, basing my discussion on a descriptive framework I am developing which uses Halliday's (1994) metafunctions of language as its starting point. This framework, which arises from my work on the stylistic aspects of critical discourse analysis (CDA; Jeffries 2010b), has the potential to relate many of the existing descriptive frameworks in linguistics to each other. The aim is to provide a place in linguistic theory for the specific kind of meaning to be found in texts, whether they are written or spoken, lasting or ephemeral, literary or non-literary. I will also use in new ways some long-standing distinctions in linguistics between *langue* and *parole* (Saussure 1959) and between *locution*, *illocution* and *perlocution* (Austin 1962). Combined, these dimensions allow for an integrated model of textual meaning, which will be illustrated through the analysis of a poem.

Interpretation and readings

This chapter sets out a framework for language that sets textual meaning in context and draws on some of the main theories and models of language that have been influential in the approximately 100-year period since the rise of modern linguistics. I make the assumption that there are (at least) two sorts of textual significance produced during the process of reading (or listening) and that, although these may be closely integrated in the reader's experience, they are not fundamentally the same. So, on the one hand I do not think we can understand textual meaning without theoretical recognition of some kind of consensual meaning of texts, which I link to the word 'interpretation'. On the other hand, there must also be a more personal kind of textually prompted significance which will vary almost as much as the individual readers do. It is important, however, to recognise that what I have called 'consensual' meaning is not therefore singular, automatically 'decoded' in some robotic manner or even fixed.

Short (2008: 13) argues strongly against the idea that texts can mean an almost infinite number of different things, although he notes that texts also rarely have one single interpretation. When discussing the multiple meanings of texts, he notes that analysts need some way to understand 'what counts as a different interpretation and what counts as a different instantiation of the same interpretation'. For Short, the term 'reading' is unhelpful in trying to understand this distinction because it does not elucidate the difference between individual response and post-processed interpretation. Short's argument is dismissive of the word 'reading', and I share some of his discomfort with the overuse of this word in sanctioning unsystematic responses to texts as though they were the same as interpretations. However, I think we could make use of the word (readings) to refer precisely to the kinds of responses that arise from readers' personal experience and can even arise from mistaken understanding of the text at times. What Short helps us see is that we need to identify the different origins of our responses to texts in order to make any progress in understanding how interpretation – and reading – work. One way to do this is to see textual interpretation as part of a larger model of language which includes how the basic elements of language work (phonology, morphology, grammar, semantics) and also how the context of language use can interact with textual features (pragmatics). The picture is not complete until we recognise a third, intermediate, aspect of language, arising from (co-)textual features of language, which produces insights into the combination of propositional meaning and style that constitutes all language use.

One of Halliday's (1994) contributions to our thinking about human language has been to propose an over-arching set of 'metafunctions' which together characterise all the different kinds of work (function) that linguistic forms can carry out. These metafunctions are labelled *textual, ideational* and *interpersonal*. What Halliday intended, within the terms of his systemic-functional linguistics model, was to identify different aspects of language structure (and use) and allocate them variously to the three metafunctions. Thus, the transitivity system, whereby verb choice is seen to influence the nature and number of participants labelled in the rest of the clause, would be considered ideational in Halliday's terms, since it is a choice from a number of alternative ways of including the same propositional content and therefore is a way of presenting the world through language. The modal system, on the other hand, is for Halliday and his followers an example of an interpersonal linguistic system, since it explicitly provides the point-of-view of the producer. The third (textual) metafunction, refers to all those features that are basic to the structure and function of a language, such as the dummy auxiliary in English, which has no other function than to provide the usual auxiliary meanings of question, emphasis or negation.

Halliday's evident insight in distinguishing the three metafunctions seems to me to serve an even better purpose if they are seen not as simple categories of language use into which the systems of a language should be fitted. If, instead, we see them as three major divisions of linguistic description, this allows us to integrate the insights from much of the work of linguistics into a single, unified model.

In Table 31.1, I have used Halliday's metafunctions as generalised labels for the different kinds of meaning produced by language. While I value his distinction, since I am using it rather differently anyway, I will replace his term 'textual' with 'linguistic'. The reason for this apparently cosmetic alteration is that I want to allocate to this type of meaning production only the de-contextual meaning that is recognised as basic to all language use, if difficult to isolate from its co-textual and contextual use. Unlike Toolan (1996:125), I do not believe that this context-free aspect of linguistic meaning is needed only for descriptive convenience and will demonstrate the theoretical need to recognise the linguistic metafunction below. I reserve the word 'textual' for the meanings produced when linguistic forms are combined into text.

Though Halliday's original metafunctions are envisaged as being on the same plane, I suggest that the linguistic metafunction can be seen as underlying the other two metafunctions as they rely on the basics of

Table 31.1 The metafunctions and their relationship to linguistic form and meaning.

Textual metafunction	Ideational metafunction	Interpersonal metafunction
De-contextual form and meaning	Co-textual form and meaning	Contextual form and meaning
Semantic meaning	Textual/conceptual meaning	Pragmatic meaning

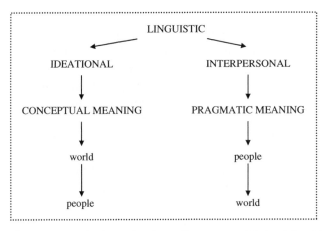

Figure 31.1: Revised metafunctions of language and their relationship to meaning

language, albeit in different and varying ways, for their ideational and interpersonal functions to be carried out. Let us therefore propose a slightly different alignment of the three metafunctions as shown in Figure 31.1.

Figure 31.1 suggests that the language system is the foundation of all language activity, but is not directly accessed by users who are engaged in simultaneously presenting (and/or receiving) a version of the world (or text-world) as they see it and also interacting with others. The first layer of effect, then, as seen in Figure 31.1, is for the ideational metafunction to produce conceptual meaning and cause the text to represent the world (the 'real' or a fictional world) in some way, and for the interpersonal metafunction to produce pragmatic meaning and cause the text to 'act upon' other people, either directly (spoken or immediate writing) or indirectly (written or remote speech). While not being definitively intentional or necessarily conscious, this level of meaning tends to indicate the viewpoint of the producer (or, if it is relevant, the author, narrator, etc.). At a secondary level, the text may have an effect on the world under the interpersonal metafunction by the recipient's acceptance or rejection of the illocutionary force (or other pragmatic meaning) and an effect on the recipient under the ideational metafunction as she or he reads with or against the ideational or ideological grain of the text and accepts or rejects the construction of the world or text-world represented there.

The linguistic underpinning of text interpretation

Having renamed Halliday's 'textual metafunction' a 'linguistic metafunction' and considering it as vital to the use of language, even if it is mostly operating beneath the level of conscious notice, we can see that it covers all that would have been covered in structuralist accounts of language by phonetics, phonology, morphology, syntax and semantics. Whether you adhere to this formalist view of the basis of language or take a more dynamic (transformational-generative) or even cognitive view of the basics, some such description of the fundamental particles of language and their behaviour is needed, whatever else you build upon it. Though Halliday's model is intended to be functional at *every* level, the meaning of 'function' within this linguistic metafunction is not so different from the meaning it holds in more formalist accounts. The many different theories and models of this general level of language description may contribute different insights to our understanding of human language, but they all operate at a similar level.

Interpersonal meanings of texts

Under the new version of the interpersonal metafunction lie all of the features usually covered by the term *pragmatics*. Thus, *implicatures* and politeness/impoliteness phenomena such as *positive and negative face threats* would feature here as would features of interaction such as turn-taking, openings, closings and all the other observed patterns figuring in the endeavours of *conversation analysis*. Early pragmatic concepts such as *speech acts* (e.g. agreeing, warning, instructing, requesting and apologising) are also interpersonal; as I wish to use speech act theory in developing my framework in the next section, I will explore it a little further here as a prime example of the interpersonal metafunction of language. Readers may be familiar with the three simultaneous 'actions' which Austin (1962), and later Searle (1969), proposed (Figure 31.2).

Though speech act theory is now largely the background against which other pragmatic developments take place, the reason that this distinction has been so powerful and has become axiomatic for pragmatic theories is that it helps us to understand why there are sometimes apparent mismatches between the superficial form of a text or utterance and its contexualised meaning. The utterance 'I feel awful' *seems* to simply describe the feelings of a person, and in another context it may do just that (for example, if they are feeling ill). But in the context of something having been done which is perceived as wrong by both the speaker and the addressee, it has the illocutionary force of an apology. The perlocution – whether the addressee accepts the apology as an apology – is not certain

Locution	'I feel awful'
Illocution	I am sorry / I apologise
Perlocution	Apology enacted and accepted – or not accepted.

Figure 31.2: Locution, illocution and perlocution

and will depend on individual circumstances, personalities, personal histories and so on.

What we see here, in the speech act model of interaction, is an example of what happens simultaneously at all times that language is used and received. There is no theoretical implication in this model that there are somehow three separate things going on at once which then have to be explained in terms of cognitive processing. The mistake of trying to test for the physical or literal truth of a model can often cause us to abandon models that are insightful and useful. It is worth remembering that even the most hard-science models of the universe and its constituent parts are also merely metaphors for what is going on. They can be tested, improved and sometimes also replaced entirely, but most good models provide some new insight into complex phenomena which are long-lasting even when superseded in some fashion.

In the next section, I will attempt to apply a three-way distinction similar to the speech act trio of locution–illocution–perlocution to the ideational metafunction of language and see what insights it affords us.

Ideational metafunctions of texts

Applying the three-way distinction inspired by speech act theory to the ideational metafunction of language creates some parallels between the two metafunctions, each of which has three co-occurring levels of action. In Table 31.2, I have used speech acts as the exemplar of pragmatic meaning and the construction of opposites (Jeffries 2010a) as an example of ideational meaning. They are illustrated using an example from *The Big Bang Theory*, a US sitcom that focuses on the life and personal relationships of a group of young scientists. One of the scientists, Sheldon, represents a fairly extreme version of the nerdy

Table 31.2 Interpersonal and ideational metafunctions of textual meaning.

Interpersonal metafunction	Speech act (denial/refusal)	Ideational metafunction	Construction of opposites
Locution	'I'm a physicist, not a hippy'	Form/meaning (code)	'I'm a physicist, not a hippy'
Illocution	Denial: I have not spoken to Amy about how I feel – and don't intend to	Textual/conceptual function	Physicists are the opposite of hippies
Perlocution	Leonard either accepts or opposes Sheldon's refusal to speak to Amy.	Conceptual effect	Leonard either agrees or contests Sheldon's view that these are opposites.

stereotype, and his relationships with women are therefore fraught with misunderstanding and stress. One day, his girlfriend asks him (on Skype) whether he would be willing to meet her mother and he panics, not quite understanding what this signifies, but aware that it is meaningful. He asks his friend Leonard for help, and Leonard responds by his asking whether he has talked about how he is feeling to his girlfriend. He replies 'Leonard, I'm a physicist, not a hippy.'

The first row in Table 31.2 is not really a feature of texts at all in my framework, but refers to the underlying linguistic structures and meanings that inform the textual meanings and effects. Speech act theory refers to this as 'locution', a term which emphasises the production of some kind of linguistic structure(s). It is not, however, very different from a simple admission that we cannot – and should not – ignore the basic linguistics of the text.

The second row of the table explains Sheldon's utterance in terms of its illocutionary force on the interpersonal level though the utterance supplies not the actual denial ('No, I will not talk to Amy') but an implicit denial based on the fact that only hippies (and not physicists) talk about their feelings. On the ideational level, the text can be seen to produce a 'constructed' opposite between physicist and hippies which is the basis of the illocutionary force, as the implied world view is that you cannot be both at once. Thus, the text is concurrently constructing a world in which physicists and hippies are somehow complementary opposites (as evidenced by their differing levels of emotional literacy) and also producing a denial from Sheldon in response to Leonard's suggestion that he should talk to Amy about how he feels.

The third row of the table is at the level of effect or perlocution. On the one hand, Leonard has to decide how to deal with the speech act of denial or refusal in coping with his very difficult friend. He can either accept that Sheldon will not change, or he can try further to persuade him. On the other hand, Leonard may or may not consciously realise that, in performing the denial or refusal, Sheldon is constructing a one-off opposite between physicists and hippies. If he notices this opposition construction, he might deliberately contradict (or accept) the contrast between hippies and physicists in relation to their emotional behaviour. He might find it amusing, as the sitcom audience is certainly intended to do – and does. Even if he does not consciously acknowledge the ideational force of Sheldon's utterance, at some level he will certainly understand that the construction of this opposition is intended to perform the function of denial/refusal. At this junction between the ideational and the interpersonal, then, Sheldon's utterance is unified, even though we as analysts, and Leonard as his addressee, can see the distinction between *what* Sheldon is saying and *how* he is presenting the world in order to do so.

Textual–conceptual functions

In my (2010b) model of textual meaning, I attempted to develop a text-based methodology for CDA. In doing so, I adopted the ideational meta-function as an umbrella term to cover a range of linguistic features, some of them already familiar from systemic-functional linguistics, and used regularly by CDA practitioners, but others newly included. Thus, I attempted to find a set of ideational functions that were performed by the language of texts and utterances which would explain how the text was constructing the world (or a fictional world) conceptually. In some ways, this was no more than bringing together ideas already well established and recognised in stylistics and CDA, but it seemed to me important to bring them under a more general umbrella of ideational meaning in order to help explain textual meaning more fully.

The result of this process was a list of a number of ways in which texts fulfil the ideational metafunction, which I label 'textual-conceptual functions'. Some of these textual-conceptual functions overlap in particular ways, but since this is not intended to be a model of either the production or reception of language, such overlaps are not theoretically problematic. Here is the current list of textual-conceptual functions:

- naming and describing
- representing actions/events/states
- equating and contrasting
- exemplifying and enumerating
- prioritising
- implying and assuming
- negating
- hypothesising
- presenting others' speech and thoughts
- representing time, space and society

The use of everyday phrases (e.g. naming and describing) to refer to quite technically complex linguistic features is not intended to dumb down the field nor to patronise students. The intention of these naming devices was rather to demonstrate that they refer to *what texts are doing in constructing their view of the world*, irrespective of the formal structures used to carry out this ideational representation.

The mechanisms by which texts carry out these textual-conceptual functions is a matter which links the ideational to the linguistic metafunction since it is through the underlying systems and structures that the textual-conceptual functions are produced. Though many of them have a prototypical delivery mechanism, they can also have a wide range of optional forms varying in their distance from the prototype. For example, negating is prototypically carried by the particles *no* or *not*, though its potential forms include morphological negation (*un-, dis-*), lexical negation (*never, fail*) and of course also paralinguistic gestures such as shaking the head or shrugging. Similarly, there are prototypical forms of deixis which deliver the time, space and social envelope in which a text-world functions, though there is no clear cut-off as to the kinds of linguistic items that can participate in this activity. This lack of one-to-one form-function relationship is, of course, fundamental to our understanding of how human language works. If all forms had one and only one function, and all functions only one form, we would live in a clear, but much impoverished world where lying and mis-leading might be absent, but so too would poetry and comedy.

Before I return to consider what this framework might tell us about interpretation, I will use one of the additional (non-Hallidayan) textual-conceptual functions to illustrate why I think that textual meaning is both separate from and reliant upon the meanings produced by the linguistic metafunction. When I first noticed the textual construction of (often temporary) opposites, it struck me that there was no place in the frame-works provided by linguistics for this phenomenon. The Larkin poem ('Is it a trick or a trysting-place / These woods we have found to walk'; Larkin 1990: 296) and Conservative Party poster ('Labour say he's black. Tories say he's British') that first alerted me to constructed opposites (*trick/trysting-place* and *black/British*) confirmed for me that the same meaning construc-tion processes work in both literary and non-literary genres. This sug-gested that textual construction of meaning may form part of linguistic meaning in general. However, the question remained whether we should replace the de-contextual frameworks of linguistic structure and meaning entirely as a result of recognising the online construction of meaning that takes place in texts and utterances.

The answer, it seemed to me, was no. The only way that textually constructed opposites could possibly be understood by text recipients was by reference to the prior existence of prototypical lexical opposites (e.g. *hot/cold, right/wrong*) as the model on which constructed opposites could be processed. This is not to deny the contingent nature of the conventional opposites that have to be taught to children and are clearly therefore not 'natural' in any biologically determined way. But the very fact that the interpretation of textually constructed opposites is dependent on an idealised form of opposition is enough to suggest that the linguistic metafunction and the structures and units that it subsumes (however you choose to theorise them) are psychologically real to language users as well as being convenient for descriptive linguistics.

A unified model of textual meaning

Here, I will try to formulate a simple picture of how the two important strands of meaning, conceptual and pragmatic, sit alongside each other in

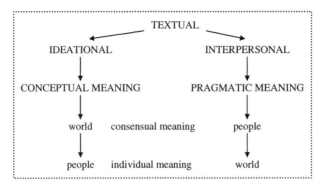

Figure 31.3: Consensual and individual meaning

the interpretation of texts, which will (incidentally) demonstrate that stylistics truly does sit at the centre of linguistic concerns and not at its periphery.

By revisiting Figure 31.1 (see Figure 31.3 above), the two different levels of effect of the conceptual and pragmatic meaning can be linked to consensual and individual meaning respectively. Thus, although all pragmatic meaning is necessarily linked to context, there is a level at which even pragmatic meaning will be largely shared by a language community, and there is also a level at which the text or utterance is received by individual recipients that is less predictable from socially shared understanding and schematic knowledge alone and draws on their individual circumstances. Likewise with ideational meaning, there will be a level of meaning which is agreed on the whole by most readers because the text has constructed a particular text-world, whether fictional or non-fictional, and a level at which readers' responses will be much more personal and individual and thus less predictable from the text itself.

In the next section I will demonstrate these different aspects of meaning in relation to a poem. Here, I would point out that Figure 31.3 helps us to differentiate between the text's putative construction of meaning and the reader's potential response to that meaning. This, it seems to me, is more useful than simply asserting that there is an infinite and infinitely variable range of possible responses to any text, even though that is ultimately true. The point of scientific approaches to understanding natural phenomena, including language, is to produce a model of what is happening which will explain the phenomenon by focusing on significant patterns rather than reproducing the full complexity of the original data. Thus, while a reader who has certain schematic knowledge (of, for example, the architecture and layout of the city of Bath) might add a layer of personal meaning to their reading of Jane Austen's *Northanger Abbey* that would not be shared by a reader who has never been there, there is, nevertheless, a level at which the text of that novel provides information for all readers to construct a mental image of (eighteenth-century) Bath that is adequate for reading the novel. Likewise, the reader of a piece of extremist propaganda may have a personal and sometimes strong (positive or negative) reaction to the text-world constructed there if it tries to naturalise, for example, a racist ideology. But readers with either kind of reaction would very probably agree on what it is that the text is *doing*, ideologically speaking.

Though I am making a distinction between consensual and individual meaning which is linked to textual features, there may also be some consensus among readers on their individual responses to the text. Thus, contemporary readers of Jane Austen will inevitably have had shared schematic knowledge of the social context of the time that is not available to the twenty-first-century reader and this will affect the range of personal readings that attach to *Northanger Abbey*. Even then, there would presumably be different possible kinds of reaction to Austen's satirical view of her society, depending on the experience and ideology (and gender, class, etc.) of the reader. This variation in the reception of texts is certainly interesting, and in some areas of literary studies it is central to the examination of literary (and also non-literary) texts, but, in order to make any headway at all in analysing the text itself, it helps to make this distinction.

Short's (2008) view that there are limited interpretations of literary texts fits with the framework I have introduced above where there are limits to the possible interpretations of literary texts which are largely derived from the textual features. This does not mean that there will be only one interpretation or that there will be no arguments about interpretation. There can also be better and worse – or even wrong – interpretations that can be discussed, evidence produced and changes of opinion brought about. Any teacher of literature will recognise that this is one of the processes of the classroom.

Short (forthcoming) is of the view, and I agree, that 'the popularity of "reading", like the popularity of "intertextuality", has resulted in an unfortunate lack of descriptive precision'. He adds that the interpretations should be 'carefully considered, dispassionate, post-processed (and ideally post-analysis) accounts of texts, whereas readings can be more off-the-cuff (post-processed but less considered or less dispassionate), or related to a pre-existing ideological viewpoint (e.g. Marxist, feminist) and/or personal'. Short's list of characteristics of interpretations versus readings may be reinterpreted themselves in the light of the framework presented in this chapter, so that the distinctions between the two can be cast in terms of the distinction between social/consensual textual meaning and personal/private.

Short claims that interpretations are produced by the kind of textual analysis that brings evidence to bear on the interpretative points being

Table 31.3 Interpretations versus readings.

Interpretations	Readings
Social/consensual	Personal/private or ideological
Text-centred	Text-derived
Illocutionary	Perlocutionary
With text	With and/or against text

made by reference to features in the text itself and that the analyst has no pre-existing frame of reference (except a linguistic one) to inform the analysis. Of course, the analyst may well have a hypothesis about the ideology of a text or the particular features of a literary work that they expect to find, but this does not influence the actual analysis, only the reason for doing the analysis in the first place. It is a kind of objective/subjective distinction, which is one of the ideological differences between stylistics and many of the literary and cultural studies approaches to the text.

Table 31.3 allows us to make a distinction between the meanings that are created by features of texts themselves and those that are linked more closely to the readership, with all the variation that this implies. It should not, however, be seen as distinguishing between text and reader in any absolute or reactionary way. The left-hand column of this table can have just as much to do with cognition as the right-hand column; the difference is that the left-hand column refers to the processing of text which will be shared by most reasonably competent readers (possibly at a subconscious level) and stylisticians (at a conscious level). The columns in Table 31.3 are identical to the two levels of effect in Figures 31.1 and 31.3, so that the term 'consensual' in Figure 31.3 can be replaced by 'interpretation', and 'individual' by 'reading'. In other words, both types of meaning can apply to both the conceptual and the pragmatic meaning. There are relatively agreed (or at least evidenced) interpretative features of texts which can be said to be either ideational or interpersonal, and there are also more individualised readings of texts which depend a little on the text itself but as much on the context of situation, the participant roles of producer and recipient and also their relationship, history, backgrounds and so on.

What should be added here, before I offer an analysis of a poem informed by the framework presented above, is that the interpretative process may, of course, be contextualised by a more individual goal, such as the desire felt by many CDA practitioners to critique public discourse or the enthusiasm felt by a literary researcher for a particular author's works. As in the use of language in everyday life, the systematic and the personal are entwined. The duty of the researcher is to tease out the strands as clearly as possible.

Hardly Worth Mentioning

except there was blood, quite a lot
staining the table beside the coaster
thoughtfully provided, you might have thought,
to rest a cut hand on, gripping the fingers
to staunch it while you worked out what to do.

It didn't seem much, but when I showed them
they were alarmed, said 'Casualty'; and then
my finger, only the little finger actually
of my left hand, lay beside the coaster –
a joke-shop replica, staining the table more.

It didn't hurt. I thought how sharp
the blade must have been, precision-tooled:
I pictured sparks at a whetstone
(though I suppose it was a factory)
and they could think of nothing to say but
'It's serious.' I said, 'Well then, I shall faint'
and did. Their voices reached me
down a corridor of doors that echoed closed
on a picnic with the girl who lost the child
and there was an end of it; and at once
I was back in the office still in this
ludicrous predicament, but now

aware I'd wet myself. 'I will never play
the piano again,' I said and no one laughed.
They took me to the car, talking about shock,
and with my finger in a Strepsils tin.
'They'll sew it back on,' they said;
'they can do it really easily these days.'

They couldn't though. Look.

from Peter Sansom, January (Sansom 1994: 56)

The first time I read this poem I was surprised. I had never noticed that my friend Peter (Sansom) had lost a finger. Such is the strength of the poetic voice that I honestly believed that this was something that had happened to him – perhaps in an earlier part of his life when he worked in a factory for a holiday job. Of course, it turned out to be not exactly his story (though there was an accident on a football field involving fingers) but one that he had adapted from a mixture of experience and other sources (perhaps half-remembered news articles) and chose to write in the first person. This is the first observation to make about the division between personal and consensual meaning. Readers not personally familiar with the poet may not be quite as focused as I was on the question of whose story this was, though they may also have thought subconsciously that it might be the poet's own story. Neither of these trains of thought about the poem are part of its interpretation, in my view, though they may well make up part of the *experience* of reading the poem.

Slightly less personal, but not textually significant in interpretative terms, is the mention of a particular kind of sore-throat tablet, Strepsils. Many readers will perhaps not be familiar with these soothing sweets but their lack of specific knowledge will be enough to provide them with the scenario – a tin has been found in the office which is large enough to hold the severed finger. Those who know Strepsils will perhaps produce a more vivid mental picture of the scene, with the logo and colour of the tin more clearly marked, but that is not the role of the proper noun here. Its use, as with many other particulars in contemporary poetry, is to provide authentic detail which the reader can supplant with their own imagined version. Thus, to say 'a tin' would be less likely to produce the right image for the reader than 'a Strepsils tin' even if the actual reader produces an image instead of a tin of Buttercup Lozenges or Tyrozets.

The kind of background knowledge of particular items such as Strepsils is only different in specificity from the other background knowledge needed to be able to picture, for example, the 'sparks at a whetstone' that crosses the narrator's mind as he goes in and out of consciousness in shock. It certainly enhances the reading of a text to know as much as possible about the reference of the lexical items used and it can produce incorrect interpretations if some of those references are misunderstood. The reference of linguistic items is, however, not the core of textual meaning as described in the framework above. The question is rather what the text is doing ideationally in presenting this particular world. Even in the process of naming, the text is making stylistic choices between options, and it is this choice that is central to stylistics and to text interpretation as well.

Hardly Worth Mentioning: an analysis

In this section, I will use the list of textual-conceptual functions presented above as a checklist to consider the ideational construction of the poem. It is, of course, also possible to look at the interpersonal aspects of any text, including poetry. However, it is generally assumed that the social purpose of poetry and similar literary genres is more conceptual than interpersonal, though of course one only has to consider love poetry or even the possible social intentions of Jane Austen's novels, to see that all texts have both types of meaning. There are also, of course, features of poetic language that are best captured by reference to the linguistic metafunction (Halliday's textual metafunction), and these form the basis of much traditional stylistic analysis of poetry, including my own (Jeffries 1993). Though the analytical process under the ideational metafunction would normally be carried out by using each textual-conceptual function in turn, the presentation of the results is often integrated in practice, to show how they combine in a text. Because the text is a reasonably short poem, I will discuss it mostly in stanza order.

Stanza 1

The first stanza continues the syntax of the title, so they are considered together. The lexical choice of the first word (*Hardly*) enacts the textual-conceptual function of negation, which has the effect of making the question of whether this story is *worth mentioning* the uppermost consideration for the reader at the outset.

The representation of processes (transitivity) together with prioritisation (subordination) shows few intentional material actions at the higher levels of the syntax and as a result creates an effect of the static scene just after an accident has happened. The title has an ellipted subject and verb (*It is*) which leave the whole of the first sentence without an explicit main verb. The effect of this is to dislocate the described scene from any sense of real time (the narrator's or reader's time) and leave it as a past-tense story but with little sense of time passing within the scene itself. The first level of subordination in the sentence produces an intensive relational verb (*was*), which means that the top two levels (including the elided verb) are relatively static descriptions with little activity implied. Lower levels of subordination do show more in the way of action (*to rest*, *gripping*, *to staunch*) though they are all subordinate to *staining*, which is an event rather than an action, having, as it does, an inanimate subject (*blood*).

The naming here is mainly of the inanimate objects (*the coaster*, *the table*) and the only personal reference is made by the pronoun *you*, which refers to the generic 'one' as a result of participating in a hypothetical world produced by the modal auxiliary *might* with the mental cognition verb *thought*. The final three lines of this stanza, then, take the text into a hypothetical mental space where the narrator seems to be avoiding thinking too much about the actual situation by producing a hypothetical world in which an ordinary object on office tables (*the coaster*) is actually provided to staunch blood in the case of accidents.

Stanzas 2 and 3

These stanzas each begin with a negated clause (*It didn't seem much* / *It didn't hurt*). In both cases, this use of negation produces conceptually a parallel situation to the one asserted where in fact it *does* seem quite an event and where it *might actually* hurt (Nahajec 2012). These parallel scenarios underlie the rest of these stanzas where the only material action of the narrator in the whole poem (*showed*) is overshadowed by the many verbs which lack any sense of intentional action in response to the accident. Thus the verb choices here are intensive relational (*were*), verbalisation (*said*, *say*), mental cognition (*thought*, *think*, *suppose*), event (*lay*) and mental perception (*pictured*).

The post-accident situation, then, is not exactly full of activity to deal with what turns out to be quite a serious consequence for the narrator.

Negation features again in stanza 3 when the narrator points out how unhelpful the co-workers are when 'they could think of nothing to say but / "It's serious."' This negation (*nothing*) produces the concept of a situation in which they said something less self-evident than 'It's serious', which underlines the frozen shock of all those involved in the situation.

Stanza 3, in addition to the transitivity choices mentioned above, makes use of modal forms (*thought, must, suppose, could*) to produce a hypothetical world, this time imagining the *factory* that produced the blade which caused the accident. There is also a created opposition here between the likely factory and the more romanticised image of a *whetstone* from the pre-industrial era. Like the earlier hypothetical world where coasters are provided to staunch blood rather than catch coffee drips, this is a conscious daydream rather than a hallucination. They both have the modality signals which demonstrate that this is an imagined situation in the mind of a rational human being who is coping with the dramatic events by focusing on how knife blades are produced – and how they were produced in the past.

Stanza 4

The hypothetical world of the next stanza, however, is neither modal nor seemingly rational. The text becomes incoherent as the narrator wakes up from a faint. The voices of the co-workers 'reached me / down a corridor of doors that echoed closed / on a picnic with the girl who lost the child'. None of these clauses are modal and they are all presented as factual. This indicates the more comatose state of the narrator and his experience of trying to link up some kind of anxiety dream (about *the girl*) with the voices of his colleagues (the use of a male pronoun here reflects my inability to let go of the author as narrator in this instance). It is notable that the transitivity choices here are also lacking in intentional material actions as the events (*reached, echoed*) and the supervention (*lost*) underscore the narrator's feeling of lack of control over his situation. Even when he gains consciousness again in the last two lines, he is not in control but is simply described by a relational circumstantial verb (*was*) as *back in the office* and *still in this ludicrous predicament*.

The naming patterns in this poem are striking because the people who figure in the poem are anonymous and referred to only by pronouns. The narrator and victim of the accident is *I*, the co-workers are *they* and only *the girl who lost the child* is drawn with a little more detail by the post-modified noun phrase. This patterning foregrounds the girl, as she is internally deviant by contrast with the other people in the poem. Though she is a shadowy figure in the unconscious narrator's dream, the shock of the accident brings to the surface something that is very important to the narrator, though left unexplained.

By contrast with the naming of people, the naming of objects is either matter-of-fact and everyday (*the table, the coaster, the blade*) or extensively modified and therefore foregrounded: *a corridor of doors that echoed closed | on a picnic with the girl who lost the child*. The effect is to focus on this longer noun phrase which, though referring to a dream-sequence, has more significance than all the participants in the scene itself as a result of the foregrounding.

Stanza 5

While the whole poem is a straightforward past-tense narrative, with only a couple of diversions into hypothetical worlds, the adverbial (*now*) at the end of stanza 4 nevertheless causes the last part of the poem to seem more immediate, though the verbs remain past tense (*'d wet, said, laughed*). Though *now* is normally seen as bringing the text into the deictic present, this clearly remains a past narrative, but with more sense of progression as the adverb presupposes that there was a time before his awareness of having wet himself.

The stanza also contains a clichéd joke ('I'll never play the piano again'), which is dependent on the negation (*never*) and the presupposition that the speaker has played the piano before (triggered by the iterative adverb *again*). The joke is either not recognised or seen as inappropriate by the onlookers as we are told that *no one laughed*. This negation conceptually produces both the actual (negated) and also the positive situation in which people do laugh at jokes, emphasising by this contrast the unusual solemnity of the situation and the slightly hysterical gabbling of the narrator.

The transitivity choices in this final stanza suddenly become more active (*took, sew, do*) though the latter two are subordinated to verbalisations, which are equally frequent. There is, then, finally some activity to treat this injured person, though there is still delay being caused by a lot of talking as underlined by the final two lines of the stanza, which are direct speech (*They'll sew it back on*) and free direct speech (*they can do it really easily these days*) respectively.

The final line of the poem introduces a new dimension to the text as it uses modality (*couldn't*) and an ellipted clause (*do it easily*) to bring the text into a present tense made real by the final minor sentence in the form of an imperative (*Look*). This has the effect of creating an interpersonal link between the narrator and the addressee which the reader is conditioned to feel is him- or herself. This speech act (instruction) is foregrounded by its internal deviation from the rest of the poem, where there is no acknowledgement of the presence of an addressee and its effect is to make the reader shift from a spectator to a participant. It is at this point that the pragmatic meaning will make most readers wonder whether it is the poet who has lost a finger at the consensual level of interpersonal meaning, and it is also the trigger for a much more personal reaction to the poem for me as a friend of the poet.

Conclusions

This chapter has introduced a new framework for bringing together much of what we know and understand about human language into an integrated model of communication that acknowledges the place of the producer and the recipient in making meaning while also positioning the text itself as a central component of the process of communicating. For obvious reasons, the priority of the text is more evident when the producer and recipient may be at some distance from each other and/or unknown to each other, so literary works benefit from a model that places the text centrally. However, the increasing interest shown in the ideological potential of texts to influence readers (through CDA, for example) also makes this framework fit for the interpretation of non-literary texts, using the same set of textual-conceptual functions as for literary works.

Interpretation is a common word with many popular meanings and yet it is also used frequently in academic discourse, very often with an assumed rather than a defined meaning. This chapter has attempted to mark out the territory of interpretation as being analogous to the illocutionary level of meaning as defined in relation to speech acts, but relating in this case to the ideational rather than the interpersonal metafunction of language.

32

A portrait of historical stylistics

Joe Bray

Introduction

This chapter examines the assumptions of historical stylistics, noting that the term has the potential to be used somewhat loosely, to cover a wide range of practices. If it refers simply to the application of stylistic tools to texts from any period other than the present day, then most work in stylistics would fall into this category, there being no obvious reason why late twentieth-century texts, for example, should not also be judged 'historical'. This chapter makes the case instead for a more radical understanding of the term, arguing that to be properly historical, stylistic analysis must undertake a thorough investigation of its own practice, and the key methods and concepts it employs. Taking as an exemplary case the study of character, I show how the category itself was undergoing far-reaching changes at a particular point in its history, and how these can and should affect any discussion of character in texts from this period. A fully informed stylistic analysis, this chapter claims, needs to be aware not just of the particularity and contingency of the texts it investigates, but also of the means by which it does so.

(New) historical stylistics

Historical stylistics is a broad and not easily defined field, though one central strand has involved the use of corpora to investigate how styles change over time. A key article in this respect is Biber and Finegan (1989a), which charts, based on a selection of linguistic features in a sample of fiction, essays and letters from the eighteenth to the twentieth centuries, a gradual shift from literate to oral styles. This kind of quantitative approach (see also Biber and Finegan 1988) has obvious parallels with the use of corpora in historical linguistics, historical sociolinguistics and historical pragmatics, all of which have blossomed since the early 1980s, especially with the advent of electronic resources such as the Helsinki and ARCHER corpora (see, for example, Fitzmaurice and Taavitsainen 2007; Mair 2008; Nevalainen and Raumolin-Brunberg 2003; for a good recent survey see Kytö 2011). The difficulties, as well as the advantages, of using such large databases have frequently been highlighted, however, and stylisticians have tended either to stress that quantitative approaches must be combined with qualitative ones (see, for example, Semino and Short 2004), or to eschew the quantitative altogether as not providing an explanation for the '*motives* or *mechanisms*' of historical changes (S. Adamson 1999: 592). For all the recent developments in corpus linguistics, there remains a lack of a theoretical framework through which these could be harnessed in the service of stylistics, or, as Beatrix Busse puts it, 'the potential of historical corpora for an *explicit historical stylistic* investigation has only rather tentatively been exploited' (2010a: 33, though see Mahlberg 2010 and 2013a).

Busse herself calls for a 'New Historical Stylistics', which will 'explore styles (in the broadest sense of the term) within larger quantitative and qualitative frameworks' (2010a: 33). She defines this new 'diachronic turn' as 'the application of the complex approaches, tools, methods, and theories from stylistics to historical (literary) texts' (2010a: 34), identifying two main aims, one of which is 'to investigate diachronically changing or stable and/or foregrounded styles in historical (literary) texts, in a particular situation, in a particular genre, writer, and so on', while new historical stylistics 'also includes the synchronic investigation of particular historical (literary) texts from a stylistic perspective' (2010a: 34). According to Busse, a 'New Historical Stylistic perspective' will combine 'the analytical potential recently offered to us by historical corpus linguistics' with 'an informed, systematic, and detailed microlinguistically oriented and qualitative analysis' (2010a: 34). She elaborates that 'A New Historical Stylistic analysis of texts from older stages of the English language presupposes a comprehensive knowledge of the period, the context, and the language in which the text was produced', pointing to the 'variety of contextual information which guides our reading: generic knowledge, encyclopaedic background knowledge, and knowledge of scripts and schemas' (2010a: 35).

Some of the most compelling work in historical stylistics has demonstrated the benefits of just such contextual knowledge. Indeed, this kind of approach is valuable for any kind of stylistic practice. The term 'historical' is of course slippery and vague, as indicated by Busse's 'analysis of texts from older stages of the English language'. Just how old does a text have to be to be historical? A case could be made for many twentieth-, even twenty-first-century texts being further from the contemporary reader's familiar experience, and hence requiring more 'encyclopaedic background knowledge' than, for example, the nineteenth-century realist novel. Some of the most striking and influential work in stylistics has involved bringing the kind of contextualisation that Busse calls for to bear on relatively

recent examples (see, for example, Simpson 2000). Yet, beyond this difficulty with the term 'historical', there is a strong case for arguing that
historical stylistics should involve more than the application of the tools
of stylistics to texts, with knowledge of the context of the period in which
the texts were written. To be properly 'historical', a stylistic analysis needs
to interrogate fully its own critical practice, and consider diachronic
changes in the meaning of the methods and concepts it employs.

Character and characterisation

As an example case-study, the rest of this chapter will consider the stylistic
treatment of character, and the process of characterisation. In his discussion of the need for more harmony between literary and linguistic
approaches in the integration of formal and contextual analysis, Willie
van Peer draws attention to 'a frequently addressed issue in literary
studies, i.e. that of character' (1988: 9). Noting that 'character, it can hardly
be denied, is what readers infer from words, sentences, paragraphs and
textual composition depicting, describing or suggesting actions, thoughts,
utterances or feelings of a protagonist', and that 'the linguistic organization of a text will predetermine to a certain degree the kind of "picture"
one may compose of a protagonist', van Peer laments that 'at present there
is hardly a theoretical framework' for the study of 'the particular *forms* by
which this is achieved' (1988: 9). This lack has been partially remedied
in the subsequent decades, for example by Jonathan Culpeper, who sets
out to 'describe both the textual factors and the cognitive factors that
jointly lead a reader to have a particular impression of a character' (2001:
11). Culpeper thus brings into play recent developments in the emerging
field of cognitive stylistics, such as schema theory and situation models,
in an attempt to show that characters are 'part of what goes on in a
comprehender's mind' (2001: 27), and that 'one's impression of a character
is formed in the interaction between the text and the interpreter's
background knowledge; in other words, as a result of both bottom-up
and top-down processes' (2001: 28).

Yet for all the innovation and sophistication of Culpeper's framework,
his approach to characterisation does not greatly vary according to the
period of the text he is analysing. Though he admits that 'if we have
identified a play as a Morality Play (for example *Everyman*, c.1500), then
we are likely to retrieve and use our knowledge about personified vices
and virtues such as the fictional Seven Deadly Sins; whereas if we have
identified a play as a "kitchen sink drama" (for example Arnold Wesker's
plays), then we are likely to give more weight to our knowledge about real
people' (2001: 36–7), the actual concept of character with which he is
working does not change; as he explains, this is 'a pragmatic view', according to which character is 'a sub-set of context, broadly understood to be the

assumptions that interact with an utterance in the generation of meaning'
(2001: 25). Culpeper's methodology embodies, in other words, Busse's
ideal of 'the synchronic investigation of particular historical (literary)
texts from a stylistic perspective' coupled with 'a comprehensive knowledge of the period, the context, and the language in which the text was
produced.'

Yet 'character' can be not just 'a sub-set of context' in the pragmatic
sense, but also a shifting, unstable category through which context is
continually created and recreated. As van Peer notes in passing, 'the very
concept of character is itself susceptible to historical change' (1988: 9), and
these changes have an impact on the way characters are formed, both
on the page and in the mind. I argue that a diachronic consideration of
the meaning of character, and the process of characterisation, needs to
inform any stylistic analysis of, in van Peer's terms, the 'forms' by which
the 'picture' of a protagonist is composed. Indeed, as I will show, this
metaphor of character as a picture or portrait is fundamental to late eight-
eenth- and early nineteenth-century understanding of the concept, and
sheds light on its constantly changing complexity in this period.

Character and caricature in *Emma*

What, for example, is the stylistician to make of the following passage
from Jane Austen's *Emma* (1816):

> Emma's politeness was at hand directly, to say, with smiling interest –
>   'Have you heard from Miss Fairfax so lately? I am extremely happy.
> I hope she is well?'
>   'Thank you. You are so kind!' replied the happily deceived aunt, while
> eagerly hunting for the letter. – 'Oh! here it is. I was sure it could not be
> far off; but I had put my huswife upon it, you see, without being aware, and
> so it was quite hid, but I had it in my hand so very lately that I was almost
> sure it must be on the table. I was reading it to Mrs. Cole, and since she
> went away, I was reading it again to my mother, for it is such a pleasure to
> her – a letter from Jane – that she can never hear it often enough; so I knew
> it could not be far off, and here it is, only just under my huswife – and since
> you are so kind as to wish to hear what she says; – but, first of all, I really
> must, in justice to Jane, apologise for her writing so short a letter – only
> two pages you see – hardly two – and in general she fills the whole paper
> and crosses half. My mother often wonders that I can make it out so well.
> She often says, when the letter is first opened, "Well, Hetty, now I think
> you will be put to it to make out all that chequer-work" – don't you,
> ma'am? – And then I tell her, I am sure she would contrive to make it out
> herself, if she had nobody to do it for her – every word of it – I am sure she
> would pore over it till she had made out every word. And, indeed, though

my mother's eyes are not so good as they were, she can see amazingly
well still, thank God! with the help of spectacles. It is such a blessing!
My mother's are really very good indeed. Jane often says, when she is here,
"I am sure, grandmamma you must have had very strong eyes to see as
you do – and so much fine work as you have done too! – I only wish my eyes
may last me as well."'

 All this spoken extremely fast obliged Miss Bates to stop for breath; and
Emma said something very civil about the excellence of Miss Fairfax's
handwriting.   *(Austen 1996: 130–1)*

This scene comes from Emma's first visit in the novel to the house of
Mrs and Miss Bates. Though Emma generally finds such visits 'very
disagreeable, – a waste of time – tiresome women' (1996: 129), while on a
walk with Harriet she makes a 'sudden resolution' to call on them, spurred
on perhaps by 'many a hint from Mr. Knightley, and some from her own
heart, as to her deficiency' (1996: 129). The conversation soon turns from
'thanks for their visit, solicitude for their shoes, anxious inquiries after
Mr. Woodhouse's health, cheerful communication about her mother's,
and sweet-cake from the beaufet' (1996: 129–30), to Jane Fairfax, Miss
Bates's niece and her favourite topic. Emma's decision to drop in is partly
based on her reasoning that, as she puts it to Harriet, 'as well as she could
calculate, they were just now quite safe from any letter from Jane Fairfax'
(1996: 129), yet to her dismay, masked by smiling politeness, it turns out
she is mistaken.

 As the reader's first sustained exposure to Miss Bates, the passage plays a
key role in establishing what van Peer calls the 'picture' of her character.
Those searching for what he terms 'the particular *forms* by which this is
achieved' might focus on some or all of the following: her initial failure to
pick up on Emma's ironic politeness, ensuring she remains 'happily
deceived'; her inability to stay on the topic of the letter, drifting instead
into a discussion of her mother's eyesight; her direct quotation of the
speech of both her mother and Jane; her references to her mother in
both the second and third person, often in close proximity ('don't you,
ma'am? – And then I tell her'), her verbose, repetitive style ('And then I tell
her, I am sure she would contrive to make it out herself, if she had nobody
to do it for her – every word of it – I am sure she would pore over it till
she had made out every word'); the use of dashes and exclamation marks
to convey the breathless speed of her delivery ('I really must, in justice to
Jane, apologise for her writing so short a letter – only two pages you see –
hardly two – '). Taken together, these features reinforce the impression of
Miss Bates given by the narrator's early description: 'She was a great talker
upon little matters, which exactly suited Mr. Woodhouse, full of trivial
communications and harmless gossip' (1996: 20).

 At this point in his or her reading of the novel the reader may thus agree
with Emma that Miss Bates is a rather tiresome old lady, tediously

preoccupied with the accomplishments of her niece, and the trivial concerns of the neighbourhood; a caricature of a gossip. Like many of Austen's apparently secondary characters, she does not seem central to the plot, or the heroine's moral development. In a 1940 essay entitled 'Character and caricature in Jane Austen', the psychologist and critic D. W. Harding attempts to draw a line between Austen's 'characters' and her 'caricatures'. While the former are 'full and natural portraits of imaginable people', the latter 'while certainly referring to types of people we might easily have come across are yet presented with such exaggeration and simplification that our response to them is expected to be rather different' (Harding 1998: 80). With her caricatures, he claims, 'attention is . . . concentrated on a few features or a small segment of the personality to the neglect of much that would make the figure a full human being, and the understanding is that the reader will accept this convention and not inquire closely into the areas of behaviour and personality that the author chooses to avoid' (1998: 87). In a passage that encapsulates Emma's attitude to Miss Bates at this point in the novel Harding adds that

> There is in fact a close relation between the handling of a fictional figure as caricature and the clinical attitude that we adopt in real life towards someone who is drunk, very ignorant, irritable with tiredness, or in some other way less than an equal companion. We have to pull our punches. Our forbearance, justifiable though it may be, reduces his interpersonal status; his actions are no longer allowed full social relevance, we belittle him by humouring him.
> *(Harding 1998: 91)*

Harding does admit, however, that 'transitional forms may occur on the borderline between character and caricature, and that there is occasionally a mixture of the two techniques in one figure' (1998: 82). As an example he gives sustained attention to Miss Bates. Though he observes that she is given typical features of Austen's caricatures, such as lengthy, uninterrupted speeches, she is a key demonstration, for him, of her ability to add 'fuller human relevance as the outer layers are penetrated and less grotesque features of personality are indicated' (1998: 102). 'It is in Miss Bates', he claims, 'that Jane Austen exploits most delicately the technique of going beyond the ridiculous features of the caricature' (1998: 102). Emma's cutting remark on Box Hill, after Frank Churchill has proposed a group game to please her, has a small, but noticeable effect:

> '. . . I shall be sure to say three dull things as soon as ever I open my mouth, shan't I? – (looking round with the most good-humoured dependence on every body's assent) – Do not you all think I shall?'
>   Emma could not resist.
>   'Ah, ma'am, but there may be a difficulty. Pardon me – but you will be limited as to number – only three at once.'

> Miss Bates, deceived by the mock ceremony of her manner, did not immediately catch her meaning; but, when it burst upon her, it could not anger, though a slight blush showed that it could pain her.
>
> *(Austen 1996: 306)*

This moment is a reminder to both the reader and Emma that Miss Bates is, in Harding's words, not simply 'a figure of fun, something to caricature', but 'after all a person' (1998: 103). After Mr Knightley's famous reproach ('She is poor; she has sunk from the comforts she was born to; and, if she live to old age, must probably sink more. Her situation should secure your compassion. It was badly done indeed!' (1996: 309)), Emma is overcome with 'anger against herself' on the carriage ride home:

> Never had she felt so agitated, mortified, grieved, at any circumstance in her life. She was most forcibly struck. The truth of his representation there was no denying. She felt it at her heart. How could she have been so brutal, so cruel to Miss Bates!
>
> *(1996: 310)*

As many critics have noted, the Box Hill episode marks a crucial point in Emma's increasing self-awareness and knowledge of her own feelings, not least for Knightley. That evening she reflects that 'she had often been remiss, her conscience told her so; remiss, perhaps, more in thought than fact; scornful, ungracious' (1996: 311), and resolves to pay a visit to Miss Bates and her mother the next morning.

The way that Miss Bates moves from being a tiresome caricature, an exaggerated figure of fun, into a character deserving sympathy and under-standing, hints then that caricature may be a more complex form of representation than might first appear, and that its dividing line with character may be hard to draw. Turning to the original context of the term helps to explore its potential complexities further. Consideration of contemporary artistic treatments of 'caricature' in fact reveals that its relationship to portraiture is somewhat fraught in this period, and that the ability of both to represent character is newly up for debate.

The Age of Caricature

The reign of George III (1760–1820) has often been designated the 'Age of Caricature'. There was a huge upsurge in graphic satire, both political and social, in this period; the British Museum alone holds over ten thousand satirical etchings from the period of George III's reign, and there would also of course have been numerous re-issues, pirated cheap copies and lost woodcuts, as well as adaptations in other forms. The most prolific and celebrated caricaturists included Thomas Rowlandson (1757–1827) and James Gillray (1756–1815). While Rowlandson's drawings are often concerned with the comedy of social life, and revel in the ridiculous and the ribald, by the tumultuous decade of the 1790s Gillray had established himself as the period's foremost political caricaturist. His prints were coveted by many of those who he satirised, including politicians such as Fox and Sheridan, and often valued more highly than the more formal portraits that could be seen at the Royal Academy exhibitions. Diana Donald notes that 'One writer after another praised [Gillray's] grasp of characteristic expression and gait which enabled the artist to convey character more tellingly than a conventional portraitist, and transformed caricature from a game into a dramatic art form' (1996: 39). This notion of a 'more telling' representation of character is also current in modern criticism of caricature. Amelia Rauser points to the 'fascinatingly para-doxical' operation of the form, pointing out that 'Caricature deforms the exterior appearance of a person, selecting and exaggerating certain nota-ble elements of his or her visage; yet this exaggeration and deformation paradoxically makes a more-like likeness, a truer portrait. Furthermore, at least in a good caricature, the elements selected and deformed also, paradoxically, reveal a truth about the subject's interior life, even though they are themselves only elements that lie on the surface of the person' (2008: 15). For her, caricature is thus 'preoccupied with unmasking the authentic truth of subjective individuals' (2008: 15), and goes hand in hand with the emergence of what she calls 'the modern notion of selfhood – with its "golden nugget" of identity deep within and its valor-ization of private authenticity, individualism, and consistency across time' (2008: 15).

Yet this emphasis on caricature's ability to unmask the 'authentic truth' of selfhood only tells part of the story. The term itself was applied loosely in the period of its heyday, to refer to any kind of satirical print. At one end were the crude, cheap etchings which poked fun at the low sexual and political scandals of the day; at the other were often very elaborate engrav-ings which brought caricature much nearer to 'high' art. It has always to be remembered that the 'Age of Caricature' coincided with the emergence of a national tradition in art, under the influence in particular of the Royal Academy, founded in 1768, and its first President, Sir Joshua Reynolds. Both Rowlandson and Gillray learned their trade as artists in the Academy schools, and, however far from the works of Reynolds and Gainsborough the satirical counter-culture of the 1780s and 1790s might have seemed, its leading proponents were always working in their shadow.

Some of Gillray's more elaborate caricatures in particular achieved an artistic complexity, and a reputation, parallel, if not equivalent to the 'history paintings' of his more illustrious contemporaries. As an example, his *Sin, Death, and the Devil* (1792) presents Pitt and his recently dismissed Lord Chancellor, Edward Thurlow, with whom he had been feuding, as the warring figures of Death and the Devil from *Paradise Lost*. They are kept apart by the snaky sorceress Sin, a representation of Queen Charlotte, who was scurrilously rumoured to be Pitt's secret lover and protector. As the grotesque figure of Thurlow – winged and be-wigged – approaches the Gate of Hell, bearing a broken mace and a shield decorated with the seal of his old office, the Queen's withered torso rises from the ground and her hand shields Pitt, though there is a crude suggestion that it may be doing more. As well as its obvious allusion to *Paradise Lost*, the etching also refers to Hogarth's painting *Satan, Sin and Death*, executed many decades earlier, but recently reproduced as an engraving by Rowlandson and John Ogborne. Furthermore, as a sentence that slithers along the bottom of Gillray's image makes clear, his caricature also offers a satirical response to the modern pictorial representations of Milton's poem being produced by Henry Fuseli and others.

Sin, Death, and the Devil is not alone among Gillray's caricatures in being full of intertextual allusions and suggestions. Such works deliberately echo, indeed satirise, the 'grand style' of Reynolds and others, with their emphasis on classical models and abstract, universal ideals. The creation of 'more-like likeness' hardly seems the main point; the caricature's meaning depends instead on a complex web of political and cultural signification. In other words, caricature can be used for more ends than simply 'unmasking the authentic truth of subjective individuals' as Rauser puts it. Furthermore, the potential ambiguity of 'likeness' illustrates the changing nature of portraiture more generally in the period, and signals a wider uncertainty surrounding the representation of character.

Character in art: the changing face of the portrait

According to the leading art critic Shearer West, between 1790 and 1815 'portraiture began to be a less defined art, as it took on the qualities of history or genre painting' (1996: 76). Influenced by the theory and practice of Reynolds in particular, the boundary between the portrait and the history painting became increasingly blurred, such that the traditional association of the portrait with the accurate representation of its subject began to be questioned, or, as Shearer West puts it, 'likeness was no longer the primary concern of the portraitist' (1996: 76). For Reynolds in the *Discourses*, the most important feature of 'grand style' is that it 'does not consist in mere imitation': 'I will now add that Nature herself is not to be too closely copied. There are excellencies in the art of painting beyond what is commonly called the imitation of nature: and these excellencies I wish to point out' (1975: 41). 'The true test of all the arts', Reynolds argues in the thirteenth Discourse, 'is not solely whether the production is a true copy of nature, but whether it answers the end of art, which is to produce a pleasing effect upon the mind' (1975: 241). In the fourth Discourse he notes that 'even in portraits, the grace, and, we may add, the likeness, consists more in taking the general air, than in observing the exact similitude of every feature' (1975: 59). Such comments are evidence, for John Barrell, of 'an insistence that portraiture should aim, as far as possible, at the excellencies of the grand style, and so at a clarity of marking though not at a laboured fidelity' (1986: 123), or, as Marcia Pointon observes, 'likeness', is 'a shifting commodity, not an absolute point of reference; it is an idea to be annexed, rather than a standard by which to measure reality' (1993: 9).

This shifting conception of 'likeness' in late eighteenth-century portraiture had consequences for the understanding and interpretation of character. Nicholas Penny quotes the comment of one contemporary that 'in the male portraits Reynolds sometimes "lost likeness" in his endeavour to "give character where it did not exist"' (1986: 17). 'Character' is here, as elsewhere in the period, held to be in opposition to, or tension with, 'likeness'. In *A Poetical Epistle to Sir Joshua Reynolds* (1777) William Combe, having observed that 'this seems to be a *Portrait-painting* Age', and that 'a Portrait is now interesting even to the stranger' puts the form's popularity down to its attempt to match the history-painting: 'this Addition of Character, whether Historical, Allegorical, Domestic, or Professional, calls forth new sentiments to the Picture; for by seeing Persons represented with an appearance suited to them, or in employments natural to their situation, our ideas are multiplied, and branch forth into a pleasing variety, which a representation of a formal Figure, however strong the resemblance might be, can never afford' (1777: ii). According to Combe, then, 'the Addition of Character' to the portrait, and the resultant shift away from 'the representation of a formal Figure', means that its 'likeness' to its subject is of secondary importance: 'this interesting Cast of Character gives, to the well-painted Portrait, a right to demand a place in the Collection of those who are not only ignorant of the Original, but are careless about it' (1777: ii).

The term 'character' itself has a long and complex association with the portrait. Writers on portraiture in the early eighteenth century were confident about the form's ability to represent the subject's 'character' comprehensively and accurately. The portrait-painter Jonathan Richardson claimed in 1719 that 'A Portrait is a Sort of General History of the Life of the Person it represents, not only to Him who is acquainted with it, but to Many Others, who upon Occasion of seeing it are frequently told, of what is most Material concerning Them, or their General Character at least; The Face; and Figure is also Describ'd and as much of the Character as appears by These, which oftentimes is here seen in a very great Degree' (1719: 45). The portrait's ability to represent 'Character' to 'a very great degree' became something of a commonplace, as Nadia Tscherny notes: 'the connection between portraiture and biography has a history in British eighteenth-century thought' as 'it became fashionable to speak of written characterisations in the vocabulary of painting and vice-versa' (1986: 8). In *An Essay on the Theory of Painting* (1725), Richardson develops the analogy further, claiming that 'upon the sight of a Portrait the Character, and Master-strokes of the History of the Person it represents are apt to flow in upon the Mind, and to be the Subject of Conversation: So that to sit for one's Picture, is to have an Abstract of one's Life written, and published, and ourselves thus consign'd over to Honour, or Infamy' (1725: 13–14). Indeed, Richardson even suggests that the portrait can give a clearer representation of 'Character' than the written biography:

> Painting gives us not only the Persons, but the Characters of Great Men. The Air of the Head, and the Mien in general, gives strong Indications of the Mind, and illustrates what the Historian says more expressly, and particularly. Let a Man read a Character in my Lord Clarendon, (and certainly never was there a better Painter in that kind) he will find it improv'd by seeing a Picture of the same Person by Van Dyck.
>
> *(Richardson 1725: 10)*

A portrait by van Dyck can then, according to Richardson, illustrate 'character' both 'more expressly' and 'particularly' than the best efforts of the historian. Yet this early eighteenth-century confidence in the portrait's representative ability has faded by the end of the century, partly because the notion of 'character' itself has become subject to greater scrutiny. Deidre Lynch outlines an early eighteenth-century typographical culture that has 'an investment in the eloquence of the material surface – the face of the page, the outside of the body – and their culture's idealization of what was graphically self-evident' (1998: 38). 'Characters' can therefore be found on the body, as well as on the page and the coin; as writers 'seem eager to understand faces less as natural facts and more as signs, prototypical reading matter' (1998: 30). According to Lynch, there arose 'an ideal of a legible, tell-tale body, one marked with characters that externalize character' (2000: 354). As Lisa Freeman has observed, however, 'the term "character" underwent a radical semantic transformation' in the eighteenth century, as it 'experienced an explosion in the number of figurative meanings with which it was associated' (2002: 20, 22). Freeman claims that 'the one-to-one correspondence between signifier and signified that had once been embodied by this term was cleaved apart because the outside of a "character" no longer bore any necessary or meaningful resemblance to its inside', and that 'character lost its self-evident or transparent signature and entered into the grey area of fiction, fabrication, forgery, and fraud' (2002: 22). As a result, according to Freeman, 'understanding "character" now required skills in observation, penetration, and interpretation' (2002: 22).

By the time that Jane Austen was beginning her career as a novelist, in other words, 'character' was a hotly debated, often problematic concept. Portrait-painters, and writers on portraiture, were no longer confident about the form's ability to capture character fully and accurately, and the blurring of the boundary with caricature was a further complication.

All her heroines struggle, in different ways, to read the 'pictures' of those around them; indeed, these struggles are the central theme of her novels. No protagonist makes more mistakes in the interpretation of character than the one she feared her readers would like least, Emma Woodhouse, and thus it is fitting that in the final novel to be published in her lifetime the metaphor of character as a portrait, so central to late eighteenth- and early nineteenth-century culture, is actually made literal.

The portrait in *Emma*

As an example of the distinction between a caricature and a character, Harding (1998) points to the contrast between Mrs Elton and Harriet Smith in *Emma*. While the former is revealed on her first visit to Hartfield as 'a pushing, ill-judging woman' by her long, uninterrupted speeches comparing Hartfield to Maple Grove and singing the praises of Bath and Jane Fairfax, Harriet's presentation is, he claims, very different. Though he admits she is 'exposed to our laughter' at various points in the novel, she is still, he says, 'presented as a character, a full portrait': 'Her speeches are always part of a true conversational interchange, and her absurdity (such as her treasuring up laughably trivial mementoes of Mr Elton) arises out of her particularized experience in the story and is not tacked on to her as if it were one of the identifying tags by which she is to be recognized' (Harding 1998: 91, 87).

Harriet's 'character' is indeed the subject of much detailed discussion in the novel. In an early conversation, for example, Mr Elton praises Emma for 'the striking improvement of Harriet's manner, since her introduction at Hartfield', observing that 'You have given Miss Smith all that she required ... you have made her graceful and easy. She was a beautiful creature when she came to you, but, in my opinion, the attractions you have added are infinitely superior to what she received from nature' (1996: 37). Emma replies that 'Harriet only wanted drawing out' and 'I have done very little', though she does admit that 'I have perhaps given her a little more decision of character, have taught her to think on points which had not fallen in her way before' (1996: 37). The language of art criticism, which has been lurking under the surface of their conversation, then emerges clearly:

> 'Exactly so; that is what principally strikes me. So much superadded decision of character! Skilful has been the hand.'
>
> 'Great has been the pleasure, I am sure. I never met with a disposition more truly amiable.'
>
> 'I have no doubt of it.' And it was spoken with a sort of sighing animation which had a vast deal of the lover.   *(1996: 37)*

Mr Elton is thus suggesting here that Emma has been to some degree responsible for the moulding of Harriet's 'character', comparing here to a painter who has not just 'drawn her out', but even 'drawn her', adding 'character' to make her into the 'full portrait' that Harding describes.

And of course Emma does indeed literally draw Harriet in the novel, in a famous episode which highlights some of the difficulties involved in representing and assessing 'character'. Her proposal to attempt the 'likeness' of her friend earns Mr Elton's instant enthusiasm. Believing that he is in love with Harriet, Emma is confused by his praise for her drawing: 'Yes, good man! – thought Emma – but what has all that to do with taking likenesses? You know nothing of drawing. Don't pretend to be in raptures about mine. Keep your raptures for Harriet's face' (1996: 38). As the drawing of the portrait progresses, Emma fails to see that it is her supposed skill at 'taking likenesses' rather than Harriet's 'likeness' that Mr Elton admires. She is forced to admit that 'There was no being displeased with such an encourager, for his admiration made him discern a likeness almost before it was possible. She could not respect his eye, but his love and his complaisance were unexceptionable' (1996: 41).

When the portrait is finished Elton is in 'continual raptures' and defends it 'through every criticism' (1996: 41). He is particularly insistent on its 'likeness'. To Mrs Weston's observations that 'Miss Woodhouse has given her friend the only beauty she wanted' and 'The expression of the eye is most correct, but Miss Smith has not those eye-brows and eye-lashes. It is the fault of her face that she has them not', he replies 'I cannot agree with you. It appears to me a most perfect resemblance in every feature. I never saw such a likeness in my life. We must allow for the effect of shade, you know' (1996: 41). Similarly, when Mr Woodhouse expresses his anxiety that Harriet appears to be sitting out of doors, Mr Elton is fervent in his praise:

> 'You, sir, may say any thing,' cried Mr. Elton; 'but I must confess that I regard it as a most happy thought, the placing of Miss Smith out of doors; and the tree is touched with such inimitable spirit! Any other situation would have been much less in character. The naïveté of Miss Smith's manners – and altogether – Oh, it is most admirable! I cannot keep my eyes from it. I never saw such a likeness.'   *(1996: 42)*

Mr Elton's repeated praise for the 'likeness' of the drawing is further evidence of the fact that, in Pointon's words, this is 'a shifting commodity, not an absolute point of reference; it is an idea to be annexed, rather than a standard by which to measure reality' (1993: 9). It is his partiality which makes him see 'likeness' where others, even the artist herself, do not. After the first day's sketch Emma judges that although there is 'no want of likeness', 'she meant to throw in a little improvement to the figure, to give a little more height, and considerably more elegance' (1996: 41), and she later acknowledges to herself the truth of Knightley's criticism that she has made Harriet 'too tall': 'Emma knew that she had, but would not own it' (1996: 41).

The term 'likeness' in *Emma* is not, however, restricted to this episode. The novel also foregrounds the subjectivity involved in assessing 'likeness' in a broader sense; that is, the difficulty of judging whether characters are 'like' one another. The novel suggests how hard it is for characters to assess others in relation to themselves, to 'unmask' individual subjectivity and achieve 'a more-like likeness', in Rauser's terms. The term usually occurs in *Emma* in the context of a comparison of two characters. For example, Emma is eager to stress what she and Frank Churchill have in common, after Frank's engagement to Jane Fairfax has come to light. Though he at first rebuffs her suggestion that 'in the midst of your perplexities at that time, you had very great amusement in tricking us all', she persists with her interpretation:

> 'I am sure it was a source of high entertainment to you, to feel that you were taking us all in. – Perhaps I am readier to suspect, because, to tell you the truth, I think it might have been some amusement to myself in the same situation. I think there is a little likeness between us.'
>
> He bowed.
>
> 'If not in our disposition,' she presently added, with a look of true sensibility, 'there is a likeness in our destiny; the destiny which bids fair to connect us with two characters so much superior to our own.'
>
> *(1996: 391–2)*

Frank's lack of response, coupled with Emma's stagey 'look of true sensibility', invites the reader to question this comparison, especially given that Frank is eventually shown to have behaved almost as openly towards Jane as circumstances would permit. Emma's assessment of 'likeness' here again illustrates the slipperiness and subjectivity of the concept.

In contrast, she is determined not to see a likeness between her and one other character in particular. When Harriet suggests to her that she will be 'an old maid at last, like Miss Bates!' after her friend has told her that she has 'very little intention of ever marrying at all', Emma's characterisation (or caricaturisation?) of Miss Bates is withering:

> 'That is as formidable an image as you could present, Harriet; and if I thought I should ever be like Miss Bates! so silly – so satisfied – so smiling – so prosing – so undistinguishing and fastidious – and so apt to tell every thing relative to every body about me, I would marry tomorrow. But between us, I am convinced there never can be any likeness, except in being unmarried.' *(1996: 73)*

The reader is perhaps less likely to dismiss this 'likeness' given Emma's self-satisfied behaviour towards Harriet early in the novel. The style of the passage also subtly suggests the mistakenness of her interpretation. For the way that Emma dismisses Miss Bates here ironically mimics the patterns of Miss Bates's own speech, with its exclamation, its dashes and its repetition (see the discussion, above, of the passage describing her first visit to Miss Bates in the novel). Austen cleverly hints here then that the gap between Miss Bates and her may not be as great as Emma wishes, and that Harriet's assessment of a 'likeness' may not be far from the truth.

Conclusion

The 'picture' of Miss Bates in *Emma* can thus, I have argued, only be fully understood through an investigation of the cultural meanings of 'character' at the time, and the way it is represented in other art forms. The changing nature of portraiture in the late eighteenth and early nineteenth centuries, coupled with its complex relationship to caricature, reveals a shifting, increasingly uncertain attitude towards character which pervades much literature of the period, and especially Austen's novels. Any stylistic analysis of the means by which she constructs character would benefit from taking account of these fundamental changes, which were transforming the concept itself. The historical stylistician typically deploys the contents of his or her tool-kit judiciously, with due regard for context. At least occasionally, however, it might be worth considering whether the tools themselves need reconfiguring.

Part V

Extensions of stylistics

33

Media stylistics

Marina Lambrou and Alan Durant

Linguistic analysis of media discourse is often described as 'media stylistics'. This may seem an obvious choice of expression, but unless examined it can obscure complexity in what such approaches to the analysis of media consist of, as well as what they are for. 'Media stylistics' is of interest, it is suggested in this chapter, because it throws light on an especially influential but also contested field of language use (Durant and Lambrou 2009). This area of stylistics is also interesting theoretically, in that it exposes for reflection a number of different facets of and approaches to stylistic investigation more widely.

The chapter begins by reviewing the general concept of 'media stylistics'. We disentangle some of the polysemy of the two terms which, when combined, describe work in this area, and discuss some key themes and concerns which emerge. In brief commentary on two short extracts of media discourse in English, we elaborate a distinction between two alternative emphases: study of media language as concerned with general capabilities associated with changing technologies for conveying linguistic messages (e.g. language use in telegraphy, radio or instant messaging); and study of media language as critical commentary on modern society's dominant communication forms, which tend to take an electronic, 'media' form. In the first emphasis, media discourse has implications as regards the social functions of language and as regards social change (as Eisenstein (1979) and others have argued in relation to the advent of print in the Middle Ages, and as Ong (1982) has proposed for broadcast speech-as-a-kind-of-writing, or 'secondary orality', in the mid-twentieth century). In the second emphasis, media language is viewed as a matter of linguistic resources used to communicate within an array of available contemporary media choices whose general existence is simply taken as a social fact. It would be easy to overstate such a distinction. So we also explore interaction between these different emphases, especially at the level of media 'genres'. In the formation of genres, patterns of linguistic choice are superimposed on a given technical infrastructure and history of media capabilities; distinctive media styles gradually evolve from each combination to serve specific and changing expressive and communicative purposes.

The 'media' and 'stylistics' in 'media stylistics'

Each of the two words that combine in the expression 'media stylistics' introduces complexity into how we understand this stylistic sub-field. Let us consider each separately to begin with.

Media

The word *media* is used to describe many different kinds of contemporary discourse, including in an ever-increasing number of compounds and combinations. In some of those combinations, other words pre-modify *media* as indications of media-type (e.g. *analogue media*, *e-media*); other combinations use *media* as the modifier, indicating agents, functions and consequences (e.g. *media blitz*, *media hype*, *media conglomerate*, *media revolution*). Such verbal creativity is common; less common, perhaps, is reflection on what precisely we mean when we use *media* itself in these ways.

The English word *media* has its origins in Latin 'medium', meaning 'middle', and comes into English in the late sixteenth century. As applied to communication, early uses of 'medium' implied what is usually called a 'communication model' of language: a speaker addresses a hearer by means of a channel, 'in between', which carries a message from one to the other; roles are then reversed, as speaker becomes hearer (Mattelart and Mattelart 1998). With a complicated social history surrounding them, the two linguistic modes, or 'mediums' (sometimes, carrying over the Latin plural, *media*), are in this conception speech and writing (Briggs and Burke 2005; Gelb 1952; Goody 1987). As Raymond Williams (1983) shows in his *Keywords* entry for *media*, and as Katie Wales (2007) elaborates in her account of more recent changes in the word, *media* has changed in meaning subsequently and acquired new meanings closely linked to the social history of which it is part.

Simplifying considerably, three senses relevant to media stylistics are important. The first is the continuing sense of *media* as communication modes or channels, between people or organisations. This sense has broadened, from writing through various forms of print publication such as newspapers and magazines into audio and audio-visual electronic formats including telegraph, telephone, film, television, radio and more recently a range of new digital media. Subject to shifts of spatialisation, such *media* provide a foundation, vehicle or platform for achieving communicative purposes (including advertising, artistic expression, and propaganda). A second meaning emerges by metonymy applied to the first. Since the mid-twentieth century (and earlier in an animate sense associated with spiritualism), *media* now also means people and institutions involved in production and ownership of the historically varying technological channels of communication denoted by the first sense. So for instance we have collective plural *media* denoting journalists, paparazzi, newsreaders and editors. A third strand of meaning introduces affective or symbolic loading into the other two meanings: *media* acquire a mythical character based either favourably on associations of celebrity, glamour and social influence, or unfavourably based on associations including sensationalism, intrusiveness and manipulation. Each meaning, along with related strands in the word, could be analysed in greater depth. Their significance as range and alternative in the context of media stylistics is that what we look for when analysing 'media language' will vary, depending on which sense dominates in any given analysis or for a particular analyst.

Stylistics

The other word in the expression 'media stylistics' – *stylistics* – is examined from different perspectives throughout this volume. As has long been recognised, the word's general difficulty is its relation to *style*. Two views in relation to media 'stylistics' are relevant. The first involves general description of 'style', widespread from the 1960s onwards (see Crystal and Davy 1969; O'Donnell and Todd 1980, and more recently Crystal 2006 and Biber and Conrad 2009). On this understanding, style is a matter of the variables which function together to characterise often readily identifiable kinds of language use: for media, these are either kinds of media discourse in general, for instance in contrast with print publications, or some particular form or genre (such as the newspaper headline, email, text message, TV documentary voice-over, or blog). This broad sense of *style* has been usefully subclassified by Conrad and Biber (2009) as the combined effect of genre, register and style considerations, which may be distinguished from one another on the basis on how pervasive or episodic particular features are, and whether they are functional or not. A contrasting view of stylistics foregrounds interpretation. It traces how discourse choices cause or at least shape the meanings a text conveys. For example, an analysis may show how a particular documentary voice-over exhibits racist overtones, how women were side-lined in a studio discussion, or how an email thread conveys or fails to convey intimacy, distance or respect. This sense comes closer to more general discourse analysis and critical interpretation found in literary and cultural studies and is best described as discourse stylistics (see Lambrou 2014b; Simpson and Hall 2002). Nothing prevents descriptive and interpretive approaches combining, in the form of interpretive claims supported by linguistic evidence. Difficulties have been extensively discussed in the field, however, regarding how far textual elements may be thought to *determine* meaning, especially in the context of increased recognition of the importance of pragmatic strategies in assigning meaning (Fish 1980).

Table 33.1 Concerns and aims of media stylistics.

1a. examination of particular, individual texts	1b. examination of a selected corpus of texts, identifying pervasive features of the type of text represented by the sample
2a. investigation of media language aiming to enhance understanding of particular discourse features or techniques	2b. application of linguistic techniques in order to illuminate extra-linguistic, cultural or political topics (as for instance in critical discourse analysis (CDA))
3a. textual description	3b. textual interpretation (and assessment of textual effects)

Media stylistics

When the words *media* and *stylistics* are combined as description of an approach to the analysis of the media, a number of alternative concerns and aims come into view. These can be tabulated in a somewhat simplified grid, as shown in Table 33.1.

Whether aspects are listed left or right in the two vertical columns does not imply how they should combine. It is easy to imagine a study which looks at a single text in order to illuminate some cultural or political point. Equally, it is easy to conceive of a study of a corpus of texts designed to investigate particular linguistic features or techniques. What may be significant, however, is that the sense of 'interpretation', as an element of contrast in the third row, shifts both as regards *what* is being interpreted and also what such an interpretation *shows*, depending on which other two choices are made.

Survey and key concepts

Questions about the scope and ambitions of media stylistics may be treated as abstract, theoretical considerations (as they are in the Table 33.1). But the range of approaches being typified emerges from a particular historical formation, something that is felt most when work is read from different periods, or when wider aims and methods are generalised from particular studies.

For example, how the beginnings of media stylistics are dated will depend partly on the meanings given to the terms *media* and *stylistics* discussed above. If we take *media* to include 'speech' and 'writing', rather than only modern electronic media, then *all* stylistics is in some sense media stylistics. Stylistics on this understanding is closely intertwined with rhetoric, which has a 2,500-year history ranging across both oratory (speech) and composition (writing). Stylistic studies inevitably investigate variation in relation to an over-arching contrast between the two mediums: the dimension of register traditionally known in Halliday's three-way classification as 'mode' (Halliday 1978). In their 1960s study, Crystal and Davy even claim a central importance for considerations of medium (speech/writing) and participation (monologue/dialogue) as defining dimensions of media discourse (1969: 68). Stylistic work can compare techniques used in the 'media' of speech and writing explicitly, or it must presume their general characteristics simply as a backdrop to more specific stylistic choices made *within* one medium or the other. With modern media, the second approach is problematic. Many such media exhibit complex crossover between characteristics associated with speech and with writing (e.g. in terms of production circumstances such as simultaneity and co-presence of participants or spontaneity versus revision and editing; in terms of the durability or evanescence of the message; and in terms of the relative prominence of involvement strategies marked by first- and second-person pronouns, modal auxiliaries of subjective attitude, contractions and hedging). This is a major significance of Naomi Baron's 'continuum' rather than 'opposition' view of speech and writing (Baron 2000, 2008), and presents a challenge in law and social policy when questions are raised regarding what is speech and what is writing (e.g. for the purpose of distinguishing slander and libel). Different answers may be arrived at for film dialogue, live studio discussion and internet messaging, for instance.

What we tend now to think of as 'media stylistics' emerges most distinctly in the course of the twentieth century. Concern was initially with the rise of influential *mass media*, from the 1920s onwards (radio, then early television), especially with how such media were affecting language use through increased influence of expanding twentieth-century professions including advertising, political propaganda and public relations (Briggs and Burke 2005; L'Etang 2004). Early exploration of media language can be found in work by writers in the tradition of general semantics, for example, such as Chase (1938) and Hayakawa (1939), as well as in Osgood et al. (1957), whose efforts to 'measure meaning' extended into investigation of discourse fields including advertising. In Britain, Raymond Williams's *Communications* (1962), which related analysis of the changing broadcast environment of the time to both historical and theoretical perspectives on communication, is a notable, early British examination of modern forms of 'media' communication. Particularly influential internationally has been Marshall McLuhan's *Understanding Media* (1964), which includes among its essays an analysis of how technical capability and format (which are specific media attributes) affect not only the reach or circulation of a discourse but also its significance and implications: famously, in McLuhan's words, 'the medium is the message'.

During the later 1960s, as part of a significant growth in stylistic enquiry, work on media language can be found in for instance Leech's concern with the language of advertising (1966a), in Crystal and Davy's (1969) early work on news reporting, and in the work of a number of other writers. While some of this analysis was less critically engaged than earlier concern in general semantics to expose discourse power as projected in Communism and Fascism, it was more systematically descriptive and linked more closely with other fields of linguistic enquiry. Two generalisations might be made about subsequent lines of development. First, from an early focus on grammar, vocabulary and pronunciation there has been increased emphasis on topics in discourse analysis and pragmatics, leading for example to innovative studies of media speech participation and interaction (O'Keeffe 2006), and, following Goffman (1981), of different speaker and hearer roles when production is by teams and comprehension is by large but internally varying audiences (Allan Bell 1991). Second, more detailed connections have been developed between the linguistics involved in media stylistics and social and political aspects of discourse circulation, for instance in investigations of power relations expressed in radio discourse (Hutchby 1996), regarding ideology in general (Hodge and Kress 1988), and to do with specific issues related to racism and gender discrimination (van Dijk 1988).

Key topics and developing approaches

Two media forms in particular have been prominent in shaping present understanding of media stylistics: investigation of broadcast news (on radio and television) and investigation of advertisements (usually in magazines or on television). Some features of the development of approaches to analysing each of these kinds of discourse are outlined below. Significant amounts of related work have also been undertaken on a third media format, broadcast media interviews (Allan Bell and van Leeuwen 1994; Clayman and Heritage 2002; Montgomery 2007), with studies covering in-depth news and analysis pieces, political studio discussion formats, and celebrity and chat show interviews.

News

Analysis of broadcast news discourse has been especially important because of the social significance of the format during the main period of mass broadcast media. From the 1940s until the 1990s a restricted number of media channels was generally available because of the limited broadcast spectrum, which created a climate of special influence and contentiousness surrounding what was said in radio and television programming and created a bottleneck in public discourse that had to be addressed by regulation in the form of ownership controls, mandatory programme standards and a complex concept of balance. Following the rise of satellite, cable and more recently internet TV, forms such as rolling 24-hour news and individualised newsfeeds to portable devices (e.g.

smartphones) have challenged the dominance of broadcast news as the main public source of information and opinion, a historical position taken over from print media and radio. During the main period of centralised, mass broadcasting, however, radio and television news functioned – as they still do in some circumstances – as the main forum for negotiation of public meanings and values.

The news formats that developed in television news emerged out of earlier forms of radio news, propaganda films shown in cinemas and, before that, print news, in a phenomenon McLuhan (1964) called 'rear mirrorism'. But the formats developed in new directions. Alongside the political impact of its communicated content and reception, therefore, television news became of special interest to stylistics because of how its continuously developing techniques contributed to the formation of political ideology.

Within print media, one particular focus of study, especially in the early period of stylistics, has been on newspaper discourse (Reah 2002), including newspaper headlines (Aitchison 2007; Biber 2003; Crystal and Davy 1969; O'Donnell and Todd 1980). According to Biber (2003), a 'dramatic' stylistic change occurred in the register of newspapers as a whole following the eighteenth and nineteenth centuries, when newspaper prose had been 'similar to academic prose in developing an increasingly dense use of passive verbs, relative clause constructions and elaborated nouns phrases' (2003: 170). The shift Biber notes is towards a more oral style, achieved by changes including more marked use of first- and second-person pronouns, contractions and phrasal verbs in an apparent effort to widen the appeal of newspapers. By means of a corpus-based study Biber identifies in linguistic patterns which make up newspaper prose, and especially headlines, a distinctive role played by compressed noun-phrase structures (Table 33.2).

As information is packed into fewer words – a phenomenon echoed in some commercial discourse types – Biber points out that the meaning relationship expressed by *noun–noun* sequences can lead to interpretive confusion or indeterminacy, even if readers are expected to draw on pragmatic knowledge to help them. Biber concludes his study with the view that, while newspapers have developed a more oral style, they have simultaneously been 'innovative in developing literate styles with extreme reliance on compressed noun-phrase structures' (2003: 179).

Table 33.2 Compressed noun-phrase structures in newspaper prose (Biber 2003).

Noun–noun sequence	Meaning relationship
air disaster	N1 expresses the location of N2
reprisal raid	N1 expresses the purpose of N2
Etc.	Etc.

Headline style of this kind might be thought to be merely an ornamental preference. Or, alternatively, it might appear functional, depending on the view we take of the interrelation between information density, copy length, page layout and ease of reading. Stylistic work is required first to research what the relevant patterns are, then how they have changed (e.g. by means of a time-series study), and then how they might be functional in virtue of an adapted suitability to production and reception conditions, or anticipated effects and uses.

With both print and broadcast news, much of the early stylistic interest centred on transitivity (R. Fowler 1991; Hodge and Kress 1988). Transitivity is concerned, effectively, with who does what to whom, as reflected in argument structures linked to verbs (for instance when the subject of an active verb is made an optional agent in a related passive construction that has made the object of that active construction the subject of the passive one). Different transitivity patterns make available alternative ways of depicting social agency in spheres of conflict – for instance, conflict between police and unions, between different political parties or between warring countries (Toolan 2001). Work on this theme has grown into more complex studies of focalisation, as well as wider critical linguistic studies of the ideological content of news texts, which Simpson (1993: 6) points out is a 'central component of the critical linguistic creed'. Related critical approaches to news texts include K. Clark's (1992) discussion of the representation of women in news, which applies a transitivity model to examine violence towards women through the lens of how meaning is represented at the level of the linguistic clause.

As might be expected, news media continue to be a major topic in critical discourse analysis (CDA). Various linguistic levels in a text are correlated in this field with wider sociocultural dimensions of a news story, such as poverty, misery or social change. Fairclough (1995b) and van Dijk (2008) see CDA as what Fairclough calls a form of 'critical social research' (1995b: 202), forging links between linguistics and social analysis in an effort to understand the power relations inherent in news discourse and to make transparent the ideologies of professional news practices.

Building further connection between professional news practices and linguistic style, Allan Bell's (1991) study of news stories as narratives, developing earlier work by Galtang and Ruge (1973), explores the qualities that make a news story 'newsworthy'. Bell proposes a list of twelve features which serve as implicit editorial criteria: *negativity, recency, proximity, consonance, unambiguity, unexpectedness, superlativeness, relevance, personalisation, eliteness, attribution* and *facticity* (1991: 156–8). He proposes that an action or event which contains more of these qualities, or only some of them but in a pronounced form, is more likely to be worthy of media attention than other kinds of story.

Studies such as Bell's, and Fairclough's, have had considerable influence on the concept of media literacy: the development in education of skills of understanding not only what is said in the media but why it is said and whose interest such statements serve. Now that readers and viewers have access to vast numbers of news stories online and make extensive use of social media, however, they may wish to re-evaluate Bell's twelve features. Defining news in an era of blogs, Facebook posts and Twitter messages about everyday personal activities – and in a context of increased use by newspapers and broadcast media of amateur contributors, witnesses to events and crowd-sourced material – is something Bednarek and Caple seek to do in *News Discourse* (2012: 2). It might be argued that, if the idea of news authors is changing, then the critical agenda of media stylistics may also need to adapt. Researching linguistic underpinnings of balance and bias, for example – with its valorisation of distortion and other kinds of deviation from such principles – was an important feature of broadcast media in the pre-digital age. But such concepts, and the pressure towards negotiation of common public meanings implicit in them, may be less crucial in a multimedia news environment shaped by a more pluralistic 'marketplace of ideas', by online self-publication, and by user-chosen news feeds and algorithmic recommendation engines.

Advertisements

An important parallel development in linguistic analysis of media discourse concerns the language of advertising. In fact, the phrase 'the language of advertising' provided the title of the influential linguistic study by Geoffrey Leech (1966b) that set out to describe the main linguistic features of British television advertisements of the mid-1960s. To take simply one illustration, Leech examined hyperbolic use of words in his sample of advertisements and drew up a list of the twenty most frequent laudatory adjectives (Table 33.3).

Laudatory terms are significant in advertising, and Leech's study asks what those terms are and how they are used. As with news, two major directions follow from such early descriptive research. The first involves extension in the range and complexity of linguistic features taken into account. The

Table 33.3 The twenty most frequent laudatory adjectives found by Leech (1966b).

1 new	11 crisp
2 good/better/best	12 fine
3 free	13 big
4 fresh	14 great
5 delicious	15 real
6 full	16 easy
7 sure	17 bright
8 clean	18 extra
9 wonderful	19 safe
10 special	20 rich

themes of Leech's work, for example, have been extended into an accessible and comprehensive exposition by Myers (1994), who identified creative linguistic devices such as sound patterning (alliteration, assonance, rhyme), parallelism (lexical/syntactical repetition), and catchy tunes and intonation, as well as innovative use of graphology including unpredictable spelling. Slightly earlier than Myers, Geis's influential study *The Language of Television Advertising* (1982) took analysis of advertising claims in a different direction, bringing to bear principles of Gricean pragmatics and especially the notion of conversational implicature. Geis condemns use of poetic devices in advertisements, including metaphor and metonymy, and draws particular attention to a disparity between logical/factual propositions and what is conveyed by looser, inferential interpretation. For example, he responds to a cereal advertisement that begins 'Mother Nature sweetens apples for two good reasons' with the judgement that 'Everything claimed is false, for there is no such thing as Mother Nature' (1982: 88). A large number of studies have subsequently discussed the verbal styles of advertising (e.g. G. Cook 2001; Goddard 2002), focusing especially on advertising discourse that communicates promotional messages indirectly.

The second main direction in stylistic treatments of advertising, as with news, has been closer engagement between linguistic aspects of analysis and forms of sociocultural critique, foreshadowed by Williamson's analysis of gender in advertisements (1978; see also G. Cook 2001 for a summary of Geis and Williamson). Myers's own second book on advertising (1999) is also a notably wider analysis of promotional language linked to a discussion of professional practice, bringing media stylistic investigation of advertisements closer to the vast literatures on advertising in fields including marketing and media regulation (Durant 2010; Preston 1994).

In a further parallel with media news, advertising as an industry is currently undergoing a major upheaval in response to the rise of digital and online media. A great deal of advertising is migrating online, for example, and some of the attention-grabbing work performed in print by design and verbal artifice is now achieved algorithmically by advertising keywords (words which trigger advertisements related to browser search terms). Many promotional functions are also fulfilled now by other, often oblique kinds of promotional activity, including staged events and public relations communications (Wernick 1991). Much of the analysis developed in media stylistics so far, accordingly, may fit better with classic print and broadcast media advertising than with the challenges of a wider and rapidly changing field of commercial speech.

Digital media and multimodality

Arguably the two areas of stylistic study described above, news and advertisements, should be thought of as products of a particular period of media and media institutions: a world of mass media broadcasting and large-circulation print advertising, which prevailed during the second half of the twentieth century. The media forms of this period were centre-periphery in character (i.e. mass address to a large, distributed audience; see McQuail and Windahl 1993); this shaped the direction in which early stylistic work evolved, as is evident in the simultaneous concern with theories of reception and what are called new audience studies in media studies that began in the 1980s and 1990s (Morley 1992). The impact of electronically mediated communication since the 1980s may, however, be considered quite fundamental (Scollon and Levine 2004). For instance, new media often have different and rapidly changing capabilities and characteristics: low entry-cost and technical proficiency required in production, extending access and text authorship; a delayering of editorial processes between initial composition and publication (sometimes affecting citizen journalism and celebrity tweets controversially); and varying authority associated with what is said, ranging from innocent error, through disguised commercial promotion, to passing-off and fraud. Such new discourse structures pose a new challenge to ideas of media literacy, and rapid expansion of digital media may call for new terminology and forms of analysis more suited to what is often described as an information age, digital economy or 'open society'.

One important research concern related to such developments is investigation of the texture of multimodal discourse. In such discourse, verbal text interacts with images, animation, voiceovers and typography to create various levels of meaning that interact as effectively a single message. Illustrations of one kind or another have been part of newspapers since early in their history, but the relationship and proportion between text and image in print news has gradually changed, especially with the development of new image-printing technologies (see Bednarek and Caple 2012, who also provide a useful timeline of technological advances in photographic reproduction from the 1800s onwards). In online news, photo galleries, video clips and hyperlinks to additional news images and photos – often with narration and music – are included and calculated to appeal to an audience accustomed to interactive engagement typified by use of recent technologies such as smartphones and iPads.

What response can media stylistics make to changes such as these? Multimedia involve new technical capabilities, especially a capacity to juxtapose and link text segments in different formats. Among the most influential research into such capabilities has been writing by Kress and van Leeuwen (2001), who set out to analyse how, in multimodal communication, 'common semiotic principles operate in and across different modes, and … it is therefore quite possible for music to encode action, or images to encode emotion' (2001: 1). By comparison with traditional linguistic approaches to textual meaning, in which meaning is thought of as articulated only once, Kress and van Leeuwen see multimodal texts as 'making meaning in multiple articulations'. They propose four domains of practice, or strata, in which meanings are constructed – discourse, design, production and distribution – and their work sets out a framework describing the relative prominence or salience of features in different contributing media. Further work in this area seems likely to be needed as increased attention is given to electronic multimedia texts not only in practical settings but also in professional and social contexts where critical discussion of their meanings and effects is necessary.

Two miniature examples

In this section, we look briefly at two short passages in order to illustrate a contrast we have drawn above: that between interest in media discourse which is influential simply because it is presented on a mediatised platform (on television, on screen as a web page or tweet, etc.) and media discourse as a kind of discourse whose existence in a particular media format itself has a bearing on the meaning and significance likely to be attributed to it.

Loose Women interview

The transcript shown in Figure 33.1 was made of one section from a popular British daily current affairs programme, *Loose Women* (aired in 2011). It presents an informal interactional style commonly associated with 'this type of programme', where 'type of programme' is a broad description begging exactly a set of stylistic questions about what variables go into constituting a media format or genre. One question worth pursuing is whether the language used differs significantly from everyday face-to-face interaction: that is, whether a style emerges that is specific to this variety of media discourse, while drawing on but also adapting prevailing conventions of face-to-face, 'non-media' spoken interaction.

As a stretch of spoken media discourse, the excerpt can be analysed at different levels, by applying linguistic frameworks and models also deployed in investigating non-mediated, face-to-face discourse. Topics might include:

- interactional style, using conversation analysis, perhaps with a special focus on turn-taking, adjacency pairs, or topic changes
- features of a conventional interview as a speech event, using frameworks developed in the ethnography of speaking
- dialect, register and style considerations, focusing on non-standard English and register changes
- lexical deviation, such as *vajazzle* (neologism) and *well jel*: words foregrounded by their use in the introductory remarks and by the applause that follows them)

Line	Speaker	
1	AMc	(*Directly to camera*) What do these three following words have in common?
2	CMc	Sha-up
3	DW	Well jel
4	CB	Vajazzle
5		(*Laughter and clapping from audience*)
6	AMc	Now these are three catchphrases from a docusoap that has made stars out
7		of our next two guests. Who would've thought that a small county to the East
8		of London would have had such an effect on our lives. Now that the second
9		series has come to an end we're all in mourning for *The Only Way is Essex*.
10		Let's take a look at what the fuss is about. (*Shows clip from the show*).
11	AMc	Please welcome Sam and Billy Faiers.
12	All	(*Clapping and cheering from the audience and panel*)
13	AMc	Hello girls, hello, nice to see you. Now the second series is over how does
14		that feel to have it behind you?
15	Sam	It's been really good hasn't it (*to Billy*) it's been amazing
16	Billy	Yeah we're we're just sort of I dunno it's been mad at the moment it's been
17		lots of press and this an that
18	AMc	And do they film quite close up to transmission?
19	Billy	Yeah it's like they do three days filming and then the show's on the air on
20		Wednesday then we'll be filming for the Sunday episodes so a really really
21		quick turnaround
22	AMc	OK
23	CMc	Now Sam you're you're a bit more used to it I suppose cause you're in the
24		first series and Billy you're new to the second. How how are you getting on
25		with it?
26	Billy	Yeah I'm really enjoying it it's been so much fun
27	CMc	I mean it's bigger I mean you can't go anywhere now really cause everybody
28		knows who you are
29	Billy	Everyone recognises you do get recognised
30	Sam	Yeah
31	Billy	I fink you get we get recognised a lot together
32	Sam	Yeah
33	Billy	Cause I still feel like I'm not I'm not famous I feel like no one's going to
34		recognise me cause we're only in the second series I don't I dunno it's weird
35		isn't it? (*To Sam*)

Figure 33.1: Transcript from *Loose Women* television programme
Interview from *Loose Women* (ITV1), presented by Andrea McClean (AMc) with panel members
Carol McGiffin (CMc), Denise Welch (DW) and Cilla Black (CB) (May 2011). The guests on the
show are sisters Sam and Billy Faiers, stars of the docusoap / reality television show *The Only Way
is Essex* (commonly abbreviated as TOWIE)

- lexical cohesion, including semantic fields (e.g. use of 'media' terminology such as *second series*, *on air*, *transmission*, etc., and celebrity terminology such as *lot of press*, *famous*, *recognise me*)

Both the guests and the chat-show panel members in this extract make
extensive use of non-standard speech patterns which resemble face-to-face
conversational style. Despite this apparently informal structure, however,
interaction still keeps to the question–answer format of an interview. The
presenter dominates as main interviewer (ll.1, 6, 11, 13, 18) and another
member of the panel takes over this role two-thirds of the way through (ll.
23, 27). What does such a mix of styles suggest? There is no apparent style-
shift by the guests to a more formal register, as might be thought conventional in a televised interview. Their use of *dunno* (l. 16), *fink* (l. 31) and *yeah*
(ll. 26, 30, 32) suggests preference for their everyday vernacular, despite
being in the studio. At the same time, it will be noted that the guests
are known for their 'Essex' dialect (Essex is a county to the East of
London, associated with a variety of English known as Estuary English).
Foregrounding dialect features is not only indexical, however, reflecting
social origins; it forms part of the media personae of the interviewees, and
both maintain this identity through use of linguistic markers of place and
class. Moreover, recognition by both panel members and audience of
particular words associated with the programme *The Only Way is Essex*
(such as *sha-up* (l. 2), *well jel* (l. 3) and the neologism *vajazzle* (l. 4)) suggests
shared common knowledge between all the participants in this speech
event that is media-specific, in referring both to the status of the speakers
as TV personalities and to the style and mood of the programme in which
they appear.

  This brief example begins to show how media discourses can draw selectively on speech styles to create nuanced registers matched to programme
type and audience expectations: news, chat show, reality programme,
sports commentary and so on. The development of such styles involves
both technical and linguistic processes: in this case, a long-term shift in
television discourse from formal public address to acceptance of non-
standard linguistic forms and more intimate forms of onscreen conversation. Such genre formation involves several factors simultaneously: a changing, relative embeddedness and accessibility of media technologies in
everyday life (such that watching TV may be an individual online activity,
a family activity with everyone sitting in front of the television, or background viewing in a public place such as a waiting room or bar), the relative
rarity or ordinariness involved in participating in a given media format (as a
changing mix of professional and amateur participants in a broadcast programme), and changing conventions governing performance of public and
private personality (including observance and breaking of social taboos).
Importantly, this history of media style formation is not finished, but rather
undergoing a volatile and rapid period of continuing change.

Joke or threat? A tweet that led to prosecution

In January 2010 Paul Chambers, a 27-year-old trainee accountant, was arrested, convicted and fined after tweeting a message out of frustration at airport delays. He had been due to meet his girlfriend but found that his local airport was closed, and tweeted the following to 600 followers (Twitter is an online social networking service which allows users to text short messages, or 'tweets', to the public):

> Crap! Robin Hood airport is closed. You've got a week and a bit to get your shit together otherwise I'm blowing the airport sky high!!

Chambers was prosecuted in May 2010 (under section 127(1) of the Communications Act 2003, which prohibits sending 'by means of a public electronic communications network a message or other matter that is grossly offensive or of an indecent, obscene or menacing character'). In arriving at its judgment, the court had to decide whether Chambers's electronic communication represented a credible and serious threat. Airport staff did not believe it was. Doubt as to the seriousness of such a verbally direct threat nevertheless raised the question of what could make it acceptable to appear to threaten in the medium of Twitter, when analogous words used in a different context would be likely to have more serious consequences.

In Chambers's defence, it was argued that his words were a joke, as if said out loud to friends, rather than a genuine threat of violent action. The defendant's use of swear words, for example – *crap* and *shit* – reflects a type of language typically used casually in face-to-face interaction, rather than in a public forum. Other aspects of the language used suggest pastiche, as ironic self-dramatisation as a filmic 'avenging angel' character, working to the loose schedule of 'a week and a bit', and the message was tweeted to friends rather than sent to its addressee, the 'threatened' airport. Interpretations along such lines appeal to an audience's perception of echoic reference in discourse style, which tweet followers might view as citing rather than seriously adopting language choices.

During the case a number of well-known comedians and television presenters, who viewed the case as absurd and a threat to free speech, rallied in support of Chambers. In July 2012, he won his appeal and his conviction was overturned. The import of the verdict remains ambivalent, nevertheless. While to many it seemed a triumph of common sense, the appeal verdict suggests that even in cases where issues of security and public safety could be at stake, comments may be considered harmless if interpreted in the specialised context of online social media communication.

The import of this brief illustration for stylistics is more straightforward. Some degree of sensitivity needs to be exercised in assessing linguistic practices in a rapidly changing electronic communication environment.

The tweet is not only a technical format that can be described in terms of its maximum number of characters (140), but a format whose linguistic style and existence within a wider genre of tweets plays a part in determining *what it means*. Other areas in which similar considerations arise include how to deal with celebrity tweets that present themselves as personal messages but function as a new zone of unregulated advertising, and assessment of the point at which online messages become defamatory statements rather than ill-judged expressions of honest comment in an online climate of increasingly robust, personalised review that goes beyond 'like' and 'dislike'. Such questions will in the long term not only be topics for special consideration by online communities and regulators. Gradually online discourse styles have a knock-on effect on the repertoire of choices available in print media and public forms of face-to-face discourse.

Conclusion: what can stylistics tell us about media language?

Across its contributing sub-fields, the potential application and usefulness of different kinds of stylistic work varies. Analysis of a particular text can help a reader to clarify his or her interpretation, by linking meaning to detailed formal description which functions as discussable evidence. Stylistic commentary can draw attention to techniques that the reader of the analysis, once aware of, will notice in future in other texts. In this respect, stylistic analysis contributes to the development of new kinds of literacy.

Stylistic analysis of a corpus of media texts, selected to represent a media *genre*, can contribute to a wider debate about the relationship between technological forms of communication and social behaviour. Prominent among the questions to be addressed are issues to do with habits of reading (of short or long stretches of text, of pages in print and on screen, and in audio-book format), and whether language as a social form of exchange and interaction is now directed less towards agreement over, or at least negotiation of, common meanings by the proliferation of personalised, on-demand electronic communication formats.

In an influential discussion of how to analyse media language, Fairclough (1995a) proposes that it should be 'an objective of media education to ensure that students can answer four questions about any media text' (1995a: 201). Fairclough's questions require that students should be able to compare and contrast media text design, a text's production and interpretation, what he calls its order of discourse, and wider sociocultural processes such as the text's likely effects. The first two of these questions have virtually the same force now as they did when Fairclough formulated them, even if answers will differ as a result of both technological and genre changes affecting the media landscape he was discussing. To Fairclough's important questions for students, however, media stylisticians should add another: what new issues need to be defined as we move from analysis of the linear, broadcast era into contemporary social media and a world of time-shifted and on-demand programming rather than centrally broadcast scheduled content?

34

Advertising culture

Rodney H. Jones

In the summer of 2012, Nike became the first company to have its Twitter campaign banned by the Advertising Standards Authority (ASA) of the United Kingdom (Sweney 2012). The action came as a result of complaints from the public about two particular tweets from footballers Wayne Rooney and Jack Wilshire. The tweets were part of the sportswear manufacturer's '#makeitcount' campaign, launched at the beginning of the year to promote a new range of products which included the Nike+ Fuelband, a device which tracks users' physical activity and automatically sends updates to social networking sites such as Facebook and Twitter. The campaign urged customers to tweet about their New Year's resolutions. Rooney's tweet read:

> My resolution – to start the year as a champion, and finish it as a champion…#makeitcount gonike.me/makeitcount

And Wilshire tweeted:

> In 2012, I will come back for my club – and be ready for my country. #makeitcount gonike.me/makeitcount

The essence of the ruling by the Advertising Standards Authority was that Nike had violated the Consumer Protection from Unfair Trading Regulations (2008) which prohibits 'using editorial content in the media to promote a product where a trader has paid for the promotion without making that clear in the content or by images or sounds clearly identifiable by the consumer'. In other words, because the tweets were not clearly identifiable as advertisements, they violated the law.

Nike countered that although the footballers were sponsored by the company, they were free as part of the campaign to tweet about their New Year's resolutions just like the thousands of customers who had sent similar tweets. Besides, they argued, Nike's sponsorship of Rooney and Wilshire was a well-known fact among their Twitter followers, and the inclusion of the 'hashtag' #makeitcount and the address of the campaign's website made the promotional nature of the tweets obvious. But the ASA disagreed. They contended that the average Twitter user scrolls through many tweets a day and might not make the connection between the hashtag and the campaign. They also pointed out that representatives from Nike had discussed with Rooney and Wilshire the content of their messages before they tweeted them, calling into question their authenticity as spontaneous communications.

This case was not the first time the ASA had investigated a complaint involving promotional tweets. Several months before, the confectionery manufacturer Mars Corporation hired celebrity model Katie Price and footballer Rio Ferdinand to make five tweets. The first four were statements seemingly incongruous with the stars' personalities, Rio Ferdinand, for example, tweeting 'can't wait to get home from training and finish that cardigan', and Price tweeting 'Large scale quantitative easing in 2012 could distort liquidity in the govt. bond market.' These seeming non-sequiturs were followed by both sending the same tweet: 'You're not you when you're hungry @SnickersUK#hungry#spon lockerz.com/s/ 177408824'. Unlike the Nike case, however, the ASA ruled that this use of Twitter was acceptable since Ferdinand and Price had added the hashtag #spon to their last tweets. When critics pointed out that the tweets leading up to them did not bear this hashtag, the Authority argued that most consumers would read the 'stream' of tweets as a single unit.

These two examples dramatically illustrate some of the legal and ethical challenges introduced by new trends in advertising culture brought about by digital media. What is interesting to note for readers of this *Handbook* is that, at the heart of these legal and ethical questions are issues which are central to the study of stylistics and discourse analysis, issues having to do with how linguistic features of texts signal things like authorship, 'authenticity', the author's intentions and even what sort of text a text is taken to be, as well as questions about how readers process and understand texts and what kinds of responses they have to them.

This chapter will examine how concepts from stylistics and discourse analysis can shed light on the kinds of texts and communicative situations created by a new generation of advertisers who are rapidly abandoning traditional print and broadcast genres and turning to techniques of social media marketing in which our understanding of what is an advertisement and what is not, and of who is an advertiser and who is a customer, are no longer simple and straightforward.

Stylistics and advertising in the twenty-first century

Over the years, stylistics has made a significant contribution to our understanding of advertising discourse (G. Cook 1992; Vestergaard and Schrøder

1985). Along the way, advertising culture has challenged stylistics to rethink some of its most basic assumptions about things such as 'literariness' (Carter and Nash 1983), and what constitutes a 'text' (Glasser 1998), and to develop new analytical tools to deal with features of advertising discourse such as multimodal design (Kress and van Leeuwen 1996).

The American Marketing Association (2012) defines advertising as 'the placement of announcements and persuasive messages in time or space purchased in any of the mass media by business firms, nonprofit organizations, government agencies, and individuals who seek to inform and/or persuade members of a particular target market or audience about their products, services, organizations, or ideas.' Different approaches to stylistics and discourse analysis provide insights into different aspects of this definition.

Traditional literary stylistics, which sees style chiefly as a matter of linguistic choice, takes as its task the description of the uniqueness of a text or kind of text by examining features of lexis, syntax and graphology. Perhaps the most famous example of this approach in the study of advertising is Leech's (1966a) *English in Advertising*, in which he argues that advertising has created a special style of English marked by features such as the frequent use of adjectives, short sentences, and imperative and interrogative clauses. Others, such as Myers (1994), have explored the rhetorical devices used by advertisers from the creative language play of puns and metaphors to the adoption of everyday conversational language.

Other schools of discourse analysis and stylistics have focused on the broader aspects of advertising texts. Genre analysts such as Bhatia (1993), for example, have attempted to identify the conventional structure of advertising and promotional discourse, seeing it in terms of 'moves' arranged in certain predictable sequences. Perhaps the most interesting insights of such work are related to what Bhatia calls 'strategic interdiscursivity', the appropriation by advertisers of conventional generic resources from *other* kinds of texts (such as personal letters, literary works and newspaper articles). Such insights, along with similar points about the generic 'instability' of advertising discourse (see for example G. Cook 1992), are especially relevant to cases such as those described above in which whether or not an advertisement is legal or not depends on readers being able to identify these conventional features.

Scholars interested in the pragmatic aspects of communication have focused more on how advertisers create meaning indirectly, and how customers make sense of these meanings. Particularly notable is the work of Tanaka (1994), who, drawing on the *relevance theory* of Sperber and Wilson (1995), argues that much of the communication in advertising is *covert* rather than *overt*. In overt communication, the communicator wants not only to convey a message, but also to convey that he or she wants the reader or hearer to recover this message. In covert communication, on the other hand, the communicator wants to convey a message, but at the same time wishes to hide the fact that they wish the reader or hearer to recover the message, thus avoiding being held responsible for it. An example of this can be seen when food manufacturers make health or content claims about their products indirectly so as to avoid being held accountable for making false or questionable claims (R. H. Jones et al. 2011).

Of particular interest when it comes to advertising is work which explores the cognitive dimensions of discourse and style. Advertising, in fact, is often described by marketers themselves in terms of the four functions of the AIDA model (attention, interest, desire and action) (Russell 1921), the first three of which are essentially cognitive processes. Scholars from the fields of cognitive linguistics and cognitive stylistics have explored a range of ways in which readers process advertising discourse, from the effects of metaphor and metonymy, both verbal (Ungerer 2000) and pictorial (Forceville 1996), to the activation by advertisements of cognitive schema (Jeffries 2001; Stockwell 2002), or 'text worlds' (Hidalgo Downing 2000b) in which readers' previous expectations are either reinforced or challenged in some way.

Finally, scholars of stylistics and discourse analysis have considered how advertising texts interact with the wider sociocultural contexts in which they are produced and consumed, how they construct certain kinds of readers (Allan Bell 1984) and how they reinforce certain ideologies and social relationships (Simpson 1993; Vestergaard and Schrøder 1985). Particular attention has been paid to the construction of gender in advertisements (Mills 1995), and to the relationship between code choice and social identity (Piller 2001).

The culture of advertising, however, has changed dramatically since many of these studies were carried out, so much so, in fact, that the definition of advertising I quoted above no longer seems adequate. Many of the texts which function as advertisements in the digital age do not constitute discrete 'announcements' placed 'in time or space', but rather are more like what Dawkins (2006) calls 'memes': ideas, phrases and scraps of text that circulate freely through online networks. Neither are they necessarily 'purchased in the mass media by business firms, nonprofit organizations, [or] government agencies'. Often, in fact, they are spread by customers themselves for free through their social networks. Finally, many advertising texts nowadays do not seem to have the traditional functions of 'inform(ing) and/or persuad(ing)' readers, but instead function more like 'phatic' communication (Malinowski 1923), designed chiefly to facilitate the formation of social ties not just between advertisers and customers but also among customers themselves.

These new forms of advertising include such things as social marketing campaigns using platforms such as Twitter and Facebook; 'viral marketing', in which provocative content is introduced into the media environment by an unidentified source and then spread from user to user; 'buzz marketing', in which influential individuals are hired to covertly promote products within their social circles; and consumer-generated advertising, in which consumers themselves produce promotional messages either intentionally or automatically when they use a certain product. Many of these new forms of advertising have altered traditional participation frameworks (Goffman 1981) associated with promotional discourse: no longer are advertisements seen as one-way communication; now they are sites of *interaction* between advertisers and customers in which advertisers routinely gather as much information about customers as customers gather about products. In fact, the main purpose of much contemporary advertising is not to encourage potential customers to buy a product but to encourage them to give up more and more information about themselves, making them more efficient targets for future advertising (McStay 2011).

Underlying most of these approaches is the strategy of advertising through 'non-advertising', a strategy born of the realisation that customers are increasingly sceptical of traditional advertising discourse and are more likely to be convinced to buy products based on the experiences of 'real people', preferably people in their own social networks whom they trust (Chaney 2009). This strategy of dressing up advertising as something else, of course, is not new. Perhaps the most famous example occurred as far back as 1929 when the Great American Tobacco Company hired young women to stage a demonstration for 'equal rights' in which they smoked their 'torches of freedom' (Lucky Strike cigarettes), an event which generated widespread newspaper coverage and shifted the terms of the debate about the social acceptability of women smoking (Amos and Haglund 2000). With the rise of social media and Web 2.0, however, such strategies have become much more widespread and sophisticated, partly because of the resources web-based communication makes available for spreading messages quickly, for remixing messages, for obscuring the connection between messages and their sources, and for helping to foster the creation of social networks and affinity groups around particular kinds of social practices, lifestyles, products and texts (R. H. Jones and Hafner 2012).

The Nike '#makeitcount' campaign, which ran during the first few months of 2012, provides an excellent example of this new type of advertising. The campaign combined traditional marketing elements such as print advertisements, television commercials and celebrity endorsements with less traditional forms of viral marketing, crowd sourcing and customer engagement (Gerard 2012). At the heart of this effort was the generation of advertising texts which, through their source, placement, and linguistic and semiotic features, 'impersonated' other kinds of texts. By encouraging its fans to tweet about their New Year's resolutions using the hashtag '#makeitcount', for example, the company was able to transform a positive, motivational phrase into a 'brand', and, more importantly, to transform people's acts of motivating themselves and others into acts which also marketed their products. Customers themselves did not even have to make much of an effort to become marketers of Nike products.

Just by wearing the Nike+ Fuelband or using the Nike+ smartphone app and setting them to automatically generate tweets like 'I just finished a 3.4 KM run with Nike+ GPS #nikeplus #makeitcount', users of the products became 'automatic' marketers. In other words, Nike managed to produce a product whose function was not only to motivate users to continue to use it, but also to generate a stream of free advertising whenever it was used.

Campaigns such as Nike's '#makeitcount' campaign and Snickers's '#hungry' campaign highlight the limitations of more traditional tools of text analysis in understanding how meanings are produced and circulated in new advertising cultures. Discourse analysis and stylistics, however, have, over the years, developed a number of broader analytical concepts which can help us to understand how these new kinds of advertising texts work. These concepts are:

1) the concept of *genre*, with its questions about what specific features in a text signal that it is a particular *type* of text, and about how different text types interact with one another;
2) the concept of *authenticity*, with its questions about who is speaking in a particular text, and about the 'truth' or 'sincerity' of the authorial voice; and
3) the concept of *context*, with its questions about how texts are part of and, in many cases, help to create social occasions and social relationships, and how these social occasions and relationships affect how meanings are produced and understood.

In what follows I will discuss both how these three concepts from stylistics can help us to understand new kinds of advertising texts such as those I described above, and also how such texts might challenge scholars in stylistics and discourse analysis to think about and apply these concepts in new ways.

Genre

As I mentioned above, the question of 'what makes an ad an ad' is not a new one. Advertisers have long endeavoured to disguise advertisements as something else, not necessarily to deceive customers, but often simply to surprise or amuse them. In fact, in most places like the UK, it is illegal for advertisers to intentionally deceive customers about the nature of the texts they produce. According to the UK Codes of Broadcast and Non-Broadcast Advertising (CAP 2012), for example, 'Unsolicited ... marketing communications must be obviously identifiable as marketing communications without the need to open them [and] ... Marketers and publishers must make clear that advertorials are marketing communications; for example, by heading them "advertisement feature".'

Even without explicit labels such as 'advertisement feature', most consumers find it easy to spot advertisements in traditional media. One reason for this is the *interruptive* nature of most advertising. It is by their physical placement within texts that are *not* advertising, and their discernible differences in style and content from the surrounding text that people are able to identify most advertisements (G. Cook 1992). It is only when these differences are blurred, when, for example, the style and the content of the ad are so close to that of the surrounding text that it becomes difficult to make distinctions that advertisers must explicitly alert readers that what they are reading is an ad.

This usually works out quite well when it comes to television and print advertising because advertisers, broadcasters, consumers and regulators all share a common understanding of the generic conventions of advertisements vis-à-vis other texts such as TV dramas, documentaries, news articles and editorials. They also share similar expectations about the conventions of interdiscursivity governing these kinds of text, including things like the degree to which one type of text can borrow features from other types of text before they generically 'cross the line', and the various means texts should use to signal this borrowing through things like style, placement, or the use of explicit labels or disclaimers. Much of our understanding of these conventions is enshrined in laws and regulations such as the UK Codes of Broadcast and Non-Broadcast Advertising. Most of our understanding of them, however, is implicit, the product of deeper cultural assumptions about discourse that we are socialised into as members of our societies.

Part of the difficulty in evaluating the generic status of social media advertisements, either legally or linguistically, is that they are integrated within relatively new genres, such as 'tweets' and 'status updates', the generic conventions and canons of interdiscursivity of which are still emergent and unstable, yet to be fully conventionalised (Santini 2006). In many ways, in fact, the genre of the 'tweet' is very similar to the genre of the advertisement in terms of linguistic features, placement in relation to other texts, and the intention of the authors. Page (2012b), in fact, refers to Twitter as a kind of 'linguistic market' in which the chief function of most texts is promotional rather than informational.

Stylistically, the tweet must operate within many of the same kinds of linguistic constraints that most advertising texts must work within, chiefly the demand to attract the greatest amount of attention from readers in the shortest amount of space (Grosser 1995). This linguistic efficiency is sometimes achieved through the use of abbreviations and the kind of telegraphic style associated with newspaper headlines or the 'simplified register' that scholars such as Bruthiaux (1996) have identified in classified advertisements (Zappavigna 2011). Linguistic efficiency, however, is not enough for either advertisers or 'tweeters' – they must also make their messages 'attention grabbing' and memorable. They often do this through the creative use of prosody, the establishment of associative links with common proverbs or other set phraseological units (Naciscione 2010), or the use of seeming 'non-sequiturs' that force readers to work to create logical connections, as with the statement:

> You wouldn't take your dog to the prom. Don't take a test without
> CliffsNotes. *(Dziura 2006)*

Non-sequiturs are often treated by critics of advertising as a 'logical fallacy' or deceptive technique. But often advertisers use the obviously fallacious logic or apparent 'randomness' of non-sequiturs for humorous affect. The exploitation of apparent 'randomness' is also an important part of social media communication. In fact, it has been observed that much of the 'art' of Twitter is in mastering the rhetoric of the random (Joel 2011). This is one reason the Snickers campaign featuring the apparently random comments of Katie Price and Rio Ferdinand fit in so well with the medium of Twitter and functioned so well as promotional discourse. The trick for both advertisers and tweeters is to come up with phrases that are random enough that they create curiosity while at the same time activating knowledge schema that allow readers to make the kinds of logical leaps necessary to make sense of them.

Another important linguistic similarity between tweets and advertisements is grammatical. Analyses of advertisements have revealed a higher proportion of imperative clauses than in other discourse types (Leech 1966a; Myers 1994). Given that the main purpose of advertisements is to get people to do something (specifically buy a product), the frequent use of imperatives (such as 'Just do it') is not surprising. Despite the fact that the ostensible purpose of 'tweets' is to tell people 'what you are doing' or (as the question was later revised) 'what's happening', a purpose that one would expect to generate declarative clauses, a large number of clauses in tweets are also imperative. In a study of the grammar of tweets by different kinds of Twitter users, Page (2012a) found a high proportion of imperative clauses, especially in tweets from celebrities.

This predilection for imperatives can be seen in the tweets customers contributed to Nike's '#makeitcount' campaign. Although the instruction given to participants was to tweet about their New Year's resolutions, many tweets carrying this hashtag, rather than describing what the writer was going to do, encourage the reader to take some kind of action:

> Don't cry over the past, it's gone. Don't stress about the future, it hasn't
> arrived. Live in the present and #makeitcount.
>
> You're only young once, so be bad, break the rules, get caught, &
> #makeitcount.
>
> You really do only live once. #MakeItCount

Even declarative and interrogative clauses in these tweets often have an imperative function:

> You Have 3 Choices In #Life: Give Up, Give In or Give It Your All.......What is your choice? #MakeItCount

Of course, the fact that the hashtag itself (#makeitcount) is an imperative no doubt contributed to the generation of imperative clauses in the tweets carrying this tag, especially when the hashtag was grammatically embedded in the tweet. The most important thing about this proliferation of imperative clauses is that it served the promotional interests of the company. Rather than telling its customers what to do, Nike managed to create a discursive environment in which customers told one another what to do, and the advice they gave broadly mirrored the goals of the company and the image it desired to promote.

Finally, tweets resemble advertisements in terms of the generic 'moves' normally included in them. Nearly all advertisements, from classified ads to television commercials, contain at least three moves: 'messaging', the giving of information about a product; 'branding', the promotion of the name of the product or the seller, or of a memorable slogan or a logo associated with the product or seller (such as the phrase 'Just do it' or the Nike 'swoosh'); and 'connecting', the provision of some means by which the seller and the buyer can be connected and the sale can be made (such as information on where the product is available, or the telephone number, address or website of the seller). That is not to say that all ads have to perform these three moves explicitly. In cases where the product is easily and widely attainable, for example, the third move might be left out.

Tweets similarly often consist of three moves: 'messaging', the actual message being sent; 'branding', usually in the form of a 'hashtag', which indicates what the tweet is about and how users are meant to classify it; and 'connecting', performed through the automatic inclusion of the Twitter address of the sender plus sometimes the inclusion of a shortened URL of a webpage recommended (or owned) by the sender. In the tweet below, for example, sent during the Iranian protests of 2009, the Twitter address '@persiankiwi' connects the reader to the sender, the sentence below it about the state of the Iranian Government conveys the 'message', and the hashtag #Iranelections 'brands' the tweet as a certain kind of tweet associated with a particular topic, at the same time promoting other tweets with this hashtag.

> @persiankiwi
> The Gov is colapsing [sic] and the system of control is fast breaking down –
> #Iranelection

This structure makes tweets particularly suited for promotional discourse. Below is an example of a tweet from British Airways that exploits this three–move structure:

> @British_Airways
> Our ad shows our plane in London. But it can go all over the UK. Enter FY14BJ & see where we are now taxi.ba.com #HomeAdvantage

In this tweet the 'connecting' function is performed by the Twitter address of British Airways and the link ('taxi.ba.com') to a page that allows visitors to track the flight paths of British Airways planes. The 'branding' function is performed not just by the inclusion in the name of the Airline in the Twitter address, but also by the hashtag #HomeAdvantage, which is the name of the advertising campaign that British Airways ran during the 2012 London Olympics.

This last point highlights the importance of one particular linguistic feature of tweets that makes them different from traditional promotional discourse: the hashtag. Above I assigned to the hashtag the function of 'branding', since, especially in promotional tweets, hashtags usually promote either the name of a product or company (e.g. #Nike, #Snickers) or a phrase or slogan that users are meant to associate with the product or company (e.g. #makeitcount, #hungry). Actually, however, the function of hashtags is much more complex, integrating the moves of messaging, branding and connecting.

In her study of the uses of hashtags in tweets by corporations, celebrities and 'ordinary' users, Page (2012b) assigns to the hashtag a primarily promotional purpose. When used by corporations and celebrities, she notes, hashtags serve to make visible (and *searchable*) company and product names, slogans and messages that seek to engage customers or fans. But even when they are used by 'ordinary' people, she argues, they fulfil an essentially promotional function, serving as a resource for users to promote and amplify their tweets by associating them with particular 'brands' of messages, and to promote themselves as affiliated with particular topics, or social or professional groups.

The best possible outcome for tweeters, whether they are corporations, celebrities or 'ordinary' people, is that the hashtags they use come to be 'hypercharged' with meaning, so strongly associated with certain kinds of social practices and certain kinds of social identities that they come to be considered 'microgenres' (Zappavigna 2012). This is what happened with the hashtag #fail, which came to be associated with (often humorous) complaints about mistakes one has made or something that fails to work, as in:

> Vista spent 45 minutes installing updates.. only to say after rebooting that the update has failed and all changes are rolled back. #fail

and

> I'm mexican and I have nothing mexican to wear for tomorrow lol #fail

This is also, to some extent what Nike was able to accomplish with the hashtag #makeitcount – the creation of a 'microgenre' associated with the social practice of giving and receiving encouragement. This is in part what was behind Nike's assertion that by using the hashtag #makeitcount, Rooney and Wilshire were participating in a kind of *community of practice*

(Lave and Wenger 1991) rather than in a promotional campaign. Similarly, what was behind the ASA's ruling *against* Nike was their assertion that the tweets in question actually belonged to a different microgenre, one that should be signalled by the #spon hashtag.

Insofar as hashtags work to produce 'microgenres', they also work to strengthen connections among those who make use of these genres, and here is where the unique potential of social media marketing becomes particularly evident. Because hashtags both render tweets searchable and serve to signal users' affiliation with the particular values or attitudes implied by the tag, hashtags help to create what Zappavigna (2011, 2012) calls 'ambient affiliation networks'. 'The social function of the hashtag', she writes, 'is to provide an easy means of grouping tweets, and in turn, creating ad hoc social groups or sub-communities'.

In other words, hashtags, when cleverly used by marketers, become labels not just for particular companies or products or campaigns, but for particular kinds of people. Of course, the building of communities of customers bonded together by 'brand loyalty' ('Marlboro smokers', 'Mac users') has long been an important aim of marketing. In social media marketing, however, it has become the *primary* aim. So it matters little whether users of the hashtag #makeitcount are tweeting about exercise and Nike products or about their love lives, their jobs or their plans to write the great American novel. Whenever they use the hashtag, they are affiliating themselves with a group of 'like-minded' people whose attitude and lifestyle Nike has co-opted. With the hashtag #makeitcount, Nike has made optimism and perseverance its brand.

Authenticity

Along with upholding the charge that the tweets by Rooney and Wilshire did not sufficiently signal their promotional nature to readers, the ASA also based its ruling on the charge that they were somehow 'inauthentic', that they did not represent the 'true' and spontaneous thoughts of their authors since their contents were decided upon 'with the help of a member of the Nike marketing team' (Advertising Standards Authority 2012). At the same time, however, many of the tweets bearing the hashtag '#makeitcount' from users of the Nike+ Fuelband and smartphone app (such as 'I just finished a 5.06 km run with Nike+ GPS. #nikeplus #makeitcount') are *entirely* authored by the company (automatically generated by the product), and yet they are not subject to the same charge of inauthenticity.

The notion of 'authenticity' in texts has long been a preoccupation of stylistics, where it has usually meant the verification of a text's authorship. More recently in media and discourse studies, authenticity has come to be associated with a wider range of attributes of texts such as their credibility, their historical accuracy and the sincerity of their authors (van Leeuwen

2001). In everyday parlance, authenticity has come to be used to describe discourse that is 'real', 'uncontrived', 'unscripted'. It has also come to be associated with the discourse of 'ordinary people' rather than that of governments, institutions, corporations or celebrities.

For stylistics the question is how this newer sense of 'authenticity' – meaning 'sincerity' or 'honesty' – is actually realised in discourse. Coupland (2010: 6) claims that authenticity is essentially a kind of discursive 'tactic' 'through which people ... make claims about their own or others' statuses as authentic ... members of social groups'. In other words, authenticity centrally depends on one's ability to use one's 'speech style as an anchor for solidarity and local affiliation' (Coupland 2003: 420). For others, however, most notably Goffman (1981), authenticity is less a function of one's affiliation with one's audience as it is a function of what he calls 'footing', the position one takes up vis-à-vis one's message. For Goffman, there are three possible roles speakers or writers can take up in relation to their words – the role of animator (he who merely speaks or 'animates' the words), the role of author (he who composes the words), and the role of principle (he whose thoughts are represented in the words). What most people regard as 'authentic' talk – what Goffman calls 'fresh talk' (1981: 172) – occurs when these three roles are seen to coincide, when the speaker or writer is perceived as representing his or her 'own thoughts' in his or her 'own words'. For Goffman, however, this is always only a perception – 'fresh talk' is never really as 'fresh' as it seems.

Testimonials in advertising are in many ways about *performing* authenticity (even when, for many, just the fact of sponsorship is enough to undermine it). In the past such performances mainly depended on the authority of the speaker – the authenticity of the testimonial had very much to do with the reputation of the person delivering it. More recently, as the public has become increasingly sceptical of authority, the locus of authenticity has shifted to the nature of the talk itself. To be deemed authentic, talk must be 'true to a certain conception of talk in its natural state – not scripted or rehearsed but fresh and spontaneous' (Montgomery 2001). To be believable, celebrities and authorities must 'be themselves', which often means talking more like 'ordinary people'.

Both of these themes – the performance of 'natural' talk and the communication of in-group solidarity as markers of authenticity – come together in social media campaigns in which stars post status updates and tweets in the same vernacular used by their fans, and often about the same mundane topics. One of the best examples of this form of stylised authenticity can be seen in a component of the Nike campaign that did not use social media *per se*, but still made use of many of the techniques of social media marketing, namely the component of the '#makeitcount' campaign in which Olympic athletes were asked to write short messages (not unlike tweets) in their own handwriting on black and white photographs of themselves followed by their Twitter addresses and the hashtag

Figure 34.1: Mo Farah Nike advertisement

'#makeitcount'. Poster-sized versions of the photos, like the one of runner Mo Farah shown in Figure 34.1, were displayed at Nike shops throughout Great Britain.

What gives to these messages an air of authenticity is that they are perceived to be the athletes' genuine thoughts about their actual hopes and aspirations (as opposed to the kinds of sportswear they prefer), and this sense of authenticity is increased by the fact that the messages are written in (what is perceived to be) their own handwriting. Perhaps the most clever move, however, came when customers themselves at Nike's flagship London shops in Westfield Stratford City and Oxford Street were photographed and asked to compose their own handwritten pledges. By inviting ordinary people to engage in the same acts of testimonial as the athletes, the company was able not just to make customers feel more like celebrities, but also to make their celebrity spokespeople seem like 'ordinary' people.

A similar strategy was used in the Twitter component of the campaign: when both celebrities and customers were asked to produce the same kinds of tweets, the celebrities were able to claim the status of 'authentic' customers. In doing so, the marketing strategists successfully blurred the boundaries between promotional discourse and everyday language, allowing them to argue (as Nike did when challenged by the ASA) that the celebrity tweets were no different from those posted by genuine customers. As Dan McLaren (2012) blogged for the UK Sports Network, 'with people tweeting about different elements of their lives, including products and services that they are using on a daily basis where is the line to be drawn. If an athlete says "hey, just been to pick up my new XYZ car. It's amazing!!" – and the car company is a sponsor of theirs, does this constitute a marketing message or is it just natural commentary of their life?'

Context

In arguing against the ASA's ruling, Nike said that the tweets from Rooney and Wilshire 'should be viewed in the *context* in which they appeared' (ASA 2012, emphasis added). Twitter, they contended, is not a broadcast channel in the same way television and radio are, but more a means of direct communication between specific parties (like the telephone). Rooney and Wilshire, they argued, were communicating not to the general public, but to their 'followers', and since both footballers were known by their 'followers' to be sponsored by Nike, they would not be misled by the advertisements.

The notion that context plays an important role in determining textual meanings is not new to stylistics and discourse analysis (see, for example, Schirato and Yell 1997; Toolan 1992). By *context*, what I primarily mean is the 'social occasion' within which a text is used (and which, to some degree, the text itself helps create), which includes the time, place, medium and perceived purpose of the communication as well as the pattern of relationships or the 'interaction order' (Goffman 1983) that it constructs.

Traditional advertising typically follows a one-way interruptive format. That is to say, it relies on a model of interrupting a potential customer's engagement with some other text (a television show, a newspaper, a web page). Customers accept such disruptions because they see them as 'necessary evils' which allow them to access media content free of charge. The challenge, then, for traditional advertisements, is to attract and hold people's attention within contexts in which (for the most part) they would rather pay attention to something else. Traditional advertising is also 'one-way' communication. The roles of author and reader (or viewer) are relatively fixed, and customers typically do not have the opportunity to engage in conversations with advertisers.

Social-media marketing has dramatically changed the context in which advertising communication takes place. First, messages are more integrated into the primary media experiences of users: whether it is a tweet from my favourite athlete about his New Year's resolution, or from my favourite singer about her eating habits, or an update from my cousin telling me how many kilometres he ran today, or a Facebook photo of my friend showing off her new Nike Lunarglide running shoes. In successful social-media marketing, the boundaries between the advertisement and the surrounding discourse – between the 'text' and the 'context' – are erased, and brand engagement occurs as customers begin to subtly and often subconsciously combine the advertisement's messages with their own media consumption and text-making practices (Tuten 2008).

Social-media advertisement is less about 'passive consumption of packaged content' and more about 'conversations, connections, and shared control' (Tuten 2008: 30). This two-way communication even occurs when customers are not conscious of it when, for example, the products they use (like the Nike+ Fuelband) send out automated advertisements, or when the information they share with friends on social networking sites is used to determine which products to market to them and which strategies will be most effective. Within these new participation structures (Goffman 1981), not only are the boundaries between texts and contexts breaking down, but so are the boundaries between marketers and customers. One of the key pillars of the Advertising Standards Code in the UK and elsewhere is that this boundary must be maintained. 'Marketing communications', the code stipulates, 'must not falsely claim or imply that the marketer is acting as a consumer' (CAP 2012). What the code does not address is the situation created in social-media marketing in which customers come to act (sometimes unawares) as marketers.

In many ways, the internet and social media have fundamentally altered the relationship between messages and contexts, with messages and the ways we interact with them taking an unprecedented role in constructing and constraining context. In his book *The Filter Bubble: What the Internet is Hiding From You*, Eli Pariser (2011) discusses how things such as cookies, personalised search algorithms and selective information feeds have conspired to make everybody's experience of the internet intensely personal – and disturbingly limited. Search engines return results based on the previous behaviour and 'interests' of their users, and weblogs and Twitter feeds become 'echo chambers' for the opinions of like-minded people. Social media sites such as Facebook allow users to create 'discursive worlds' complete with people, stories and values, and then feed back these worlds to users. As Rettberg (2009: 451) puts it, 'social media represent our lives by filtering the data we feed into them through templates and by displaying simplified patterns, visualizations and narratives back to us'.

What this means for advertising culture is that advertisers are no longer in the business of peddling messages to customers in the form of 'identities' and 'narratives', but rather in the business of providing tools (such as hashtags and automatic updates and opportunities for 'ambient affiliation') through which customers create their own identities and write their own narratives. In this regard, the Nike+ Fuelband is the prototypical marketing tool of the future, a device that customers wear on their bodies which, every time they use it, automatically creates a new 'episode' in their life stories as told on their Twitter feeds or Facebook timelines, life stories which themselves carry the Nike brand.

Conclusion

In this chapter I have tried to outline some of the ways advertising culture has changed from the days when scholars such as Leech (1966a) and G. Cook (1992) undertook their seminal studies, and to show how concepts from stylistics and discourse analysis can be applied to understand new forms of advertising in which what constitutes an 'ad' is no longer straight-forward and the relationship between advertisers and customers has become, to use the terminology of Facebook, 'complicated'.

I began the chapter by bringing up some of the legal and ethical issues surrounding social media marketing, illustrated by recent rulings by the UK's ASA, and then proceeded to demonstrate how tools from stylistics and discourse analysis can help shed light on these issues. What I have also demonstrated, I hope, is how a critical stylistic analysis raises even further ethical issues that advertisers, regulators, customers and scholars will need to grapple with in the coming years: issues about the authorship and ownership of texts, issues about the erosion of the line between the public and the private, and issues about the degree of control people have over the texts they generate in their daily lives.

35

Political style

Jonathan Charteris-Black

Introduction: what is style?

'Style' is a notoriously elusive word to define. The word has a broad range of meanings with positive associations in creative areas of cultural activity such as art, design, architecture, fashion, leadership or drama – as well as in literature and language use. Style is self-expression through any symbolic mode. Although the meanings expressed by style are personal and unique, the symbols through which these meanings are communicated depend on the pre-existing values that are attached to them. Style, and the semiotic resources on which it relies, therefore arises from an interaction between the personal and social. Style is closely related to 'identity' and is the habitual means of self-expression that marks an individual as distinct and relies on shared knowledge of the values attached to the symbolic resources through which this identity is expressed. If we describe someone as having a 'metropolitan style' because this person wears Levi jeans, Rayban sunglasses and uses an iPhone, this evaluation relies on the social values attached to these symbolic resources.

Style is essential in creating political meaning; as Hariman (1995: 3) puts it: 'To the extent that politics is an art, matters of style must be crucial to its practice'. The word 'style' originates in the Latin 'stilus' – an instrument for writing on a wax tablet (with a sharp end for inscription and a blunt one for erasure) – which reminds us that style was used in relation to language before the other expressive domains to which it has become extended. 'Stylistics' retains this earlier linguistic sense of 'style' and carries with it connotations of aesthetic value. In this chapter on political style I will focus on this narrower sense of style, although this is not to claim that language is any more persuasive than other symbolic choices (Charteris-Black 2007). Political style arises from a complex interaction of verbal and non-verbal semiotic modes through which a politician conveys socially shared meanings, but language is often more available for analysis than the other components of style.

I will first trace the origin of political style in classical rhetoric and compare this with broader, contemporary semiotic approaches that integrate verbal and non-verbal modes of expression. I will then outline a lexically based method for investigating linguistic style that corresponds well with earlier classical understanding of style. The study then applies this method to the speeches of the British Prime Minister at the time of writing – David Cameron.

Political style, past and present

Hariman (1995: 4) defines political style as follows: 'a coherent repertoire of rhetorical conventions depending on aesthetic reactions for political effect'; he identifies four styles: the realist, the courtly, the republican and the bureaucratic. In Ancient Greece 'style' referred to the selection of words that ensured a suitable balance between clarity and elevation for a particular oratorical setting. Ordinary words and simpler phrases contributed to a plain style while less familiar words and more elaborate expressions contributed to an elevated style (Fortenbaugh 2007). The choice of a plain or elaborate style would depend on the purpose and setting. Simpler words encouraged ease of comprehension while more complex words encouraged admiration and wonder – although they may be understood less easily. The simple or 'Attic' style contrasted with the elevated or 'Asianic' style – although there was also a middle style that integrated elements of both.

Classical rhetoricians differentiated between 'style' – actual word choices as well as 'delivery' (the control of voice, gesture, facial expression, etc.) – and 'memory'. They argued that style, delivery and memory were equally important in persuasion. Choice of style would be influenced by the branch of oratory; forensic rhetoric required simplicity, whereas a more elevated style might be preferred for settings requiring epideictic rhetoric. Potentially elaborate figures of speech – such as metaphor – would be more appropriate in epideictic rhetoric, while simpler figures – such as repetition – would be appropriate in forensic rhetoric (Fortenbaugh 2007). Classical rhetoricians emphasised that the most essential consideration was to fit the style to the occasion so that what was most effective at a specific point in a speech would depend on the speaker's assessment of both topic and audience.

Contemporary approaches show similarities and differences from the classical views on style. For example, in leadership studies the 'style' approach emphasises the importance of adopting behaviours that are most likely to be effective in a particular situation. It proposes that a blend of 'task' and 'relationship' behaviours should vary according to the communicative requirements of the leadership context. This follows the classical view and, as in classical times, politicians are necessarily concerned to differentiate themselves from others since the creation of style is crucial in developing a recognisable persona to attract voters. However, contemporary approaches do not treat 'style' as distinct from 'delivery' and integrate analysis of non-verbal features – such as appearance, and symbolic action – with verbal features such as speech style, metaphor and the level of conviction expressed through use of modality. Politicians draw on semiotic resources other than language, and there are potentially 'grammars' for each of the modes of communication (sight, sound, touch, etc.). As Hariman (1995: 7) summarises: 'each political style draws on universal elements of the human condition and symbolic repertoire but organizes them into a limited, customary set of communicative designs'.

Charteris-Black (2007, 2011) presents a semiotic account of political communication to explain how these various verbal and non-verbal modes are integrated in a particular 'design'. I argue that linguistically politicians communicate their legitimacy – what I refer to as 'being right' – through language that describes their values and their visions. They establish their ethical integrity by showing that they 'have the right intentions' and their logical ability through arguments supported by evidence showing that they can 'think right'. They also establish their legitimacy by 'sounding right' – for example, by creating empathy through personalisation, humour and other verbal means for engaging with an audience's feelings. Finally, they need 'to tell the right story' by engaging with established narrative frames for 'us' and 'them' roles that an audience will recognise on the basis of shared views about what is heroic and villainous.

Equally important in identifying political style are the range of semiotic modes – physical appearance, dress, body language, artefacts and symbolic actions – that together constitute the 'symbolic repertoire' through which political meaning is formed. Although these might be included in the notion of 'delivery', in the classical epoch there were not the theoretical or formal frameworks for analysing multimodal aspects of political communication. Growing technological sophistication in the evolution of media – radio, television, the internet – has necessarily led to increasing complexity in meaning-making resources. The expansion of the media – in terms of scope, range and potential for influence – has changed the way that political style is created. It has also led to the development of a new class of professional expert – skilled in the dark arts of spin. However, technological developments have also created opportunities for shining light into the darkness. Corpus-based critical perspectives offer new insight into political style. In the next section I will explain corpus methods for the analysis of political style.

Researching style – comparative keyword analysis

Political speeches offer one of the most accessible sources of data since they are readily available via the internet and can be treated as in the public domain. British parliamentary debates are recorded in Hansard that has an online version; Charteris-Black (2009) demonstrates how this can be used to investigate gender differences in the use of metaphor by politicians. The method of comparing word frequency in two research corpora that I will describe here differs from critical metaphor analysis but provides alternative insights into style that can supplement metaphor analysis in situations where metaphors do not occur – perhaps because they are deliberately avoided. The method is known as comparative keyword analysis (P. Baker 2006; Seale and Charteris-Black 2010; Seale et al. 2006).

I will demonstrate how comparative keyword analysis provides a method for investigating political style by identifying keywords that form the basis for a qualitative investigation. The method compares any two sets of data to establish which words occur with a statistically higher frequency in one set (A) as compared with the other (B). In the case I am going to describe here, (A) is a corpus of speeches by David Cameron (see the list at the end of the chapter) and (B) is a reference corpus comprising a representative sample of speeches by other British politicians (summarised in Table 35.1). The purpose of the comparison is to identify the lexical and phrasal choices of David Cameron that are distinctive and contribute to his style.

The sample is selected according to a number of criteria: that the politicians are well known, experienced (and therefore familiar with the genre), that there is a gender balance and that both major parties are represented. The number of words varies according to the status of the politician, their influence and their length of time in leadership roles. The reference corpus can be added to and developed over time to accommodate to diachronic change. An earlier version of this corpus included a smaller number of speeches by David Cameron – since he was the focus of this study

Table 35.1 British politicians' speeches.

Politician	Speeches	Words
Tony Blair	26	101,533
David Cameron	30	83,361
Margaret Thatcher	11	73,421
Enoch Powell	26	50,904
Winston Churchill	25	32,217
Hazel Blears	6	17,297
Peter Hain	6	16,510
Harriet Harman	6	15,101
Alan Johnson	6	15,314
TOTAL	142	405,658

I included additional speeches; I also decided to include his speeches in the reference corpus. Since the measure of comparison is based on *statistical difference* between corpus A and B, in a balanced corpus the inclusion of A within B will not significantly affect calculation of this difference.

The method proceeds by using Wordsmith Tools software (Scott 2005) to create a list of all of the words in A and B. Comparison is then made of the two wordlists to show the words that are more frequently used in A (speeches by David Cameron) as compared with B (the reference corpus of British politicians). When examined critically, these so-called keywords provide insight into David Cameron's rhetorical style. For example, the word 'love' occurs 28 times in the speeches by David Cameron; this is more than the combined uses (27) of all other politicians in the reference corpus – 'love' is therefore a 'positive keyword' for David Cameron. We can interpret this rhetorically as an attempt to represent himself as a contemporary, modern man who is emotionally open about his feelings because he is prepared to talk about them explicitly in public. Winston Churchill or Enoch Powell did not talk in public about what they 'love': political style necessarily seeks to integrate individual style with what is perceived as socially appealing; this will change over time, and in David Cameron's case this is for men to be emotionally expressive.

Keywords are helpful in identifying salient differences between groups of texts. A point worth noting is that when investigating style it is often *lower*-frequency keywords that are more revealing; for example, 'love' is ranked in position 112 of Cameron's keywords, whereas 'growth' is ranked ninth – however, 'love' tells us more about Cameron's style, because 'growth' only tells about current political preoccupations. However, this is only established by qualitative analysis of keywords.

Keyword clusters formed by two or three words that occur in adjacent positions to a keyword can also be examined. For example, Cameron uses the phrase 'I love' eleven times whereas it only occurs once elsewhere in the reference corpus. Moreover, some important markers of style occur primarily in phrases. For example, when we examine 'big society' we find that *no* other politician in the reference corpus has used this phrase – it is therefore a key phrase that is worth investigating further.

Examination of these words and word clusters in context offers insight into rhetorical style. The software enables us to examine how particular words were used by providing a 'keyword in context' display of concordance lines (known as a KWIC display) that gives every instance of the word occurring in the research corpus and shows the words occurring on either side of it each time it occurs. This allows the contextual meaning of particular words to be explored; Figure 35.1 shows a KWIC display for the phrase 'I love' in the Cameron corpus.

The concordance lines show the entities that David Cameron 'loves' include: 'this/my country' (× 4); 'the NHS' (× 2); 'our character' (× 1), 'our people' (×1), 'this party' (×1) and 'our countryside' (× 1). We can return to

N Concordance

1	today. I came into politics because	I **love**	being last night to Her Majesty – how much able to say that – and she
2	today. I came into politics because	I **love**	this country. I think its best days
3	means for conservation. Let me tell you:	I **love**	this country. I think its best days
4	talking down the NHS. I'll say it again –	I **love**	our countryside and there's
5	it? But this is the point: It's because	I **love**	the NHS. And yes, in many ways
6	this party because I love my country.	I **love**	the NHS so much that I want to
7	, ever again. I joined this party because	I **love**	our character. I love our people,
8	hate the party, and its traditions. I don't.	I **love**	my country. I love our character. I
9	that matters and that is that the people	I **love**	this party. There's only one
10	beliefs. I am not a complicated person.	I **love**	are healthy and well. My family
11	I love my country. I love our character.	I **love**	this country and the things it
12		I **love**	our people, our history, our role in

Figure 35.1: KWIC display for 'I love' in Cameron corpus

the full transcripts of speeches to see the full context of how the keywords were used. In addition, collocates of words can be shown (the words most frequently occurring to the left or right of the word in question) and two-, three- or four-word clusters that are frequent in the text can be displayed. This was an important stage in the classification of keywords because it is through analysis of the context of use that we can identify higher levels of meaning – semantic prosody and communicative purposes.

Deciding which keywords to report, or to analyse further, was not done on purely statistical grounds. Some keywords, though highly significant numerically, are of trivial importance for research into style. For example, as we will see in the next section, many of the keywords in the Cameron corpus related to political issues that were salient at the time of his leadership; these were content keywords such as 'deficit', 'growth', 'Eurozone', 'banks', 'Libya' and so on. However, these were not especially relevant to an investigation of his rhetorical style, though they might be of interest to a political scientist who is interested in identifying the dominant areas of policy. The sort of keywords that are relevant to the investigation of communication style – what I refer to as 'style keywords' are often *not* nouns, but – in Cameron's case – words such as 'actually' or 'let's' that provide subtle insight into *how* arguments were communicated rhetorically. Choosing the keywords that best bring out the characteristics of a particular text is, then, a qualitative judgement, informed by examination of the meanings that these words have in the texts concerned and relating this to the purpose of the analysis. Comparative keyword analysis is therefore a conjoint qualitative and quantitative analytic method.

A few qualifying points need to be made. Firstly, it is important to ensure that both A and B are 'representative' – that is, the speeches should control for genre – so in this case as mentioned above these were higher-stakes speeches such as party conference speeches, policy statement speeches or speeches preceding a major vote in an elected assembly. We can expect the speaker to have had a higher involvement in their authorship (even though advice on drafts will certainly have been offered). Issues of authorship are discussed in more detail in Charteris-Black (2011: 6), the primary point being that, though politicians do not author all their speeches, the words that are put into their mouths by speech writers are intended to fit their style of leadership. Although speech writers are marketing a political 'brand', the copyright on this brand is owned by the politician.

Secondly, a focus on word choices does not preclude identification and analysis of other language variables. A premise underlying my work on the metaphors used by individual politicians (Charteris-Black 2011) is that metaphors are insightful in the expression of rhetorical style. Identifying, classifying and analysing such metaphors contribute to the identification of the underlying narrative structures that I refer to as 'myths' but that have also been described as scenarios (Musolff 2006) or systematic metaphors (L. Cameron 2010) using related frameworks. I also argue that metaphors work through interaction with other rhetorical features such as schemes and metonyms as well as lexis. The more complex such interaction the less likely explicit attention will be drawn to any one feature – thereby evading the sensibility of an audience that they are being consciously worked upon. However, sometimes metaphors are deliberately avoided – for example in a plain style – and so other technologies for language analysis can assist in identifying word and phrase choices. The approach described above could also be used to examine the style of the same leader in different speech situations or to examine shifts in a leader's style by comparing different time periods.

The study

Findings

Analysis of keywords and key phrases suggested that initially they could be divided into two major groupings – one primarily related to content and the other to style. These are shown in Tables 35.2 and 35.3. The content of political language is likely to concern the various political and economic issues that have dominated public policy discussions. They reflect major policy areas and the perspective taken on these by the party rather than the personal style of the politician. By contrast, style-related keywords are more revealing of the politician's stylistic resources for persuasion and are therefore more relevant to the topic of this study.

It is perhaps not surprising that Table 35.2 shows a large number of keywords relating to economic policy, because of the global financial crisis that has dominated nearly every aspect of current affairs since Cameron came into office. The keywords are mainly nouns and indicate political objectives relating to overcoming national indebtedness by reviving the economy through stimulating the private sector and incurring short-term hardships for 'long-term' economic stability. Other

Table 35.2 Cameron's content-related keywords and phrases.

Purpose of content keywords and phrases	Related keywords	Related key phrases
Explaining economic policy	Growth, economy, deficit, business, crisis, businesses, debt, Eurozone, banks, money, term, entrepreneurs, innovation, financial, competitive, tax, taxes, expenses	the long term
Explaining political policy	Coalition, government, country, plan, green, government, politics, EU, Libya, reforming, Whitehall	national interest
Social objectives	Family, marriage, people	

Table 35.3 Cameron's style-related keywords and phrases.

Rhetorical purpose	Related keywords	Related key phrases
Establishing consensus	Got, get, need	We've got (to), we have to, we need to, let's,
	I, I've, we'll, we're	I want to, I know that, I think that, I think we
	yes, going	To make sure, going to be
	Our, you, your	In this together
Intensifying	Really, incredibly, actually, today	Really want/need
Appealing to morals	Big, society things bigger, stronger, responsibility, broken	the right thing, big society, power and control, system (political, tax), broken society
Describing political actions	Want, make, change, build, doing, help, getting, do, drive, asking	Make it happen
Creating contrasts	Just	not just about
Drawing conclusions	So, because, that's	So we, that's why

groups of keywords occur where political policy is being explained – for example, as typical for Conservative governments, the view that society is rooted in 'marriage' and the 'family'.

A general point about content keywords is that they do not identify much that intuition alone would not have identified, based on an awareness of contemporary economic, political and social issues. They provide a snapshot overview of contemporary political concerns and are not particularly interesting from the perspective of analysing style. Corpus linguistics seeks to identify that which is not accessible from intuition alone, and this is why we need to make qualitative judgements that identify 'style' keywords as separate from such 'content' keywords. These are shown in Table 35.3.

Table 35.3 shows a range of words and expressions that are more revealing of Cameron's political style – his personal linguistic resources for conveying a persuasive message. These keywords and phrases have been grouped together to identify a range of rhetorical purposes, which are shown in the left-hand column. The rhetorical purposes were identified from analysis of keywords and key phrases – rather than the other way round, though contextual knowledge complemented the empirical findings. For reasons of space I will only focus here on the first three rhetorical strategies.

Establishing consensus and modality

The 2010 election had led to a hung parliament as the Conservatives fell 20 seats short of the 326 seats required to have a majority government. As a result, a coalition was formed with the Liberal Democrats, whose leader Nick Clegg had been widely perceived as the most successful performer in the televised debates between the party leaders – the first ever in a British general election campaign. Politically, therefore, it was essential that David Cameron was able to establish a consensus to ensure the survival of his government – especially since the only previous hung parliament in the post-war period (in 1974) had only lasted a few months. However, given the volatility of the financial markets there has been a strong rhetorical incentive to appear strong and unified so as to ensure international credibility and avoid the cataclysm of a collapse in confidence in the UK economy. Against this background the somewhat paradoxical rhetorical objective has been to appear strong while being in a politically vulnerable position.

To achieve this challenging objective Cameron draws on the resources of modality with the rhetorical purpose of establishing consensus. Theories of modality differentiate between deontic and epistemic modality as follows: 'deontic modality is concerned with the necessity or possibility of acts performed by morally responsible agents' (Lyons 1977: 823), while epistemic modality is 'concerned with matters of knowledge and belief' of the speaker (Lyons 1977: 793). Deontic modality is the linguistic means for imposing obligations and granting permission while epistemic modality is the means by which propositions can be expressed as being possible or probable. Epistemic modality is 'concerned with the speaker's assumptions or assessment of possibilities . . . and indicates the speaker's confidence or lack of confidence in the truth of the proposition expressed' (J. Coates 1987: 112).

Cameron's style uses 'we' for the subject of verbs expressing a high degree of moral legitimacy for political actions, while he uses 'I' as a subject pronoun when making deontic assertions with a high level of confidence in the actions he advocates. The following examples illustrate this with the key phrases 'we need to. . .' and 'I want to. . .':

> Just as in Britain *we need to deal with* the deficit and restore competitiveness, so the same is true of Europe.   *(17 May 2012)*

> But *we need to do more*, embedding high quality vocational education, which is why we are creating University Technical Colleges for 14–19 year olds. . .
> *(17 May 2012)*

> Before we get into the detail *I want to say this.*
> I believe passionately in the NHS.   *(6 April 2011)*

Table 35.4 compares Cameron's key phrases using deontic modality with the British politicians' corpus. The numbers in the central columns show the frequency per 10,000 words and the lower number and the number of occurrences; the right-hand column shows the level of significance calculated using the log-likelihood test.

Table 35.4 Deontic modality: Cameron compared with other British politicians.

	Cameron (per 10,000 words)	British politicians (excluding Cameron) per 10,000 words	Level of significance
We need to	9.35 (n=78)	2.79 (n=90)	P <0.0001
We've got to/ we have got to	3.96 (n=33)	0.19 (n=6)	P <0.0001
We have to	3.72 (n=31)	2.39 (n=77)	P <0.05
Let's	5.28 (n=44)	0.65 (n=21)	P <0.0001
I want to	8.39 (n=70)	2.34 (n=72)	P <0.0001

The table shows that Cameron uses first-person plural forms in phrases expressing some form of necessity or obligation statistically more than is common in British political speeches. He uses 'we need to' over three times more frequently, 'we've / we have got to' around twenty times more frequently and 'let's' over eight times more frequently. For reasons of space I will focus on 'we need to', 'let's' and 'I want to'.

In a study of the language of people experiencing illness I found that 'need' statements were more characteristic of a feminine style in expressions starting with 'need to' and that such expressions characterise a style of high modality that positions a perspective around the speaker's needs (Charteris-Black and Seale 2010). Cameron's political style could be described as realist when his arguments are based on necessity, but it also reflects contemporary styles that are traditionally more associated with women (D. Cameron 2003).

In political contexts a 'feminine' style is effective in avoiding confrontational styles – such as the adversarial style of Prime Minister's question time – that are viewed as embodying an aggressive masculinity. Expressing directives using 'need' statements imposes an obligation on the part of the hearer because denying the recommended action would also imply a rejection of the moral premises on which it was based. 'Need' statements do not specify rhetorical perspective and therefore convey ethical legitimacy, as in the following:

> But *we need to tell the truth* about the overall economic situation.
>
> *(5 October 2011)*

> The dangers of climate change are stark and very real. If we don't act now, and act quickly, we could face disaster. Yes, *we need to change the way we live*. *(8 October 2009)*

> And in this world of unease as well as freedom *we need to do more to support* the family, and again the old politics are failing. *(3 October 2007)*

A similar concealment of rhetorical perspective that imposes moral obligation occurs in the phrase 'we've got to'. In Cameron's rhetoric it is more common than 'we have to' – the insertion of 'got' heightens the level of modal certainty and is a directive with a higher degree of obligation, as in the following:

> But to those who just oppose everything we're doing, my message is this: Take your arguments down to the job centre. *We've got to get Britain back to work.*   (5 October 2011)

Sometimes the two types of modal expression occur in close proximity:

> But if we want our country to carry on with this proud, open tradition, *we've got to understand* the pressures of mass immigration and that's why *we need to put* limits on it.   (8 October 2009)

When Cameron issues directives with a lower modality and emphasises the collaborative nature of his directives, he uses the more informal 'let's' as this implies willing participation on the part of the hearer. 'Let's' was not common in the British politician's corpus – for example, it was not used at all by either Powell or Churchill – and this more informal way of expressing collaboration seems to have been first introduced by Thatcher. Cameron typically uses 'let's' in conjunction with 'together' to emphasise the collaborative nature of his directives:

> Well, here is a progressive reform plan for Europe. *Let's work together* on the things where the EU can really help, like combating climate change, fighting global poverty and spreading free and fair trade.   (1 October 2008)

He also often repeats the phrase 'let's':

> Half the world is booming – *let's go and sell to them.* So many of our communities are thriving – *let's make the rest like them.* There's so much that's great about our country.   (5 October 2011)

This informal register perhaps changes the level of directness so that his directives are represented as invitations to participate. On occasions Cameron ends a speech with a triple repetition (tricolon) that includes 'let's':

> So *let's see* an optimistic future. *Let's show* the world some fight. *Let's pull* together, work together. And together lead Britain to better days.
>
> (5 October 2011)

> So *let's build* together a new generation of Conservatives. *Let's switch* a new generation on to Conservative ideas. *Let's dream* a new generation of Conservative dreams.   (4 October 2005)

When using deontic modality more forcefully Cameron switches from plural to singular pronoun, so he talks about what 'I want to see' and what 'I want to say':

You've heard me talk about social responsibility so let me say this. *I want to see* private schools start Academies, and sponsor Academies in the state system.   *(5 October 2011)*

These forms are more emphatic as they express Cameron's personal commitment to a particular policy; one phrase he uses in conjunction with some form of moral directive is to preface it with 'I want to say' followed by the deictic 'this', as in the following:

The last thing *I wanted to say* to you today is simply this: I am very aware that as the British Prime Minister, I can expect incredible things from you. Dedication, bravery, courage, service. *I want to say* what you can expect from me.   *(24 June 2010)*

These deictic speech acts serve to emphasise the assertions that follows and transform them into exhortations expressing a high degree of speaker involvement.

Cameron's political style in phrases such as 'we need to' and 'let's' needs to establish consensus and accommodate to his relatively fragile political position. However, the risk of a style that is *too* consensual is that it sounds weak and this may explain a stylistic counterpoint to consensual language in his use of 'I want to say' and other forms that convey higher epistemic modality when making assertions. These are shown in Table 35.5.

When using first-person singular pronouns to convey epistemic statements Cameron uses modal forms to show that his assertions carry conviction. This is to counterbalance the relative mitigation that occurs when using form such as 'let's'. A style that is generally associated with a high level of self-confidence and self-conviction has been associated with both Margaret Thatcher and Tony Blair; it is sometimes described as 'conviction rhetoric' (e.g. Charteris-Black 2011: 10). The following examples illustrate Cameron's conviction style:

So let me face head-on the question of faith schools. *I know that people feel strongly about this issue.*   *(4 October 2006)*

I know that working longer will be tough for many people. But it will also allow us to help pensioners more.   *(8 October 2009)*

Table 35.5 Epistemic phrases: Cameron compared with other British politicians.

	Cameron (per 10,000 words)	British politicians (excluding Cameron) per 10,000 words	Level of significance
I know that	2.28 (n=19)	0.65 (n=21)	P <0.001
I think that	1.80 (n=15)	0.15 (n=5)	P <0.0001

Having worked as a special advisor 20 years ago, having watched
government over the last 20 years, *I know that the British Civil Service is an
incredible machine.* (13 May 2010)

By making assertions emphatically he represents himself as well informed,
convinced and convincing – as well as being in touch with public opinion,
rhetorical goals that are necessary in establishing consensus.

Intensifiers and a feminine style

Emotional expressivity is often claimed to be associated with traditional
ways of performing femininity; for example:

> Femininity and female roles are associated with the ability to experience,
> express, and communicate emotions to others, and to empathize with
> others' feelings, whereas masculinity and male roles are defined as the
> ability to suppress and control one's emotions.
>
> *(Fischer and Manstead 2000: 91)*

However, Cameron's biographers claim that in this respect Cameron does
not follow traditional masculine roles:

> Many of his friends speak of how candid, how unEnglish, he is about
> his emotions. Frequently he will be in tears at the end of a play or film, and
> be quite open and willing to talk about it. This is no wheeze: he is confident
> enough not to regard it as a sign of weakness.
>
> *(Elliott and Hanning 2012: 63)*

There is evidence in Cameron's use of intensifiers that they contribute to
emotional expressivity in a style that is traditionally considered feminine.
For example, assertions commencing with 'I think that…' are usually
followed by an intensifier that heightens its epistemic modality: we see
this in the following where intensifiers are underlined:

> I'd say that bank lending is still a very big issue for small businesses, but I
> think that next is absolutely red tape. (6 January 2011)

> I think that is incredibly misguided and I think it denies the evidence,
> because if you don't have a plan to balance the books, you have no
> confidence; and if you don't have confidence, you won't have growth. It is
> as simple as that. (6 January 2011)

> We will also make the necessary preparations in order to set up sanctions
> in Iran and I think that this is going to be a very honest, a very candid
> partnership, one that is characterised by a deep sense of friendship.
>
> (20 May 2010)

This type of emotional talk is designed to establish consensus by hyperbole – as if the strength of the opinions being expressed can compensate

Table 35.6 Intensifiers: Cameron compared with other British politicians.

	Cameron (per 10,000 words)	British politicians (excluding Cameron) per 10,000 words	Level of significance
Incredibly	1.80 (n=15)	0.03 (n=1)	P <0.0001
Really	9.50 (n=79)	2.32 (n=75)	P <0.0001
Actually	5.53 (n=46)	1.37 (n=44)	P <0.0001

for the underlying political vulnerability. By talking with conviction Cameron is able to represent himself as what he would like to be: the leader of a majority government. A similar purpose underlies his use of other intensifiers, which are summarised in Table 35.6.

Cameron uses 'really' and 'actually' around four times more frequently, and there is only a single instance of other British politicians using the intensifier 'incredibly', whereas for Cameron it is something of a style marker:

> In doing so, you've got *an incredibly talented team* of ministers. Vince Cable is an absolute star in terms of economic policy and economic thinking;
> *(13 May 2010)*

> ... some of the fastest broadband speeds in the world. *This is incredibly exciting* – and a clear demonstration of how determined we are to work with you to build the right framework for growth in Britain. *(25 October 2010)*

He uses 'really' with same hyperbolic intention:

> A big part of that answer is the Big Society. I think we are on to a really big idea, *a really exciting* future for our country ... *(19 July 2010)*

> To get our society working, and in a year – the Olympics year – when the world will be watching us, to show everyone what Great Britain *really means*.
> *(5 October 2011)*

In the literature use of hyperbole when making positive evaluations is associated with a feminine style (e.g. R. Lakoff 1975). However, in a gender-based study of people who had experienced illness I found that intensifiers such as 'very' and 'absolutely' were used more frequently by lower-class women and by higher-class men (Charteris-Black and Seale 2010). The reason for this convergence seems to be that emotional disclosure through hyperbole and intensifiers that is typically used as part of a feminine discursive style is a style that higher-class men adopt as part of an emotionally influential repertoire.

Findings for 'actually' provide further evidence that Cameron's style combines the dual advantages of a higher-class masculine style with a feminine one – 'actually' is an intensifier but it is one that also socially positions the speaker as higher class. Figure 35.2 shows evidence of this.

'Actually' does not add to the propositional content of what is said but enhances the speaker's commitment and emotional force; as with other modal choices Cameron's use of 'actually' heightens the level of self-assuredness one might expect of an old Etonian. Cameron's hyperbole combines class advantage with the benefits of sounding like a modern man who is not afraid to demonstrate emotionality in public – thereby rejecting gender stereotypes. However, in other respects Cameron's style is rather conventionally masculine – nowhere more so than his use of the word 'big'.

Appealing to morals and 'big talk'

According to Elliott and Hanning (2012) it was Cameron's director of strategy Steve Hilton who authored the phrase 'Big Society'; however, his media advisor Andy Coulson advised him successfully against using the phrase in the 2010 election campaign because focus groups showed that many people were uncertain about what it meant. However, although it was not used in the election campaign, Cameron subsequently re-introduced the phrase – 'insisting that while deficit reduction was his "duty", building a bigger society was his "passion"' (Asthana 2012). The phrase perhaps unconsciously sought to address people's belief that Conservative governments did not care about 'society' because of Margaret Thatcher's famous statement: 'There is no such thing as society' (see Keay 1987). Perhaps also Cameron wanted to distance himself from Reagan's 'Small Government' – a low degree of government control over business.

Such nominal metaphors are often described as 'sound bites' because they are designed to be short, memorable and readily packaged for distribution through the media. There is the possibility that a powerful metaphor will become a catchphrase that serves as a shorthand for the political tone of an era – as happened with 'The Iron Curtain' or 'The War on Terror'. Sound bites serve as banners around which supporters can rally. Political advertising is no different from advertising in general – it fails if nobody notices it and it is possible that Cameron deliberately intended 'The Big Society' to be ambiguous so as to attract media attention and provide a rhetorical opportunity for him to define it:

> The Big Society is about a huge culture change ... where people, in their everyday lives, in their homes, in their neighbourhoods, in their workplace ... don't always turn to officials, local authorities or central government for answers to the problems they face ... but instead feel

N Concordance

```
 1                  we see matters in common, but first we  actually  swapped news about coalitions
 2                 programme managed to do, which is  actually  re-instil pride in the estate, and,
 3                 that the opposition parties did not  actually  meet their European
 4                 - which were in danger of spiralling -  actually  fall. All this has happened not
 5                 truth is that we need a government that  actually  helps to build up the Big
 6            using different words for a long time and  actually  mean the same thing.
 7               and passing laws and regulations; and,  actually,  I profoundly believe that if we
 8                   that the first part that we publish is  actually  that part about the Big Society
 9                  more community organisers, to help  actually  create the social action of the
10              what I would most like to be a legacy is  actually  helping to build the Big Society
11                , where we take 16-year-olds, and  actually  have a programme for them,
12              . *  Set a new and tougher target to  actually  reduce the total regulatory
13   or that facility,' it was simple things like  actually  making sure you can fill in a
14              people come to Britain?' And it wasn't,  actually,  'Spend a bit more money on
15              people together is stronger. Where we  actually  think about people's well-being
```

Figure 35.2: KWIC display for 'actually' in Cameron corpus

both free and powerful enough to help themselves and their own communities. It's about people setting up great new schools. Businesses helping people getting trained for work. Charities working to rehabilitate offenders.   *(19 July 2010)*

Analysis of the phrase in context shows that 'The Big Society' in fact ideologically resembles what Reagan meant by 'Small Government', but in such a way to fit with an image of a caring and emotionally involved and 'big-hearted' leader. Evidence for this is that the phrases 'The Big Society' and 'big government' have *contrary* meanings in the Cameron corpus. Cameron uses 'big government' with a completely opposite semantic prosody from 'Big Society', as we see by comparing Figures 35.3 and 35.4.

The collocations of 'big government' are entirely negative as it is something that has failed and leaves people powerless whereas 'Big Society' is empowering and collocates with positive words such as 'success', 'build', 'create' and so on. This is supported by the claim that the phrase originated as one-half of a soundbite, 'Big society, not big government', which was supposedly coined by Samantha Cameron (Elliott and Hanning 2012: 427). Significant public figures such as Rowan Williams, the former Archbishop of Canterbury, have denounced the term 'Big Society' as deceptive since:

> Big society rhetoric is all too often heard by many therefore as aspirational waffle designed to conceal a deeply damaging withdrawal of the state from its responsibilities to the most vulnerable.   *(The Observer, 24 June 2012)*

In Cameron's rhetoric the opposite of 'The Big Society' is not 'small society' (which he does not use), but 'broken society' as in Figure 35.5.

This metaphor alludes to a phrase first introduced under New Labour that Britain is 'broken', but the phrase 'broken society' occurs for the first time in the Cameron corpus. Among earlier politicians in the British corpus 'promises' were typically 'broken', and therefore the word delegitimises by implying a lack of morality. Its reification in 'broken society' is therefore intended to contribute to Cameron's ethical credibility, and it is perhaps for this reason that the former Archbishop of Canterbury was keen to expose the deception involved in terms such as 'Big Society'.

An essential component of Cameron's political style is an effort to establish ethical credibility by claiming the moral high ground. Demonstrating ethical credibility is necessary for establishing trust based in a belief that government is in the interests of the people rather than personal interest. Building trust is a prerequisite of political success – especially because of increasing awareness of manipulation of public opinion through media presentation and the 'massaging' of consent. In modern democracies speakers need to convince followers that they and their policies can be trusted; but evidently trust is a quality that it is hard to earn and harder still to retain when in power.

N Concordance

```
 1  prisons ... is failing under the weight of big government targets and bureaucracy.
 2  who work in the NHS. The fault lies with big government. With their endless
 3  in the opposite direction. In welfare, big government has failed people in a
 4  ones around it will want to improve. Big government has totally failed in
 5      aren't simply about cutting back big government and hoping civic society
 6  care for those who can't. So if we cut big government back. If we move
 7  that people have been left powerless by big government. So it is time to shake
 8      has failed to solve these problems. Big government has all too often helped
 9  responsibility. The clearest sign of big government irresponsibility is the
10  Do you know the worst thing about their big government? It's not the cost,
11  . And we will have to tear down Labour's big government bureaucracy, ripping up
12  year, but for every year. Cutting back on big government is not just about
13  homes. The truth is, it's not just that big government has failed to solve these
14  is a dark side as well. After 12 years of big government, we still have those
15  clear where growth will come from. Not big government, with its Regional
```

Figure 35.3: KWIC display for 'big government' in Cameron corpus

```
N  Concordance
1             if these are the three strands of the Big Society agenda, there are also
2                . First, social action. The success of the Big Society will depend on the daily
3        and ultra local power is a reality – and the Big Society is built. They are all
4             that we will leverage, will mean that the Big Society Bank will – over time –
5         is no one lever we can pull to create the Big Society in our country. And we
6                       , top-down government schemes. The Big Society is that something
7        . And these are the three big strands of the Big Society agenda. First, social
8                     that actually helps to build up the Big Society. This means a whole
9        problems. A big part of that answer is the Big Society. I think we are on to a
10  country, and it's a vital part of building the Big Society. Taking responsibility
11          the modern way, the 21st century way, the Big Society way. By opening up
12                  about more than cuts? Yes. Is the Big Society some optional extra? No
13      can be enormous. That's a big part of the Big Society. I didn't invent the idea.
14                    should hope to achieve. So the Big Society is not some fluffy
```

Figure 35.4: KWIC display for 'the Big Society' in Cameron corpus

```
N   Concordance
 1     extending opportunity, and repairing our broken society. READY FOR CHANGE
 2          who say that all of this - mending the broken society - will require state action,
 3          our bureaucratised NHS. Repairing our broken society. That is our plan for
 4          debt for decades to come. Mending our broken society because unless we do,
 5          together all our work to help mend the broken society. Labour still have the
 6     Conservative government: to repair our broken society. NO TIME FOR MORE
 7          we need, but change. To repair our broken society, it's not more of the
 8     reform. That's how we plan to repair our broken society. BROKEN SOCIETY I
 9          , they're right. We'll never mend the broken society without a clear barrier
10          we plan to repair our broken society. BROKEN SOCIETY I know this is a
```

Figure 35.5: KWIC display for 'broken society' in Cameron corpus

Conclusion

In this study of political style I have sought to illustrate how the linguistic components of political style can be identified and analysed in choices at the level of word and phrase. I have also tried to show how groups of related words and phrases can be used to identify a range of rhetorical purposes. In the case of David Cameron I have illustrated how key phrases such as 'We need to', 'let's' and 'I want to' sought to establish consensus by drawing on deontic modality. I have suggested that this is part of a feminine style that emphasises emotional expressivity for which there is further evidence in phrases such as 'I love' and intensifiers such as 'really', 'actually' and 'incredibly' that he uses much more frequently than other British politicians. In this respect the findings are in line with those of Charteris-Black and Seale (2009: 108):

> The new ideal is for men who combine conventional 'masculine' qualities with a command of a more 'feminine' language of emotional expressiveness...

However, the risk of appearing rhetorically weak that may arise from using 'feminine' language is compensated for by his 'big talk'; this shows in assertions such as 'I know that' and in his position statement of 'The Big Society', which he has developed as an antonym for 'the broken society'. This paper has hoped to demonstrate how computational software and refined methodologies that draw on small-scale language corpora can be used more generally for an investigation of political style that offers many future possibilities.

Speeches in the Cameron corpus

4 October 2005 Conference Speech
4 October 2006 Conference Speech
3 October 2007 Conservative Party Conference
1 October 2008 Conservative conference
26 May 2009 'Fixing broken politics' speech

8 October 2009 Conservative Party conference address

11 May 2010 Downing Street

12 May 2010 David Cameron's speech outside 10 Downing Street as Prime Minister

13 May 2010 the Department of Business, Innovation and Skills

14 May 2010 the Department of Energy and Climate Change

18 May 2010 PM speech at Big Society launch

20 May 2010 Press conference on The Coalition: our programme for government

21 May 2010 Joint press conference with Chancellor Merkel, Berlin

25 May 2010 Queen's Speech

28 May 2010 Transforming the British economy: Coalition strategy for economic growth

24 June 2010 HMS Ark Royal, in Halifax, Nova Scotia

19 July 2010 the Big Society

15 November 2010 A transcript of Prime Minister David Cameron's foreign policy speech to the Lord Mayor's Banquet in London

6 January 2011 Manchester on economic growth

28 January 2011 'A Confident Future for Europe' World Economic Forum, Switzerland

29 March 2011 PM's speech at London Conference on Libya

6 April 2011 PM's speech on NHS Reform

16 May 2011 PM's speech on the NHS

23 May 2011 Speech on the Big Society

25 May 2011 Press conference with President Barack Obama at Lancaster House in London

5 October 2011 Party Conference Speech, Manchester 'Leadership for a better Britain'

17 May 2012 A Speech on the Economy

23 May 2012 statement to the House of Commons regarding G8 and NATO

15 June 2012 Speech to the Falkland Islands Government reception in London.

36

The stylistics of relationships

Sara Mills

Introduction

A great deal of stylistics work has centred on the analysis of linguistic choice, particularly in relation to vocabulary. There has been a certain amount of work which has focused on characterisation (Culpeper 2001), and on agency and transitivity (Burton 1982; Wareing 1994). What I would like to do in this chapter is to take that work further to analyse relations between characters. I find stylistic analysis which focuses on representation generally problematic, because of the assumptions which are made about the correspondence between characters and real people. There is an assumption that what is discovered in relation to the linguistic constitution of characters is in some ways instantly of value when discussing people. I would contest that assumption as, after all, characters in texts, literary or otherwise, are simply representations. Generally, theorists argue that people, just like literary characters, are textually constructed, formed through discourse, and therefore if we can begin to unpick the constitution of characters in texts, we can also begin to unpick the constitution of individual subjectivity. I would argue that this too easy slippage between characters and people needs to be questioned.

Characters in literary texts are not like humans in that they tend not to be internally contradictory, they are represented as speaking in fully formed, grammatical sentences, they do not interrupt each other and so on. However, that does not mean to say that representations of characters have *no* relation to people. It is precisely because they are ideological, in Althusser's (1984) sense, that these representations are interesting. They are representations which are presented to the reader from a particular perspective, and as such these representations are presented as propositions about the world, which the reader may be led to challenge, disbelieve or empathise with. These encoded representations have an impact on what readers assume is 'common-sense', 'natural' or stereotypical, and thus they are part of the construction of constraints on the way that subjects assume that they can fashion themselves.

In analysis of characters so far, the focus has very much been on individual characters, particularly in relation to the types of actions that they take. However, in this chapter, I would like to extend this work to an analysis of relationships between characters, and in order to do this I will draw on work in feminist critical discourse analysis (CDA), which focuses on transitivity and agency, together with work in politeness theory, which focuses on the linguistic work that individuals do to maintain or challenge their relationships. I bring these two positions together in order to analyse the power relations and stereotypical roles that are played out within literary texts. I also analyse the perspective that is taken on male and female characters; thus, these stereotypical views are not simply presented neutrally to the reader; the male stereotypes are often viewed fairly uncritically, while the females behaving stereotypically are often negatively evaluated.

Theoretical and methodological position

Representation

Althusser (1984: 20) asserts that ideology is the 'imaginary representation of the real relations of production'. Literary texts, just like other texts, are part of that masking of the way things really are. In literary texts, characters are presented to the reader as simplified schemas from a particular perspective, and readers can pick up on which characters are being presented to them as 'good' and which are 'bad', because of linguistic signals from the narrator. Althusser (1984) has argued that texts often present the reader with 'common sense' – those ideological propositions about the world which we assume that everyone can agree on. In texts where there are stereotypical representations, this type of proposition is generally presented without narratorial evaluation. That is not to say that readers are simply dupes of the narrator's perspective, but the dominant reading is the one which the narrator presents to the reader as self-evidently one which is not to be questioned. A resisting reader, however, challenges those common-sense representations (Mills 1994, 2012). These questions of representation may seem a little dated, since they raged in literary circles from the 1970s to 1990s, but I would argue that there are very good reasons to be concerned about representations, particularly when readers are presented with profoundly ideological messages about women without those views being questioned or challenged.

Feminist critical discourse analysis: transitivity and agency

The analysis of transitivity, or who does what to whom, has a long history, within both CDA (Halliday 1976) and feminist textual analysis

(Burton 1982; Wareing 1994). In essence, theorists interested in transitivity are concerned to map out, drawing on Halliday's model, the characters who are represented as acting and those who are represented as acted upon. Burton (1982) analyses a passage from Sylvia Plath's novella *The Bell Jar* and discovers that the central character is represented as acted upon rather than acting in her own right. Burton argues that this representation of a character who is subjected to the action of other characters is problematic, since she argues that this is 'disenabling'. For Burton, the fact that women read novels which represent female characters who are acted upon rather than acting has profound implications for the way that women see themselves and think about what actions are possible for them. Wareing (1994) has used Burton's work to analyse the representations of women characters in a range of novels by women. She has shown that strong female characters, who throughout a literary text act upon other characters and who are not represented as the recipient of actions, are represented as passive and acted upon when they are represented in sex scenes with male characters. Thus, this work on agency – who acts and who is acted upon – is of use when analysing relationships between characters.

However, this work has largely focused on the actions of female characters and has not systematically investigated the relations between characters and the patterns of actions between characters, which is the focus of this chapter. It is worth observing that CDA has had a slightly troubled relationship with feminism, largely because of its tendency to foreground issues of class over those of gender, but there are many feminist theorists working within CDA – for example, Michelle Lazar (2005), Joanna Thornborrow (2001) and Ruth Wodak (1998) – who have seen gender as one of the elements that must be integrated into a wider political scope.

Politeness and relational work

Politeness theory is concerned to analyse the way that individuals negotiate their position in relation to others and demonstrate both their care and respect for others and their awareness of their own position within the social hierarchy (Mills 2011). These two aspects of politeness are equally important: in using linguistic formulae such as 'Could you possibly...' an individual is, at one and the same time, showing that they are aware of a need to indicate respect for the other person, and also that they are aware that perhaps their position in the hierarchy necessitates that they use a deferent form of request. (For a further, more complex view of politeness and impoliteness, see Linguistic Politeness Research Group 2011). Locher and Watts (2005) have argued that, in order to move research beyond a simple concern with the intentions of the speaker (P. Brown and Levinson 1987), we should focus instead on the way that individuals negotiate their relations with others through what they term 'relational work' (also called 'rapport management' by Spencer-Oatey 2001). It is this process of drawing on resources of politeness in order to negotiate one's relationships with others that I will be using to describe relations between characters within a novel.

Analysis of roles and relationships

In order to test out how this type of theory might be put to work on a literary text, I will now turn to an analysis of Christos Tsiolkas's book *The Slap*, which was first published in 2008. This book was long-listed for the Booker Prize in 2010, and the reviews of the book on the cover draw attention to the 'realness' of this representation – 'shockingly lucid and real', 'Tsiolkas puts a microscope to family life and presents us with a vision both of unflinching honesty and great tenderness'. The novel has 'peeled eyeball candour, the characters are driven by their appetites into a thrilling, vital approximation of what it is to be alive'. Thus, the book is presented by reviewers as an analysis of current family life and is praised for its honesty in its representations. It was also televised as a series on Australian television, which became available in the UK in 2011. What struck me when I first read the book was how stereotypical the roles of male and female characters were, and the impact that this might have in a novel which was published very recently on the many people who have read it.

The book is concerned with the depiction of the members of a Greek-Australian family and their friends. The main focus of the book is an incident where one of the male characters slaps someone else's child because of their bad behaviour. Because of this one action, a great number of relationships are transformed, some of the characters refusing to speak to others – all of them taking up a position on the incident and cementing alliances with others through the position they take in relation to it. The narrative is relayed to the reader through a largely third-person narration, with some free indirect discourse. The chapters are presented from a range of character perspectives, some from the perspective of Hector, his father (Manolis) and his wife (Aisha), and others from the perspective of Rosie, the mother of the child who was slapped, and Harry, the man who slaps him. It is the representation of the relationships and the stereotypical nature of the roles that characters adopt in these relationships that I will focus on, as it seems to me that the unquestioned nature of these representations presents female characters as taking up submissive roles and in fact enjoying those roles. This perspective on these characters obviously constructs a set of propositions about the world.

On the back cover of *The Slap*, the plot is described as 'A man slaps an unruly boy. It's a single act of violence. But the event reverberates through the lives of everyone who witnesses it happen.' This is a not a neutral description of the plot, and perhaps we come to a sense of 'what the book is about' through a process whereby we assess the patterns of transitivity and agency choices as a whole. Thus, this assessment of the meaning of the book is that it is the character of the child who is at fault (he is 'unruly'). The violence is described as a 'single act of violence' suggesting that the only violence represented in this novel is that between the man and the boy, and that this act is in some way understandable or justifiable, because it only happens on this one occasion as a result of a loss of temper. What I have found is that there is a disjuncture between this view of what the novel is about and the patterns of transitivity choices overall, particularly in the way that male and female characters interact. Thus, based on an analysis of transitivity patterns, an alternative evaluation of the plot might be instead: 'A man, who, like all of the other male characters, has anger management issues, gets away with slapping a spoilt child and with beating his wife. His wife, just like all the other female characters assents to this violence.' This overall assessment of the plot is based on the types of transitivity and relational politeness patterns that we can find in the novel.

Words associated with female characters

There are words that are associated with female characters throughout the novel: for example, *prude, cooking, appearance, puritan, self-righteous, patience, reproach, orderly, safe, meticulous, efficiency, calm, steadiness, intelligence, mediate, bitch, chatter, sow, gossip*. In general, these words are ones associated with the domestic sphere or the moral sphere. Female characters are often judged harshly by male characters. For example, female characters are represented as a constraint on male behaviour. The book opens with a description of the main character, Hector, meditating on the things that he cannot do because of the presence of his wife, Aisha: 'Through the years he had learned to rein his body in, to allow himself to only let go in solitude; farting and pissing in the shower, burping alone in the car, not washing or brushing his teeth all weekend when she was away at conferences' (Tsiolkas 2008: 1). Hector is represented as being continually reprimanded by Aisha for smoking in the house. Males are thus characterised as constrained by females. Aisha forces Hector to buy a dependable car. 'She wanted something safe and less expensive to run. Reluctantly Hector had agreed. But he still dreamed of another Valiant – or a two door Ute, or an old EJ Holden' (2008: 11). Manolis, Hector's father, states that he 'doubted that there had been a day in his forties and most of his fifties that did not pass without him regretting ever marrying, without him cursing the terrible burden of having a wife and family' (2008: 295). There is nothing in the novel as a whole that would challenge this 'common-sensical' view of females, even in the chapters that are focused on female characters.

Words associated with male characters

There are words that are associated with male characters throughout the book: for example, *smell, exercise, sex, jump, force, grab, push up, stretch, walk, buy, challenge, barrel through, leap, switch off, addicted, lazy, vain, passive, selfish, chaotic, danger, impulsive, smash, masturbate, throwing, burns, parties, drunk, taking drugs, chatting up, fights, swung, punch, animal.* These words seem to characterise male characters as active, violent and supremely individualistic.

Males are represented as not looking after children. Instead, the roles that women characters have in the book are largely to do with looking after children and cooking, despite the fact that they all have careers. Children are represented as solely the preserve of women. When Hugo, a friend's child who behaves badly, kicks Aisha when she is looking after him, Hector takes him to a bedroom, throws him onto the bed and bellows at him, scaring him. Hector states: 'He was fucking sick of children, let the women sort it out' (2008: 35).

Males are presented as individualised. It is only the females who are discussed in general terms and as such are largely undifferentiated. Hector fantasises about other women while making love to his wife. Hector thinks: 'He simply loved women. Young, old, those just starting to blossom and those beginning to fade. And sheepishly, almost embarrassed at his own vanity, he knew that women loved him. Women *loved* him' (2008: 1). Hector is an individual 'he' here, but as in many other parts of the book, women are simply described as a plural 'they'.

I would like now to discuss the patterns in the way that actions are represented.

a) Male characters decide what happens

M:	suggests doing something.
F:	says that she doesn't want to do that.
They do the action that the M suggested.	

In an interaction between Hector and his wife, 'Aisha was breaking eggs over a frying pan and he kissed her neck … He switched off the radio in mid-crescendo. "Hey I was listening to that". Hector flicked through a nest of CDs stacked clumsily next to the CD player … He kissed his wife's neck again. "It's got to be Satchmo today", he whispered to her. "It's got to be West End blues"' (2008: 3).

This phrase, 'it's got to be…' is one which appears frequently throughout the novel when associated with male desires. The female is represented as challenging this action, but as in the end acquiescing in what the male wants to do.

A further example of this pattern is when Aisha meets a man at a conference. She says 'Maybe I'll have an early night tonight', but he laughs and gives her some pills 'For when we go dancing'. Aisha says 'Are we going out dancing, are we?' 'Sure we are. There's no early night for you' (2008: 361). She then says that she 'has no interest in taking drugs'. Later 'they did go dancing. Of course they did' (2008: 362), and they did take drugs.

A further example can be seen when Aisha comments on Hector, when they are on holiday together: 'He was a child every time he did not get his own way. He wanted her to agree to the beach, he obviously wanted a cigarette, he wanted everything to go his way ... She had suggested going to La Luna for dinner. It was expensive ... but the food was excellent and she loved that the balcony looked over the hothouse lushness of the river. Hector groaned at the suggestion. "Again. We've already been there for dinner and once for lunch. I want to do something different." "Fine ... we'll find somewhere else"' (2008: 380–1). Thus, as all the female characters, she complains about his selfishness, but allows him to dictate what they do.

b) Males watch women

All of the male characters are represented as watching women; they see women as sexualised exteriors. When Hector sees Connie, the young girl that he is having an affair with, he comments: 'Through the surgery window he watched her smoke, drinking in every aspect of her. The thick fair hair, the plump bottom and long strong legs in too tight black jeans' (2008: 14). At the market, Hector watches a Vietnamese woman: 'The young woman walking in front of him had denim jeans tightly cupping her round, tantalisingly small buttocks. She had long, swinging straight black hair and Hector guessed she was Vietnamese ... all that existed was the perfect sashaying arse before him' (2008: 11). Females are described from a male perspective, while no male characters are described from a female perspective in this sexualised way.

c) Males are violent; women accept that violence

F:	'provoke' violence (within the masculinist terms of the book).
M:	express anger; are violent – this is presented as 'natural', calming and pleasurable for males.
F:	accept their anger and apologise for their own behaviour which 'provoked' the anger/violence.

Male characters express a great deal of violence throughout the novel; for example, Harry the character who slapped the child, Hugo, says: 'He couldn't decide who he hated more: the hysterical wife who had hissed at him with unconcealed contempt, the drunk weak faggot of a husband, or the whining little prick he had slapped. He wished the three of them were dead. Fuck the lawyer. If he had real balls he'd take his shotgun and fire three quick bullets in each of their heads ... They were trash, should've been sterilised at birth. He shouldn't have slapped the child, he should have grabbed the bat off him and smashed it once, twice, a hundred times into the little fucker's head, made him pulp and blood. Almost tasting the blood, seeing the boy's face collapse into jutting bones and squashed muscle, Harry felt calm for the first time' (2008: 87). Violence is represented as 'normal' for these male characters; expressing violent feelings and thoughts is represented as unproblematically pleasurable for the male characters. Hector, commenting on the slapping of the child says: 'He wanted his wife to intervene because she would be calm, fair and just. He could not forget the exhilaration he had felt when the sound of the slap slammed through his body. It had been electric, fiery exciting. It has nearly made him hard. It was the slap he wished he had delivered. He was glad the boy had been punished, glad he was crying, shocked and terrified' (2008: 41).

When Aisha says something which annoys her father-in-law, Manolis, the novel narrates: 'He straightened his back. He must have looked fierce because instantly she perceived her mistake and recoiled from him. He wanted to grab her hair, pull her face to the table, beat her as if she was a little girl' (2008: 338). Later he says 'He wished he could slap her' (2008: 339). He also thinks about Rosie, the mother of the boy who was slapped: 'He should have grabbed the *poutana* by the hair, and shouted at her, You created this, you dragged us all into this. You are a bad mother' (2008: 339).

Women are represented as enjoying and submitting to violence. In a chapter focused on Harry, Hector's cousin, the narration states about Harry's mother: 'His mother would always start the fights. You're an animal she would suddenly announce over a meal. You're a rapist, a degenerate. Her husband would continue to eat his meal silently ... And Harry would wait for the moment that his father would rise and hit her. He'd pray then that one punch or slap would be enough ... One day you'll understand, he would often say to his child, women are the form the Devil takes here on earth ... When he emerged back into the main part of the house, his father would be sitting in front of the television; his mother would be ironing or sewing in the kitchen. There might be a rip in his mother's blouse, blood in the corner of her mouth, but the shouting, the tearing into each other had stopped' (2008: 92). Here Harry's mother is represented as being guilty of starting the fight by insulting her husband and thus the father's responsibility for the violence is diminished. The fact that the violence is described so dispassionately seems to represent male violence as normal and as a part of normal life. The mother's acceptance of the violence is represented by the fact that she continues to sew or iron, even though she is bleeding or has a torn blouse.

Harry exhibits just the same type of behaviour with his wife: he finds that his wife, Sandi, has talked about something to Hector without telling him; he continues to serve food calmly so as 'not to lose it and snap, and grab his wife and shake the stupid bitch over and over until he could hear her teeth rattle in her head, till he could see her eyes bulge, till he had her crying for forgiveness on her fucking knees. On. Her. Fucking. Knees' (2008: 124). Later when he is talking alone to his wife, he thinks: 'He could kick her in the face right now' and when she realises he is angry 'He saw fear spread across her features and a surge of excitement flooded through him. He grabbed her hair and tilted her head towards him. "How fucking dare you?" She went limp. She did not struggle. "Harry, I was going to tell you." ... He could hit her now, he could, like his father would have, to see how far he could go, how far she'd let him and how far he'd let himself ... He freed her hair from his hand, pulled her into his arms and hugged her hard ... "I'm sorry" she kept repeating, "I'm so sorry Harry". "It's alright", he kissed the top of her head ... he was reminded of a faithful dumb animal' (2008: 125). So, rather than violence being the responsibility of the males, it is seen as a joint enterprise where females are also represented as being responsible rather than just being victims. It is the female who apologises for the violence and the male who accepts that apology. Female characters are represented as 'letting' the male character be violent, just as the male characters 'let' themselves be violent.

Another example where females accept the violence of their husband occurs when Harry hits Sandi; Aisha comments 'They heard the car's brakes in the driveway and when Sandi had emerged, the blood thick and black on her shirt and pants, they had thought her drunk. Then they realised her nose was broken, her lips split, her jaw so dislocated she couldn't speak. She fell on Hector and two teeth dropped on the ground. Leave him, Aisha said, almost making it an order. But Sandi had not left him' (2008: 407).

There is also a slight variant on this pattern:

| M: | try to provoke an argument. |
| F: | do not respond; keep silent. |

For example, Sandi asks her husband, Harry '"Have you called the lawyer?" He groaned out loud at the question. "Have you?" "I'll do it tomorrow". He watched her warily. Sandi rarely argued with him. She had learned early in their courtship that he reacted to direct confrontation by a woman with implacable stubbornness. She nodded, unsmiling. Fuck. You. "I promise". Her face relaxed into a warm smile and she leant over and kissed him on the lips' (2008: 86). Thus, here the female character asks a question and the male does not initially respond, but on being pressed, he promises to call the lawyer at the same time thinking 'Fuck.You'. She is silent until he promises. Female characters do not provoke arguments in this way and the males do not try to avoid arguments or conflict. There is only one representation of a woman slapping a male and that is when Richie's mother slaps him when he reveals that Hector has had an affair with Connie; she immediately apologises for her violence. Richie says 'It stung. But it was just' (2008: 466).

d) Males want sex and women submit to sex

M:	wants to have sex.
F:	submits to sex while resisting superficially.

Sex is represented consistently as something which men do to women characters, and which concerns male sexual pleasure and needs. For example, Hector and Aisha:

> 'They're not asleep yet.' 'I don't fucking care,' he whispered. His cock was hard and he took one of her hands and placed it on his crotch. She giggled. . . . He pulled her top up and first cupped, then he began kissing her breasts. She tried to pull away from him but he would not let her. His lips closed over stiffening, obliging nipple, then he was sucking it, biting it, till Aisha let out a small whimper of pain and reluctantly he stopped. He straightened, faced her, her eyes were sparkling, and then suddenly, they were both giggling.   *(2008: 48–9)*

In this passage, Hector acts on Aisha (*took, placed, pulled, cupped, began kissing, not let, closed, sucking, biting, stopped, straightened, faced*) and some of these actions are quite violent (*pulled, biting*) and when she cries out in pain he only 'reluctantly' stops. All of these actions have an impact on Aisha. Her actions, however, are more complex; for while she is represented as the recipient of actions, she is also represented as resisting those actions, not wishing to have sex while their children are still awake. A further level of complexity is that despite the fact that she resists being bitten, her body is represented as willing to have sex – her nipple is represented as 'stiffening' and 'obliging'; her eyes are 'sparkling' and then on two occasions she giggles – thus her outward protestations 'They're not asleep yet' and her 'whimper of pain' are disregarded by Hector, and they proceed to have sex.

(There is one female character, Anouk, who explicitly models her sexual desires on male sexuality: 'Fuck me, she ordered him sharply now and she wondered. Is this the way a man understands sex?' (2008: 60). Thus in a sense she does not challenge the pattern 'M desires sex and acts on that desire', and 'F does not desire sex but submits to sex'; she simply uses the male model. This shows that women characters can act on men sexually, but they can only do it by acting explicitly as men.)

When Aisha has sex with Art, a man she meets at a conference, 'She had allowed him to lead their lovemaking, had submitted to the sureness of his desire' (2008: 370). When Hector and Aisha then have sex afterwards: 'She had submitted to his lovemaking' (2008: 379), 'her husband mounted her' (2008: 379), 'Hector was now fucking her like a whore' (2008: 379).

When Rosie has sex with someone called Qui, 'He *had* been brutal; he had been dirty: on waking she had felt unclean. The way he had often made her feel' (2008: 239).

A variant on this pattern is:

e) Females initiate sex but are rebuffed

F: initiate sex for the benefit of male (in response to gift/money).
M: is grateful but does not reciprocate.

When Harry gives his wife Sandi a music box, she whispers 'I want you to come in my mouth. I want you to fuck my mouth'; she then performs oral sex on him and afterwards he says 'That couldn't have been much fun for you', acknowledging that the act was concerned only with his sexual pleasure, and she responds 'I enjoy making love to you. You don't have to thank me. You're my husband' (2008: 113). There is no further sexual activity; instead she carries on with her domestic routines.

With his mistress, Kelly, the sexual dynamics are much the same. Harry enters her apartment while Kelly is talking on the phone to her mother, and her children are in their room '"Sure Ma" she said in English "I'll bring them over Sunday." With her free hand, she started tickling his balls, then slowly her fingers tapped along the shaft of his fattening cock. "Of course I won't fucking forget." Harry looked up at the Madonna staring down disapprovingly at him on the kitchen wall. He closed his hand around Kelly's fingers to tighten her grip around his cock ... he pulled at her nipple, twisting it till she slapped his hand away. He was conscious of the young girl watching television behind the wall. He could smell his lover's sweat and he kissed her arm, her neck, her hair as she finished her conversation. He shuddered, stifled his groan and blew into her hand. Kelly put down the phone' (2008: 98). Immediately after this, she makes him coffee, but there is no reciprocal sex. He leaves her money. Later Harry comments 'She was so good Kelly, she asked no questions, demanded nothing of him. Why couldn't all women be like Kelly?' (2008: 134). She draws attention to this explicitly saying, when he leaves her $200, 'Harry I'm not a whore' (2008: 134). However, she does take $50.

On the rare occasions where females initiate sex and the males do not want sex, then they do not have sex. 'Kelly reached for his crotch. He slapped her hand away. "I'm not into it." "Okay"' (2008: 134). When women are represented as sexual they are viewed negatively: Connie, a young female character who has a relationship with Hector, accuses him of rape, even though they have not slept together. She does this because he wants to end their relationship. Rosie, the mother of Hugo, the child who was slapped, characterises herself in the following terms when, in the past, girls at her school had stopped talking to her because she 'was a slut': 'she got back at them by sleeping with their boyfriends, with their brothers. She fucked their fathers. She continued doing it at the new school, the state school, full of boys to fuck. She had fucked and fucked, one night allowing herself to be fucked by seven of them, each taking turns. She had bled, her cunt had been torn. Everyone knew what she was. The new girl was a slut' (2008: 289). While sex for men is thus represented as simply a 'natural' drive, for women it is seen as a response to troubles: 'She was a slut. That was what she had become when her father left, when they lost the house' (2008: 300). The implicit causative link between 'her father left … they lost the house' and 'she was a slut' underpins a number of representations of female sexuality.

Politeness

In analysing this book from the perspective of politeness and relational work – that is, the work that individual interactants do to maintain or disrupt relationships – we can see that the male characters in the novel are generally blunt and rude (what P. Brown and Levinson (1987) term a *bald, on-record* face-threat) and the females accept that rudeness by giggling or by silence (Mills 2003). The male characters consistently use face-threatening acts (FTA) – that is, they behave in a way which challenges the composure of the other person – and the females respond with negative politeness – that is, politeness which is concerned to re-establish the equilibrium between the characters, and which stresses deference towards the male characters, thus displaying a subservient position.

f) Males are rude and females acquiesce

M:	rudeness, FTA (powerful).
F:	acquiesce in the rudeness / try to pretend it has not happened; negative politeness (powerless).

For example, when Harry is buying a music box for his wife which has Sanskrit writing on it, he asks the shop assistant what the writing says: 'He had no concern about showing his ignorance. He knew his education was limited … He had money and that's all that mattered …' "You don't know what it says?" The girl bit her bottom lip apologetically and shook her head. Harry smiled at her and picked up the box. "It probably says *Fuck you, Yank*". The girl's mouth formed a shocked perfect circle and then she laughed out loud. Harry winked at her. "Wrap it up for me honey, make it look nice. It's a gift for the ball and chain"' (2008: 102). This type of politeness routine where the males are rude and the female characters acquiesce in their rudeness by laughing or being silent characterises most of the male–female character relationships throughout the novel.

When Gary and Rosie, the parents of the child who was slapped, lose their court case against Harry for his violence towards their son, their lawyer Margaret 'was slowly walking up to them: "I'm sorry". Gary gave a harsh laugh. "You're a cunt"' (2008: 280). The lawyer does not respond at all.

A further example is when Hector is in a restaurant with Aisha: 'The waitress inquired about what they would like to eat and Hector slapped the menu on the table. "Give us a bloody moment". The girl, shocked, embarrassed, stared at him and then hung her head and bowed. Aisha could not bring herself to look at him' (2008: 384). However, her silence is an example of female characters who, by their silence, are indicating their deference towards the male character.

Another pattern in the politeness used by characters throughout the narrative is:

g) Males use FTAs and women are compliant

M:	FTA command
F:	silence/compliance

For example, Thanassis, a friend of Hector's family, 'banged his fist on the table, upsetting Koula's coffee. Thanassis, apologising, called out to the kitchen. "Zaita, bring us a cloth"' (2008: 304). There is no representation of Zaita's response or action – we are to assume that Zaita complied with this command.

Manolis, Hector's father, commands his wife, Koula, in a similar fashion: '"The Devil take you. Make me a coffee". "I'm getting lunch ready". "I want another coffee". "Are you going to talk to her?" Manolis looked around the kitchen . . . "Make me a damn coffee". Manolis rubbed his calf. "Are you in pain?"' (2008: 299). Here, Koula is represented as asking questions and giving sympathy, and Manolis is represented as commanding her to make him coffee. At the end of the extract, he announces he is going to a funeral, but before that he sits down in his armchair, and we are to assume that Koula makes him a coffee.

Perspective

We are given the perspectives of eight of the characters on these events. Four of the chapters are from the perspective of male characters and four are from females' perspectives, in the following order: Hector, Anouk, Harry, Connie, Rosie, Manolis, Aisha, Richie. However, often the female characters are judged explicitly by the narratorial voice in a different way from the male characters. The male characters are largely unevaluated, but, for example, Anouk, one of Aisha's female friends, when taking a taxi:

'Should they take the tunnel?' Her mind cleared, irritability smacking away the fog and she replied bitchily, 'You're the driver, shouldn't you know the best route to take? Isn't that why I'm paying you?' (2008: 61)

The critical element in this passage is the adverb 'bitchily' where Anouk's comments are evaluated. Female characters, even when they are the narrator, are evaluated by an external omniscient narrator.

While the chapters are focused on individual characters, there is a great deal of free indirect discourse (FID). The thoughts and speech of the male characters particularly are represented through FID, which results in the perspective of the external narrator merging with that of the male characters. The male characters watch women characters in the street: for example, when Harry is waiting at a garage, 'Harry saw Alex at the pump. A young woman had stepped out of a scarlet Toyota Corolla and was looking around. She was Asian, young and up herself, clutching a handbag with pink and yellow roses imprinted on the cloth, her chin raised in haughty expectation. Wait all you like, darling' (2008: 94). Here the extract starts with the narrator describing Harry and his assistant Alex at a petrol station; then an Asian woman is described. Harry's perspective begins and this section becomes FID when evaluation from Harry's perspective is introduced 'young and up herself ... her chin raised in haughty expectation'. Thus Harry's evaluation of the woman, through the merging into FID, is affirmed by the narrator.

With the character of Manolis, Hector's father, there is a similar use of FID; in the chapter which is focused on Manolis: 'Not for the first time he sighed inwardly at the innate conservatism of women. It was as if being a mother, the agony of birth, rooted them eternally to the world, made them complicit in the foibles and errors and rank stupidity of men. Women were incapable of camaraderie, their own children would always come first ... Women were mothers, and as mothers they were selfish, uninterested, unmoved by the world' (2008: 325). These statements about women in the merged voice of narrator and Manolis tie in views represented throughout the novel of the undifferentiated nature of women. Male characters are not referred to in this undifferentiated way, nor is there the same use of FID with the women characters.

h) Male thoughts contrast with their speech/action

M:	think violent thoughts.
M:	do not express their violent thoughts, but say what they think is expected by women.

There is often a contrast between what the male characters are represented as thinking and what they then go on to express, because of the constraints imposed by the female characters. For example, when Harry, the man who has slapped the child, Hugo, goes to see the child's mother, Rosie, to apologise. Rosie is breastfeeding Hugo. He says: '"I'm sorry I hit Hugo. I shouldn't have done it. You've got to understand it was because I was scared for Rocco." She interrupted him. "Your son is twice his size", she sneered. And thank you *Panagia* that he is my son rather than that little faggot you are breeding on your tittie there. Why had he come? He just wanted to belt the silly cow' (2008: 129). Thus what we see in this contrast between the thoughts of the male characters and what they actually say are the genuine wishes of the male characters, which are often very violent in comparison to what they say. Female characters' thoughts are not represented in contrast to their acts or speech.

Conclusions

Thus, we can see that, although the book is on the surface about 'a man hitting an unruly boy', in fact along the way a great deal of other ideological information is presented to the reader as part of common-sense background information: for example, that women enjoy violence and will submit to it, that women enjoy and will submit to sex when they don't want it, that children and cooking are women's jobs, that men should be allowed to have sex whenever they like, and that men should decide what happens. The book appears on the surface to be a book that narrates this story from a range of different perspectives; however, the overriding perspective is largely that of the male characters. This book thus presents to the reader stereotypical views on male and female characters which are differently evaluated: the female characters are represented in a fairly negative way as stereotypically submissive and acquiescing in their subjection, whereas the male characters are represented as stereotypically violent and demanding, and this representation is shown neutrally or positively. These propositions about the world and about what is acceptable for males and females are ones that the reader is encouraged to evaluate in line with the narrator's position. However, readers may well find that the position of comprehension that is proffered to them by the narrator is not one that they can in fact take up. Instead, they may well take up the role of the resisting reader who questions these stereotypes of females and males.

By bringing together a feminist CDA analysis of transitivity and a focus on relational work, I have shown that it is possible to analyse the relationships between characters. When this approach is used with a focus on point of view and evaluation, it is possible to examine the way that common-sense knowledge and stereotypical views of gender are presented in the novel. Because of this focus on the transitivity and politeness patterns that occur consistently throughout the book – in terms of what the female characters do when interacting with the male characters, and how those actions are evaluated – it is possible to challenge what is presented as the theme of the book by publishers and reviewers. The transitivity and politeness analysis allows us to examine the way that the book presents stereotypical gender character traits, and perhaps also enables us to see that these ideologies of submissive women and violent men are not a thing of the past, but are still very much still in play in the culture as a whole.

37

Stylistics in translation

Benedict Lin

Translation, most intuitively, is about conveying in another language what the translator considers to be the essential meaning of the text. But what constitutes this 'essential meaning' is not a simple matter. For many everyday functional texts, such as a set of instructions for setting up a piece of equipment or a weather report, this unproblematically is concerned with the purely referential meaning. Translate this referential meaning adequately, and the translated text performs the same function as the original text.

For a good number of text types, however, meaning beyond the referential may be considered 'essential'. Critical discourse analysts, for instance, would argue that news reports and historical accounts embed attitudes and implied meanings, through how content is ordered, and through their linguistic or lexicogrammatical selections – in other words, through *how* something is said, or through *style*, and not just through what is said. Even more clearly, it is through style that literary texts construct what Hasan (1989) has called a second level of semiosis, to convey what might be called second-order 'thematic' meanings. As Boase-Beier (2011: 72) remarks, it is also through their 'stylistic signals' that literary texts 'indicate to the reader that the text is to be read as literary, that is, as a fictional text that demands extensive engagement on the reader's part and that in turn can have profound effects on the way the reader sees the world'.

Translating such texts, then, must involve attention to matters of style. Or as Boase-Beier (2011: 72–3) points out, 'any translation, whether aiming to preserve or change the text-type of the original, will need to interact closely with the style of the text'. In particular, literary translators would need close awareness and understanding of stylistic patterns and issues in their source texts, in order to consider the stylistic effects they wish to (re)create in their target texts.

It would seem clear then, that stylistics can make significant contributions to translation theory and practice. And yet, few stylisticians have engaged to any extent with translation. Recognising the potential significance of stylistics in translation, the leading stylistics journal *Language and Literature* did devote a special issue in 2004 (13: 1) to papers on translation and style, Boase-Beier in her introduction noting the previous lack of interaction between stylistics and translation studies in general and expressing a hope that the special issue would 'provide impetus for further study' (2004a: 11). Yet only one other study (Ji 2009) has appeared in the journal since. Indeed, the only major systematic study in English to integrate stylistic theory with translation appears to be Boase-Beier (2006). Otherwise, the preoccupations of English-using stylisticians have been stolidly monolingual, leading Boase-Beier (2011: 71) to refer in her opening subheading to 'The Strange Paradox of Stylistics and Translation'.

Style and stylistics in translation studies

This is not to say that translation studies itself has not engaged in matters of style and stylistics. As Munday (2008b: 28) notes, 'style periodically, and even frequently, appears in discussions in translation theory'. However, it seems to have been rarely explored systematically (Boase-Beier 2006: 1). Discussions of literary translation mentioning the role of style, such as Munday (2008b), M. Baker (2000), Parks (2007) are among the exceptions.

For Boase-Beier (2006, 2011), one main reason for translation studies not engaging stylistics is that the linguistics with which stylistics is often associated is that of structuralist linguistics. Such a stylistics did have resonance with early preoccupations in translation theory that centred around notions such as *equivalence* between source text (ST) and target text (TT) (Nida 1964), and translation *shifts* (Catford 1965). Structuralist stylistics offered a basis for systematic comparative analyses between STs and TTs to enable, for instance, development of detailed taxonomies of small linguistic changes ('shifts') when experienced translators translate between two given languages. This made it possible to identify equivalences and differences between the two languages, and hence provide guidance for future translators.

However, translation studies has moved beyond a focus on equivalence and shifts in the linguistic texts alone, to more contextualised concerns. These concerns include what cognitive processes are involved in the process of translation, how translations act as forms of intercultural communication, how translation strategy is determined by the purpose for the translation and the function of the translated text in the target culture, how social and ideological power is negotiated and communicated in translation, and how translated works of literature are positioned as a whole in the historical and literary systems of the target culture. (See Munday 2008a for a survey of translation theories and approaches, and the issues that have been raised in translation studies.)

For all of these concerns, stylistic analysis of both source and translated texts can provide illumination in more than just ad hoc ways, but the stylistics involved must come from theoretical orientations that embrace variables other than just text. And Boase-Beier (2006) suggests that the broadening of stylistics away from narrow formalism/structuralism to encompass social, historical, psychological and pragmatic aspects of style means that contemporary stylistics therefore has much to offer to the understanding and practice of translation.

Boase-Beier (2004b, 2006, 2011) herself, for instance, has argued for and demonstrated a case for cognitive stylistics playing a significant role in the practice of literary translation. In Boase-Beier (2004b: 29), she notes that a literary translator needs first to read and interpret the source text before creating a new text, the translated text. In such close reading, she argues, the translator cannot avoid the question of the author's intentions, and for this, the translator must use clues in the style of the poem to provide answers: a poet's style, she notes, is central in conveying attitudes, states of mind and hence intentions. It is style, as well, that creates the 'poetic effects' that 'make readers re-examine their knowledge of the world'. Consequently, then, it is the translator's task to reconstruct the author's intention as he or she has interpreted it. In doing this, the translator in turn has to make his or her own style choices 'which will ... similarly exercise the reader of the translation'.

Boase-Beier demonstrates how a cognitive stylistic analysis can help a translator in this process. In her own analysis of the German poem, 'Beim lesen der Zeitung' ('While Reading the Paper') (2004b: 29–33), she shows how a missing auxiliary for the perfect tense is used as an accepted poetic device in German with 'a strange and significant consequence': it creates 'an ambiguity about the speaker's position' as to whether the murderers during the Jewish Holocaust could be believed to have known nothing about what they were doing. She argues that it is this moment of ambiguity that engages the reader cognitively, inviting the reader to seek a literary interpretation. She then shows how a translator, as reader, can arrive at such an interpretation through relating this ambiguity to allusions in the co-text of the poem, as well as to intertextual knowledge of 'the expressed views of perpetrators and participants in the atrocities of the Holocaust'. Thus, the elided auxiliary is 'the main textual clue' to the author's intention, interacting 'not only with the context supplied by the rest of the poem, but also with an individual translator's background knowledge and interests'.

Consequently, the translator's task, she argues, is to create a similar ambiguity 'so as to force the reader to experience the ambiguity of thought' (2004b: 33) that would achieve the same poetic effects. She demonstrates how this can be done through her own English translation that, while 'noticeably different from the original', has similar effects. This involves two stylistic choices: the elision of the verb *to be* to create ambiguity for the clause which in the original contained the elision of the auxiliary, and a lexical variant from the original ('butchers', where a literal translation would have called for 'murderer'). Translation here thus becomes a creative rather than merely reproductive enterprise.

Here, of course, she goes beyond demonstrating the worth of cognitive stylistic analysis to translation practice, to suggesting a theoretical point for poetic translation: if the aim of the translation is to produce a similar effect to the original, then perhaps creative liberties might need to be taken with regard to lexicogrammatical equivalence. And yet, the translated text itself will always remain an interpretation of the original, a creative work in its own right.

Aesthetic construction in poetic translation: a functional stylistics model

The example given above of Boase-Beier's work reflects the centrality of the notions of deviation, foregrounding and deautomatisation in stylistic analysis, and how these need to be attended to in the translation of a poem, if the translation aims to reflect what the translator believes to be the intention of the poet. It would be argued, however, that the focus remains too much on individual linguistic choices that deviate from general language norms within a poem: while accounting for their cognitive ramifications, such a focus does not sufficiently consider how these choices interpattern into the artistic whole of the text.

What will now be offered therefore is an analysis of a Chinese poem and one of its English translations that attempts to consider the overall aesthetic construction of thematic meaning in a whole text, through different levels of linguistic patterning – that is, how style choices across a text coalesce into an artistic ensemble that articulates the 'eye' of the text. The framework used is Hasan's (1989) systemic-functional linguistics (SFL) based model of verbal art, which, it is argued, also has the potential to account for complex considerations of context and translation purpose.

In this model, what distinguishes verbal art in literary works from other forms of discourse is that it has two levels of semiosis (see Figure 37.1):

- The first level projects the discourse represented *in* the poem. Here, verbal art works in the same way as everyday discourse. It is the lexicogrammar itself that encodes meanings construing potential contexts of situation. But note that these are meanings and contexts represented *in* the poem – in other words, who is saying what, to whom, where and so on.
- The second level produces a discourse *between* the text and reader. This is the level that verbal art possesses which other forms of

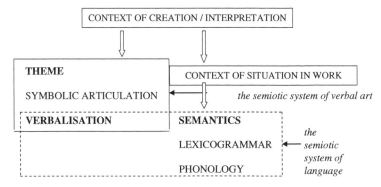

Figure 37.1: Hasan's (1989) model elaborated to show context of situation

discourse generally do not. This second level is achieved through the 'verbalisation' at first-level semiosis encoding some form of *symbolic articulation* that yields potential 'thematic sayings' from the text to the reader – for instance, a 'moral' that may be read into a story, or a statement about the human condition or about society.

Symbolic articulation is achieved through skilful interpatterning of lexicogrammatical patterns, in such a way as to consistently fore-ground some part of the text through its deviations from the text's norms. This draws attention to that part, suggesting its symbolic significance, and hence inviting interpretation of 'deeper' meaning(s) or 'thematic saying(s)', which is inevitably influenced by the context of interpretation.

To probe aesthetic construction and verbal artistry in a poem and its translations, one first conducts lexicogrammatical analysis, and then examines closely the lexicogrammatical patterns for interpatterning and consistent foregrounding. Consequently, potential (for) thematic sayings may be explored in relation to particular contexts of interpretation situated in particular contexts of culture. Hence, one can probe issues related to aesthetic (re)constructions to better evaluate the poem and its translations.

The analysis that follows proceeds along the lines described, employing the lexicogrammatical categories outlined in Halliday (1994), and assum-ing some reader familiarity with these categories.

The analysis: verbal artistry in a Tang poem

Original (by Jia Dao)
寻隐者不遇
贾岛

松下问童子
song xia wen tong zi
言师采药去
yan shi cai yao qu
只在此山中
zhi zai ci shan zhong
云深不知处
yun shen bu zhi chu

Gloss
寻 隐者 不 遇
Seek recluse not meet
松 下 问 童子
pine under ask youth
言 师 采 药 去
says master pick herbs go
只 在 此 山 中
only in this mountain midst
云 深 不 知 处
clouds deep not know where

An Unsuccessful Visit to an Absent Recluse
Translation by Wang Dakang (王大濂)

Beneath pine trees I asked your lad nearby.
'My master's gone for herbs,' was the reply.
'He's only in this mountain somewhere 'round.
In heavy mists he's nowhere to be found.'

Initial reading

Jia Dao's poem is a well-known Tang dynasty classic, which elementary school students across China are often made to memorise and recite. It tells of a failed visit by a seeker to a recluse, a common narrative trope in Chinese poetry (Varsano 1999: 41). This poem specifically records a snippet of a conversation between the seeker and a *tong zi* (童子), literally a youth, presumably related to the recluse (e.g. a servant boy or young disciple).

The narrative itself would seem trivial and not worthy of attention. Thus, it would appear that Jia Dao's poem has achieved its canonical status only because it suggests potential profound 'thematic sayings'. Indeed, literary commentaries have discussed the poem as an expression of Taoist thought and attitude, Varsano (1999), for instance, seeing the poem as expressing 'a momentary brush with enlightenment' when 'not knowing has replaced, and thus become, knowing at its most profound'. Interestingly, in relation to the analysis that will follow, she locates the 'source triggers' of this reading in the last line of the poem ('云深不知处' – '(The) clouds (are) deep, (I) know not where'), the most oft-quoted of the poem. She also recognises that while this 'ineffable meaning' comes from a realm beyond language, it is at least in part made *through language*.

Wang's translation, on the other hand, appears not to go beyond the trivial. Although the references to a reclusive 'Master' may in themselves suggest the theme of truth, the translation does seem to be merely a light rhyming verse, doing little more than recounting a short personal tale of the 'unsuccessful visit'. It may, indeed, be dismissed as doggerel.

What might be the reasons why the translation appears to fail? The analysis explores this question and, consequently, discusses issues related to poetic translation.

Jia Dao's poem

To begin with, dividing Jia Dao's poem into clauses, the patterns in Figure 37.2 may be identified.

The poem appears to have two interwoven metastructures: a bipartite division into two parallel halves (the first two lines comprising clauses 1–3 and the last two comprising clauses 4–6), and a story-within-a-story (clauses 1 and 2 providing the framing story and clauses 3 to 6 the framed story). While the bipartite division is to be expected within Chinese poetic conventions, note that clause-complexing patterns neatly reinforce this.

From the perspective of the story-within-a-story metastructure, it might be claimed that clauses 5–6 ('云深不知处' – '[the] clouds [are] deep [I] know not where') is foregrounded, since they form the only clause complex within the framed story. As the ensuing analysis unfolds, this foregrounding soon emerges to be significant.

Moving on to the first of SFL's three metafunctional perspectives, the transitivity patterns that realise the ideational metafunction may be analysed. The analysis here is based on Li's (2007) SFL account of Chinese grammar, and yields the Participant–Process configuration in Figure 37.3.

Line	Cl. no.	Clause	Patterns (1)	Patterns (2)	
1	1	松下问童子	Cl. Simplex	Cl. Simplex	Cls.1-2: Q&A– Framing 'Story'
2	2	言	Cl. Complex: Projection	Cl. Simplex	
2	3	师采药去。		Cl. Simplex	Cls.3-6: (Arguably) A SINGLE projection of Cl.2: Framed 'Story within a story'
3	4	只在此山中，	Cl. Simplex	Cl. Simplex	
4	5	云深	Cl. Complex: Projection	**Cl. Complex: Projection**	
4	6	不知处。			

Figure 37.2: Clause divisions in Jia Dao's poem

Line	Cl.no.	Participants	Process	Circumstance
1	1	(Narrator – Sayer) 童子- Receiver	问- Verbal	松下- Location
2	2	(童子– Sayer)	言 - Verbal	-
2	3	师–Actor; 药–Goal	采...去–Material	-
3	4	(师– Carrier)	只在此山中Relational (Circumstantial)	-
4	5	云- Carrier	深–Relational (Ascriptive)/Attribute	-
4	6	(童子–Senser) 处- Phenomenon	不知- Mental	

Figure 37.3: Transitivity selections in Jia Dao's poem

As can be seen, the configuration suggests the same interwoven meta-structures as does the clause-complexing configuration. Clauses in the first two lines encode 'events' in the outer reality of the material world, while the clauses in the last two lines encode more abstract worlds of being and knowing, thereby suggesting a bipartite division again. On the other hand, clauses 1 and 2 encode the Verbal exchange between two Sayers constituting the framing story, while clauses 3 to 6 encode the framed story's world as one from which the narrator is excluded as Participant, and in which there is a silence where no Verbal exchanges take place.

From the perspective of the bipartite metastructure, clauses 3 and 6 are foregrounded through Process differentiation from more dominant Processes. More generally, clause 5 may also be seen to be foregrounded, since 云 ('clouds'), as Carrier of an Attribute, is the only non-human Participant in what Hasan (1989) calls an '-er' role. At this point of the analysis then, clauses 5 and 6 seem to be emerging as being more consistently foregrounded, since clause-complexing patterns also appear to foreground them.

Considering next SFL's textual metafunction, and analysing the poem in terms of its Theme–Rheme choices, where Theme is the speaker's 'point of departure' and 'what the clause is to be about' (Halliday 1994), the selections in Figure 37.4 (taking into account possible ellipsis) may be identified.

The arrows in Figure 37.4 indicate the semantic links and 'drifts' between Theme and Rheme elements. As can be seen, the links reinforce the sense of a 'story-within-a-story' metastructure, the framed story of clauses 3 to 6 bound by a semantic chain starting with 师 ('Master') in clause 3, yet clearly tied to the framing story (which is unified by the Rheme to Theme chain in clauses 1 and 2) through the Thematic link between clause 2 and clause 6.

Clause 5 stands apart from all the Theme and Rheme links: its cohesion with the rest of the text depends on its logico-semantic link with clause 6 through clause complexing. Moreover, apart from the not-unexpected

Line	Cl. no.	Theme (all Topical)	Rheme
1	1	松下 (Under pine tree(s)	问童子
2	2	[童子(Lad/Youth)] 言	
2	3	师 (Master/Teacher)	采药去。
3	4	[师 (Master/Teacher)]	只在此山中，
4	**5**	云 (Clouds)	深
4	6	[童子(Lad/Youth)/Everybody??]	不知处。

Figure 37.4: Theme–rheme selections and links in Jia Dao's poem

Line	Cl. no.	Theme (all Topical)	Rheme
Title		寻 (seeking) 不遇 (not meeting)	隐者
1	1	松下 (Under pine tree(s)	问童子
2	2	言 (Saying)	
2	3	师 (Master/Teacher)	采药去。
3	4	只在此山中(Only in the midst of the mountain)	
4	5	云 (Clouds)	深
4	6	不知 (Not knowing)	处。

Figure 37.5: Theme–rheme in Jia Dao's poem (alternative)

Circumstance of Location (松下 – 'Beneath pine trees') as Theme in the opening clause of the narrative, 云 ('clouds') stands out as the only Theme that does not refer to 师('Master') or 童子 (the youth). Clause 6, conversely, then stands out as the clause with the most links to other clauses. Clauses 5 and 6, then, appear to be foregrounded again through Theme–Rheme selections.

An alternative Theme–Rheme analysis, where ellipsis is ignored, yields Figure 37.5. Here, the Theme choices suggest, through semantic and phonological pairings as shown in Figure 37.6, the bipartite metastructure identified earlier.

Taken together, the two possibilities of Theme–Rheme analysis thus suggest the same two possible interleaving metastructures. Moreover, Figure 37.6 suggests a possible symbolic reading of what a journey in the search for truth might result in, since it suggests a movement from certainty to uncertainty in the two halves of the poem. Furthermore, abstracting the Themes in this second interpretation, the following pattern of what is 'textually prominent' (Li 2007) emerges: 松下 ('Beneath pine trees') → 言(say) → 师 ('Master'/Teacher) →只在此山中

Line 1: 松下 (definite, located point; height & security?)	Line 3: 只在此山中 (indefinite location in expanse of wilderness)
Line 2: 言 *yan2* (clear assertive pronouncement)	Line 4: 云 *yun2* (cloudiness, ineffability?)
Line 2: 师 *shi* (authoritative knower)	Line 4: 不知 *zhi* (not knowing)

Figure 37.6: Semantic and phonological pairings of possible themes in Jia Dao's poem

Line	Cl. No.	Analysis of Mood Elements
1	1	松下 (我=narrator?) 问 童子 Adjunct (Subject) Predicator Complement
2	2	(童子) 言 ( ) (Subject) Predicator (Complement)
2	3	师 采 药 去 **Subject** **Predi-..** **Complement** **..cator**
3	4	(师) 只 在此山中 (Subject) Adjunct Predicator
4	5	云 深 **Subject** **Predicator**
4	6	(我) 不 知 处 (Subject) **NEGATIVE** **Predicator** **Complement**

Figure 37.7: Mood element choices in Jia Dao's poem

('only in this mountain') → 云 ('clouds') → 不知 ('know not'). These selections may be said to have semantic links to pronouncements (言), teaching (师), knowledge (不知), clarity (云), reach(ability) (height of the pine trees, clouds). Especially considered in the light of the Themes in the two-clause title (寻 'seeking' and 不遇 'not meeting'), the textual emphasis, it might be argued, suggests bigger philosophical ruminations beyond the event, and hence a second order of semiosis.

Finally, examining choices in the interpersonal grammar through considering choices in the Mood structure (see Figure 37.7), one finds Subject ellipsis pervasive. The dominance – and pattern – of Subject ellipsis has potential semantic consequences. It has been assumed thus far that the interlocutors in the framing story are the narrator and the recluse master/teacher's youth or 'lad' (童子), but the ellipsed Subjects and absence of first and second pronouns leave deictic reference ambiguous: the interlocutors can, in fact, be anyone – the questioner in clause 1 need not be the speaker in the poem, for example, and the youth (童子), the natural Subject of clause 2, need not be the recluse's 童子. The addressee of the poem also remains ambiguous. This potentially universalises the framing discourse, suggesting that the encounter has a universal symbolic significance.

Even more importantly, the mood element choices suggest once again a coalescing with the patterns of other lexicogrammatical patterns. Non-ellipsis of Subject foregrounds clauses 3 (师 'Master' as Subject) and 5 (云, 'clouds' as Subject). Clause 6 is also foregrounded as the only clause with negative polarity (encoded in 不知 'know not'). Hence, once again, clauses 5 and 6 are foregrounded, making these two clauses that constitute the last line of the poem clearly now the most consistently foregrounded across all perspectives and aspects of the lexicogrammar.

It would seem clear then, that in Jia Dao's poem, lexicogrammatical patterns from the three different metafunctional perspectives have been intricately interpatterned to consistently foreground clauses 5 and 6, making line 4 (云深不知处 – The clouds (are) deep, (I) know not where) the most textually prominent line of the poem. This subliminally draws attention to the line (perhaps accounting for why it is the most oft-quoted) and hence suggests its potential significance. In particular, highlighting the clouds (云), which would otherwise not be a key Participant in the story, and linking them through clause complexing to the potentially philosophical notion of not knowing (不知), calls for the ascription of symbolism that Varsano (1999) claims is one of the 'source triggers' of her thematic reading. As part of the aesthetic construction, specific elements of the grammar (e.g. Thematic selection and depersonalisation) add to the suggestion of a symbolic reading of the poem, with the last line as the key.

As suggested by Hasan's model, each reader's interpretation of theme is dependent on the context of his or her interpretation, thus leading to subjective differences. But whatever the interpretation, it is the aesthetic construction through linguistic choices leading to consistent foregrounding that accounts for such second level reading.

The translation

Turning now to the translation, a very different picture emerges. Figure 37.8 presents the clauses in Wang's translation. The clause-complexing patterns in the translation do not suggest a clear metastructure, although a bipartite division into two halves is suggested through the rhyme scheme. The story-within-a-story is also disrupted through the interjection of the second part of clause 2 ('was the reply'). The intricate metastructuring of the original, in other words, is not replicated.

Moreover, the second line (clause 2 in the translation, the equivalent of clauses 2 and 3 in the original) is now foregrounded instead of the last, through being the only clause embedding a rankshifted clause.

The transitivity configuration in the translation (see Figure 37.9) again does not suggest the same possible intertwined metastructures as Jia Dao's original: at best, it only suggests weakly a bipartite division between the first

Line no.	Clause no.	Clause	Patterns	Comparison with equivalent clauses in Jia Dao's original
1	1	Beneath pine trees I asked your lad near<u>by</u>	Cl. Simplex	(Cl. 1 松下问童子) Similar
2	2a	*['My master's gone for herbs,']*	*[Cl. Simplex]*	(Cl. 3 师采药去 → Cl. 2言)
2	2	**[2a] was the re<u>ply</u>.**	**Cl. Simplex**	• Changed order • Projected clause becomes rankshifted [2a]: Cl. Complex becomes Simplex OR 2 Cl. Simplex become 1 (with embedded Cl. Simplex)
3	3	'He's only in this mountain somewhere 'round	Cl. Simplex	(Cl. 4 只在此山中) Similar
4	4	In heavy mists he's nowhere to be found.'	Cl. Simplex	(Cl. 5-6 云深不知处) Cl. Complex becomes Cl. Simplex

Figure 37.8: Clause division in Wang's translation

two lines and the last two lines, since clauses 3 and 4 (lines 3 and 4) possess similar Process types, whereas clauses 1 and 2 (lines 1 and 2) do not.

Clause 1 and the embedded clause 2a also now appear foregrounded through Process differentiation from a background of dominant Relational processes, as does clause 2 as a whole again, through being the only clause with a rankshifted clause functioning as a Participant. As with clause-complexing selections, clause 2 again appears more strongly foregrounded.

Examination of the Theme–Rheme selections of the translation fails to reveal clear patterning. Indeed, as suggested by the arrows in Figure 37.10, the Thematic 'flow' appears erratic, and it would seem difficult to identify clear metastructure.

In terms of Theme choices, it is again clause 2, containing the only Theme that is a rankshifted clause (clause 2a), that can be regarded as foregrounded. Clause 2, hence, is emerging as the most consistently fore-grounded clause in the translation.

The Thematic emphasis (Circumstance of location in clauses 1 and 4, the 'master' in clause 3 and news about him in clause 2) also fails to suggest any possible symbolic articulation beyond the immediate narrative, especially since there are no possible alternative readings of Theme.

Figure 37.11 presents the Mood selections in the translation.

In contrast to Jia Dao's original, the absence of Subject elision and the use of first and second personal pronouns make the interlocutors much more specific, thus defining the exchange as a localised event. Such local-ising potentially suggests that the poem is a mere recount or narrative lacking the further symbolic significance of Jia Dao's original.

Line	Cl.no.	Participants	Process	Circumstance
1	1	*I* - **Sayer** *your lad nearby* - **Receiver**	*asked* - **Verbal**	*Beneath pine trees* – location
2	[2a]	[*My master* – **Actor**]	[*'s gone* – **Material**]	[*for herbs* – **purpose**] * (Goal of Material Action in clause 3 in the original)
2	2	[2a] – **Identifier**	*was* – **Relational** * (Verbal Process in clause	
		the reply - **Identified**	3, the equivalent in the original, with 童子, the youth, as implied Sayer)	
3	3	*He* – **Carrier** *only in this mountain somewhere 'round.* – **Attribute**	*'s* - Relational (Circumstantial)	
4	4	*He* – **Carrier** * (Change of Participant.童子, the youth, is the most likely implied '-er' Participant, i.e. the Senser, in equivalent clause 6 in the original)	*'s* – Relational (Circumstantial) * (Mental Process in clause 6 in the original)	*In heavy mists* - location * (Realised as clause in the original, i.e. clause 5. Note also the lexical changes – 云 or 'clouds' becomes 'mists' and 深 or 'deep' becomes
		nowhere to be found – **Attribute** * (Phenomenon in the original)		'heavy')

Figure 37.9: Transitivity selections in Wang's translation

Line	Cl. no.	Theme (all Topical)	Rheme
Title		*An Unsuccessful Visit to an Absent Recluse*	
1	1	Beneath pine trees	I asked your lad nearby
2	2	"My master's gone for herbs"	was the reply.
3	3	"He'	s only in this mountain somewhere 'round.
4	4	In heavy mists	he's nowhere to be found."

Figure 37.10: Theme–rheme selections in Wang's translation

Moreover, the 'master' is clearly the dominant Subject, and positive polarity prevails throughout all clauses. Through Subject selection differentiation, then, clause 1 ('I' as Subject) and, once again, clause 2 (with the rankshifted clause 2a as Subject) are foregrounded: clause 2 is now clearly

Line	Cl. no.	Analysis of Mood Elements
1	1	Beneath pine trees I asked your lad nearby. Adjunct Subject Finite/Predicator Complement
[2	2a	'My master 's gone for herbs,'] Subject Finite Predicator Adjunct
2	2	[2a] was the reply. Subject Finite/Predicator Complement
3	3	'He 's only in this mountain somewhere 'round. Subject Finite/Predicator Adjunct Complement
4	4	In heavy mists he 's nowhere to be found.' Adjunct Subject Finite/Predicator Complement

Figure 37.11: Mood element choices in Wang's translation

the most consistently foregrounded clause in Wang's translation. However, it should be noted that, in every instance, the foregrounding has been for the very same reason – that clause 2a is a rankshifted clause functioning as a clausal element – whereas in Jia Dao's poem foregrounding of clauses 5 and 6 occur for quite different reasons in each lexicogrammatical perspective, drawing attention to different facets of the clause semantics.

The translation thus foregrounds consistently quite a different part of the poem – clause 2, which translates line 2 of Jia Dao's original. Any possible thematic saying would hence be also quite different, in the first place. But as has been seen, clause 2 is foregrounded primarily only because clause 2a ('My master's gone for herbs') functions as a rankshifted clause element, whichever lexicogrammatical perspective is taken, so the foregrounding may be considered weaker. Moreover, unlike Jia Dao's calling attention to the clouds and to a potential philosophical notion, there is nothing standing obviously outside the main narrative or suggestive of more abstract ideas in this clause to invite a symbolic reading. There also appears little else in the lexicogrammatical patterns to suggest much more than a mere narrative.

In short, beyond the facile aesthetics of regular rhyme and rhythm, no doubt meant as a formal literary equivalence to the prosody of Tang regulated-verse quatrains, there is insufficient sophistication in lexicogrammatical patterning to call for more than a first-level reading of the poem. This perhaps accounts for Wang's translation seeming little more than simple rhyming verse.

Suggested contributions of stylistics to translation

The foregoing analysis suggests again some ways in which stylistics can contribute to translation, literary translation in particular. Most immediately, the comparative analysis demonstrates how a suitable model can provide a more founded, rigorous descriptive basis for evaluating a translation. If recreating and suggesting the aesthetic achievement of Jia Dao's poem were the aim of the translation, then the translation's failure lies perhaps in having too superfical a view of the aesthetics of verbal art, seeing it only in terms of formal tropes and literary devices. What the translator has failed to do is to fashion through interpatterning of English lexicogrammatical patterns a level of symbolic articulation that may construe potential thematic sayings. And the analysis points to the lexicogrammatical patterning details that demonstrate this, so that the evaluation can be argued for in grounded terms.

But beyond providing a descriptive basis for looking at translation – and, in this instance, thereby enabling more fine-grained evaluation – stylistics can provide insights that contribute to theorising translation. The foregoing analysis demonstrates the challenge that translators of poetry face – the perception and then re-creation of artful interpatterning to produce consistent foregrounding of some element of the poem. Such reproduction of verbal artistry is not easily done in translation, since the range of lexicogrammatical resources available in different languages differ – the artistry in Jia Dao's poem results in part from the pervasive possibility of pronominal ellipsis in Chinese that is far less available in English. Moreover, it is an artistry that involves complex interpatterning over a whole text – merely considering isolated deviations from general linguistic norms that draw attention and force the reader to reflect is not enough. In addition, as already discussed, the mere use of poetic tropes and tools from the target language's literary tradition to achieve a superficial sense of literary equivalence is facile.

(Re-)producing the verbal artistry of a successful poem such as Jia Dao's is therefore a highly complex matter, perhaps too complex to be replicated in a translation using the different resources of a different language. To be able to represent fully the aesthetic achievement and sayings of a successful poem in translation is likely a fictional translation goal. Translations that achieve a good degree of verbal artistry are perhaps then necessarily the translators' creative (re-)construals, rather than faithful representations, of the aesthetic and culture of the original poems, as Bassnett and Lefèvre (1998) suggest collectively of all literary translations.

Otherwise, in both the practice and evaluation of poetic translation, the goals and agendas of each translation effort must be taken into account. For instance, translations may serve to provide merely a literal sense of first-level meanings for bilingual readers such as English-speaking students of Chinese. Such readers may have some proficiency in the language of the original text, but need some help from a translation, and with the help may grow to appreciate and understand the original more deeply and richly. In such a case, the translation does not have to be an aesthetically well-constructed effort: there need be no pretensions to this, and the translator's job becomes perhaps easier. The translation should likewise be evaluated not in aesthetic terms, but for its sufficiency in conveying possible first-level meanings. If ambiguities exist, perhaps multiple, variant translations may be needed. Similarly, if a translation is to serve the purposes of cultural studies, a sufficient focus on first-level accuracy may do, perhaps supplemented with glosses and explanations.

Translations that purport to attempt to represent the aesthetic achievement of the original should then aspire to be poetic creations in their own right, the translator perhaps, for instance, starting from his or her interpretation of semantic possibilities at the symbolic second level of discourse, and then artistically fashioning a poem in the target language with the 'content' of original. In such a case, liberties may be taken, à la Ezra Pound, but there can be no pretensions to faithful representation of the original. Evaluations of such translations, then, may focus on the aesthetic achievement itself, and the image of the original that is subjectively constructed.

The basis for these theoretical arguments comes from what the analysis has demonstrated of the challenges of poetic translation, and perhaps for those in translation studies many of these arguments are not new. Skopos theory in translation studies (see Munday 2008a: 79–80 for a sketch of this theory proposed by Vemeer in the 1970s), for instance, argues more broadly that the form of any translation must be determined by its *skopos* – that is, the purpose of the translation and the function of the translated text in the target culture. What has been argued above is the particular case of poetic translation, and what the stylistic analysis has demonstrated are some firm grounds for skopos theory in this case.

In summary, stylistics can make important contributions to translation studies, particularly literary translation, in the following ways:

- *Descriptive*: providing tool-kits, based on whatever theoretical model is suitable, for rigorous descriptive analysis of both source texts and target texts. In itself, this is valuable for *descriptive translation studies*, where, for instance, the concern might be with discovering existing norms and practices in a set of translated texts at a particular time and place, or with identifying particular translators' stylistic peculiarities *vis-à-vis* the source texts.
- *Theoretical*: applying suitable theoretical approaches to comparative stylistic analysis, so as to unveil issues inherent in translation, as demonstrated above. This enables contributions to debates in translation theory by providing detailed evidential support for arguments.
- *Applied*: using descriptive analysis to provide a grounded, more rigorous basis for evaluating translations. Perhaps even more usefully, as Boase-Beier has demonstrated, stylistic analysis before translation can enable more nuanced, effective translations of style. Logically, then, stylistics should be a key part of a translator's training and education. At the very

least it will help to raise translators' awareness of very important considerations in their practice, even if it is impracticable for them to analyse stylistically every text to be translated.

Possible future directions for stylisticians

The examples in this chapter have illustrated the potential contributions of cognitive and functional stylistics to translation. Boase-Beier's contribution from cognitive stylistics is well established, while the analysis using Hasan's (1989) SFL-based framework is relatively novel, and seeks to suggest a wider exploration of the application of this model to translation studies. Munday (2008b) is a more extensive work employing the general SFL linguistic framework to explore ideology in translation of fiction, picking up on the more general influence that SFL has played in translation studies (see Munday 2008a: 89–104 for an overview). Clearly, there is also much potential for contributions from corpus stylistics – M. Baker (2000), Malmkjaer (2003, 2004) and Ji (2009) being examples – and for addressing questions not addressed in the examples in the chapter (e.g. identifying a translator's particular tendencies in a range of work).

But the potential for stylistics to contribute to the understanding of translation, especially literary translation, surely extends to other approaches as well. Herein is a space where non-monolingual stylisticians can extend their usefulness, through engaging with those in translation studies, so that the natural affinity between the two disciplines can be more fully realised.

38

The stylistics of everyday talk

David Peplow

Introduction

Stylistics is commonly concerned with the analysis of literary texts. For stylisticians, literary texts are complex and constructed works that produce aesthetic effects in readers. Typically, the stylistician's job is to explain these effects through recourse to a text's linguistic features. This may involve consideration of, say, patterns in foregrounding, conceptual metaphor and/or narrative voice. As the carefully constructed product of an author or a heteronomous object that produces aesthetic effects in readers (see Ingarden 1973), literary texts are deemed to be worthy of close, stylistic analysis, and this perception of worthiness is well-established.

By contrast, everyday talk has not always been perceived as deserving of close analysis. For a long time, everyday talk was not subjected to analysis at all. Everyday interactions between people were regarded by scholars as so unglamorous that such talk was not seen as a legitimate area of academic study. Chomsky, for instance, felt that naturally occurring conversation was too messy and disordered to base linguistic rules around. He infamously stated that:

> A record of natural speech will show numerous false starts, deviations from rules, changes of plan in mid-course, and so on . . . Observed use of language or hypothesized dispositions to respond, habits, and so on, may provide evidence as to the nature of this mental reality, but surely cannot constitute the actual subject matter of linguistics, if it is to be a serious discipline.
> *(Chomsky 1965: 4)*

Although such opinions are in the minority now, everyday talk is still seen by some as mundane and primarily phatic, and not as naturally worthy of study as interaction within institutional settings, for instance.

In this chapter, I seek to demonstrate that everyday talk is a legitimate and, furthermore, potentially fascinating area of academic and stylistic study. I show that there is a rich (albeit relatively short) history of detailed and rigorous stylistic-like analysis of everyday talk within linguistics and sociology. I present some case-studies from my own research on group-talk, demonstrating the importance of close analysis to an understanding of social interaction.

Definitions and previous research

Before proceeding it is worth establishing some working definitions of the key terms used in this chapter; firstly, *everyday talk*. By definition, we engage in everyday talk on a regular basis, often with people with whom we are familiar. As a result, the term 'everyday talk' covers a wide range of interactions, so offering a satisfactory definition is problematic. The line dividing everyday talk from *not*-everyday talk is fine: a weekly chat in the pub with friends might be 'everyday', while the interactions that constitute a first date in the same pub might not be classed as 'everyday'. Everyday talk may be a sufficiently slippery and vague term that the only way to define it may be to say what it is *not*.

Definitions of everyday talk often contrast it with institutional talk. For example, Levinson defines everyday talk as

> that familiar predominant kind of talk in which two or more participants freely alternate in speaking which generally occurs outside specific institutional settings like religious services, law courts, classrooms and the like. *(Levinson 1983: 284)*

For Levinson, everyday talk is defined in opposition to talk that occurs in institutions (e.g. schools and law courts). Levinson's definition also describes the typical participants engaged in everyday talk and some of the possible features of this talk. The participants 'freely alternate' turns with one another, so that discourse roles and institutional roles of the speakers do not prescribe a particular kind of power-laden talk. In contrast to typical institutional talk, participants in everyday talk tend to have symmetrical speaking rights and generally engage in this talk in order to strengthen social bonds rather than to convey information to each other.

Having said this, it is important to recognise that the distinction between institutional and everyday talk is not absolute. This is a point made by McElhinny (1997) and is demonstrated across a number of empirical studies: for example, Stokoe's (2000) analysis of university seminars, Drew and Sorjonen's (1997) consideration of workplace interaction, and ten Have's (1991) analysis of questioning in typically institutional settings. McElhinny (1997) argues that the terms 'institutional' and 'everyday' are porous, meaning that seemingly institutional interactional contexts usually contain a good deal of everyday social talk, and vice versa. She specifically focuses on family talk, arguing that this setting encodes a series of hierarchies and institutional power relations (McElhinny 1997). As I go on to suggest later when I present my own research into book groups, it may be better to see 'everyday talk' and 'institutional talk' as idealised categories existing on two ends of a cline. This affords us the opportunity to see many real-life instances of talk as being hybrid, containing features of prototypically everyday talk and prototypically institutional talk.

If we accept that much everyday talk is social and phatic in nature, then such interaction can appear aimless and content-light. Sociologist Georg Simmel makes the point that in such sociable conversation 'the content is merely the indispensable carrier of the stimulation' (1997: 126). The degree to which an everyday conversation is aimless and content-light clearly varies from one conversation to the next, but if this kind of talk tends to be more concerned with phatic communion than with the transfer of information then it is legitimate to focus analysis on the *form* that the talk assumes rather than concentrating on the *content*. As a 'method of textual interpretation in which primacy of place is assigned to *language*' (Simpson 2004: 2), stylistics is typically concerned with analysing form over content, suggesting that the application of a stylistic approach to everyday talk may be valuable.

For the remainder of this section, I outline relevant previous research working at the interface between stylistics and the study of everyday talk: the creativity of everyday talk (Carter 2004), work in conversation analysis which considers everyday talk as highly ordered and structured (e.g. Edwards 1997; Schegloff 1997), and the concept of 'style' within sociolinguistics (e.g. Coupland 2007; Kirkham 2011; Snell 2010). These three areas of research inform my own approach, which I detail in the second half of this chapter.

In acknowledging the relevance of stylistic approaches to various forms of discourse, Simpson (2004: 2–3) notes that 'even casual conversation' can be highly creative, displaying 'stylistic dexterity'. In this vein, Carter's (2004) work on the 'art of common talk' explores some of the stylistic features evident in everyday talk. Carter argues that everyday talk is replete with examples of repetition, idiom, metaphor, morphological innovation and punning. Regardless of how this linguistic creativity is manifest, Carter argues that it 'grows from mutual interaction rather than from individual innovation' (2004: 102). The creativity evident in everyday talk is rarely just the product of the individual genius raconteur. It is, instead, co-produced between multiple participants in the process of interaction. The necessary co-production of conversation means that any stylistic approach must be somewhat different from a piece of literary stylistics, which tends to be focused on an *individual* writer's style and creativity.

Carter (2004) argues that discursive creativity is context-dependent. What counts as creative varies according to the discourse situation: the roles of the respective speakers and the purpose of the interaction. Therefore, the linguistic creativity valued in a job interview is likely to be very different from that valued in talk at the pub between friends. Carter (2004) goes on to suggest that particular contexts of talk are more likely to facilitate linguistic creativity over others. He argues that spoken creativity grows 'organically from those contexts which best support such dialogue and in which meanings are made interpersonally as well as conveyed transactionally' (Carter 2004: 111). Using the two speech contexts given as examples above, friendly pub-talk is likely therefore to contain a higher number of, and richer, instances of creativity than talk in a job interview. Friends talking in a pub are likely to have more symmetrical speaking rights than participants in a job interview, and as such the topics of conversation are likely to be less formalised and more focused on phatic, interpersonal tasks. Carter's work (2004) shows that linguistic creativity is not just the preserve of literary texts or particular speech acts (e.g. jokes). Everyday talk displays a wealth of linguistic creativity, as speakers co-construct intricate patterns of talk between each other in interaction and negotiate meaning on a turn-by-turn basis.

Just as literary stylistics has considered the language of poems, prose and plays as meriting close and detailed study, the field of conversation analysis (CA) has argued for the systematic and close analysis of talk. CA is the study of naturally occurring conversation, and at its inception CA researchers broke new ground merely by considering casual conversation an appropriate area of study. In the late 1960s when CA pioneer Harvey Sacks delivered his famous series of lectures (collected in Sacks 1992), much of the research conducted in linguistics and in the sociology of language was highly influenced by Chomskyan transformational grammar (Chomsky 1965, 1975), which stressed the need for language to be studied in the abstract. As noted earlier, Chomsky felt that naturally occurring conversation was too messy and disordered to base linguistic rules around (1965: 4). Contra Chomsky, Sacks believed that conversation was worth studying, precisely because there *is* 'order at all points' underlying human activity:

> [If] we figure or guess or decide that whatever humans do, they are just another animal after all, maybe more complicated than others but perhaps not noticeably so, then whatever humans do can be examined to discover some way they do it.   *(Sacks 1984: 22)*

CA researchers do not consider naturally occurring conversation to be merely the transference of content-laden messages from one speaker to another, but a highly organised structural system (Edwards 1997: 85–6). CA researchers, therefore, tend to be more concerned with the structural elements of conversation, such as turn-taking and adjacency pairs. At the centre of the CA paradigm is the belief that the practical effect of an utterance depends on its sequential position in the particular stretch of talk (ten Have 1999: 6). In this way, it is possible to identify similarities between the methods of literary stylistics and CA: both are mainly interested in structural features over content, both attempt to be rigorous and systematic in analysis, and neither (traditionally) seeks to be associated with particular critical ideologies favoured by alternative methodologies. These similarities between stylistics and CA are brought into relief when we consider the background and academic career path of leading CA researcher Emmanuel Schegloff.

Schegloff discusses the reasons for his adherence to CA in his famous paper in *Discourse and Society* (1997). The purpose of his article is to criticise the methods of critical discourse analysis (CDA: an alternative, more theory-driven approach to discourse). Schegloff's polemic led to responses defending CDA from Wetherell (1998) and Billig (1999), and further replies from Schegloff (1998, 1999). The debate between CA and CDA as to which is the 'better' method for analysing naturally occurring conversation is well documented elsewhere (e.g. Hammersley 2003; Hutchby and Wooffitt 2008), and I will not give it further treatment here. For our present purposes, the main interest of Schegloff's paper (1997) lies in the implicit similarities that he draws between the methods of CA and the close textual analysis valued by literary stylistics.

Schegloff (1997) describes the process of writing his Masters thesis in the Department of Sociology at the University of California. Schegloff's thesis focused on the debate within American literary criticism between socially oriented scholars of literature (e.g. Lionel Trilling and Irving Howe) and the more formalist New Critics (e.g. Allen Tate and Robert Penn Warren). Writing about his time studying sociology at Berkeley, Schegloff describes his initial belief that the former, socially oriented group of critics were the 'good guys' and that the New Critics were the 'bad guys' (1997: 169). However, Schegloff describes becoming increasingly dissatisfied with the work of the sociocultural critics because, for him, their arguments 'presupposed' that students possessed skills in basic, formal textual analysis; a presupposition Schegloff felt was without justification (1997: 169). As a result of his dissatisfaction with the socioculturally aligned critics, Schegloff describes moving towards the critical practices of the more formalist and proto-stylistic New Critics, because the latter understood the need to study 'objects in their own right' (1997: 170) rather than presupposing contexts and results.

Schegloff (1997) tells this story because he sees the analytical shortcomings of the socially oriented literary critics as analogous to the problems he associates with similar, theory-driven scholarship in other academic areas. Within stylistics proper, literary linguists have levelled similar criticisms at traditional literary scholarship: for instance, Simpson (2004: 4) chastises literary critics for drawing too readily on 'untested or untestable intuition', while Stockwell (2002: 152) argues that this group of scholars has gone about their task 'impressionistically, either using ill-defined terms or producing personal responses that are often poetic and insightful in their own right but hardly analytical or accessible for discussion'. It is possible, therefore, to see CA and literary stylistics as united in their task of searching for patterns in the fine detail of language use (whether studying naturally occurring interaction or literary texts) and bound together by their rejection of approaches that take macro-level, theory-driven approaches at the expense of formalist analysis. Due to this similarity in methods, adopting a version of a CA approach may be a way of accounting for the stylistics of everyday talk.

The concept of 'style' within sociolinguistics is the third area of research I wish to draw on in this review. For sociolinguists, style is an increasingly important focus of study (see Moore 2012 for a review). In sociolinguistics, a person or group's style is 'a variable, as distinctive as class, region or gender' (Wales 2011: 397). This issue of distinctiveness is important in the sociolinguistic conception of style; an individual or group's style is what makes their talk characteristic and distinct from other individuals and groups that are otherwise similar (Irvine 2001). Compared with other sociolinguistic variables (e.g. gender and class), style is more under the control of the speaker and can demonstrate an individual's desire to belong to a group or wish to be distinct.

Coupland defines the sociolinguistic concept of style as 'a way of doing something' (2007: 1). Style is an individual or group's particular way of achieving interactional aims, producing an identity, or conducting a particular type of talk. Style in sociolinguistics denotes distinctiveness, so the sociolinguistic study of style considers individual and group shifts in language use that transcend prototypical usage and the social meaning this may have (Moore 2004: 376). I now go on to describe two recent studies that offer sociolinguistic analyses of style: Snell's (2010) study of Teesside English and Kirkham's (2011) analysis of university classroom discourse.

Snell (2010) studies the use of the possessive form of 'me' in the Teesside dialect (e.g. 'that's me pencil'). Her ethnographic study comprises extensive recordings and observations of children from two primary schools in different socioeconomic areas of Teesside. Snell's decision to look in detail at the children's use of the possessive 'me' was prompted not just by the data she collected, but also by the folk-linguistic assumption that this feature is a linguistic marker of Teesside identity (Snell 2010: 634).

Following quantitative and qualitative analysis of the children's talk, Snell found that across a variety of different contexts the children used the possessive 'me' in stylised, 'foregrounded' (2010: 650) forms in order to perform particular interactional work:

> possessive 'me' was consistently used to index a specific kind of interactional stance. Further, these stances often involved . . . self-conscious performance, a form of stance-taking that I will refer to as 'stylisation'.
>
> *(Snell 2010: 632)*

'Stylisation' is defined as 'the knowing deployment of culturally familiar styles and identities that are marked as deviating from those predictably associated with the current speaking context' (Coupland 2001: 345). Through analysis of a number of transcripts, Snell shows that the purposes of these stylised forms of the possessive 'me' can be to impress peers, display sexuality and create social alliances (Snell 2010: 640–8). As a 'self-conscious performance', this stylisation is a matter of choice for the participants and is something that distinguishes themselves from their peers. Now I move on to give an example from Snell's study.

Snell (2010: 640) argues that the following excerpt of transcript provides an example of the possessive 'me' being used in a stylised manner to impress peers. In this interaction, friends Harry and David are playing in the playground. Harry has just been given the radio-microphone by the researcher:

5	Harry:	ah(hhh hhhh)
6		can you get me some budweiser (.)
7		f- they're only er tr-
8		er one pound fifty a pack (.)
9		so get me: ten packs (.)
10		because I've got a budweiser thing here (.)
11		**I LO::VE MY [mi] (.) <u>BUDWEISER</u>**

Snell remarks that this kind of performance was 'not unusual for Harry' (2010: 640). Clearly, the subject matter of beer consumption is a deviant and somewhat risky topic for a 9-year-old child to broach, especially when being recorded by an adult. The stylised nature of the utterance at line 11 is also suggested in the manner of articulation, with the drawn-out vowel on 'LO::VE' and the increase in volume. However, Snell is centrally concerned with the use of the possessive 'me' on this line, which she argues is a key part of Harry's performance and his movement into a play frame (2010: 641). Snell argues that the children in her data only used the possessive 'me' in this kind of stylised, performative and foregrounded manner (2010: 647). She goes on to posit that use of these stylised forms is 'motivated by immediate interactional and relational goals' (2010: 651) – in Harry's case, to impress his peers with his knowledge of adult culture.

The second sociolinguistic study of style relevant to the present chapter is Kirkham's (2011) analysis of student talk. Kirkham recorded and observed classroom discourse in an undergraduate English literature seminar group. The recordings were taken from classes from a third-year module on American sports literature, with Kirkham focusing on how two particular students in the class used the epistemic phrases 'I don't know' and 'I think'. In the present review I shall only look at Kirkham's analysis of the occurrences of 'I don't know'. His decision to concentrate on these epistemic phrases was prompted by his observation that the two students used these markers very differently from one another. The fact that these markers were employed so distinctively suggests that these expressions had different values in the individual's stylistic repertoires (Kirkham 2011: 205).

The two students are referred to as Tom and Elle. Tom was a British male student who 'stood out as one of the more confident students' (Kirkham 2011: 205), while Elle was a Canadian exchange student who was a markedly less confident student. Elle produced the lowest number of words of the students who regularly attended the classes. Kirkham initially gives a quantitative analysis of his classroom data, subsequently complementing this with a qualitative analysis of his transcripts. Focusing on the use of 'I don't know', Kirkham found that Tom and Elle used this phrase in very distinct ways and to achieve very different interactional aims. Elle's uses of 'I don't know' repeatedly communicated an 'explicitly unknowledgeable stance' towards the topics being discussed in class. For example, here Elle is discussing the reason why she liked one particular book studied on the module over the others:

```
5    Elle:     and I found with the- a lot of the other books
6              um (.) I'm not (.) I'm not very-
7              I don't know a lot like the rules or like the
8              [plays] and so I can't (.)
9    Tutor:    [mm ]
10   Elle:     I can't picture it or understand it as well as I
11             could this one
12   Tutor:    okay
```

(Kirkham 2011: 207)

Elle's 'I don't know' at line 7 performs its basic propositional task of playing down her knowledge of the sporting subject matter of the texts being studied, which Kirkham found to be typical of Elle's usage of the phrase.

By contrast, Tom's use of 'I don't know' often performs face-work to his classmates, playing down his right to have the definitive say on an issue. Discussing basketball player Dennis Rodman's autobiography, Tom remarks:

```
1    Tom:     I kinda thought that (.)
2             I don't know loads about basketball but I (.)
3             obviously since like the (.)eighties and the
4             inter nineties it's kinda-
5             the culture's changed and now (.) players like
6             Rodman (.) things like- things like his life being
7             so much a part of the game it's kind of more
8             common now because (.) I don't know maybe
9             it wasn't like that in the seventies and sixties
```

(Kirkham 2011: 208)

Tom's 'I don't know' on lines 2 and 8 act as disclaimers and, on one level, play down his claim to possessing knowledge on the topic of basketball. However, from what he says in the remainder of this extract, it would appear that Tom does actually possess a good understanding of basketball culture. Therefore, the phrase 'I don't know' is not used in its literal sense. Instead, it carries out other work, conveying a personal identity that is not 'too geeky or too knowledgeable' (Kirkham 2011: 208) and performing negative politeness so that others in the class feel permitted to have their say on the issue.

In the data that Kirkham (2011) presents, Elle uses the epistemic phrases to display uncertainty and tentativeness. By contrast, Tom employs the same expressions in a less clearly propositional way – to perform negative politeness and to manage his own identity in the classroom. Kirkham concludes from his analysis that particular phrases do not have fixed meanings and can have various meanings depending on who is speaking and on the context of the utterance:

> individuals engaged in classroom discussion may draw upon similar
> resources, such as I think and I don't know, but ... these forms are
> ultimately indeterminate without a consideration of (i) the specific
> interactional context in which they take place; and (ii) the place of those
> forms in an individual's stylistic repertoire.   *(Kirkham 2011: 213)*

For each student, their different repeated uses of the phrase 'I don't know' form part of their individual stylistic repertoire.

In discussing the sociolinguistic concept of 'style', it may seem that we have moved away somewhat from the consideration of literary style. In many respects, we are talking about very different phenomena when we discuss literature and everyday talk, and it would be wrong to assume that the notion of 'style' is the same in literary texts as it is in interaction. However, this brief account of style in sociolinguistics suggests that *distinctiveness* might be the underlying quality that unites the literary stylistic concept of style and the sociolinguistic concept of style. Literary writers are associated with particular styles through being distinct from other writers, and this is not so different from the language choices of individuals or groups who, at times, seek to differentiate themselves from other individuals or other groups of people. In Snell's (2010) study, a particular linguistic item was repeatedly used in a stylised form by children to add distinctiveness to what was being said and to further fulfil particular interactional aims. In Kirkham's (2011) study, the same expressions were used to different effects by two speakers. These two speakers had stylistic repertoires that were distinct from one another, and these stylistic differences between the two speakers ultimately reflected the distinct classroom identities that the two students assumed.

The stylistics of everyday talk: case-studies

Building on the areas of research outlined in the previous sections, I will now discuss case-studies from my own ethnographic research into everyday talk. I am particularly interested in the analysis of collaborative talk in group contexts, and my approach could be considered a contribution to the 'stylistics of everyday talk'. Within this field, my research has focused specifically on the discourse of reading groups. A reading group (otherwise known as a book club or book group) describes a collective of people who meet regularly to discuss a book that all members have read. Although my focus is on face-to-face book groups, online groups and book forums are an increasingly popular phenomenon on the internet (Rehberg Sedo 2003; Trimarco 2011). Typically, face-to-face groups meet once a month, so that members have time in between meetings to read the book and formulate their views on it. Groups organised through institutions such as libraries, schools, prisons and workplaces tend to hold their meetings in these institutions, typically at a fixed time each month. For private or 'closed' groups that have grown out of a friendship group, members may take turns at hosting or may meet in a pub, bar or restaurant (see Hartley 2001 for a comprehensive survey of UK reading groups).

Over a period of several months I observed and recorded six reading groups – all of which existed prior to my study. Following other ethnographic studies of book groups (e.g. Benwell 2009; Swann and Allington 2009), I take a discursive approach to my reading groups, focusing on the ways in which the readers go about discussing literary texts (e.g. how argumentation and agreement over interpretations and evaluations are achieved in this context). I am also interested in how the personal identities of readers operate in reading groups and whether different book clubs establish particular group identities and styles. In order to look at these issues in detail, I have used a CA-inspired form of close analysis and also draw on some of the terms used in discursive psychology (Edwards and Potter 1992; J. Potter 1996). As mentioned above, a CA-inspired analysis of transcript is, in many respects, analogous to a stylistic account of a literary text.

As an example, I shall now focus on one of the reading groups, presenting some of the data from this group's meetings. I concentrate on how recurrent patterns of interaction reflected and created a particular style, or a 'way of doing something' (Coupland 2007: 1) in this group. I refer to this group as *OCBC*. At the time of recording, this group had been running for four years, meeting in a member's living room roughly once every six weeks. The hosting member changed with each meeting. In terms of book selection, the group moved through aesthetic/historical movements. Before I began recording, the group had read a series of Victorian novels. In the first three recorded meetings, the group had moved onto modernist short stories. The group then read some contemporary popular fiction, mainly as a respite from reading high modernism!

There is a question as to whether the discourse in book groups can be categorised as everyday talk. I have discussed this at length elsewhere

(Peplow 2012), and my feeling is that the extent to which a reading group conforms to institutional talk or everyday talk depends very much on how the group is organised, where it meets, and how well the members know each other. Book groups that meet in libraries, for instance, often have a librarian facilitator who 'runs' the meetings, and the members of these groups may not know each as intimately as in a closed group comprising long-term friends. The *OCBC* members had known each other for a number of years and engage in a form of talk that is quite informal and not governed by prescribed institutional roles. Having said this, *OCBC* is highly focused on the discussion of texts, meaning that particular types of informal talk (e.g. gossip) are not permitted during the meeting proper. Recalling the everyday/institutional cline mentioned earlier, it is best to think of *OCBC*'s talk as occupying a place on the 'everyday' end of the cline, yet containing some typically 'institutional' features (Peplow 2012).

Most of the *OCBC* members share the ideal that the book group should be a site of education – an ideal possibly resulting from the fact that three of the eight members are retired teachers. For example, in the following passage of talk the group is discussing the benefits of reading 'challenging' texts (in this particular meeting the group had read Joyce's *Dubliners*):

Extract 1

1	Jackie:	so I mean are they (0.5) because I mean I must admit I've learnt quite a lot
2		this evening haha almost feel like reading it again
3	Sue:	=[exactly]
4	Alex:	=[exactly]
5	Carol:	=[exactly]
6	Jackie:	but I mean are they designed (0.5) is it part of you know his er wanting to do
7		it in this way er I mean they are quite good for discussion really aren't they
8	Alex:	=mmm very challenging

This idea that 'challenging' (l. 8) books are often 'good for discussion' (l. 7) is shared by the group, and is testament to *OCBC*'s somewhat serious approach to reading in the group context.

Further evidence for the group's view of itself as seriously engaged in the discussion of books comes from the group interview I conducted at the end of the project. Members reported taking pride in how focused they are on the 'task at hand', as they perceived it. Here, Alex is discussing the two book groups to which she currently belongs, comparing these groups to less focused groups:

Extract 2

1	Alex:	I wouldn't have said that we had (0.5) cos there erm I know some people I
2		know (.) I've got a friend who meets in the afternoons (.) and it's all ladies (.)
3		>my other book group's all ladies<
4		mmm
5	Alex:	but they have tea and cake and I honestly don't think they do much book
6		discussion
7	Carol:	mmm
8		[yeah xxxxxxxxxxxxxxx]
9	Alex:	[whereas in both both] groups that I belong to (0.5) we actually do erm (.)
10		very good (.) book discussions you know we concentrate at the task in hand
11		(.) for a good level of time (.) and then we might finish up having a gossip at
12		the end
13	Roger:	=mmm
14	Alex:	but we do spend (.) y'know an hour between an hour and two (0.5) at my
15		other book group cos we're quite local and everything (0.5) erm (.) y'know
16		focused on the book

This extract shows the production of a group identity for *OCBC* that presents them as seriously engaged in the discussion of literary texts. Purely sociable talk was allowed during the meetings but was only tolerated up to a point, with most members preferring this kind of talk to be confined to the time before or after the meetings had begun (Peplow 2012).

As *OCBC* members were interested in conducting their meetings in ways that facilitated the serious discussion of literary texts, there was a good deal of competitive talk in the meetings. Most members in the group were keen to offer their interpretation and evaluation of the text under discussion. In this intellectually charged context, particular members of the group were also eager to stress that their interpretation(s) of the text under discussion was superior to others' interpretations. As a result, I found that particular particles of speech and specific rhetorical constructions were recurrent in the group's talk. These rhetorical features were key to the readers' competitions over knowledge-rights. These were the 'oh' particle, 'X then Y' structures, and category entitlements (Peplow 2011). I consider the uses of the 'oh' particle in one of the group's meetings in the following analysis.

'Oh' may seem an innocuous particle, but it serves important pragmatic functions in conversation. 'Oh' is particularly important in interlocutors' displays of knowledge states. CA researcher Heritage has looked in detail at the functions of 'oh', theorising it as a 'change of state' marker (Heritage 1984: 299) that displays the knowledge state of a speaker. For Heritage, 'oh' is:

> heavily deployed in interactions involving information transfer and in interactional events that involve the embodiment of cognitive events such as noticing, remembering and understanding   *(Heritage 2005: 188)*

Here, Heritage is discussing the use of 'oh' in its prototypical and most common form, as in the following, where the second speaker does not already possess the information that the first speaker divulges:

A: We've bought a kitten.
B: Oh really! What's its name?

'Oh' is so important for signalling this change in epistemic state, co-occurring often with the receipt of news, that Heritage goes as far as to say that interlocutors who have experienced an epistemic shift are under 'interactional obligation' to embody it (2005: 191).

In addition to this common use of 'oh', Heritage found that the particle has other pragmatic functions. It is also used in situations where the speaker is already in possession of some information another speaker is imparting. Similar to the common, news-receipt form, the function of 'oh' in these instances is to display knowledge state. The difference in these other cases is that the speaker already possesses the knowledge being passed on to him or her, so 'oh' is used to indicate their prior ownership of that knowledge. The prevalence of this particular form of 'oh' formed part of *OCBC*'s stylistic repertoire.

In extract 3, the 'oh' particle is used in this secondary way – to display the speaker's prior knowledge. For this particular meeting the group had short stories from Joyce's *Dubliners* collection (Joyce 2006). In the brief interaction reproduced below, the final story, 'The Dead', is being discussed. At this point, readers in the group are debating protagonist Gabriel at length and, in particular, his supposed 'epiphany' at the end of the story. Roger strongly believes that Gabriel experiences an epiphany, while Connie is less sure:

Extract 3
1   Roger: but don't you think that the fact that his anger (0.5) and
2   embarrassment over Michael Furey turns into an
             <u>understanding</u>
3   Jackie: =mmm
4   Connie: **oh** I think he has an understanding

In this brief extract taken from a longer interaction, Roger assumes the role of questioner and Connie that of answerer. Roger structures his turn as a negative interrogative, probing the basis of Connie's interpretation and, by implication, questioning why she has not adopted the same view as him on the issue of Gabriel's character. The question presents Roger's reading of Gabriel as default and normative, making it difficult to dispute. Indeed, Heritage and Raymond (2005: 22) argue that negative interrogatives strongly invite agreement.

In response, Connie uses an 'oh'-prefaced turn offering partial agreement with Roger's negative interrogative. This is only partial agreement because we would expect Connie to foreground an agreement token (e.g. 'yes') if she agreed definitively with Roger. Absolute agreements usually emphasise agreement in the turn design in this way (Pomerantz 1984: 64–8; Sacks 1987: 62). The 'oh' allows Connie to acknowledge the correctness of the view embedded in Roger's question (thereby avoiding the potentially tricky business of articulating a 'dispreferred' disagreement, Pomerantz 1984) *and* show that she had independently arrived at the view that Gabriel had an 'understanding' of his wife's situation prior to Roger's question. Connie's turn, therefore, is interesting in terms of its recipient design – appeasing Roger by agreeing with him, while also showing that she is capable of reaching her own interpretation.

Other instances of the 'oh'-preface functioning as a marker of preexisting knowledge from *OCBC*'s discussion of *Dubliners* include the following:

Extract 4

1	Jackie:	and he was very touched when she came up to him and kissed him [so]
2	Sue:	[yes]
3	Jackie:	=there's obviously (0.5) love you know (0.5) going on
4	Connie:	=**oh** I think he loved her

Extract 5

1	Connie:	like like him being on a <u>stage</u> [you know]
2	Sue:	[oh yes]
3	Connie:	=an actor on a stage and that's mentioned lots and lots
4	Sue:	**oh** yes even at the beginning isn't it
5	Connie:	=exactly

As these examples show, 'oh' is highly prevalent in this discussion, often indexing a speaker's claim to greater rights to interpret through prior knowledge. Giving an assessment in the second position (i.e. after another has given a first assessment) can be problematic, especially if this second assessment is an agreement (Heritage and Raymond 2005; Raymond and Heritage 2006). In the reading group, 'oh'-prefaces appear frequently in sections of the meeting where multiple speakers collaboratively build an interpretation or where there are competing interpretations at play. Extracts 3 through to 5 demonstrate this.

In addition to enjoying competitive debates over interpretation, *OCBC* engages in a lot of collaborative talk in their meetings. The group is, in a sense, collaboratively competitive in its talk about books, and the collaborative features of the group's discourse are evident through close analysis. As with the competitive talk, the collaborative talk (and the co-constructed interpretations and evaluations of texts) is evident in the *form* that the interaction takes as much as in the *content*. The degree to which the talk in this group is collaborative is fascinating and demonstrates the extent to which the interpretations and evaluations of texts are co-produced by various readers in this context.

In the following analysis I offer several examples of the highly collaborative discourse typical of *OCBC*'s meetings. In the first two examples, the speakers engage in what Jennifer Coates (1996: 118–20) refers to as 'jointly-constructed utterances'. Coates defines this phenomenon as occasions when speakers 'work together so that their voices combine to produce a single utterance or utterances' (1996: 118).

Extract 6
```
1   Peter:    somebody would discover and
2   Connie:   =take the baby away
```

For instance, in Extract 6 Connie successfully projects the end of Peter's utterance and completes it by latching onto his utterance mid-turn. A similar instance of joint construction occurs between Alex and Carol in Extract 7. On this occasion, however, there is simultaneous and overlapping talk between the two speakers:

Extract 7
```
1   Alex:    so the implication was that he might have done
2            [something that would've prevented him]
3   Carol:   [something that would've prevented him]
4
```

This extract is particularly interesting, not just because Alex and Carol make exactly the same point, with Carol successfully predicting the completion of Alex's turn, but because what is said in the simultaneous speech spans an entire clausal element – a phenomenon Coates found in her data too (1996: 119). Coates argues that both forms of jointly constructed utterance illustrated above 'can only be achieved when speakers pay extremely close attention to each other, at all linguistic levels' (1996: 119). Analysing similar cases of turn completion between speakers, Lerner refers to this as 'co-production', arguing that it can display 'understanding, affiliation, and agreement' between speakers (G. Lerner 2002: 250).

As a final example of collaborative talk from *OCBC* I offer a slightly longer excerpt. This passage of talk, taken from *OCBC*'s meeting on *The Book Thief* (Zusak 2005), contains several overlaps and jointly constructed utterances. In this extract, the group is discussing the personal qualities of Death, the narrator of the novel:

Extract 8

1	Roger:	because he's a compassionate (.) [entity]
2	Carol:	[yes and he's]
		having to pick up all
3		[BAD stuff that's going]
4	Roger:	[having to pick up all the bad stuff]
5		
6	Carol:	=ro[und]
7	Roger:	[and] the good stu[ff]
8	Carol:	[an] and the good st[uff as well]
9	Peter:	[and the good st]
		uff (.) but (.) all
10		the bad stuff
11	Carol:	=yeah

There is evidently a high degree of agreement between the speakers in this passage of talk. However, this is displayed not simply in the agreement tokens 'yes' (l. 2) and 'yeah' (l. 11), but also more subtly in the structure of the turns between the speakers and the degree of turn-sharing. There is a considerable amount of overlapping talk, with the group members pursuing 'a theme simultaneously, saying different, but related things' (Coates 1996: 131). Within this overlapping there are plenty of examples of echoing (G. Lerner 2002), as the speakers display agreement and actively co-construct a shared sense of what is happening in the narrative. For instance, the phrase 'the good stuff' is uttered by three different speakers (at lines 7, 8, 9), as is 'bad stuff' (ll. 2–3, 5, 10). This echoing shows 'understanding, affiliation, and agreement' between speakers (G. Lerner 2002: 250).

This form of highly co-constructed talk helps to produce a certain style and identity for *OCBC* that is both seriously engaged in the discussion of literary texts and collaborative. The repetition of phrases, overlapping and frequent joint construction of meaning between the readers establish 'patterns' of talk (Carter 2004: 164–5) that are intricate and elaborate. Meaning is created as a group, and this is demonstrated in the formal features of the talk as much as in the content of the talk. Paying close attention to the linguistic features of group interaction illuminates important aspects of competitive and collaborative meaning-making, thus confirming the value of considering the stylistics of everyday talk.

Conclusion

This chapter started by exploring the issues around the stylistics of everyday talk in an expansive way, considering research that approaches interaction in a way that is analogous to the traditional literary stylistic approach to texts. Following this, I presented some examples of my own research that has been influenced by these approaches to everyday talk. I focused on the style of a particular reading group, analysing the recurrent use of a particle of speech by group members ('oh') and its role in competitive talk, while also accounting for the intricate ways in which highly collaborative talk is conducted in this group's discussions.

Unlike a literary text, everyday talk is not usually constructed to have specific aesthetic effects on its recipients or audience. However, the patterns that are formed in this kind of interaction (and the spontaneity with which these are formed) mean that everyday talk is more than worthy of the close analysis we associate with stylistics. Undertaking this analysis is markedly different from conducting traditional stylistic analysis of literary texts, but a stylistic focus on language form and structure has much to offer our analysis of the interactions we engage in day-to-day.

39

Coda: the practice of stylistics

Peter Stockwell and Sara Whiteley

In this final chapter, the editors of the *Handbook* reflect on the state of the discipline of stylistics in the world.

Handbook of Stylistics: *Is stylistics now a discipline, rather than an interdiscipline?*

Peter Stockwell: We are so used to thinking of stylistics as an interdiscipline and as interdisciplinarity as an inherently good thing that I think we have missed the fact that – some time since the 1990s – stylistics has matured into a single coherent discipline. This *Handbook* is partly evidence of that. It strikes me as odd now that we used to think of stylistics as the application of the discipline of linguistics to the separate field of literary studies: since literature is fundamentally a matter of language in its broadest conception, essentially literary studies should primarily be regarded as a special form of applied linguistics! In fact, it is the range of practices in literary scholarship in the institutional mainstream that is interdisciplinary: literary studies draws on history, or sociology, or economics, or politics, or philosophy, or creative art. Only stylistics directly faces the literary work in its own terms. I am often in discussions around questions such as 'what can stylistics offer to cognitive linguistics?', or 'what can stylistics bring to literary criticism?', whereas in fact I am increasingly insistent that the only question should be a simple 'what can stylistics do?' The payoffs for those other disciplines are of secondary importance.

Sara Whiteley: I agree that stylistics is now best thought of as a discipline. I think I realise this most in my teaching and in the fact that there are now undergraduate degrees in stylistics. Students are quick to realise that stylistic methods and approaches are not simply quirky or innovative combinations of language and literature – they are much more than that, sophisticated and productive in their own right. That said, I think stylistics as a discipline is also uniquely outward-looking. Practitioners are generally not content to simply 'do' stylistics, and are also attentive to current developments in a range of related fields such as linguistics, psychology, cognitive science, education and beyond. As a stylistician, you are still highly likely to find yourself flitting between library shelves to reach many sections of the Dewey-decimal system! And I think that some of the most fascinating and challenging stylistic work is still that which tests the boundaries and crossing-points between stylistics and other fields.

Handbook: *What is the relationship now (and in the future) between stylistics and literary scholarship?*

SW: In stylistics' transition from an interdiscipline to a discipline, I think a sense of division from mainstream literary scholarship has been an important identity-forming force. Many stylisticians, myself included, came into stylistics through a sense of dissatisfaction with other less rigorous approaches to literary analysis. Indeed, inherent within the stylistic commitment to systematicity in analysis and clarity in argument is a critique of some of the more impressionistic and pretentious forms of mainstream literary criticism. At present, I get the impression that stylistics is seen as a strange offshoot of literary scholarship by those who do not practise it. Stylistics is often unrepresented in university English departments, and where it is present, it is regarded as a minority interest. Now that it is a recognisable, coherent discipline, in the future I would like to see stylistics taking a central place in mainstream literary study. As we stated in the introduction to this volume, stylistics *is* the proper study of literature. And as this *Handbook* demonstrates, it excels at addressing issues central to literary scholarship such as composition, representation, meaning, effect, the style and craft of the author, and literature's significance for readers. Like other modes of literary scholarship, stylistic investigation stems from a researcher's intuitive responses to a text, and stylistic methods enable the systematic and rigorous examination of that text. As such, stylistics can both strengthen literary-critical arguments and shed new light on the way texts work. It is difficult to conceive of a form of literary scholarship which does not involve some analysis of texts (novels, poems, plays, letters, diary entries, manuscripts and so on), and which therefore would not benefit from stylistics. Making this change happen at an institutional level is where the challenge lies, however. Foundational modules in stylistics as the norm for all undergraduate literature degrees would be a big step forward, for instance.

PS: It's not that the various current practices of literary scholarship are pointless or valueless – there is a great deal of richness and value in this large body of work. I simply believe that every single example of literary scholarship would be better than it is if it included a greater stylistic sensibility. In a sense, the true measure of the success of stylistics would be when it was regarded as an inherent part of the basic training of a literary scholar. It's probably also true to say that stylistics – or at least a form of detailed and systematic attention to textuality – is more an implicit norm in the second-language literature classroom: if you are studying a literature in a foreign language, then you necessarily have to be a stylistician. And of course we're talking about something more systematic and, well, disciplined than an amateurish close-reading, however sensitive it is.

Essentially, stylistics is work. You have to have some training in what you're doing, and you have to go through the actual difficult process of sketching the analysis with a pencil or keyboard, or running a concordance or database search, or pursuing a great deal of empirical research publications in other fields before you can then do the hard intellectual work of adapting this material for literary analysis. A stylistic analysis is not simply something that you can have an opinion about – there is a basic level at which you simply have to do it right. Of course, there is a lot more ideology, argument and interpretation built on top of that. It's also important to recognise, though, that some of the brilliant textbooks and courses in stylistics around the world mean that the journey from being a new student to being able to do some really quite smart stylistics is very short. This is enormously empowering.

Handbook*: Though contributions to this volume encompass a range of literature, would you say that some literary texts are more suitable for stylistic analysis than others?*

PS: I think in the early days of stylistics there was a temptation to explore texts that were strikingly deviant or odd in some way. So writers such as e. e. cummings, Hemingway, Joyce or Hopkins were disproportionately popular. This was perhaps because the linguistic tools of the day naturally lent themselves to these sorts of texts. I think stylistics now is much more expansive, and I can't imagine any literary work that would be of no interest to the stylistician. I think the question is more about the literature than the stylistic selection: some literary texts offer more to say than others. Without getting into questions of canon and better and worse literature (on which stylistics has a great deal to contribute, of course), it's obvious that some literary works are rich and others are less so.

It strikes me that stylistics at heart is doing something rather old-fashioned but still valuable: appreciation. Mick Short has made this point several times – we are able to account for how some literary works are valued, prized and loved, and (in the other sense of 'appreciate') the value of the text increases as we gain a better understanding of how complex or clever it is. On a related theme, Paul Simpson has said that the test of a good stylistics talk is that it should make you want to go and read the literary text that has been discussed. Certainly most stylisticians choose to analyse texts that are significant either for themselves or more broadly socially, and so the analysis is properly motivated. The analysis itself is the thing, not the aggrandisement of the stylistician. In general, it seems to me that stylisticians are relatively non-egotistical. Perhaps with one or two (nameless!) exceptions, there is in general a loose ethos that we are engaged in a collective enterprise aimed at improving our understanding of how literature works. So stylistics does not usually aim for an eccentric but pyrotechnic innovation in interpretation – newness for its own sake – but is often concerned more with explaining existing or mainstream readings. Occasionally, of course, the practice of stylistics brings you to a revelatory moment in a reading that is an exciting new insight, but that moment is not the primary objective as it might be in traditional literary criticism.

SW: I agree that all literary works (indeed, all texts!) should hold some interest for a stylistician, though some offer richer pickings than others. In order to examine a text stylistically, you have to have some personal experience of its meaning or effects. Like other forms of literary scholarship, your choice of the text you analyse (or the period or genre you specialise in) is often motivated by your own personal preferences and interests. Because textual choice is so central to stylistic practice as it currently stands, I do think it would be interesting to disrupt this convention a little and see what consequences it had for the stylistic method. Discovering and analysing unfamiliar texts could be a good way for stylisticians to further test and refresh their stylistic tool-kits.

PS: I agree with this, though I also think stylistics offers a way of gaining access to and appreciation of the reading responses, feelings and interpretations of other analysts too. This is where stylistics is particularly intersubjective. I have read literary texts and not really known what to make of them, but have then been led by the hand by a stylistic account that has brought the literary work to life. Again, the test of good stylistics is the extent to which the literary text in focus appreciates in value as a result.

Handbook: *Is the contemporary shift from print to screen in the reading and sharing of literature a problem for stylistics?*

PS: I'm not sure this is as radical or new as we like to think. Text is still text whether accessed by codex or screen, and the sorts of things that people do with literature are the same as we have always done, but perhaps quicker and shared with a greater range of people. Stylistics has always had such close contact with semiotics, discourse analysis and media studies that rich multimodal literary works have not been a particularly difficult problem. In fact, I think the best work on multimodal literature has been done within a stylistics tradition. In the past, the performative and experiential aspects of literary consumption have been the challenge for stylistics. For the most part, stylistics has had most success with poetry and prose and has had problems with theatre and drama. This is to do with the nature of the performed object as an experience rather than the fixed playtext. However, I think much of the work on embodiment, experientialism and situatedness coming out of cognitive poetics offers us a chance of making great advances even here.

SW: The shift from print to screen in the reading and sharing of literature is more a shift in context than text – the text is the same but presented differently (on paper or monitors or e-readers). Cognitive poetic approaches do have the most potential for describing the effect of context on literary reading, but I think there is still much more work to be done in this area. Regardless of recent shifts in technology, I would say that the discussion of context – things like location, attention and motivation (which are often tied up in debates about the differences between print and screen, or print and audio before this) – *are* still 'a problem' in cognitive poetics. Deeper understanding of how these phenomena work and how they might relate to cognitive poetic frameworks is needed. So, I think the contemporary shift from print to screen (or the more familiar shift from print to audio) is only a problem for stylistics in so far as it highlights gaps in our current understanding of context and its impact on literary reading which need filling with further research.

Handbook: *What is the role of stylistics in pedagogy and the EFL classroom?*

SW: In university teaching, I think stylistics has an important role to play in providing students with a 'way in' to texts which may at first seem challenging, and encouraging greater awareness of and confidence in their own intuitions. Stylistics also provides a method for developing systematic, well-evidenced and clearly expressed arguments, which is an essential skill, as well as a greater sense of the way literary study intersects with other disciplines.

PS: I can't see how the study of a foreign literature can be anything other than stylistic, though of course I know that there is an awful lot of rather uninspiring and dull teaching of literature as culture. We have had many academic visitors from around the world pass through Nottingham, who have taken their training in stylistics back to their own countries, adapting it for their own purposes and revivifying their language classrooms. The relationship between stylistics and applied linguistics has been very close, as Ron Carter points out in this *Handbook* (Chapter 6). A student encountering a foreign literature in a foreign language such as English, for the first time, often feels daunted by their lack of cultural and contextual knowledge, and too often this is the cue for their teachers to embark on a long and tedious tour of British or American culture, and the literary work gets lost in a different sort of activity. However, that student has probably a very recent and highly foregrounded sense of the language patterns in English, and will often notice key stylistic features of a piece of English literature that a native English speaker might well miss or overlook. A teacher who shows such students that they are in an advantageous position and can go a long way with some very modest linguistic knowledge will be an inspirational classroom presence, and that teacher is likely to be a stylistician.

Handbook: *What are your views on the global reach of stylistics?*

PS: Though there is still probably a European centre of gravity, stylistics can be found everywhere in the world. I have seen enough work on the stylistics of translation and by scholars around the world applying the stylistic method to their own literature to be convinced that stylistics can profitably be used to understand any world literature better. There is, of course, a preponderance of stylistic analyses of British, Irish and American literature, but this is largely a historical consequence of the institutional success of stylistics in these parts of the world. Whenever I have had the privilege of taking stylistics to colleagues in South America, China or south-east Asia, there has been extraordinary interest and a desire to adapt stylistics for local purposes. It seems to me there is as much dissatisfaction in many parts of the world with the stuffy and inward-looking field of literary studies as I have felt over the years.

SW: The global reach of stylistics is also demonstrated by the international and ever-growing membership of the Poetics and Linguistics Association (PALA). At their conferences and through their website there is a clear sense of an international community engaged in stylistics.

PS: Yes, and I think it is important not to be proprietorial about it. Stylistics does not belong to any one nationality or school of thought. It's clear that the sorts of things our colleagues in Japan, or in America, for example, do with stylistics is often rather different from what might happen in Britain. One thing that has been apparent from PALA events over the decades is the fact that stylistics is a very broad church, not only in the incredibly rich range of literatures that have appeared but also in terms of the different linguistic approaches adapted for stylistic analysis. This said, if you were to create a database of stylistic analyses of different literary texts, you would find an overwhelming preponderance of English literature from the British Isles (including Irish literature), with some north American texts, but a relative neglect even of other English literatures, let alone world literatures in other languages. This is a situation that is being remedied by our colleagues around the world right now, but it remains an unrepresentative body of work at the moment.

Handbook: *Are there any areas of literary study that stylistics can't or shouldn't move into?*

SW: Because of its focus on textuality, stylistics should be a core feature of literary scholarship. As it can usefully underpin much literary research, and is also a progressive discipline whose capabilities are continually being expanded and improved, I wouldn't want to say that there are areas which stylistics *can't* or *shouldn't* enter into. That said, I think it is also important not to apply stylistics' text-grounded focus too reductively in our conception of literary study. In some areas of what I would like to think of as 'literary study' it is important to be able to conceive of literature beyond or outside of the text. For example, I think literary study should involve the study of readers and reading, but not all the things which readers do with literature are necessarily text-focused or interpretative. Reading groups engage in 'off-book' discussion around a text, and individual readers use internet sites to list, rank, rate and share their reading history. These extra-textual and evaluative practices are areas which I believe currently stretch the boundaries of stylistic understanding because they are not text-grounded in the usual stylistic sense of the word. Yet I still see them as relevant for the study of literature. Similarly, an understanding of authorial biography or the wider contexts of literary production are obviously important in literary study, but cannot always be grounded in a text in a stylistic sense. An approach that claimed it was wholly able to address *everything* currently encompassed by 'literary study' would only do so at the expense of rigour and principles. As the proper way to study literature, stylistics does many things very well, but it still needs to exist in symbiotic dialogue with the areas of literary study that necessarily segue into other disciplines such as history, cultural studies and sociology.

PS: I think all of these areas can be better understood with some stylistic input. Joe Bray and Violeta Sotirova have shown how really sharp stylistic analysis can shed light on authorial choices. Similarly I have always thought there is a natural affinity with creative writing as a university practice: both of us are concerned with the effects of careful stylistic choices. In my view, the best creative writing course would be one co-taught by writers and stylisticians. I also think stylisticians should not shy away from deploying their analyses in order to advance their own evaluations – it's better to be explicit about this, and recognise that stylisticians are not robots but readers of literature as well.

I agree that nothing should be off-limits, but there are of course boundaries to the discipline otherwise it would not be a discipline but a cult! I have had several researchers wanting to explore a possible integration between the approach to language offered by stylistics and the ideas about language offered by poststructuralist deconstruction. I think this is simply impossible, because both traditions are founded on radically opposed basic principles; both could offer critiques of the other, but that would be a different thing. I think in this area, you simply have to take a side and there is – for good theoretical reasons – no possibility of an accommodation. Moreover, I don't see much value in making one. I'm aware that some of the finest stylisticians in the world (Derek Attridge and Geoff Hall, to take two leading examples) don't agree with me, and in fact I would be delighted to be proven wrong on this.

Handbook: *What is the role of non-literary stylistics in the future of stylistics?*

SW: The organisation of this handbook reflects the general bias towards literary stylistics in the field as it stands – arguably because literary language often contains particularly interesting or playful linguistic features. But essentially all texts – spoken and written – are valid sites of stylistic analysis – and I think that literary stylistics has a lot to learn from the application of its tool-kit beyond the realm of literature. So I think, in the future, study of the 'non-literary' should play a greater role in stylistics. The mark of a stylistician should be their ability to turn their hand to analysing any text, however it is classified.

PS: The history of the discipline has seen the consensus swing from the search for a literary language or key to literariness, right across to the notion that the language of literature is in a seamless continuum with everyday examples of language use – and then all the way back again to argue for the special status of literary textuality, and back again to suggest that literature is composed of everyday language but deploys it and frames it in a special way. As someone who has spent time drawing on cognitivist linguistic principles, I'm inclined towards the view that language is language, but the particular situation conditions its use and effects. So literature is special, but the specialness is not exclusive. That means that a stylistician has to be of the world not apart from it. Fortunately, many of the best stylisticans of literature also have another history in different areas of applied linguistics, discourse analysis, text linguistics, educational linguistics, or as grammarians, creative writers, or as cinema, theatre or art critics. As a stylistician, you have licence to roam across any literature from any period of history and from any culture – I sometimes feel claustrophobic sympathy for literary critics cribbed in by their periodisation. The danger – they might retort – is that the stylistician can look like a jack-of-all-trades, but if you are genuinely a master of one (stylistics itself), then I have found that it is a relatively simple matter of hard work to catch up with the literary criticism in a particular area. I am also fortunate in having understanding literary colleagues who are happy to share their expertise so that I hope I avoid making simplistic or outdated assertions. Just as it is important to be in communication with literary scholars, it is also important to talk to those who work in media studies, language acquisition, sociology, economics and so on.

Handbook: *Besides the corpus and cognitive revolutions, are there any other new notable directions in stylistics?*

SW: The scope and reach of both these revolutions is far from over, and many exciting directions in stylistics are still emerging from within these general areas. I think one interesting methodological direction is towards the greater reliance on formal reader response data and the way it is being used to support and direct stylistic analyses. It is becoming more common to refer to data such as questionnaires, interviews, discussions and online postings in the framing of stylistic analyses. Through collaboration with researchers in other disciplines, there are also even greater connections being made between non-verbal data (such as response times and eye movements) and traditional stylistic concerns. Stylisticians are becoming more proficient in the collection and analysis of this kind of extra-textual data, which is a notable future direction in the field. Greater attention to aesthetics and phenomenological or experiential aspects of reading is another notable new direction that has evolved from the cognitive revolution.

PS: Yes, these are all the things you are interested in! But of course they are all areas of great potential right now. As I've said before, it strikes me increasingly that there is much common cause between stylistics and the way creative writing is (or could be) taught in universities. I have learnt a lot from practising professional writers who talk about their work in terms of detailed textural choices, and such people are almost without exception interested in the sorts of things stylisticians do. It is especially awkward and insightful to produce a stylistic analysis of a colleague's own writing and discuss its effects.

My sense of the future is that stylistics will continue to move towards the centre of the institution of literary scholarship. There is some resistance from the middle of this institution, of course, but in fact the driver for change is not coming from there but from below and from above. The demand from below lies in the way that 'English language' has been promoted and taught in schools, and indirectly promoted by governments who see it as more easily testable than literary cultural knowledge. Students arrive at university, as it were, already primed and ready for a focus on literary texture. From above, there are more job opportunities for trained stylisticians than for periodised literary scholars. This is because the stylistician is usually highly adaptable and can teach both literature and language. When I got my first university job 25 years ago, there was barely any such thing as a lectureship in stylistics (I was employed as a sociolinguist!): nowadays an appointment in one of the many diverse areas of stylistic-related work is regarded as normal.

Undoubtedly there will be another revolution in the study of language after the cognitivist turn. Perhaps the increase in computational power and methods will accelerate corpus stylistics into a form unimaginable today. I hope I will still be adaptable enough and enthusiastic enough to embrace whatever comes along next, not simply for the sake of intellectual fashion but because there will be new opportunities to move towards better descriptions and understanding of literary works, creativity, readers and reading.

References

Aarts, J. (2000) 'Towards a new generation of corpus-based grammars', in B. Lewandowska-Tomaszczyk and P. Melia (eds) *PALC'99: Practical Applications in Language Corpora*, Frankfurt: Peter Lang, pp. 17–63.

Abercrombie, D. (1973) 'Paralinguistic communication', in J. P. B. Allen (ed.) *The Edinburgh Course in Applied Linguistics*, Vol. 2, Oxford University Press, pp. 31–7.

Abrams, J. (2010) 'State of the nation: new British theatre', *Performing Arts Journal* 95: 8–10.

Abrams, M. H. (with Harpham, G. G.) (2005) 'Imagery', in *A Glossary of Literary Terms* (8th edn), Boston: Thomson, pp. 128–30.

Adams, M. (2009) 'Multi various outcomes' and 'What participants experience' (video interviews): available under 'Interviews' at: www.dlwp.com/dlwpinternational/venice/index.html

Adamson, J., Freadman, R. and Parker, D. (eds) (1998) *Renegotiating Ethics in Literature, Philosophy and Theory*. Cambridge University Press.

Adamson, S. M. (1999) 'Literary language', in S. Romaine (ed.) *The Cambridge History of the English Language, Vol. 4: 1776–1997*. Cambridge University Press, pp. 591–690.

Adamson, S. M., Hunter, L., Magnusson, L., Thompson, A. and Wales, K. (eds) (2001) *Reading Shakespeare's Dramatic Language: A Guide*. London: Thomson Learning.

Adey, P. (2010) *Mobility*. London: Routledge.

Adiga, A. (2008) *The White Tiger*. London: Atlantic Books.

Advertising Standards Authority (2012) 'ASA adjudication on Nike (UK) Ltd', available at: www.asa.org.uk/Rulings/Adjudications/2012/6/Nike-(UK)-Ltd/SHP_ADJ_183247.aspx

Aitchison, J. (2007) *The Word Weavers: Newshounds and Wordsmiths*. Cambridge University Press.

Albright, D. (1991) *W. B. Yeats: The Poems*. New York: Simon and Schuster.

Alexander, M. (2006) *Cognitive-Linguistic Manipulation and Persuasion in Agatha Christie*. Unpublished MPhil thesis, University of Glasgow.

Alford, M. H. T. (1971) 'Computer assistance in language learning', in R. A. Wisbey (ed.) *The Computer in Literary and Linguistic Research*, Cambridge University Press, pp. 77–86.

Allington, D. (2011) '"It actually painted a picture of the village and the sea and the bottom of the sea": reading groups, cultural legitimacy, and description in narrative (with particular reference to John Steinbeck's *The Pearl*)', *Language and Literature* 20 (4): 317–32.

Allington, D. (2012) 'Private experience, textual analysis, and institutional authority: the discursive practice of critical interpretation and its enactment in literary training', *Language and Literature* 21 (2): 211–25.

Allington, D. and Swann, J. (2009) 'Researching literary reading as social practice', *Language and Literature* 18 (3): 219–30.

Alter, R. (1986) 'Daniel Martin and the mimetic task', in E. Pifer (ed.) *Critical Essays on John Fowles*, Boston: G. K. Hall, pp. 150–62.

Althusser, L. (1984) *Essays in Ideology*. London: Verso.

American Marketing Association (2012) 'Dictionary of marketing terms', available at: www.marketingpower.com/_layouts/Dictionary.aspx.

Amos, A. and Haglund, M. (2000) 'From social taboo to "torch of freedom": the marketing of cigarettes to women', *Tobacco Control* 9: 3–8.

Anderson, B. (1983) *Imagined Communities: Reflections on the Origin and Spread of Nationalism*. London: Verso.

Anderson, J. R. (1983) *The Architecture of Cognition*. Cambridge, MA: Harvard University Press.

Andringa, E. (1996) 'Effects of "narrative distance" on readers' emotional involvement and response', *Poetics* 23 (6): 431–52.

Archer, D. (2007) 'Computer assisted literary stylistics: the state of the field', in M. Lambrou and P. Stockwell (eds) *Contemporary Stylistics*, London: Continuum, pp. 244–56.

Archer, D. and Bousfield, D. (2010) '"See better, Lear? See Lear better!" A corpus-based pragma-stylistic investigation of Shakespeare's *King Lear*', in D. McIntyre and B. Busse (eds), *Language and Style*, London: Palgrave Macmillan, pp. 183–203.

Archer, D, Culpeper, J. and Rayson, P. (2010) '"Love – a familiar or a devil"?: An exploration of key domains in Shakespeare's comedies and tragedies', in D. Archer (ed.) (2010) *What's In a Word List?: Investigating Word Frequency and Keyword Extraction*, London: Ashgate, pp. 137–58.

Aristotle (1954) *Rhetoric and Poetics* (trans. W. R. Roberts). New York: Modern Library.

Arizti, B. and Martinez-Falquina, S. (2007) (eds) *On the Turn: The Ethics of Fiction in Contemporary Narrative in English*. Newcastle: Cambridge Scholars Publishing.

Askehave, I. and Swales, J. M. (2001) 'Genre identification and communicative purpose: a problem and a possible solution', *Applied Linguistics* 22 (2): 195–212.

Asthana, A. (2012) 'The real David Cameron', *Public Policy Research*, 19: 64–6.

Atherton, C. (2005) *Defining Literary Criticism: Scholarship, Authority and the Possession of Literary Knowledge, 1880–2002*. Basingstoke: Palgrave Macmillan.

Attridge, D. (1996) 'Closing statement: linguistics and poetics in retrospect', in N. Fabb, D. Attridge, A. Durant and C. MacCabe (eds) *The Linguistics of Writing*, Manchester University Press (2nd edn) [original 1987], pp. 15–32.

Attridge, D. (2005) 'Keats and beats, or what can we say about rhythm?' in D. Thomières (ed.) *Le Rythme dans les littératures de langue anglaise*, Presses Universitaires de Reims, pp. 99–116.

Austen, J. (1995) *Sense and Sensibility* [original 1811]. London: Penguin.

Austen, J. (1996) *Emma* (ed. F. Stafford) [original 1816]. London: Penguin.

Austin, J. L. (1962) *How to Do Things With Words*. Oxford University Press.

Ayscough, S. (1790) *An Index to the Remarkable Passages and Words made use of by Shakspeare; Calculated to Point out the Different Meanings to which the Words are Applied*. London: Stockdale.

Baars, B. J. and Gage, N. M. (2010) *Cognition, Brain, and Consciousness: Introduction to Cognitive Neuroscience* (2nd edn). London: Elsevier Academic Press.

Backhaus, P. (2007) *Linguistic Landscapes: A Comparative Study of Urban Multilingualism in Tokyo*. Clevedon: Multilingual Matters.

Baker, L. and Wagner, J. L. (1987) 'Evaluating information for truthfulness: the effects of logical subordination', *Memory and Cognition* 15 (3): 247–55.

Baker, M. (2000) 'Towards a methodology for investigating the style of a literary translation', *Target* 12 (2): 241–66.

Baker, P. (2006) *Using Corpora in Discourse Analysis*. London: Continuum.

Bakhtin, M. M. (1973) *Problems of Dostoevsky's Poetics*. Ann Arbor: Ardis.

Bakhtin, M. M. (1981) *The Dialogic Imagination: Four Essays* (ed. M. Holquist, trans. C. Emerson and M. Holquist). Austin: University of Texas Press.

Bakhtin, M. M. (1986) 'The problem of speech genres', in C. Emerson and M. Holquist (eds) *Speech Genres and Other Late Essays*, Austin: University of Texas Press, pp. 60–102.

Bally, C. (1909) *Traité de stylistique française*. Heidelberg: Carl Winters.

Barnbrook, G. and Sinclair, J. (1995) 'Parsing Cobuild entries', in J. Sinclair, M. Hoelter and C. Peters (eds) *The Languages of Definition: The Formalization of Dictionary Definitions for Natural Language Processing*, Luxembourg: Office for Official Publications of the European Communities, pp. 13–58.

Baron, N. (2000) *Alphabet to Email*. London: Routledge.

Baron, N. (2008) *Always On: Language in an Online and Mobile World*. Oxford University Press.

Barrell, J. (1986) *The Political Theory of Painting from Reynolds to Hazlitt: 'The Body of the Public'*. New Haven: Yale University Press.

Barrie, J. M. (1904) *Peter Pan (or The Boy Who Wouldn't Grow Up)*. London: Hodder and Stoughton.

Barry, P. (2007) *Literature in Contexts*. Manchester University Press.

Barry, P. (2009) *Beginning Theory: An Introduction to Literary and Cultural Theory* (2nd edn). Manchester University Press.

Barsalou, L. W. (1999) 'Perceptual symbol systems', *Behavioral and Brain Sciences* 22: 577–609.

Barsalou, L. W. (2003) 'Situated simulation in the human conceptual system', *Language and Cognitive Processes* 18 (5–6): 513–62.

Barsalou, L. W. (2009) 'Simulation, situated conceptualization, and prediction', *Philosophical Transactions of the Royal Society of London, Series B: Biological Sciences* 364 (1521): 1281–9.

Barsalou, L. W., Solomon, K. O. and Wu, L.-L. (1999) 'Perceptual simulation in conceptual tasks', in M. K. Hiraga, C. Sinha and S. Wilcox (eds) *Cultural, Psychological and Typological Issues in Cognitive Linguistics*, Amsterdam: John Benjamins, pp. 209–28.

Barthes, R. (1977) *Image, Music, Text* (ed. and trans. S. Heath). London: Fontana Press.

Bartlett, F. (1932) *Remembering: A Study in Experimental and Social Psychology*. Cambridge University Press.

Barton, S. B. and Sanford, A. J. (1993) 'A case study of anomaly detection: shallow semantic processing and cohesion establishment', *Memory and Cognition* 21 (4): 477–87.

Bassnett, S. and Lefèvre, A. (1998) *Constructing Cultures: Essays on Literary Translation*. Clevedon: Multilingual Matters.

Bate, J. (2010) *English Literature: A Very Short Introduction*. Oxford University Press.

Bateson, F. W. (1934) *English Poetry and the English Language*. Manchester University Press.

Bean, R. (2009) *England People Very Nice*. London: Oberon.

de Beaugrande, R. (1991) *Linguistic Theory: The Discourse of Fundamental Works*. London: Longman.

de Beaugrande, R. and Dressler, W. U. (1981) *Introduction to Text Linguistics*. London: Longman.

Bednarek, M. and Caple, H. (2012) *News Discourse*. London: Continuum.

Bell, Alice and Ensslin, A. (2011) '"I know what it was. You know what it was": second-person narration in hypertext fiction', *Narrative* 19 (3): 311–29.

Bell, Allan (1984) 'Language style as audience design', *Language in Society* 13: 145–204.

Bell, Allan (1991) *The Language of News Media*. Oxford: Blackwell.

Bell, Allan and van Leeuwen, T. (1994) *The Media Interview: Confession, Contest, Conversation*. Sydney: New South Wales University Press.

Belsey, C. (2011) *A Future for Criticism*. Oxford: Wiley-Blackwell.

Benford, S., Crabtree, A., Reeves, S., Flintham, M., Drozd, A., Sheridan, J. and Dix, A. (2006) 'The frame of the game: blurring the boundary between fiction and reality in mobile experiences', *Proceedings of ACM CHI 2006 Conference on Human Factors in Computing Systems* 1: 427–36.

Benjamin, W. (1979) 'A small history of photography', in *'One-Way Street' and Other Writings* (trans. E. Jephcott and K. Shorter) [original 1931], London: NLB, pp. 240–57.

Benwell, B. (2009) '"A pathetic and racist and awful character": ethnomethodological approaches to the reception of diasporic fiction', *Language and Literature* 18 (3): 300–15.

Berkenkotter, C. and Huckin, T. N. (1995) *Genre Knowledge in Disciplinary Communication: Cognition/Culture/Power*. Mahwah: Lawrence Erlbaum Associates.

Bernières, L. de (2004) *Birds Without Wings*. London: Secker and Warburg.

Bernières, L. de (2009) *A Partisan's Daughter*. London: Vintage.

Bex, A. R. (1994) 'The relevance of genre', in R. D. Sell and P. Verdonk (eds) *Literature and the New Interdisciplinarity: Poetics, Linguistics, History*, Amsterdam: Rodopi, pp. 107–29.

Bhatia, V. K. (1993) *Analysing Genre: Language Use in Professional Settings*. London: Longman.

Biber, D. (1998) *Variation across Speech and Writing*. Cambridge University Press.

Biber, D. (2003) 'Compressed noun-phrase structures in newspaper discourse: the competing demands of popularization vs. economy', in J. Aitchison and D. M. Lewis (eds) *New Media Language*, London: Routledge, pp. 169–81.

Biber, D. (2011) 'Register', in P. C. Hogan (ed.) *The Cambridge Encyclopedia of the Language Sciences*, Cambridge University Press, pp. 707–8.

Biber, D. and Conrad, S. (2009) *Register, Genre, and Style*. Cambridge University Press.

Biber, D. and Finegan, E. (1988) 'Drift in three English genres from the 18th to the 20th centuries: a multidimensional approach', in M. Kytö, O. Ihalainen and M. Rissanen (eds) *Corpus Linguistics, Hard and Soft*, Amsterdam: Rodopi, pp. 83–101.

Biber, D. and Finegan, E. (1989a) 'Drift and the evolution of English style: a history of three genres', *Language* 65 (3): 487–517.

Biber, D., and Finegan, E. (1989b) 'Styles of stance in English: lexical and grammatical marking of evidentiality and affect', *Text* 9 (1): 93–124.

Biber, D., Conrad, S. and Reppen, R. (1998) *Corpus Linguistics*. Cambridge University Press.

Biber, D., Finegan, E., Johansson, S., Conrad, S. and Leech, G. (1999) *Longman Grammar of Spoken and Written English*. Harlow: Longman.

Billig, M. (1999) 'Whose terms? Whose ordinariness? Rhetoric and ideology in conversation analysis', *Discourse and Society* 10 (4): 543–58.

Billington, M. (2009) 'Review of *England People Very Nice*', *The Guardian*, 12 February.

Black, S. (2009) 'Ishiguro's inhuman aesthetics', *Modern Fiction Studies* 55 (4): 785–807.

Blakemore, D. and Carston, R. (2004) 'The pragmatics of sentential coordination with *and*', *Lingua* 115 (4): 569–89.

Blast Theory (2009) *Ulrike and Eamon Compliant*. Mobile narrative. Script produced by Blast Theory, available at: www.dlwp.com/dlwpinterna tional/venice/index.html

Bloom, H. (1973) *The Anxiety of Influence: A Theory of Poetry*. Oxford University Press.

Bloom, H. (1995) *The Western Canon*. New York: Riverhead Books.

Boase-Beier, J. (2004a) 'Translation and style: a brief introduction', *Language and Literature* 13 (1): 9–11.

Boase-Beier, J. (2004b) 'Knowing and not knowing: style, intention and the translation of a Holocaust poem', *Language and Literature* 13 (1): 25–35.

Boase-Beier, J. (2006) *Stylistic Approaches to Translation*. Manchester: St Jerome Publishing.

Boase-Beier, J. (2011) 'Stylistics and translation', in K. Malmkjaer and J. Windle (eds) *The Oxford Handbook of Translation Studies*, New York: Oxford University Press, pp. 71–82.

Bockting, I. (1994) 'Mind style as an interdisciplinary approach to characterisation in Faulkner', *Language and Literature* 3 (3): 157–74.

Bonheim, H. (1982) *The Narrative Mode*. Cambridge: D. S. Brewer.

Bono, E. de (1967) *The Use of Lateral Thinking*. London: Jonathan Cape.

Booth, W. C. (1988) *The Company We Keep: An Ethics of Fiction*. Berkeley: University of California Press.

Booth, W. C. (1991) *The Rhetoric of Fiction*. Harmondsworth: Penguin.

Bortolussi, M. and Dixon, P. (2003) *Psychonarratology: Foundations for the Empirical Study of Literary Response*. Cambridge University Press.

Bousfield, D. (2007) '"Never a truer word said in jest": A pragmastylistic analysis of impoliteness as banter in *Henry IV, Part I*', in M. Lambrou and P. Stockwell (eds) *Contemporary Stylistics*, London: Continuum, pp. 209–20.

Bousfield, D. (2008) *Impoliteness in Interaction*. Amsterdam: John Benjamins.

Bowles, H. (2010) *Storytelling and Drama*. Amsterdam: John Benjamins.

Box, G. E. P. and Draper, N. R. (1987) *Empirical Model-Building and Response Surfaces*. New York: Wiley.

Boyne, J. (2006a) *The Boy in the Striped Pajamas: A Fable*. New York: Ember.

Boyne, J. (2006b) 'An interview with John Boyne', in J. Boyne (ed.) *The Boy in the Striped Pajamas: A Fable*. New York: Ember, pp. 4–10.

Bradley, A. C. (1965) *Shakespearean Tragedy: Lectures on Hamlet, Othello, King Lear, Macbeth* [original 1904]. London: Macmillan.

Bray, J. (2007) 'The "dual voice" of free indirect discourse: a reading experiment', *Language and Literature* 16 (1): 37–52.

Bréal, M. (1897) *Essai de sémantique*. Paris: Hachette [translated as *Semantics: Studies in the Science of Meaning*. New York: Dover, 1964].

Brecht, B. (1977) 'The exception and the rule', in *The Measures Taken and Other Lehrstücke*, London: Methuen, pp. 35–60.

Briggs, A. and Burke, P. (2005) *A Social History of the Media: From Gutenberg to the Internet* (2nd edn). Cambridge: Polity.

Brock, T. C. and Green, M. C. (2005) *Persuasion: Psychological Insights and Perspectives*. London: Sage.

Brône, G. and Vandaele, J. (eds) (2009) *Cognitive Poetics: Goals, Gains, and Gaps*. Berlin: Mouton de Gruyter.

Brooks, D. (2006) *Steve and Me: My Friendship with Stephen Lawrence and the Search For Justice*. London: Abacus Books.

Brown, G. (1990) *Listening to Spoken English* [original 1977]. London: Longman.

Brown, P. and Levinson, S. (1978) 'Universals in language usage: politeness phenomena', in E. N. Goody (ed.) *Questions and Politeness*, Cambridge University Press, pp. 56–324.

Brown, P. and Levinson, S. (1987) *Politeness: Some Universals in Language Usage*. Cambridge University Press.

Brumfit, C. J. and Carter R. (eds) (1986) *Literature and Language Teaching*. Oxford University Press.

Bruthiaux, P. (1996) *The Discourse of Classified Advertising: Exploring the Nature of Linguistic Simplicity*. New York: Oxford University Press.

Buckland, W. (2009) 'Making sense of *Lost Highway*', in W. Buckland (ed.) *Puzzle Films: Complex Storytelling in Contemporary Cinema*. Oxford: Wiley-Blackwell, pp. 42–61.

Bühler, K. (1982) 'The deictic field of language and deictic worlds', in R. J. Jarvella and W. Klein (eds) *Speech, Place and Action: Studies in Deixis and Related Topics*, Chichester: John Wiley, pp. 9–30.

Burke, M. (2005) 'How cognition can augment stylistic analysis', *European Journal of English Studies* 9 (2): 185–95.

Burke, M. (2010a) 'Rhetorical pedagogy: teaching students to write a stylistics paper', *Language and Literature* 19 (1): 77–98.

Burke, M. (2010b) *Literary Reading, Cognition and Emotion: An Exploration of the Oceanic Mind*. London: Routledge.

Burroughs, W. (1959) *Naked Lunch*. New York: Grove Press.

Burrows, J. F. (1987) *Computation into Criticism: A Study of Jane Austen's Novels and an Experiment in Method*. Oxford: Clarendon.

Burrows, J. F. (1992) 'Computers and the study of literature', in C. Butler (ed.) *Computers and Written Texts*, Oxford: Blackwell, pp. 176–204.

Burton, D. (1980) *Dialogue and Discourse*. London: Routledge.

Burton, D. (1982) 'Through glass darkly: through dark glasses', in R. Carter (ed.) *Language and Literature: An Introductory Reader in Stylistics*, London: Allen and Unwin, pp. 195–214.

Busa, R. (2007) 'Foreword: perspectives in the digital humanities', in S. Schreibman, R. G. Siemens and J. Unsworth (eds) *A Companion to Digital Humanities*, Oxford: Blackwell, pp. xvi–xxi.

Busse, B. (2010a) 'Recent trends in historical stylistics', in D. McIntyre and B. Busse (eds), *Language and Style*, Basingstoke: Palgrave, pp. 32–54.

Busse, B. (2010b) 'Non-literary language: a stylistic investigation of the cover pages of the British satirical magazine *Private Eye*', in D. McIntyre and B. Busse (eds) *Language and Style*, London: Palgrave, pp. 468–97.

Busse, B. (2010c) 'Recent trends in new historical stylistics', in D. McIntyre and B. Busse (eds) *Language and Style*, London: Palgrave, pp. 32–54.

Busse, B. (forthcoming) 'Enregistering urban space in Brooklyn, New York', *Journal of Sociolinguistics*, in prep.

Butterworth, J. (2009) *Jerusalem*. London: Nick Hern Books.

Cameron, D. (2003) 'Gender and language ideologies', in J. Holmes and M. Meyerhoff (eds) *The Handbook of Language and Gender*, Oxford: Blackwell, pp. 447–67.

Cameron, D. (2011) 'Evolution, science and the study of literature', *Language and Literature* 20 (1): 59–72.

Cameron, D. (2012) *Verbal Hygiene: The Politics of Language* (2nd edn). London: Routledge.

Cameron, L. (2008) 'Metaphor and talk', in R. Gibbs (ed.) *The Cambridge Handbook of Metaphor and Thought*, Cambridge University Press, pp. 197–211.

Cameron, L. (2010) 'The discourse dynamics framework for metaphor', in L. Cameron and R. Maslen (eds) *Metaphor Analysis*, London: Equinox, pp. 77–94.

Cameron, L. and Larsen-Freeman, D. (2008) *Complex Systems and Applied Linguistics*. Oxford University Press.

Camus, A. (1946) *The Stranger (or The Outsider)* (trans. S. Gilbert). New York: Alfred Knopf.

CAP (2012) 'UK Codes of Broadcast and Non-Broadcast Advertising', available at: www.cap.org.uk/Advertising-Codes.aspx

Carnap, R. (1947) *Meaning and Necessity* [original 1928]. University of Chicago Press.

Carper, T. and Attridge, D. (2003) *Meter and Meaning: An Introduction to Rhythm in Poetry*. London: Routledge.

le Carré, J. (2007) *The Constant Gardener*. London: Hodder.

Carrol, L. (1992) *Alice in Wonderland* [original 1865]. Hertfordshire: Wordsworth Classic Books.

Carston, R. (2002) *Thoughts and Utterances*. Oxford: Wiley-Blackwell.

Carston, R. (2012) 'Negation, "presupposition" and the semantics / pragmatics distinction', available at: www.phon.ucl.ac.uk/home/robyn/pdf/negationsemprag.pdf

Carter, R. (1982) 'Style and interpretation in Hemingway's "Cat in the Rain"', in R. Carter (ed.) *Language and Literature: An Introductory Reader in Stylistics*, London: Allen and Unwin, pp. 65–82.

Carter, R. (2004) *Language and Creativity: The Art of Common Talk*. London: Routledge.

Carter, R. (2010) 'Methodologies for stylistic analysis: practices and pedagogies', in D. McIntyre and B. Busse (eds) *Language and Style*, London: Palgrave, pp. 55–70.

Carter, R. (2012) 'Coda: some rubber bullet points', *Language and Literature* 21 (1): 106–14.

Carter, R. and McCarthy, M. (2006) *Cambridge Grammar of English. A Comprehensive Guide. Spoken and Written English. Grammar and Usage.* Cambridge University Press.

Carter, R. and McRae, J. (eds) (1996) *Language, Literature and the Learner: Creative Classroom Practice.* London: Longman.

Carter, R. and Nash, W. (1983) 'Language and literariness', *Prose Studies* 6 (2): 124–41.

Carter, R. and Simpson, P. (1989) 'Introduction', in R. Carter and P. Simpson (eds) *Language, Discourse and Literature,* London: Unwin Hyman, pp. 1–20.

Carter, R. and Stockwell, P. (eds) (2008) *The Language and Literature Reader.* London: Routledge.

Catford, J. C. (1965) *A Linguistic Theory of Translation.* Oxford University Press.

Cathcart, B. (2003) *The Case of Stephen Lawrence.* London: Penguin.

Chandler, R. (1943) *The Lady in the Lake.* New York: Knopf.

Chaney, P. (2009) *The Digital Handshake: Seven Proven Strategies to Grow Your Business Using Social Media.* Hoboken: John Wiley.

Chapman, R. (1994) *Forms of Speech in Victorian Fiction.* London: Longman.

Chapman, S. (2012) 'Towards a neo-Gricean pragmatics: implicature in Dorothy L. Sayers's *Gaudy Night*', *Journal of Literary Semantics* 41 (2): 139–53.

Charteris-Black, J. (2007) *The Communication of Leadership: The Design of Leadership Style.* London: Routledge.

Charteris-Black, J. (2009) 'Metaphor and gender in British parliamentary debates', in K. Ahrens (ed.) *Politics, Gender and Conceptual Metaphor.* Amsterdam: Benjamins, pp. 196–234.

Charteris-Black, J. (2011) *Politicians and Rhetoric: The Persuasive Power of Metaphor* (2nd edn). Basingstoke: Palgrave Macmillan.

Charteris-Black, J. and Seale C. (2009) 'Men and emotion talk: evidence from the experience of illness', *Gender & Language* 3: 81–113.

Charteris-Black, J. and Seale, C. (2010) *Gender and the Language of Illness.* Basingstoke: Palgrave Macmillan.

Chase, S. (1938) *The Tyranny of Words.* New York: Harvest Books.

Chatman, S. (1978) *Story and Discourse: Narrative Structure in Fiction and Film.* Ithaca: Cornell University Press.

Chbosky, S. (1999) *The Perks of Being a Wallflower.* New York: MTV Books/ Pocket Books.

Chomsky, N. (1965) *Aspects of the Theory of Syntax.* Boston: MIT Press.

Chomsky, N. (1975) *The Logical Structure of Linguistic Theory.* London: Plenum Press.

Christie, A. (1958) *Dumb Witness* [original 1937]. London: Fontana.

Christie, A. (1964) 'Murder in the mews', in A. Christie, *Murder in the Mews and Other Stories* [original 1937], London: Fontana, pp. 7–55.

Christie, A. (1972) *Hallowe'en Party* [original 1969]. London: Fontana.

Clark, B. (1996) 'Stylistic analysis and relevance theory', *Language and Literature* 5 (3): 163–78.

Clark, B. (2009) 'Salient inferences: pragmatics and *The Inheritors*', *Language and Literature* 18 (2): 173–212.

Clark, B. (2012) 'Beginning with "One more thing": pragmatics and editorial intervention in the work of Raymond Carver', *Journal of Literary Semantics* 41 (2): 155–74.

Clark, B. (2013) *Relevance Theory*. Cambridge University Press.

Clark, B. (2014) 'Stylistics and relevance theory', in M. Burke (ed.) *The Routledge Handbook of Stylistics*, London: Routledge.

Clark, B. and Owtram, N. T. (2012) 'Imagined inference: teaching writers to think like readers', in M. Burke, S. Czabo, L. Week and J. Zerkowitz (eds) *Current Trends in Pedagogical Stylistics*, London: Continuum, pp. 126–41.

Clark, K. (1992) 'The linguistics of blame' in M. Toolan (ed.) *Language, Text and Context*, London: Routledge.

Clayman, S. and Heritage, J. (2002) *The News Interview: Journalists and Public Figures on the Air*. Cambridge University Press.

Clement, T. and Gueguen, G. (2008) 'Annotated overview of selected electronic resources', in S. Schreibman and R. Siemens (eds) *A Companion to Digital Literary Studies*, Oxford: Blackwell, available at: www.digitalhumanities.org/companionDLS

Close, A. J. (1976) 'Don Quixote and the "intentionalist fallacy"', in D. N. de Molina (ed.) *On Literary Intention*, Edinburgh University Press, pp. 174–93.

Cluysenaar, A. (1976) *Introduction to Literary Stylistics*. London: Batsford.

Coates, J. (1987) 'Epistemic modality and spoken discourse', *Transactions of the Philological Society* 85 (1): 110–31.

Coates, J. (1996) *Women Talk: Conversation Between Women Friends*. Oxford: Blackwell.

Coates, R. (1987) 'Pragmatic sources of analogical reformation', *Journal of Linguistics* 23: 319–40.

Cockcroft, R. (2003) *Rhetorical Affect in Early Modern Writing*. Basingstoke: Palgrave Macmillan.

Cockcroft, R. and Cockcroft, S. (2005) *Persuading People* (2nd edn). Basingstoke: Macmillan.

Cohn, D. (1990) 'Signposts of fictionality: a narratological perspective', *Poetics Today* 11 (4): 775–804.

Cohn, D. (1999) *The Distinction of Fiction*. Baltimore: The Johns Hopkins University Press.

Collie, J. and Slater, S. (1987) *Literature in the Language Classroom*. Cambridge University Press.

Collins, B. (1999) 'Forgetfulness', in *Questions about Angels*, University of Pittsburgh Press, p. 20.

Combe, W. (1777) *A Poetical Epistle to Sir Joshua Reynolds*. London: Fielding and Walker.

Connor, S. (1985) *Charles Dickens*. Oxford: Blackwell.

Conrad, J. (1999) *Chance* [original 1913]. Oxford University Press.

Conrad, S. and Biber, D. (2009) *Real Grammar: A Corpus-Based Approach to English*. London: Pearson Longman.

Cook, A. (2011) 'Cognitive interplay: how blending theory and cognitive science reread Shakespeare', in M. Ravassat and J. Culpeper (eds) *Stylistics and Shakespeare: Transdisciplinary Approaches*, New York: Continuum, pp. 246–68.

Cook, G. (1992) *The Discourse of Advertising*. London: Routledge.

Cook, G. (1994) *Discourse and Literature: The Interplay of Form and Mind*. Oxford University Press.

Cook, G. (2000) *Language Play, Language Learning*. Oxford University Press.

Cook, G. (2001) *The Discourse of Advertising* (2nd edn). London: Routledge.

Cook, G. (2011) 'In defence of genius', in J. Swann, R. Pope and R. Carter (eds) *Creativity in Language and Literature: The State of the Art*, Basingstoke: Palgrave, pp. 290–303.

Copeland, R. and Sluiter, I. (2009) (eds) *Medieval Grammar and Rhetoric: Language Arts and Literary Theory, AD 300–1475*. Oxford University Press.

Corbett, J. (2006) 'Genre and genre analysis', in K. Brown (ed.) *The Encyclopedia of Language and Linguistics*, Vol. 5, Amsterdam: Elsevier, pp. 26–32.

Coulthard, M. and Johnson, A. (2007) *An Introduction to Forensic Linguistics*. London: Routledge.

Coupland, N. (2001) 'Dialect stylisation in radio talk', *Language in Society*, 30 (3): 345–75.

Coupland, N. (2003) 'Sociolinguistic authenticities', *Journal of Sociolinguistics* 7 (3): 417–31.

Coupland, N. (2007) *Style: Language, Variation and Identity*. Cambridge University Press.

Coupland, N. (2010) 'The authentic speaker and the speech community', in C. Llamas and D. Watts (eds) *Language and Identities*, Edinburgh University Press, pp. 99–112.

Coveney, M. (2009) 'Review of "Jerusalem"', *The Independent*, 20 July.

Cresswell, T. (2006) *On the Move: Mobility in the Modern Western World*. London: Routledge.

Crompton, S. (2012) 'A burning desire to change the world', *Daily Telegraph*, 30 July.

Crowley, S. and Hawhee, D. (1999) *Ancient Rhetorics for Contemporary Students* (2nd edn). Boston: Allan and Bacon.

Cruden, A. (1737) *A Complete Concordance to the Holy Scriptures*. London: Frederick Warne.

Cruden, A. (1741) *A Verbal Index to Milton's Paradise Lost*. London: W. Innys and D. Browne.

Cruickshank, T. and Lahey, E. (2010) 'Building the stages of drama: towards a Text World Theory account of dramatic play texts', *Journal of Literary Semantics* 39 (1): 67–92.

Crystal, D. (1963) 'A perspective for paralanguage', *Le maître phonétique* 120: 25–9.

Crystal, D. (1975) *The English Tone of Voice*. London: Arnold.

Crystal, D. (1997) *A Dictionary of Linguistics and Phonetics*. Oxford: Blackwell.

Crystal, D. (2003) *The Cambridge Encyclopedia of the English Language* (2nd edn). Cambridge University Press.

Crystal, D. (2006) *Language and the Internet* (2nd edn). Cambridge University Press.

Crystal, D. and Davy, D. (1969) *Investigating English Style*. London: Longman.

Crystal, D. and Quirk, R. (1964) *Systems of Prosodic and Paralinguistic Features in English*. London: Mouton and Co.

Culpeper, J. (1994) *Language and Characterisation with Special Reference to Shakespeare's Plays*. Unpublished PhD thesis, Lancaster University.

Culpeper, J. (1998) '(Im)politeness in dramatic dialogue', in J. Culpeper, M. Short and P. Verdonk (eds) *Exploring the Language of Drama: From Text to Context*, London: Routledge, pp. 83–95.

Culpeper, J. (2001) *Language and Characterisation: People in Plays and Other Texts*. Harlow: Longman.

Culpeper, J. (2009) 'Keyness: words, parts-of-speech and semantic categories in the character-talk of Shakespeare's *Romeo and Juliet*'. *International Journal of Corpus Linguistics*, 14 (1): 29–59.

Culpeper, J. (2011) *Impoliteness*. Cambridge University Press.

Culpeper, J. and McIntyre, D. (2010) 'Activity types and characterisation in dramatic discourse', in J. Eder, F. Jannidis and R. Schneider (eds), *Characters in Fictional Worlds: Understanding Imaginary Beings in Literature, Film and Other Media*, Berlin: De Gruyter, pp. 176–207.

Culpeper, J., Hoover, D. and Louw, W. (2010) *Approaches to Corpus Stylistics: The Corpus, the Computer and the Study of Literature*. London: Routledge.

Cureton, R. (1980) 'Poetic syntax and aesthetic form', *Style* 14: 318–40.

Cureton, R. (2001) *Telling Time: Toward a Temporal Poetics*. Odense: University of Southern Denmark.

Curry, A. (2010) 'The "blind space" that lies beyond the frame: Anne Provoost's *Falling* (1997) and John Boyne's *The Boy in the Striped Pajamas* (2006)', *International Research in Children's Literature* 3 (1): 61–74.

Dahl, R. (1979) *My Uncle Oswald*. London: Michael Joseph.

Damasio, A. (1999) *The Feeling of What Happens: Body and Emotions in the Making of Consciousness*. New York: Harcourt Brace.

Damasio, A. (2003) *Looking for Spinoza: Joy, Sorrow, and the Feeling Brain*. New York: Houghton Mifflin Harcourt.

Dancygier, B. (2012) *The Language of Stories: A Cognitive Approach*. Cambridge University Press.

Dancygier, B. and Sweetser, E. (eds) (2012) *Viewpoint in Language: A Multimodal Perspective*. Cambridge University Press.

Dancygier, B. and Vandelanotte, L. (2009) 'Judging distances: mental spaces, distance, and viewpoint in literary discourse', in G. Brône and

J. Vandaele (eds) *Cognitive Poetics: Goals, Gains, and Gaps*, Berlin: Mouton de Gruyter, pp. 319–70.

Daniels, L. (2004) *Batman: The Complete History*. San Francisco: Chronicle Books.

Darling, J. (2003) 'Chemotherapy', in *Sudden Collapses in Public Places*, Todmorden: Arc Publications.

Das, S. (2005) *Touch and Intimacy in First World War Literature*. Cambridge University Press.

Davis, T.F. and Womack, K. (2001) (eds) *Mapping the Ethical Turn*. Charlottesville: University Press of Virginia.

Dawkins, R. (2006) *The Selfish Gene: 30th Anniversary Edition*. Oxford University Press.

Deggan, M. (2013) 'What is literary "atmosphere"? The role of fictive motion in understanding ambience in fiction', in M. Borkent, B. Dancygier and J. Hinnell (eds) *Language in the Creative Mind*, Stanford: CSLI.

Derrida, J. (1997) *Limited Inc.* [original 1977]. Evanston: Northwestern University Press.

Detroit Free Press (2012) 'Student-teacher nexus is still the key to achievement', *The Detroit Free Press*, 3 September.

Dickinson, E. (1990) *Selected Poems*. Mineola: Dover Publications.

van Dijk, T. (1988) *News as Discourse*. London: Lawrence Erlbaum Associates.

van Dijk, T. (2008) *Discourse Power*. Basingstoke: Palgrave Macmillan.

van Dijk, T.A. and Kintsch, W. (1983) *Strategies of Discourse Comprehension*. New York: Academic Press.

van Dine, S.S. (2012) 'Twenty rules for writing detective stories' [original 1928]. Available at: http://gaslight.mtroyal.ab.ca/vandine.htm

Donald, D. (1996) *The Age of Caricature: Satirical Prints in the Reign of George III*. New Haven: Yale University Press.

Dorst, A.G. (2011) *Metaphor in Fiction: Language, Thought, and Communication*. Oisterwijk: BOX Press.

Douthwaite, J. (2000) *Towards a Linguistic Theory of Foregrounding*. Turin: Edizioni dell'Orso.

Doyle, A.C. (1981) 'Silver blaze', in *The Penguin Complete Sherlock Holmes*, Harmondsworth: Penguin, pp. 335–50.

Drew, P. and Sorjonen, M. (1997) 'Institutional dialogue', in T. van Dijk (ed.) *Discourse as Social Interaction*, London: Sage, pp. 92–118.

Duchan, J.F., Bruder, G.A. and Hewitt, L.E. (1995) *Deixis in Narrative: A Cognitive Science Perspective*. Hillsdale: Lawrence Erlbaum.

Duffy, C.A. (2012) 'Stephen Lawrence', *The Guardian*, 6 January.

Durant, A. (2010) *Meaning in the Media: Discourse, Controversy and Debate*. Cambridge University Press.

Durant, A. and Lambrou, M. (2009) *Language and Media*. London: Routledge.

Duranti, A. and Goodwin, C. (1992) *Rethinking Context: Language as an Interactive Phenomenon*. Cambridge University Press.

Dziura, J. (2006) 'Non-sequitur advertising masquerading as analogous reasoning', available at: www.jenisfamous.com/2006/04/non-sequitur-advertising-masquerading.html

Eaglestone, R. (2007) 'Boyne's dangerous tale', *Jewish Chronicle*, March: 53.

Eagleton, T. (1983) *Literary Theory: An Introduction*. Oxford: Blackwell.

Eagleton, T. (2007) *How to Read a Poem*. Oxford: Blackwell.

Eder, J., Jannidis, F. and Schneider, R. (2010) 'Characters in fictional worlds: an introduction', in J. Eder, F. Jannidis and R. Schneider (eds) *Characters in Fictional Worlds: Understanding Imaginary Beings in Literature, Film and Other Media*, Berlin: De Gruyter, pp. 3–64.

Edwards, D. (1997) *Discourse and Cognition*. London: Sage.

Edwards, D. and Potter, J. (1992) *Discursive Psychology*. London: Sage.

Eggins, S. (2005) *An Introduction to Systemic Functional Linguistics* (2nd edn). London: Pinter.

Eggins, S. and Martin, J. R. (1997) 'Genres and registers of discourse', in T. van Dijk (ed.) *Discourse Studies: A Multidisciplinary Introduction*, London: Sage, pp. 230–56.

Eggins, S. and Slade, D. (1997) *Analysing Casual Conversation*. London: Cassell.

Eisenstein, E. (1979) *The Printing Press as an Agent of Social Change: Communications and Cultural Transformations in Early Modern Europe*. Cambridge University Press.

Eliot, T. S. (1922) 'The Waste Land', in *The Waste Land and Other Poems*, London: Faber and Faber, pp. 21–46.

Eliot, T. S. (1964) *The Use of Poetry and The Use of Criticism* [original 1933]. London: Faber and Faber.

Eliot, T. S. (1966) *Selected Essays*. London: Faber and Faber.

Elliott, F. and Hanning, J. (2012) *Cameron: Practically a Conservative*. London: Fourth Estate.

Ellis, B. E. (1991) *American Psycho*. London: Picador.

Ellis, R. D. (2005) *Curious Emotions: Experiencing and the Creation of Meaning*. Amsterdam: John Benjamins.

Emmott, C. (1997) *Narrative Comprehension: A Discourse Perspective*. Oxford: Clarendon Press.

Emmott, C. (2002) 'Responding to style: cohesion, foregrounding and thematic interpretation', in M. Louwerse and W. van Peer (eds) *Thematics: Interdisciplinary Studies*, Amsterdam: John Benjamins, pp. 91–117.

Emmott, C. and Alexander, M. (2010) 'Detective fiction, plot construction, and reader manipulation: rhetorical control and cognitive misdirection in Agatha Christie's *Sparkling Cyanide*', in D. McIntyre and B. Busse (eds) *Language and Style*, Basingstoke: Palgrave Macmillan, pp. 328–46.

Emmott, C., Sanford, A. J. and Morrow, L. I. (2006) 'Capturing the attention of readers? Stylistic and psychological perspectives on the use and effect of text fragmentation in narratives', *Journal of Literary Semantics* 35 (1): 1–30.

Emmott, C., Sanford, A. J. and Dawydiak, E. (2007) 'Stylistics meets cognitive science: studying style in fiction and readers' attention from an interdisciplinary perspective', *Style* 41 (2): 204–26.

Emmott, C., Sanford, A. J. and Alexander, M. (2010) 'Scenarios, characters' roles and plot status: readers' assumptions and writers' manipulations of assumptions in narrative texts', in J. Eder, F. Jannidis and R. Schneider (eds) *Characters in Fictional Worlds: Understanding Imaginary Beings in Literature, Film and Other Media*, Berlin: De Gruyter, pp. 377–99.

Emmott, C., Sanford, A. J. and Alexander, M. (2013) 'Rhetorical control of readers' attention: psychological and stylistic perspectives on foreground and background in narrative', in L. Bernaerts, D. de Geest, L. Herman and B. Vervaeck (eds) *Stories and Minds: Cognitive Approaches to Literary Narrative*, Lincoln: University of Nebraska Press, pp. 39–57.

Empson, W. (1930) *Seven Types of Ambiguity*. London: Chatto and Windus.

Empson, W. (1935) *The Structure of Complex Words*. London: Chatto and Windus.

Enkvist, N. E. (1987) 'Text strategies: single, dual, multiple', in R. Steele and T. Threadgold (eds) *Language Topics: Essays in Honour of Michael Halliday*, Vol. 2, Amsterdam: Benjamins, pp. 203–11.

Ensslin, A. and Bell, A. (2012) '"Click = Kill": textual *you* in ludic digital fiction', *StoryWorlds* 4: 49–73.

Eskin, M. (2004) 'On literature and ethics', *Poetics Today* 24 (4): 573–94.

Evans, V. (2006) 'Lexical concepts, cognitive models and meaning-construction', *Cognitive Linguistics* 17 (4): 491–534.

Evans, V. (2009) *How Words Mean: Lexical Concepts, Cognitive Models, and Meaning Construction*. Oxford University Press.

Evans, V. and Green, M. (2006) *Cognitive Linguistics: An Introduction*. London: Routledge.

Evert, S. (2008) 'Corpora and collocations', in A. Lüdeling and M. Kytö (eds) *Corpus Linguistics: An International Handbook*, Berlin: Mouton de Gruyter, pp. 803–21.

Eysteinsson, Á. (1990) *The Concept of Modernism*. Ithaca: Cornell University Press.

Fabb, N., Halle, M. and Piera, C. (2008) *Meter in Poetry: A New Theory*. Cambridge University Press.

Fahnestock, J. (2005) 'Rhetorical stylistics', *Language and Literature* 14 (3): 215–30.

Fahnestock, J. (2011) *Rhetorical Style: The Uses of Language in Persuasion*. Oxford University Press.

Fairclough, N. (1995a) *Media Discourse*. London: Arnold.

Fairclough, N. (1995b) *Critical Discourse Analysis: The Critical Study of Language*. London: Longman.

Fairclough, N. (2003) *Analysing Discourse: Textual Analysis for Social Research*. London: Routledge.

Fauconnier, G. and Turner, M. (2002) *The Way We Think: Conceptual Blending and The Mind's Hidden Complexities*. New York: Basic Books.

Faulks, S. (1994) *Birdsong*. London: Vintage Books.

Ferrari, G. R. F. (1997) 'Plato and poetry', in G. A. Kennedy (ed.) *The Cambridge History of Literary Criticism, Vol. 1: Classical Criticism*, Cambridge University Press, pp. 92–148.

Fillmore, C. (1982) 'Frame semantics', in Linguistic Society of Korea (ed.) *Linguistics in the Morning Calm*, Seoul: Hanshin, pp. 111–37.

Fillmore, C. (1985) 'Frames and the semantics of understanding', *Quaderni de Semantica* 6 (2): 222–54.

Fillmore, C. J. (2006) 'Frame semantics', in D. Geererts (ed.) *Cognitive Linguistics: Basic Readings*, Berlin: Mouton de Gruyter, pp. 373–400.

Firth, J. R. (1957) *Papers in Linguistics 1934–1951*. Oxford University Press.

Fischer, A. (1999) 'Graphological iconicity in print advertising', in M. Nänny and O. Fischer (eds) *Form Miming Meaning: Iconicity in Language and Literature 2*, Amsterdam: John Benjamins, pp. 251–83.

Fischer, A. H. and Manstead, A. S. R. (2000) 'Gender differences in emotion across cultures', in A. H. Fischer (ed.) *Emotion and Gender: Social Psychological Perspectives*, Cambridge University Press, pp. 91–7.

Fischer, O. and Nänny, M. (eds) (2001) *The Motivated Form: Iconicity in Language and Literature 2*. Amsterdam: John Benjamins.

Fischer-Starcke, B. (2010) *Corpus Linguistics in Literary Analysis: Jane Austen and her Contemporaries*. London: Continuum.

Fish, S. (1973) 'What is stylistics and why are they saying such terrible things about it?' in S. Chatman (ed.) *Approaches to Poetics*, New York: Columbia University Press, pp. 109–52.

Fish, S. (1980) *Is There a Text in This Class?* Cambridge, MA: Harvard University Press.

Fitzgerald, F. S. (1920) *This Side of Paradise*. New York: Scribner.

Fitzgerald, F. S. (1925) *The Great Gatsby*. New York: Scribner.

Fitzgerald, F. S. (1986) *Tender is the Night* [original 1934]. London: Penguin.

Fitzmaurice, S. M. and Taavitsainen, I. (eds) (2007) *Methods in Historical Pragmatics*. New York: Mouton de Gruyter.

Fludernik, M. (1993) *The Fictions of Language and the Languages of Fiction: The Linguistic Representation of Consciousness*. London: Routledge.

Fludernik, M. (1995) 'Pronouns of address and "odd" third person forms: the mechanics of involvement in fiction', in K. Green (ed.) *New Essays in Deixis: Discourse, Narrative, Literature*, Amsterdam: Rodopi, pp. 99–129.

Flynn, G. (2006) *Sharp Objects*. London: Phoenix.

Forceville, C. (1996) *Pictorial Metaphor in Advertising*. London: Routledge.

Forster, E. M. (1976) *Where Angels Fear to Tread* [original 1905]. Harmondsworth: Penguin.

Fortenbaugh, W. W. (2007) 'Aristotle's *Art of Rhetoric*', in I. Worthington (ed.) *A Companion to Greek Rhetoric*, Oxford: Blackwell, pp. 107–23.

Foucault, M. (1984) 'What is an author?', in P. Rabinow (ed.) *The Foucault Reader* [original 1969], New York: Pantheon Books, pp. 101–20.

Fowler, A. (1982) *Kinds of Literature: An Introduction to the Theory of Genres and Modes*. Oxford: Clarendon Press.

Fowler, R. (1971) *The Languages of Literature*. London: Barnes and Noble.

Fowler, R. (1977) *Linguistics and the Novel*. London: Methuen.

Fowler, R. (1981) *Linguistic Criticism*. Oxford University Press.

Fowler, R. (1991) *Language in the News: Discourse and Ideology in the British Press*. London: Routledge.

Fowles, J. (1977) *Daniel Martin*. London: Jonathan Cape.

Francis, G., Hunston, S. and Manning, E. (1996) *Grammar Patterns 1: Verbs*. London: HarperCollins.

Francis, G., Hunston, S. and Manning, E. (1998) *Grammar Patterns 2: Nouns and Adjectives*. London: HarperCollins.

Freeman, D. C. (1993) '"According to my bond": *King Lear* and re-cognition', *Language and Literature* 2 (1): 1–18.

Freeman, D. C. (1995) '"Catch[ing] the nearest way": *Macbeth* and cognitive metaphor', *Journal of Pragmatics* 24: 689–708.

Freeman, D. C. (1999) '"The rack dislimns": schema and rhetorical pattern in *Antony and Cleopatra*', *Poetics Today* 20: 443–60.

Freeman, L. A. (2002) *Character's Theater: Genre and Identity on the Eighteenth-Century English Stage*. Philadelphia: University of Pennsylvania Press.

Frye, N. (1957) *Anatomy of Criticism: Four Essays*. Princeton University Press.

Frye, N., Baker, S. and Perkins, G. (1985) *The Harper Handbook to Literature*. New York: Harper and Row.

Furlong, A. (1996) *Relevance Theory and Literary Interpretation*. Unpublished Ph.D. thesis, University College London.

Gallagher, S. (2005) *How the Body Shapes the Mind*. New York: Oxford University Press.

Galtang, J. and Ruge, M. (1973) 'Structuring and selecting news', in S. Cohn and J. Young (eds) *The Manufacture of News: Social Problems, Deviance, and the Class Media*, London: Constable, pp. 62–7.

Garvin, P. L. (ed.) (1964) *A Prague School Reader on Esthetics, Literary Structure and Style*. Washington: Georgetown University Press.

Gavins, J. (2007) *Text-World Theory: An Introduction*. Edinburgh University Press.

Gavins, J. (2013) *Reading the Absurd*. Edinburgh University Press.

Gavins, J. and Steen, G. (eds) (2003) *Cognitive Poetics in Practice*. London: Routledge.

Geertz, C. (1983) *Local Knowledge: Further Essays in Interpretive Anthropology*. New York: Basic Books.

Geis, M. (1982) *The Language of Television Advertising*. New York: Academic Press.

Gelb, I. (1952) *A Study of Writing*. University of Chicago Press.

Genette, G. (1979) *The Architext: An Introduction* (trans. J. E. Lewin). Berkeley: University of California Press.

Genette, G. (1980) *Narrative Discourse: An Essay in Method* (trans. J. E. Lewin). Ithaca: Cornell University Press.

Gerard, S. (2012) 'Nike continues branding dominance with #makeitcount and @Nikefuel', available at: www.linkbuildr.com/nike-continues-brand ing-dominance-with-makeitcount-and-nikefuel

Gerrig, R. J. (1993) *Experiencing Narrative Worlds: On the Psychological Activities of Reading*. New Haven: Westview Press.

Gibbons, A. (2012a) *Multimodality, Cognition, and Experimental Literature*. London: Routledge.

Gibbons, A. (2012b) '"You've never experienced a novel like this": time and interaction when reading TOC', *Electronic Book Review*, available at: www. electronicbookreview.com/thread/fictionspresent/linear

Gibbs, R. W. (1992) 'What do idioms really mean?' *Journal of Memory and Language* 31 (4): 485–506.

Gibbs, R. W. (2003) 'Embodied experience and linguistic meaning', *Brain and Language* 84 (1): 1–15.

Gibbs, R. W. (2005) *Embodiment and Cognitive Science*. Cambridge University Press.

Gibbs, R. W. (ed.) (2008) *The Cambridge Handbook of Metaphor and Thought*. New York: Cambridge University Press.

Gibbs, R. W. (2011) 'Are deliberate metaphors really deliberate? A question of human consciousness and action', *Metaphor and the Social World* 1: 26–52.

Gibbs, R. W. and Matlock, T. (1999) 'Psycholinguistics and mental repre- sentations', *Cognitive Linguistics* 10 (3): 263–70.

Giddens, A. (1984) *The Constitution of Society: Outline of the Theory of Structuration*. Cambridge: Polity Press.

Gifford, D. with Seidman, R. (1988) *Ulysses Annotated: Notes for James Joyce's Ulysses* (2nd edn). Berkeley: University of California Press.

Gilbert R. (2010) 'Grasping the unimaginable: recent holocaust novels for children by Morris Gleitzman and John Boyne', *Children's Literature in Education* 41: 355–66.

Giovanelli, M. (2013) *Text World Theory and Keats' Poetry*. London: Bloomsbury.

Givón, T. (1987) 'Beyond foreground and background', in R. S. Tomlin (ed.) *Coherence and Grounding in Discourse*, Amsterdam: John Benjamins, pp. 175–88.

Givón, T. (1993) *English Grammar: A Function-Based Approach*. Philadelphia: John Benjamins.

Glasser, R. A. (1998) 'A plea for phraseo-stylistics', in T. Kakietek (ed.) *Topics in Phraseology*, Vol. 1, Katowice: Wydawnictwo Uniwersytetu Śląskigro, pp. 22–31.

Glenberg, A. (1999) 'Why mental models must be embodied', in G. Rickheit and C. Habel (eds) *Mental Models in Discourse Processing and Reasoning*, Amsterdam: Elsevier, pp. 77–90.

Glenberg, A. and Robertson, D. (2000) 'Symbol grounding and meaning: a comparison of high-dimensional and embodied theories of meaning', *Journal of Memory and Language* 43 (3): 379–401.

Glock, H.-J. (2005) *A Wittgenstein Dictionary*. Oxford: Blackwell.

Goddard, A. (2002) *The Language of Advertising*. London: Routledge.

Goffman, E. (1981) *Forms of Talk*. Oxford: Blackwell.

Goffman, E. (1983) 'The interaction order: American Sociological Association, 1982 presidential address', *American Sociological Review* 48 (1): 1–17.

Goh, R. (2001) 'Iconicity in advertising signs: motive and method in miming "the Body"', in O. Fischer and M. Nänny (eds), *The Motivated Sign: Iconicity in Language and Literature 2*, Amsterdam: John Benjamins, pp. 189–210.

Golding, W. (1958) *The Lord of the Flies*. London: Faber and Faber.

Goodreads (2012) *Goodreads homepage*, available at: www.goodreads.com.

Goody, J. (1987) *The Interface between the Written and the Oral*. Cambridge University Press.

Gottschall, J. (2008a) 'Measure for measure', *The Boston Globe*, 11 May.

Gottschall, J. (2008b) *Literature, Science and a New Humanities*. New York: Palgrave Macmillan.

Gray, B. (1973) 'Stylistics: the end of a tradition', *Journal of Aesthetics and Art Criticism* 31 (4): 501–12.

Greaves, C. (2009) *ConcGram 1.0.* (software). Amsterdam: Benjamins.

Green, K. (1992) 'Deixis and the poetic persona', *Language and Literature* 1 (2): 121–34.

Green, K. (1995) (ed.) *New Essays in Deixis: Discourse, Narrative, Literature*. Amsterdam: Rodopi.

Green, M. C. (2004) 'Transportation into narrative worlds: the role of prior knowledge and perceived realism', *Discourse Processes* 38 (2): 247–66.

Green, M. C. and Brock, T. C. (2000) 'The role of transportation in the persuasiveness of public narratives', *Journal of Personality and Social Psychology* 79: 701–21.

Green, M. C., Brock, T. C. and Kaufman, G. F. (2004) 'Understanding media enjoyment: the role of transportation into narrative worlds', *Communication Theory* 14 (4): 311–27.

Greene, G. (1973) 'The innocent', in *Collected Stories* [original 1937], New York: Viking, pp. 451–6.

Gregoriou, C. (2007) *Deviance in Contemporary Crime Fiction*. Basingstoke: Palgrave.

Gregoriou, C. (2009) *English Literary Stylistics*. London: Palgrave Macmillan.

Gregoriou, C. (2011a) *Language, Ideology and Identity in Serial Killer Narratives*. London: Routledge.

Gregoriou, C. (2011b) 'Poetics of deviance in *The Curious Incident*', in M. Effron (ed.) *The Millennial Detective: Essays on Trends in Crime Fiction, Film and Television, 1990-2010*, Jefferson: McFarland, pp. 97–111.

Gregory, M. (1998) "Ethical criticism: what it is and why it matters", *Style* 32 (2): 194–220.

Grice, H. P. (1975) 'Logic and conversation', in P. Cole and J. L. Morgan (eds) *Syntax and Semantics*, Vol. 3: *Speech Acts*. New York: Academic Press, pp. 41–58.

Grice, H. P. (1989) *Studies in the Way of Words*. Cambridge, MA: Harvard University Press.

Gries, S. (2008) 'Dispersions and adjusted frequencies in corpora', *International Journal of Corpus Linguistics* 13 (4): 403–37.

Griffin, G. (2009) 'Science and the cultural imaginary: the case of Kazuo Ishiguro's *Never Let Me Go*', *Textual Practice* 23 (4): 645–63.

Griffin, J. (1964) *Wittgenstein's Logical Atomism*. Oxford University Press.

Griffiths, P. E. (1997) *What Emotions Really Are: The Problem of Psychological Categories*. University of Chicago Press.

Grisakova, M. and Ryan, M.-L. (2010) *Intermediality and Storytelling*. Berlin: Walter de Gruyter.

Grosser, W. (1995) 'Style in advertising', in W. Grosser, J. Hogg and K. Hubmayer (eds) *Style: Literary and Non-Literary*, Salzburg: Edwin Mellen Press, pp. 265–85.

Guéraud, S., Tapiero, I. and O'Brien, E. J. (2008) 'Context and the activation of predictive inferences', *Psychonomic Bulletin and Review* 15: 351–6.

Haiman, J. (1980) 'The iconicity of grammar: isomorphism and motivation', *Language* 56: 515–40.

Haiman, J. (1985) *Natural Syntax: Iconicity and Erosion*. Cambridge University Press.

Haining, P. (1990) *Agatha Christie: Murder in Four Acts*. London: Virgin Books.

Hall, G. (2005) *Literature in Language Education*. London: Palgrave.

Hall, G. (2008) 'A grammarian's funeral: on Browning, post-structuralism, and the state of stylistics', in G. Watson (ed.) *The State of Stylistics*, Amsterdam: Benjamins, pp. 31–44.

Hall, G. (2010) 'Stylistics, linguistics and literature: short afterword', in D. McIntyre and B. Busse (eds) *Language and Style*, Basingstoke: Palgrave Macmillan, pp. 501–7.

Halliday, M. A. K. (1964) 'Descriptive linguistics in literary studies', in M. A. K. Halliday and A. McIntosh (eds) *Patterns of Language: Papers in General, Descriptive and Applied Linguistics*, London: Longman, pp. 56–69.

Halliday, M. A. K. (1971) 'Linguistic function and literary style: an inquiry into the language of William Golding's *The Inheritors*', in S. Chatman (ed.) *Literary Style: A Symposium*, New York University Press, pp. 330–68.

Halliday, M. A. K. (1976) 'Antilanguages', *American Anthropologist* 78 (3): 570–84.

Halliday, M. A. K. (1978) *Language as Social Semiotic*. London: Edward Arnold.

Halliday, M. A. K. (1985) *An Introduction to Functional Grammar* (2nd edn). London: Hodder Arnold.

Halliday, M. A. K. (1994) *An Introduction to Functional Grammar* (3rd edn). London: Arnold.

Halliday, M. A. K. and Hasan, R. (1976) *Cohesion in English*. London: Longman.

Halliday, M. A. K. and Hasan, R. (1989) *Language, Context, and Context: Aspects of Language in a Social-Semiotic Perspective*. Oxford University Press.

Halliday, M. A. K. and Matthiessen, C. (2004) *An Introduction to Functional Grammar*. London: Hodder.

Halliwell, S. (1986) *Aristotle's Poetics*. London: Duckworth.

Hamilton, C. (2008) 'Rhetoric and stylistics in Anglo-Saxon countries in the 20th and 21st centuries', in U. Fix, A. Gardt and J. Knape (eds) *Rhetoric and Stylistics: An International Handbook*, Vol. 1, Berlin: Mouton de Gruyter, pp. 245–63.

Hammersley, M. (2003) 'Conversation analysis and discourse analysis: methods or paradigms?', *Discourse and Society* 14 (6): 751–81.

Hanauer, D. (1998) 'Reading poetry: an empirical investigation of formalist, stylistic, and conventionalist claims', *Poetics Today* 19 (4): 565–80.

Hanauer, D. (2001) 'The task of poetry reading and second language learning', *Applied Linguistics* 22 (3): 295–323.

Hanks, P. (1988) 'Typicality and meaning potentials', in M. Snell-Hornby (ed.) *ZüriLEX '86 Proceedings*, Tübingen: Francke.

Harding, D. W. (1998) [1940] 'Character and caricature in Jane Austen', in M. Lawlor (ed.) *Regulated Hatred and Other Essays on Jane Austen*, London: Athlone Press, pp. 80–105.

Hardy, D. (2003) *Narrating Knowledge in Flannery O'Connor's Fiction*. Columbia: University of South Carolina Press.

Hardy, D. (2005) 'Towards a typology of narrative gaps: knowledge gapping in Flannery O'Connor's fiction', *Language and Literature* 14 (4): 363–75.

Hariman, R. (1995) *Political Style: The Artistry of Power*. University of Chicago Press.

Harpin, A. (2011) 'Land of hope and glory: Jez Butterworth's tragic landscapes', *Studies in Theatre and Performance*, 31 (1): 61–73.

Harris, R. (1981) *The Language Myth*. London: Duckworth.

Harris, R. (1987) *The Language Machine*. London: Duckworth.

Harrison, M. J. (2005) 'Clone alone', *The Guardian*, 26 February, available at: www.guardian.co.uk/books/2005/feb/26/bookerprize2005.bookerprize

Hartley, J. (2001) *Reading Groups*. Oxford University Press.

Hasan, R. (1978) 'Text in the systemic-functional model', in W. U. Dressler (ed.) *Current Trends in Textlinguistics*, Berlin: Walter de Gruyter, pp. 228–46.

Hasan, R. (1989) *Linguistics, Language and Verbal Art*. Oxford University Press.

Haskel, P. I. (1971) 'Collocations as a measure of stylistic variety', in R. A. Wisbey (ed.) *The Computer in Literary and Linguistic Research*, Cambridge University Press, pp. 159–68.

Hatherley, O. (2010) *A Guide to the New Ruins of Great Britain*. New York: Verso.

ten Have, P. (1991) 'Talk and institution: a reconsideration of the "asymmetry" of doctor-patient interaction', in D. Boden and D. H. Zimmerman (eds) *Talk and Social Structure: Studies in Ethnomethodology and Conversation Analysis*, Cambridge: Polity Press, pp. 138–63.

ten Have, P. (1999) *Doing Conversation Analysis: A Practical Guide*. London: Sage.

Havránek, B. (1964) 'The functional differentiation of the standard language', in P. L. Garvin (ed.) *A Prague School Reader on Esthetics, Literary*

Structure and Style [original 1932], Washington: Georgetown University Press, pp. 3–16.

Hayakawa, S. (1939) *Language in Thought and Action*. New York: Harvest Books.

Heaney, S. (1990) *New Selected Poems 1966–1987*. London: Faber.

Hemingway, E. (1995) *A Farewell to Arms* [original 1929]. New York: Charles Scribner.

Heritage, J. (1984) 'A change-of-state token and aspects of its sequential placement', in M. Atkinson and J. Heritage (eds) *Structures of Social Action: Studies in Conversation Analysis*, Cambridge University Press, pp. 299–345.

Heritage, J. (2005) 'Cognition in discourse', in H. te Molder and J. Potter (eds) *Conversation and Cognition*, Cambridge University Press, pp. 184–202.

Heritage, J. and Raymond, G. (2005) 'The terms of agreement: indexing epistemic authority and subordination in talk-in-interaction', *Social Psychology Quarterly* 68 (1): 15–38.

Herman, D. (1994) 'Textual "you" and double deixis in Edna O'Brien's *A Pagan Place*', *Style* 28 (3): 378–410.

Herman, D. (1999) *Narratologies*. Columbus: Ohio State University Press.

Herman, D. (2002) *Story Logic: Problems and Possibilities of Narrative*. Lincoln: University of Nebraska Press.

Herman, D. (2004) 'Steps toward a transmedial narratology', in M.-L. Ryan (ed.) *Narrative Across Media: The Languages of Storytelling*, Lincoln: University of Nebraska Press, pp. 47–75.

Herman, D. (2008) 'Narrative theory and the intentional stance', *Partial Answers: Journal of Literature and the History of Ideas* 6 (2): 233–60.

Herman, D., Jahn, M. and Ryan, M. L. (eds) (2005) *Routledge Encyclopedia of Narrative Theory*. London: Routledge.

Herman, L. and Vervaeck, B. (2005) *Handbook of Narrative Analysis*. Lincoln: University of Nebraska Press.

Herman, M. (dir.) (2008) *The Boy in the Striped Pajamas*, screenplay: M. Herman.

Herman, V. (1995) *Dramatic Discourse: Dialogue as Interaction in Plays*. London: Routledge.

Herrick, J. (2001) *The History and Theory of Rhetoric* (2nd edn). Boston: Allan and Bacon.

Herrmann, J. B. (2013) *Metaphor in Academic Discourse: Linguistic Forms, Conceptual Structures, Communicative Functions and Cognitive Representations*. Amsterdam: VU Press.

Hidalgo Downing, L. (2000a) *Negation, Text Worlds and Discourse: The Pragmatics of Fiction*. Stamford: Ablex.

Hidalgo Downing, L. (2000b) 'Text world creation in advertising discourse', *Revista alicantina de estudios ingleses* 13: 67–88.

Hirsch, E. D. (1967) *Validity in Interpretation*. New Haven: Yale University Press.

Hirsch, E. D. (1976) 'Objective interpretation', in D. N. de Molina (ed.) *On Literary Intention*, Edinburgh University Press, pp. 26–54.

Hirsch, E. D. (1992) 'In defence of the author', in G. Iseminger (ed.) *Intention and Interpretation*, Philadelphia: Temple University Press, pp. 11–23.

Hodge, R. and Kress, G. (1988) *Social Semiotics*. Cambridge: Polity Press.

Hoey, M. (2001) *Textual Interaction: An Introduction to Written Discourse*. London: Routledge.

Hoey, M. (2005) *Lexical Priming: A New Theory of Words and Language*. London: Routledge.

Hoey, M. (2013) 'Lexical priming', in C. A. Chapelle (ed.) *The Encyclopedia of Applied Linguistics*, Oxford: Blackwell.

Hoffmann, S., Evert, S., Smith, N., Lee, D. and Berglund-Prytz, Y. (2008) *Corpus Linguistics with BNCweb: A Practical Guide*. Frankfurt: Lang.

Hogan, P. C. (1995) *Joyce, Milton, and the Theory of Influence*. Gainesville: University Press of Florida.

Hogan, P. C. (2003) *The Mind and its Stories: Narrative Universals and Human Emotion*. Cambridge University Press.

Hogan, P. C. (2011a) *Affective Narratology: The Emotional Structure of Stories*. Lincoln: University of Nebraska Press.

Hogan, P. C. (2011b) 'Characters and their plots', in J. Eder, F. Jannidis and R. Schneider (eds) *Characters in Fictional Worlds: Understanding Imaginary Beings in Literature, Film and Other Media*, Berlin: De Gruyter, pp. 134–54.

Hogan, P. C. (2013) *How Authors' Minds Make Stories*. New York: Cambridge University Press.

Honeck, R. P. and Hoffman, R. R. (eds) (1980) *Cognition and Figurative Language*. Hillsdale: Lawrence Erlbaum.

Hoover, D. L. (1990) *Language and Style in 'The Inheritors'*. Lanham: University Press of America.

Hoover, D. L. (2008) 'Quantitative analysis and literary studies', in S. Schreibman and R. Siemens (eds) *A Companion to Digital Literary Studies*. Oxford: Blackwell, available at: www.digitalhumanities.org/companionDLS

Hopkins, G. M. (1918) *Poems*. London: Humphrey Milford.

Hopper, P. J. and Thompson, S. A. (1980) 'Transitivity in grammar and discourse', *Language* 56: 251–99.

Horn, L. R. (1984) 'Towards a new taxonomy for pragmatic inference: Q- and R-based implicature', in D. Schiffrin (ed.) *Meaning, Form, and Use in Context*, Washington: Georgetown University Press, pp. 11–42.

Horn, L. R. (1988) 'Pragmatic theory', in F. Newmeyer (ed.) *Linguistics: The Cambridge Survey*, Vol. 1: *Linguistic Theory: Foundations*, Cambridge University Press, pp. 113–45.

Horn, L. R. (1989) *A Natural History of Negation*. University of Chicago Press.

Horn, L. R. (2004) 'Implicature', in L. R. Horn and G. Ward (eds) *The Handbook of Pragmatics*, Oxford: Blackwell, pp. 3–28.

Hunston, S. (2002) *Corpora in Applied Linguistics*. Cambridge University Press.

Hunston, S. and Francis, G. (2000) *Pattern Grammar: A Corpus-Driven Approach to the Lexical Grammar of English*. Amsterdam: John Benjamins.

Hunston, S. and Sinclair, J. (2000) 'A local grammar of evaluation', in S. Hunston and G. Thompson (eds) *Evaluation in Text: Authorial Stance and the Construction of Discourse*, Oxford University Press, pp. 74–101.

Hunt, R. and Vipond, D. (1985) 'Crash-testing a transactional model of literary reading', *Reader: Essays in Reader-Oriented Theory, Criticism, and Pedagogy* 14: 23–39.

Hutchby, I. (1996) *Confrontation Talk: Arguments, Asymmetries and Power on Talk Radio*. Mahwah: Lawrence Erlbaum.

Hutchby, I. and Wooffitt, R. (2008) *Conversation Analysis*. Cambridge: Polity Press.

Hutcheon, L. (2006) *A Theory of Adaptation*. London: Routledge.

Ingarden, R. (1973) *The Cognition of the Literary Work of Art* (trans. G. G. Grabowicz). Evanston: Northwestern University Press.

Irvine, J. (2001) '"Style" as distinctiveness: the culture and ideology of linguistic differentiation,' in P. Eckert and J. R. Rickford (eds) *Style and Sociolinguistic Variation*, Cambridge University Press, pp. 21–43.

Iser, W. (1978) *The Act of Reading: A Theory of Aesthetic Response*. London: Routledge and Kegan Paul.

Iser, W. (1993) *The Fictive and The Imaginary: Charting Literary Anthropology*. Baltimore: The Johns Hopkins University Press.

Ishiguro, K. (2005) *Never Let Me Go*. London: Faber and Faber.

Jackson, P. (dir.) (2009) *The Lovely Bones*, screenplay: F. Walsh, P. Boyen and P. Jackson.

Jakobson, R. (1960) 'Closing statement: linguistics and poetics', in T. A. Sebeok (ed.) *Style and Language*, Cambridge, MA: MIT Press, pp. 350–77.

Jakobson, R. (1966) 'Grammatic parallelism and its Russian facet', *Language* 42: 399–429.

Jakobson, R. (1968) 'Poetry of grammar and grammar of poetry', *Lingua* 21: 597–609.

Jakobson, R. and Jones, L. (1970) *Shakespeare's Verbal Art in 'Th' Expense of Spirit'*. The Hague: Mouton.

Jakobson, R. and Lévi-Strauss, C. (1962) '"Les Chats" de Charles Baudelaire', *L'Homme: revue française d'anthropologie* 2: 5–21 [trans. K. Furness-Lane, reprinted in M. Lane (ed.) (1970) *Structuralism: A Reader*, London: Jonathan Cape, pp. 202–21].

James, H. (1994) *The Turn of the Screw* [original 1898]. Harmondsworth: Penguin.

James, H. (2003) *The Portrait of a Lady* [original 1881]. Harmondsworth: Penguin.

James, H. (2007) *The Europeans* [original 1878]. Harmondsworth: Penguin.

Jauss, H. R. (1970) *Literaturgeschichte als Provokation*. Frankfurt: Suhrkamp.

Jaworski, A. and Thurlow, C. (eds) (2010) *Semiotic Landscapes: Language, Image, Space*. London: Continuum.

Jeffries, L. (1993) *The Language of Twentieth Century Poetry*. Basingstoke: Palgrave Macmillan.

Jeffries, L. (2001) 'Schema affirmation and *White Asparagus*: cultural multilingualism among readers of texts', *Language and Literature* 10 (4): 325–43.

Jeffries, L. (2010a) *Opposition in Discourse*. London: Continuum.

Jeffries, L. (2010b) *Critical Stylistics*. Basingstoke: Palgrave.

Jeffries, L. and McIntyre, D. (2010) *Stylistics*. Cambridge University Press.

Jerng, M. (2008) 'Giving form to life: cloning and narrative expectations of the human', *Partial Answers: Journal of Literature and the History of Ideas*, 6 (2): 369–91.

Ji, M. (2009) 'Corpus stylistics in translation studies: two modern Chinese translations of *Don Quixote*', *Language and Literature* 18 (1): 61–74.

Jobert, M. (2003) *Le Texte et la voix: étude des traits paralinguistiques vocaux dans les romans d'Edith Wharton*. Lille: ANRT.

Joel, M. (2011) 'Twitter is random', available at: www.twistimage.com/blog/ archives/twitter-is-random

Johansen, J. D. (1993) *Dialogic Semiosis: An Essay on Signs and Meaning*. Bloomington and Indianapolis: Indiana University Press.

Johansen, J. D. (1996) 'Iconicity in literature', *Semiotica* 110: 37–55.

Johnstone, B. (2009) 'Pittsburghese shirts: commodification and the enregisterment of an urban dialect', *American Speech* 84 (2): 157–75.

Joly, A. and O'Kelly, D. (1989) *L'Analyse linguistique des textes anglais*. Paris: Nathan.

Jones, G. (1999) *Strange Talk: The Politics of Dialect Literature in Gilded Age America*. Berkeley: University of California Press.

Jones, R. H. and Hafner, C. A. (2012) *Understanding Digital Literacies: A Practical Introduction*. London: Routledge.

Jones, R., Bhatia, V. K., Bhatia, A. and Vyas-Ngarkar, R. (2011) 'Nutritional labeling as social interaction', Paper presented at the 12th International Pragmatics Conference, Manchester, UK.

Jost, W. and Olmstead, W. (eds) (2004) *A Companion to Rhetoric and Rhetorical Criticism*. Oxford: Blackwell.

Joyce, J. (1986) *Ulysses* (ed. H. W. Gabler with W. Steppe and C. Melchior). New York: Vintage Books.

Joyce, J. (2006) *Dubliners* [original 1914]. London: W. W. Norton.

Joyce, J. (2008) *The Dead* (ed. T. Fasano) [original 1914]. Claremont: Coyote Canyon Press.

Jucker, A. H. and Taavitsainen, I. (2013) *English Historical Pragmatics*. Edinburgh University Press.

July, M. (2007) 'The swim team', in *No One Belongs Here More than You*, New York: Scribner, pp. 13–18.

Kaal, A. A. (2012) *Metaphor in Conversation*. Oisterwijk: BOX Press.

Kālidāsa (1969) *The Abhijñānaśākuntalam of Kālidāsa* (ed. M. R. Kale, 10th edn). Delhi: Motilal Banarsidass.

Keats, J. (1973) *The Complete Poems* (ed. J. Barnard). Harmondsworth: Penguin.

Keay, D. (1987) 'Interview with Margaret Thatcher 23 Sep 1987', *Woman's Own* 31 October: 8–10.

Keefe, D. E. and McDaniel, M. A. (1993) 'The time course and durability of predictive inferences', *Journal of Memory and Language* 32 (4): 446–63.

Keen, S. (2007) *Empathy and the Novel*. Oxford University Press.

Kelley, T. M. (1987) 'Poetics and the politics of reception: Keats's "La Belle Dame Sans Merci"', *ELH* 54 (2): 333–62.

Kelman, J. (1998) *How Late it Was, How Late* [original 1994]. London: Vintage Books.

Kennedy, C. (1982) 'Systemic grammar and its use in literary analysis', in R. Carter (ed.) *Language and Literature*, London: Unwin Hyman, pp. 83–100.

Kennedy, G. (1998) *An Introduction to Corpus Linguistics*. London: Longman.

Kennedy, G. (ed.) (1997) *The Cambridge History of Literary Criticism*, Vol. 1: *Classical Criticism*. Cambridge University Press.

Kenny, A. (1992) *Computers and the Humanities*. London: British Library.

Kermode, F. (2005) 'Outrageous game', *London Review of Books* 27 (8): 21–2.

Kerouac, J. (1957) *On the Road*. New York: Viking Press.

Kerouac, J. (1980) *Visions of Cody* [original 1960]. London: Granada Books.

Kerr, S. (2005) '*Never Let Me Go*: when they were orphans', *The New York Times*, 17 April.

Kintsch, W. and Keenan, J. (1973) 'Reading rate and retention as a function of the number of propositions in the base structure of sentences', *Cognitive Psychology* 5: 257–74.

Kiparsky, P. (1987) 'On theory and interpretation', in N. Fabb, D. Attridge, A. Durant and C. MacCabe (eds) *The Linguistics of Writing: Arguments between Language and Literature*, Manchester University Press, pp. 185–98.

Kirkham, S. (2011) 'Personal style and epistemic stance in classroom discussion', *Language and Literature* 20 (3): 201–17.

Klingberg, T. (2009) *The Overflowing Brain: Information Overload and the Limits of Working Memory*. Oxford University Press.

Knights, L. C. (1946) *Explorations: Essays in Criticism Mainly on the Literature of the Seventeenth Century*. London: Chatto and Windus.

Kövecses, Z. (2000) *Metaphor and Emotion: Language, Culture, and Body in Human Feeling*. Cambridge University Press.

Kövecses, Z. (2010) *Metaphor: A Practical Introduction* (2nd edn). New York: Oxford University Press.

Kramsch, C. (1993) *Context and Culture in Language Teaching*. Oxford University Press.

Kramsch, C. (2000) 'Social discursive constructions of self in L2 learning', in J. P. Lantolf (ed.) *Sociocultural Theory and Second Language Learning*, Oxford University Press, pp. 133–54.

Kramsch, C. and Kramsch, O. (2000) 'The avatars of literature in language study', *Modern Language Journal* 84: 533–73.

Krennmayr, T. (2011) *Metaphor in Newspapers*. Utrecht: LOT dissertation series, 276.

Kress, G. (ed.) (1976) *Halliday: System and Function in Language: Selected Papers.* Oxford University Press.

Kress, G. (1985) *Linguistic Processes in Sociocultural Practice.* Oxford University Press.

Kress, G. and van Leeuwen, T. (1996) *Reading Images: The Grammar of Visual design.* London: Routledge.

Kress, G. and van Leeuwen, T. (2001) *Multimodal Discourse: The Modes and Media of Contemporary Communication.* London: Arnold.

Kristeva, J. (1980) *Desire in Language: A Semiotic Approach to Literature and Art* (ed. L. S. Roudiez, trans. T. Gora, A. Jardine and L. S. Roudiez). New York: Columbia University Press.

Kristeva, J. (1981) 'Word, dialogue and novel', in *A Semiotic Approach to Literature and Art*, Oxford: Blackwell, pp. 64–91.

Krog, A. (2006) *Verweerskrif [Body Bereft].* Roggebaai: Umuzi.

Kuiken, D., Miall, D. S. and Sikora, S. (2004) 'Forms of self-implication in literary reading', *Poetics Today* 25 (2): 171–203.

Kytö, M. (2011) 'Corpora and historical linguistics', *Revista Brasileira de Linguística Aplicada*, 11 (2): np.

L'Etang, J. (2004) *Public Relations in Britain: A History of Professional Practice in the 20th Century.* London: Lawrence Erlbaum.

Labov, W. (1966) *The Social Stratification of English in New York City.* Washington: Center for Applied Linguistics.

Labov, W. (1972) *Language in the Inner City.* Philadelphia: University of Pennsylvania Press.

Labov, W. and Waletzky, J. (1967) 'Narrative analysis: oral versions of personal experience', in J. Helm (ed.) *Essays on Verbal and Visual Arts*, Seattle: University of Washington Press, pp. 12–44.

Lahey, E. (2005) *Text World Landscapes and English-Canadian National Identity in the Poetry of Al Purdy, Alden Nowlan and Milton Acorn.* Unpublished Ph.D. thesis, University of Nottingham.

Lakoff, G. (1987) *Women, Fire, and Dangerous Things: What Categories Reveal About the Mind.* University of Chicago Press.

Lakoff, G. (2004) *Don't Think of an Elephant: Know Your Values and Frame the Debate.* White River Junction: Chelsea Green.

Lakoff, G. and Johnson, M. (1980) *Metaphors We Live By.* University of Chicago Press.

Lakoff, G. and Johnson, M. (1999) *Philosophy in the Flesh: The Embodied Mind and Its Challenge to Western Thought.* New York: Basic Books.

Lakoff, G. and Turner, M. (1989) *More Than Cool Reason: A Field Guide to Poetic Metaphor.* University of Chicago Press.

Lakoff, R. (1975) *Language and Women's Place.* New York: Harper and Row.

Lambert, M. (1981) *Dickens and the Suspended Quotation.* New Haven: Yale University Press.

Lambrou, M. (2014a) 'Stylistics, conversation analysis and the co-operative principle', in M. Burke (ed.) *The Routledge Handbook of Stylistics*, London: Routledge.

Lambrou, M. (2014b) 'Discourse stylistics', in V. Sotirova (ed.) *The Bloomsbury Companion to Stylistics*, London: Bloomsbury.

Lambrou, M. and Stockwell, P. (eds) (2007) *Contemporary Stylistics*. London: Continuum.

Landsberg, M. E. (ed.) (1995) *Syntactic Iconicity and Linguistic Freezes: The Human Dimension*. Berlin: Mouton de Gruyter.

Lang, B. (ed.) (1987) *The Concept of Style*. Ithaca: Cornell University Press.

Langacker, R. (1987) *Foundations of Cognitive Grammar*, Vol. 1: *Theoretical Prerequisites*. Stanford University Press.

Langacker, R. (2008) *Cognitive Grammar: A Basic Introduction*. New York: Oxford University Press.

Lanham, R. (1991) *Handlist of Rhetorical Terms* (2nd edn). Berkeley: University of California Press.

Lantolf, J. P. (ed.) (2000) *Sociocultural Theory and Second Language Learning*. New York: Oxford University Press.

Larkin, P. (1955) *The Less Deceived*. Hessle: Marvell Press.

Larkin, P. (1977) 'Aubade', *The Times Literary Supplement*, 23 December.

Larkin, P. (1990) *Collected Poems* (ed. A. Thwaite). London: Faber and Faber.

Lasdun, J. (1995) 'Plague Years', in *The Revenant*, London: Jonathan Cape.

Lave, J. and Wenger, E. (1991) *Situated Learning: Legitimate Peripheral Participation*. Cambridge University Press.

Laver, J. (1994) *Elements of Phonetics*. Cambridge University Press.

Lawrence, D. H. (1986) *The Rainbow* [original 1915]. London: Penguin.

Lazar, M. (ed.) (2005) *Feminist Critical Discourse Analysis: Gender, Power and Ideology in Discourse*. Basingstoke: Palgrave.

Lecercle, J.-J. (1990) *The Violence of Language*. London: Routledge.

Lee, H. (1960) *To Kill a Mockingbird*. New York: J. B. Lippincott.

Leech, G. (1969) *A Linguistic Guide to English Poetry*. London: Longman.

Leech, G. (1966a) *English in Advertising: A Linguistic Study of Advertising in Great Britain*. London: Longman.

Leech, G. (1966b) 'Linguistics and the figures of rhetoric', in R. Fowler (ed.) *Essays on Style and Language*, London: Routledge and Kegan Paul, pp. 135–56.

Leech, G. (1970) '"This bread I break": language and interpretation', in D. C. Freeman (ed.) *Linguistics and Literary Style*, New York: Holt, Rinehart and Winston, pp. 119–28.

Leech, G. (1983) *Principles of Pragmatics*. London: Longman.

Leech, G. (1992) 'Pragmatic principles in Shaw's *You Never Can Tell*', in M. Toolan (ed.) *Language, Text and Context*, London: Routledge, pp. 259–78.

Leech, G. (2006) 'Politeness: is there an East-West divide?', *Journal of Politeness Research* 3 (2): 167–206.

Leech, G. (2008) *Language in Literature: Style and Foregrounding*. London: Longman.

Leech, G. (2010) 'Analysing literature through language: two Shakespearean speeches', in D. McIntyre and B. Busse (eds) *Language and Style*, London: Palgrave Macmillan, pp. 15–31.

Leech, G. and Short, M. (1981) *Style in Fiction*. London: Longman.

Leech, G. and Short, M. (2007) *Style in Fiction: A Linguistic Introduction to English Fictional Prose* (2nd edn). London: Longman.

van Leeuwen, T. (2001) 'What is authenticity?', *Discourse Studies*, 3 (4): 392–7.

Lennard, J. (2006) *The Poetry Handbook*. Oxford University Press.

Léon, P. (1993) *Précis de Phonostylistique, parole et expressivité*. Paris: Nathan Université.

Lerner, G. (2002) 'Turn-sharing: the choral co-production of talk-in-interaction', in C. A. Ford, B. A. Fox and S. A. Thompson (eds) *The Language of Turn and Sequence*, Oxford University Press, pp. 225–56.

Lerner, I., Bentin, S. and Shriki, O. (2012) 'Spreading activation in an attractor network with latching dynamics: automatic semantic priming revisited', *Cognitive Science* 36 (8): 1339–82.

Lévi-Strauss, C. (1955) 'The structural study of myth', *The Journal of American Folklore* 68 (270): 428–44.

Levin, S. R. (1962) *Linguistic Structures in Poetry*. The Hague: Mouton.

Levinson, S. C. (1983) *Pragmatics*. Cambridge University Press.

Levinson, S. C. (1987) 'Minimization and conversational inference', in J. Verschueren and M. Bertuccelli-Papi (eds) *The Pragmatic Perspective*, Amsterdam: John Benjamins, pp. 61–129.

Levinson, S. C. (2000) *Presumptive Meanings: The Theory of Generalised Conversational Implicature*. Cambridge, MA: MIT Press.

Li, E. S. H. (2007) *A Systemic Functional Grammar of Chinese*. London: Continuum.

LibraryThing (2012) *LibraryThing homepage*, available at: www.librarything.com

Lindquist, H. (2009) *Corpus Linguistics and the Description of English*. Edinburgh University Press.

Linguistic Politeness Research Group (eds) (2011) *Discursive Approaches to Politeness and Impoliteness*. Berlin: Mouton de Gruyter.

Liu Hsieh (1959) *The Literary Mind and the Carving of Dragons* (trans. V. Y. Shih). New York: Columbia University Press.

Locher, M. and Watts, R. (2005) 'Politeness theory and relational work', *Journal of Politeness Research*, 1 (1): 9–33.

Lodge, D. (1966) *The Language of Fiction*. London: Routledge and Kegan Paul.

Lodge, D. (1977) *The Modes of Modern Writing: Metaphor, Metonymy and the Typology of Modern Literature*. London: Arnold.

Lodge, D. (1980) *How Far Can You Go?* London: Secker and Warburg.

Loftus, E. F. and Loftus, G. R. (1980) 'On the permanence of stored information in the human brain', *American Psychologist*: 35, 409–20.

Lombard, B. L. (1998) 'Ontologies of events', in S. Laurence and C. Macdonald (eds) *Contemporary Readings in the Foundations of Metaphysics*, Oxford: Blackwell, pp. 277–94.

Longacre, R. E. (1983) *The Grammar of Discourse*. New York: Plenum Press.

Louw, W. E. (1993) 'Irony in the text or insincerity in the writer? The diagnostic potential of semantic prosodies', in M. Baker, G. Francis and E. Tognini-Bonelli (eds) *Text and Technology*, Amsterdam: Benjamins, pp. 157–76.

Louw, W. E. (1997) 'The role of corpora in critical literary appreciation', in A. Wichmann, S. Fligelstone, T. McEnery and G. Knowles (eds) *Teaching and Language Corpora*, London: Longman, pp. 240–51.

Louw, W. E. (2009) 'Consolidating empirical method in data-assisted stylistics: towards a corpus-attested glossary of literary terms', in V. Viana and S. Zyngier (eds) *Directions in Empirical Literary Studies: In Honour of Willie van Peer*, Amsterdam: John Benjamins, pp. 56–84.

Louw, W. E. (2010a) 'Collocation as instrumentation for meaning: a scientific fact', in W. van Peer, V. Viana and S. Zyngier (eds) *Literary Education and Digital Learning: Methods and Technologies for Humanities Studies*, Hershey: IGI Global, pp. 79–101.

Louw, W. E. (2010b) 'Automating the extraction of literary worlds and their subtexts from the poetry of William Butler Yeats', in M. Falces Sierra, E. Hidalgo Tenorio, J. Santana Lario and S. Valera Hernández (eds) *Para por y sobre Luis Quereda*, Granada University Press, pp. 24–51.

Louw, W. E. and Milojkovic, M. (forthcoming) *Literary Worlds as Contextual Prosodic Theory and Subtext*. Amsterdam: John Benjamins.

Lüdeling, A. (2008) 'Three views on corpora: corpus linguistics, literary computing, and computational linguistics', http://computerphilologie.tu-darmstadt.de/jg07/luedzeldes.html#FNRef1

Luyken, G. (1991) *Overcoming Language Barriers in Television: Dubbing and Subtitling for the European Audience*. Manchester: European Institute for the Media.

Lynch, D. (dir.) (1997) *Lost Highway*. October Films.

Lynch, D. (dir.) (2001) *Mulholland Dr.* Universal Pictures.

Lynch, D. S. (1998) *The Economy of Character: Novels, Market Culture, and the Business of Inner Meaning*. University of Chicago Press.

Lynch, D. S. (2000) 'Personal effects and sentimental fictions', *Eighteenth-Century Fiction* 12 (2–3): 345–68.

Lyons, J. (1972) 'Human language', in R. A. Hinde (ed.) *Non-Verbal Communication*, Cambridge University Press, pp. 49–85.

Lyons, J. (1977). *Semantics*. Cambridge University Press.

McCall Smith, A. (1998) *The No. 1 Ladies' Detective Agency*. Edinburgh: Polygon.

McCann, C. (2009) 'Miró, Miró, on the wall', in *Let the Great World Spin*, London: Bloomsbury, pp. 73–114.

McConachie, B. (2008) *Engaging Audiences: A Critical Approach to Spectating in the Theatre*. New York: Palgrave.

McConachie, B. and Hart, E. (2006) *Performance and Cognition: Theatre Studies After the Cognitive Turn.* Oxford: Taylor and Francis.

McElhinny, B. (1997) 'Ideologies of public and private language in sociolinguistics', in R. Wodak (ed.) *Gender and Discourse*, London: Sage, pp. 106–39.

McEwan, I. (2005) *Saturday.* London: Vintage Books.

McHale, B. (1987) *Postmodernist Fiction.* London: Routledge.

McIntyre, D. (2006) *Point of View in Plays: A Cognitive Stylistic Approach to Viewpoint in Drama and Other Text-Types.* Amsterdam: John Benjamins.

McIntyre, D. (2008) 'Integrating multimodal analysis and the stylistics of drama: a multimodal perspective on Ian McKellen's Richard III', *Language and Literature* 17 (4): 309–34.

McIntyre, D. and Culpeper, J. (2010) 'Activity types, incongruity and humour in dramatic discourse', in D. McIntyre and B. Busse (eds) *Language and Style*, London: Palgrave Macmillan, pp. 204–22.

McLaren, D. (2012) 'What does the ASA ruling on Rooney / Wilshere Tweets mean?', available at: www.theuksportsnetwork.com/what-does-the-asa-ruling-on-rooney-wilshere-tweets-mean

MacLaverty, B. (1983) *Cal.* Harmondsworth: Penguin.

McLuhan, M. (1964) *Understanding Media: The Extensions of Man.* London: Ark.

MacMahon, B. (1996) 'Indirectness, rhetoric and interpretive use: communicative strategies in Browning's "My Last Duchess"', *Language and Literature* 5 (3): 209–23.

MacMahon, B. (2006) 'Relevance theory: stylistic applications', in K. Brown (ed.) *Encyclopedia of Language and Linguistics*, Oxford: Elsevier, pp. 519–22.

McNeillie, A. (1994) *The Essays of Virginia Woolf,* Vol. 4: *1925–1928.* London: The Hogarth Press.

Macpherson, W. (1999) *The Stephen Lawrence Inquiry.* London: The Stationery Office.

McQuail, D. and Windahl, S. (1993) *Communication Models for the Study of Mass Communication.* London: Pearson.

McRae, K. and Boisvert, S. (1998) 'Automatic semantic similarity priming', *Journal of Experimental Psychology: Learning, Memory and Cognition* 24: 558–72.

McStay, A. (2011) *The Mood of Information: A Critique of Online Behavioural Advertising.* London: Continuum.

Mahlberg, M. (2005). *English General Nouns: A Corpus Theoretical Approach.* Amsterdam: John Benjamins.

Mahlberg, M. (2007a) 'Corpus stylistics: bridging the gap between linguistics and literary studies', in M. Hoey, M. Mahlberg, M. Stubbs and W. Teubert *Text, Discourse and Corpora*, London: Continuum, pp. 219–46.

Mahlberg, M. (2007b) 'Lexical items in discourse: identifying local textual functions of sustainable development', in M. Hoey, M. Mahlberg, M. Stubbs and W. Teubert *Text, Discourse and Corpora: Theory and Analysis*, London: Continuum, pp. 191–218.

Mahlberg, M. (2010) 'Corpus linguistics and the study of nineteenth century fiction', *Journal of Victorian Culture* 15 (2): 292–8.

Mahlberg, M. (2012) 'Corpus stylistics: Dickens, text-drivenness and the fictional world', in J. John (ed.) *Dickens and Modernity*, Cambridge: Brewer, pp. 94–114.

Mahlberg, M. (2013a) *Corpus Stylistics and Dickens's Fiction*. London: Routledge.

Mahlberg, M. (2013b) 'Corpus analysis of literary texts', in C. Chapelle (ed.) *The Encyclopedia of Applied Linguistics*, Boston: Wiley-Blackwell.

Mahlberg, M. and Smith, C. (2010) 'Corpus approaches to prose fiction: civility and body language in *Pride and Prejudice*', in D. McIntyre and B. Busse (eds) *Language and Style*, Basingstoke: Palgrave Macmillan, pp. 449–67.

Mahlberg, M. and Smith, C. (2012) 'Dickens, the suspended quotation and the corpus', *Language and Literature* 21 (1): 51–65.

Mair, C. (2008) 'Corpora and the study of recent change in language', in A. Lüdeling and M. Kytö (eds), *Corpus Linguistics: An International Handbook*, Berlin and New York: Walter de Gruyter, pp. 1109–25.

Malinowski, B. (1923) 'The problem of meaning in primitive languages,' in C. K. Ogden and I. A. Richards (eds) *The Meaning Of Meaning: A Study of the Influence of Language Upon Thought and of the Science of Symbolism*, London: Routledge, pp. 296–336.

Malmkjaer, K. (2003) 'What happened to God and the angels: H. W. Dulken's translations of Hans Christian Andersen's stories in Victorian Britain *or* an exercise in translation stylistics', *Target* 15 (1): 13–24.

Malmkjaer, K. (2004) 'Translational stylistics: Dulken's translations of Hans Christian Andersen', *Language and Literature* 13 (1): 13–24.

Manguel, A. (1997) *A History of Reading*. London: Flamingo.

Manning, C. D. and Schütze, H. (1999) *Foundations of Statistical Natural Language Processing*. Cambridge, MA: MIT Press.

Marsh, J. (2008) (dir.) *Man on Wire*, Magnolia Pictures (USA), Icon Productions (UK).

Marsh, R. C. (ed.) (1956) *Logic and Knowledge*. London: Allen and Unwin.

Marshall, D. L. (2010) *Vico and the Transformation of Rhetoric in Early Modern Europe*. Cambridge University Press.

Martin, A. (2004) *The Blackpool Highflyer*. London: Faber and Faber.

Martin, J. R. and Plum, G. A. (1997) 'Construing experience: some story genres', *Journal of Narrative and Life History* 7 (1–4): 299–308.

Martin, J. R. and Rothery, J. (1981) 'The ontogenesis of written genre', *Working Papers in Linguistics* 2, Department of Linguistics, University of Sydney.

Martin, J. R., Matthiesson, C. M. I. M. and Painter, C. (1997) *Working with Functional Grammar*. London: Edward Arnold.

Martin, W. (2000) 'Criticism and the academy', in A. W. Litz, L. Menand and L. Rainey (eds) *The Cambridge History of Literary Criticism*, Vol. 7: *Modernism and the New Criticism*, Cambridge University Press, pp. 269–321.

Mason, B. and Thomas, S. (2008) 'A million penguins research report', available at: www.ioct.dmu.ac.uk/documents/amillionpenguinsreport.pdf

Mason, J. (2012) 'Narrative interrelation: the reality of intertextuality', *First Annual Nottingham-Birmingham-Warwick ESRC DTC Conference*, Nottingham, UK, 14 November.

Masuda, K. (2003) 'What imitates birdcalls?: two experiments on birdcalls and their linguistic representations', in W. G. Müller and O. Fischer (eds) *From Sign to Signing: Iconicity in Language and Literature 3*, Amsterdam: John Benjamins, pp. 77–102.

Mattelart, A. and Mattelart, M. (1998) *Theories of Communication: A Short Introduction*. London: Sage.

Mautner, T. (2000) *The Penguin Dictionary of Philosophy*. Harmondsworth: Penguin.

Melville, H. (1990) *Bartleby, The Scrivener* [original 1853]. London: Dover Books.

Menand, L. (2000) 'T. S. Eliot', in A. W. Litz, L. Menand and L. Rainey (eds) *The Cambridge History of Literary Criticism*, Vol. 7: *Modernism and the New Criticism*, Cambridge University Press, pp. 17–56.

Merrin, J. (2002) 'Art over easy', *The Southern Review* 38 (1): 202–14.

Miall, D. S. (2006) *Literary Reading: Empirical and Theoretical Studies*. New York: Peter Lang.

Miall, D. S. (2007) 'Foregrounding and the sublime: Shelley in Chamonix', *Language and Literature* 16 (2): 155–68.

Miall, D. S. (2008) 'Feeling from the perspective of the empirical study of literature', *Journal of Literary Theory* 1 (2): 377–93.

Miall, D. S. (2011) 'Emotions and the structuring of narrative response', *Poetics Today* 32 (2): 323–48.

Miall, D. S. (2012) 'How does it feel? Attending to the unreliable narrator', *Fictions* 11: 41–57.

Miall, D. S. and Kuiken, D. (1994) 'Foregrounding, defamiliarization, and affect: response to literary stories', *Poetics* 22 (5): 389–407.

Miall, D. S. and Kuiken, D. (1999) 'What is literariness? Three components of literary reading', *Discourse Processes* 28 (2): 121–38.

Miall, D. S. and Kuiken, D. (2002a) 'A feeling for fiction: becoming what we behold', *Poetics* 30 (4): 221–41.

Miall, D. S. and Kuiken, D. (2002b) 'The effects of local phonetic contrasts in readers' responses to a short story', *Empirical Studies of the Arts* 20 (2): 157–75.

Miller, C. (2012) 'From Homer to the urban poor: review of Vico and Naples by Barbara Ann Naddeo (Cornell UP, 2010) and Vico and the Transformation of Rhetoric in Early Modern Europe by David Marshall (CUP, 2010)', *Times Literary Supplement*, 3 August, p. 24.

Miller, G. A. (1956) 'The magical number seven, plus or minus two: some limits on our capacity for processing information', *Psychological Review* 63 (2): 81–97.

Mills, S. (ed.) (1994) *Gendering the Reader*. London: Harvester Wheatsheaf.

Mills, S. (1995) *Feminist Stylistics*. London: Routledge.

Mills, S. (2003) *Gender and Politeness*. Cambridge University Press.

Mills, S. (2011) 'Discursive approaches to politeness and impoliteness', in Linguistic Politeness Research Group (eds) *Discursive Approaches to Politeness*, Berlin: Mouton De Gruyter, pp. 19–57.

Mills, S. (2012) *Gender Matters: Feminist Linguistic Analysis*. London: Equinox.

Milojkovic, M. (2012) 'Time and transitions in Larkin's poetry', *NAWA: Journal of Language and Communication* 6 (1): 102–26, and available at: [www.pala.ac.uk/resources/proceedings/2011/milojkovic2011.pdf]

Milojkovic, M. (2013) 'Is corpus stylistics bent on self-improvement? The role of reference corpora 20 years after the advent of semantic prosody', *Journal of Literary Semantics* 42 (1): 59–78.

Miner, E., Odagiri, H. and Morrell, M. (1985) *The Princeton Companion to Classical Japanese Literature*. Princeton University Press.

Minnis, A. (2010) *Medieval Theory of Authorship: Scholastic Literary Attitudes in the Later Middle Ages* (2nd edn). Philadelphia: University of Pennsylvania Press.

Mirsky, M. (2006) 'Notes on reading Kazuo Ishiguro's *Never Let Me Go*', *Perspectives in Biology and Medicine* 49 (4): 628–30.

Mitchell, D. (2004) *Cloud Atlas*. London: Sceptre.

Mitchell, K. (2008) *Intention and Text: Towards an Intentionality of Literary Form*. London: Continuum.

Mitchell, W. J. T. (1986) 'What is an image?' *Iconology: Image, Text, Ideology*, University of Chicago Press, pp. 7–46.

Mitchell, W. J. T. (1993) 'Image', in A. Preminger and E. Miner (eds) *The New Princeton Encyclopedia of Poetry and Poetics*, Princeton University Press, pp. 556–9.

Mitchell, W. J. T. (1994) *Picture Theory: Essays on Verbal and Visual Representation*. University of Chicago Press.

Mitscherling, J., DiTommaso, T. and Nayed, A. (2004) *The Author's Intention*. Lanham: Lexington Books.

Moessner, L. (ed.) (2001) 'Genre, text type, style, register: a terminological maze?' *European Journal of English Studies* 5 (2): 131–8.

Molinié, G. (1997) *La Stylistique* (4th edn). Paris: Presses Universitaires de France.

Montaigne, M. (1877) *Essays of Montaigne* (trans. C. Cotton, ed. W. Hazlitt) [original 1580]. London: Reeves and Turner.

Montello, M. (2005) 'Novel perspectives on bioethics', *The Chronicle of Higher Education* 51 (6): 6.

Montgomery, M. (2001) 'The uses of authenticity: "Speaking from experience" in a U.K. election broadcast', *Communication Review* 4 (4): 447–62.

Montgomery, M. (2007) *The Discourse of Broadcast News: A Linguistic Approach*. London: Routledge.

Montoro, R. (2011) 'Multimodal realisations of mind style in *Enduring Love*', in R. Piazza, M. Bednarek and F. Rossi (eds) *Telecinematic Discourse:*

Approaches to the Language of Films and Television Series, Amsterdam: John Benjamins, pp. 69–83.

Moon, R. (2007) 'Words, frequencies and texts (particularly Conrad)', *Journal of Literary Semantics* 36: 1–33.

Moore, E. (2004) 'Sociolinguistic style: a multidimensional resource for shared identity creation', *Canadian Journal of Linguistics* 49: 375–96.

Moore, E. (2012) 'The social life of style', *Language and Literature* 21 (1): 66–83.

Moran, J. (2012) 'Reflections on the first onstage protest at the Royal National Theatre: what is the problem with Richard Bean's recent work?', *Studies in Theatre and Performance*, 32 (1): 15–28.

Morini, M. (2010) 'The poetics of disengagement: Jane Austen and echoic irony', *Language and Literature* 19 (4): 339–56.

Morley, D. (1992) *Television, Audience and Cultural Studies*. London: Routledge.

Moulin, C., Nyhan, J., Ciula, A., Kelleher, M., Mittler, E., Tadić, M. and Kuutma, K. (2011) *Research Infrastructures in the Digital Humanities* (Science Policy Briefing 42). Strasbourg: European Science Foundation.

Mukařovský, J. (1964a) 'Standard language and poetic language', in P. L. Garvin (ed.) *A Prague School Reader on Esthetics, Literary Structure and Style* [original 1932], Washington: Georgetown University Press, pp. 17–30.

Mukařovský, J. (1964b) 'The Esthetics of Language', in P. L. Garvin (ed.) *A Prague School Reader on Esthetics, Literary Structure and Style* [original in Czech 1932], Washington: Georgetown University Press, pp. 31–69.

Mukařovský, J. (1970) *Aesthetic Function, Norm and Value as Social Fact* (trans. E. Suino Mark) [original 1936]. Ann Arbor: University of Michigan Press.

Mukařovský, J. (1976) *On Poetic Language*. Lisse: Peter de Ridder Press.

Müller, W. G. (2001) 'Iconicity and rhetoric: a note on the iconic force of rhetorical figures in Shakespeare', in O. Fischer and M. Nänny (eds) *The Motivated Form: Iconicity in Language and Literature 2*, Amsterdam: John Benjamins, pp. 305–22.

Munday, J. (2008a) *Introducing Translation Studies: Theories and Applications* (2nd edn). London: Routledge.

Munday, J. (2008b) *Style and Ideology in Translation: Latin American Writing in English*. London: Routledge.

Musolff, A. (2004) *Metaphor and Political Discourse: Analogical Reasoning in Debates about Europe*. Basingstoke: Palgrave Macmillan.

Musolff, A. (2006) 'Metaphor scenarios in public discourse', *Metaphor and Symbol* 21 (1): 23–38.

Myers, G. (1994) *Words in Ads*. London: Arnold.

Myers, G. (1999) *Ad Worlds: Brands, Media, Audiences*. London: Arnold.

Myers, G. (2010) *The Discourse of Blogs and Wikis*. London: Continuum.

Naciscione, A. (2010) *Stylistic Use of Phraseological Units in Discourse*. Amsterdam: John Benjamins.

Nagy, G. (2005) *A Cognitive Theory of Style*. Berne: Peter Lang.

Nahajec, L. (2012) *Evoking the Possibility of Presence: Textual and Ideological Effects of Linguistic Negation in Written Discourse*, unpublished PhD thesis, University of Huddersfield.

Nänny, M. and Fischer, O. (eds) (1999) *Form Miming Meaning: Iconicity in Language and Literature*. Amsterdam: Benjamins.

Nänny, M. and Fischer, O. (2006) 'Iconicity: literary texts', in K. Brown (ed.) *Encyclopedia of Language and Linguistics* (2nd edn). Oxford: Elsevier, pp. 462–72.

Nell, V. (1988) *Lost in a Book: The Psychology of Reading for Pleasure*. New Haven: Yale University Press.

Nevalainen, T. and Raumolin-Brunberg, H. (2003) *Historical Sociolinguistics: Language Change in Tudor and Stuart England*. London, New York and Toronto: Pearson Education.

Newland, P. (2008) *The Cultural Construction of London's East End: Urban Iconography, Modernity and the Spatialisation of Englishness*. Amsterdam: Rodopi.

Newton, A. Z. (1995) *Narrative Ethics*. Cambridge, MA: Harvard University Press.

Nida, E. A. (1964) *Towards a Science of Translating*. Leiden: E. J. Brill.

Nightingale, B. (2009) 'Review of "Jerusalem"', *The Times*, 16 July.

Nørgaard, N. (2010) 'Multimodality and the literary text: making sense of Safran Foer's *Extremely Loud and Incredibly Close*', in R. Page (ed.) *New Perspectives on Narrative and Multimodality*, London: Routledge, pp. 115–26.

Nørgaard, N., Busse, B. and Montoro, R. (2010) *Key Terms in Stylistics*. London: Continuum.

Nöth, W. (2001) 'Semiotic foundations of iconicity in language and literature', in O. Fischer and M. Nänny (eds) *The Motivated Form: Iconicity in Language and Literature 2*, Amsterdam: John Benjamins, pp. 17–28.

Nowottny, W. (1962) *The Language Poets Use*. London: Athlone Press.

Nünning, A. (2003) 'Narratology or narratologies? Taking stock of recent developments, critique and modest proposals for future usages of the term', in T. Kindt and H. H. Müller (eds) *What is Narratology?*, Berlin: De Gruyter, pp. 56–76.

O'Donnell, W. R. and Todd, L. (1980) *Variety in Contemporary English*. London: Allen and Unwin.

O'Halloran, K. A. (2007) 'The subconscious in James Joyce's "Eveline": a corpus stylistic analysis which chews on the "Fish hook"', *Language and Literature* 16 (3): 227–44.

O'Keeffe, A. (2006) *Investigating Media Discourse*. London: Routledge.

Ochs, E. and Capps, L. (2001) *Living Narrative: Creating Lives in Everyday Storytelling*. Cambridge, MA: Harvard University Press.

Ong, W. (1968) 'Tudor writings on rhetoric', *Studies in the Renaissance* 15: 39–69.

Ong, W. (1982) *Orality and Literacy: The Technologizing of the Word*. London: Routledge.

Ortony, A. (ed.) (1979) *Metaphor and Thought*. Cambridge University Press.

Osgood, C., Suci, G. and Tannenbaum, P. (1957) *The Measurement of Meaning*. Chicago: University of Illinois Press.

Osherson, S. (2009) 'Book forum: *The Boy in the Striped Pajamas*', *Journal of the American Academy of Child and Adolescent Psychiatry* 48 (1): 456–7.

Owtram, N. T. (2010) *The Pragmatics of Academic Writing: A Relevance Approach to the Analysis of Research Article Introductions*. Oxford: Peter Lang.

Page, R. (2010) *New Perspectives on Narrative and Multimodality*. London: Routledge.

Page, R. (2012a) *Stories and Social Media: Identities and Interaction*. New York: Routledge.

Page, R. (2012b) 'The linguistics of self-branding and micro-celebrity in Twitter: the role of hashtags', *Discourse and Communication* 6 (2): 181–201.

Pahta, P. and Taavitsainen, I. (2010) 'Introducing Early Modern English Medical Texts', in I. Taavitsainen and P. Pahta (eds) *Early Modern Medical Texts: Corpus Description and Studies*, Amsterdam: John Benjamins, pp. 1–10.

Palmer, A. (2004) *Fictional Minds*. Lincoln: University of Nebraska Press.

Palmer, A. (2007) 'Attribution Theory: action and emotion in Dickens and Pynchon', in M. Lambrou and P. Stockwell (eds) *Contemporary Stylistics*. London: Continuum, pp. 81–92.

Panksepp, J. (1998) *Affective Neuroscience: The Foundations of Human and Animal Emotions*. Oxford University Press.

Paran, A. (2006) *Literature in Teaching and Learning*. Alexandria: TESOL Publications.

Pariser, E. (2011) *The Filter Bubble: What the Internet Is Hiding from You*. New York: Penguin.

Parks, T. (2007) *Translating Style: The English Modernists and their Italian Translations* (2nd edn). Manchester: St Jerome.

Partington, A. (1998) *Patterns and Meaning*. Amsterdam: John Benjamins.

Patterson, A. (2009) *Milton's Words*. Oxford University Press.

Pecher, D. and Zwaan, R. (2005a) 'Introduction', in *Grounding Cognition: The Role of Perception and Action in Memory, Language, and Thinking*, Cambridge University Press pp. 1–8.

Pecher, D. and Zwaan, R. (eds) (2005b) *Grounding Cognition: The Role of Perception and Action in Memory, Language, and Thinking*. Cambridge University Press.

Pennies from Heaven (1978), dir. Piers Haggard, London: BBC [DVD].

van Peer, W. (1986) *Stylistics and Psychology: Investigations of Foregrounding*. London: Croom Helm.

van Peer, W. (1988) 'Introduction', in *The Taming of the Text*, London: Routledge, pp. 1–14.

van Peer, W. (1993) 'Typographic foregrounding', *Language and Literature* 2: 49–61.

van Peer, W. (ed.) (2007) 'Special issue on foregrounding', *Language and Literature* 16 (2).

van Peer, W. and Andringa, E. (1990) 'Stylistic intuitions: an empirical study', *Language and Style* 23 (2): 235–46.

van Peer, W. and Hakemulder, J. (2006) 'Foregrounding', in K. Brown (ed.) *The Encyclopedia of Language and Linguistics*, Vol. 4, Oxford: Elsevier, pp. 546–51.

van Peer, W., Hakemulder, F., Hakemulder, J. and Zyngier, S. (eds) (2007) *Muses and Measures: Empirical Research Methods for the Humanities*. Newcastle upon Tyne: Cambridge Scholars.

van Peer, W., Hakemulder, F. and Zyngier, S. (2012) *Scientific Methods for the Humanities*. Amsterdam: John Benjamins Publishing.

Penny, N. (1986) 'An ambitious man: the career and achievement of Sir Joshua Reynolds', in N. Penny (ed.) *Reynolds*, London: Royal Academy of Arts, pp. 17–42.

Peplow, D. (2011) '"Oh, I've known a lot of Irish people": reading groups and the negotiation of literary interpretation', *Language and Literature* 20 (4): 295–315.

Peplow, D. (2012) *Negotiating Literary Interpretations in the Reading Group*, unpublished PhD thesis, University of Nottingham.

Perelman, C. and Olbrechts-Tyteca, L. (1969) *The New Rhetoric*. University of Notre Dame Press.

Pfister, M. (1988) *The Theory and Analysis of Drama*. Cambridge University Press.

Phelan, J. (1996) *Narrative as Rhetoric: Technique, Audiences, Ethics, and Ideology*. Columbus: Ohio State University Press.

Phelan, J. (2001) 'Sethe's choice: *Beloved* and the ethics of reading', in T. F. Davis and K. Womack (eds), *Mapping the Ethical Turn: A Reader in Ethics, Culture, and Literary Theory*, Charlottesville: University Press of Virginia, pp. 93–109.

Phelan, J. (2004) 'Rhetorical literary ethics and lyric narrative: Robert Frost's "Home Burial"', *Poetics Today* 25 (4): 627–51.

Phelan, J. (2005) *Living to Tell about It: A Rhetoric and Ethics of Character Narration*. Ithaca: Cornell University Press.

Phelan, J. (2007a) *Experiencing Fiction: Judgments, Progressions, and the Rhetorical Theory of Narrative*. Columbus: Ohio State University Press.

Phelan, J. (2007b) 'Rhetoric/ethics', in D. Herman (ed.) *The Cambridge Companion to Narrative*, Cambridge University Press, pp. 203–16.

Phillips, M. (1989) *Lexical Structure of Text* (Discourse Analysis Monograph 12). English Language Research, University of Birmingham.

Pilkington, A. (2000) *Poetic Effects: A Relevance Theory Perspective*. Amsterdam: John Benjamins.

Piller, I. (2001) 'Identity construction in multilingual advertising', *Language in Society*, 30: 153–86.

Pointon, M. (1993) *Hanging the Head: Portraiture and Social Formation in Eighteenth-Century England*. New Haven: Yale University Press.

Pomerantz, A. (1984) 'Agreeing and disagreeing with assessments: some features of preferred/dispreferred turn shapes', in J. M. Atkinson and

J. Heritage (eds) *Structures of Social Action: Studies in Conversation Analysis,* Cambridge University Press, pp. 57–101.

Pope, A. (1980) *Collected Poems* (ed. B. Dobrée) [original 1711]. London: Dent Everyman.

Pope, R. (1995) *Textual Intervention.* London: Routledge.

Pope, R. (2002) *The English Studies Book* (2nd edn). London: Routledge.

Popova, Y. (2003) '"The fool sees with his nose": metaphoric mappings in the sense of smell in Patrick Süskind's *Perfume*', *Language and Literature* 12 (2): 135–51.

Porter Abott, H. (2002) *The Cambridge Introduction to Narrative.* Cambridge University Press.

Potter, D. (1996) *Pennies from Heaven.* London: Faber and Faber.

Potter, J. (1996) *Representing Reality: Discourse, Rhetoric and Social Construction.* London: Sage.

Poyatos, F. (1993) *Paralanguage: A Linguistic and Interdisciplinary Approach to Interactive Speech and Sound.* Amsterdam: John Benjamins.

Pratt, M. L. (1977) *Toward a Speech Act Theory of Literary Discourse.* Bloomington: Indiana University Press.

Premchand, M. (2004) *Godān.* New Delhi: Rūpa.

Preston, I. (1994) *The Tangled Web They Weave: Truth, Falsity, and Advertisers.* Madison: University of Wisconsin Press.

Prince, G. (1987) *A Dictionary of Narratology.* Lincoln: University of Nebraska Press.

Prince, G. (1988) 'The disnarrated', *Style* 22: 1–8.

Prince, G. (1991) *A Dictionary of Narratology.* Aldershot: Scolar Press.

Prince, G. (1999) 'Revisiting narrativity', in W. Grünzweig and A. Solbach (eds) *Transcending Boundaries: Narratology in Context,* Tübingen: Gunter Narr Verlag, pp. 43–51.

Prince, G. (2006) 'The disnarrated', in D. Herman, M. Jahn, and M.-L. Ryan (eds) *The Routledge Encyclopaedia of Narrative Theory,* New York: Routledge, p. 118.

Prinz, J. J. (2002) *Furnishing the Mind: Concepts and their Perceptual Basis.* Cambridge, MA: The MIT Press.

Prinz, J. J. (2004) *Gut Reactions: A Perceptual Theory of Emotion.* New York: Oxford University Press.

Propp, V. (1968) *Morphology of the Folktale* (2nd edn, trans. L. Scott, rev. L. A. Wagner) [original 1928]. Austin: University of Texas Press.

Punday, D. (2010) *Five Strands of Fictionality: The Institutional Construction of Contemporary American Fiction.* Columbus: Ohio State University Press.

Rabinowitz, P. J. (1998) *Before Reading: Narrative Conventions and the Politics of Interpretation.* Columbus: Ohio State University Press.

Rachel (2012) *A Review of 'Sailing Alone Around the Room: New and Selected Poems',* available at: www.goodreads.com/review/show/401661630

Raley, R. (2010) 'Walk this way: mobile narrative as composed experience', in J. Scäfer and P. Gendolla (eds) *Beyond the Screen: Transformations of*

Literary Structures, Interfaces and Genres, Bielefeld: Transcript Verlag, pp. 299–316.

Ramsay, S. (2008) 'Algorithmic criticism', in S. Schreibman and R. Siemens (eds) *A Companion to Digital Literary Studies*, Oxford: Blackwell, pp. 477–92.

Rand, A. (1943) *The Fountainhead*. New York: Bobbs Merrill.

Rauser, A. (2008) *Irony, Authenticity, and Individualism in Eighteenth-Century English Prints*. Newark: University of Delaware Press.

Raymond, G. and Heritage, J. (2006) 'The epistemics of social relations: owning grandchildren', *Language in Society* 35 (5): 677–705.

Reah, D. (2002) *The Language of Newspapers*. London: Routledge.

rebeccareid (2009) *Reviews: 'Sailing Alone Around the Room: New and Selected Poems by Billy Collins'*, available at: www.librarything.com/work/11852

Redpath, T. (1976) 'The meaning of a poem', in D. N. de Molina (ed.) *On Literary Intention*, Edinburgh University Press, pp. 14–25.

Rehberg Sedo, D. (2003) 'Readers in reading groups: an online survey of face-to-face and virtual book clubs', *Convergence* 9 (1): 66–90.

Reicher, M. (2010) 'The ontology of fictional characters', in J. Eder, F. Jannidis and R. Schneider (eds) *Characters in Fictional Worlds: Understanding Imaginary Beings in Literature, Film and Other Media*, Berlin: de Gruyter, pp. 111–33.

Reinelt, J. (2006) 'Towards a poetics of theatre and public events in the case of Stephen Lawrence' *The Drama Review* 50 (3): 69–87.

Rettberg, J. W. (2009) '"Freshly generated for you, and Barack Obama": how social media represent your life', *European Journal of Communication*, 24 (4): 451–66.

Reynolds, J. (1975) *Discourses on Art* (ed. R. R. Wark) [original 1797]. New Haven: Yale University Press.

Richards, I. A. (1929) *Practical Criticism*. London: Kegan Paul.

Richardson, J. (1719) *Two Discourses*. London: W. Churchill [reprinted Menston: Scolar Press, 1972].

Richardson, J. (1725) *An Essay on the Theory of Painting*. London: A. C. Bettesworth.

Richman, P. (ed.) (1991) *Many Rāmāyaṇas: The Diversity of a Narrative Tradition in South Asia*. Berkeley: University of California Press.

Ricks, C. (1964) *Milton's Grand Style*. Oxford: Clarendon Press.

Ricks, C. (1984) *The Force of Poetry*. Oxford: Clarendon Press.

Ricks, C. (2002) *Allusion to the Poets*. Oxford University Press.

Rickson, I. (dir.) (2011) *Jerusalem*, The Apollo Theatre, London, 2011–12.

Ricoeur, P. (1984) *Time and Narrative*, Vol. 1 (trans. K. McLaughlin and D. Pellauer). University of Chicago Press.

Riffaterre, M. (1966) 'Describing poetic structures: two approaches to Baudelaire's "Les Chats"', in J. Tompkins (ed.) *Reader-Response Criticism*, Baltimore: The Johns Hopkins University Press, pp. 200–42.

Riffaterre, M. (1990) 'Compulsory reader response: the intertextual drive' in M. Worton and J. Still (eds) *Intertextuality: Theories and Practices*, Manchester University Press, pp. 56–78.

Rimmon, S. (1977) *The Concept of Ambiguity: The Example of James*. Chicago University Press.

Rivara, R. (2000) *La Langue du récit: Introduction à la narratologie énonciative*. Paris: L'Harmattan.

Robbins, B. (2007) 'Cruelty is bad: banality and proximity in *Never Let Me Go*', *Novel: A Forum on Fiction* 40 (3): 289–302.

Robson, M. and Stockwell, P. (2005) *Language in Theory: A Resource Book for Students*. London: Routledge.

Romaine, S. (2010) '19th century key words, key semantic domains and affect: "In the rich vocabulary of love 'most dearest' be a superlative"', *Studia Neophilologica* 82: 12–48.

Roos, H. (2008) '"Not properly human": literary and cinematic narratives about human harvesting', *Journal of Literary Studies* 24 (3): 40–53.

Rosch, E. (1975) 'Cognitive representations of semantic categories', *Journal of Experimental Psychology (General)* 104: 192–233.

Rosenthal, M. L. (1962) 'Glossary of names and places', in *W. B. Yeats: Selected Poems and Three Plays* (3rd edn, ed. M. L. Rosenthal), New York: Collier. pp. 235–41.

Ross, D. (2009) *Critical Companion to William Butler Yeats: A Literary Reference to His Life and Work*. New York: Facts on File Inc.

Roudiez, L. S. (1980) 'Introduction', in J. Kristeva *Desire in Language: A Semiotic Approach to Literature and Art* (ed. L. S. Roudiez, trans. T. Gora, A. Jardine and L. S. Roudiez), New York: Columbia University Press, pp. 1–20.

Rowling, J. K. (2012) *The Casual Vacancy*. New York: Little, Brown.

Rumelhart, D. E. (1975) 'Notes on a schema for stories', in D. G. Bobrow and A. Collins (eds) *Representation and Understanding: Studies in Cognitive Science*, New York: Academic Press, pp. 211–36.

Russell, C. P. (1921) 'How to write a sales-marketing letter', *Printers' Ink*, 2 June.

Ryan, M.-L. (2006) *Avatars of Story*. Minneapolis: University of Minnesota Press.

Ryan, M.-L. (1991a) *Possible Worlds, Artificial Intelligence and Narrative Theory*. Bloomington and Indianapolis: Indiana University Press.

Ryan, M.-L. (1991b) 'Possible worlds and accessibility relations: a semantics typology of fiction', *Poetics Today* 12 (3): 553–76.

Ryan, M.-L. (1998) 'The text as world versus the text as game: possible worlds semantics and postmodern theory', *Journal of Literary Semantics* 27 (3): 137–63.

Sacks, H. (1984) 'Notes on methodology', in J. M. Atkinson and J. Heritage (eds) *Structures of Social Action: Studies in Conversation Analysis*, Cambridge University Press, pp. 21–7.

Sacks, H. (1987) 'On the preferences for agreement and contiguity in sequences in conversation', in G. Button and J. R. E. Lee (eds) *Talk and Social Organisation*, Clevedon: Multilingual Matters, pp. 54–69.

Sacks, H. (1992) *Lectures on Conversation*. Oxford: Blackwell.

Salinger, J. D. (1951) *The Catcher in the Rye*. New York: Little, Brown.

Sampson, G. (2007) 'Grammar without grammaticality', *Corpus Linguistics and Linguistic Theory* 3 (1): 1–32.

Sanford, A. J. (2002) 'Context, attention and depth of processing during interpretation', *Mind and Language* 17 (1–2): 188–206.

Sanford, A. J. and Emmott, C. (2012) *Mind, Brain and Narrative*. Cambridge University Press.

Sanford, A. J. and Garrod, S. C. (1981) *Understanding Written Language: Explorations in Comprehension Beyond the Sentence*. Chichester: John Wiley.

Sanford, A. J. and Sturt, P. (2002) 'Depth of processing in language comprehension: not noticing the evidence', *Trends in Cognitive Sciences* 6 (9): 382–6.

Sanford, A. J. S., Sanford, A. J., Molle, J. and Emmott, C. (2006) 'Shallow processing and attention capture in written and spoken discourse', *Discourse Processes* 42 (2): 109–30.

Sanford, A. J. S., Price, J. and Sanford, A. J. (2009) 'Enhancement and suppression effects resulting from information structuring in sentences', *Memory and Cognition* 37 (6): 880–8.

Sansom, P. (1994) *January*. Manchester: Carcanet Books.

Santini, M. (2006) 'Interpreting genre evolution on the web: preliminary results', paper presented at the 11th Conference of the European Chapter of the Association for Computational Linguistics, Trento, Italy, 4 April.

Sapir, E. (1921) *Language*. New York: Harcourt, Brace and Co.

Sapir, E. (1929) 'The status of linguistics as a science', *Language* 5: 207–14.

Sargent, S. (2001) 'Tz'u', in V. Mair (ed.) *The Columbia History of Chinese Literature*, New York: Columbia University Press, pp. 314–36.

Sarker, S. K. (2002) *W. B. Yeats: Poetry and Plays*. New York: Atlantic.

Saussure, F. de (1959) *Course in General Linguistics* [original 1916]. New York: McGraw-Hill.

Saussure, F. de (1983) *Course in General Linguistics* (trans. R. Harris) [original 1922]. London: Duckworth.

Scarry, E. (1999) *Dreaming by the Book*. New York: Farrar, Straus and Giroux.

Schank, R. (1982a) *Dynamic Memory: A Theory of Reminding and Learning in Computers and People*. Cambridge University Press.

Schank, R. (1982b) *Reading and Understanding: Teaching from the Perspective of Artificial Intelligence*. Mahwah: Lawrence Erlbaum Associates.

Schank, R. (1984) *The Cognitive Computer*. Reading: Addison-Wesley.

Schank, R. (1986) *Explanation Patterns*. Mahwah: Lawrence Erlbaum Associates.

Schank, R. and Abelson, R. (1977) *Scripts, Plans, Goals, and Understanding: An Inquiry into Human Knowledge Structures*. Hillsdale: Lawrence Erlbaum.

Schechner, R. (1985) *Between Theater and Anthropology*. Philadelphia: University of Pennsylvania Press.

Schegloff, E. A. (1997) 'Whose text? Whose context?', *Discourse and Society* 8 (2): 165–87.

Schegloff, E. A. (1998) 'Reply to Wetherell', *Discourse and Society* 9 (3): 413–16.

Schegloff, E. A. (1999) '"Schegloff's texts" as "Billig's data": a critical reply', *Discourse and Society* 10 (4): 558–72.

Schirato, T. and Yell, S. (1997) *Cultural Literacies*. London: Allen and Unwin.

Schmidt, S. J. (1982) *Foundations for the Empirical Study of Literature: The Components of a Basic Theory* (trans. R. de Beaugrande). Hamburg: Helmut Buske Verlag.

Schneider, R. (2000) *Grundriß zur kognitiven Theorie der Figurenrezeption am Beispiel des viktorianischen Romans*. Tübingen: Stauffenburg.

Schneider, R. (2001) 'Toward a cognitive theory of literary character: the dynamics of mental-model construction', *Style* 35: 607–40.

Schötz, S. (2002) *Paralinguistic Phonetics in NLP Models and Methods, NLP Term Paper*. Lund: Department of Linguistics and Phonetics.

Schreibman, S. and R. Siemens (eds) (2007) *A Companion to Digital Literary Studies* (2nd edn). Oxford: Blackwell.

Schreibman, S., Siemens, R. G. and Unsworth, J. (eds) (2004) *A Companion to Digital Humanities*. Oxford: Blackwell.

Schwartz, D. R. (2001) 'A humanistic ethics of reading', in T. F. Davis and K. Womack (eds) *Mapping the Ethical Turn: A Reader in Ethics, Culture, and Literary Theory*, Charlottesville: University Press of Virginia, pp. 3–15.

Scocca, T. (2012) 'Don Draper's shocking secret: he doesn't exist', *Slate*, 8 June, available at: www.slate.com

Scollon, R. and Levine, P. (2004) *Discourse and Technology: Multimodal Discourse Analysis*. Washington: Georgetown University Press.

Scott, M. (1996) *WordSmith Tools*. Oxford University Press.

Scott, M. (2005) *Wordsmith Tools 4.0*. Oxford University Press.

Scott, M. and Tribble, C. (2006) *Textual Patterns*. Amsterdam: Benjamins.

Seale, C. and Charteris-Black, J. (2010) 'Interviews and internet forums: a comparison of two sources of data for qualitative research,' *Qualitative Health Research* 20 (5): 595–606.

Seale, C., Charteris-Black, J. and Ziebland, S. (2006) 'Gender, cancer experience and internet use: a comparative keyword analysis of interviews and online cancer support groups', *Social Science and Medicine* 62 (10): 2577–90.

Searle, J. R. (1969) *Speech Acts: An Essay in the Philosophy of Language*. Cambridge University Press.

Sebold, A. (2002) *The Lovely Bones*. London: Picador.

Sedo, D. R. (2003) 'Readers in reading groups: an online survey of face-to-face and virtual book clubs', *Convergence: The International Journal of Research into New Media Technologies* 9 (1): 66–90.

Segal, E. (1995) 'Narrative comprehension and the role of deictic shift theory', in J. F. Duchan, G. A. Bruder and L. E. Hewitt (eds) *Deixis in Narrative: A Cognitive Science Perspective*, Hillsdale: Lawrence Erlbaum, pp. 3–17.

Semino, E. (1995) 'Schema theory and the analysis of text worlds in poetry', *Language and Literature* 4 (2): 79–108.

Semino, E. (2002) 'A cognitive approach to mind style in narrative fiction', in E. Semino and J. Culpeper (eds) *Cognitive Stylistics*, Amsterdam: John Benjamins, pp. 95–122.

Semino, E. (2004) 'Representing characters' speech and thought in narrative fiction: a study of *England, England* by Julian Barnes', *Style* 38 (4): 428–51.

Semino, E. (2007) 'Mind style 25 years on', *Style* 41 (2): 153–203.

Semino, E. (2008) *Metaphor in Discourse*. Cambridge University Press.

Semino, E. (forthcoming) 'Language, mind and autism in Mark Haddon's *The Curious Incident of the Dog in the Night-Time*', in M. Fludernik and D. Jacob (eds) *Linguistics and Literary Studies*, Berlin: de Gruyter.

Semino, E. and Short, M. (2004) *Corpus Stylistics: Speech, Writing and Thought Presentation in a Corpus of English Narratives*. London: Routledge.

Semino, E., Short, M. and Wynne, M. (1999) 'Hypothetical words and thoughts in contemporary British narratives', *Narrative* 7 (3): 307–34.

Semino, E. and Swindlehurst, K. (1996) 'Metaphor and mind style in Ken Kesey's *One Flew Over the Cuckoo's Nest*', *Style* 30 (1): 143–66.

Seuren, P. A. M. (1988) 'Presupposition and negation', *Journal of Semantics* 6 (1): 175–226.

Shakespeare, W. (2004) *Antony and Cleopatra*, London: Arden.

Sheldrake, R. (2012) *The Science Delusion: Freeing the Spirit of Enquiry*. London: Coronet.

Shelfari (2012) *Shelfari homepage*, available at: www.shelfari.com

Shen, D. (1988) 'Stylistics, objectivity and convention', *Poetics* 17 (3): 221–38.

Shivani, A. (2006) 'American poetry in an age of constriction', *The Cambridge Quarterly* 35 (3): 205–30.

Shklovsky, V. (1965) 'Art as technique', in L. T. Lemon and M. J. Reiss (eds) *Russian Formalist Criticism: Four Essays*, Lincoln: University of Nebraska Press, pp. 3–24.

Short, M. (1973) 'Some thoughts on foregrounding and interpretation', *Language and Style* 6: 97–108.

Short, M. (ed.) (1989) *Reading, Analysing and Teaching Literature*. Harlow: Longman.

Short, M. (1996) *Exploring the Language of Poems, Plays and Prose*. Harlow: Longman.

Short, M. (2007) 'Thought presentation 25 years on', *Style* 41 (2): 225–41.

Short, M. (2008) '"Where are you going to my pretty maid?" "For detailed analysis, sir", she said', in G. Watson (ed.) *The State of Stylistics*, Amsterdam: Rodopi, pp. 1–29.

Short, M. (2012) 'Discourse presentation and speech (and writing, but not thought) summary', *Language and Literature* 21 (1): 18–31.

Short, M. (forthcoming) 'Stylistics and "He wishes for the cloths of heaven" by W. B. Yeats', in V. Sotirova (ed.) *Companion to Stylistics*, London: Continuum.

Sim, W.-C. (2006) *Globalisation and Dislocation in the Novels of Kazuo Ishiguro*. Lewiston: Edwin Mellen Press.

Simmel, G. (1997) 'The sociology of sociability', in D. Frisby and M. Featherstone (eds) *Simmel on Culture: Selected Writings*, London: Sage, pp. 120–9.

Simone, R. (ed.) (1994) *Iconicity in Language*. Amsterdam: John Benjamins.

Simpson, P. (1993) *Language, Ideology and Point of View*. London: Routledge.

Simpson, P. (2000) 'Satirical humour and cultural context: with a note on the curious case of Father Todd Unctuous,' in T. Bex, M. Burke and P. Stockwell (eds) *Contextualised Stylistics*, Amsterdam: Rodopi, pp. 243–66.

Simpson, P. (2004) *Stylistics: A Resource Book for Students*. London: Routledge.

Simpson, P. and Hall, D. (2002) 'Discourse analysis and stylistics', *Annual Review of Applied Linguistics* 22: 136–49.

Sinclair, J. (1966). 'Taking a poem to pieces', in R. Fowler (ed.) *Essays on Style and Language*, London: Routledge, pp. 68–81.

Sinclair, J. (1991) *Corpus, Concordance, Collocation*. Oxford University Press.

Sinclair, J. (1993) 'Fictional worlds revisited', paper presented at *Le transformazioni del narrare*, 14–16 October. Italy: Schena Editore.

Sinclair, J. M. (2003) *Reading Concordances*. London: Longman.

Sinclair, J. (2004) *Trust the Text*. London: Routledge.

Sinclair, J. (2006) *Phrasebite*. Pescia: TWC.

Sinclair, J. (2007) 'The exploitation of meaning: literary texts and local grammars', in I. Bas and D. C. Freeman (eds) *Challenging the Boundaries*, Amsterdam: Rodopi, pp. 1–35.

Sinclair, J. and Coulthard, R. M. (1975) *Towards an Analysis of Discourse*. Oxford University Press.

Singh, K. (1989) *Train to Pakistan*. New Delhi: Time Books International.

Sklar, H. (2013) *The Art of Sympathy: Forms of Moral and Emotional Persuasion in Fiction*. Amsterdam: John Benjamins.

Snell, J. (2010) 'From sociolinguistic variation to socially strategic stylization', *Journal of Sociolinguistics* 14 (5): 630–56.

Sontag, S. (1978) *Illness as Metaphor*. New York: Farrar, Straus and Giroux.

Sorescu, M. (2004) 'Pure pain' (trans. A. Sorkin and L. Vance) in *The Bridge*, Tarset: Bloodaxe Books.

Sotirova, V. (2006) 'Reader responses to narrative point of view', *Poetics* 3 (2): 108–33.

Sotirova. V. (2010) 'The roots of a literary style: Joyce's presentation of consciousness in Ulysses', *Language and Literature* 19 (2): 131–49.

Sotirova, V. (2013) *Consciousness in Modernist Fiction: A Stylistic Study*. Basingstoke: Palgrave.

Spencer, C. (2009) 'Review of *England People Very Nice*', *The Telegraph*, 12 February.

Spencer-Oatey, H. (ed.) (2001) *Culturally Speaking*. London: Continuum.

Sperber, D. (1995) 'How do we communicate?' in J. Brockman and K. Matson (eds) *How Things Are: A Science Toolkit for the Mind*, New York: Morrow, pp. 191–9.

Sperber, D. and Wilson, D. (1990) 'Rhetoric and relevance', in J. Bender and D. Wellbery (eds) *The Ends of Rhetoric*, Palo Alto: Stanford University Press, pp. 140–55.

Sperber, D. and Wilson, D. (1995) *Relevance: Communication and Cognition* (2nd edn). Oxford: Wiley-Blackwell.

Starr, G. G. (2010) 'Multisensory imagery', in L. Zunshine (ed.) *Introduction to Cognitive Cultural Studies*, Baltimore: The Johns Hopkins University Press, pp. 275–91.

States, B. O. (1985) *Great Reckonings in Little Rooms: On The Phenomenology Of Theatre*. Berkeley: University of California Press.

Steen, G. J. (2011a) 'The contemporary theory of metaphor: now new and improved!', *Review of Cognitive Linguistics* 9 (1): 26–64.

Steen, G. J. (2011b) 'Genre between the humanities and the sciences', in M. Callies, W. R. Keller and A. Lohöfer (eds) *Bi-Directionality in the Cognitive Sciences: Examining the Interdisciplinary Potential of Cognitive Approaches in Linguistics and Literary Studies*, Amsterdam: John Benjamins, pp. 21–42.

Steen, G. J., Dorst, A. G., Herrmann, J. B., Kaal, A. A. and Krennmayr, T. (2010a) 'Metaphor in usage', *Cognitive Linguistics* 21 (4): 765–96.

Steen, G. J., Dorst, A. G., Herrmann, J. B., Kaal, A. A., Krennmayr, T. and Pasma, T. (2010b) *A Method for Linguistic Metaphor Identification: From MIP to MIPVU*. Amsterdam: John Benjamins.

Sternberg, R. (2011) *Cognitive Psychology* (6th edn). New York: Wadsworth.

Stewart, D. (2010) *Semantic Prosody: A Critical Evaluation*. London: Routledge.

Stockwell, P. (2002) *Cognitive Poetics: An Introduction*, London: Routledge.

Stockwell, P. (2003) 'Schema poetics and speculative cosmology', *Language and Literature* 12 (3): 252–71.

Stockwell, P. (2005) 'Texture and identification', *European Journal of English Studies* 9 (2): 143–53.

Stockwell, P. (2009) *Texture: A Cognitive Aesthetics of Reading*. Edinburgh University Press.

Stockwell, P. (2010) 'The eleventh checksheet of the apocalypse', in D. McIntyre and B. Busse (eds) *Language and Style: In Honour of Mick Short*, London: Palgrave Macmillan, pp. 419–32.

Stockwell, P. (2012) 'The reader's paradox', in M. Burke, S. Csabi, L. Week and J. Zerkowitz (eds) *Pedagogical Stylistics*, London: Continuum, pp. 45–57.

Stokoe, E. H. (2000) 'Constructing topicality in university students' small-group discussion: a conversation analytic approach', *Language and Education* 14 (3): 184–203.

Stubbs, M. (2001) *Words and Phrases: Corpus Studies of Lexical Semantics*. Oxford: Blackwell.

Stubbs, M. (2005) 'Conrad in the computer: examples of quantitative stylistic methods', *Language and Literature* 14 (1): 5–24.

Stubbs, M. (2008) 'The turn of the linguists: text, analysis, interpretation', in A. Müller Wood (ed.) *Texting Culture Culturing Texts*, Trier: WVT, pp. 1–14.

SunnyPetunia (2008) *Review of 'Sailing Alone Around the Room: New and Selected Poems'*, available at: www.librarything.com/work/11852/reviews/36001731

Swales, J. M. (1990) *Genre Analysis: English in Academic and Research Settings.* Cambridge University Press.

Swann, J. and Allington, D. (2009) 'Reading groups and the language of literary texts: a case study in social reading', *Language and Literature* 18 (3): 247–64.

Swann, J. and Maybin, J. (2007) 'Introduction: language creativity in every-day contexts', *Applied Linguistics* 28 (4): 491–6.

Swann, J., Deumert, A., Lillis, T. and Mesthrie, R. (2004) 'Genre', in J. Swann (ed.) *A Dictionary of Sociolinguistics*, Edinburgh University Press, pp. 123–4.

Swann, J., Pope, R. and Carter, R. (eds) (2010) *Creativity in Language and Literature: The State of the Art.* London: Palgrave.

Sweney, M. (2012) 'Nike becomes the first UK company to have Twitter campaign banned', *The Guardian*, 20 June, available at: www.guardian.co.uk/media/2012/jun/20/nike-twitter-campaign-banned

Swift, G. (1992) *Waterland* [original 1982]. London: Picador.

Szymborska, W. (1998) *Poems New and Collected* (trans. S. Barańczak and C. Cavanagh). New York: Harcourt.

Taavitsainen, I. (1999) 'Personality and style of affect in *The Canterbury Tales*', in G. Lester (ed.) *Chaucer in Perspective: Middle English Essays in Honour of Norman Blake*, Sheffield Academic Press, pp. 218–34.

Taavitsainen, I. (2001) 'Changing conventions of writing: the dynamics of genres, text types, and text traditions', *European Journal of English Studies* 5 (2): 139–50.

Taavitsainen, I. (2002) 'Historical discourse analysis: scientific language and changing thought-styles', in T. Fanego, B. Méndez-Naya and E. Seoane (eds) *Sounds, Words, Text and Change: Selected Papers from 11 ICEHL, Santiago de Compostela, 7–11 September 2000*, Amsterdam: John Benjamins, pp. 201–26.

Taavitsainen, I. (2009) 'The pragmatics of knowledge and meaning: corpus linguistic approaches to changing thought-styles in Early Modern medical discourse', in A. H. Jucker, D. Schreier and M. Hundt (eds) *Corpora: Pragmatics and Discourse*, Amsterdam: Rodopi, pp. 37–62.

Tabakowska, E. (1999) 'Linguistic expression of perceptual relationships: iconicity as a principle of text organization (a case study)', in M. Nänny and O. Fischer (eds) *Form Miming Meaning: Iconicity in Language and Literature*, Amsterdam: John Benjamins, pp. 409–22.

Tagg, C. (2011) 'Wot did he say or could u not c him 4 dust? Written and spoken creativity in text messaging', in C. L. Ho, K. T. Anderson and A. P. Leong (eds) *Transforming Literacies and Language: Multimodality and Literacy in the New Media Age*, London: Continuum, pp. 223–36.

Tanaka, K. (1994) *Advertising Language: A Pragmatic Approach to Advertisements in Britain and Japan*. London: Routledge.

Tarbox, K. (1988) *The Art of John Fowles*. Athens: University of Georgia Press.

Thomas, B. (2012) *Fictional Dialogue: Speech and Conversation in the Modern and Post Modern Novel*. Lincoln: University of Nebraska Press.

Thomas, J. (1995) *Meaning in Interaction: An Introduction to Pragmatics*. London: Longman.

Thompson, G. (1996) *Introducing Functional Linguistics*. London: Edward Arnold.

Thompson, S. A. (1987) '"Subordination" and narrative event structure', in R. S. Tomlin (ed.) *Coherence and Grounding in Discourse*, Amsterdam: John Benjamins, pp. 435–54.

Thornborrow, J. (2001) *Power Talk: Language and Interaction in Institutional Discourse*. Harlow: Longman.

Thorne, J. P. (1965) 'Stylistics and generative grammars', *Journal of Linguistics* 1 (1): 49–59.

Thorne, J. P. (1970) 'Generative grammar and stylistic analysis', in J. Lyons (ed.) *New Horizons in Linguistics*, Harmondsworth: Penguin, pp. 185–97.

Threadgold, T. (2001) 'Genre', in R. Mesthrie (ed.) *Concise Encyclopedia of Sociolinguistics*, Amsterdam: Elsevier, pp. 235–9.

Tognini-Bonelli, E. (2001) *Corpus Linguistics at Work*. Amsterdam: Benjamins.

Toker, L. and Chertoff, D. (2008) 'Reader response and the recycling of topoi in Kazuo Ishiguro's *Never Let Me Go*', *Partial Answers* 6 (1): 163–80.

Toolan, M. (1990) *The Stylistics of Fiction: A Literary-Linguistic Approach*. London: Routledge.

Toolan, M. (1992) *Language, Text and Context: Essays in Stylistics*. London: Taylor and Francis.

Toolan, M. (1996) *Total Speech: An Integrational Linguistic Approach to Language*. Durham, NC: Duke University Press.

Toolan, M. (2001) *Narrative: A Critical Linguistic Introduction* (2nd edn). London: Routledge.

Toolan, M. (2009) *Narrative Progression in the Short Story: A Corpus Stylistic Approach*. Amsterdam: Benjamins.

Toolan, M. (2010) 'What do poets show and tell linguists?' *Acta Linguistica Hafniensia* 42 (1): 189–204.

Toolan, M. (2011) 'Literary creativity in poems: marvellously repetitive', in R. Jones (ed.) *Discourse and Creativity*, London: Pearson, pp. 27–57.

TracyRowan (2009) *Review of 'Sailing Alone Around the Room: New and Selected Poems'*, available at: www.librarything.com/work/11852/reviews/36001731

Trager, G. (1958) 'Paralanguage: a first approximation', *Studies in Linguistics* 13: 1–12.

Trimarco, P. (2011) 'Literary communication online', paper presented at the Approaches to the Study of Literary Reading Conference, Open University, Milton Keynes, 18 February.

Trubetskoy, N. (1967) *Principes de phonologie*. Paris: Klincksiek.

Tscherny, N. (1986) 'Reynolds's Streatham portraits and the art of intimate biography', *The Burlington Magazine* 128 (994): 4–10.

Tsiolkas, C. (2008) *The Slap*. London: Atlantic.

Tsur, R. (2008) *Toward a Theory of Cognitive Poetics* (2nd edn). Brighton: Sussex Academic Press.

Turner, M. (1996) *The Literary Mind*. Oxford University Press.

Tuten, T. T. (2008) *Advertising 2.0: Social Media Marketing in a Web 2.0 World*. Connecticut: Praeger.

Ungerer, E. (2000) 'Muted metaphors and the activation of metonymies in advertising', in A. Barcelona (ed.) *Metaphor and Metonymy at the Crossroads*, Berlin and New York: Mouton de Gruyter, pp. 321–40.

Vālmīki (1982) *Rāmāyaṇa*, Vol. 3: *Yuddha Kānda and Uttara Kānda* (trans. N. Raghunathan). Madras: Vighneswara Publishing.

Varsano, P. M. (1999) 'Looking for the recluse and not finding him in: the rhetoric of silence in early Chinese poetry', *Asia Major* 12 (2): 39–70.

Ventola, E. (1987) *The Structure of Social Interactions: A Systemic Approach to the Semiotics of Service Encounters*. London: Frances Pinter.

Verdonk, P. (2002) *Stylistics*. Oxford University Press.

Verdonk, P. (2010) 'A cognitive stylistic reading of rhetorical patterns in Ted Hughes's "Hawk Roosting"', in D. McIntyre and B. Busse (eds), *Language and Style*, London: Palgrave Macmillan, pp. 84–94.

Vestergaard, T. and Schrøder, K. (1985) *The Language of Advertising*. London: Basil Blackwell.

Vickers, B. (1988) *In Defence of Rhetoric*. Oxford University Press.

Vieth, L. S. (1991) 'The re-humanization of art: pictorial aesthetics in John Fowles's *The Ebony Tower* and *Daniel Martin*', *MFS Modern Fiction Studies* 37 (2): 217–33.

Wales, K. (2007) 'Keywords revisited: media', *Critical Quarterly* 49 (1): 6–13.

Wales, K. (2011) *A Dictionary of Stylistics* (3rd edn.) Harlow: Pearson.

Wales, K. (2012) 'A celebration of style: retrospect and prospect', *Language and Literature* 21 (1): 9–11.

Walker, B. (2010) 'Wmatrix, key concepts and the narrators in Julian Barnes's *Talking it Over*', in D. McIntyre and B. Busse (eds) *Language and Style*, London: Palgrave Macmillan, pp. 364–87.

Walker, B. (2012) *Character and Characterisation in Julian Barnes' 'Talking It Over': A Corpus Stylistic Analysis*, unpublished PhD thesis, Lancaster University.

Wareing, S. (1994) '"And then he kissed her": the reclamation of female characters to submissive roles in contemporary fiction', in K. Wales (ed.) *Feminist Linguistics in Literary Criticism*, Woodbridge: Boydell and Brewer, pp. 117–36.

Warnke. I. (2012) 'Urbaner Diskurs und maskierter Protest: Intersektionale Feldperspektive auf Gentrifizierungsdynamiken in Berlin Kreuzberg', in K. S. Roth and C. Spiegel (eds) *Angewandte Diskurslinguistik. Felder. Probleme. Perspektiven*, Berlin: Akademie Verlag, pp. 189–221.

Watson, G. (1999) 'Evidentiality and affect: a quantitative approach', *Language and Literature* 8 (3): 217–40.

Watson, G. and Zyngier, S. (eds) (2007) *Literature and Stylistics for Language Learners: Theory and Practice*. London: Palgrave Macmillan.

Werlich, E. (1976) *A Text Grammar of English*. Heidelberg: Quelle und Meyer.

Wernick, A. (1991) *Promotional Culture: Advertising, Ideology and Symbolic Expression*. London: Sage.

Werth, P. (1976) 'Roman Jakobson's verbal analysis of poetry', *Journal of Linguistics* 12: 21–74.

Werth, P. (1995) 'How to build a world (in a lot less than six days and using only what's in your head)', in K. Green (ed.) *New Essays on Deixis: Discourse, Narrative, Literature*, Amsterdam: Rodopi, pp. 48–80.

Werth, P. (1999) *Text Worlds: Representing Conceptual Space in Discourse*. Harlow: Longman.

West, D. (2013) *I.A. Richards and the Rise of Cognitive Stylistics*. London: Continuum.

West, S. (1996) 'Portraiture: likeness and identity', in S. West (ed.) *Guide to Art*, London: Bloomsbury, pp. 71–83.

Wetherell, M. (1998) 'Positioning and interpretive repertoires: conversation analysis and post-structuralism in dialogue', *Discourse and Society* 9: 387–412.

Wharton, E. (1990) *The Muse's Tragedy and Other Stories*. Harmondsworth: Penguin.

Wharton, E. (1997) *The Writing of Fiction* [original 1924]. New York: Touchstone.

Whissell, C. (1999) 'Phonosymbolism and the emotional nature of sounds: evidence of the preferential use of particular phonemes in texts of differing emotional tone', *Perceptual and Motor Skills* 89 (1): 19–48.

Whissell, C. (2001) 'The emotionality of William Blake's poems: a quantitative comparison of *Songs of Innocence* with *Songs of Experience*', *Perceptual and Motor Skills* 92 (2): 459–67.

Whissell, C. (2004a) '"The sound must seem an echo to the sense": Pope's use of sound to convey meaning in his translation of Homer's *Iliad*', *Perceptual and Motor Skills* 98 (3): 859–64.

Whissell, C. (2004b) 'Poetic emotion and poetic style: the 100 poems most frequently included in anthologies and the work of Emily Dickinson', *Empirical Studies of the Arts* 22 (1): 55–75.

Whissell C. (2006) 'Serial publication and the emotional associations of words in Dickens' *David Copperfield*', *Psychological Reports* 99 (3): 751–61.

Whissell C. (2011) 'Sound and emotion in Milton's *Paradise Lost*', *Perceptual and Motor Skills* 113 (1): 257–67.

Whitehead, B.M. (2008) *A Rhetorical Analysis of John Fowles's 'Daniel Martin'*, unpublished doctoral thesis, Purdue University.

Whiteley, S. (2010) *Text World Theory and the Emotional Experience of Literary Discourse*, unpublished PhD thesis, University of Sheffield.

Whiteley, S. (2011a) 'Text world theory, real readers and emotional responses to The Remains of the Day', *Language and Literature* 20 (1): 23–42.

Whiteley, S. (2011b) 'Talking about "An Accommodation": the implications of discussion group data for community engagement and pedagogy', *Language and Literature* 20 (3): 236–56.

Whitney, S. (2010) 'Uneasy lie the bones: Alice Sebold's postfeminist gothic', *Tulsa Studies in Women's Literature* 29 (2): 351–73.

Whorf, B. L. (1956) 'Science and linguistics', in J. B. Carroll (ed.) *Language, Thought and Reality: Selected Writings of Benjamin Lee Whorf*. Cambridge, MA: MIT Press, pp. 207–19.

Widdowson, H. G. (1975) *Stylistics and the Teaching of Literature*. London: Longman.

Widdowson, H. G. (2008) 'The novel features of text: corpus analysis and stylistics', in A. Gerbig and O. Mason (eds) *Language, People, Numbers: Corpus Linguistics and Society*, Amsterdam: Rodopi, pp. 293–304.

Williams, R. (1962) *Communications*. Harmondsworth: Penguin.

Williams, R. (1983) *Keywords: A Vocabulary of Culture and Society* (2nd edn). Oxford University Press.

Williamson, J. (1978) *Decoding Advertisements*. London: Newbury House.

Wilson, D. (2011) 'Relevance and the interpretation of literary works', *UCL Working Papers in Linguistics* 23: 69–80.

Wilson, D. and Sperber, D. (2004) 'Relevance theory', in L. R. Horn and G. Ward (eds) *Handbook of Pragmatics*, Oxford: Wiley-Blackwell, pp. 607–32.

Wilson, D. and Sperber, D. (2012) 'Explaining irony', in D. Wilson and D. Sperber (eds) *Meaning and Relevance*, Cambridge University Press, pp. 123–45.

Wimsatt, W. K. and Beardsley, M. C. (1954) 'The intentional fallacy', in W. K. Wimsatt (ed.) *The Verbal Icon: Studies in the Meaning of Poetry*, Lexington: University of Kentucky Press, pp. 2–18.

Wittgenstein, L. (1958) *Philosophical Investigations* [original 1922]. Oxford: Basil Blackwell.

Wodak, R. (1998) *Disorders of Discourse*. Harlow: Longman.

Wolf, W. (2001) 'The emergence of experiential iconicity and spatial perspective in landscape descriptions', in O. Fischer and M. Nänny (eds) *The Motivated Sign: Iconicity in Language and Literature*, Amsterdam: John Benjamins, pp. 323–50.

Wolf, W. (2005) 'Non-supplemented blanks in works of literature as forms of "Iconicity of absence"', in C. Maeder, O. Fischer and W. J. Herlofsky (eds) *Outside-In – Inside-Out: Iconicity in Language and Literature 4*, Amsterdam: John Benjamins, pp. 113–32.

Wood, M. (2000) 'William Empson', in A. W. Litz, L. Menand and L. Rainey (eds) *The Cambridge History of Literary Criticism*, Vol. 7: *Modernism and the New Criticism*. Cambridge University Press, pp. 219–34.

Woods, M. (2013) 'Mid-term break', *Sheer Poetry*, available at www.sheerpoetry. co.uk/gcse/seamus-heaney/notes-on-selected-poems/mid-term-break

Woolf, V. (1969) *Mrs Dalloway*. Harmondsworth: Penguin.

Woolf, V. (1989) 'Together and apart' [original 1944], in S. Dick (ed.) *The Complete Short Fiction*, San Diego: Harcourt Brace, pp. 189–94.

Woolf, V. (1992) *To the Lighthouse* [original Hogarth Press, 1927]. London: Vintage.

Wussow, H. M. (ed.) (2010) *Virginia Woolf: 'The Hours'. The British Museum Manuscript of 'Mrs Dalloway'*. New York: Pace University Press.

Wynne, M. (2006) 'Stylistics: corpus approaches', in K. Brown (ed.) *Encyclopedia of Language and Linguistics* (2nd edn), Oxford: Elsevier, pp. 223–6.

Yates, J. and Orlikowski, W. J. (1992) 'Genres of organizational communication: a structurational approach to studying communication and media', *Academy of Management Review* 17 (2): 299–326.

Yeats, W. B. (1939) *Last Poems*. London: Macmillan.

Yeh, W. and Barsalou, L. W. (2006) 'The situated nature of concepts', *American Journal of Psychology* 119 (3): 349–84.

Youmans, G. (1990) 'Measuring lexical style and competence: the type-token vocabulary curve', *Style* 24 (4): 584–99.

Youmans, G. (1991) 'A new tool for discourse analysis: the vocabulary-management profile', *Language* 67 (4): 763–89.

Youmans, G. (1994) 'The vocabulary management-profile, two stories by William Faulkner', *Empirical Studies of the Arts* 12 (2): 113–30.

Zappavigna, M. (2011) 'Ambient affiliation: a linguistic perspective on Twitter', *New Media and Society*, 13 (5): 788–806.

Zappavigna, M. (2012) *Discourse of Twitter and Social Media: How We Use Language to Create Affiliation on the Web*. London: Continuum.

Zephaniah, B. (2001) 'What Stephen Lawrence Has Taught Us', in *Too Black, Too Strong*, Highgreen: Bloodaxe Books.

Zunshine, L. (2006) *Why We Read Fiction: Theory of Mind and the Novel*. Columbus: Ohio State University Press.

Zusak, M. (2005) *The Book Thief*. London: Random House.

Zyngier, S., van Peer, W. and Hakemulder, J. (2007) 'Complexity and foregrounding: in the eye of the beholder?' *Poetics Today* 28 (4): 653–82.

Zyngier, S., Bortolussi, M., Chesnokova, A. and Auracher, J. (eds) (2008) *Directions in Empirical Literary Studies: In Honor of Willie Van Peer*. Amsterdam: John Benjamins.

Index